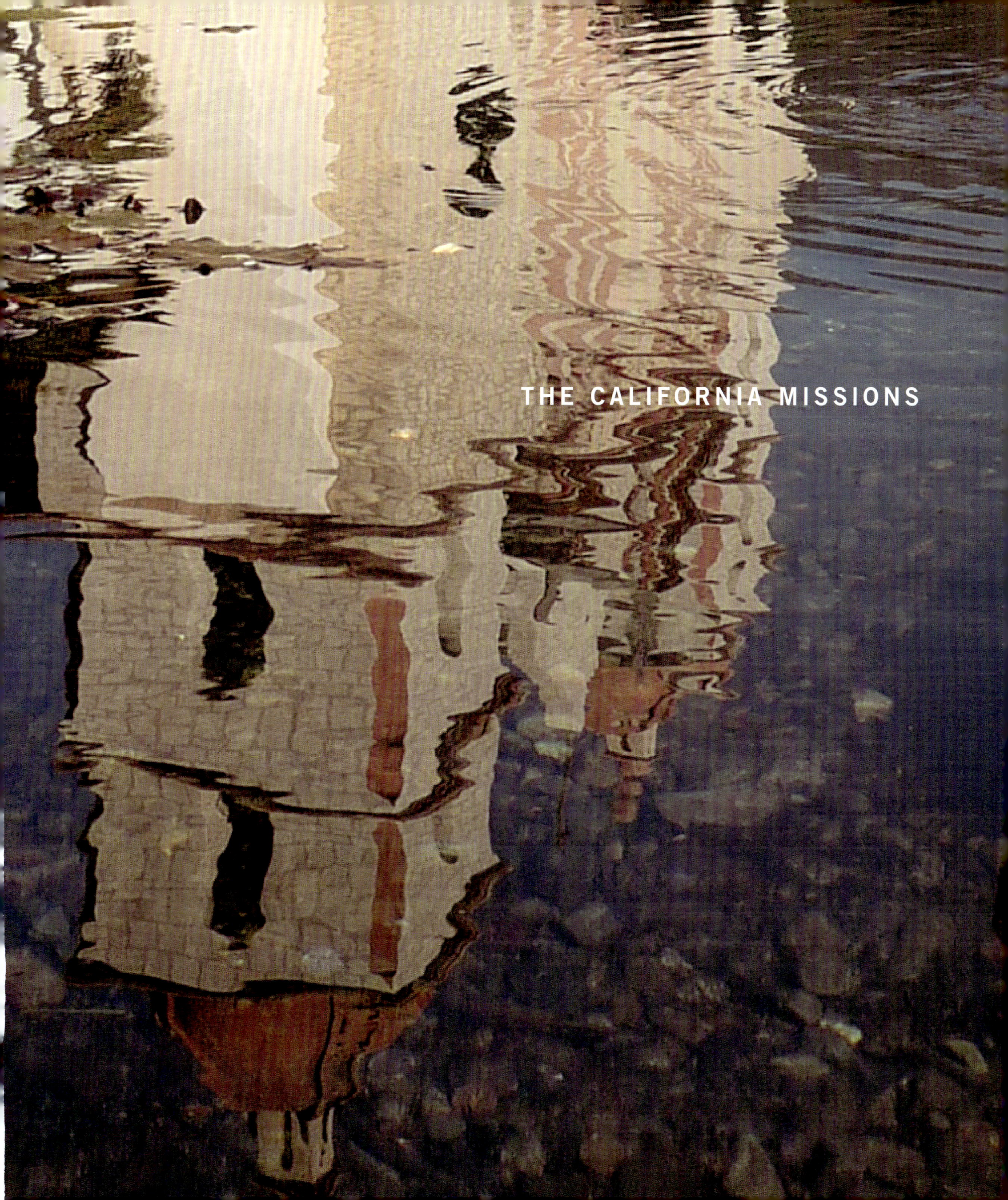

THE CALIFORNIA MISSIONS

THE CALIFORNIA
MISSIONS

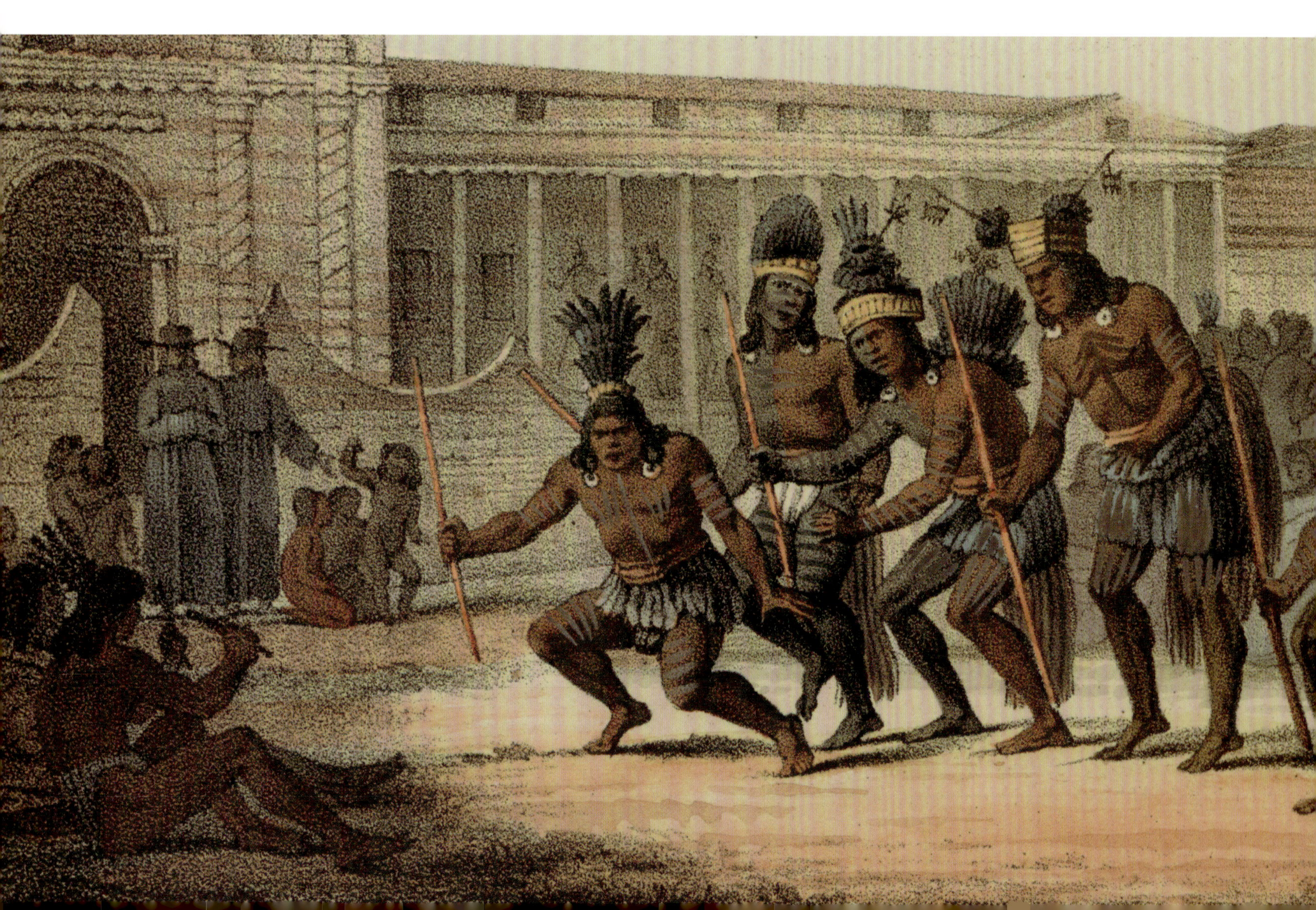

HISTORY, ART, and PRESERVATION

EDNA E. KIMBRO and JULIA G. COSTELLO with TEVVY BALL

THE GETTY CONSERVATION INSTITUTE · LOS ANGELES

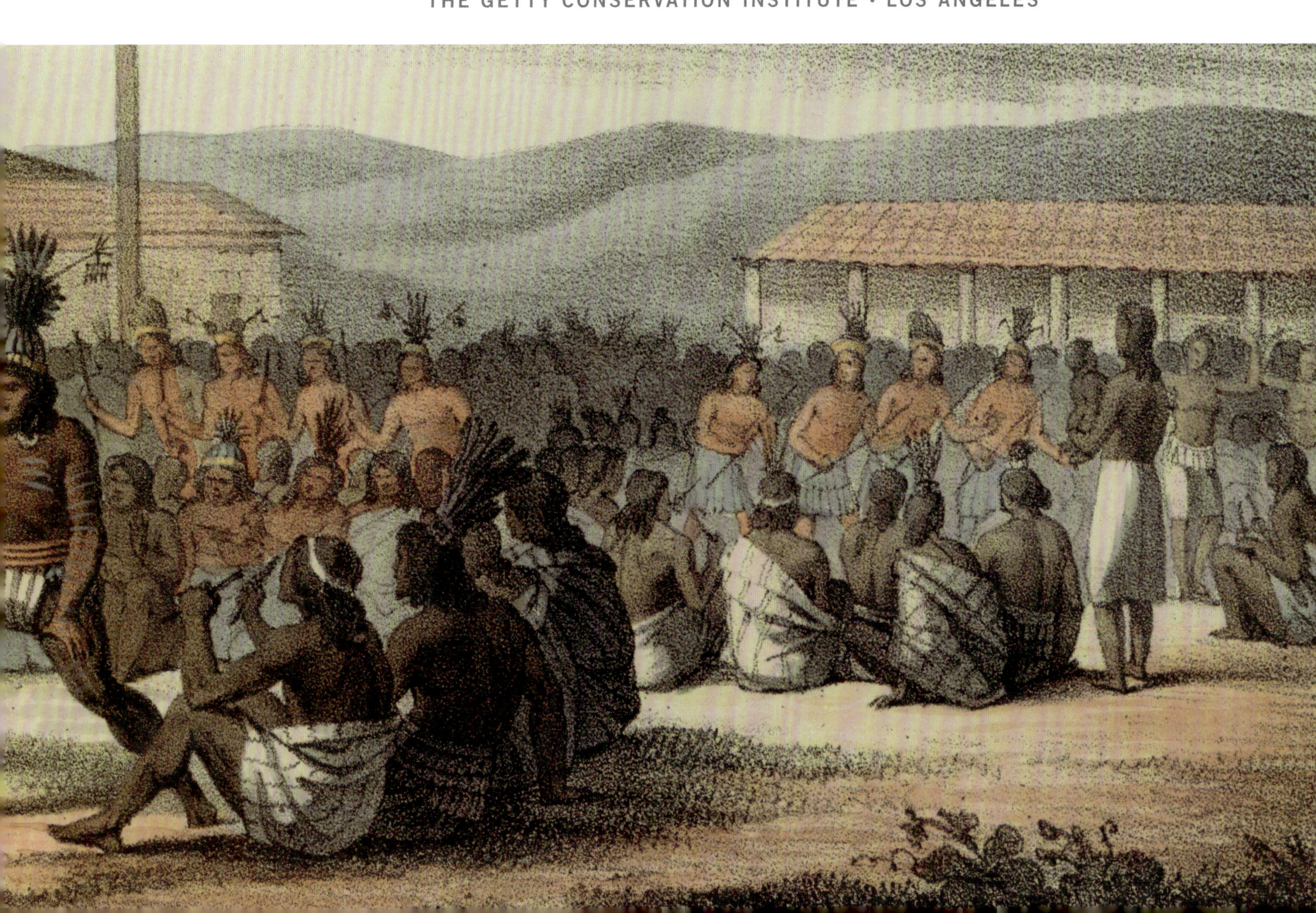

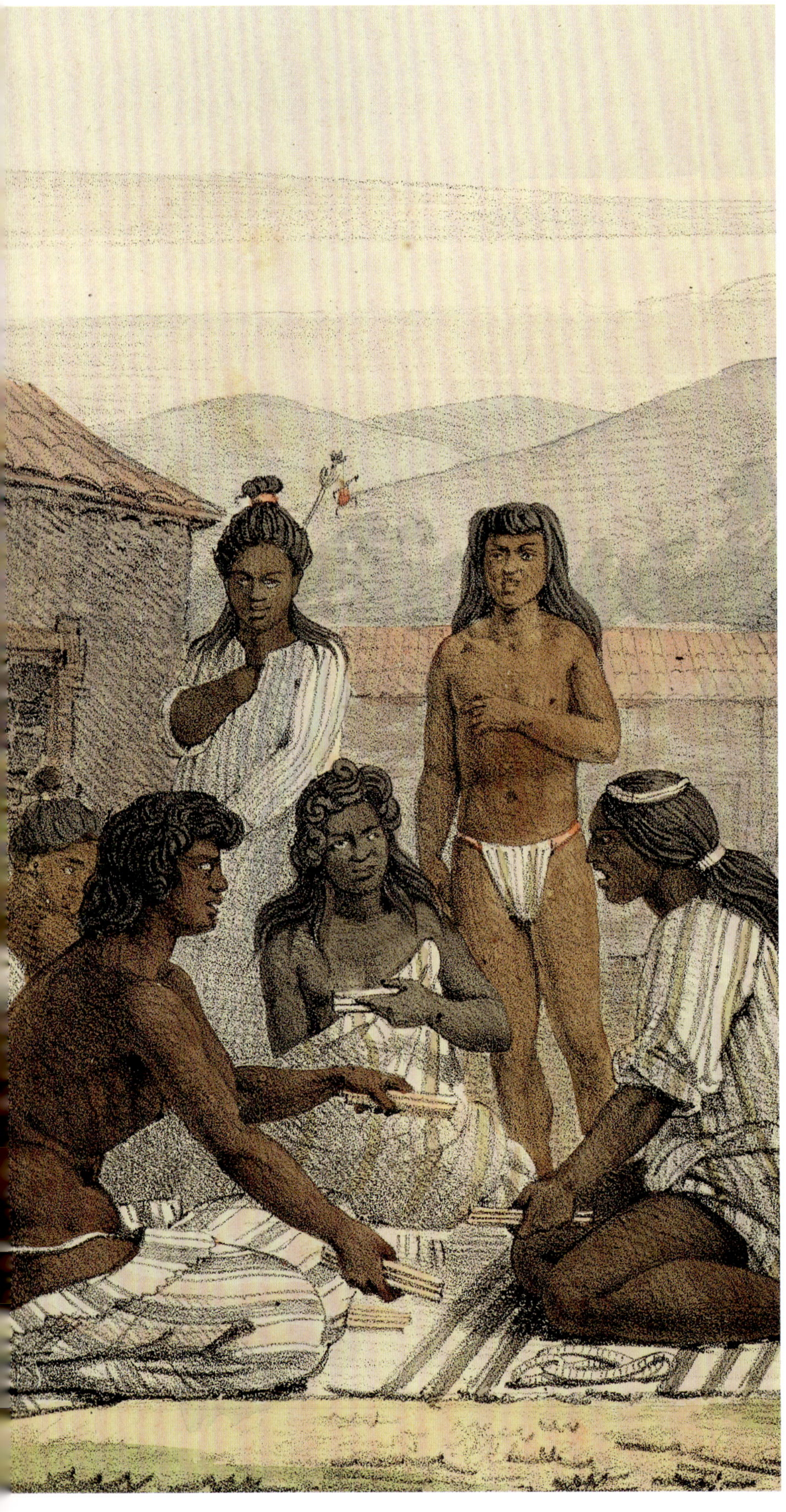

CONTENTS

PART TWO: THE MISSIONS

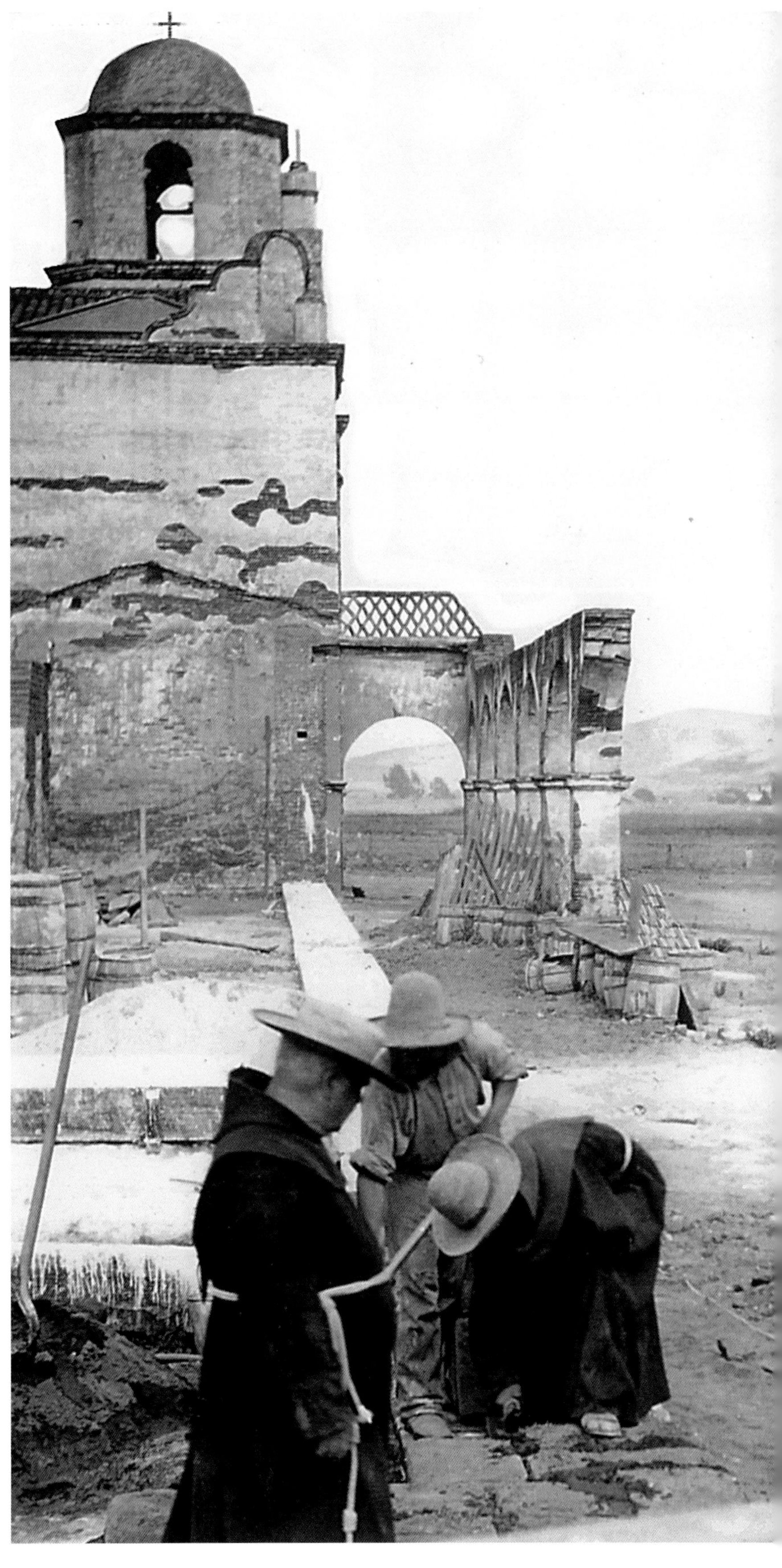

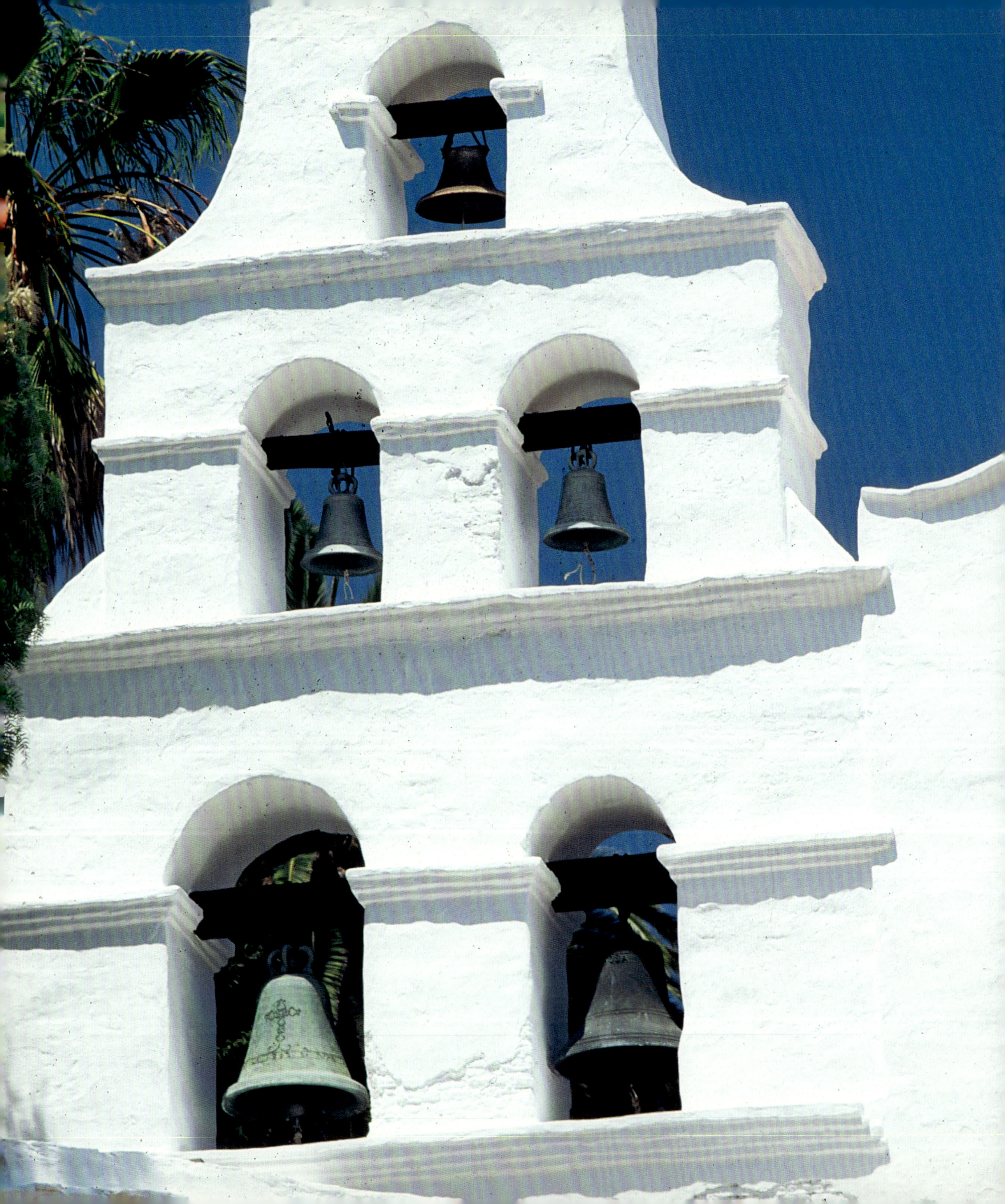

INTRODUCTION

The Spanish missions of California represent the state's oldest and richest historical legacy. Their epic story has been told many times, beginning with accounts by the missionaries themselves and followed a century later by H. H. Bancroft's voluminous history in the 1880s. Since then, countless books have promoted the romantic mission saga. In recent decades, much fine scholarship has cast new light on the mission story, illuminating the past and probing the many meanings the missions have today. So, too, have important advances been made in preserving both the venerable adobe and stone structures and the treasures they contain. Surprisingly little of this new wealth of knowledge and interpretation, however, has found its way into books for the general public. Many of these accounts also neglect to continue the narrative into the present, to explain just how the missions came to occupy such a central place in the cultural identity of California.

The present volume seeks to fill this gap by illuminating the full range of issues that have shaped their heritage—the meanings they have had in the past, their significance today, and the multifaceted legacy they bequeath to the future. We focus both on the missions' material heritage—architecture, archaeology, art—and on their larger role in shaping the region's history and culture. We begin by brushing with broad strokes the well-known story of the missions' founding and early history as outposts of the Spanish empire and Roman Catholicism, places of conversion and conquest where Spanish, Mexican, and Native American worlds mixed and mingled. Native American perspectives are incorporated into the narrative, as indigenous peoples were drawn into the growing colonial establishments and dispossessed of much of their traditional culture, laboring to erect buildings of adobe and stone, turn water to irrigation, plant orchards and fields, and learn new technologies and crafts. They left their former homes and saw their tribal lands overrun with cattle and horses. From the early days of the mission system, they also suffered the devastating European diseases that decimated the missions' indigenous populations.

It is misleading, however, to generalize too broadly, for the missions varied widely, and the story of each individual institution was complex. From San Diego to Sonoma, each had its successes and failures, colored by local administrators, tribal inclinations, and historical and environmental variables. In the 1830s the demise of the mission system was assured when its lands were distributed into private hands, the neophytes—the Native American mission converts—dispersed, and buildings abandoned. The deterioration of the missions accelerated following California statehood in 1850, when the crumbling adobe edifices were disdained by the new American arrivals as relics of a bygone civilization. By the end of the century, most of these once-vast establishments had all but melted back into their native soils.

OPPOSITE: The distinctive *espadaña* at Mission San Diego de Alcalá, reconstructed in 1931. Photograph by G. Aldana

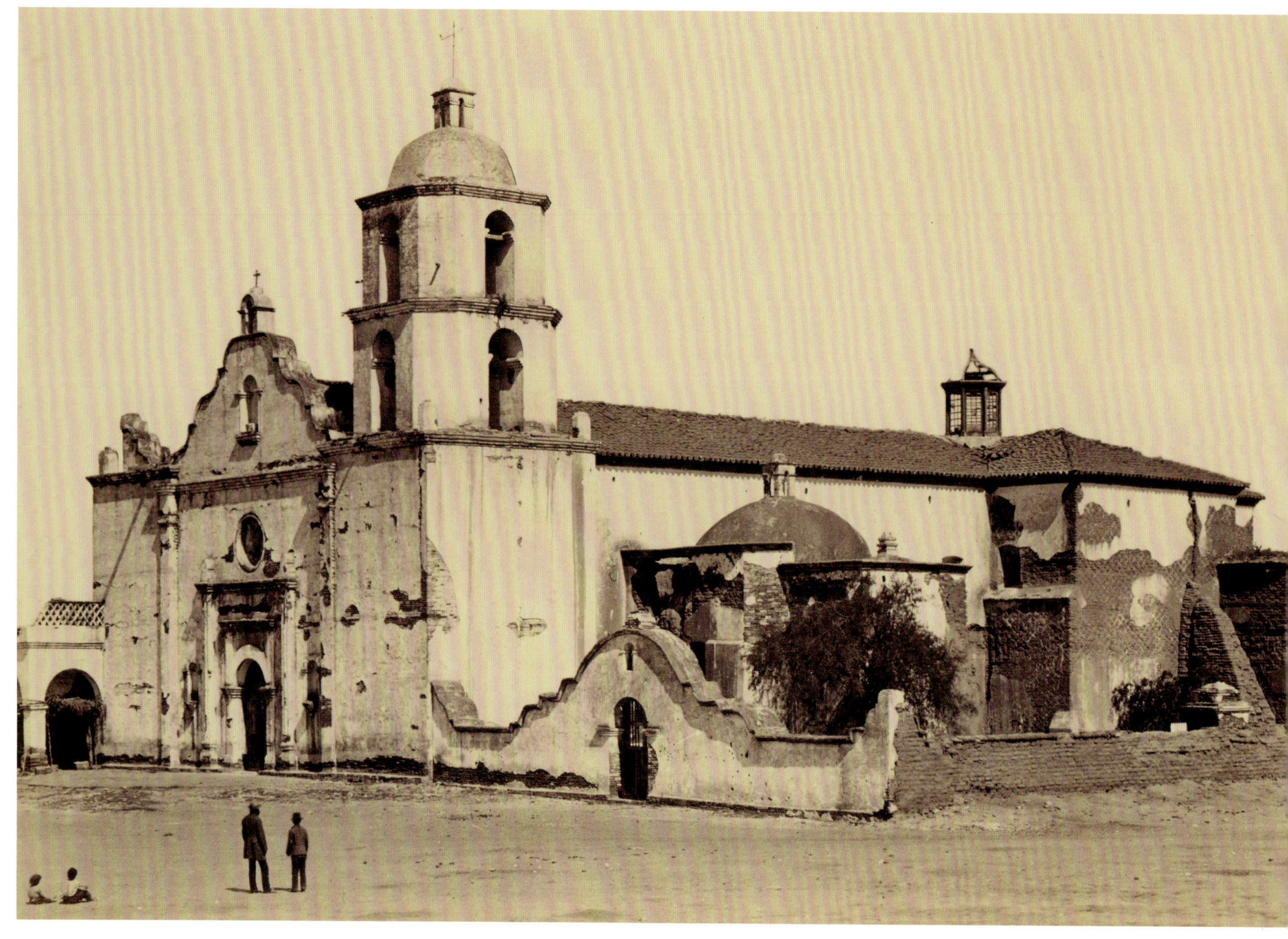

View of the church at Mission San Luis Rey de Francia, ca. 1876–80, with its striking bell tower and facade faced with *ladrillo* tiles. Photograph by Carleton Watkins. Albumen silver print. Gift in memory of Leona Naef Merrill and in honor of her sister, Gladys Porterfield. The J. Paul Getty Museum, Los Angeles. 94.XA.113.6

During these years of abandonment and neglect, however, a number of mission churches were maintained and continued to serve their local populations. Many became repositories not only of religious and secular art but also of the cultural and religious heritage of the state's almost-forgotten past. And, by the 1870s, missions and mission ruins were increasingly attracting the attention of painters and photographers such as Henry Chapman Ford and Carleton Watkins. In the decades following the 1884 publication of Helen Hunt Jackson's novel *Ramona*, the mission myth—a glorified and romanticized version of Spanish and Mexican California's history—gained widespread popularity among California's new American inhabitants. This in turn stimulated the growth of the mission preservation movement, which by the early years of the twentieth century was well under way. Subsequent decades saw a number of noteworthy restorations and reconstructions, ranging from the Civilian Conservation Corps's resurrection of Mission La Purísima, a federally funded New Deal project of the Great Depression, to the restoration of Mission San Carlos Borromeo, a labor of love carried out by the carpenter-turned-restorer Harry Downie. The New Deal also witnessed the rediscovery of the mission murals, the colorful and intricate paintings that covered the walls of churches and other buildings. Whitewashed and plastered over, or preserved as fragments in crumbling walls, these fading

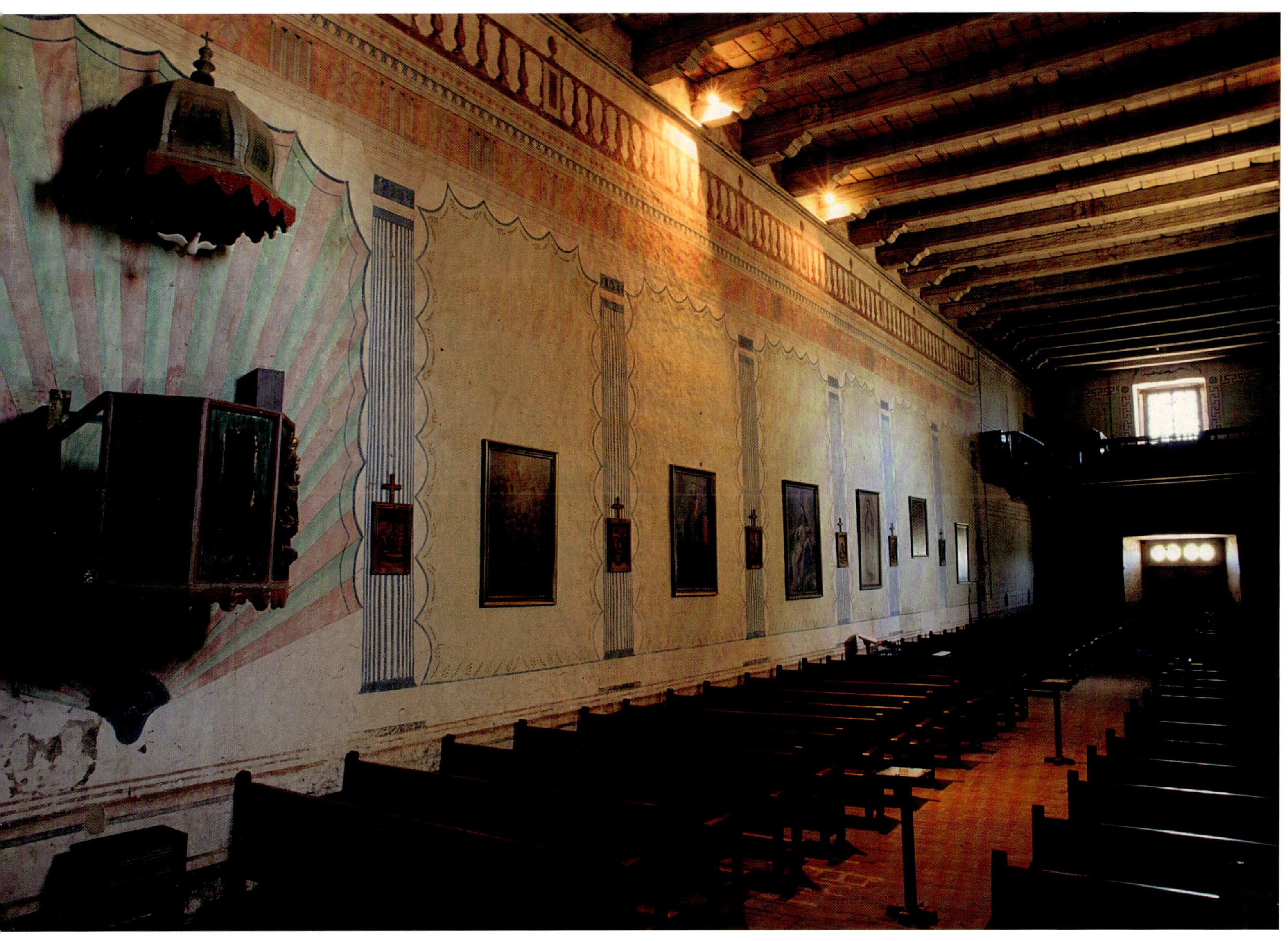

The pulpit and murals at Mission San Miguel, Arcángel, pictured here before an earthquake endangered them in 2003. This is the only completely original mission church interior in California. Photograph by G. Aldana

adornments were documented by the artists of the Index of American Design in meticulous watercolors, a selection of which is published here in full color for the first time.

In view of their complex history, it is not surprising that today the California missions represent different things to different people. Indeed, few other of the state's historical structures are imbued with a comparable richness of meanings. Founded by Spanish Franciscan missionaries, designed by artisans from Mexico and Europe, built and decorated largely by Native Americans, preserved by American newcomers, the missions possess considerable importance as symbols of the California past.

Gradually, the romantic narrative of the mission myth has been supplemented with a wide range of other perspectives, and today the mission legacy is a matter of considerable debate. Some continue to adhere to the basic tenets of the classical interpretation, maintaining that, in spite of all, the Franciscan padres and the mission system conferred on the region's native peoples the blessings of civilization—blessings fraught and shadowed, perhaps, but blessings nonetheless. Other interpretations offer starkly different views, emphasizing the mission system's catastrophic effect on indigenous populations, as well as the active role played by the missions' Native Americans not only in maintaining aspects of their traditional culture but also in actively resisting these oppressive colonial institutions.

Archaeological studies, meanwhile, have expanded our knowledge of daily life, and archives have yielded information on long-neglected artisans who designed the missions and on Native Americans who built and decorated them. The "mission story" has become complex. As one scholar has written, "Proponents of Western Civilization, of indigenous peoples, of Catholicism, or of liberal diversity... all... understand the missions in different ways, as do students of architecture, mythologies, theology, or social history."[1]

It would be misleading to suggest that a broad consensus has emerged. The mission heritage, rather, resides not in any single definitive view but in a multiplicity of often-contradictory perspectives. Today the debate continues, a fruitful probing of the missions' multifaceted history, an exploration of the many different stories that speak to us from the past. It is perhaps fitting that the missions, symbols of the heritage of California's Native American, Spanish, Mexican, and Anglo-American peoples, resist any simple, single interpretation. As the foundational institutions of California, they also represent the state as a whole in its full complexity.

Finally, the story of the missions has always been, in part, the story of their preservation, of the struggle to build them and then protect them against the many factors, natural, historical, and cultural, that have threatened them over the past two hundred years. But now only a few remnants of this epic tale remain, and it is the physical presence of these historic buildings and their precious artifacts that evokes our strong feelings of connection to the past. For some, a visit to the missions raises troubling associations related to their role as colonial institutions. Others find comfort in touching walls that were constructed by native peoples, or gazing on statues of saints that have been venerated by the faithful for centuries. Whatever view one maintains, the missions afford a profound sense of connection with those who have come before us. Today many of these historic structures of adobe or stone, along with the artistic and cultural treasures they contain, remain extremely vulnerable. Buildings and artifacts alike are subject not only to the natural processes of aging and catastrophic events such as earthquakes but also to deterioration and loss through inattention or lack of knowledge. We hope that this book will foster a renewed exploration and appreciation of the rich mission heritage, an appreciation that will promote active stewardship of these precious survivors.

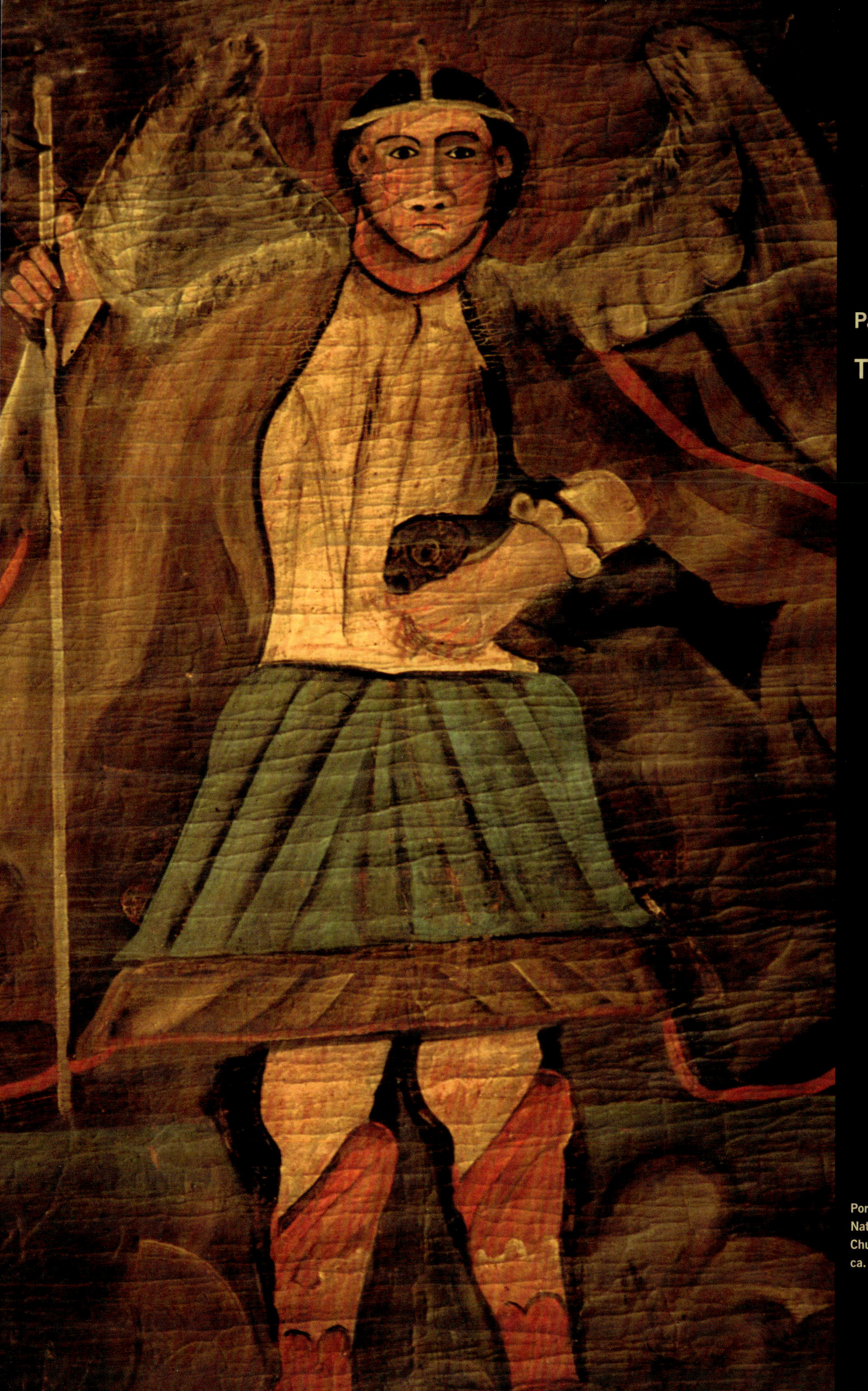

Part One

The Mission Story

Portrait of the archangel San Rafael, with Native American features, by an unknown Chumash artist at Mission Santa Inés, ca. 1820. Oil on canvas. Photograph by G. Aldana

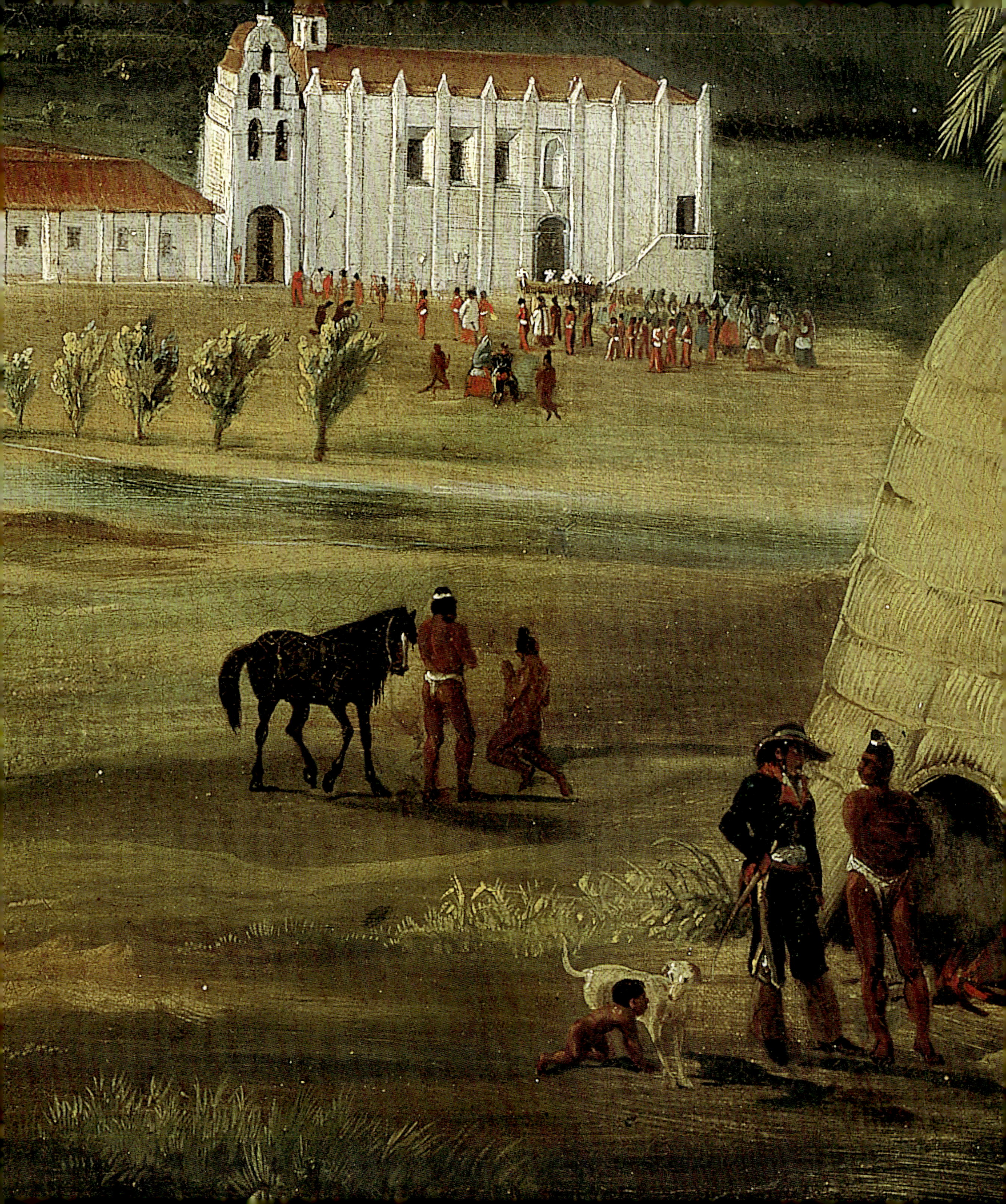

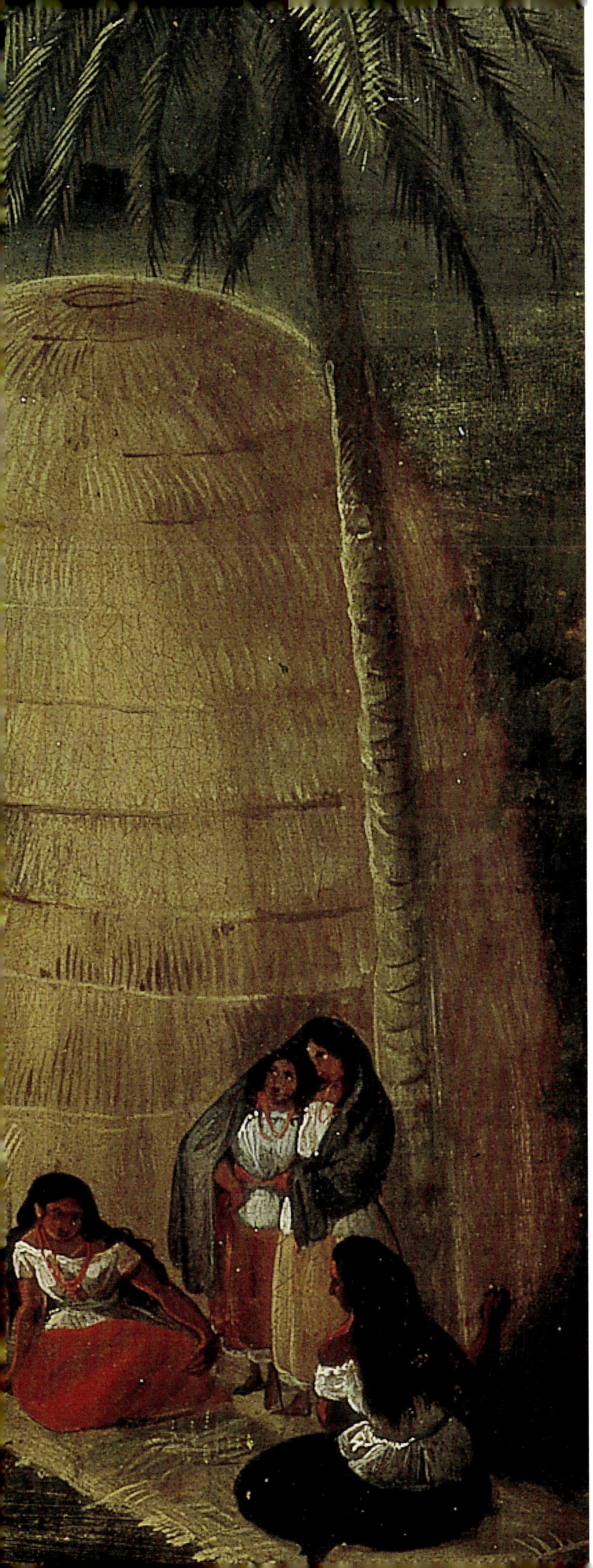

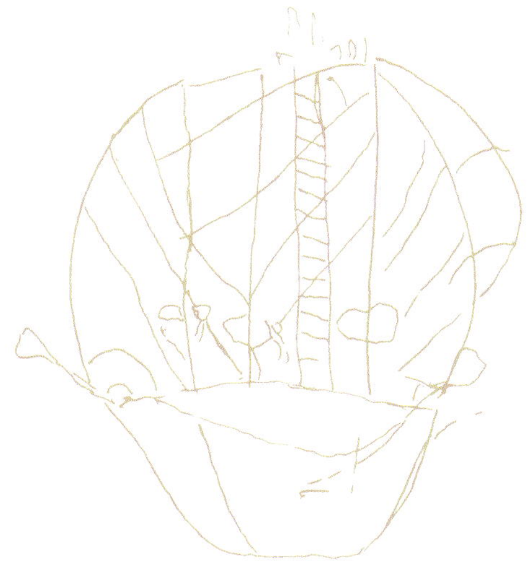

Chapter One

COLONIZING CALIFORNIA

In the oral tradition of the Kashaya Pomo, a native group living on the northern coast of what would become known as California, a narrative recounts a mysterious sighting on the sea. "In the old days, before the white people came . . . there was a boat sailing on the ocean from the south," the story relates. "Because [the people] had never seen a boat, they said, 'Our world must be coming to an end. Couldn't we do something? This big bird floating on the ocean is from somewhere, probably from up high. Let us plan a feast. Let us have a dance.' They followed its course with their eyes to see what it would do. . . . They promised Our Father [a feast]" and then "watched [the ship] sail way up north and disappear. They thought that nothing [terrible] had happened to them—the big bird person had sailed northward without doing anything—because of the promise of a feast. . . . Consequently they held a feast and a big dance."[1]

LEFT: A Gabrielino family converses with a man in Mexican dress in front of a traditional thatched house at Mission San Gabriel, ca. 1832. Ferdinand Deppe, *Mission San Gabriel* (detail). Oil on canvas. Courtesy of the Santa Bárbara Mission Archive-Library

ABOVE: Neophyte etching on a nave wall at Mission San Miguel.

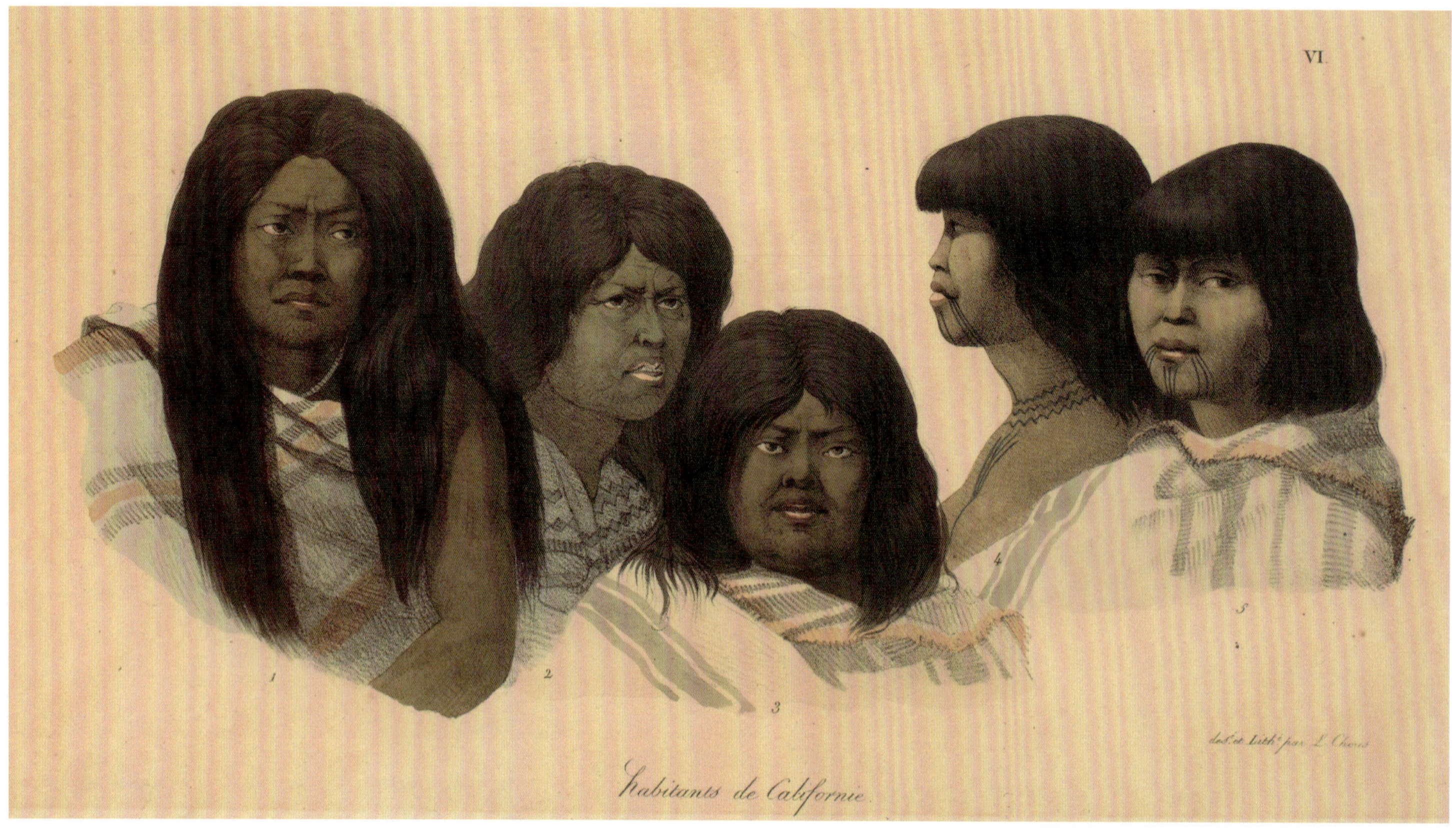

Portrait of five Native Americans by the Ukrainian artist Ludwig Choris, who accompanied a German expedition that visited California in 1816. At right: two figures with facial tattoos of the Saclan tribe, from the hills east of San Francisco Bay; second from left: a Huchiun, from the adjacent lowlands; center and left: two members of the Huimen tribe, from the southern Marin peninsula. Lithographs based on Choris's sketches first appeared in his book *Voyage pittoresque autour du monde*, which was published in Paris in 1822. Print on paper, hand-colored lithograph. Courtesy of The Bancroft Library, University of California, Berkeley

In the middle of the eighteenth century, the Kashaya Pomo were one of about eighty largely autonomous tribes living in Alta (Upper) California. Some three hundred thousand people, speaking perhaps eighty distinct languages, inhabited territories that ranged along the length of the coast (the most densely populated area in North America), stretched east over the coastal ranges and central valleys to the great Sierra Nevada, and spread southeast over the vast arid deserts to the Colorado River and beyond.[2]

The region's varied climate and terrain supported diverse ways of life. Most indigenous Californians lived in small tribes of from two hundred to five hundred members, governed by hereditary chiefs, usually male. Political entities ranged from the highly organized Chumash of the central coast to the autonomous family units prevalent among the Coast Miwok. Peoples of different regions were linked by political alliances and trading networks that shifted over time. Whereas the southernmost groups irrigated crops in riverside fields, most native Californians were hunter-gatherers who developed sophisticated systems for harvesting the resources of their tribal lands.[3] Local flora provided a variety of foods, including roots, berries, seeds, and the acorn, gathered every autumn and stored, then pounded and leached of its bitter tannin when needed. Native peoples hunted deer, elk, rabbit, waterfowl, and other game; in the north they fished for salmon and coastal groups harvested shellfish and sea mammals as well as ocean fish.

Californians were adept at working the materials at hand. Functional and decorative objects were fashioned from wood and stone, and they especially excelled at making baskets, which were used for storage, cooking, and adornment and were widely traded. The northern Pomo fashioned intricate headdresses of shell, fur, and feathers; the southern Tipai made painted pottery vessels for cooking and storage. And the Chumash built finely wrought, wooden-plank canoes, called *tomols*, which they used to fish and travel among the offshore islands. Strings of shell beads, produced on Santa Cruz Island by specialized

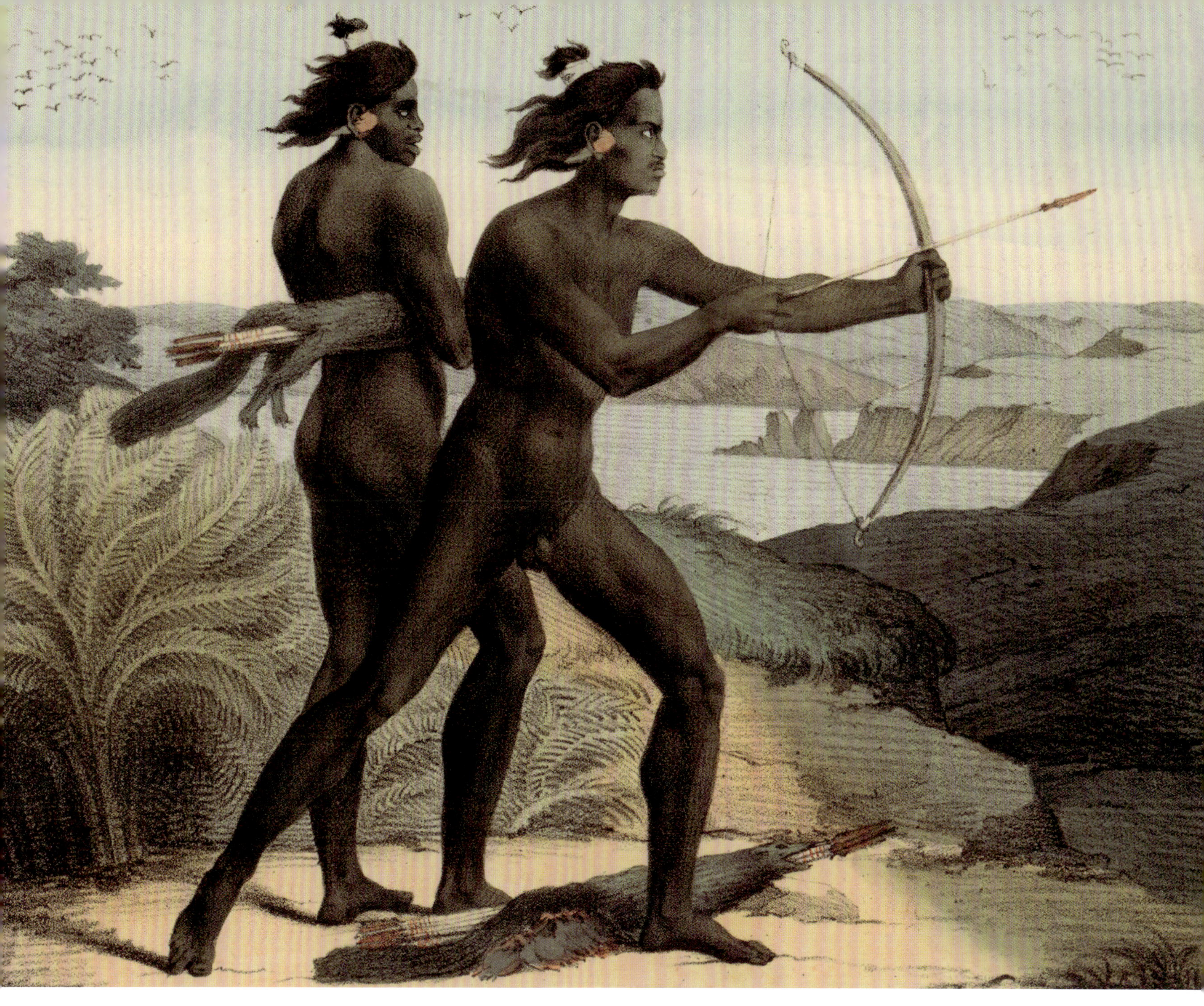

Two men from the Cholvon tribe of the northern San Joaquin River hunting near San Francisco Bay, ca. 1816. Each has a quiver made of fox skin; their bows are tipped with stone points, and they are wearing shell ornaments on their ears. Ludwig Choris, print on paper from hand-colored lithograph. Courtesy of The Bancroft Library, University of California, Berkeley

villages, were used as currency throughout the Chumash lands and were traded as far east as the Sierra Nevada.

Throughout the region, native peoples lived in an intimate relationship with the natural world: humans and trees, animals and birds, and mountains and rivers all had a spiritual existence. Human activities were governed by the rhythms of the seasons. Individual relationships with natural and spiritual forces were personal and direct, although they could be mediated through shamans, secret societies, and rituals. People joined in dances and ceremonies to celebrate the hunt, invoke victory in war, smooth ritual passages, and communicate with the vast world of the spirits. Villagers were especially bound in a sacred relationship to their long-held tribal territories, which were strictly defined and defended and which embodied significant elements of their religious and cultural history.[4] The Acjachemem people's village of Pubuna, for example, near the future site of San Juan

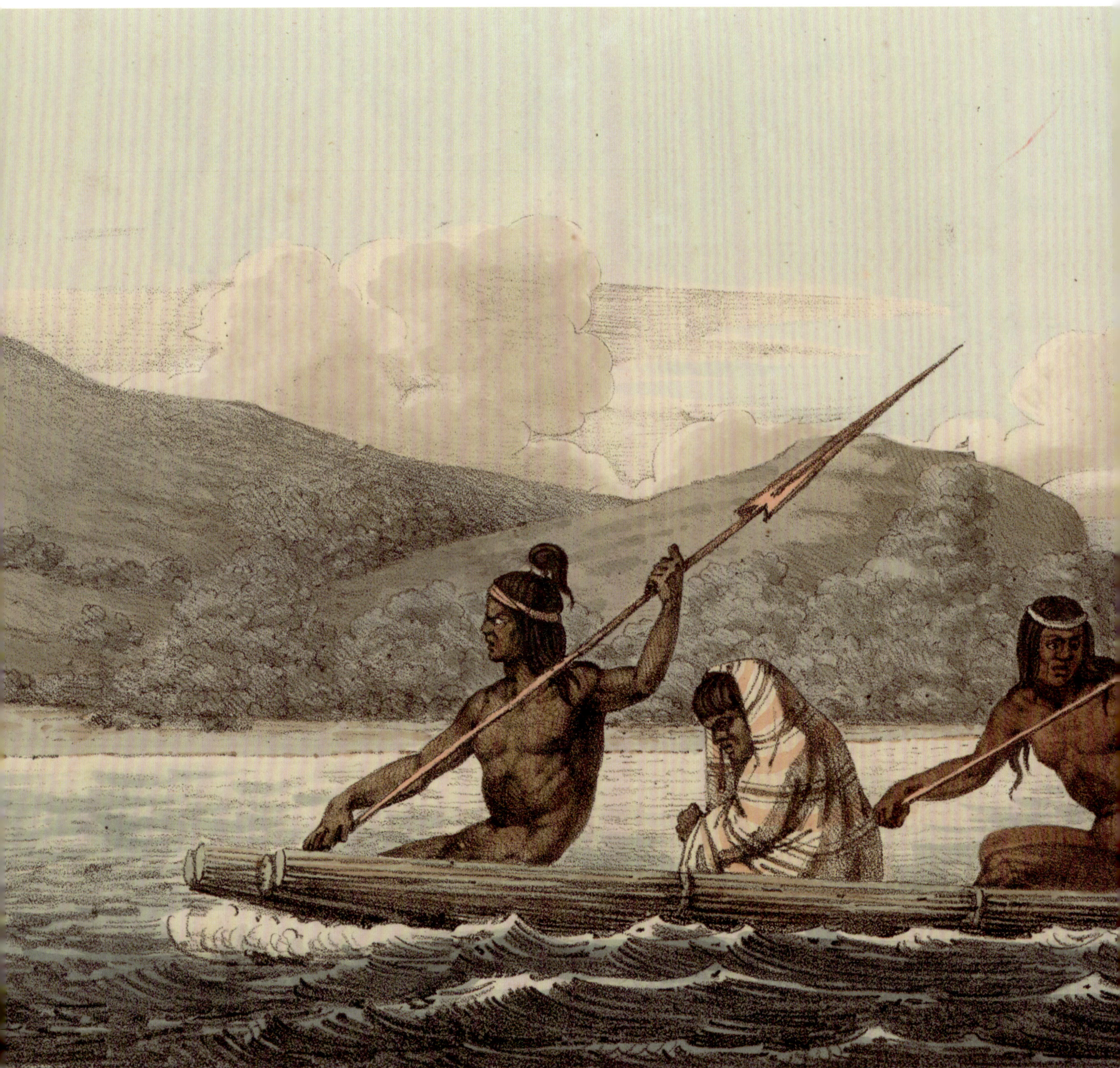

Three Costanoans cross San Francisco Bay in a boat of tule balsa, ca. 1816. This traditional craft was made of tightly bound reeds and was used for fishing and duck hunting as well as for transportation. The person in the middle is covered with a mission-made blanket of woolen cloth; baskets of native design rest in the stern. Ludwig Choris, color print. Courtesy of The Bancroft Library, University of California, Berkeley

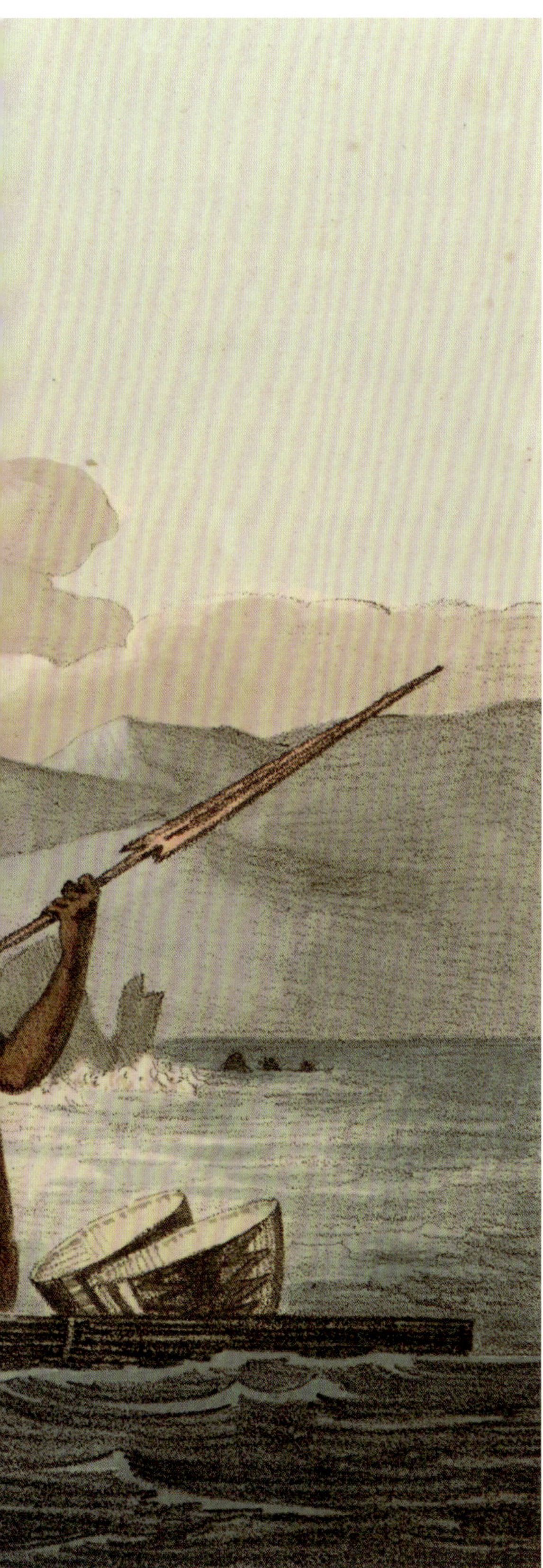

Capistrano, was said to be the birthplace of the mythical tyrant Quiot and the home of his successor, the god Chinigchinich, who was widely venerated along the southern coast. The followers of Chinigchinich built temples in the middle of their villages, where "they were extremely careful not to commit the most trivial act of irreverence."[5] The Chumash looked to Mount Pinos as the origin of the powerful religious cult *'antap* and maintained numerous shrines to local forces throughout their land.[6] And for the Ohlone of the San Francisco Bay, the world began with a terrible flood when only Coyote was left alive, standing on an island that is present-day Mount Diablo.[7]

Cultural knowledge was preserved through oral narratives recounted by memory, reinforced by physical landmarks and rituals, and passed down from generation to generation. There were stories about love and marriage, family and community, wars and alliances, rituals and dreams, death and the afterlife. Creation narratives, such as that of the Ohlone, recounted how the world and its creatures came into being, while others told of the activities of spirit forces, the origin of constellations, and calendars tracking the passing of seasons. The Ohlone believed that souls traveled westward across the ocean to the Island of the Dead, and some held the possibility that a soul might eventually return in a new body.[8] In Chumash cosmology, there were three worlds—a world above, an underworld inhabited by the *nunasis*, or angry ones, and "this world in which we live," called *Hutash*, subject to the powerful force of the sun and the cleansing properties of the moon. Humans were created after discussions among the Coyote of the Sky, the Sun, the Moon, the Morning Star, and "the great eagle that knows what is to be."[9]

From the sixteenth century, native peoples living along the coast began to have occasional contacts with men coming from other lands. Two expeditions from the colonial territory of New Spain inspected the coast of the California peninsula in the 1530s, and Spanish merchant galleons traversed coastal waters, carrying exotic goods from the Orient southward to Spanish ports. Voyages were undertaken in 1542 by the Spanish explorers Juan Rodríguez Cabrillo and in 1602 by Sebastián Vizcaíno, who praised Monterey Bay as a potential location for a naval supply base. The English explorer Francis Drake, sailing around the world in the *Golden Hind*, shored up to repair and restock his ship on the northern coast, around what is now called Drake's Bay, in 1579. Here, too, some two decades later, the Spanish galleon *San Agustín*, returning from Manila with a hold full of goods from the Far East, was driven ashore and broke up on the beach. Artifacts excavated from villages of the Coast Miwok, neighbors of the Kashaya Pomo, suggest that the local inhabitants obtained exotic goods from both ships, including stoneware and Chinese porcelain from the Ming dynasty. They could not have foreseen what cataclysms these delicate pieces would portend; nor could the Kashaya Pomo, in seeing a distant apparition of sails on the ocean horizon, have divined the momentous changes such ships, and accompanying overland expeditions, would bring to this region in the turbulent times to come.[10]

The expeditions that would alter California forever began in early 1769, dispatched by authorities in the Spanish territory of New Spain who were concerned about Russian and English expansion along the west coast of North America. The expeditions comprised soldiers and missionaries, who were to establish two outposts of settlement in the province known as Alta California, one on the bay of San Diego and the other, farther north, at Monterey Bay, which Vizcaíno had noted more than a century and a half earlier. Two groups would travel by sea and two by land, with a supply ship to follow. The first ship left La Paz, in Baja California, in January; the second followed several weeks later. Battling

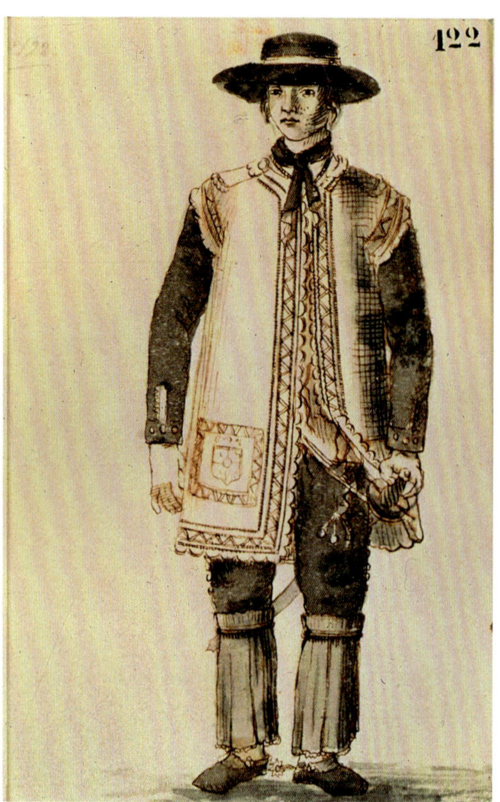

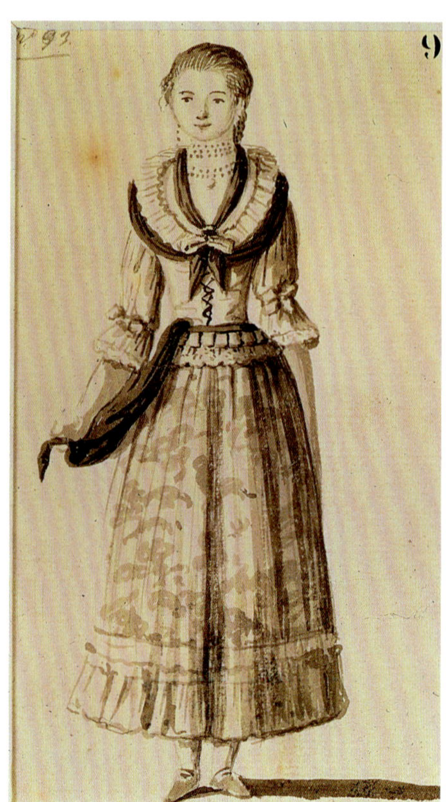

A Spanish soldier and his wife from the Monterey Presidio, wearing the traditional dress of citizens of New Spain in the 1780s. The soldiers and their families who came to Alta California were of mixed Indian, African, and Spanish ancestry and were drawn primarily from the northern provinces of what would become Mexico. Drawings ascribed to José Cardero. Courtesy Museo de América, Madrid

fierce headwinds and storms, their crews plagued by scurvy, both vessels endured arduous journeys. The land expeditions, accompanied by the Franciscan priest Junípero Serra and led by the explorer and military man Gaspar de Portolá, departed in the spring, wending their way up the rugged desert trails of the lower California peninsula. By early July all groups had arrived at San Diego Bay. Early in the morning of July 16, a crude cross was raised on a hill to mark the founding of Mission San Diego de Alcalá. The coming months brought hardship, as the Spaniards endured the continuing ravages of disease. Local natives attacked, and several men were killed before a fragile peace prevailed. The supply ship was lost at sea, and provisions ran low. At last, in March 1770, a sail appeared on the horizon, and the fledgling settlement's tenuous existence was secured. "It is a good country—distinctly better than Old [Baja] California," Father Serra wrote of the new land. For this intrepid priest and colonizer, the region, with its populous native tribes, presented "a harvest of souls that might easily be gathered into the bosom of our Holy Mother, the Church."[11]

Over the next sixty years, twenty more Franciscan missions would be established along the Alta California coast. In the mission establishments, European and native cultures would intermingle. Here, imported religion, culture, and technologies would take root and grow with a distinctly Californian character. Here, too, the traditional worlds of California's indigenous peoples would be irrevocably altered and, eventually, all but destroyed. Although revolutions in New England and New Spain would in time greatly affect the colony's future and the mission system would endure just over sixty years, mission churches and some related buildings would survive for well over two centuries, bearing the complex legacy, still resonant today, of this seminal encounter between the Old World and the New.

ca. 14,000 B.C.E.
California inhabited by Native Americans.

1492
Christopher Columbus lands on Hispaniola, claims territory for Spain.

1521
Hernán Cortés conquers the Aztec capital of Tenochtitlán.

1522
First Spanish outpost on Pacific Coast is founded at Zacatula.

1530s
Two expeditions from New Spain inspect California coast.

1533–34
Francisco Pizarro conquers the Inca kingdom.

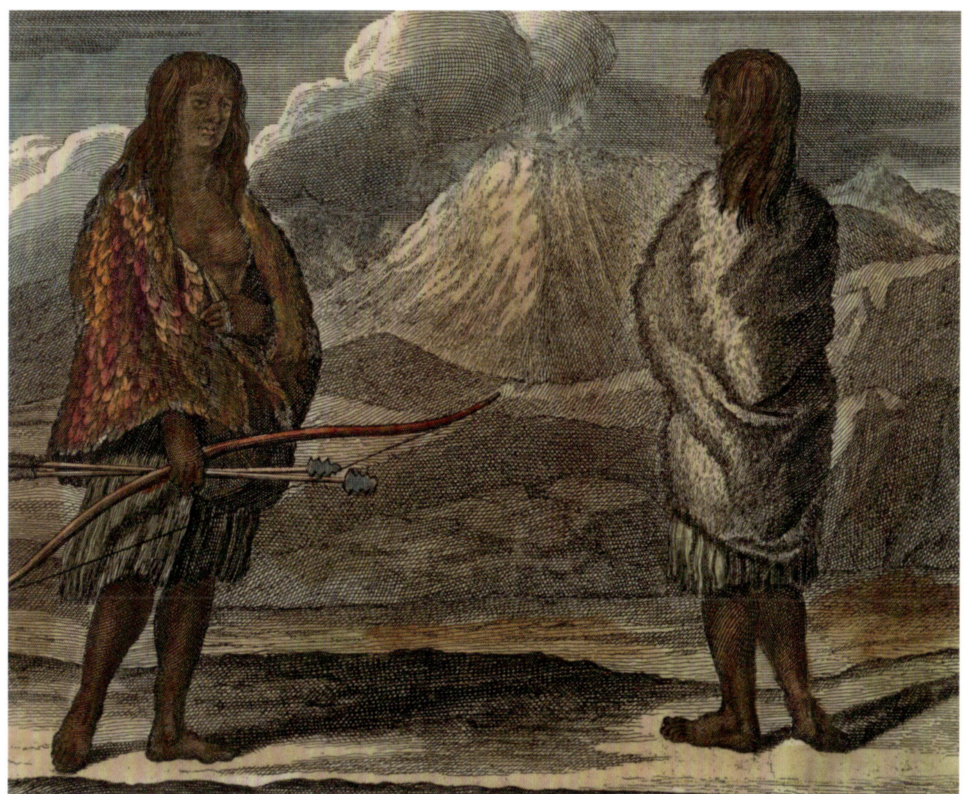

Two Native Californian women of the San Francisco Bay area are shown in traditional attire. The figure at left, likely a person of distinction, is adorned with a cape of bird feathers; the woman at right is wearing a cape of deerskin. Both are wearing skirts of split tules. Ludwig Choris, hand-colored engraving (detail). Courtesy of The Bancroft Library, University of California, Berkeley

European nations had begun carving up the Americas into spheres of influence and ownership beginning in the late fifteenth century, when Columbus, sailing under the Spanish flag, landed on the Caribbean island of Hispaniola in 1492. When the conquistadors Hernán Cortés and Francisco Pizarro subjugated the Aztecs in Mexico and the Incas in modern-day Peru, Spain strengthened its claim over the hemisphere. From these two bases Spain expanded into Florida and over much of South America. By the mid-sixteenth century its vast New World empire was governed as two large regions: the Viceroyalty of Peru, comprising what is now Panama and most of western South America; and the Viceroyalty of New Spain, encompassing Mexico, most of Central America, parts of the Caribbean, and southern North America, including the provinces of Baja and Alta California.

In its colonial enterprise, Spain sought to develop productive communities, modeled on those at home, that would hold and defend its territory. In these later years of the empire, however, the Crown's treasury was vastly depleted, and new ventures had to be carried out economically. The Spanish approach to colonization comprised three distinct institutions, which worked together: military presidios, or forts; pueblos, or civilian towns; and missions, which were under the control of the Church. The military was charged with keeping peace, guarding against foreign incursions, and controlling native populations. The Church was responsible for converting native peoples and educating them in European values. Pueblos attracted private settlers and entrepreneurs to develop industries and commercial opportunities, although mercantilist policies restricted trade with foreign nationals. The Baja California peninsula, initially thought to be an island and named "California" after a mythical land of Amazons in a popular romance, was one of the last areas to be colonized, beginning with the arrival of the Jesuits in 1697. By 1767 the Jesuits had established

1542
The Spanish explorer Juan Rodríguez Cabrillo explores California coast; sails into San Pedro Bay, claims land for king of Spain.

1565
St. Augustine founded on Florida coast—the oldest continuously occupied settlement of European origin in North America.

1579
English explorer Francis Drake, sailing around the world, lands in northern California.

1595
Spanish galleon *San Agustín* breaks up on beach near Drake's Bay.

seventeen struggling missions among the sparse population between La Paz and Rosarito, before the Spanish Crown, fearful that the Jesuit order had become too powerful, expelled them from the New World and transferred spiritual jurisdiction to the Franciscans. Shortly thereafter, Spain took steps to extend its Pacific frontier northward.

It was thus don Gaspar de Portolá, newly appointed *comandante* of the Californias, and Junípero Serra, the first father president of the Alta California missions, who opened this region to the Europeans. The Spanish plan called for first establishing outposts at San Diego and Monterey to delineate the extent of Spain's colonial territory. Presidios would be founded strategically along the coast, located on favorable harbors with access to the interior. Eventually each would become the nucleus of a town. Each presidio would have a detachment of about seventy soldiers, and *escoltas* (groups of soldier guards) would be stationed at the five to eight missions within its district. Married men with families were favored for these assignments. Their duties included protecting the colony from foreign incursions, maintaining order among the neophytes (Native American mission converts), and protecting the missions from attacks by non-Christian Indians. As the missions would support the presidios with agricultural products and workers, presidios and missions initially would be established in tandem; additional missions would be founded in areas well populated with native peoples, whom the Church regarded first and foremost as potential converts.

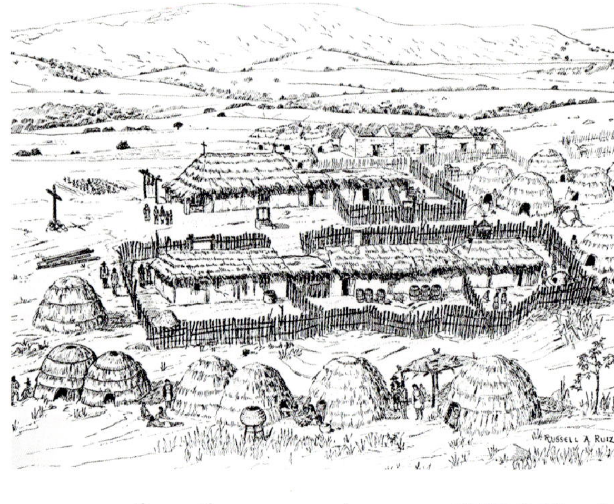

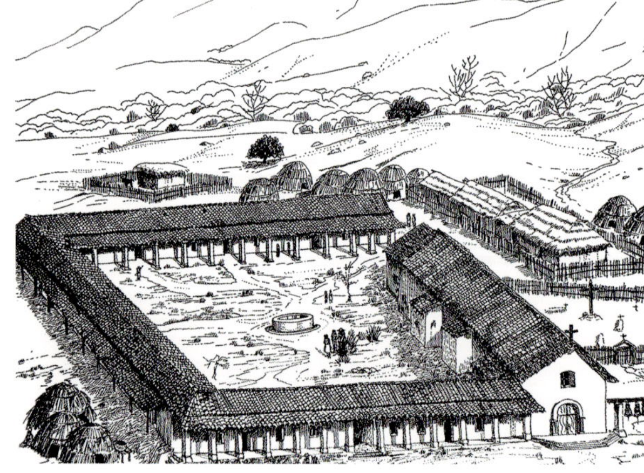

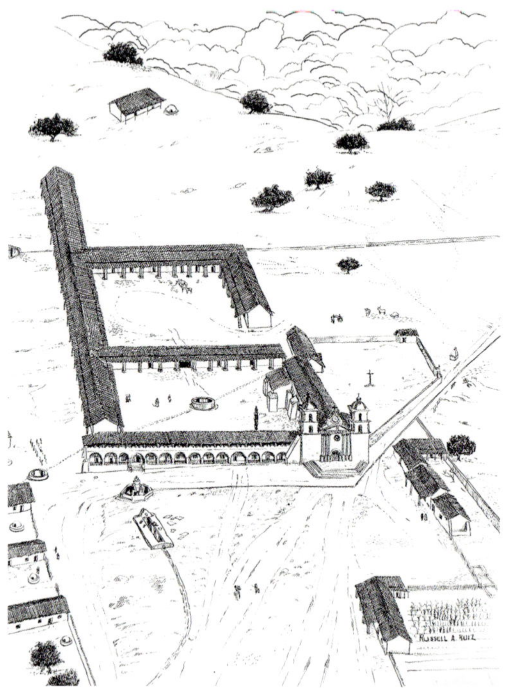

Three phases in the life of Mission Santa Bárbara, showing how the mission *casco* grew over the course of some fifty years. UPPER LEFT: The mission in 1787, one year after its founding, with thatched-roof adobe buildings; at rear is the church; in front is the *convento* and storehouses surrounded with palisade walls, along with traditional Chumash dwellings for the neophytes. LOWER LEFT: The mission in 1812, with a completed quadrangle of tile-roofed adobe buildings; at right is the church; the *convento* is in front, and the living quarters of unmarried neophyte women and workshops make up the other two sides. ABOVE: The mission in 1832; a splendid stone church has replaced the one of adobe, and the workshops and storehouses have been expanded; adobe neophyte dwellings sit to the left of the plaza, facing the soldiers' quarters on the right. Drawings by Russell Ruiz. Courtesy of the Santa Bárbara Mission Archive-Library

1602–1603
The Spanish explorer Sebastián Vizcaíno sails along the California coast.

1697–1767
Spain colonizes Baja California as Jesuits establish 17 missions.

1750
Some 300,000 Native Americans, living in about 80 autonomous tribes, inhabit the region known as Alta California.

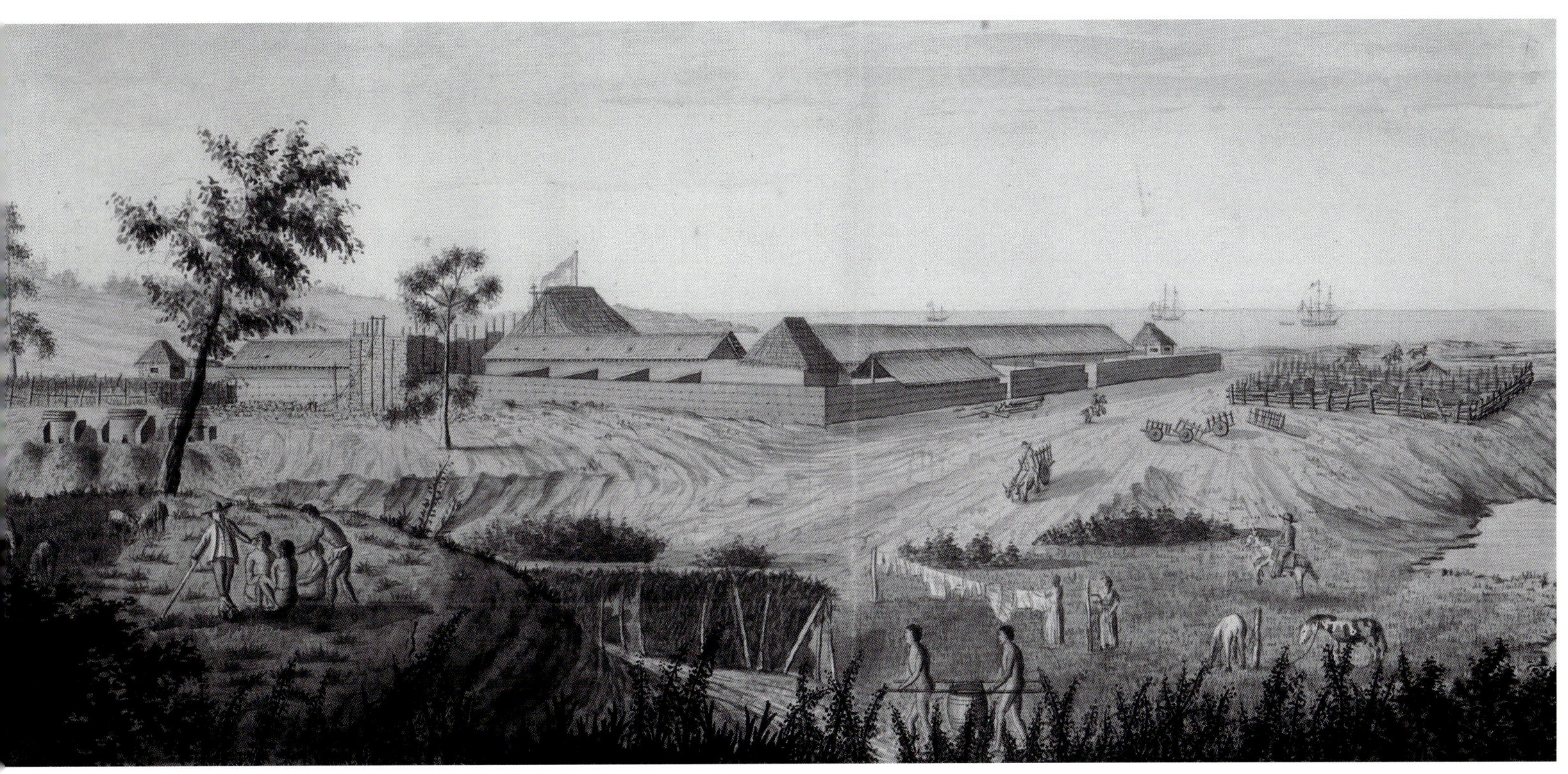

Presidios—the military component of Spanish colonization—consisted of the residences of officers, soldiers, and their families; rooms for provisions and arms; and a chapel, all enclosed within a stout defense wall. In this view of the Monterey Presidio, ca. 1792, individuals in the foreground are hanging out laundry and socializing; at the fort, the new church is under construction. Tiles are being made at kilns on the hillside. In the distance, sailing ships lie at anchor in Monterey Bay. José Cardero, ink, wash, and pencil drawing on paper (detail). Courtesy of The Bancroft Library, University of California, Berkeley

Junípero Serra, a native of Mallorca, Spain, had joined the Franciscan order at sixteen, received his doctorate, and, in 1750, volunteered for missionary work, spending the next eight or nine years in the Sierra Gorda of north-central Mexico. During the next decade he was based at the Colegio de San Fernando in Mexico City, taking various preaching expeditions to parts of Mexico. When he first walked into Alta California, he was fifty-six years old, suffering from asthma and an infected leg that troubled him the rest of his life. Serra would labor among the California missions until his death in 1784.[12]

In spring 1770, some eight months after first arriving at San Diego, Portolá set out to find Monterey Bay, a first attempt having proved unsuccessful. He headed overland while Serra sailed up the coast, and the two groups came together in June among the evergreens on the shores of Monterey Bay. There they held the ceremony whereby the Spanish explorers claimed possession of place. "In the presence of all the officers of land and sea, together with all their subordinates," Serra wrote, "an altar was prepared, the bells were hung up and rung, the hymn *Veni, Creator* was sung[,] ... the large cross and the royal standards were set up and blessed, and I said the first Mass.... Afterwards we sang the *Salve Regina* to Our Lady before a statue given by His Excellency, which stood on the altar.... The entire celebration was accompanied by frequent salvos from the guns aboard ship and ashore."[13] The Spanish flag was raised and saluted and a few additional rituals performed; then all present sat down to a feast to celebrate the founding of the Monterey Presidio and Mission San Carlos Borromeo.

Within a year, Serra decided to move the mission to a new site in the Carmel valley some five miles away, preferable for its better soil and water, proximity to native groups, and distance from the Monterey Presidio. He likely wished, in the delicate words of the historian Hubert Howe Bancroft, "to remove his little band of neophytes, and the larger flock

1767
Spain expels Jesuits from Baja California; Franciscan order assumes jurisdiction.

1769
Spanish expeditions under Gaspar de Portolá and Father Junípero Serra head north from La Paz; found San Diego Presidio and Mission San Diego de Alcalá.

1770
Monterey Presidio and Mission San Carlos Borromeo are founded.

1771
Missions San Antonio de Padua and San Gabriel Arcángel are founded.

Founding Alta California

Between 1769 and 1823, a total of four presidios, twenty-one missions, and three pueblos were established in Alta California. Missions were founded in areas where there was sufficient native population to warrant the institution, with specific locations identified for construction of the mission headquarters—the *casco*—selected for the availability both of water and of cultivable land. At each new establishment, the Franciscan fathers were forcibly educated in the nuances of the local environment. Virtually all the early missions were moved to new sites within their first few years, primarily away from floodplains. Some, such as Mission Santa Clara, were moved several times. Those missions founded later benefited from knowledge of the land obtained from earlier neighboring institutions: of the last eight missions established, none was relocated. At Mission Santa Inés, the success of the *casco* location was so assured that fields were planted, building foundations laid, and the aqueduct system begun months before the official dedication. Nearby Mission La Purísima, on the other hand, suffered twenty-five years at an unfavorable location. When most of the buildings were devastated by earthquake and floods in 1812, the padres finally abandoned the original site for sunny Los Berros Canyon, some five miles distant. The new site was not only sheltered from the chilling winds and fog of the lower Santa Ynez River valley but also closer to El Camino Real, the land link between the colony's communities.[14]

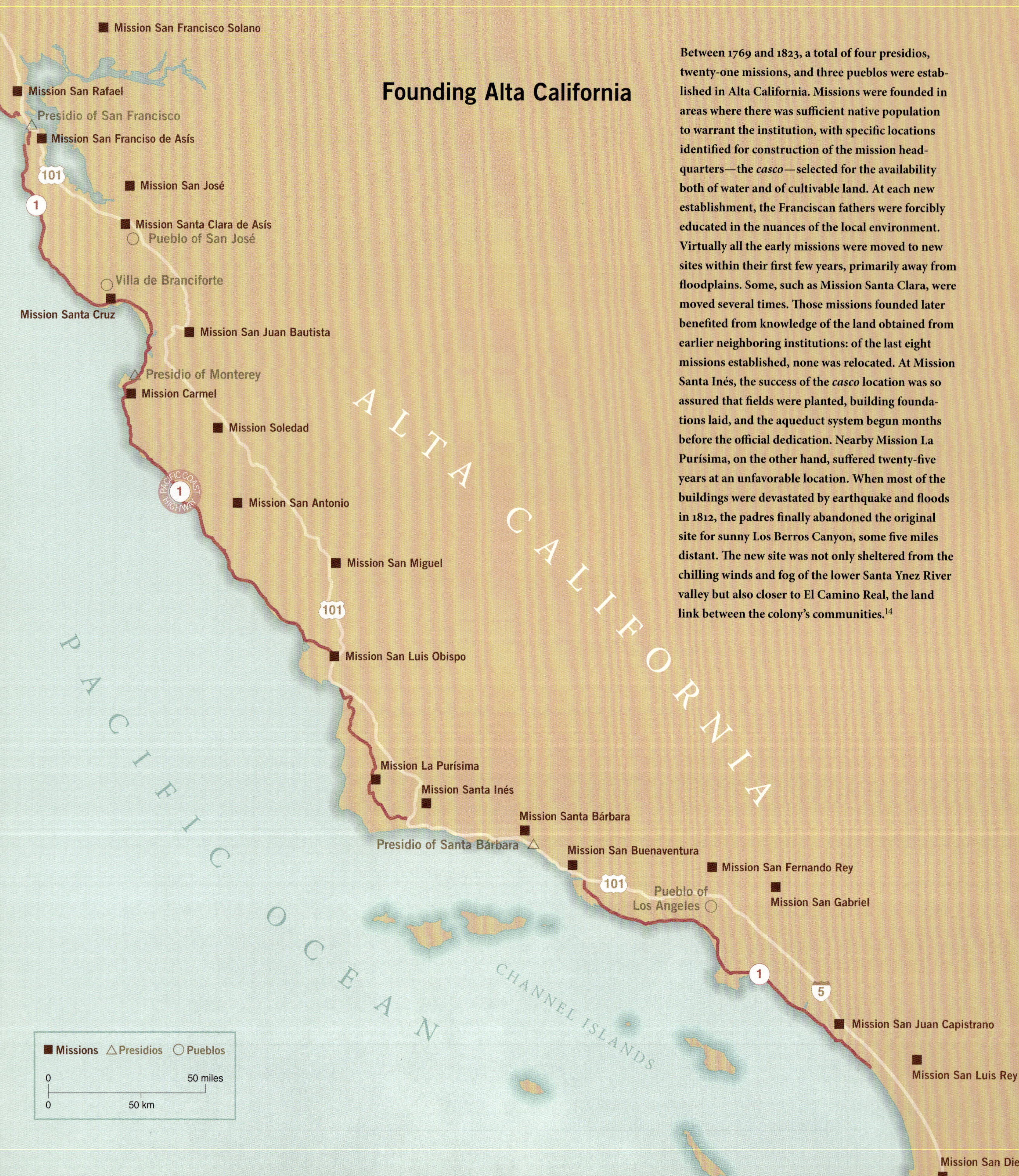

The sequence and physical location of the early missions' foundings reveal the colonizing zeal during Serra's tenure. Following upon San Diego and San Carlos Borromeo with their companion presidios, Serra founded the region's third mission, San Antonio de Padua, in 1771, in an oak-studded valley among the Salinan people. That same year Fathers Cambón and Somera founded Mission San Gabriel, Arcángel, in southern California, while Serra established Mission San Luis Obispo in northern Chumash territory in 1772. After establishing Mission San Juan Capistrano in 1776, Father Serra returned to the north, where that same year the San Francisco Presidio and its partner mission, San Francisco de Asís, were founded to protect that newly discovered bay from Russian incursions; Mission Santa Clara and its adjacent Pueblo de San José were placed at the bay's southern shore the following year. The fourth and final presidio, Santa Bárbara, was established in 1782, along with Serra's last mission, nearby San Buenaventura.

Serra was succeeded as father president by Fermín de Lasuén, who continued the settlement of California, founding Missions Santa Bárbara and, nearby, La Purísima in 1786 and 1787. Farther north, in 1791, Santa Cruz and Soledad were added to the Monterey Presidio District. In 1797, the Villa de Branciforte was founded near Mission Santa Cruz, and three more northern missions were established—San José, San Juan Bautista, and San Miguel—along with San Fernando Rey, located only twenty miles northwest of the Pueblo de la Reina de Los Angeles (founded in 1781). Nearby San Luis Rey followed the next year. In 1804 Mission Santa Inés was the last to be established south of San Francisco Bay, by the new father president, Esteban Tapis. In 1822, in the later years of the mission period, as the Spanish Alta California colony pushed northward, San Rafael, a chapel of Mission San Francisco de Asís, was granted mission status. The final and northernmost mission, San Francisco Solano, was founded at Sonoma in 1823 by Father José Altimira.

Date of Founding	Institution	Native American Groups
1769	San Diego de Alcalá	Ipai, Tipai, Luiseño, Pai Pai, Kiliwa
1770	San Carlos Borromeo del Río Carmelo	Costanoan, Esselen
1771	San Antonio de Padua	Salinan, Esselen, Yokuts
1771	San Gabriel, Arcángel	Gabrielino (Tongva), Serrano, Cahuilla
1772	San Luis Obispo de Tolosa	Northern Chumash, Yokuts
1776	San Francisco de Asís	Ohlone/Costanoan, Coast Miwok, Bay Miwok, Patwin, Wappo
1776	San Juan Capistrano	Acjachemen (Juaneño), Luiseño, Gabrielino (Tongva)
1777	Santa Clara de Asís	Ohlone/Costanoan, Yokuts, Sierra Miwok
1782	San Buenaventura	Ventureño, Island Chumash
1786	Santa Bárbara, Virgen y Mártir	Barbareño, Ineseño, and Island Chumash
1787	La Purísima Concepción de María Santísima	Purisimeño, Ineseño, and Island Chumash, Yokuts
1791	La Exaltación de la Santa Cruz	Ohlone/Costanoan, Yokuts, Sierra Miwok
1791	Nuestra Señora de la Soledad	Esselen, Ohlone/Costanoan, Yokuts, Sierra Miwok
1797	Mission del Gloriosísimo Patriarca San José	Ohlone/Costanoan, Bay Miwok, Coast Miwok, Patwin, Plains Miwok, Yokuts, Sierra Miwok, Wappo, Nisenan
1797	San Juan Bautista	Ohlone/Costanoan, Yokuts, Sierra Miwok
1797	San Miguel, Arcángel	Salinan, Yokuts
1797	San Fernando Rey de España	Fernandeño, Tataviam, Ventureño Chumash, Vanyumé, Kitanemuk
1798	San Luis Rey de Francia	Luiseño, Ipai, Cupeño, Cahuilla,
1804	Santa Inés, Virgen y Mártir	Ineseño and Island Chumash, Yokuts
1817	San Rafael, Arcángel	Coast Miwok, Wappo, Pomo
1823	San Francisco Solano	Coast Miwok, Wappo, Lake Miwok, Patwin, Pomo

Major groups are not distinguished from those with smaller representation; groups with only trace presence are not listed.[15]

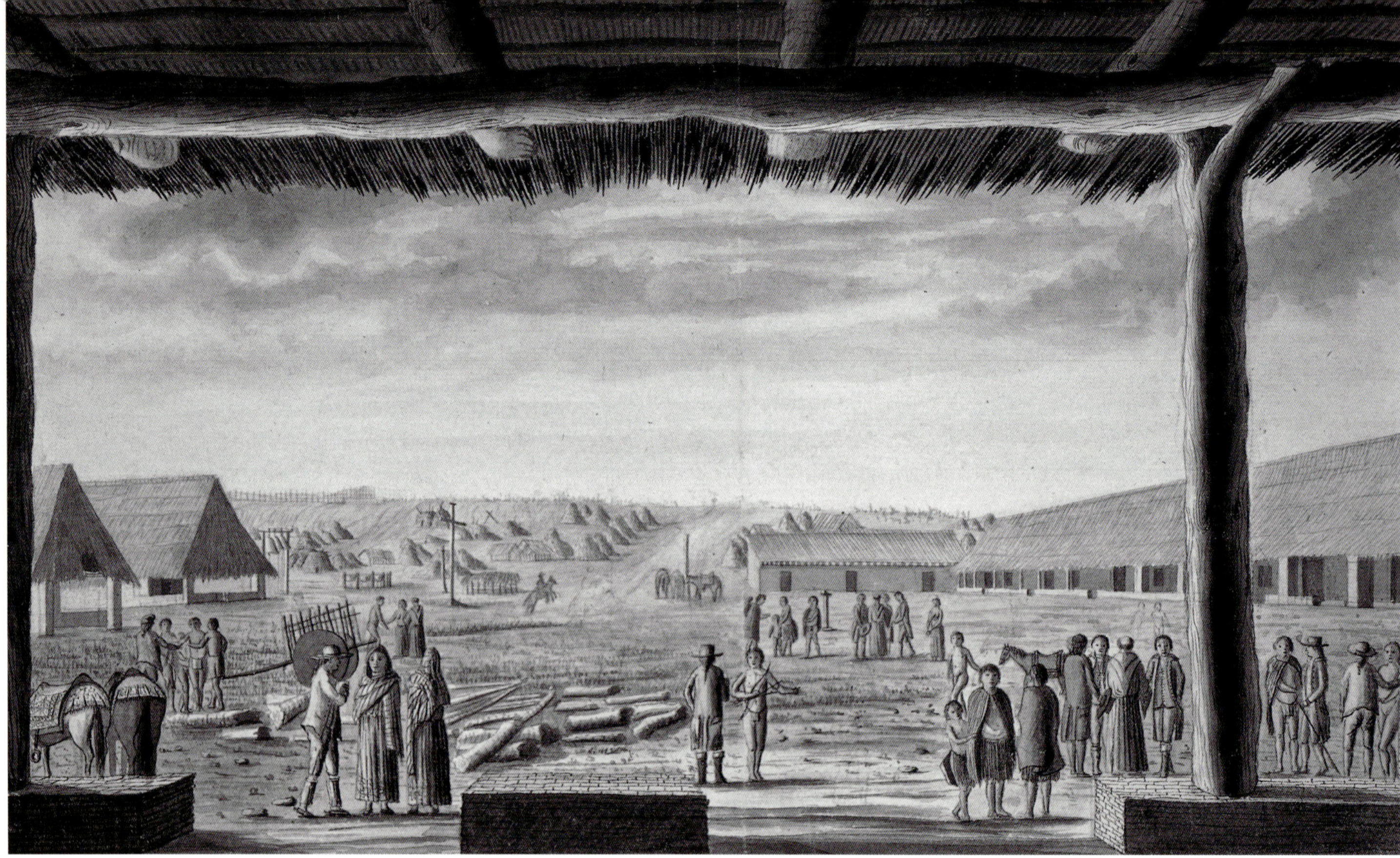

View of the church, at left, and other buildings at Mission San Carlos Borromeo, 1791. The structures are covered with thatched roofs, and the dwellings of the neophytes' *ranchería* lie in the background. Visitors from a European expedition can also be seen. José Cardero. Ink and pencil drawing on paper. Courtesy Museo de América, Madrid

he hoped to gather, from immediate contact with the presidio soldiers, always regarded by missionaries as necessary evils tending to corrupt native innocence."[16] Work began on construction of the new mission, with Indians from Baja California supplying much of the labor. Like its presidio, the mission was a simple affair: a one-room chapel of mud-covered vertical poles with a thatched roof, a four-room dwelling, a granary, and accommodations for Indians and soldiers. Within a few years, an adobe chapel and other buildings were constructed.

From his headquarters at Carmel, Father President Serra would oversee the development of the mission system, supervising resident fathers and communicating the needs of the missions to the Franciscans' home base at the Colegio de San Fernando in Mexico City. Serra also negotiated with the governor of Alta California on matters affecting the Church and its charges, in particular the generally strained relations between missions and presidios, a tension that would endure throughout the mission period. He would travel—usually on foot—throughout the mission system and beyond, returning once to Mexico City. And, of course, he would found new missions, sometimes personally, although he did not live to see the construction of the stately churches for which the California missions have become so widely known.

More than other parts of New Spain, Alta California was isolated from political, religious, and commercial centers in Mexico. Overland travel from northern Sonora was abandoned after the Colorado River Yuma revolted and drove out the Spanish in 1781, and the sea route, with its strong southerly currents and headwinds, was difficult to navigate. In good years two supply ships made the trip from San Blas; in several years none came.[17] As a result, Alta California's religious and military authorities operated without rigorous oversight and the colony was largely left to provide for its own subsistence.

1772
Mission San Luis Obispo de Tolosa is founded.

1775
Mission San Diego is attacked by native groups.

1776
San Francisco Presidio and Missions San Juan Capistrano and San Francisco de Asís are founded; native attackers set fire to Mission San Luis Obispo.

1777
Mission Santa Clara de Asís and El Pueblo de San Jose are founded.

1781
El Pueblo de Los Angeles is founded.

In other parts of the New World, conquistadors such as Cortés and Pizarro had encountered organized military empires with centralized governments and efficient systems of taxation. While conquest there involved a number of famously bloody battles and massacres, the Spanish did not have to win ultimate victory town by town. Preceded by the devastations of disease, the invaders defeated the ruling elite, installed themselves at the top, and then proceeded to govern a population accustomed to centralized authority.

In California, however, negotiations with native groups were conducted anew for the founding of each mission and presidio. The largely autonomous nature of the individual tribes determined that success with one group did not ensure acceptance by their neighbors. Spanish and native Californians experienced these initial encounters quite differently, with the Franciscans seeking religious conversions to their proffered faith and the native Californians trying to make sense of these strange beings who had arrived in their homelands. In addition, once the native peoples had come to the mission and received baptism,

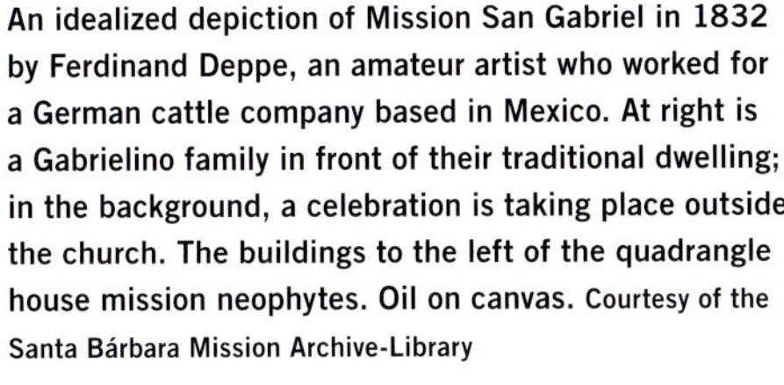

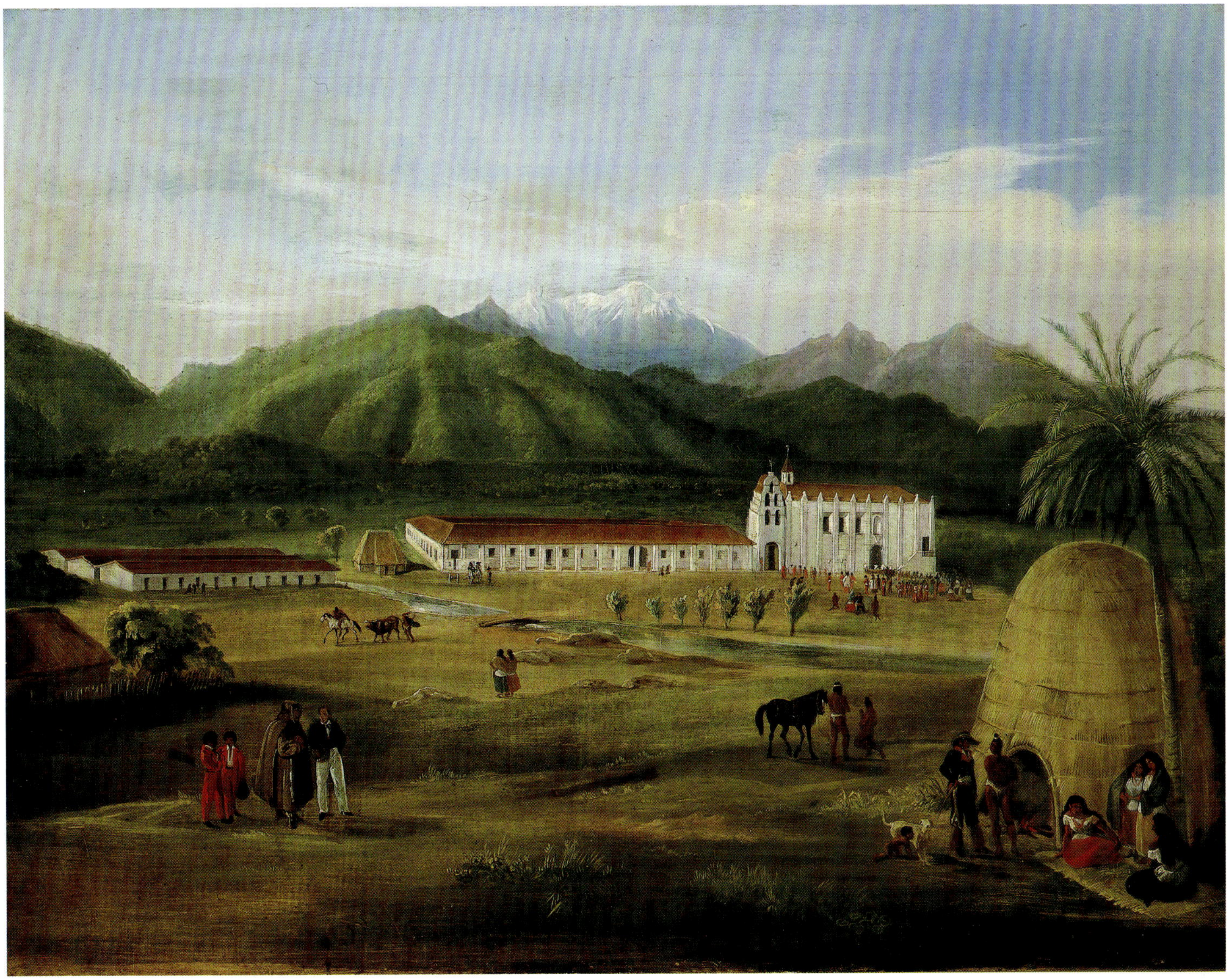

An idealized depiction of Mission San Gabriel in 1832 by Ferdinand Deppe, an amateur artist who worked for a German cattle company based in Mexico. At right is a Gabrielino family in front of their traditional dwelling; in the background, a celebration is taking place outside the church. The buildings to the left of the quadrangle house mission neophytes. Oil on canvas. Courtesy of the Santa Bárbara Mission Archive-Library

1782
Santa Bárbara Presidio and Mission San Buenaventura are founded.

1784
Father Junípero Serra dies; Father Fermín Lasuén succeeds him as head of Alta California missions.

1786
The French traveler Jean-Francois de Galaup, comte de La Pérouse and his expedition visit California; Mission Santa Bárbara is founded.

The Indians were sadly afraid when they [first] saw the Spanish arriving on horseback. Thinking them gods, the women ran to the brush, and hid themselves, while the men put out the fires in their huts. They remained still more impressed with this idea [that the Spaniards were gods], when they saw one of their guests take a flint, strike a fire and commence smoking.... An occurrence however soon convinced them that their strange visitors were, like themselves, mortals, for one of the Spaniards leveled his musket at a bird and killed it.... [The effect it produced] of taking life, led them to reason, and deduce the impossibility [that] the 'Giver of Life' [would] murder animals, as they themselves did.... They consequently put [the Spanish] down as human beings, of a nasty white color, and having ugly blue eyes.

—From a traditional Tongva narrative of an early encounter at Mission San Gabriel, as recorded by Hugo Reid

the Spanish regarded this as a definitive choice, binding for the rest of their lives and for their descendants. Along with providing a description of events, the contrasting accounts of early meetings reveal the meanings such events had for the different cultures involved.

Father Serra's first meeting with the Costanoans at Monterey Bay occurred in 1776, soon after the founding of the presidio. Francisco Palóu, Serra's first biographer, reported that "they did not show themselves during those days, since the many volleys of artillery and muskets fired by the soldiers [in celebration of the founding] had frightened them.... But they began to approach after a little while, and the Venerable Father began to offer them gifts to bring about their entrance into the fold of the Holy Church and gain their souls, which was the principal purpose of this presence."[18] Exchanging gifts on the initial meeting of different groups is a tradition as old as humanity, and glass beads had long been received by natives of North America, along with metal items such as hatchets and knives and decorative mirrors and bells. The Costanoans became friendier, Palóu later noted, "when they received the little presents... of beads and trinkets to attract them, and also of our food. They continued to visit us frequently," he reported, "bringing us presents of small value, principally shell-fish and grass seeds."[19]

One native account of early gift giving was preserved in tribal stories that Victoria Reid, Gabrielino wife of the American Hugo Reid, provided her husband and that he published as a series of letters to the *Los Angeles Star* in 1852.[20] "The presents were never refused, but only those consisting of goods were put to any use whatever," the story related. "All kinds and classes of food and eatables were rejected and held in abhorrence. — Instead therefore of partaking of them, they were buried secretly in the woods. Two old Indians... related... of having once assisted when boys to inter a quantity of *frijol* [beans] and Indian corn, just received from the whites. Some length of time afterwards, being out in the woods amusing themselves, [the Indians] came where the articles were deposited. Their surprise knew no bounds when they beheld an infinity of stalks and plants unknown to them, protruding through the earth.... [T]he wizards pronounced it *white* witchcraft!"[21]

In many instances initial interactions between Europeans and the indigenous peoples were peaceful. In others, they were not. Three times within two years of its founding, Mission San Luis Obispo de Tolosa was attacked by Indians, whose flaming arrows set the thatched roofs on fire. In 1775 a force of Tipai, who had a reputation for being combative, attacked the fledgling Mission San Diego de Alcalá, burned its structures, and killed three Spaniards, including one of the priests.[22] And often, initially peaceful relations soon gave

1787
Mission La Purísima is founded.

1790
Adobe church at Mission San Luis Obispo is completed.

1791
Missions Santa Cruz and La Soledad are founded; adobe church at Mission San Francisco de Asís is completed; skilled artisans begin arriving from New Spain.

1792–93
The British explorer George Vancouver, charting California coast, visits several missions.

[Two priests] suddenly found themselves surrounded by a numerous band of armed savages. Fearing an attack, and not knowing what else to do, one of the friars unfurled a banner, which on one side showed the picture of Our Lady of Sorrows, and held it up to the gaze of the howling Indians. No sooner had the gentiles set their eyes on the image of the Blessed Virgin than they threw down their bows and arrows. . . . The Indians from all the neighboring rancherías . . . gazed in wonder and delight at the holy Virgin.

—From an account by Francisco Palóu of an early encounter at Mission San Gabriel

way to the harsh realities of colonial subjugation. Throughout the region, according to both Spanish and native accounts, Spanish soldiers behaved brutishly toward native women. At Mission San Gabriel, according to the native narrative, shortly after the initial contact with the Tongva, "a larger party of soldiers arrived who commenced tying the hands of the adult males behind their backs; and making signs of their wish to procure women. . . . Harsh measures obtained for them what they sought, but the women were considered [by their fellow Tongva to be] contaminated and put through a long course of sweating, drinking of herbs, etc. They necessarily became accustomed to these things, but their disgust and abhorrence never left them till many years after. In fact every white child born among them for a long period was secretly strangled and buried!"[23]

Gradually, over the course of a few decades, the mission system took root in the new soil of Alta California. The mission establishments expanded, and the simple structures of pole and thatch were eventually replaced with more substantial buildings of adobe or stone. Artisans arrived in the colony to manage construction and train neophytes in the building trades. As more indigenous peoples were converted, the populations of the missions grew accordingly. By the turn of the century, for example, Mission San Carlos Borromeo had some nine hundred neophytes.

From the beginning intended to be much more than centers of religious instruction, the missions developed into expansive estates that included ranchos, farms, and centers of industry. Each mission establishment extended well beyond its *casco*, encompassing a vast agricultural enterprise of grazing lands and ranches for cattle, horses, sheep, and specialty crops. In many instances a given location was devoted exclusively to production of a single class of livestock. Mission San Gabriel, Arcángel, for example, developed seventeen ranchos for raising cattle and horses and fifteen ranchos for raising sheep, goats, and pigs.[24] Those ranchos that supported a small chapel as well as permanent residents were designated *asistencias*. At Mission Santa Bárbara's *asistencia* at Rancho San Marcos, grapes were tended and wheat cultivated. The fertile lands of the coast and central valleys soon teemed with herds of wild cattle and horses.

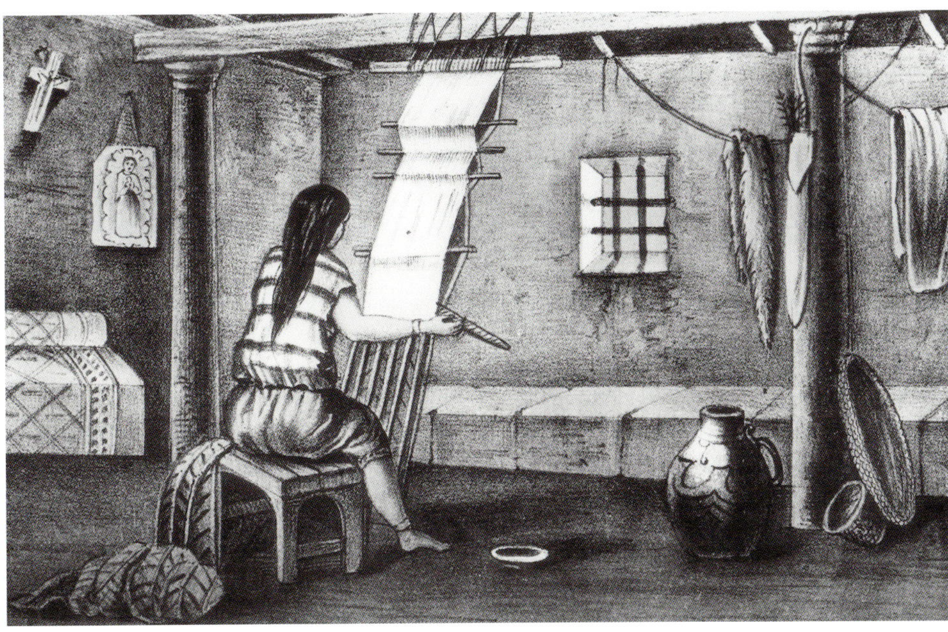

In addition to spreading the Roman Catholic faith, mission establishments were centers of industry where neophytes were taught such skills as weaving, carpentry, and leatherworking. Here a woman works at a loom weaving woolen cloth, which will be made into blankets and serapes. From the nineteenth-century book *San Fernando Rey de España*, by János Xántus. National Gallery of Art, Washington, D.C., Gallery Archives

1794
Adobe church at Mission Santa Cruz; stone church completed at Monterey Royal Presidio Chapel.

1797
Villa de Branciforte is founded; Missions San José, San Juan Bautista, San Miguel, and San Fernando Rey are founded; stone church completed at Mission San Carlos Borromeo and large adobe church at Mission La Soledad.

1798
Mission San Luis Rey is founded.

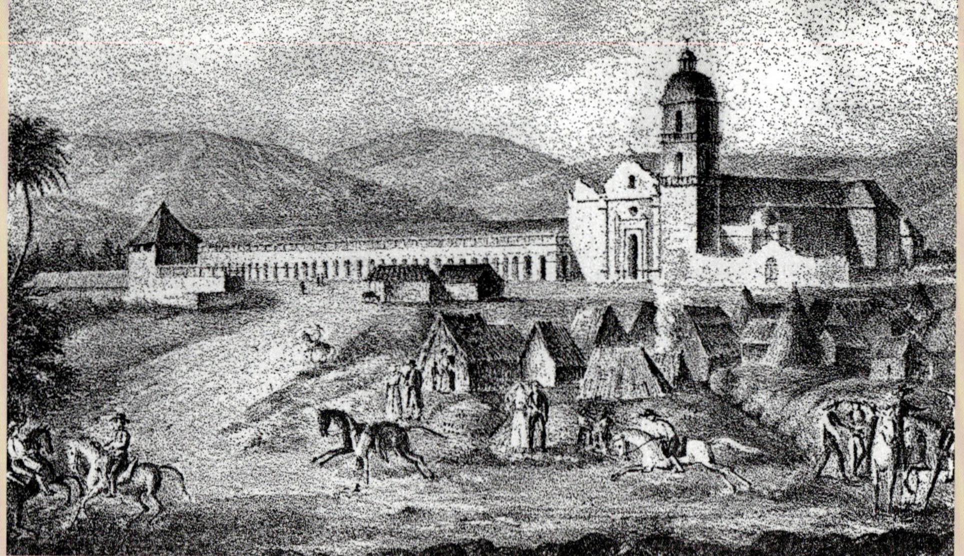

The Mission *Casco*

A mission's first buildings were simple structures, generally constructed of palisades (*palizadas*) or of forked poles with wattle-and-daub (*bajareque*) walls and roofed with thatched reeds (*tule*) or straw (*paja*). These *jacales* were mud plastered and whitewashed to resemble adobe buildings.[25] Gradually improvements were made. As a mission grew in size and resources, these early structures were replaced with ones of adobe, stone, and *ladrillos* (flat, fired construction bricks), with *tejas* (curved, fired roof tiles) laid over reeds and wood framing.

The center of the community, the *casco*, typically included a closed quadrangle of four long adobe sides, one of which was the church (a). The center of a mission's spiritual life, the church was generally the first building to be constructed of adobe.[26] Its towering facade dominated the plaza (b), where public ceremonies took place, residents socialized, and visitors arrived. The priests' residence building, the *convento*, typically flanked the church and provided the only public access to the closed quadrangle behind. Several *conventos* had two stories, and most boasted *corredores*, covered exterior walkways featuring columns of *ladrillos* or, in the north, redwood posts. The *convento* contained the *sala* (reception hall), an office with library, a kitchen, a dining room, a pantry, priests' sleeping rooms, guest rooms for visitors, storerooms, and a private chapel. Some *conventos*—for example, San Fernando, San Antonio, San Miguel, and San Gabriel—contained wineries; others had granaries.

The other two sides of the mission quadrangle—those connecting the church and *convento* wings—contained workshops, storage areas, and the *monjerío*, where the unmarried neophyte women resided under supervision. The enclosed interior patio was secured from the outside by the absence of exterior windows and doors, present only in the *convento* and church, and by a single *zaguán*, a gated access for carts and animals. This inner space teemed with the activity of cooks, weavers, leather and metal workers, and candlemakers. Today's contemplative interior mission gardens are romantic fabrications, as we will see.

The *casco* also included infrastructure and industries, and these facilities, as well as gardens and orchards (c), were scattered around the complex.[27] Water was indispensable, brought from miles away through elaborate systems of Roman design. Ditches (d) directed water to irrigate vineyards, orchards, and gardens, while penstocks powered grist mills. Potters and their assistants made ceramic kitchen wares. Construction tiles were fired in large kilns, and wool was carded, spun, and woven into cloth. Tanneries saw the processing of hides, and soap and candles were rendered from fats.

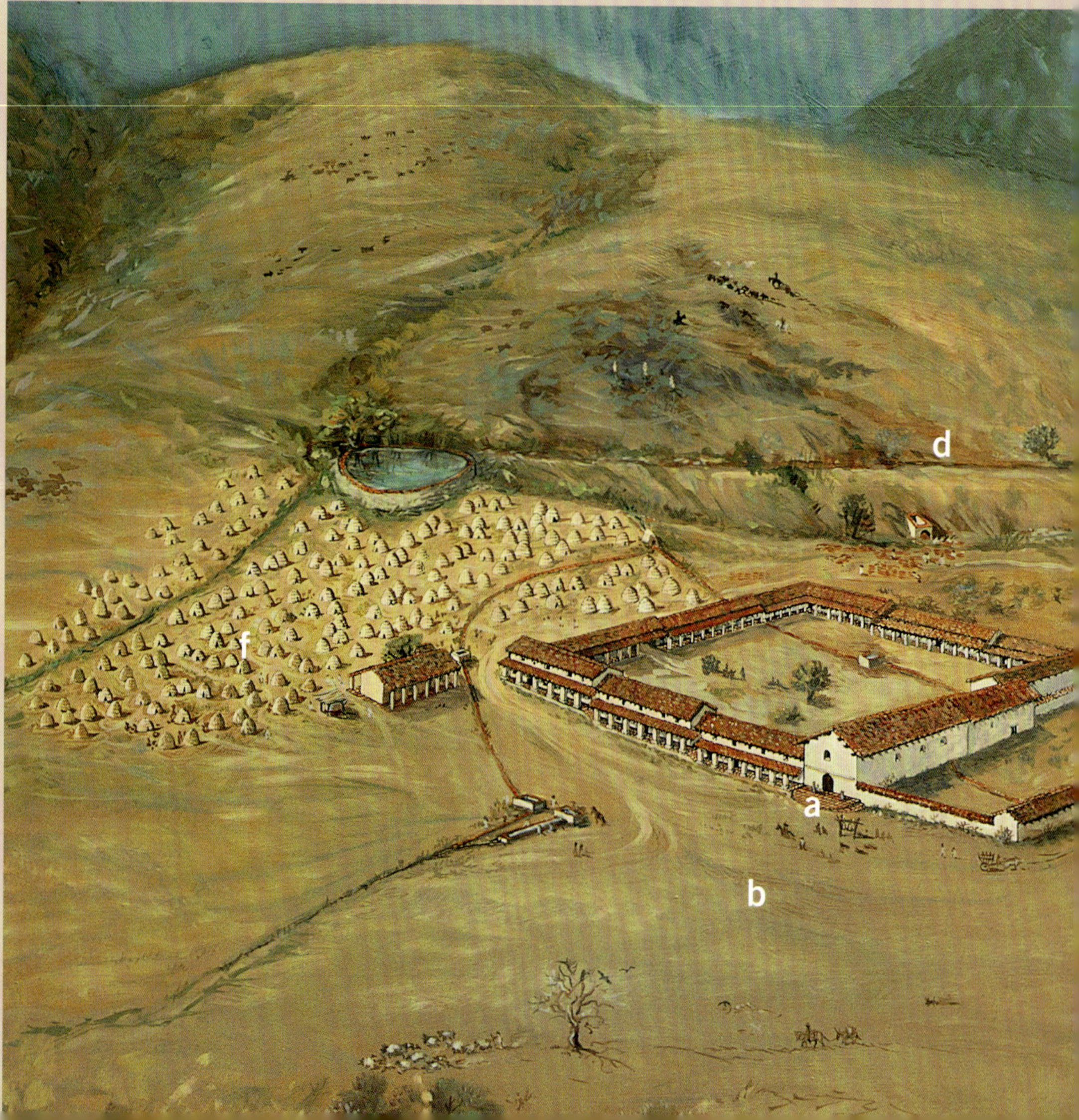

The church fronted an open plaza that featured a *lavandería* for washing clothes with a fountain for drawing water. The soldiers' quarters (e)—adobe dwellings usually built in a row with a *corredor* on the front—sat on one side of the plaza. The married neophytes' *ranchería* (f) was generally located on the other side. "Two hundred paces from the mission, [begins] the Rancheria, or village of the Indians," noted the French sea captain Auguste Bernard Duhaut-Cilly, who visited Mission San Luis Rey in the late 1820s. "It is composed of thatched huts, merely, of various shapes, the larger number conical, scattered or grouped without plan over a great extent of ground. Each one of these hovels holds a family, and all together contained at this time a population of more than two thousand persons."[28] All neophyte houses at the missions were initially of traditional construction materials and design: tule or brush over a frame of branches. As building programs at missions progressed, rows of single- or double-room adobe apartments were built, occupied by families who had distinguished themselves by service to the missionaries and the community. The Frenchman noted that often these adobe residences "did not suit the health of the Indians, accustomed to their cabins; so that many of the padres have decided to let them build themselves huts to their taste."[29]

OPPOSITE, TOP: This drawing of Mission San Luis Rey, with its imposing bell tower and arcaded *convento*, illustrated a book by the French traveler Auguste Duhaut-Cilly, who visited California in the 1820s. Neophyte houses can be seen in the foreground. Courtesy University of Southern California, on behalf of the USC Special Collections

BELOW: Overview of the first *casco* of Mission La Purísima, destroyed in the earthquake of 1812, based on recent archaeological and documentary studies. Karen Foster-Wells, oil on canvas, 1993. Courtesy of the artist

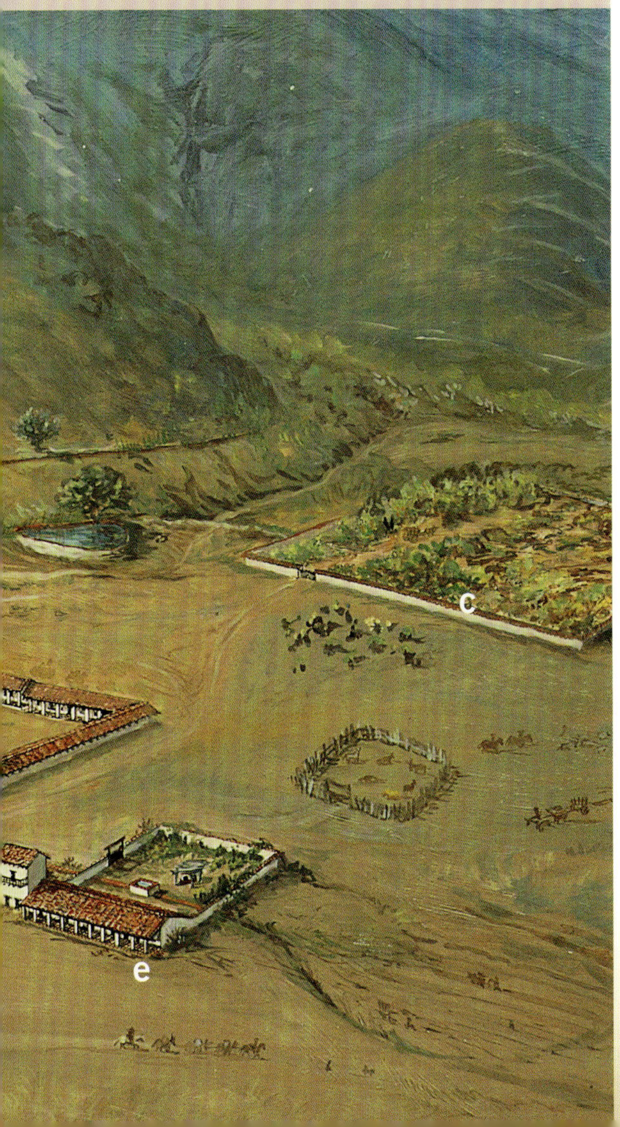

The average mission, at its peak, could claim about one thousand native men, women, and children and was administered by two Franciscan priests, with support from the small *escolta* of soldiers and their families. The missions were self-sufficient complexes, laid out according to a common plan. "The buildings in some of the missions are more extensive than in others, but they are almost alike in form," observed a San Diego resident in 1828. "In all of them are comfortable living quarters for the ministers, warehouses for the storing of goods, granaries large enough for the grain, places for making soap, rooms of weaving, carpenter shops, forges, wine presses, cellars, large patios and corrals, separate apartments for the Indian youth of both sexes, and, finally, as many workrooms as the establishment may require. Adjoining these and connected with them are the churches."[30]

By 1829 the population of Mission San Luis Rey de Francia, the largest of the mission establishments, "was about three thousand Indians, who were all employed in various occupations," wrote the American trader Alfred Robinson. "Some were engaged in agriculture, while others attended to the management of over sixty thousand head of cattle. Many were carpenters, masons, coopers, saddlers, shoemakers, weavers &c., while the females were employed in spinning and preparing wool for their looms, which produced a sufficiency of blankets for their yearly consumption. Thus every one had his particular vocation, and each department its official superintendent, or alcalde."[31]

Such descriptions of material prosperity notwithstanding, the native peoples suffered greatly from the upheaval occasioned by the mission system. Mission life constituted a profound disruption of their traditional lives, which were governed by seasonal rhythms, not a daily regimen of agricultural labor, and which involved very different ritual, sexual, and social practices from those enforced by the padres. In a practice developed in New Spain called *reducción* (literally, "reduction"), implemented in all but the southernmost Alta California establishments, baptized individuals from throughout a mission's territories were removed from their traditional homes and settled together in large *rancherías* at the mission *casco*. They were no longer free to choose their place of residence, which henceforth would be determined by the padres. As a mission's holdings expanded, converts were drawn from more distant regions. For these natives, separation from their ancestral landscapes, which were infused with an abundant richness of cultural and religious knowledge, was in itself devastating. Diverse native groups who did not speak each other's languages, and who may have been traditional enemies, were gathered into large communities and expected to live in harmony. The German traveler G. H. Frier von Langsdorff, watching an exhibition of dancing at Mission San José in 1806, noted that they were divided into groups distinguished by costumes and songs. "These people formerly lived in great enmity with each other," he wrote, "but are now united here by religion; not however so entirely but that sparks of their ancient enmity still remain alive and cannot be extinguished.... The fathers never can prevail upon them to intermarry... and [they] do not mingle in the society of the other tribes but with a certain kind of reserve."[32]

For Indian residents mission life blended Spanish and native cultures. They continued many traditional practices: they cooked over simple fire rings in familiar brush dwellings, fashioned stone tools, harvested local foods, and, for a time, maintained many of the social and political networks from their home villages. In some missions they also maintained important practices such as ceremonial dances. Europeans generally failed

1802
Epidemic decimates neophyte population at Mission Soledad.

1803–07
Expedition led by the Russian Nikolai Rezanov, with the German Georg Heinrich von Langsdorff, visits California.

1804
Mission Santa Inés is founded.

to understand the extent to which these ritual activities were important for keeping alive traditional worldviews. The Indians at Mission San José were "permitted to retain their former habits and customs not interdicted by the missioneros.... In their dances, amusements, sports, ornaments, etc., they are liberally indulged," Langsdorff noted.[33] "In their dances they remain almost always in the same place, endeavoring partly with their bows and arrows, partly with the feathers they hold in their hands and wear upon their heads... and by the variations of their countenances, to represent battles, or scenes of domestic life. Their music consists of singing, and clapping with a stick. The women have their own particular song, and their particular manner of dancing."[34]

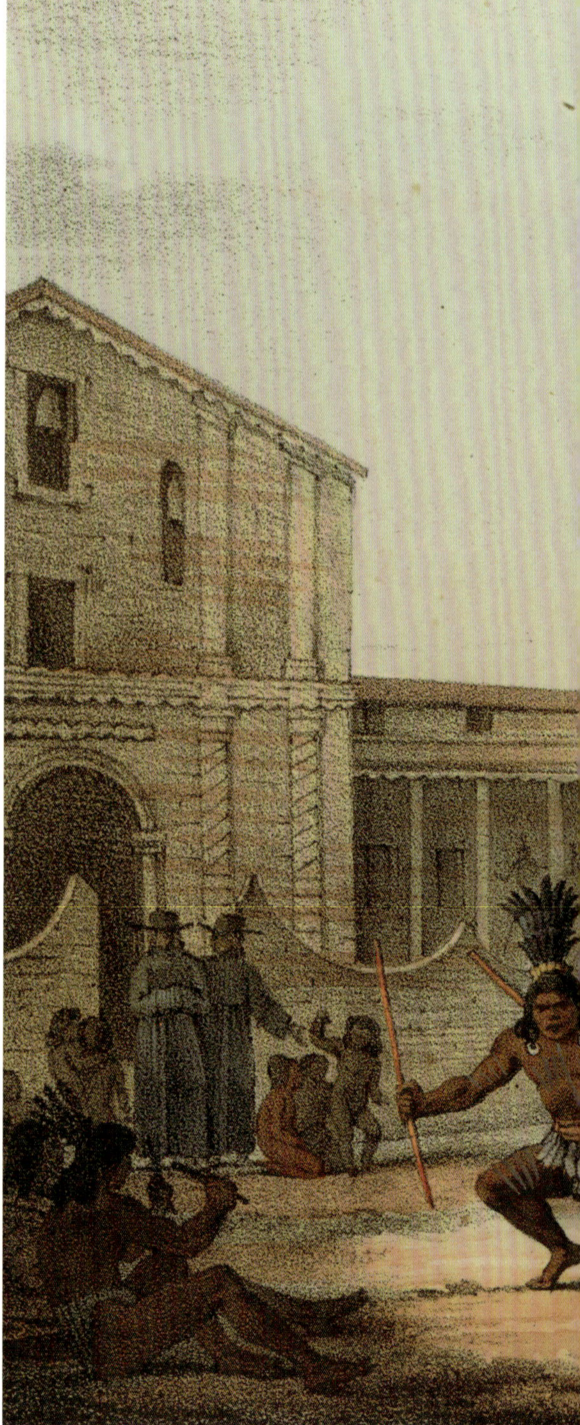

Rituals and symbols of Catholicism, meanwhile, were often accommodated by baptized converts who had little understanding of their meanings. Although attendance at services was mandatory, both the language barrier and the paucity of priests relative to the missions' indigenous populations ensured that both the substance of Catholic dogma and the inner beliefs of the neophytes were, in the beginning, mutually unintelligible.[35] Hugo Reid relates that when his wife Victoria's Gabrielino people were first converted, for example, they "had no more idea that they were worshiping God than an unborn child has of astronomy. Numbers of old men['s] and women['s]... whole stock of Spanish was contained in the never-failing address of '*Amar a Dios*!' and [their] religion, as Catholics, consisted in being able to cross themselves, under an impression it was something connected with hard work and still harder blows." They called baptism "*soyna*, 'being bathed.' And strange to say, [it] was looked upon, although such a simple ceremony, as being ignominious and degrading."[36] Eventually the priests would learn something of the local languages, and by 1815 all the missions reported presenting the catechism in local dialects.[37]

Similarly, Spanish missionaries throughout the New World tolerated local practices and deities, often with little understanding of their meanings to the local inhabitants, incorporating many into the flamboyant festivals that were abundant on the Church calendar. By 1815, more than forty years after the founding of the first missions, the traditional activities, which the padres regarded as "superstitions," still practiced by California neophytes included annual ceremonies, hunting rituals, body painting, homage to gods of nature, use of prayer poles, reading omens in dreams, shamanistic practices, and fasting.[38] The cultural meaning of these rituals eluded—or were withheld from—the padres. Fathers at Mission San Luis Rey reported, "We have made very careful inquiries as to the purpose of these ceremonies but we have never been able to obtain any information other than that they did this because their ancestors practiced it."[39] It appears quite likely, however, that these spiritual observances enabled the mission neophytes to maintain important traditional worldviews while adding elements of the new Christianity to their "store of knowledge power."[40]

Mission regulations also demanded changes in the lives of natives that drastically altered their traditional cultures. Strictly enforced routines of work and prayer produced regimented days that sharply contrasted with the relative independence of their traditional village lives. "The type of life which the natives lead in the mission is very monotonous," noted a Russian visitor in 1822. "When they get up they go to church. After having heard Mass, of which they understand not a single word, they assemble in a public place where they are given a light breakfast which is followed by hard labor until noon. At that hour the church bell beckons them and the Indians are obliged to quit work, throw themselves on their knees and enter into prayer.... After this act of devotion, each one of them, a basket in hand, comes to the common kitchen where he receives his dinner consisting of cooked

1805
Stone church completed at Mission San Gabriel.

1806
Great Stone Church dedicated at Mission San Juan Capistrano; adobe church completed at Mission San Fernando Rey; fire burns Mission San Miguel; measles epidemic at Mission San Francisco de Asís; Russian expedition under Nikolai Rezanov visits Alta California.

1809
Churches completed at Missions San Buenaventura and San José.

1810
Mexican War of Independence begins.

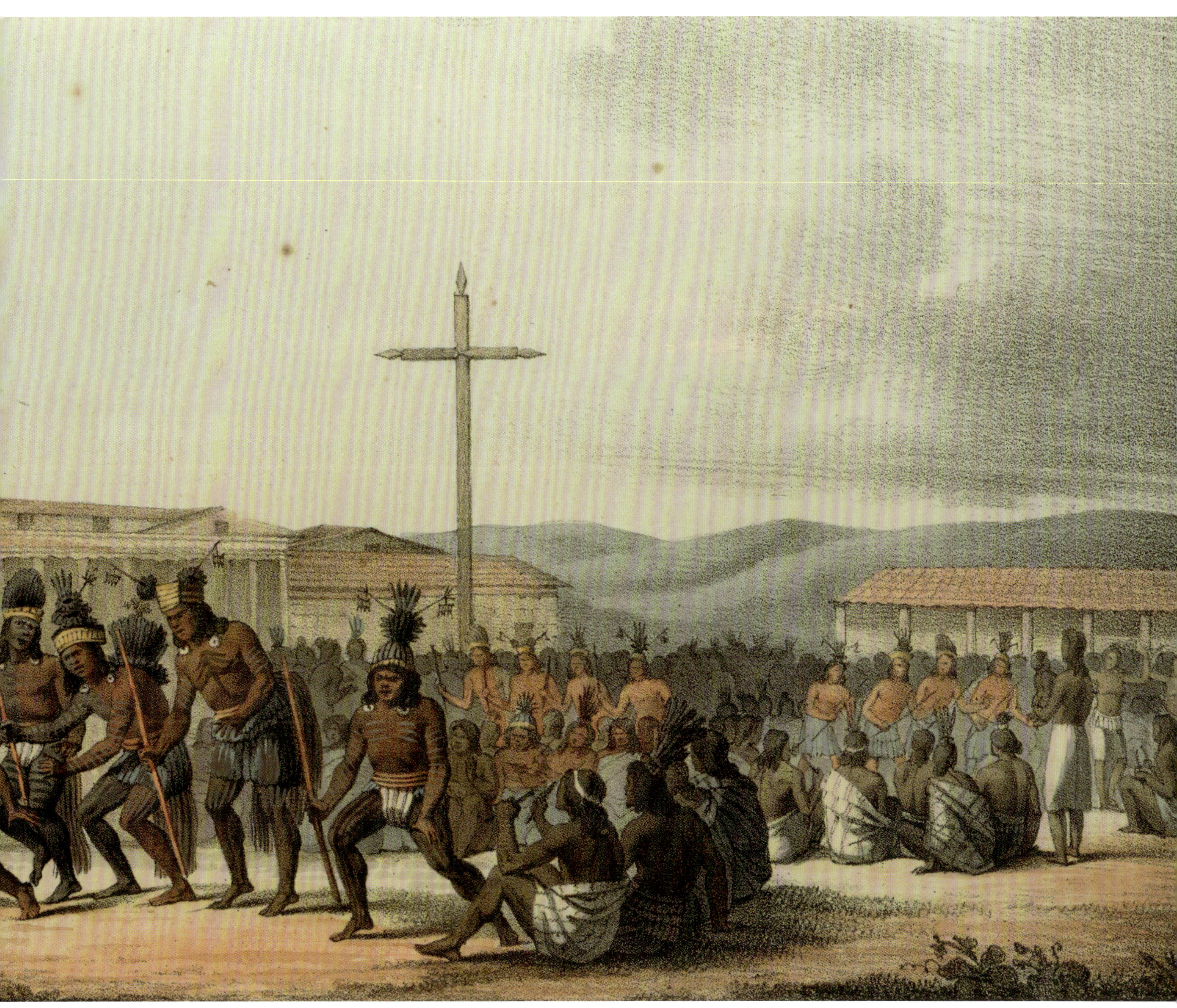

The plaza in front of the church was a mission community's public space, where gatherings and festivals were held. In this scene at Mission San Francisco de Asís in October 1816, several groups of native dancers are accompanied by musicians and singers. Such traditional rituals, tolerated by the Franciscans, played an important role in the perseverance of tribal cultures. Ludwig Choris, hand-colored engraving. Courtesy of The Bancroft Library, University of California, Berkeley

OVERLEAF: Six neophtye dancers prepare for a ceremony at Mission San José in 1806. Their body paints were made from local minerals: white from clay, red from hematite and cinnabar, and black from charcoal; one is adorned with feathers. From a book by the German traveler Georg Heinrich von Langsdorff, published in 1814. Wilhelm Gottlief Tilesius von Tilenau (attr.), ink, wash, and gouache drawing on paper (detail). Courtesy of The Bancroft Library, University of California, Berkeley

1812
Earthquake devastates Missions San Juan Capistrano, Santa Bárbara, and La Purísima; several other missions are damaged; Russian traders found Fort Ross.

1813
Adobe and ladrillo churches completed at Missions San Diego and San Antonio de Padua.

1815
Adobe and ladrillo church completed at Mission San Luis Rey.

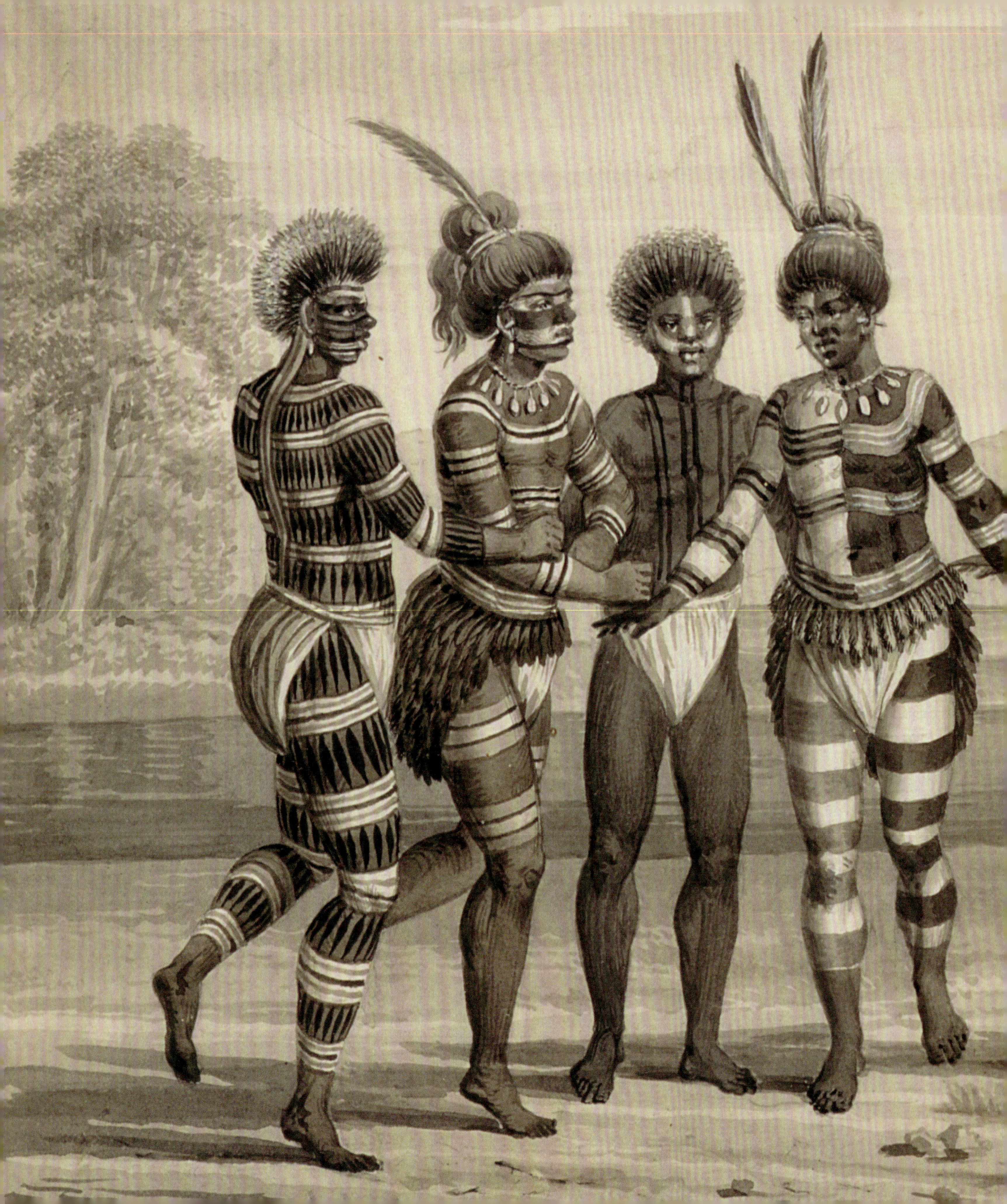

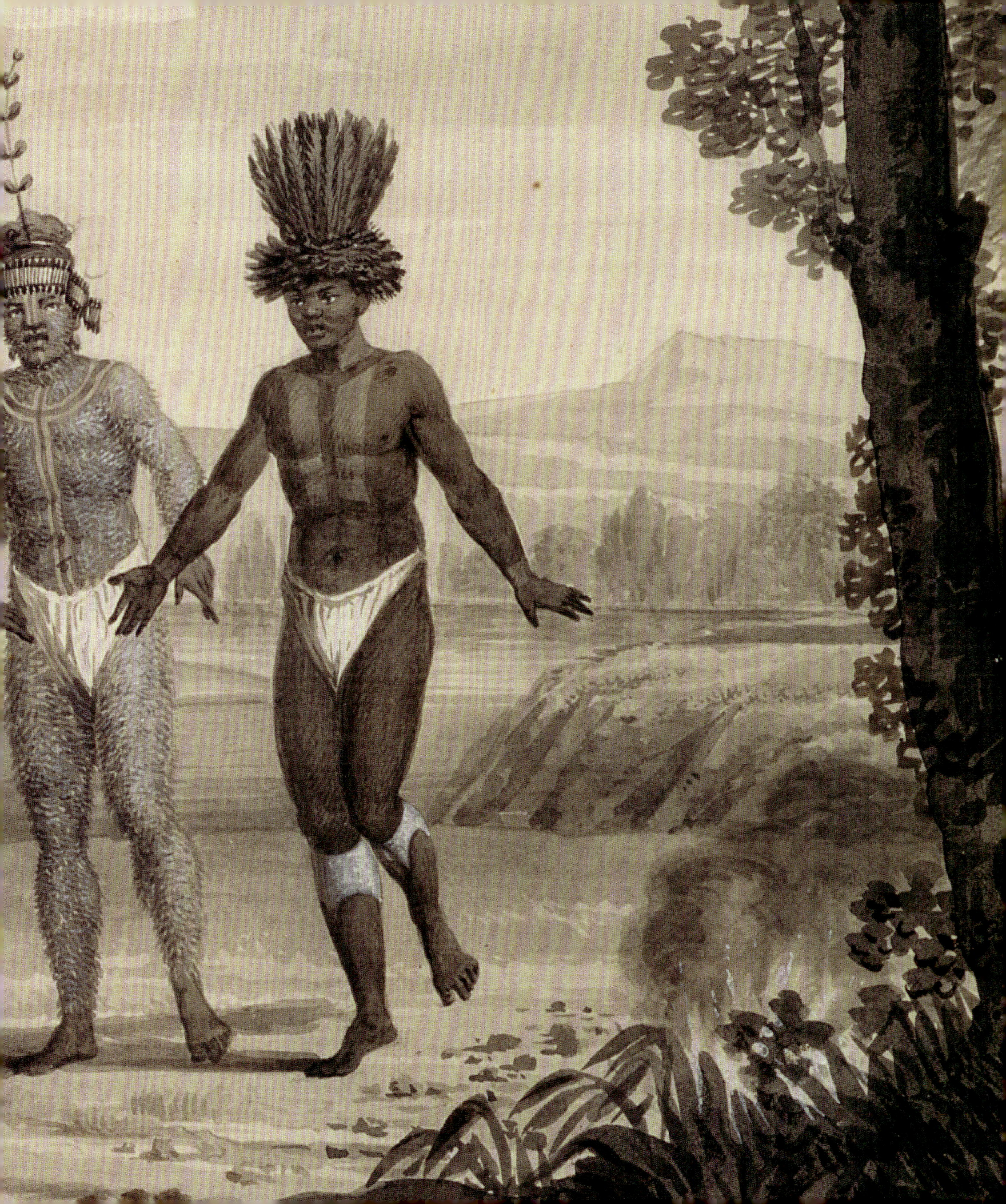

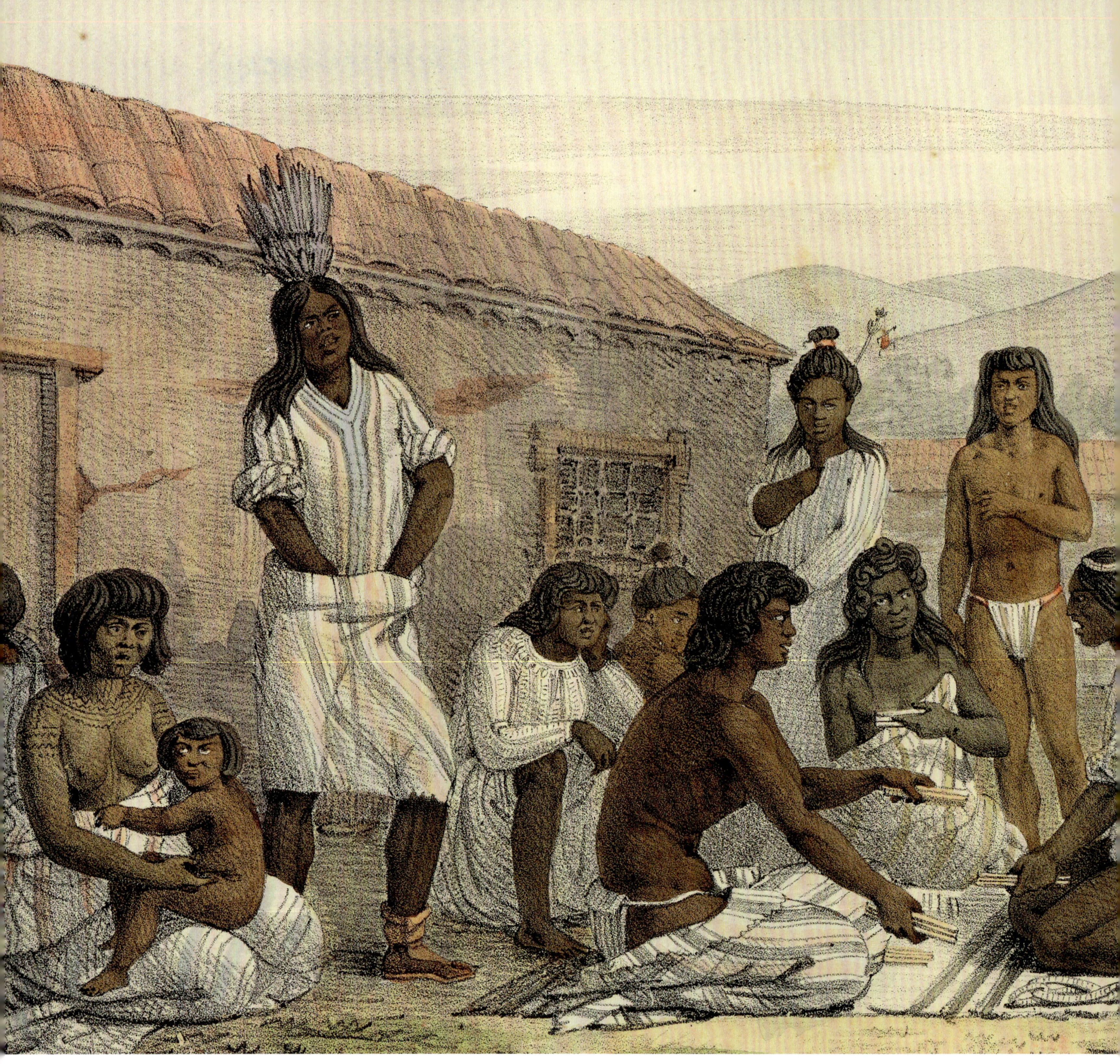

Native Californians continued traditional gambling games at the missions, an activity that helped preserve social and recreational aspects of village life. These neophytes are using gaming sticks and wagering over the string of shell beads seen on the blanket. They are clothed in woolen garments woven at the mission. Ludwig Choris, print, from *Voyage pittoresque autour du monde,* 1822. Research Library, The Getty Research Institute, Los Angeles, California

1816
Church at Pala Asistencia completed; Russian expedition led by Otto von Kotzebue visits California with the Ukranian artist Ludwig Choris, who paints and sketches native Californians.

1817
Mission San Rafael founded as an *asistencia*; Native American rebellion at Mission San José; Thomas Doak paints *reredos* at Mission San Juan Bautista; final church dedicated at Mission Santa Inés; the Chumash artist Juan Pacífico works on wall decoration at Mission San Buenaventura.

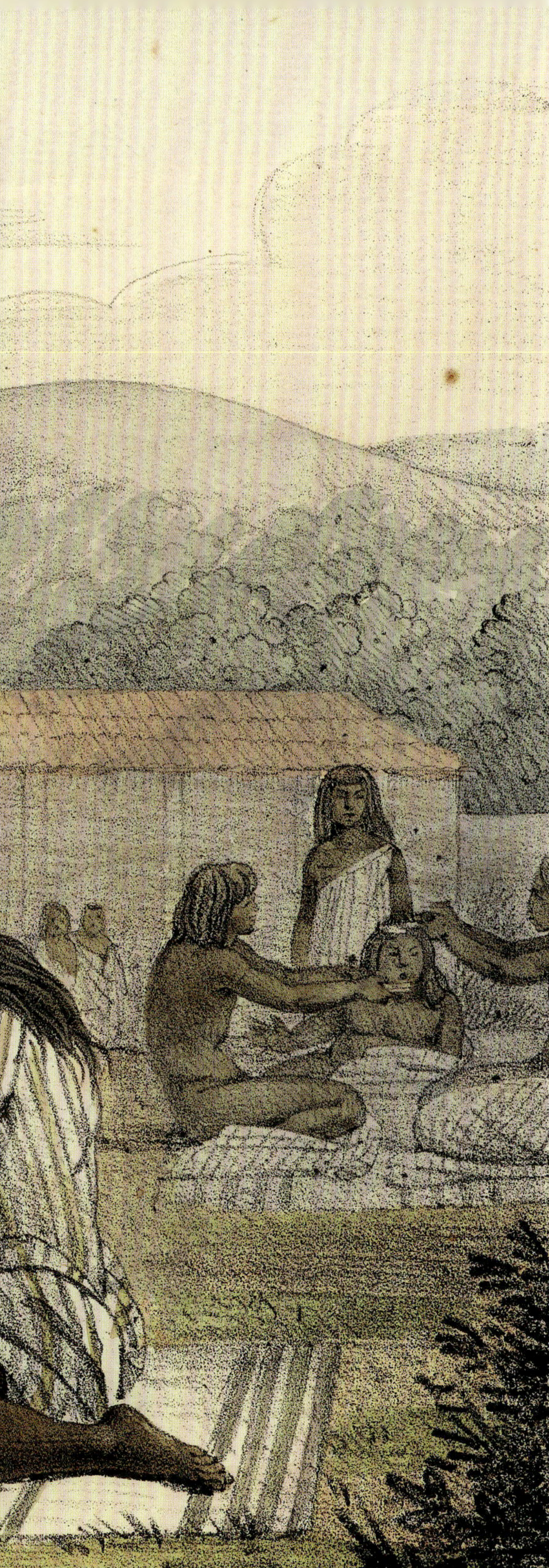

wheat grains which have been boiled in water.... Having finished the noon meal, they work until sunset. Then they go to the church, [and] from there to the kitchen to receive their supper and then they disperse to the houses."[41]

Although some traditional tribal hierarchies transferred to the missions, tribal leaders were often replaced with neophytes who catered to the demands of the Franciscans. Pablo Tac, a neophyte at Mission San Luis Rey, describes their daily routine: "With the laborers goes a Spanish majordomo and... neophyte alcaldes, to see how the work is done, to hurry them if they are lazy, so that they will soon finish what was ordered, and to punish the guilty or lazy one who leaves his plow and quits the field."[42]

Within the mission, natives developed their own social activities that took place at family meals, gambling events, and dances.[43] Neophytes often also responded to the strenuous work regimes with a passive resistance that the Spanish characterized as "indolence" or "ignorance." Native nakedness and sexual practices were viewed with considerable alarm by the padres. Their insistence on monogamous lifelong marriages, as well as on premarital abstinence, was contrary to many traditional practices, resulting in constant conflicts between the Spanish clergy and their indigenous congregations. Punishment was meted out with public lashings, a practice that, while common in Europe, appalled native peoples. Native accounts of mission life describe such punitive measures as the "punishment stocks" at Mission San Buenaventura, located in a jail just east of the mission tower. "One was shaped of wood to cover the foot like a shoe," the Chumash neophyte Fernando Librado recalled. "It was made from two pieces of wood which opened, and... were joined to a ring which went about the knee, and from this ring straps were attached to a belt that went around the waist.... Weights were fastened to the straps.... As punishment the priests would work men and women in the fields with these weighted wooden shoes."[44]

Mission Indians sometimes resisted overtly. Besides the Chumash revolt of 1824 (see p. 31), the most spectacular instance of a tribe's coordinated resistance, myriad individual acts revealed deep antipathy to the foreign occupiers. The neophyte Lorenzo Asisara related the now-well-known story in which the horsewhip tipped with iron (*cuarta de hierro*) used by Father Andrés Quintana at Mission Santa Cruz so angered his victims that, in October 1812, they waylaid and smothered him, crushing his testicles to ensure his death, then freeing the women of the *monjerío*, whereupon, according to an account given by a participant, young people of both sexes "got together and had their pleasure." The Indian rebels placed his body back in his bed, where he was found and presumed dead of natural causes. Two years later, however, the murder was revealed during an argument between several neophytes and resulted in arrests, convictions, and imprisonment.[45]

Missions varied considerably in economic productivity, their relations with native groups, and the tolerability of mission life, rendering it difficult to make generalized statements about the conditions of mission existence throughout Alta California. A visitor noted in the 1830s that some of the mission buildings "are tiled and whitewashed and look neat and comfortable; others are dirty and in disrepair and in every way uncomfortable."[46] Economic success was greatly influenced by the climate and the productivity of the land, but the personalities of the padres were of paramount importance to the tenor of mission life.[47] Resident fathers remained at their institutions for decades and were nearly autonomous in their powers. At Mission San Luis Rey, noted Pablo Tac, "the Fernandino Father is like a king. He has his pages, alcaldes, mayordomos, musicians, soldiers, gardens, ranchos,... horses by the thousand, cows, bulls by the thousand,... 12,000 lambs, 200 goats,

1818
Adobe churches are completed at Missions San Miguel and La Purisima; the French-Argentine privateer Hippolyte Bouchard raids Alta California coast.

1820
Stone church is completed at Mission Santa Bárbara.

1821
End of the Mexican War of Independence. The artist Esteban Munras, aided by neophytes, paints murals at Mission San Miguel.

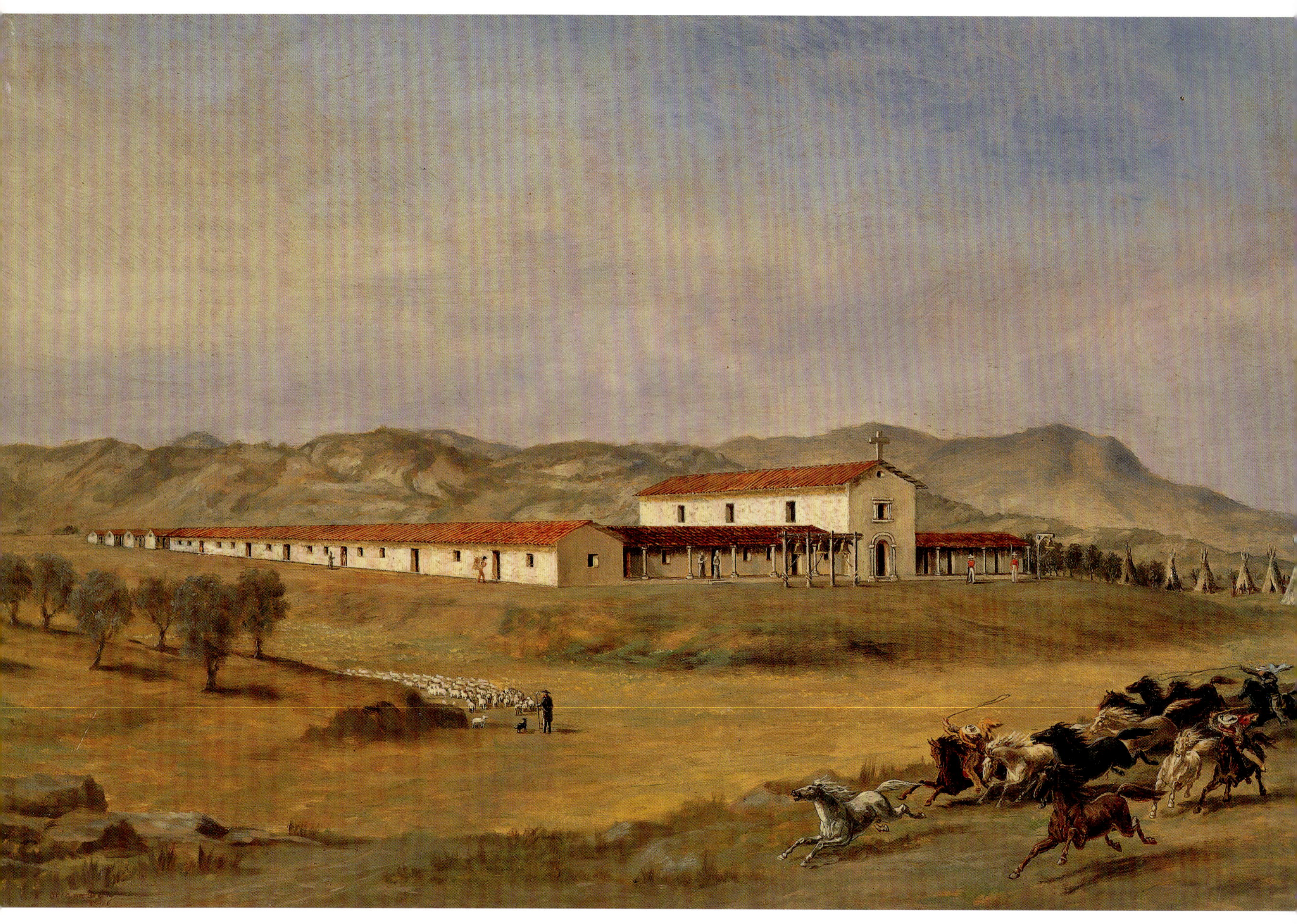

The church, *convento*, and *ranchería* of Mission Soledad, ca. 1820, as imagined by an American artist in the late nineteenth century. A flock of sheep is being tended, while neophyte riders lasso horses in the foreground. Oriana Weatherbee Day, *Mission Nuestra Señora de la Soledad*, 1877–1884. Oil on canvas, 20 × 29¾ in. Fine Arts Museums of San Francisco. Gift of Mrs. Eleanor Martin, 37565

etc."[48] When the American trader Alfred Robinson visited California in 1829, he remarked that while most mission padres were charitable and responsible, some were not, and he reserved his strongest criticism for a priest at San Fernando, whom he described as an "ugly-looking old man, whose looks did not belie his character.... The niggardly administration of this place, compared with the liberality and profusion of the other missions we had visited, presented a complete contrast."[49]

The conditions of mission life, including the practice of *reducción*, had other consequences as well. From their earliest years, most of the California missions suffered from the most devastating result of European colonization: catastrophic death rates. In addition to disrupting traditional cultural practices, the densely populated mission *rancherías* promoted rapid transmission of disease.[50] Spanish immigrants brought maladies to which the natives had no resistance. Influenza, smallpox, and typhoid raced through the villages.

1822
Adobe church completed in El Pueblo de Los Angeles

1832
Adobe chapel replaces fallen church at Mission la Soledad.

1823
Mission San Francisco Solano is founded; Mission San Rafael is granted mission status.

The Chumash Revolt of 1824

The Chumash revolt of 1824 is one of the most important incidents of armed resistance to Spanish domination in the American West. As opposed to other armed uprisings against the Spanish, which were carried out by Native Americans living in traditional villages, it arose among baptized neophytes living within the mission community. Just three years earlier Mexico had successfully wrested its independence from the oppressive hand of Spain, an example not lost on the Chumash of Alta California.

The uprising was ignited at Mission Santa Inés on Saturday, February 21, 1824, and rapidly spread to the neighboring missions of La Purísima and Santa Bárbara.[52] The revolt was apparently sparked by the beating of a neophyte from Mission La Purísima who was visiting a relative imprisoned at the Santa Inés guardhouse. Chumash attacked the soldiers with arrows and set buildings on fire, and two Chumash were killed. The priest and the soldiers and their families remained barricaded until freed the next day by troops from the Santa Bárbara Presidio. The rebels retreated to a row of adobe houses in the neophyte housing, which the soldiers burned down to flush them out. The Santa Inés Chumash insurgents then fled to Mission La Purísima.

When the uprising first began, a messenger from Santa Inés was quickly dispatched to Mission Santa Bárbara, where a general call to arms was issued by the Chumash leader. Women took the children to the mountains for safety while the men armed themselves with bows and arrows and machetes. Although the *escolta* of soldiers was initially withdrawn from Mission Santa Bárbara, an assault on the insurgents was ordered that afternoon, and a furious three-hour encounter ensued. At least two Chumash were killed and four soldiers wounded. After sacking the priests' quarters, the insurgents fled into the mountains and then deep into the interior *tulares* (marshlands). Some fifty Santa Bárbara Chumash who had formerly lived on Santa Cruz Island, meanwhile, stole the mission's two *tomols* and fled by sea to their old village. Father Ripoll, respected among the Chumash, worked to obtain amnesty for the rebels, and by summer most of those who had abandoned Mission Santa Bárbara were persuaded to return.

It was at Mission La Purísima that the armed insurgents held out longest and the punishment was most severe. Word of the Santa Inés uprising had reached the mission the day it began. When those fleeing Santa Inés arrived at La Purísima on Sunday, February 22, they joined local rebels led by the charismatic neophyte Pacomio, who had already taken possession of the mission, with one Chumash and four innocent travelers killed. La Purísima soldiers and their families were allowed to retreat to Santa Inés on February 24; one priest, Father Antonio Rodríguez, remained with his mission's insurgents. The rebel neophytes prepared for the inevitable retaliation, erecting palisade walls, cutting loopholes in the adobe walls, and mounting two small swivel guns. Nearly a month later, a force of about one hundred soldiers (and a four-pound cannon) arrived from Monterey and surrounded the fortified buildings. A morning of intense firing left sixteen Chumash dead and many wounded, along with four wounded soldiers (one mortally). A cease-fire was negotiated by Father Rodríguez, and the Chumash surrendered. Troops from Santa Bárbara arrived, depositions were taken, and sentences were pronounced. Seven Chumash were executed for the murder of the four travelers; the four leaders and eight others received prison terms of eight to ten years in Monterey. The revolt was over.[51]

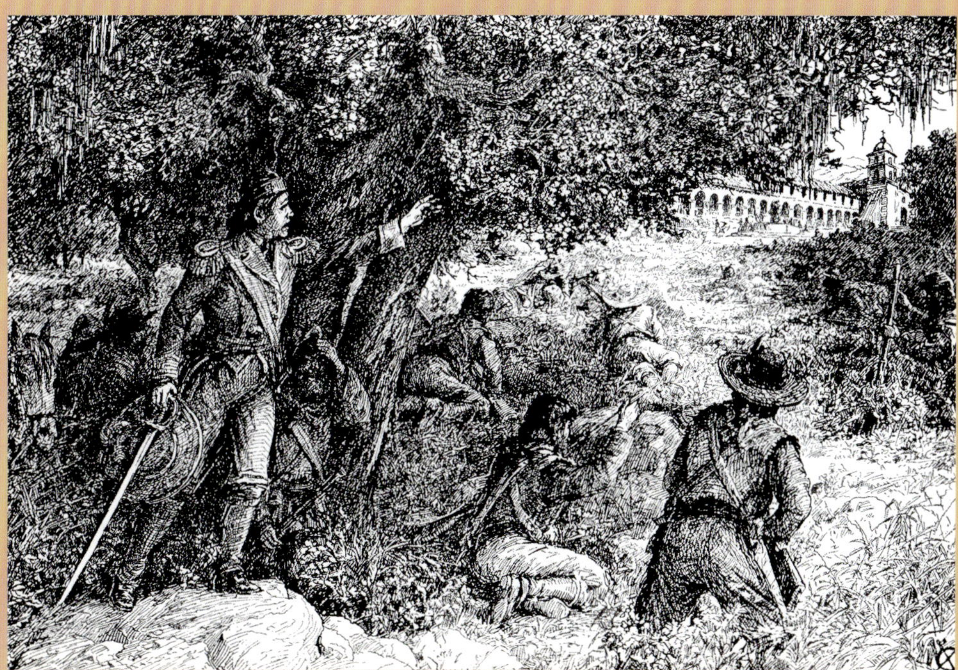

Soldiers prepare to attack rebellious Chumash at Mission Santa Bárbara. This romanticized depiction by the prominent American artist Alexander Harmer first appeared in a popular early-twentieth-century book on the missions. Courtesy Pentacle Press, www.missionscalifornia.com

ABOVE LEFT: Neophyte etching in a wall at Mission San Fernando Rey.

Rampant syphilis, initially introduced by Spanish soldiers, caused long and tragic illnesses. Birthrates dropped drastically, and established missions reached farther into the interior to replace their shrinking populations. Alta California would be as deserted as Baja California, noted a visiting ship's doctor in 1827, "if from time to time bands of Indians obliged by poverty and famine—or even sometimes taken by force to meet the need for farm labor—did not arrive to replenish the dwindling population in the European settlements."[52]

In view of such trying conditions and mistreatment, it is fair to question why the Indians stayed at the missions at all. The traveler Langsdorff pondered this dilemma when he observed in 1806, "Two or three monks, and four or five soldiers, keep in order a commu-

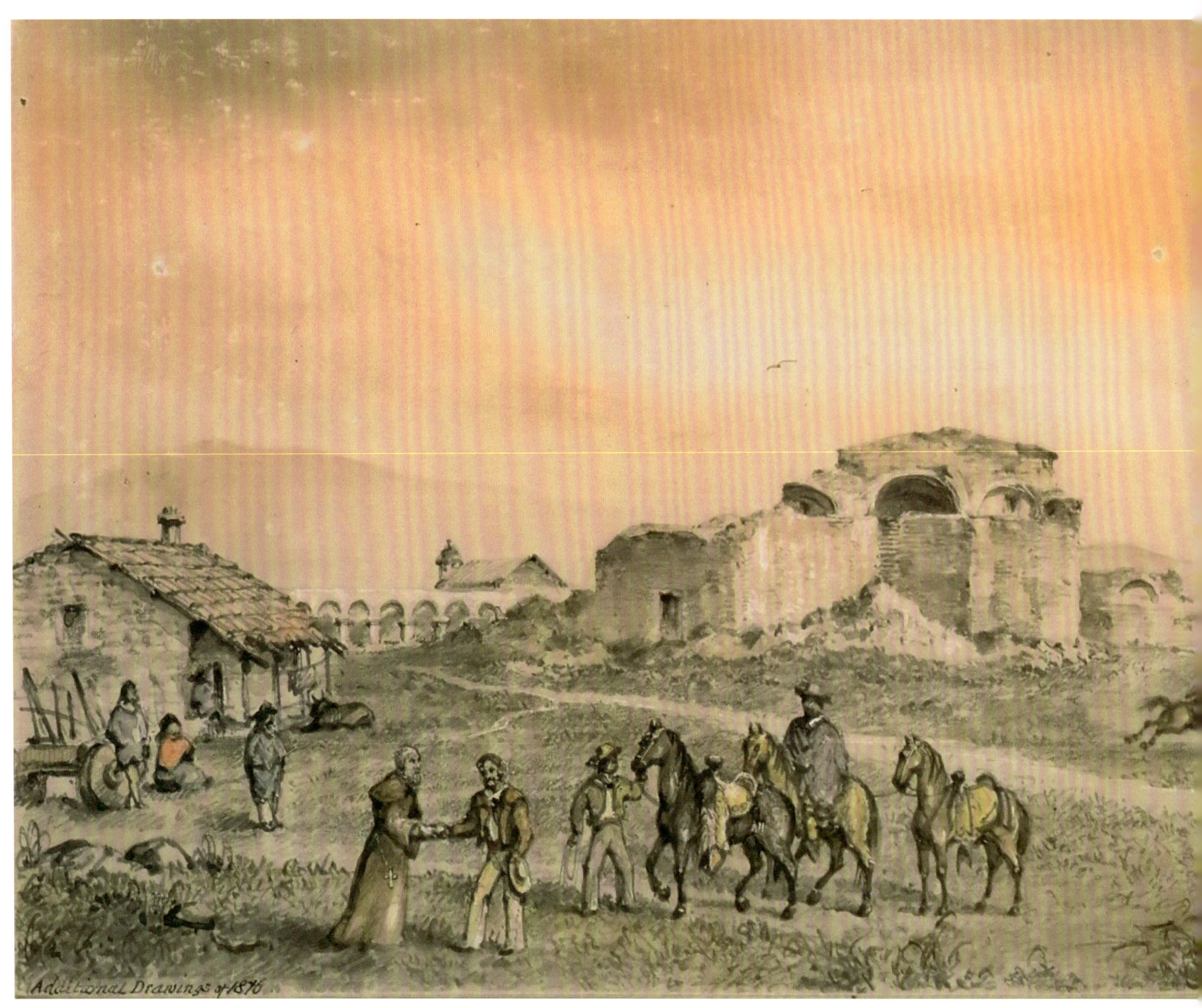

1824
Chumash neophytes revolt at Missions Santa Inés, La Purísima, and Santa Bárbara; adobe churches are completed at Missions San Francisco Solano and San Rafael.

1825
Adobe church completed at Mission Santa Clara.

1826
The American trapper Jedediah Smith visits Mission San Gabriel.

1827–28
The French traveler Auguste Bernard Duhaut-Cilly visits Missions Santa Cruz and San Luis Rey.

Following their secularization in the 1830s, the missions were generally abandoned. In this 1842 scene at Mission San Juan Capistrano, painted from memory many years later by the German American artist Edward Vischer, the ruins of the Great Stone Church, destroyed in an earthquake in 1812, are surrounded by fallen remnants of the *casco* buildings. Watercolor and pencil on paper. Courtesy of The Bancroft Library, University of California, Berkeley

nity of a thousand or fifteen hundred rough uncivilized men, making them lead a wholly different course of life from that to which they had been accustomed, without any spririt of mutiny or insurrection."[53] With such disparity between the numbers of those in power and the colonized, coercion cannot be the only explanation. One factor in the successful spread of societies with complex technologies into less developed regions is the compelling attraction of the new. The Spanish brought a cornucopia of extraordinary enticements to California: cattle and horses, incense and candles, corn and squash, guitars and trumpets, mirrors and bells, silk and iron, and even fireworks from China. Buildings made of earth rose from the ground, and water was turned from its course to make the ground bloom. As individuals and families were drawn to these apparent centers of magic and power, old village systems were destabilized. Other compelling factors in this mission migration included the increase in village deaths from new diseases, the decimation of food plants by introduced livestock, and the disruption of traditional trading alliances—against all of which traditional rituals proved ineffective. Demoralized and confused, villagers increasingly succumbed to the new life offered at the missions. Scholars have postulated that tribes reached a "tipping point" wherein those left behind could not sustain traditional ways and therefore followed their friends and relations to the mission communities.[54]

Even as the missions struggled to consolidate their existence, however, events in the larger world were beginning to foreshadow great changes in Alta California. Wars in Europe disrupted trade across the Atlantic and inspired the Spanish Crown to extract increased revenues from its territories, leading to widespread revolution in the Spanish colonies beginning in 1810. During the following decade, no more supply ships arrived in Alta California from San Blas, and communications from Spanish authorities ceased. Although the colony voiced allegiance to Spain, its residents, in need of critical supplies such as metals, arms, and sugar, and enamored of such luxuries as imported cloth, rum, and English ceramics, began to traffic with the Yankee and British traders who illegally plied the coast. And, with manufacturers in New England seeking new sources of leather, many missions negotiated contracts to supply hides from their abundant herds. The number and size of *matanzas* (slaughters of herd animals) for cattle were increased, and the hide-and-tallow industry developed into California's first major export venture.

With Mexican independence from Spain in 1821, the missions' fate was inevitable. In Mexico, the revolutionaries had demanded redistribution of the Catholic Church's vast landholdings, and the citizenry of Alta California quickly cast a covetous eye on the extensive mission lands. Indeed, the Spanish had envisioned mission institutions as a temporary stage in "civilizing" native peoples: once neophytes learned the tools of Spanish culture, the missions would be turned into pueblos, the missionaries would become parish priests, and the land would be distributed to the neophytes. The Franciscans had objected, insisting that the natives were not ready for independence, but they were ill equipped to resist the political pressure exerted by the citizens of what was now Mexican California. Retired presidio soldiers, citizens of the growing pueblos, and new foreign entrepreneurs all wanted the land. The mission era was fast coming to an end.

The mission institutions of Alta California were dismantled following the Emancipation and Secularization Decree of 1834, and within a decade some ten million acres had passed into private ownership and nearly fifteen thousand Indians were freed from mission restraints.[55] All material holdings—land, livestock, orchards, buildings, and furnishings—were transferred from the custodianship of the Church and the ownership of the

1834–36
Secularization of missions, initiating the massive dispersal of mission land into private ranchos.

1835–36
The American Richard Henry Dana visits Missions San Diego and Santa Clara; the Mexican painter Agustín Dávila paints murals and decorative furnishings at Missions Santa Clara and San José.

1838
Smallpox epidemic ravages native population at Mission San Francisco de Asís.

government and dispensed to the citizenry. The missionaries became secular priests, and each mission was put under the management of a *comisionado*, appointed by the Mexican provincial governor in Monterey. Corruption was rampant. "The priests were attached perpetually to one mission, and felt the necessity of keeping up its credit," noted the writer Richard Henry Dana, who visited California in 1835–36. "Accordingly, their debts were regularly paid, and the people were, in the main, well treated, and attached to those who had spent their whole lives among them."[56] Under the new administrators, however, most missions quickly fell into disarray, as livestock was slaughtered or neglected, fields lay fallow, and neophytes abandoned their former homes. In 1839 the *visitador general* appointed by the governor to look into these matters reported that at Mission San Diego "there was no longer anything to eat and the entire Indian community went about practically naked."[57] At San Luis Rey, the former neophyte Julio César later remembered, the administrator "left the mission stripped bare, taking everything, including the dishes and cups."[58] Even Mission Santa Bárbara, noted Dana, was transformed into "a large and deserted looking place, the out-buildings going to ruin, and everything giving one the impression of decayed grandeur."[59]

Mission lands were supposed to be allotted first to former neophytes and then as ranchos to those soldiers and citizens who had provided service to the colony. In effect, the native peoples received precious little during this massive giveaway of land to the *gente de razón* (people of reason, a term used for non-natives).[60] Before 1834 only thirty ranchos had been granted in all of Alta California; between 1835 and 1847 more than eight hundred were distributed.[61] Most Indians who obtained allotments soon sold out for needed cash or eventually lost them to legal manipulations or the schemes of greedy neighbors. Some remnant neophyte communities stayed around the old *cascos*, providing a meager congregation for those churches that retained a priest. Several mission churches survived by serving the populations of growing towns. Most of the former neophytes, however, hired out to the ranchos, or simply worked for food and lodging, while others disappeared into the interior territories.[62]

Thus arrived the rancho period, later a source of mythologies for the "era of the dons and doñas" that would permeate Californians' perception of their past. In reality, this prosperity was short-lived, lasting slightly more than a decade, from about 1835 to 1848. In that year the Treaty of Guadalupe Hidalgo ended the Mexican-American War and helped satisfy the imperial American dream of "manifest destiny" by extending the United States' borders from the Atlantic to the Pacific. When the U.S. took possession of California, most of the abandoned former mission establishments were falling to ruin.

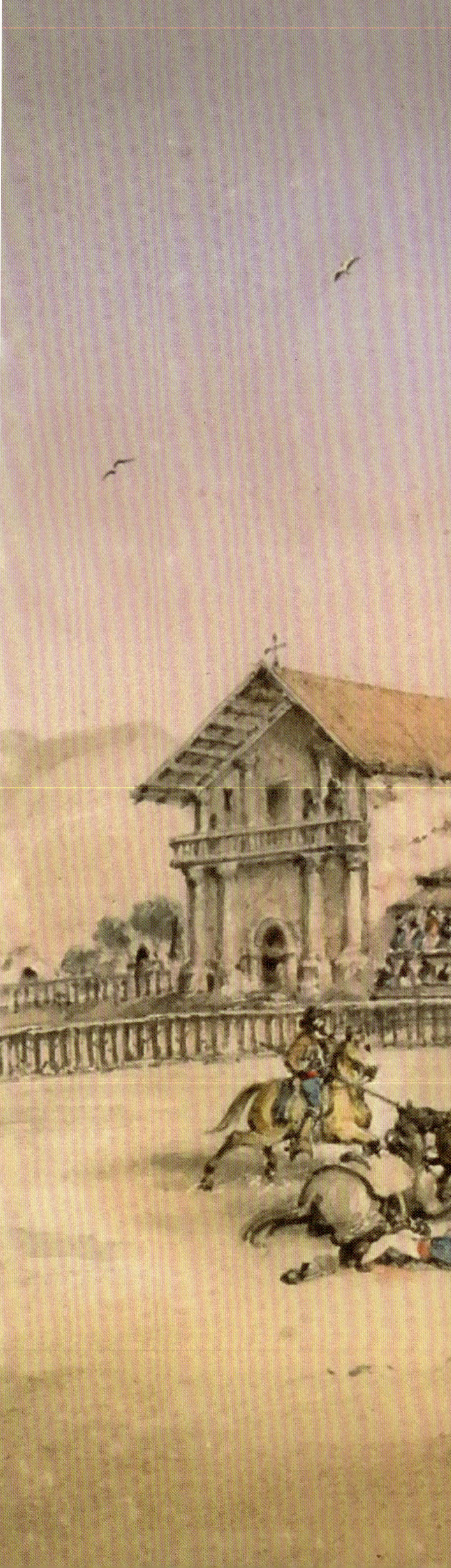

The rancho period that followed the dismantling of the mission system would come to be known as the "Days of the Dons," a romantic time of fiestas and rodeos. Seen here is Edward Vischer's reminiscence, painted years later, of an 1842 bull-and-bear fight at Mission San Francisco de Asís. Watercolor and pencil on paper, 1876. Courtesy of The Bancroft Library, University of California, Berkeley

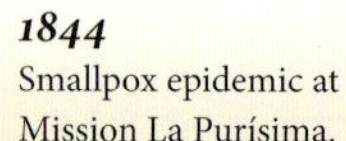

1844
Smallpox epidemic at Mission La Purísima.

1847
Bear Flag Revolt, U.S. troops occupy Mission San Luis Rey, stay ten years.

1848
Treaty of Guadalupe-Hidalgo ends Mexican American War; California annexed to the U.S.

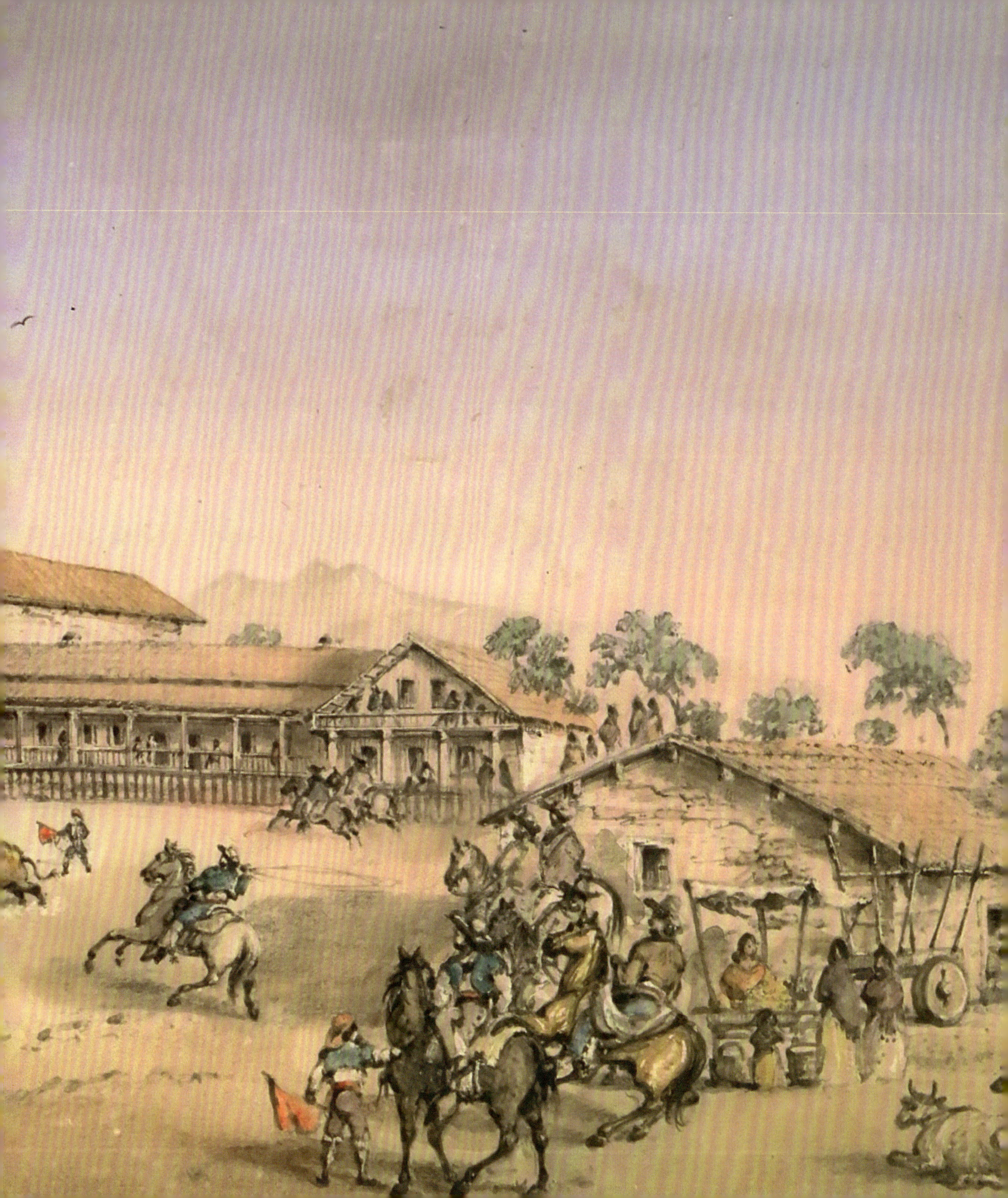

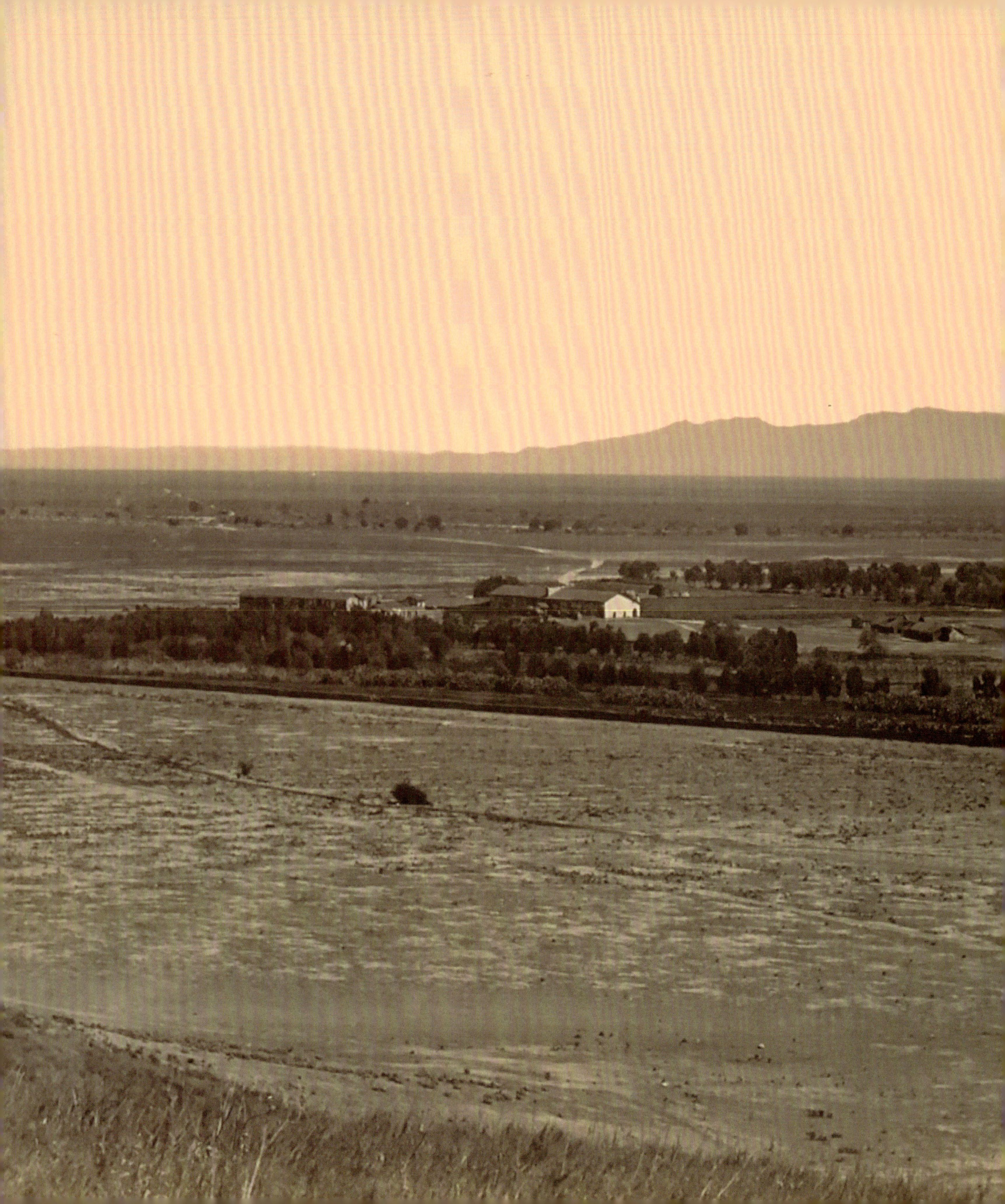

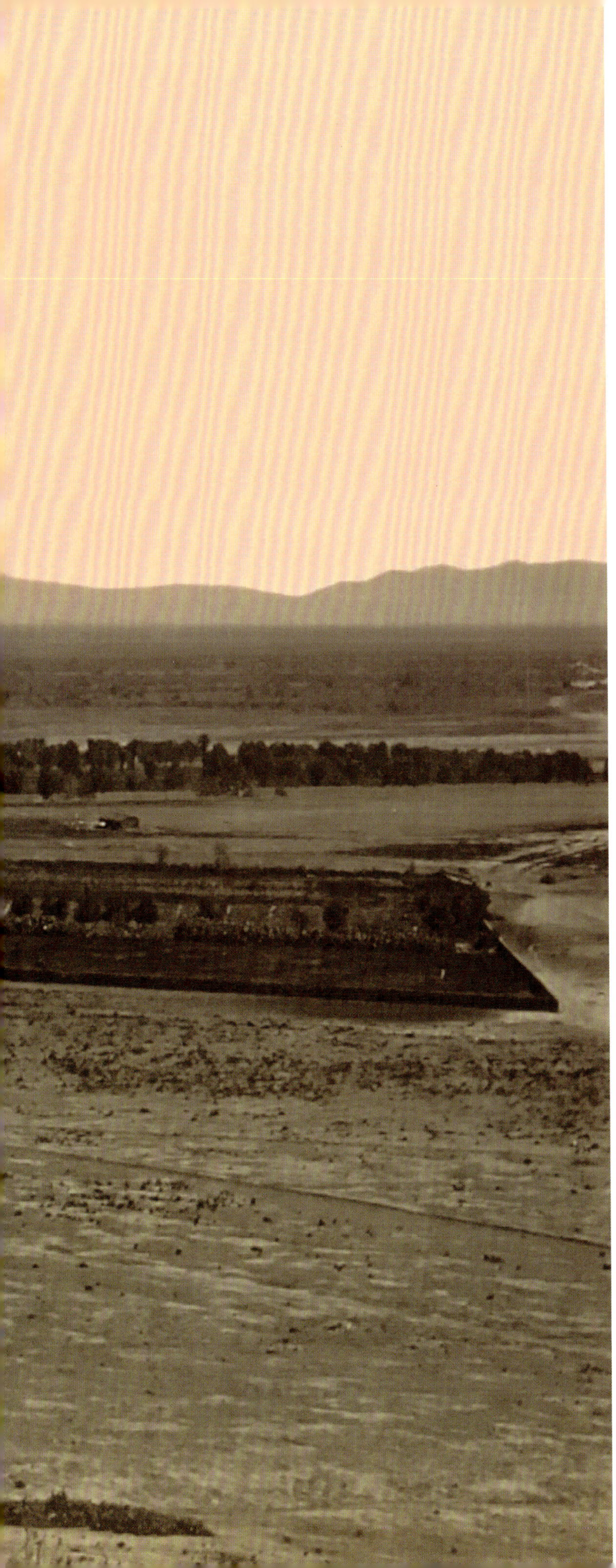

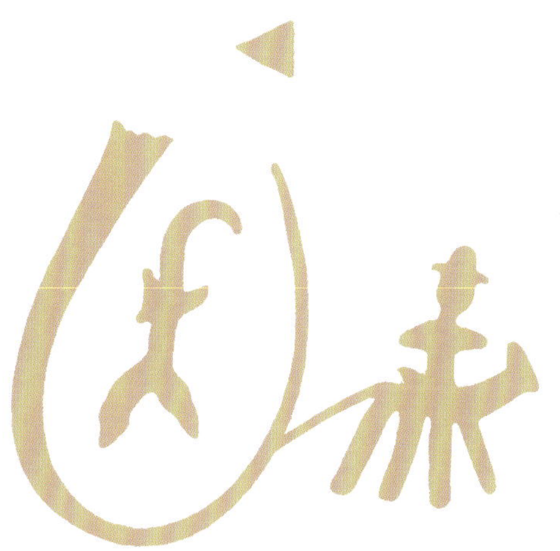

Chapter Two

RUINS, ROMANCE, AND REVIVAL

In February 1856 an obscure American artist named Henry Miller, after roaming around northern California, set out to tour the rest of the new state. Traveling by mule and sleeping "in the field," Miller intended to visit all twenty-one Spanish missions, describing and sketching each.[1] He began at Mission San Francisco de Asís, of which remained "only the Church and a building connected with it... formerly inhabited by missionaries but [now] converted into public houses where the inhabitants of San Francisco are in the habit of resorting." He then headed to Mission San José. There, he wrote, "the priest, a youth of about 18 years of age, very politely showed me around the ruins which are remaining of this once flourishing Mission.... The old adobe Church is a large building,... surrounded by ruins of a once massive edifice.... On a great part of the mission lands the farms of American squatters are found."[2]

LEFT: View of Mission San Fernando, ca. 1876–80. Photograph by Carleton Watkins. Albumen print. Courtesy of The Bancroft Library, University of California, Berkeley

ABOVE: A vaquero lassoing an animal, painted by a neophyte on a wall at Mission San Juan Capistrano.

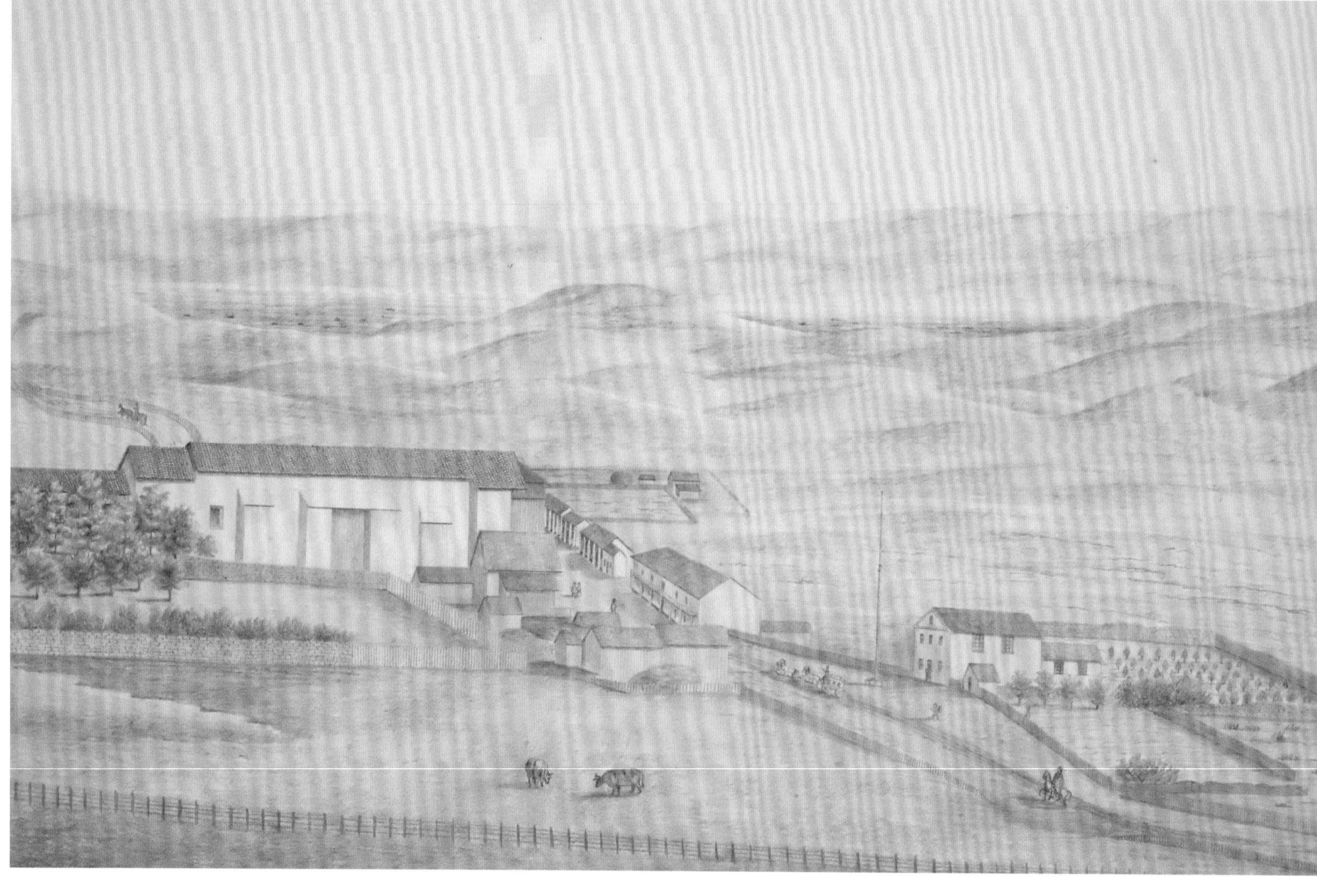

Mission San José, as depicted by the American artist Henry Miller when he toured the state to sketch the missions in 1856. At the time, the church, on the left, was still being served by a young priest, although the rest of the mission buildings were largely in ruins. The large house and garden at right were occupied by the former mission administrator. Pencil sketch on paper. Courtesy of The Bancroft Library, University of California, Berkeley

By the mid-1850s Americans were rapidly encroaching upon the landscapes of California. In February 1848, when it was annexed to the United States, California had been a quiet Mexican backwater with decaying mission establishments, newly landed families, and a scattering of Yankee and British entrepreneurs encouraging a modest trade in cattle hides and tallow. This provincial world was overwhelmed by the discovery of gold on the American River just nine days before the United States was formally ceded ownership.[3] By 1849 ninety thousand hopeful argonauts had already flooded into California, and by 1852 the number had reached a quarter million. Many then turned from the mines and spread out across the state. "Everything about California would change," one historian has observed. "In one astonishing year the place would be transformed from obscurity to world prominence;...from a society of neighbors and families to one of strangers and transients;... from Catholic to Protestant, from Latin to Anglo-Saxon."[4]

The new arrivals brought sweeping changes, as old regimes of class and ethnicity were reshuffled. The gold rush and the annexation of California coincided with the end of the Mexican-American War, and newly decommissioned soldiers flooded the mines with anti-Mexican sentiments. Following California statehood in 1850, the Foreign Miners'

1848
Discovery of gold on the American River sets off the California gold rush.

1850
California enters the U.S. as thirty-first state; Foreign Miners Tax levied on non-U.S. citizens.

1850s
Racial violence and vigilante law in San Francisco, Los Angeles, and other towns; many abandoned missions decline.

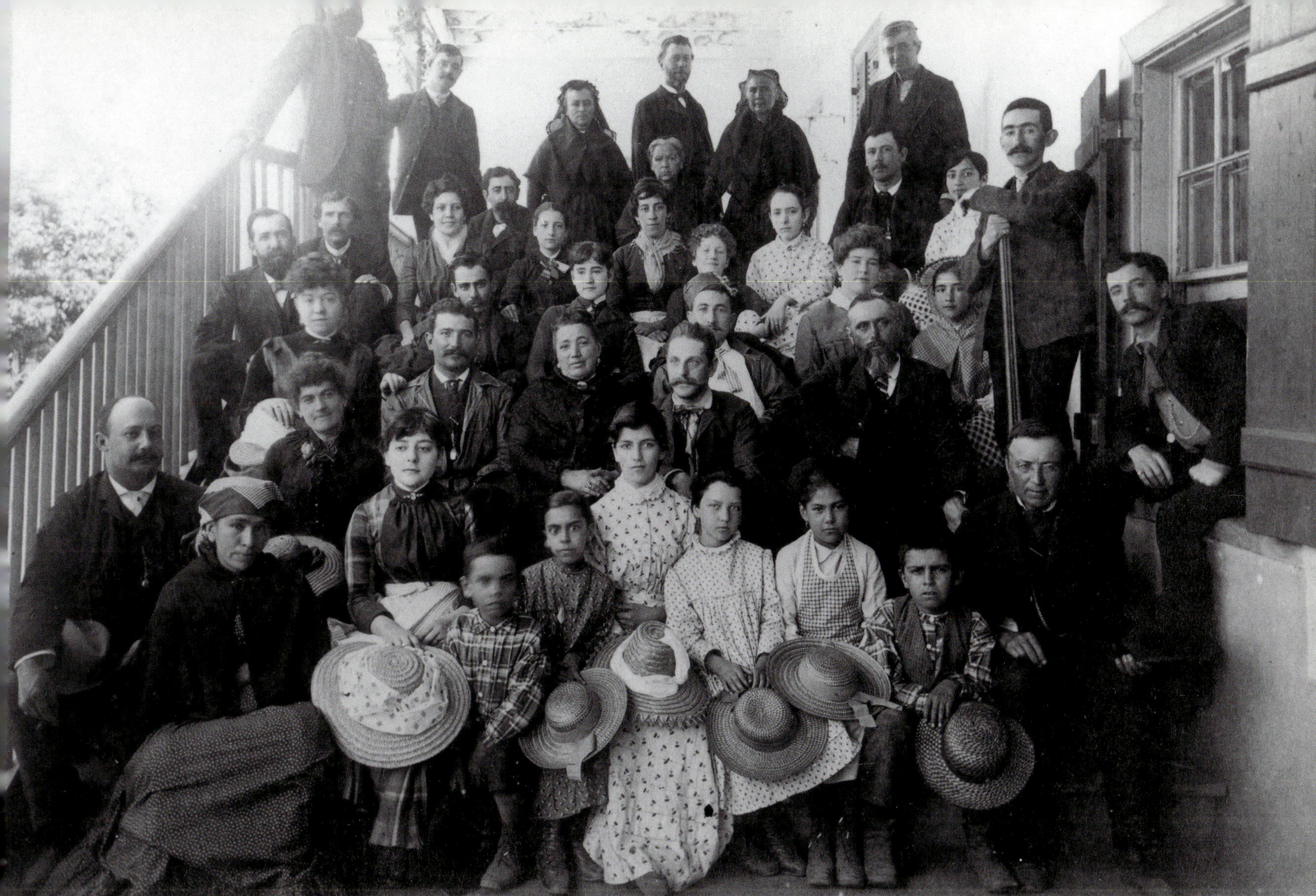

The del Valles, a prominent Californio family, seen here on the porch of their home at Rancho Camulos in the 1890s. Members of the family first arrived in California in 1819, and many would distinguish themselves through military and public service in both Mexican and American California. Rancho Camulos, near Newhall, would be an inspiration for Helen Hunt Jackson's novel *Ramona*. Seaver Center for Western History Research, Los Angeles County Museum of Natural History

Law imposed a tax on mining claims held by non-U.S. citizens, largely aimed at excluding Spanish-speaking "foreigners" from resources that only a few years earlier had belonged to the Californios, those former citizens of Mexican California. For a time in southern California—remote from the mines and prospering from running stock to feed the argonauts—Anglo and Californio elites formed alliances and intermarried, and wealthy Californios continued to be influential in political affairs. Prominent Angelenos such as Andrés Pico and Ignacio del Valle served in the state senate; another, Antonio Coronel, was elected mayor of Los Angeles. The tidal wave of argonauts in the north, however, swept up Californios with the multitudes of Sonorans and numerous Chileans who had flocked to the mines, and all Spanish-speaking residents found themselves increasingly marginalized. The 1850s saw considerable ethnic conflict, and legal proceedings were often steeped in racial and ethnic prejudice.

The new proprietors of California were hungry for land. Mission lands that had been acquired by Californio families through Mexican grants during secularization in the 1830s and 1840s were challenged in court by the Americans or, as Miller noticed at Mission San José, simply squatted on by opportunists.[5] Large rancho holdings were typically divided

1850–62
U.S. Army occupies Mission San Diego.

1851
Jesuits acquire Mission Santa Clara.

1852
Hugo Reid publishes *Letters on the Los Angeles County Indians.*

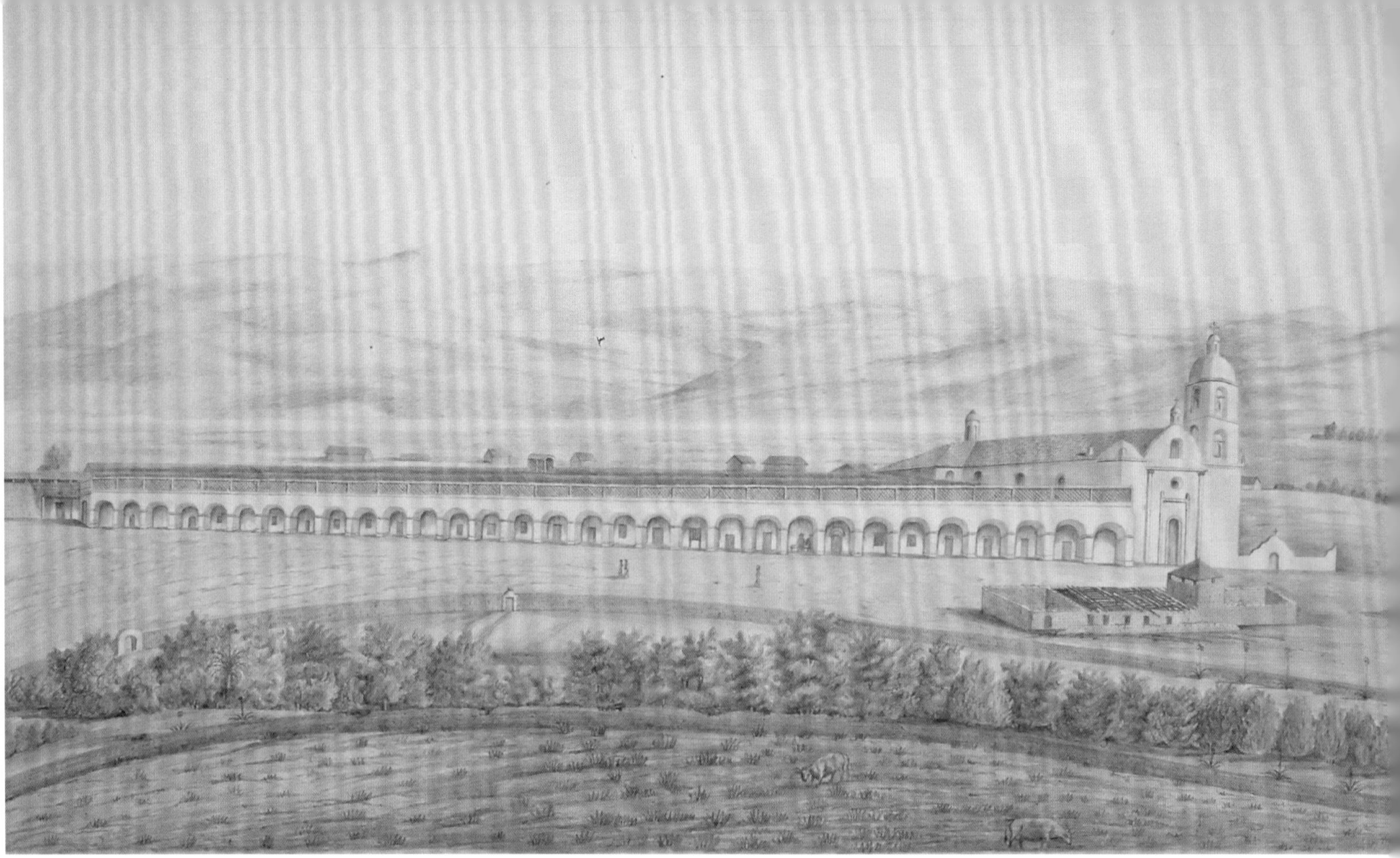

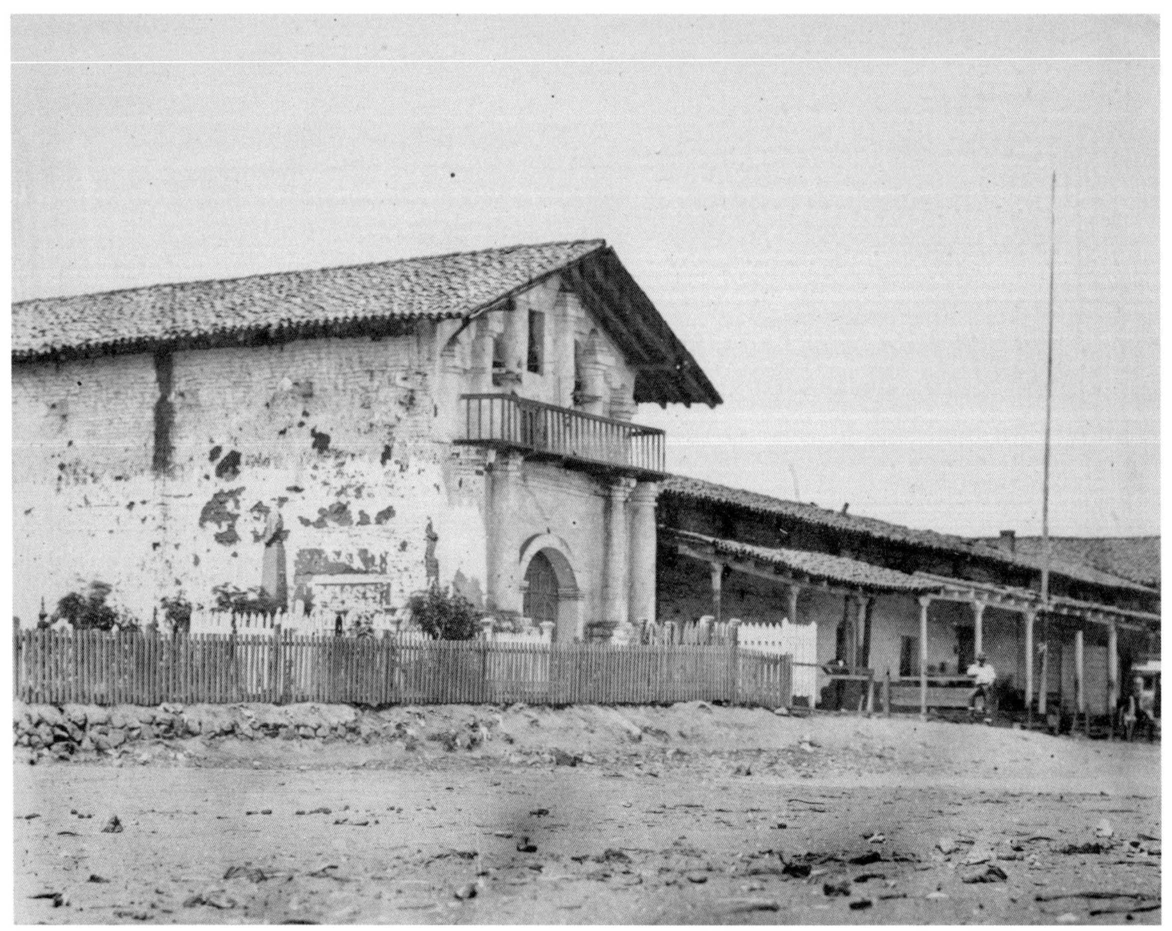

among multiple heirs, many of whom then sold portions to pay legal fees for defending ownership, lost the land for debts, or divested themselves of rural properties for opportunities in the growing towns. Although ranchos survived longer in the less populated south than in the northern portions of the state near the goldfields, it appeared that, except for some place-names, the new broom of the Americans was eventually going to sweep away all of Mexican California.

The once-dominant mission establishments, meanwhile, existed in various stages of decline. During secularization their extensive lands had been divided into private ranchos, their native populations scattered, and their assets looted and squandered.[6] The Californio rancheros' practice of scavenging roof tiles had been especially devastating. No longer produced at mission kilns, the sturdy curved tiles became a scarce commodity and were removed from mission buildings for use on the new ranchos or in towns. Once exposed to the elements, the missions' sun-dried brick walls quickly melted back into native soils. Many of these once-vast establishments had been reduced to a few buildings surrounded by neglected gardens and dissolving adobe walls, and at several northern missions earthquakes accelerated the effects of abandonment.

OPPOSITE ABOVE: **Mission San Luis Rey, as depicted by Henry Miller in 1856. "The mission buildings have a very imposing appearance and are built in the ancient Spanish style," he wrote. "On the well-preserved Church are two belfreys of considerable height." The old soldiers' quarters with guard tower, falling to ruin, can be seen in front of the mission. Pencil sketch on paper.** Courtesy of The Bancroft Library, University of California, Berkeley

Even those establishments in relatively good condition were at considerable risk. "I passed through extensive warehouses and immense rooms, once occupied for the manufacture of woolen blankets and other articles," wrote an American newspaperman who visited Mission San José in 1846. "Filth and desolation have taken the place of cleanliness and busy life." The "church and the massive two story edifices occupied by the padres during the flourishing epoch of the establishment... were in good repair.... The walls are massive, and if protected from the winter rains, will stand for ages. But if exposed to the storms by the decay of the projecting roofs, or by leaks in the main roof, they will soon crumble, or sink into shapeless heaps of mud."[7]

California's new Protestant American population generally showed little reverence for these dilapidated remnants of the state's Catholic, Spanish past. The writer Bret Harte displayed no sentimentality when he described Mission San Francisco de Asís in 1863, noting its "ragged senility contrasting with the smart spring sunshine, its two gouty pillars with the plaster dropping away like tattered bandages, its rayless windows, its crumbling entrances, and the leper spots on its whitewashed wall eating through the dark adobe."[8] Nine years later a journalist described Mission San Gabriel with similar disdain, as a "curious old relic of a by-gone civilization." "Its dinginess is hardly relieved by the bright ornamentation of the altar piece," he wrote, "and the old paintings that deck the walls are ensombered by the gloom which pervades the building."[9]

Throughout secularization, the one building that was kept in repair longest by remnant congregations at virtually all the missions was the church, and this remained true after California became part of the United States. As the spiritual heart of the mission establishment, containing the most elaborate architecture and adornments, the church now served as the last bastion of Spanish and Mexican California culture. Viewed as archaic and largely irrelevant by the new citizens of California, however, these vulnerable edifices faced a precarious future.

OPPOSITE BELOW: **Early view of Mission San Francisco de Asís, ca. 1856, showing the newly graded streets of San Francisco cutting in front of the church and convento. When Henry Miller visited, he noted that there remained "only the Church and a building connected with it... formerly inhabited by missionaries but [now] converted into public housing where the inhabitants of San Francisco are in the habit of resorting." Photograph by George R. Fardon. Salt print.** Courtesy Fraenkel Gallery, San Francisco

The first champion for the survival of the California missions was Joseph Sadoc Alemany, first archbishop of the Roman Catholic Diocese of San Francisco.[10] In 1852 he petitioned the U.S. government through the Private Land Grant Commission, arguing that under the laws of Spain and Mexico, padres' dwellings, as well as mission cemeteries,

1855–70s
Following legal petition by Joseph Alemany, portions of mission cascos returned to the Catholic Church.

1856
The American artist Henry Miller tours California, sketches the missions.

orchards, vineyards, and certain waterworks, were considered ecclesiastical property and should not have been included in private rancho grants. After some years these claims were adjudicated as valid, and between 1855 and the 1870s the church buildings and various other properties at all the California missions were deeded back to the diocese. But for many churches it was too late.

During the early period of American statehood, mission churches generally shared one of two fates: they became parish churches of towns that sprouted on former mission lands, or they languished in the countryside. Communities grew up around Missions San Francisco de Asís, Santa Clara, San Juan Bautista, San Luis Obispo, Santa Inés, Santa Bárbara, San Buenaventura, San Gabriel, and San Juan Capistrano and the Pala Asistencia.[11] In such cases, the congregations looked after their furnishings, art, and sacred objects as well as the buildings themselves, and these churches generally survived reasonably intact. When Henry Miller visited Mission San Gabriel during his leisurely tour of the missions in 1856, for example, he remarked that "the Mission Church is well preserved," even though "the other buildings... are dilapidated or totally in ruins." And at Mission Santa Bárbara, he noted, though the mission's vast landholdings had been broken up, the church, which still served the nearby town, "and adjoining house, in which the officiating priests live, are in a good state of preservation." On the Sunday he arrived, the place fairly bustled with activity, with "people from the town and ranchos... coming and going, and masses being said by the priests all day long."[12]

Andrés Pico continued to operate the former Mission San Fernando as his private rancho. When Miller visited, Pico was away, but he enjoyed dinner with the French gardener, accompanied by a few glasses of the mission's wine. "This Mission is a fine property," Miller noted. "There are a number of buildings remaining.... The Church and the building in which the proprietor... lives are in good condition." "With a good management," he added, in comments reflecting the prejudice borne by many *norteamericanos*, "the two beautiful vineyards and orchards alone, in which grow an abundance of grapes, pears, apples, apricots, peaches, figs, pomegranates, oranges, quinces, prickly pears, etc.,... would prove a fortune to the proprietor if he were a man of the Anglo Saxon stamp."[13]

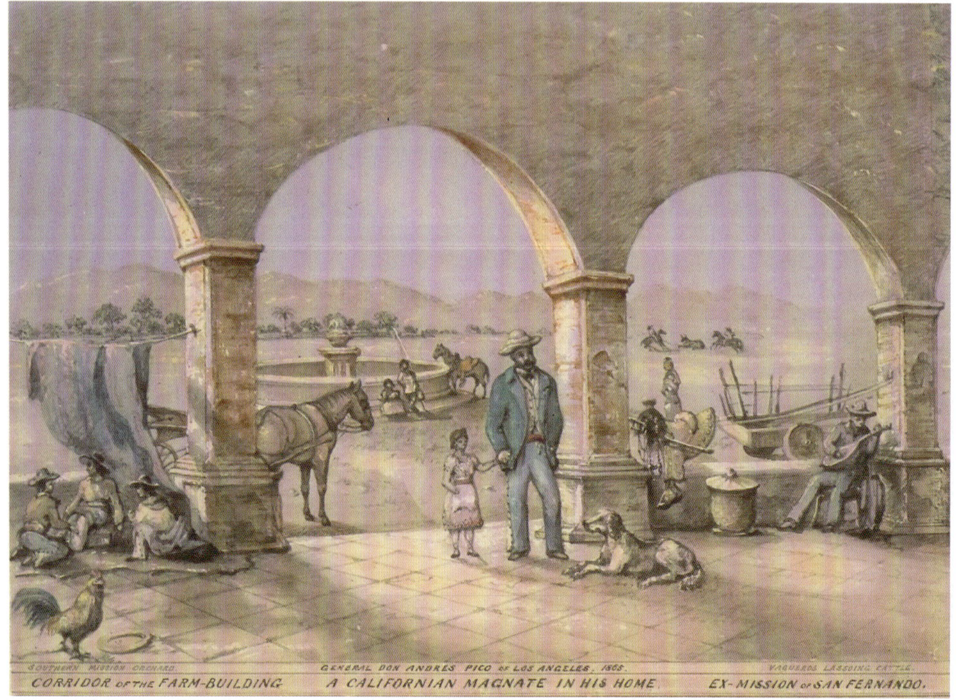

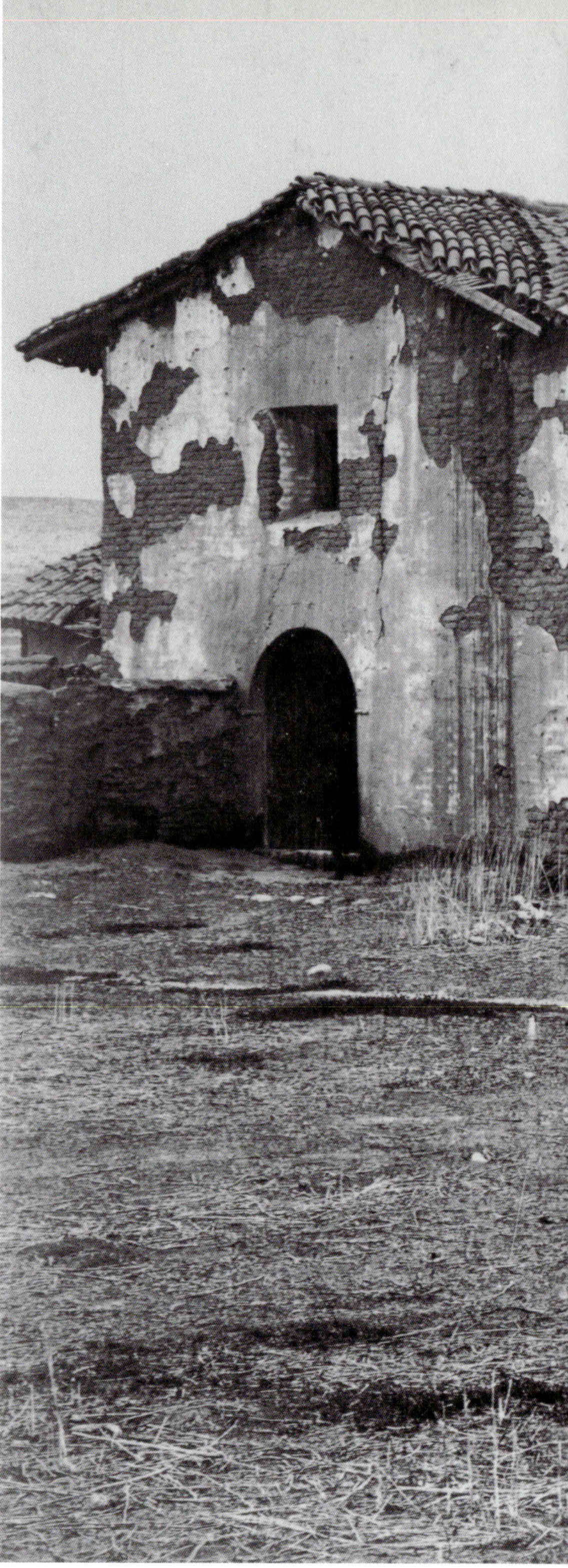

This 1865 painting by Edward Vischer portrays the Californio don Andrés Pico at his ranch, the former Mission San Fernando. Vischer was Pico's attorney and friend, and he was well acquainted with the life portrayed in this romantic scene. Vischer, *A California Magnate in his Home* (detail). Watercolor and pencil on paper. Courtesy of The Bancroft Library, University of California, Berkeley

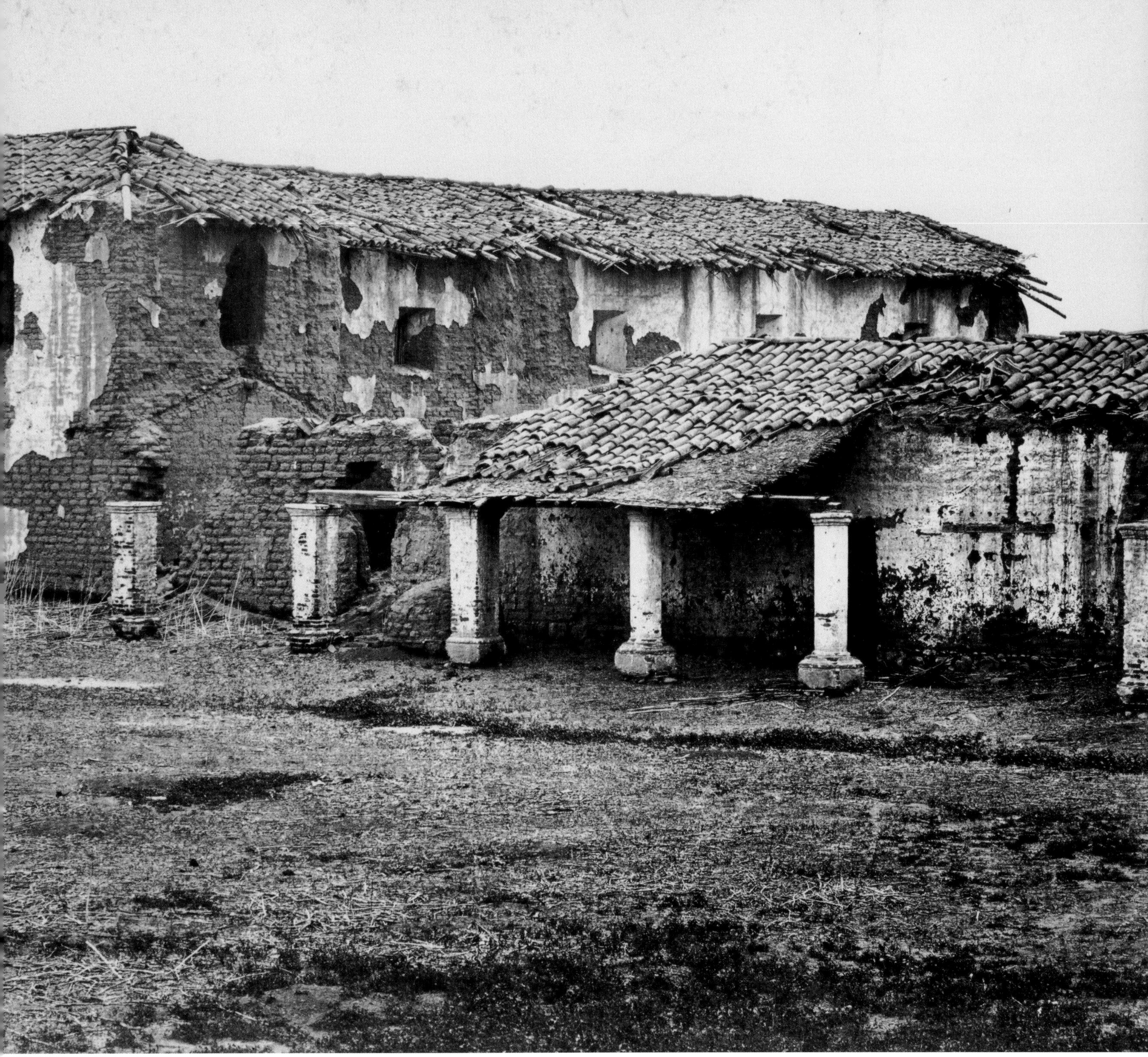

Mission San Fernando, ca. 1876–80. By the late 1870s the church, which had been in good condition when Henry Miller visited in the 1850s, was in serious disrepair, and most of the *casco* buildings had fallen to ruin. Once the fired clay tile roofs were removed, the adobe walls began to crumble. Photograph by Carleton Watkins. Albumen silver print. Gift in memory of Leona Naef Merrill and in honor of her sister, Gladys Porterfield. The J. Paul Getty Museum, Los Angeles. 94.XA.113.33

Many establishments, however, were considerably less well-off. At those in isolated locations, such as San Antonio, La Soledad, La Purísima, San Carlos Borromeo, and San Diego, the churches quickly declined. "A more desolate place than Soledad can not well be imagined," wrote an American visitor in 1849. "The old church is partially in ruins, and the adobe huts built for the Indians are roofless, and the walls tumbled about in shapeless piles."[14] The remaining buildings at many missions were taken over for uses having little to do with their original purpose. In San Luis Obispo, noted Miller, "the mission is metamorphosed into a little town at present of about 150 houses, inhabited principally by natives and Mexicans," and "the building adjoining the Church" was used as a courthouse.[15] The U.S. Army frequently appropriated empty buildings. At Mission San Diego, for example, soldiers occupied the church from about 1850 to 1862, adding a second floor loft to the interior and stabling their horses on the ground level.[16] And at San Luis Rey soldiers appropriated the abandoned ruins as an operational base from 1847 to 1857, continuing occasional use until the property was returned to the Catholic Church in 1865. Although the attendant *alcalde* tried to secure the church with locked doors, soldiers nonetheless defiled the interior. "The altar and images," noted a local newspaper, "were torn down by members of Detachment Co. E, 1st Cal., August 17th 1865."[17]

As churches closed and were abandoned, their art, books, and furnishings were often moved to neighboring missions that remained open.[18] Following American statehood, treasures from Mission San Diego were preserved in the Old Adobe Church in what is now Old Town, where the confessional and tabernacle still reside.[19] Loyal members of some congregations rescued art and sacred items from decaying churches and preserved them at their homes. At San Luis Rey, such treasures were preserved by former neophytes residing at the Pala Asistencia until they could be safely returned. Similarly, at Mission San Antonio books and other church items were stored in private homes, and the sacred vestments were secured by the priest in nearby King City. The mission statuary was stored in a livery stable there and brought back for fiestas and special events until it could be reinstated when the building was restored many years later.[20]

Although some devoted remnant congregations succeeded in staving off ruin for a while, by the 1870s even missions that had survived secularization and the early years of American statehood were on the verge of disappearing. San Fernando fell into virtually complete ruin; American settlers made off with beams and tiles, the church roof collapsed, and eventually only the walls were left standing. Earthquakes in 1857 and 1868 devastated Santa Cruz and San José, respectively. San Luis Rey was abandoned in the 1860s; the quadrangles collapsed and the roof caved in during three decades of utter neglect. The fate of Mission San Carlos Borromeo, former headquarters of the mission system, meanwhile, is evoked in this 1879 description by the Scottish writer Robert Louis Stevenson, who sojourned briefly in California:

> **The Carmel [River] runs by many pleasant farms... and at last, as it is falling towards... the great Pacific, [it] passes a ruined mission on a hill. From the mission church the eye embraces a great field of ocean, and the ear is filled with a continuous sound of distant breakers.... But the day of the Jesuit has gone by, the day of the Yankee has succeeded.... The church is roofless and ruinous, sea-breezes and sea-fogs, and the alternation of the rain and sunshine, daily widening the breaches.... As an antiquity in this new land, a quaint specimen of missionary architecture, and a memorial of good deeds, it had a triple claim to preservation from all thinking people; but neglect and abuse have been its portion. There is no sign of American interference, save where a headboard has been torn from a grave to be a mark for pistol bullets.[21]**

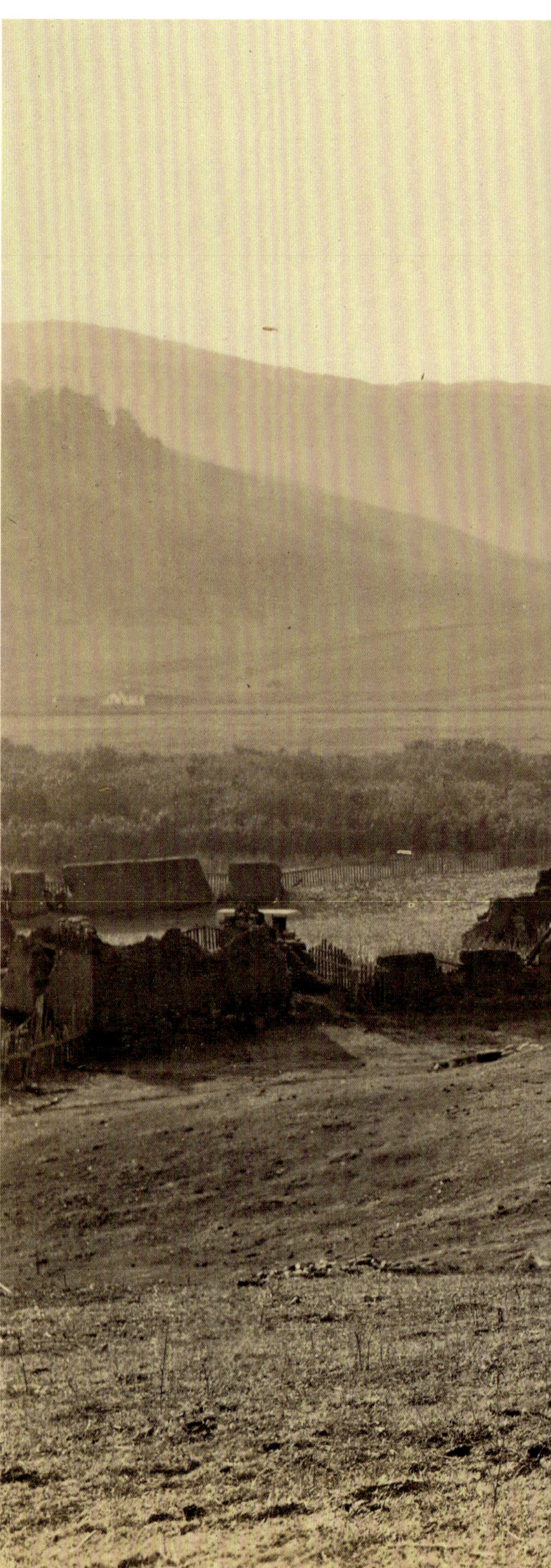

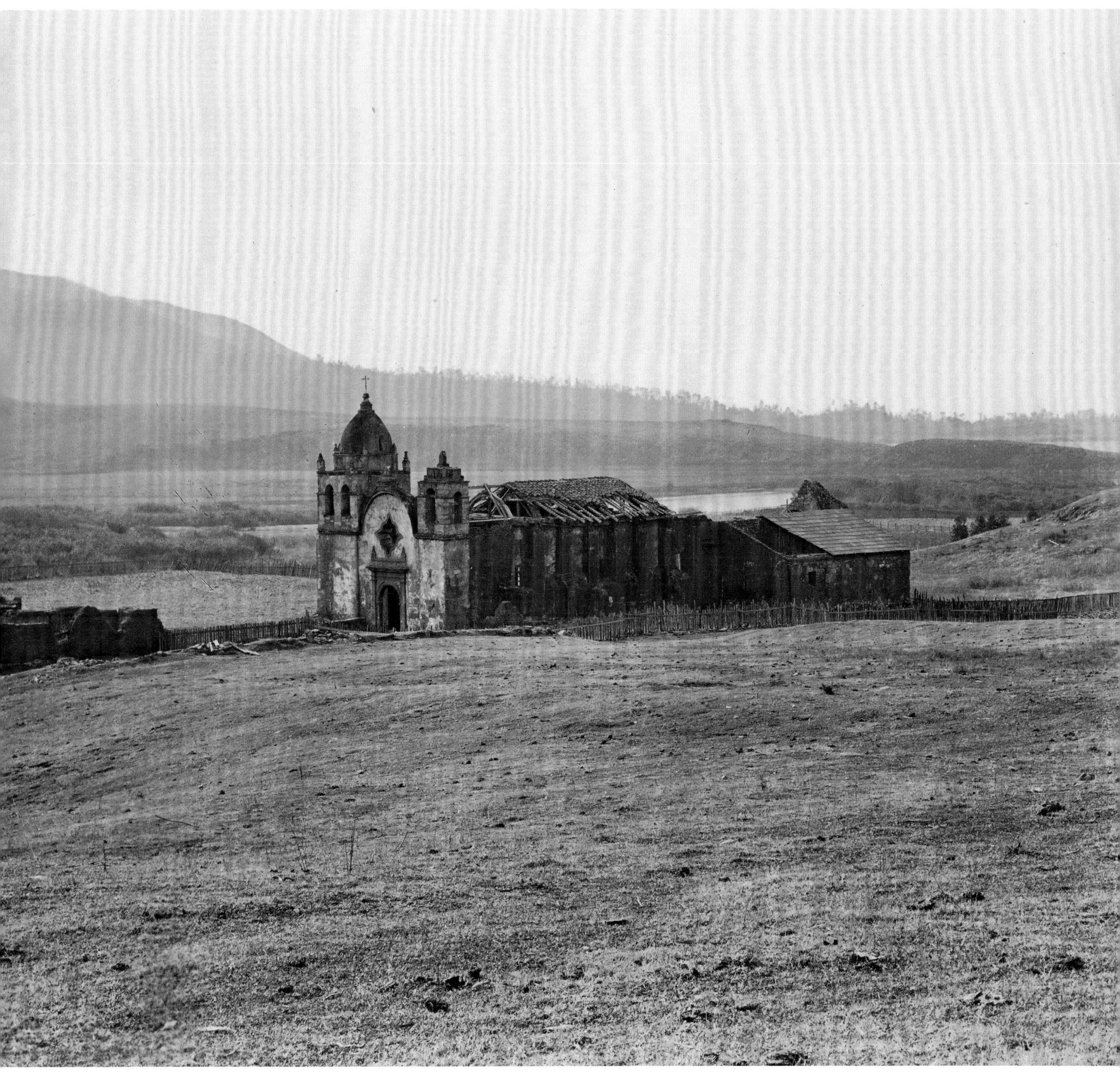

In the late nineteenth century, photographers were drawn to isolated mission ruins set in immense natural surroundings. Seen here is the ruined stone church at Mission San Carlos Borromeo, its roof caved in, ca. 1876–80. The only building still standing at the site, it is set against a backdrop of coastal hills and the glittering Carmel River. Photograph by Carleton Watkins. Albumen silver print. Gift in memory of Leona Naef Merrill and in honor of her sister, Gladys Porterfield. The J. Paul Getty Museum, Los Angeles. 94.XA.113.33

During the decades of abandonment and neglect, photographers and painters, attracted by the splendor of California's landscapes, were lured by the mission ruins, which some regarded as romantic subject matter evoking the lost grandeur of the past. The work of these artists helped foster an appreciation of the mission heritage among the general public, the most realistic of these forming a record of the physical mission establishments on which subsequent restorations and historical studies would rely (see pp. 48–49). Henry Miller's etchings would not be published until well into the twentieth century, but various other artists found an audience much earlier. Painters such as Henry Chapman Ford and Edwin Deakin produced complete series of renderings of all the missions. The first major series of mission photographs was undertaken by Carleton Watkins in about 1876, following a centennial commemoration of the founding of Mission San Francisco de Asís. Early photographs of the missions could also be found among the more than one thousand views of California available from the firm of Lawrence & Houseworth, established in the 1850s by two former gold rush miners who settled in San Francisco. By the end of the decade it was the leading purveyor of landscape photographs and stereographs of the West. Other mission photographers included Isaiah West Taber, who also arrived with the gold rush; William Henry Jackson, who executed a series of photographs between 1885 and 1890; Adam Clark Vroman, who started a mission series in the 1890s; and C. C. Pierce, who arrived in Los Angeles in the 1880s and would photograph the missions for more than half a century.

In the 1870s, meanwhile, a California travel literature began to appear, often underwritten by the railroads and other commercial interests, with the goal of acquainting the rest of the United States with the ample attractions of the new state. Books like *California for Health, Pleasure and Residence*, and *The Pacific Tourist* focused primarily on California's

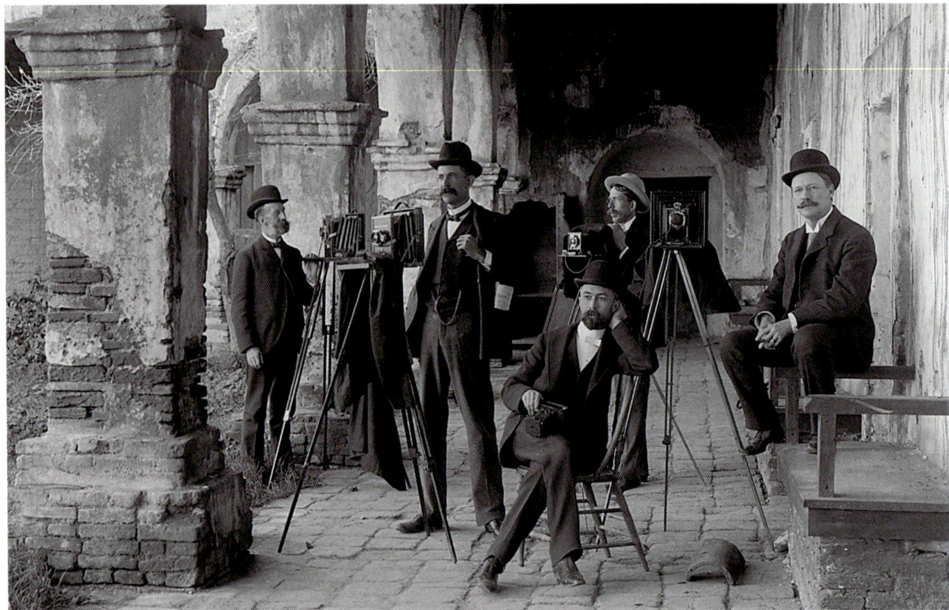

The photographer and mission enthusiast Adam Clark Vroman, seated at center, and members of his entourage, on a photography outing at Mission San Juan Capistrano in 1900. Seaver Center for Western History Research, Los Angeles County Museum of Natural History

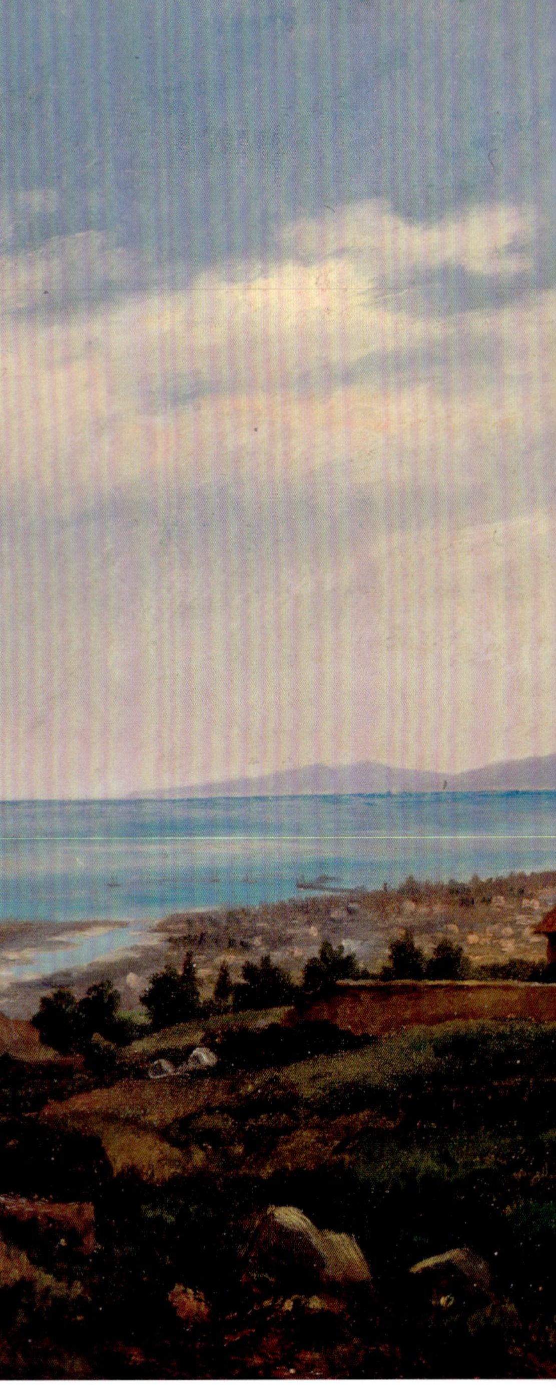

1857
Earthquake destroys church at Mission Santa Cruz.

1861
The Bavarian Edward Vischer, nearly 20 years after his first visit to California, begins painting and sketching the missions.

1865
Steeple added to church at Mission San Juan Bautista.

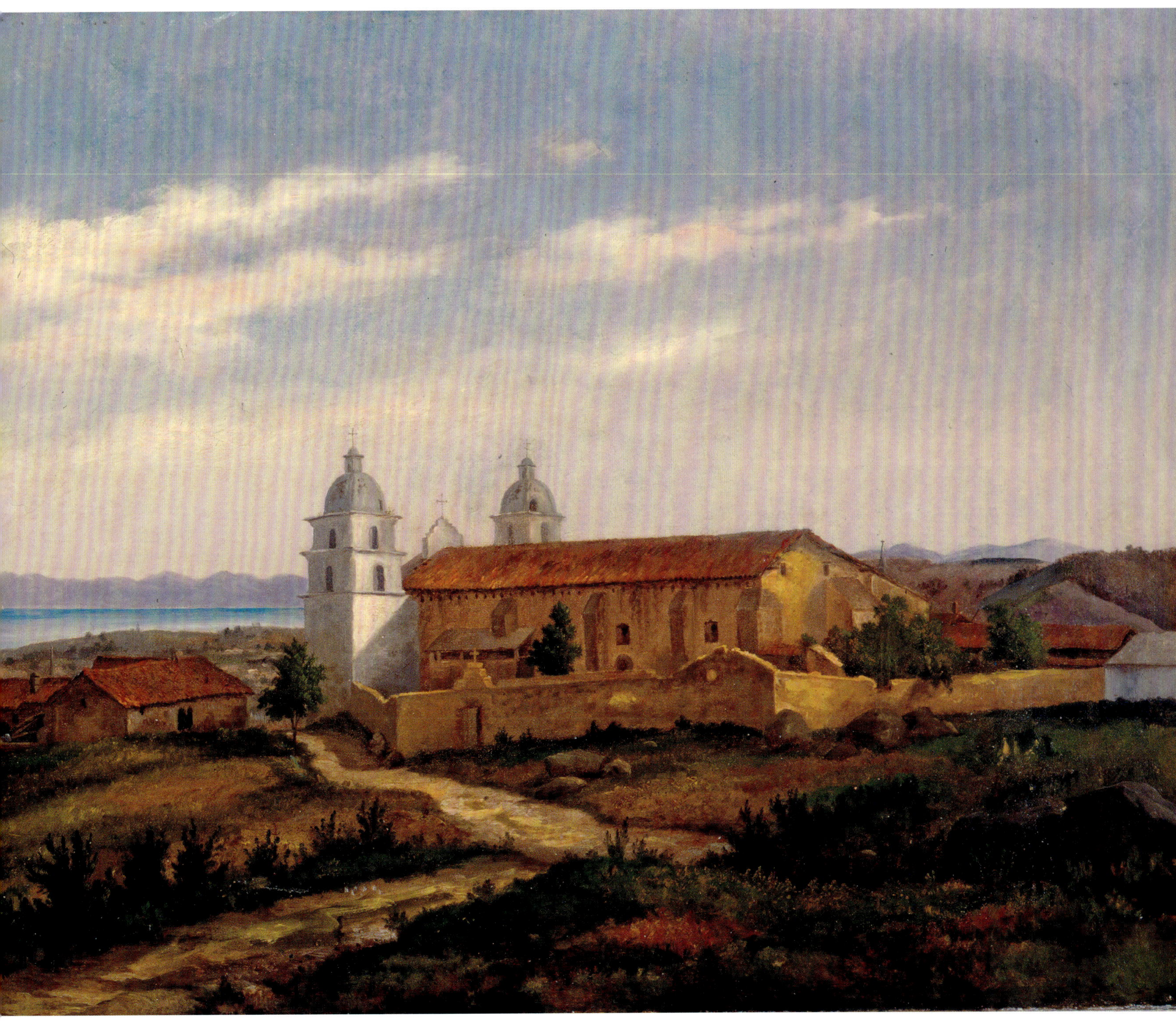

In the 1870s, an increasing number of painters began to celebrate the romantic beauty of the missions and the surrounding California landscape. This view southward of Mission Santa Bárbara depicts the mission church, with its signature bell towers, along with the walled cemetery and several outbuildings. In the distance, Santa Cruz Island seems to float on the Pacific Ocean. Henry Chapman Ford, *Mission Santa Barbara from Behind*, 1875. Oil on canvas. Courtesy of the Mission Inn Foundation and Museum, Riverside California From the collection of The Historic Mission Inn Corporation

1868
Earthquake devastates Mission San José.

1870
The church at Mission San Rafael is razed; the English artist Edwin Deakin arrives in San Francisco, begins painting the missions.

1875
The American artist Henry Chapman Ford arrives in Santa Bárbara, begins sketching and painting the missions.

The Missions in Art

In the late nineteenth and early twentieth century, a number of painters played an important role in popularizing the missions, defining the mission heritage, and encouraging the nascent mission preservation movement. In providing attractive images of the state's Spanish and Mexican heritage, these artists also helped shape the emerging identity of American California.[22]

Edward Vischer, a German who first came to California in the early 1840s, was not professionally trained; but he published in 1872 one of the first portfolios of drawings on the subject, *Missions of Upper California*. He was followed by Henry Chapman Ford, who was born in New York and had studied in Europe. Like so many others he came to California because of his health, settling in Santa Barbara in 1875. Ford visited all twenty-one missions, usually traveling by horse and buggy, and fashioned a remarkable portfolio that constituted the most accurate and artistically accomplished depictions of the missions to that time. Ford published *Etchings of the Franciscan Missions of California* in 1883 and went on to produce paintings of most of the missions. Also based in Santa Barbara was Alexander Harmer, among the most accomplished of the late-nineteenth- and early-twentieth-century California painters, who settled there in the early 1890s and spent some three decades painting California scenes.[23]

The artist who had the most significant immediate impact on public awareness of the missions may have been the English landscape painter Edwin Deakin. He first came to California in 1870, and over three decades he composed a series of paintings of all the missions, shown in a popular exhibition in San Francisco in 1900.[24] These romantic, atmospheric paintings gained wide popularity and had an appreciable influence on the growing preservation movement. "To Edwin Deakin, the 'artist historian,' is directly due the inspiration of the many clubs that are to-day enthusiastically taking up the subject of the opening and restoring of El Camino Real," commented the contemporary magazine the *Outlook*, noting that in his work Deakin sought "to perpetuate these Missions before the destroying hand of time and the vandalism of generations of robbery and abuse had utterly obliterated them."[25]

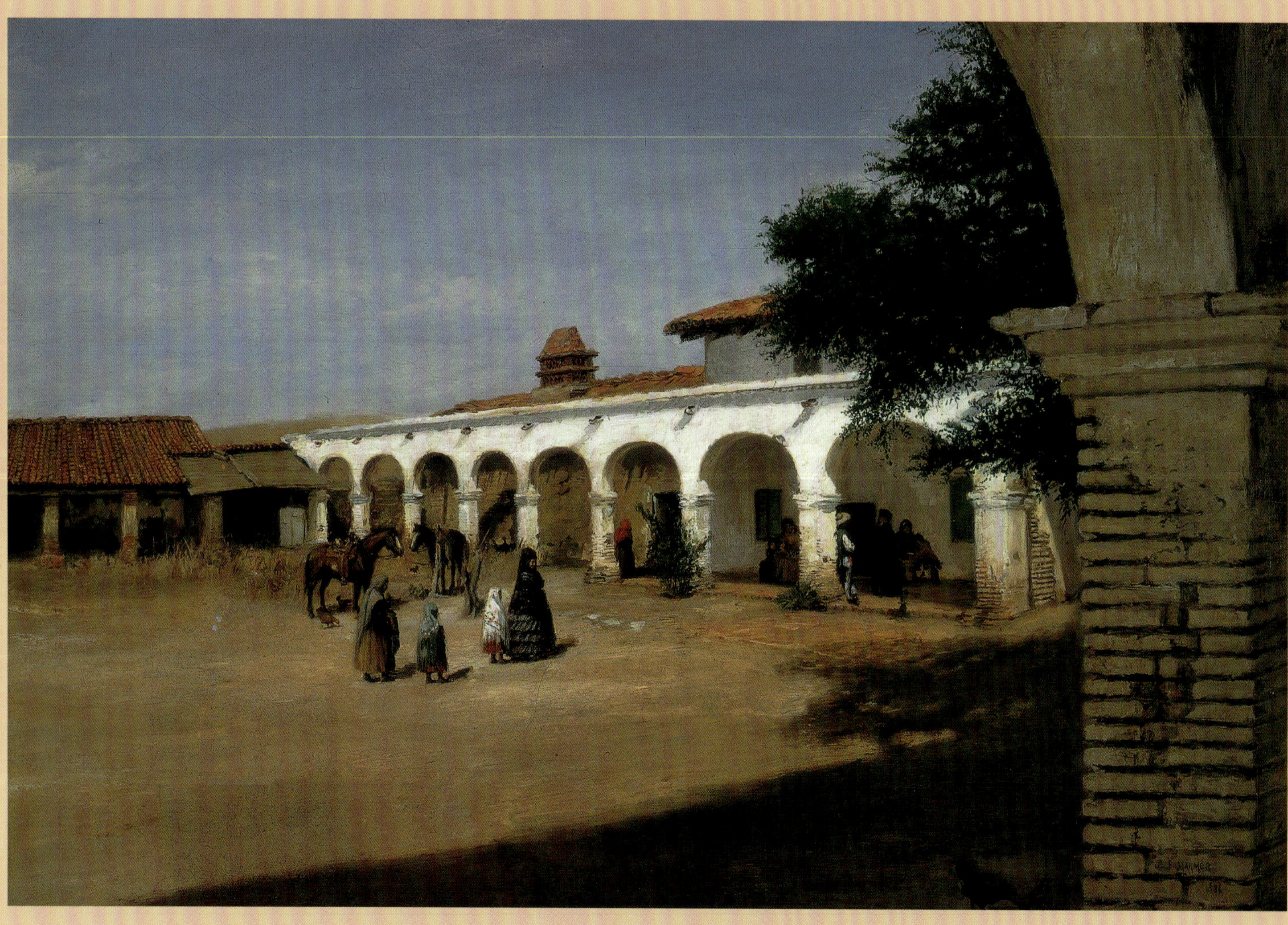

BELOW: A romantic scene of life at Mission San Juan Capistrano. A family in fine dress is crossing the quadrangle plaza, heading for the chapel; at right a priest converses with vaqueros, whose horses wait patiently nearby. Alexander Harmer, *Mission San Juan Capistrano, 1886.* Oil on canvas. Courtesy of The Irvine Museum, Irvine, California

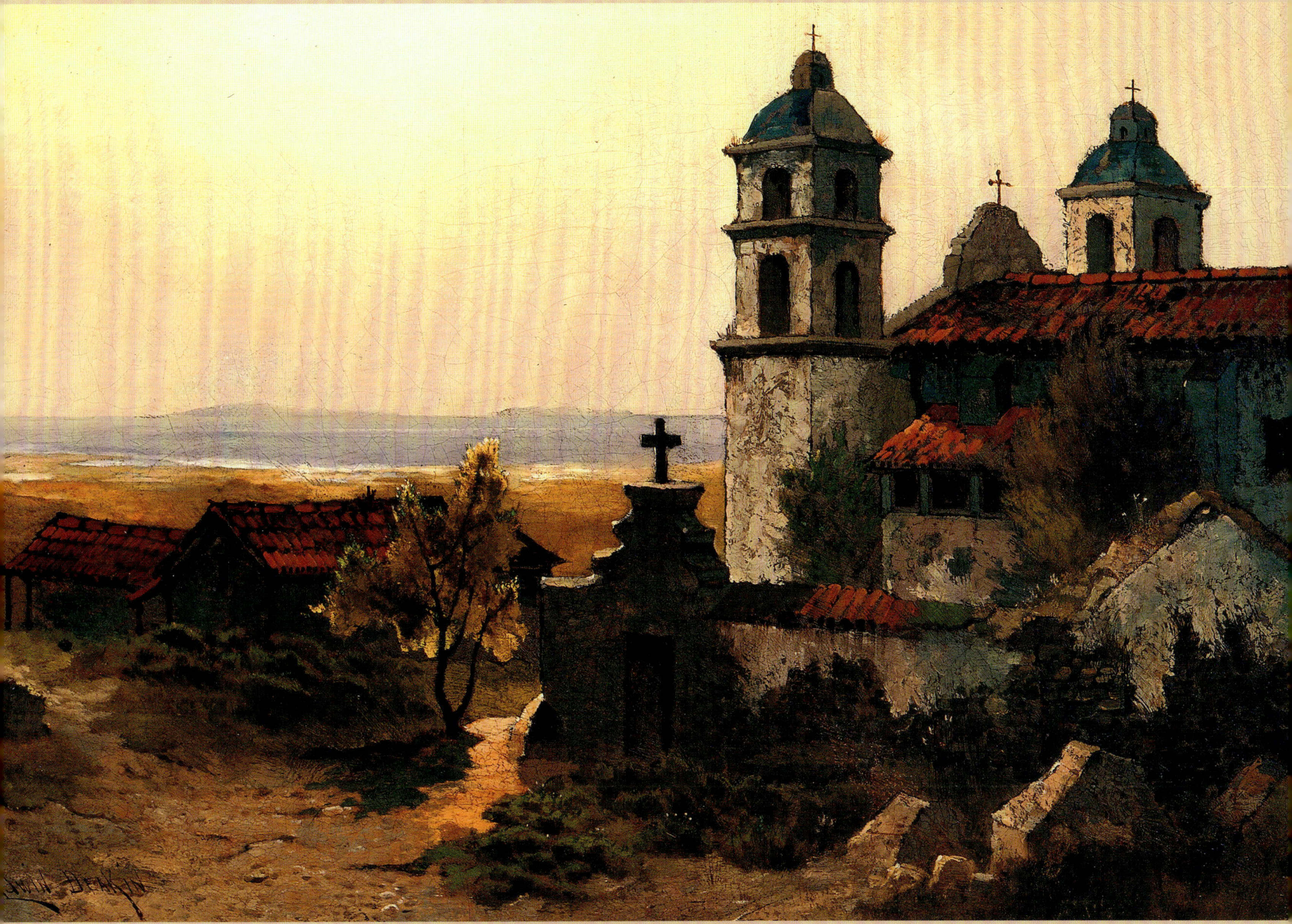

ABOVE: In this atmospheric rendering, Edwin Deakin infuses the scene with light and shortens the perspective toward the Pacific, heightening the sense of Mission Santa Bárbara's romantic isolation. Deakin, *Santa Barbara Mission*, ca. 1880. Oil on canvas. Courtesy Garzoli Gallery, San Rafael, California

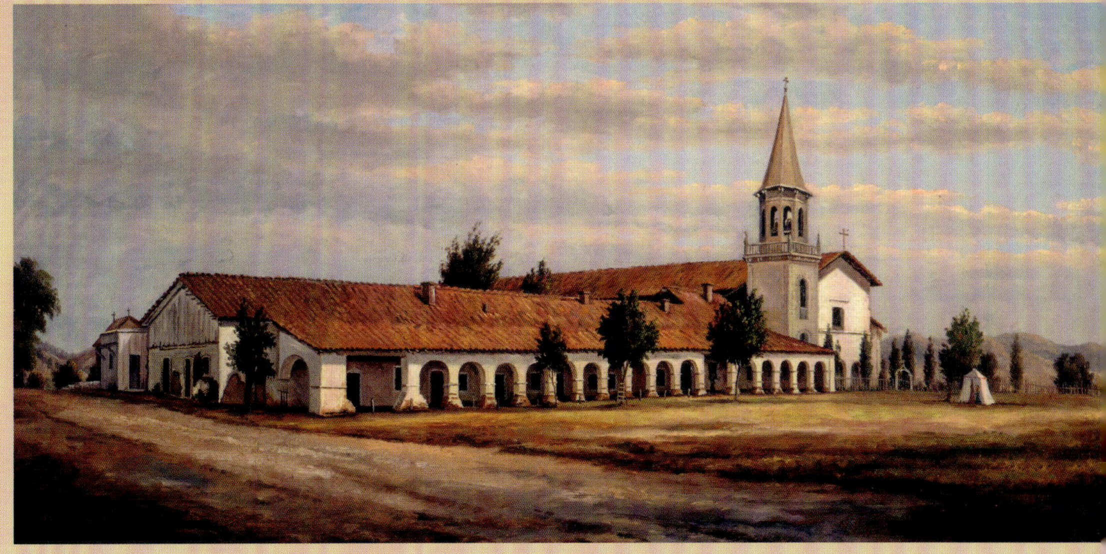

RIGHT: Henry Chapman Ford's etchings and paintings, with their technical proficiency and exacting attention to detail, provide an invaluable record of the missions in the late nineteenth century. Seen here is Mission San Juan Bautista, with its recently added Victorian tower. Ford, *Mission San Juan Bautista*, ca. 1881. Oil on canvas. Courtesy of the Mission Inn Foundation and Museum, Riverside, California. From the collection of The Historic Mission Inn Corporation

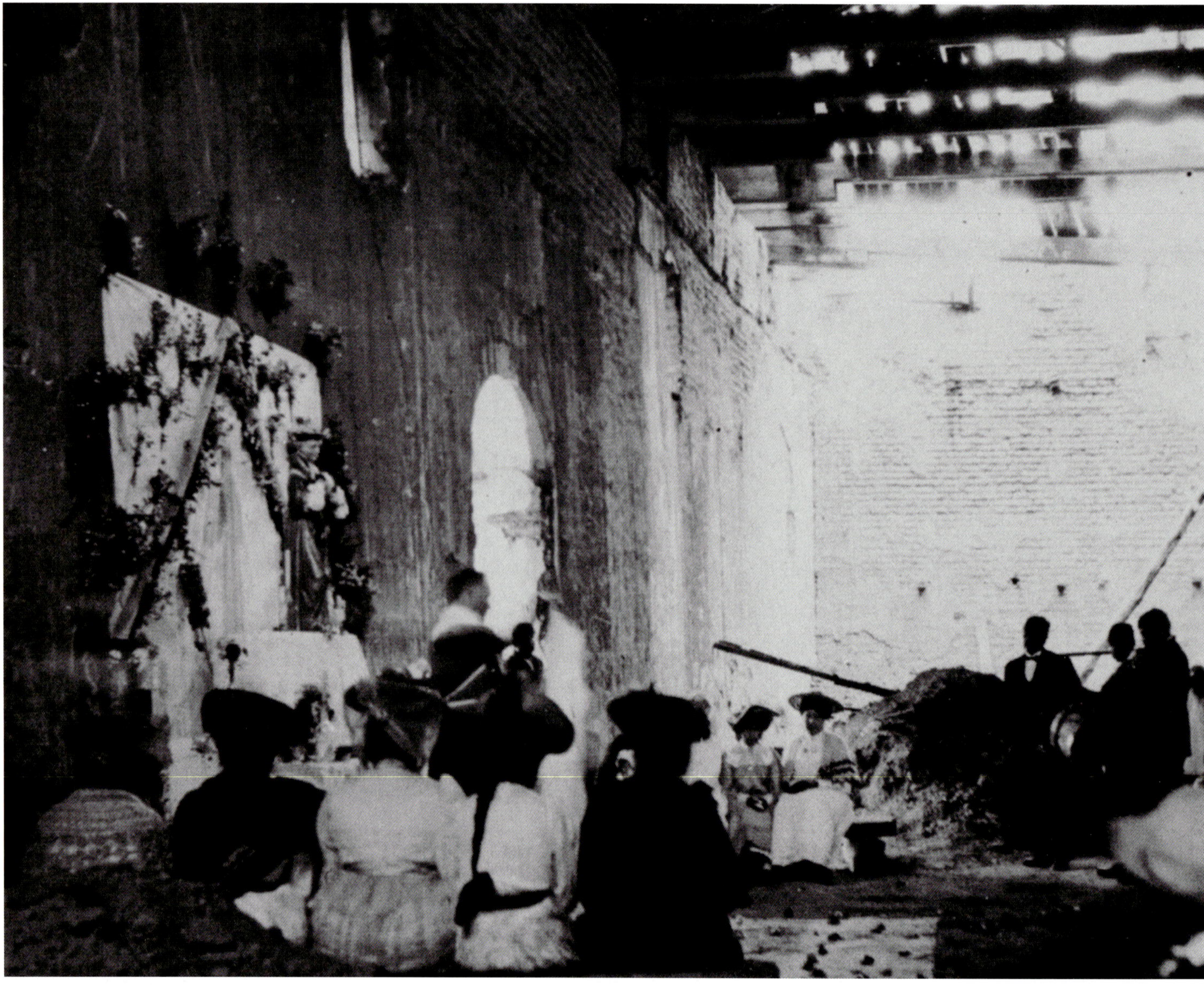

In the late nineteenth and early twentieth century, remnant congregations of mission Indians continued to worship in a number of missions. Here Saint Anthony's Day is celebrated before a makeshift altar in the ruins of Mission San Antonio, ca. 1905. At right, Indian musicians accompany the service. Courtesy Harry Downie Collection, Mission San Carlos Borromeo

climate and natural beauty, but they also mentioned the missions. In a guide titled *Semi-Tropical California*, one writer described the dilapidated "remains of the once rich and celebrated Mission of San Juan Capistrano," including "the ruins of the old Mission church, destroyed by an earthquake." Another guide included an appeal for the rescue of Mission San Carlos Borromeo: "If it be not too late, something should be done to save this noble ruin from utter destruction. It is the greatest historical monument in the State, and every Californian of whatever creed or no creed, should feel a personal interest in its preservation."[26]

One of the most forceful early voices for preservation of the missions was that of Robert Louis Stevenson, who during his stay in California explored the region's history and commented on its rapidly changing landscape. He admired the missions and their Franciscan founders, whom he preferred to the crass Americans—"sacriligious pistolshots"—now flooding the state. His description of a Mass performed in the ruins of the Carmel mission by Father Angelo Delfino Casanova, pastor at the Royal Presidio Chapel in Monterey, on

ca. 1876–82
Carleton Watkins photographs the missions.

1879
The Scottish writer Robert Louis Stevenson, sojourning in California, champions the cause of mission preservation.

the feast day of San Carlos Borromeo in 1879 poignantly captures a California in transition. He focused on the fate of the mission neophytes, uprooted from their native culture by the mission system, then expelled from their new lives, first by secularization and then by the arrival of the Americans:

> **The padre drives over the hill from Monterey; the little sacristy, which is the only covered portion of the church, is filled with seats and decorated for the service; the Indians troop together, their bright dresses contrasting with their dark and melancholy faces; and there, among a crowd of somewhat unsympathetic holiday makers, you may hear God served with perhaps more touching circumstances than in any other temple under heaven. An Indian, stone blind and about eighty years of age, conducts the singing; other Indians compose their choir; yet they have the Gregorian music at their finger ends and pronounce the Latin so correctly that I could follow the meaning as they sang.... I have never seen faces more vividly lit up with joy than the faces of these Indian singers. It was to them not only the worship of God, nor an act by which they recalled and commemorated better days, but was besides an exercise of culture, where all they knew of arts and letters was expressed.**[27]

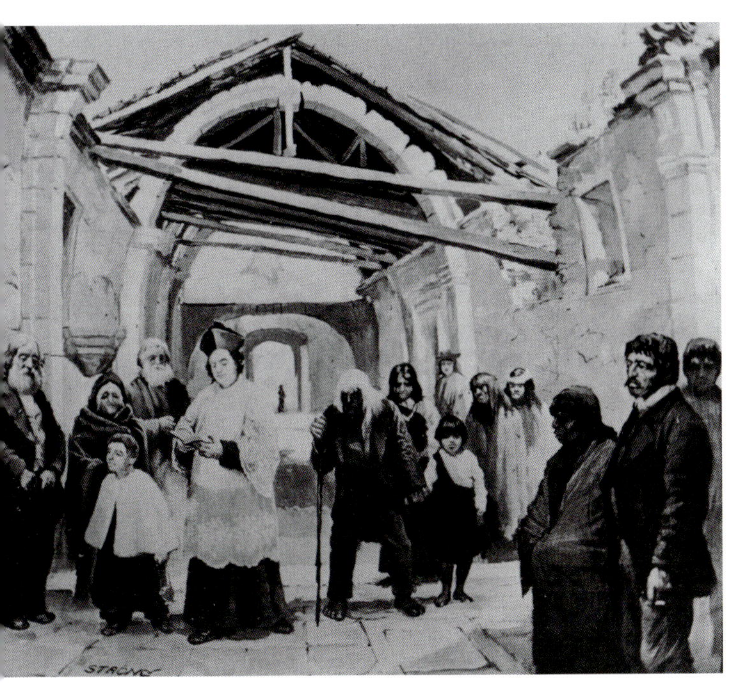

Father Angelo Casanova ministers to Native American worshippers in the ruins of Mission San Carlos Borromeo, ca. 1880. He is leading them into the sacristy, where services were still occasionally held. Courtesy of the California Historical Society

In an article published in the *Monterey Californian*, Stevenson urged that funds be raised to preserve the mission. "You have there a church of extreme interest which is going the way of all roofless and neglected buildings," he wrote. "The United States Mint can coin many million more dollar pieces, but not make a single Indian; and when Carmel Church is in the dust, not all the wealth of all the States and Territories can replace what has been lost."[28]

As popular interest in the missions began to be stirred by such appeals, local efforts to stem the deterioration of mission churches commenced in earnest. These were certainly the largest and most important buildings at the missions, the center for the spiritual life of the community and the repository of sacred and art objects. Culturally, aesthetically, and architecturally, mission churches symbolized the disappearing Spanish and Mexican heritage of California.

Individual priests were often the first to try to preserve the deteriorating structures. For the priests, concerned primarily with the churches' religious importance, historical and architectural matters were secondary, and upkeep often entailed modernization of the decor. At Santa Clara, for example, the adobe walls of the church were replaced with wider wooden ones in 1884, and at San Luis Obispo, in 1880, "the adobe walls of both the church and the residential building were boarded up, the roofs shingled, and... a modern wooden belfry and New England church steeple erected."[29]

One of the most important early preservation efforts took place at Mission San Carlos Borromeo del Río Carmelo. Once the headquarters of the California mission system and the burial place of Father Junípero Serra, the site had been abandoned from its secularization in 1834 until the early 1880s. In 1882 Father Casanova began a campaign to stop vandalism of the ruins, record the life of Serra, erect a monument over the grave, and repair the mission buildings. On July 3, 1882, a crowd of some four hundred gathered at the mission for the ceremonial opening of Father Serra's tomb. Other graves were also opened, including that of Father Juan Crespí, diarist of the Portolá expedition. Those in attendance came from all over the state. "It was an impressive and dramatic moment," the preservationist

1880–84
The writer and Indian advocate Helen Hunt Jackson makes several visits to California.

1882
Ceremonial opening of Father Serra's tomb at Mission San Carlos Borromeo awakens public awareness of need for mission preservation; Father Angelo Casanova begins restoration of the mission.

1883
Founding of the Historical Society of Southern California.

Joseph R. Knowland later recounted. "Father Serra had founded this Mission. Here he had spent many years directing, with unselfish devotion, a great work. Now, as the throng viewed his remains, they also looked upon the crumbling church walls which surrounded them. These ruins spoke impressively of neglect and indifference to the memory of an outstanding religious leader. The tragic scene not alone moved those assembled, but it awakened Californians generally."[30]

San Francisco newspapers picked up the cause, and the restoration drive captured the public's attention. More than $20,000 was raised to restore the structure—a considerable sum in the early 1880s. This early effort was unusual in that no local parish community existed to champion the work.[31] Rather, the effort to save this historic church came from the secular community and was statewide in scope. As with other early preservation efforts, authenticity was subordinated to utility: the new church roof, dedicated in 1884, had a steep pitch in the style of the eastern United States.

Perhaps the most important single cause for the "rediscovery" of Old California was the publication in 1884 of Helen Hunt Jackson's novel *Ramona.* It secured a place in the hearts of the citizenry for California's Spanish and Mexican heritage, albeit in the form of a romanticized myth that bore but an oblique relationship to historical reality. Jackson was a singular and impressive woman. After the deaths of her first husband and their two children, she remarried in Colorado, where she became what she had always laughingly derided: "a woman with a cause"—her cause being the plight of the American Indian.[32]

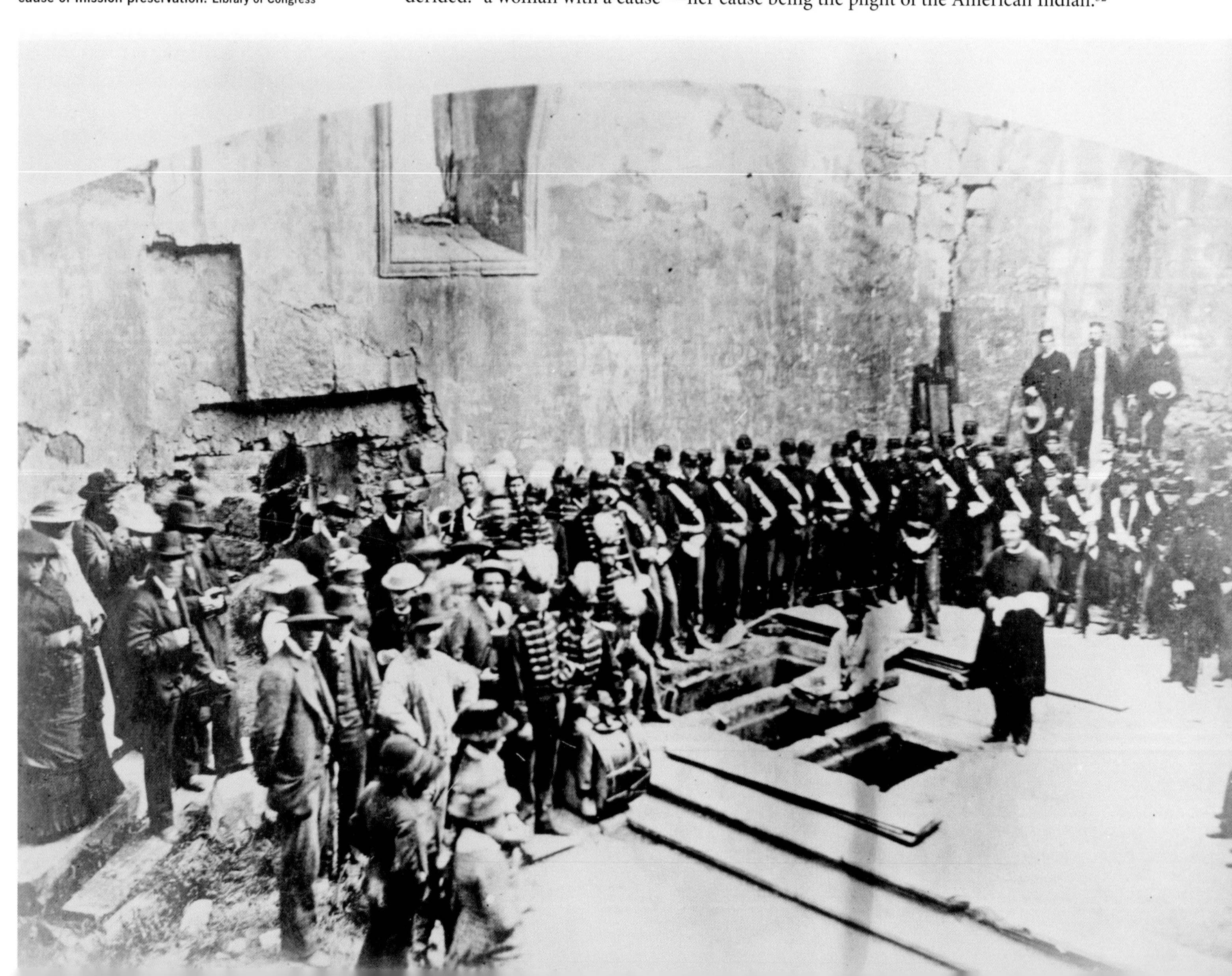

A crowd gathers within the ruins of Mission San Carlos Borromeo's church in 1882 for the ceremonial opening of the tomb of Father Serra and several of his contemporaries. A number of dignitaries witnessed the event, along with residents of Monterey and cadets from a Catholic school in San Francisco arrayed in resplendent uniforms. Father Angelo Casanova is standing next to the grave. This event, widely reported throughout the state, helped awaken the citizens of California to the cause of mission preservation. Library of Congress

Her scathing summation of the injustices inflicted on the Ponca tribe of the Dakota Territory, along with six other Native American groups, *A Century of Dishonor*, was published in 1881, and she personally sent a copy to every member of Congress.[33]

In the early 1880s she made several trips to California to write four illustrated articles for the *Century Magazine* and to investigate the condition of the former mission Indians. Driven off mission lands during secularization, they suffered an even harsher fate in American California, whose new proprietors came from a culture shaped by two centuries of Indian wars. Between 1845 and 1855 the California Indian population plummeted from 150,000 to 50,000. As Sherburne F. Cook has written, the Indians were subjected to brutal treatment at the hands of "a ruthless flood of miners and farmers who annihilated [them] without mercy or compensation. The direct causes of death were disease, the bullet, exposure, and acute starvation."[34] Those who survived endured difficult lives. Some stayed around towns or on ranchos, often working only for their keep. Others lived on isolated reservations or in small villages, where they eked out a hardscrabble existence. By 1880 only about 20,400 Native Americans were reported in the census, and the numbers continued to gradually decline through the end of the century.[35]

On her research trips, Jackson visited the Indian villages of southern California, later accompanied by her *Century* illustrator, Henry Sandham, and by Abbot Kinney, a prominent booster and supporter of Indian rights who spoke fluent Spanish and in later years would found a themed development called Venice-by-the-Sea. Near San Diego, the group traveled to the outlying hills and visited the scattered homes, the "kennels," as Jackson called them, of the poverty-stricken native people, composed of "piles of refuse and brush, old blankets, old patches of sail-cloth, old calico, dead pine boughs, and sticks all heaped together in shapeless mounds." Jackson took up the cause of the San Pasqual group who had recently been run off their land by American usurpers. In 1881 she was able to obtain

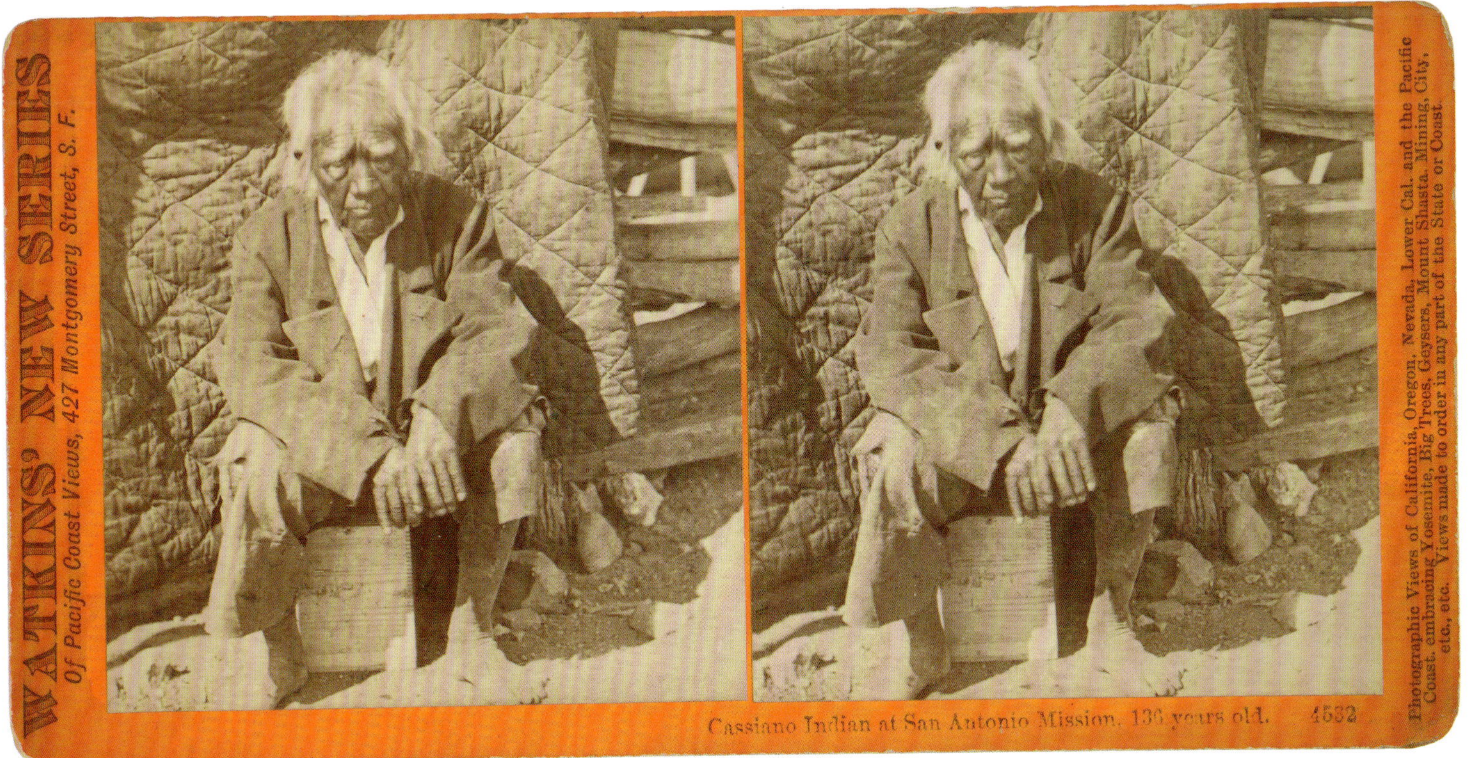

An elderly former neophyte of Mission San Antonio, ca. 1875. The estimate of his age is certainly exaggerated. Photographs by Carleton Watkins. Albumen silver print stereograph. J. Paul Getty Museum, Los Angeles. 84.XC.902.86

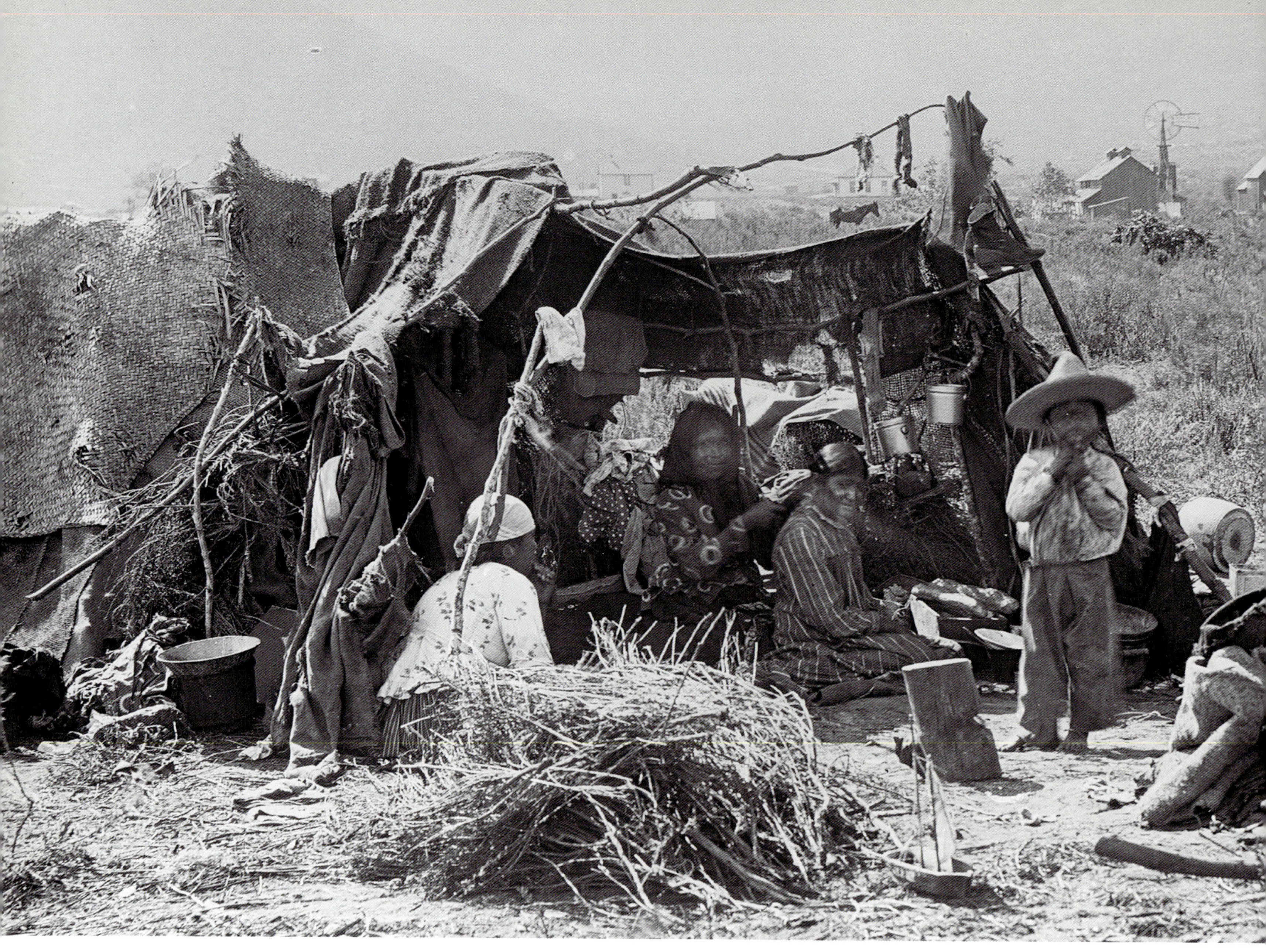

A poverty-stricken Native American family in the village of Saboba, at the foot of the San Jacinto Mountains. These people were facing eviction from lands they had occupied since the missions were secularized in the 1830s. Helen Hunt Jackson and other Indian advocates took up their cause, and in 1888 the California Supreme Court upheld their right to occupy the land, respecting the terms of a Mexican land grant from 1842. Seaver Center for Western History Research, Los Angeles County Museum of Natural History

appointments as special agents for herself and Kinney from the Commissioner of Indian Affairs. Their detailed recommendations for improving treatment of the Indians were finally implemented ten years later.[36]

Jackson sojourned at the Los Angeles home of the prominent Californios Antonio and Mariana Coronel and briefly visited the del Valle family's Rancho Camulos, near Newhall, where many customs of rancho days were still followed. She visited a number of missions, enjoying in particular the atmosphere at Mission Santa Bárbara.[37] She also visited mission ruins, which she felt infused their bucolic landscapes with an enriching sense of European tradition and which she came to view as evocative of a lost golden era. At San Juan Capistrano, she wrote in the *Century*, "the peace, silence, and beauty of the spot are brooded over by the grand gray ruin [of the stone church], lifting the whole scene into an ineffable harmony. Wandering in room after room... through corridors with red-tiled roofs and

1884
Publication of Helen Hunt Jackson's novel *Ramona* and first volumes of H. H. Bancroft's *History of California*.

1885
Santa Fe Railroad completes track to Los Angeles; resultant land boom threatens historic sites.

1886
C. C. Pierce arrives in Los Angeles, begins photographing the missions.

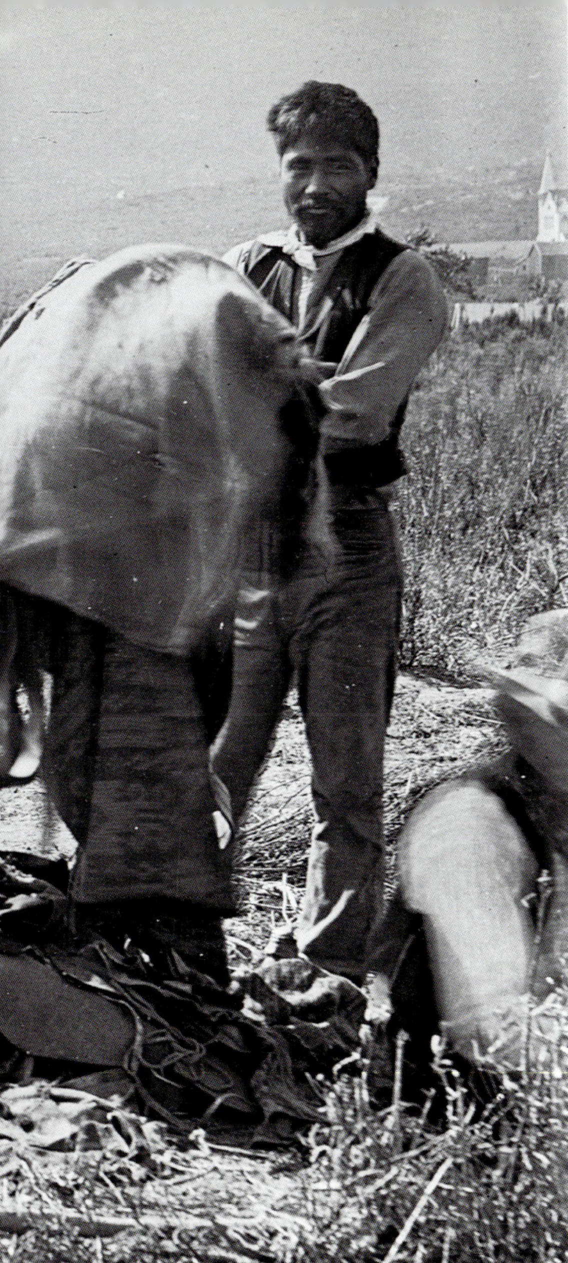

hundreds of broad Roman arches, over fallen pillars, and through carved doorways, . . . one asks oneself if he be indeed in America."[38]

Like others of her time, Jackson believed that it was the secularization of the missions, not the abuses of the mission system itself, which was responsible for the catastrophe that befell California's Native Americans. Neither she nor her contemporaries imagined a pre-Spanish California, occupied by native peoples living productive traditional lives. And it was not only Americans who were shortsighted: most Californios, and even some former neophytes, remembered life at the missions, before secularization, as the height from which they had fallen. By the 1880s few native memories reached back into the times before the Spanish came, and for some the trials and difficulties of mission life had largely faded in the light of subsequent disasters under the reign of the Americans. As early as 1872 the *San Francisco Evening Bulletin* reported that the former mission residents "who straggle around the country, here getting a job as a *vaquero*, and again herding sheep, look back at the good old times of the mission with regret."[39]

Such selective memories likely confirmed Jackson's own interpretation of the Franciscans' missionary endeavor, which she viewed with unstinting admiration. Her interviews with former mission residents seemed to reinforce this perspective. At San Juan Capistrano, she wrote, she was accompanied among the ruins by "a white-haired Mexican who in his boyhood had spent a year in the mission." He "remembered as if it were yesterday its bustling life of fifty years ago, when the arched corridor ran unbroken around the great courtyard . . . and was often filled with Indians, friars, officers, and gay Mexican ladies. . . . [E]very Sunday, came the Indians, in long procession, to get their weekly gifts. Each one received something,—a handkerchief, dress, trinket, or money." At San Juan Bautista, she said, "there are many old men and women, whose memories are like magic glasses, reproducing pictures of the past." Jackson was told that "'the Indians used to be . . . like sheep, by the thousand and thousand.' They were always good, and the padres were always kind."[40]

Frustrated with government inaction in response to her reports on the American Indians, she set out to carry her cause to the public, planning a book that she hoped would do for the Indians what *Uncle Tom's Cabin* had done for the black slaves of the South. "It is laid in So. California," she wrote to a newspaper editor, "and . . . if I can do one hundredth part for the Indians that Mrs. Stowe did for the Negro, I will be thankful."[41] She wrote the entire novel during spring 1884 from her hotel room back in New York City. *Ramona* was serialized in the *Christian Union* within two months and appeared in book form that November.

The story takes place on a fictional rancho near Los Angeles in the 1870s. The señorita Ramona, born to a Scotsman and an Indian woman, and an Indian worker named Alessandro fall in love. They endure considerable prejudice and hardship, and their story culminates in a despairing Alessandro's death at the hands of a bigoted white settler. The novel quickly became a nationwide success, and its influence on the popular culture of the time cannot be overstated. This effect, however, was quite different from what its author had intended. Jackson's romantic style and setting eclipsed her message of social oppression, and the book, instead of generating outrage at the treatment of Indians, wound up popularizing a romantic vision of life in Spanish and Mexican California.[42]

What would come to be known as the "mission myth" was shaped by *Ramona*'s evocation of a pastoral arcadia, with its whitewashed adobe walls, fragrant orchards and orange groves, and the comforting rituals of sheep-shearing time. Over the next few decades an assortment of writers, scholars, and boosters would use the book as a point of departure to

1887
Railroad arrives in San Juan Capistrano, providing easy access for artists, who often paint the mission.

ca. 1888
Tourists begin flocking to the del Valle family's Rancho Camulos, which becomes known as the "home of Ramona" after C. F. Lummis publishes booklet on Ramona myth.

1888
Association for the Preservation of the Missions founded by Los Angeles librarian Tessa L. Kelso.

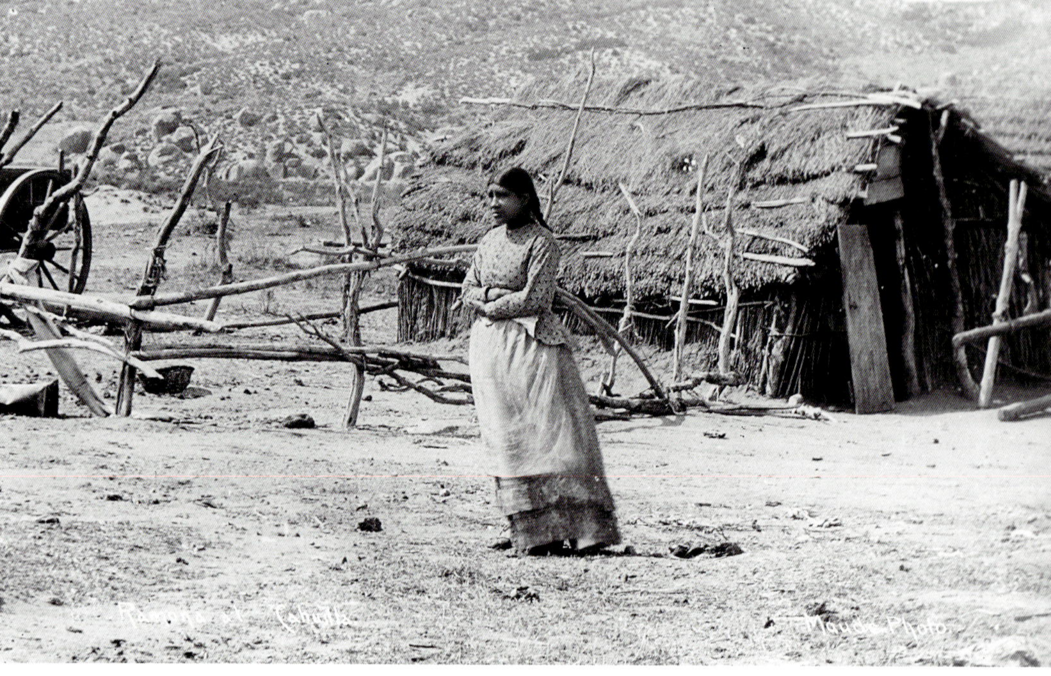

Ramona Lubo, widely assumed at the time to be the eponymous title character of Helen Hunt Jackson's novel, seen here at Cahuilla, ca. 1895. It is likely, however, that Jackson's fictional character was a composite of several people. Seaver Center for Western History Research, Los Angeles County Museum of Natural History

reinvent the heritage of an older California. Works such as D. A. Hufford's *The Real Ramona* (1900) and George Wharton James's *Through Ramona's Country* (1909) purported to trace the real-life equivalents of the novel's characters and settings. Businesses took the names of characters from the novel, and a host of towns claimed to be "authentic Ramona locales." As Dydia DeLyser has written in *Ramona Memories*, "At a time of immense social change, *Ramona*'s romanticized images of what came to be seen as southern California's 'Spanish-mission' past were blended into the region's culture, inscribed onto its landscape, and manipulated by California boosters with results far removed from the novelist's reformist intent."[43] The mission heritage would be seen as European, Mediterranean, and Spanish, not as Mexican, Indian, and mestizo. It would be transformed into an uplifting tale of kindly Franciscans bringing civilization's myriad benefits to the grateful indigenous peoples of California. The suffering of the mission Indians would not play a part in the story. The rancho period, meanwhile, would come to be popularly known by the new Americans as "the Days of the Dons," a romantic time of fiestas and rodeos featuring dashing caballeros and mantilla-clad señoritas. Ironically, this newfound passion for the Spanish past occurred at a time when California's real Spanish-speaking populations were being increasingly marginalized. "Through *Ramona*," the historian Kevin Starr has aptly noted, Americans "took some warmth from the banked fires of the culture they had displaced."[44]

The most prolific promoter of the mission myth was Harvard-educated Charles Fletcher Lummis, for a time city editor of the *Los Angeles Times*. Lummis had walked to Los Angeles from Ohio as a publicity stunt in 1884, an experience during which the landscapes and architecture of the Southwest had had an effect comparable to a religious conversion. A colorful figure, a devotee of history, anthropology, and ethnography, as well as a passionate advocate of Indian rights, Lummis often dressed in the Spanish style. He edited the magazine *Land of Sunshine*,[45] which under his tireless guidance became a showcase for southwestern art and culture. Later he founded the Southwest Museum, devoted to the study of

1892
Franciscan friars from Zacatecas, Mexico begin restoring Mission San Luis Rey.

1893
Beginning of Mission Revival movement in architecture; artist Alexander Harmer settles in Santa Barbara, begins painting California scenes.

1895
Landmarks Club founded in Los Angeles by C. F. Lummis, who becomes editor of *Land of Sunshine* and promotes cause of mission preservation.

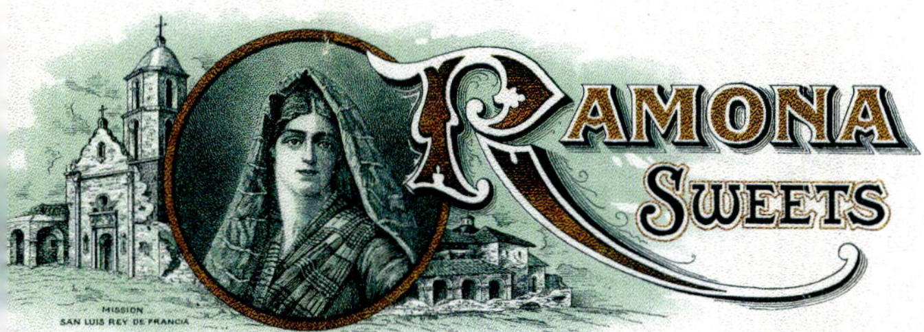

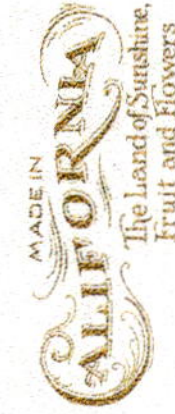

As the romantic mission myth gained popularity following the publication of *Ramona*, Jackson's heroine and the missions were featured in commercial promotions throughout California. ABOVE: A candy advertisement displaying a portrait of Ramona against a backdrop of Mission San Luis Rey. BELOW: Advertisement for the Old Mission Brand produce company portraying Mission San Carlos de Borromeo. California State Archives

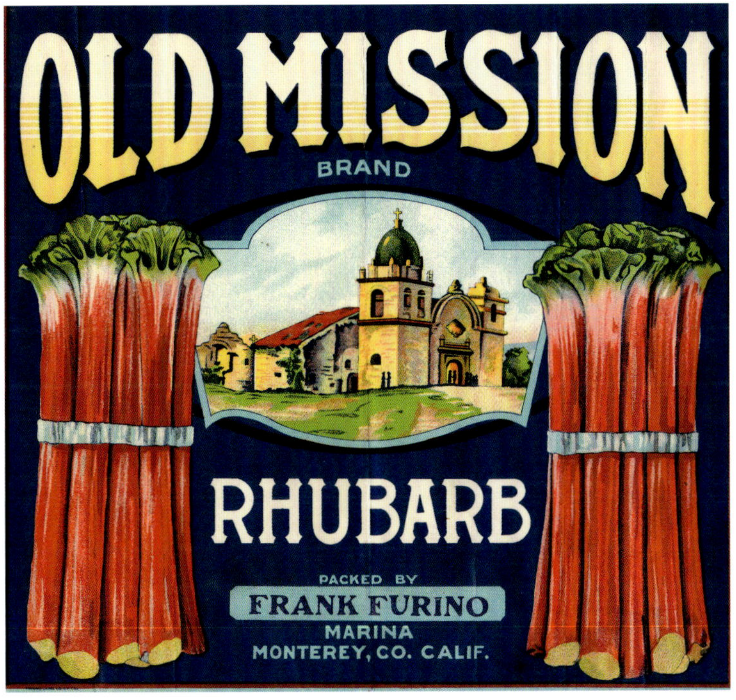

the indigenous cultures of the southwestern United States.[46] In such books as *The Spanish Pioneers*, published in 1893, and in a torrent of magazine articles, he combined a booster spirit with a fervent admiration for the legacy of the Spanish frontier. If properly appreciated, it could, he felt, provide a model for the nascent ethos of American southern California. "Next to our climate and its consequences," Lummis famously stated, the missions were "the best capital California has."[47]

Although Lummis by no means subscribed to the sentimental elements of the Ramona myth, he was a consummate pragmatist in his pursuit of heritage preservation. In 1888 he published a promotional booklet filled with photographs he had taken at Rancho Camulos, proclaiming it the home of Ramona, thereby helping to confer on the fictional story, in the minds of the public, the allure and authenticity of historical fact. The Southern Pacific Railroad put in a special stop, and members of the del Valle family became docents and character actors to accommodate the swarms of tourists that now descended to visit.

Business opportunists were quick to join the parade, and commodities from fruit crate labels to health cures took mission-related names. In Riverside an enthusiast named Frank Miller began construction of the Mission Inn, a phantasmagoria of Spanish motifs that became the unofficial headquarters of the region's mission movement. California's romanticized Spanish heritage became one of the state's sellable commodities, along with its climate, citrus farming, and oil. The del Valles themselves would market their oranges under the 'Home of Ramona' label. In later years Lummis asked Frank Miller what *Ramona* had been worth financially to California. Miller's response: "I figure that book has brought at least fifty million dollars into this region."[48] Lummis himself later confessed, "Plymouth Rock was a state of mind. So were the California Missions."[49]

The birth of the mission myth fueled California's emergence as a destination for both travel and relocation. Although Los Angeles had been connected by rail to San Francisco—and through San Francisco to the eastern United States—since 1876, the land boom of southern California awaited the arrival of the Santa Fe Railroad in 1885. It set off a fare war that was hard for midwesterners to resist. "In less than a year the Santa Fe was selling one-way tickets [to Los Angeles] from Kansas City for a low of one dollar," one historian has commented; "whole counties in the Midwest were depopulated, and sixty new communities were raised upon the ruins of the ranchos."[50]

The great land boom of the 1880s threatened historic sites that had previously been undisturbed, and those who were paying attention were alarmed. When the Historical Society

1900
Edwin Deakin holds popular exhibition of mission paintings in San Francisco.

1900–1915
Mission Revival architectural style widely used for hotels, train stations, and other tourist-related buildings, popularizing the mission theme.

of Southern California was founded in 1883, its president noted in his inaugural address that "in the midst of the inrushing flood of immigrants, old landmarks are rapidly disappearing." The society's principal mission, he announced, would be "to collect and preserve historical matter," including the missions.[51]

The 1880s, which also saw publication of Hubert Howe Bancroft's seven-volume history of California, provided fertile ground for the growth of California's early historic preservation groups. One of the first was the Association for the Preservation of the Missions, founded in 1888 by Tessa L. Kelso, of the Los Angeles Public Library.[52] The cause was taken up by popular magazines as well. "Of the many Missions and 'stations' in Southern California, the minor ones are largely

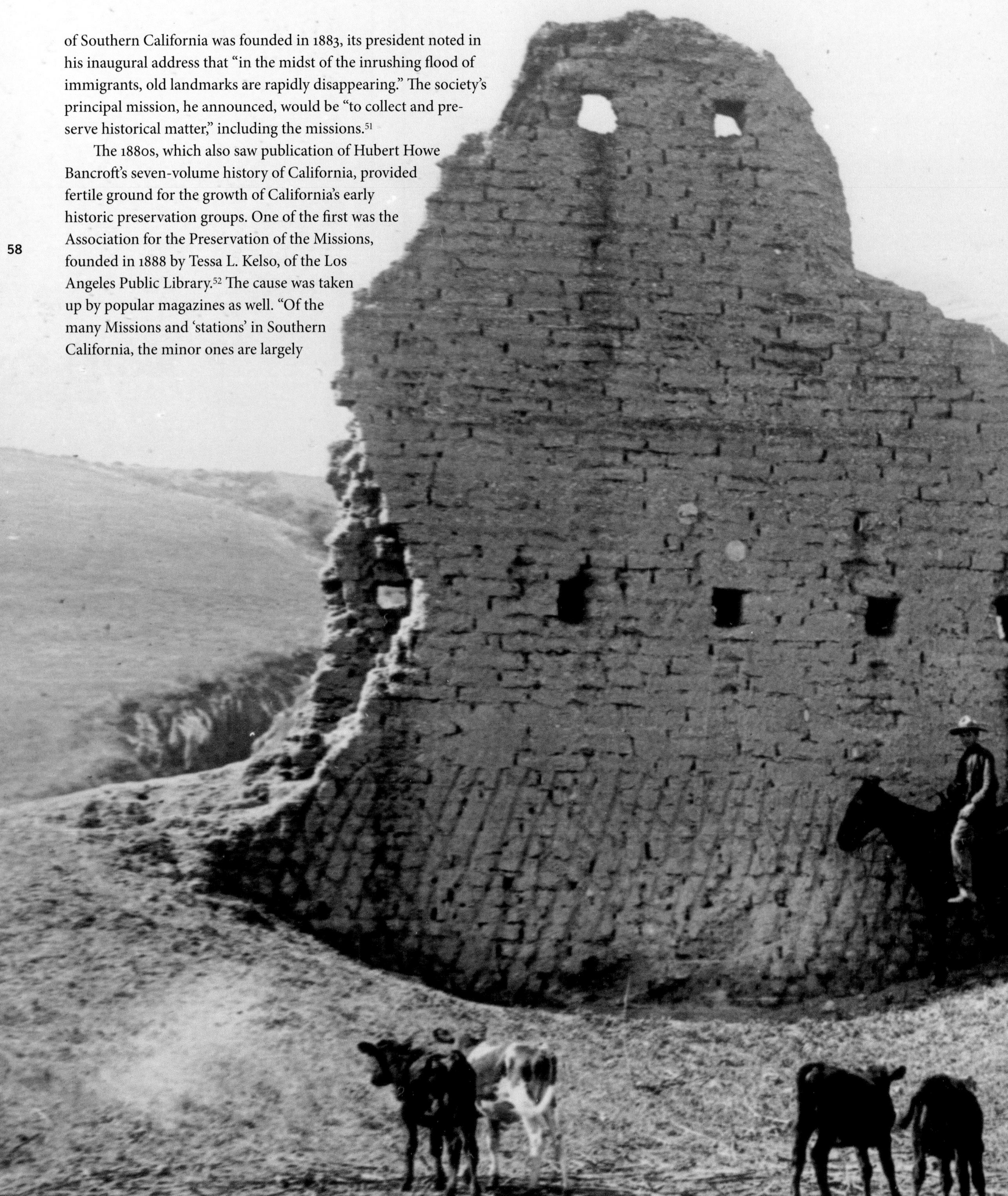

hopeless ruins, and even the more important have mostly fallen somewhat to decay," *Drakes Magazine* lamented in 1889. "In only a few are pains being taken to reserve the noble edifices from the tireless tooth of Time."[53]

Lummis cared passionately about the missions, which, he wrote, "were falling to ruin with frightful rapidity, their roofs being breached or gone, the adobe walls melting away under the winter rains."[54] He relentlessly promoted the cause of preservation in his magazine, casting his appeal so as to skirt the anti-Catholic bias of many of his readers. The missions, he explained, "belong not to the Catholic church but to you and me. . . . Let us save them—not for the Church but for Humanity."[55]

In 1895 Lummis formed the Landmarks Club of Southern California to preserve the "missions and other historical landmarks." With members both moneyed and well

The towering wall of the ruined church at the first site of Mission La Purísima shades a cowboy as he watches his cattle graze, ca. 1887. Photograph by C. C. Pierce. Courtesy University of Southern California, on behalf of the USC Special Collections

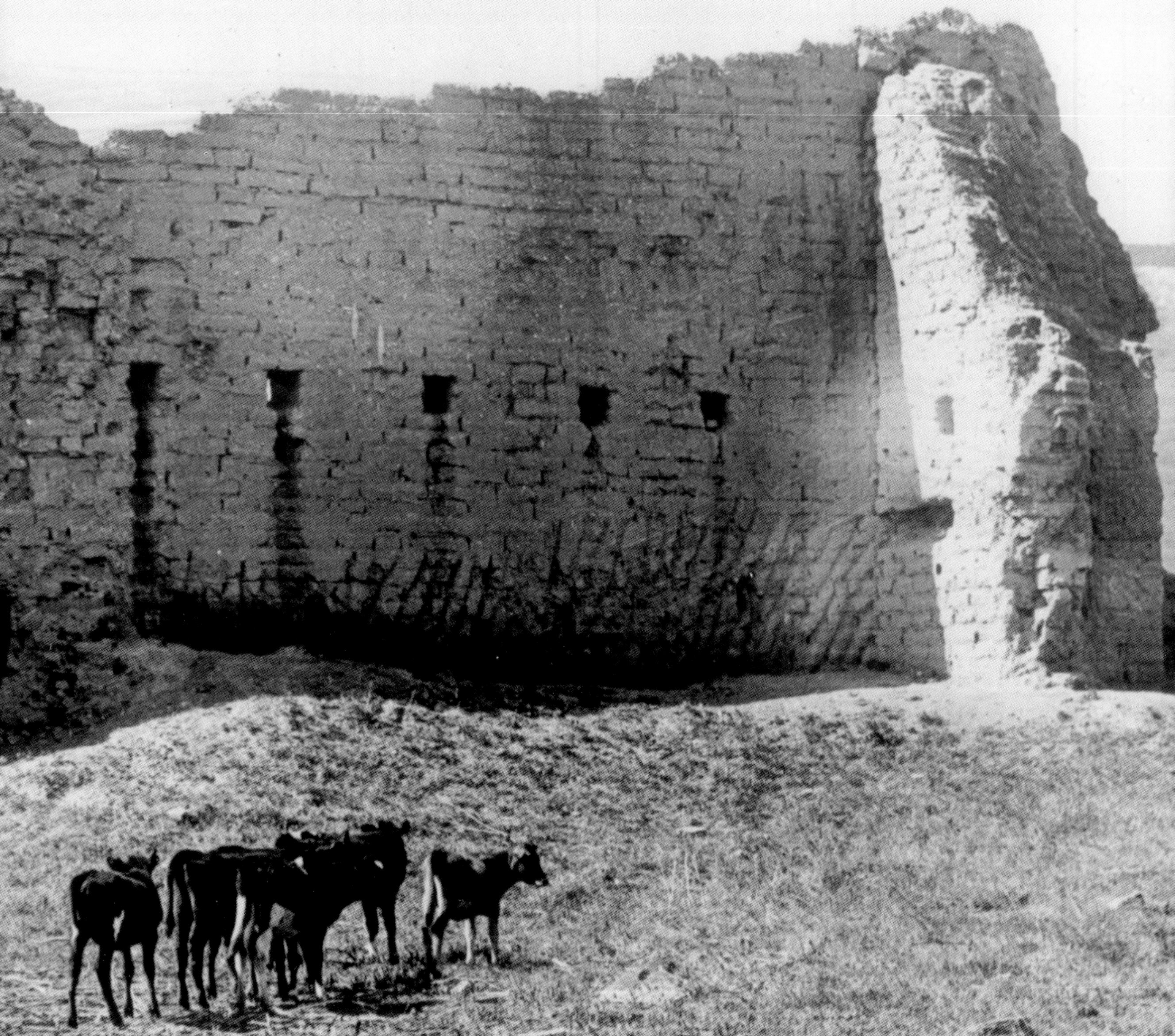

The *Mission Play*

The mission myth found perhaps its purest and most complete expression in the *Mission Play*, a historical pageant by John Steven McGroarty, a journalist for the *Los Angeles Times* who also wrote sentimental verse as well as hefty booster histories of California. It premiered in spring 1912 on the grounds of Mission San Gabriel. Underwritten in part by Henry E. Huntington, the *Mission Play* was the most popular of all the southern California outdoor drama pageants. It cost $1.5 million to mount, including the construction of the Mission Playhouse—now the San Gabriel Civic Auditorium—to house performances, and featured a cast of more than one hundred. McGroarty was advised by the noted mission historian Father Zephyrin Engelhardt, O.F.M., who told him, "I can furnish but the dry skeleton of history, because I must cling to the bare truth; but it would be like putting on flesh and skin by acting it all on the stage. This would be a supplement of priceless value."[56]

Based on the *Passion Play*, an epic of Christ's life performed annually in Oberammergau, Germany, the *Mission Play* presented a romanticized and culturally biased version of the mission saga. Its three acts dramatized Father Serra's miraculous founding of Mission San Diego de Alcalá, the conversion and civilization of the "grateful" California natives, and the tragic aftermath of secularization for the destitute—but still devoted—ex-neophyte populations. In the play's final scene, the heroine, a member of a grand Californio family, bids farewell to the ruins of her Mission San Juan Capistrano. An old Indian vaquero suggests that perhaps "the *Americanos*... will restore these broken walls." The señora responds, "Surely, when the *Americanos* are building their great cities, and their tireless hands are making California the wonder of the world, so also will they think, sometime, of these holy places where the padres toiled.... Though we may not see it,... maybe in God's good time the Mission bells will ring again their old, sweet music."

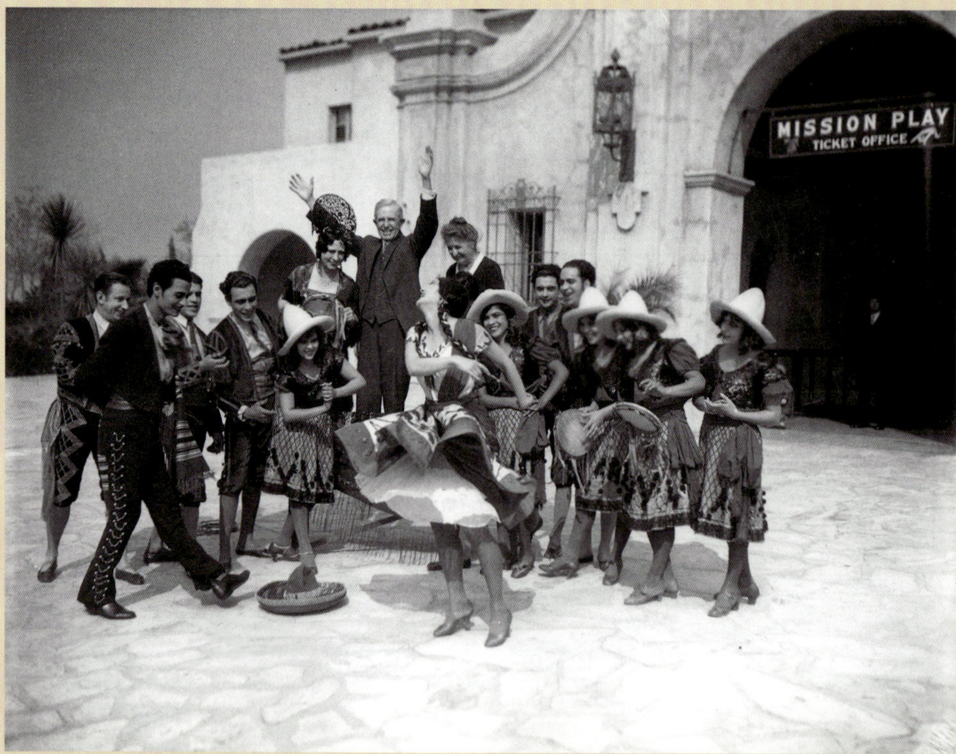

The playwright John Steven McGroarty, surrounded by actors from the *Mission Play*, ca. 1920. Security Pacific Collection, Los Angeles Public Library

The opening night performance ended in enthusiastic applause, the playwright in tears standing to accept the adulation of the audience. One critic enthused that watching the play was like witnessing history itself. Between 1912 and 1929 some 2.5 million people would attend the more than three thousand performances of this sentimental pastiche, which would occasionally be revived for performances at such venues as the Hollywood Bowl. Its author would be named poet laureate of California and would be honored by the pope and the king of Spain for promoting the state's Catholic and Spanish heritage.[57]

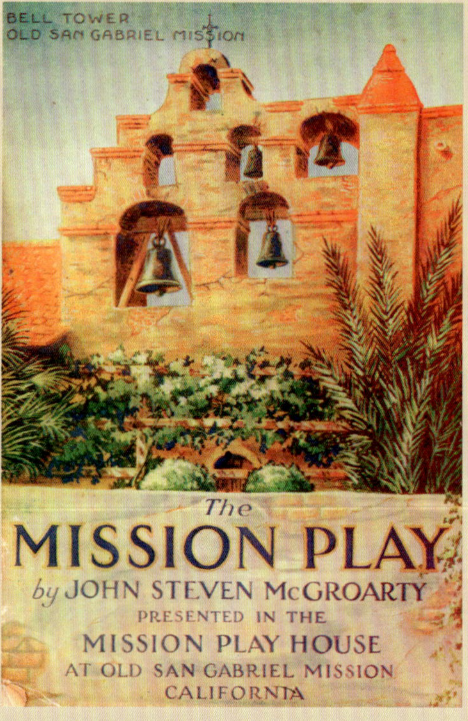

A program from the *Mission Play*. Courtesy of the Mission Inn Foundation and Museum, Riverside, California. From the collection of The Historic Mission Inn Corporation

Mission Revival Architecture

As the romantic lore of the missions spread across California, commercial, railroad, and real estate boosters increasingly used images of mission buildings on their brochures and posters, evoking concepts of the "sublime and picturesque" and the "noble bastions in the wilderness." Mission Revival architecture answered the need for a style that reflected American history "in a way that paralleled England's adoption of the Gothic Revival," observed the historian Karen Weitze. "Previously, all revivals had been imported. A mission style was indigenous."[58] Design competition for the California Building at the 1893 Columbian Exposition in Chicago brought the matter of a California style to a head, and the winning eclectic mission-style design carried the day.

The rapid development of new towns in California provided ample opportunity for architects to refine this new style. They adapted the massive buttressed walls, arched corridors with patio gardens, smooth plastered surfaces, and low-pitched tile roofs into the Mission Revival style. The architecture was compatible with the sunny, dry southern California climate and fortuitously coincided with technological advances that produced inexpensive and durable reinforced concrete structures and stucco.

The first important application of this new style was accomplished by Frederick Law Olmsted in his design of Stanford University, which opened in 1891. Subsequently, the Mission Revival style was commonly chosen for a wide range of civic buildings and commercial structures, including many of the Southern Pacific and Santa Fe railroad stations. Perhaps its most fanciful expression is seen in the Mission Inn, in Riverside, which Frank Miller expanded over the course of three decades from a small adobe hotel to "the most conspicuously elaborate, and thereafter, the most widely published, of the Mission Revival hotels."[59] Ironically, the initial turn-of-the-century renovation of the adobe involved reroofing the structure with tiles taken from the Pala Asistencia, thereby hastening the demise of an original historic building while creating a facsimile—a facsimile that has since gained renown as an important historic structure in its own right.

Although the popularity of Mission Revival declined after 1915, by 1939 more than one million Mission Revival–inspired residences graced southern California.[60] Mission Revival was succeeded by a second wave of popularity—the Spanish Colonial revival—launched by the Panama-California Exposition in San Diego's Balboa Park and enduring through the mid-1930s. Some of the most elaborate examples are found in the architecture of downtown Santa Barbara. Many architects appreciated the style's appropriateness of form and material to the western climate and landscape. Although these architectural styles have faded from popular use, the presence of key motifs of mission architecture has become common in much of California.

Between 1900 and 1915, the Mission Revival style was widely used for train stations and hotels, as mission-related iconography played an important role in California's growing prominence as a tourist destination. Seen here is the Santa Barbara railroad station, designed by Francis W. Wilson and built in 1905. Photograph © Bill Dewey

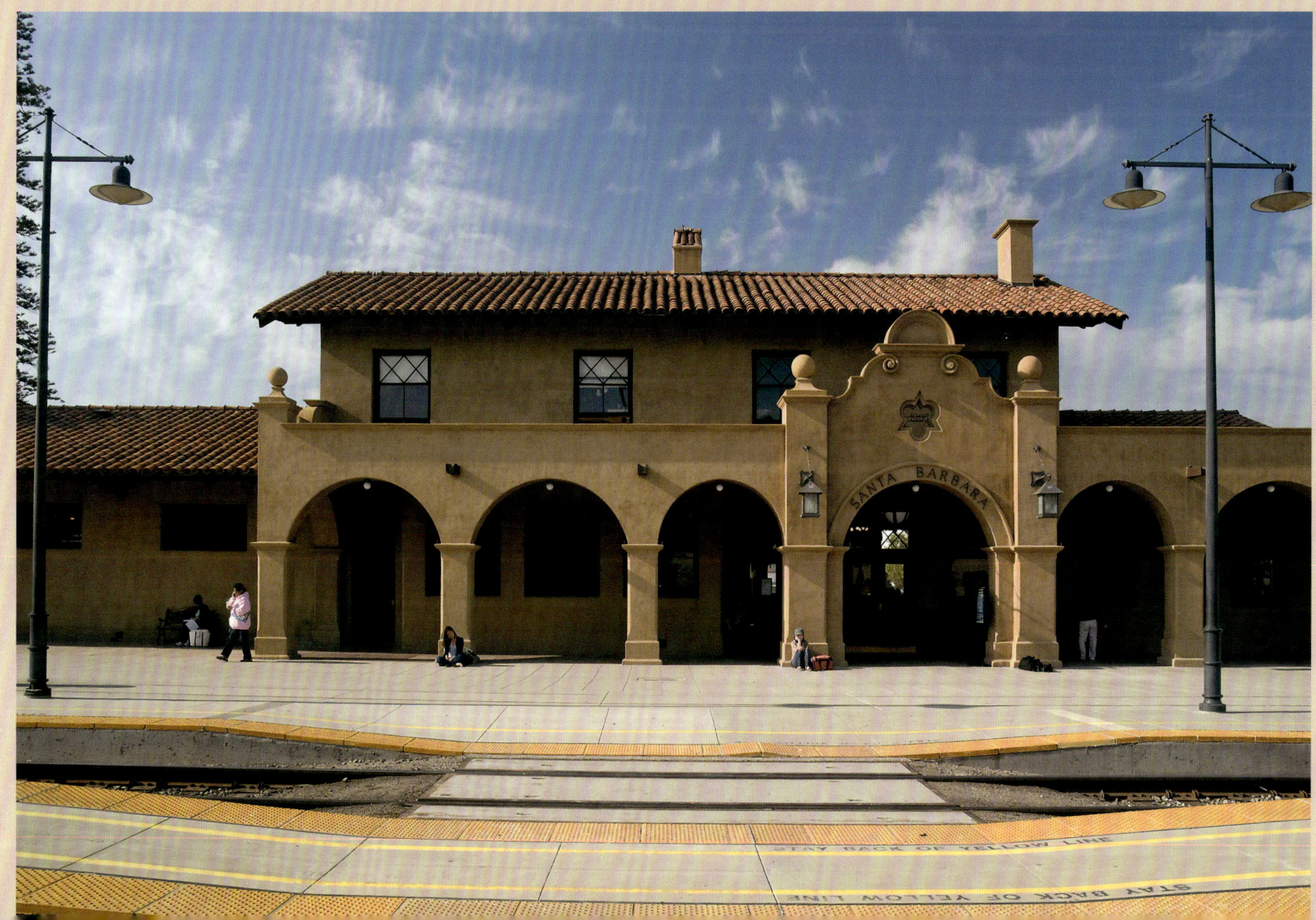

connected—including John Muir, Theodore Roosevelt Jr., and Phoebe Apperson Hearst—it appealed to individual donors through local fund-raisers, attracting support from the eastern United States and abroad. It rescued many of the state's mission sites from certain oblivion. In 1896 the club undertook preservation of the remains of San Juan Capistrano, initiating a program that was to continue for some twenty years. The following year it also began work at Mission San Fernando, reroofing the *convento* wing and stabilizing the church. Paying attention to both large and small sites, it returned Pala Asistencia to the church in 1903 through purchase from private ownership.[61]

Other groups also became involved in preservation. The Native Sons of the Golden West, a hereditary organization founded in 1875, established the Historic Landmarks Committee in 1902 to identify sites in need of preservation, with priority given, among other structures, to "the old missions of California." That same year, the Historic Landmarks League was formed, with similar preservation goals, including the protection of "structures, monuments and sites . . . [of] . . . early Spanish settlers." The chair of both these committees

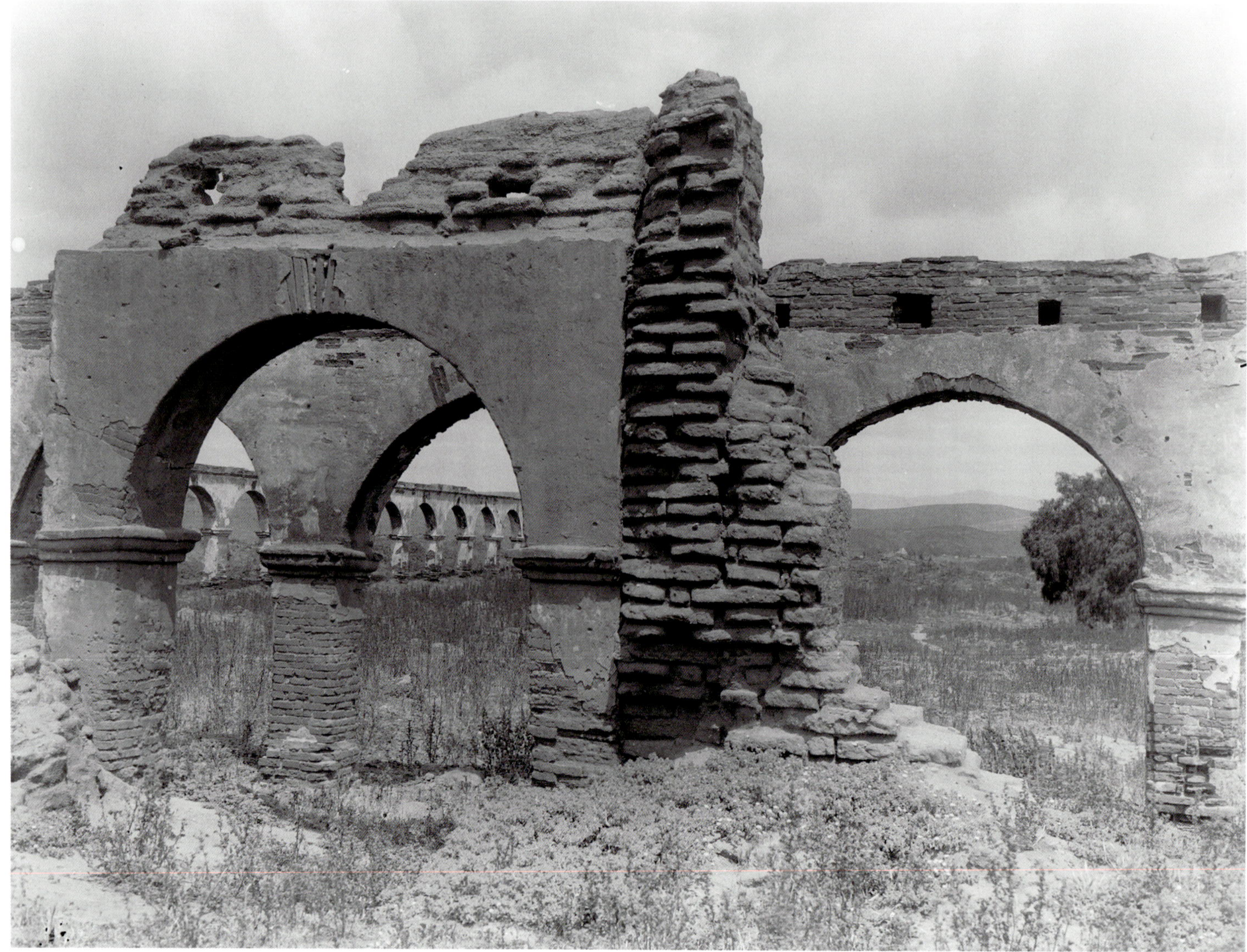

The ruins of the entrance of the inner patio at Mission San Luis Rey, ca. 1900. The arches and columns, made of fired tiles and covered with lime plaster, still survive; the adobe walls have all but melted away. Photograph by A.C. Vroman. Seaver Center for Western History Research, Los Angeles County Museum of Natural History

1902
Historic Landmarks Committee founded by Native Sons of the Golden West; Historic Landmarks League founded.

1903
Historic Landmarks League joins with William Randolph Hearst to purchase ruins of Mission San Francisco Solano.

1905
Bancroft Library established at University of California, Berkeley, with large California history collection.

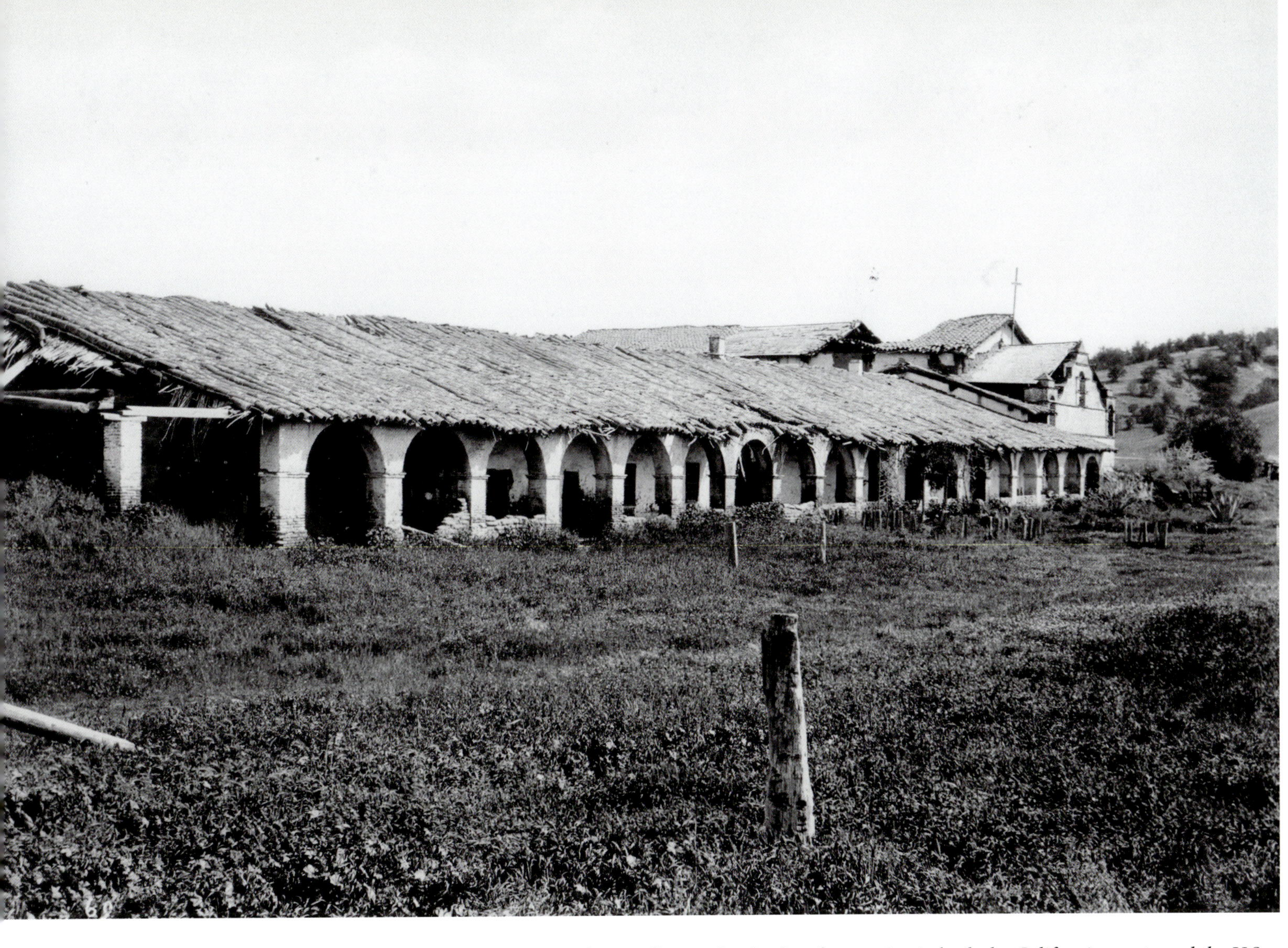

Mission San Antonio, ca. 1890. The *convento* tile roof is largely intact, and a protective wooden roof has been constructed over the atrium. Services were occasionally still held here, attended by neophyte families who continued to reside in the vicinity. Photograph by William Henry Jackson. This item is reproduced by permission of The Huntington Library, San Marino, California

was Joseph Russell Knowland, who after serving in both the California senate and the U.S. House of Representatives would become publisher of the *Oakland Tribune* and, eventually, California's preeminent preservationist.[62]

The League's first project was a 1903 campaign with William Randolph Hearst to purchase Mission San Francisco Solano, at Sonoma. Hearst's newspaper, the *San Francisco Examiner*, publicized the campaign, and in just a few months some $9,000 was raised, allowing for the purchase of the dilapidated remains, which were deeded to the state in 1906 and eventually became Sonoma State Historic Park. The League also worked on preserving Mission San Antonio, contending with heavy rains, the great San Francisco earthquake of 1906, and the difficulty of transporting building materials. That mission was once again abandoned, however, and would not be restored for nearly half a century.[63]

With less fanfare, individual mission priests continued to preserve their crumbling buildings. The restoration of Mission San Luis Rey was carried out at first entirely by the Franciscan friars from Zacatecas, Mexico, who arrived in 1892 to establish a seminary. The largest of all the California establishments, it had been reduced to a gutted church, several standing corridor arches, and acres of adobe mounds. Father Joseph Jeremiah O'Keefe,

1906
First mission bell guidepost installed at Plaza Church in Los Angeles, marking commemorative trail of El Camino Real.

1906
Remains of Mission San Francisco Solano purchased by State of California.

1907
C. F. Lummis founds Southwest Museum in Los Angeles, with large collection of Native American artifacts.

from Mission Santa Bárbara, assigned as resident pastor and translator, took charge of reconstruction. Using traditional skills they had learned in Mexico, the friars gave the church a new roof, patched and replastered adobe walls, repaired the dome, and laid a new floor. Over subsequent decades Father O'Keefe oversaw reconstruction of a portion of the quadrangle, replicating the *convento*'s two-story height and historic colonnade with balcony.[64]

The popularity of the missions, meanwhile, spread into the larger culture, aided by the technological innovations of Eastman Kodak and others that made cameras available to everyone and by the development of automobile touring clubs that allowed travelers to visit the picturesque mission ruins. A movement to commemorate El Camino Real, the complex of roads and trails linking the missions, garnered wide support from various groups, including historical societies, chambers of commerce, women's clubs, and automobile clubs. Marked by mission bell guideposts, it was, like most commemorative trails, a partly truthful, partly fanciful reconstruction, which served to extend the appeal of the missions to a broader public.[65] As delineated, it largely follows present Highway 101 from Los Angeles to Sonoma—with a stretch of State Route 82 through San Francisco—and Highway 5 south of Los Angeles. The first bell guidepost was put in place in front of the Plaza Church in Los Angeles in August 1906; over the next two decades, some 450 were set along the roadsides, where, maintained by the Automobile Club of Southern California, they would remain for many decades.[66]

In the early 1890s, friars from Zacatecas, Mexico, established a seminary at Mission San Luis Rey. Under the guidance of Father Joseph Jeremiah O'Keefe, from Mission Santa Bárbara, they set to work restoring the establishment, using traditional materials and techniques, as seen in this photograph, ca. 1900. Courtesy Pentacle Press, www.missionscalifornia.com

In early summer 1916 the Landmarks Club, briefly resurgent after a period of sporadic activity, held what was probably California's first statewide historic preservation conference at the Mission Inn in Riverside to discuss plans to resume its work. An architect emphasized the "absolute necessity" that in all preservation projects the "original style of architecture be preserved intact." There was a proposal to purchase, for promotional purposes, a copy of the recent film of *Ramona*, a one-reeler produced by D. W. Griffith's Biograph Company starring Mary Pickford in the title role. The main focus, however, was the club's upcoming "Candle Day" at Mission San Fernando, a benefit to raise funds to repair the roofs. Held on August 6, it was organized by Lucrecia del Valle, star of the *Mission Play* and great-granddaughter of the mission's last administrator. Candles were sold for a dollar, and several thousand people attended, raising sufficient money to effect needed repairs.[67] Restoration of the mission soon passed to the Catholic Church and to chambers of commerce in the San Fernando Valley, and the Landmarks Club faded from the southern California scene.

By the early decades of the twentieth century, the California missions, widely disdained in the 1850s as useless relics of a bygone civilization, had come to be venerated as iconic

1909
Publication of George Wharton James's book *Through Ramona's Country* helps perpetuate the mission myth.

1910
Father St. John O'Sullivan arrives at Mission San Juan Capistrano, where he begins a lifelong restoration effort.

1912
Premiere of the *Mission Play* in San Gabriel meets with enthusiastic reception.

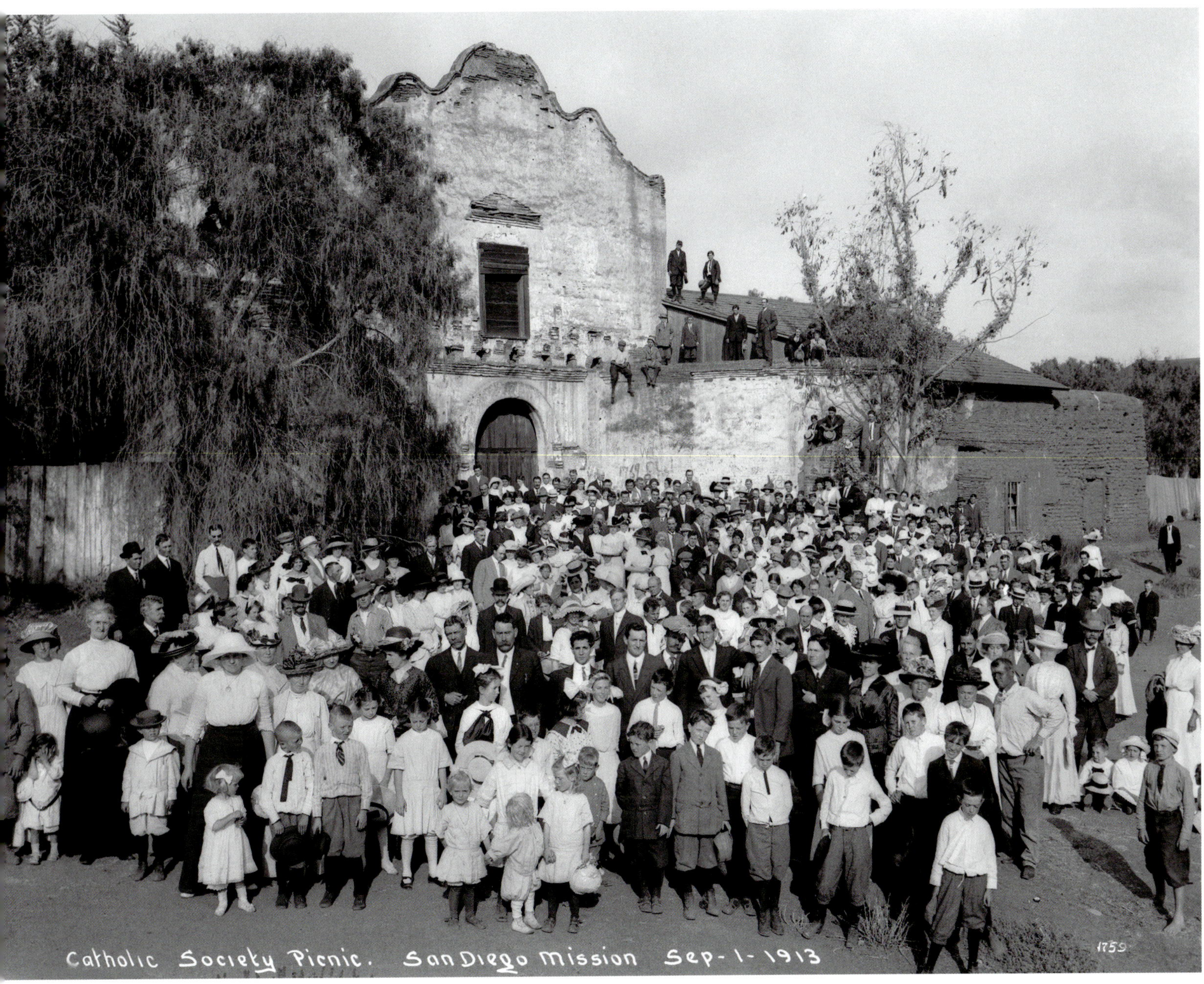

Members of the Catholic Society of San Diego enjoy a late-summer picnic in front of the mission in 1913.
© San Diego Historical Society

cornerstones of a regional identity. Promotion of a romanticized Spanish heritage was now a staple of California civic and commercial life, and a continuous flow of articles on mission ruins in magazines such as *Out West* and Union Pacific's *Sunset* kept interest alive. These were bolstered by the reprinting of Helen Hunt Jackson's *Century Magazine* articles in 1907 and the appearance of the first illustrated mission coffee-table books.[68] The Spanish Colonial revival in architecture further popularized the mission theme. Unfortunately, these developments did not ensure the success of preservation and restoration initiatives. While some mission churches continued to serve active parishes and early civic movements and individual efforts had staved off the ruination of several, a number of missions still lay in ruins, and many others faced an uncertain future.

1914
Outbreak of World War I.

1916
Candle Day at Mission San Fernando Rey, attended by several thousand people, raises money for restoration of mission.

1918
World War I ends.

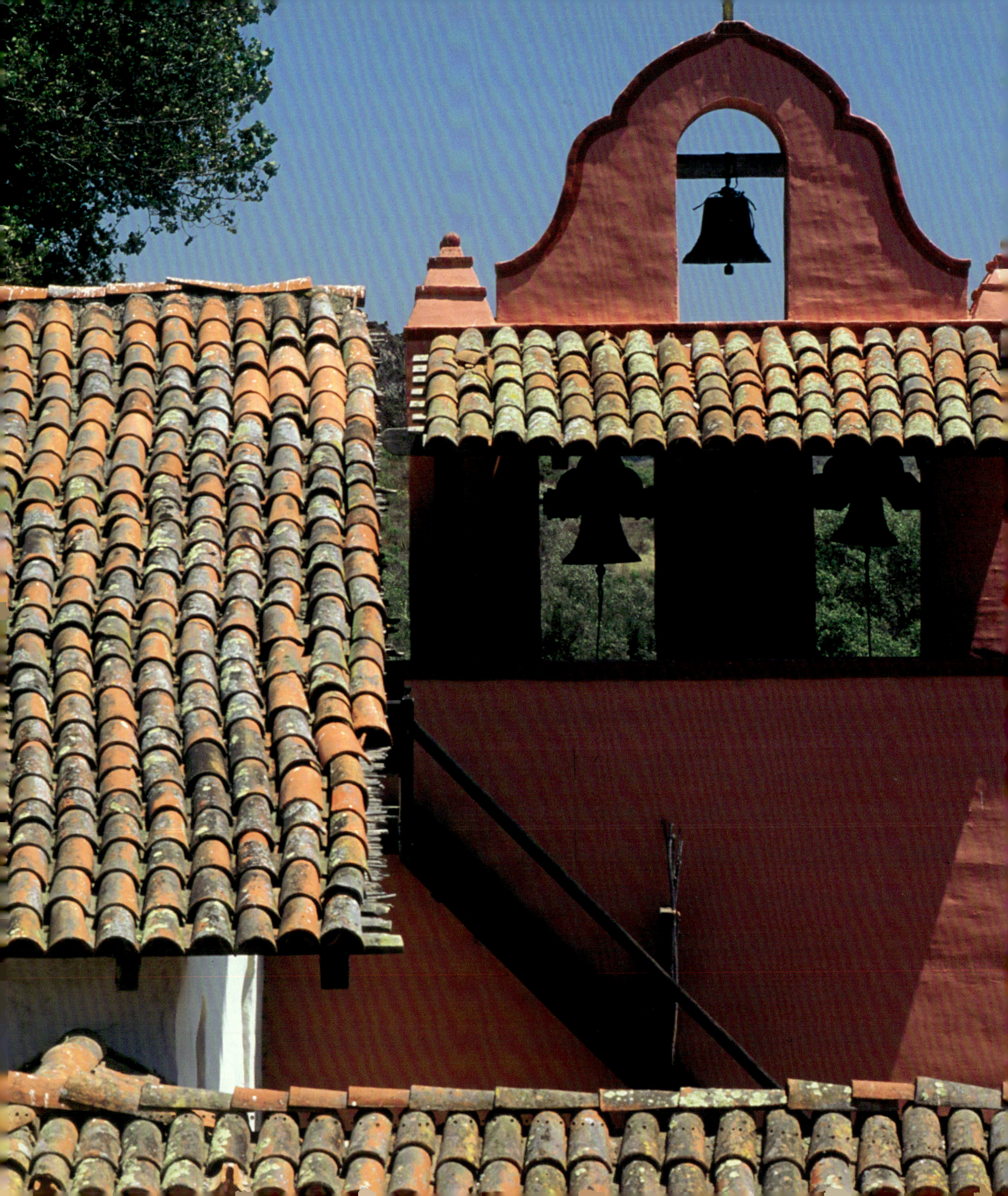

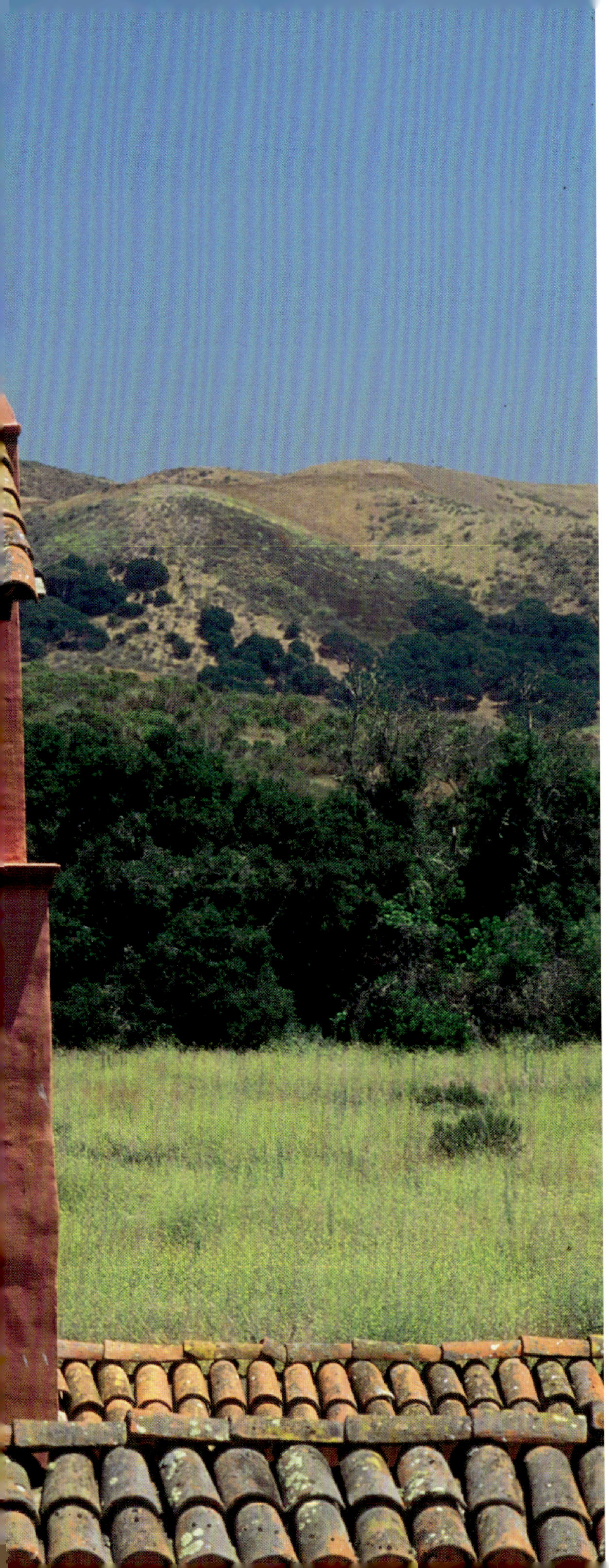

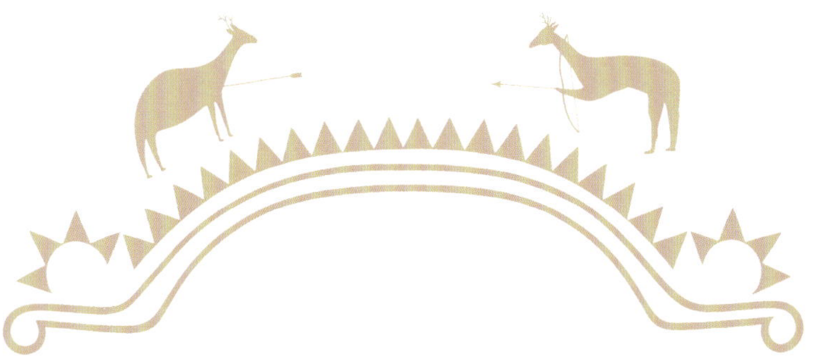

Chapter Three

RESTORATION AND RECONSTRUCTION

In spring 1934 a landscape architect named Phillip T. Primm was driving along the highway north of Santa Barbara when he noticed a decrepit sign, riddled with bullet holes, pointing to Mission La Purísima. "I turned onto a rather poor road and drove until I came to the old ruins of the mission," he recalled. "It was in a very sad state.... There had been considerable vandalism,... and there was no apparent interest by anybody as to doing anything to preserve the ruins, which had gone into decay over the better part of a century.... I got out of the car and walked about.... Many of the walls had disintegrated due to erosion by rain and wind and melted away until they appeared to be nothing but the original earth.... [I]t came to my mind that this might be a wonderful project for a CCC camp to work on."[1]

LEFT: The reconstructed *espadaña* at Mission La Purísima presides over verdant springtime fields and oak-studded hills. Photograph by G. Aldana

ABOVE: The decoration over a door at Mission San Fernando Rey includes an Indian hunter under a deerskin stalking a deer.

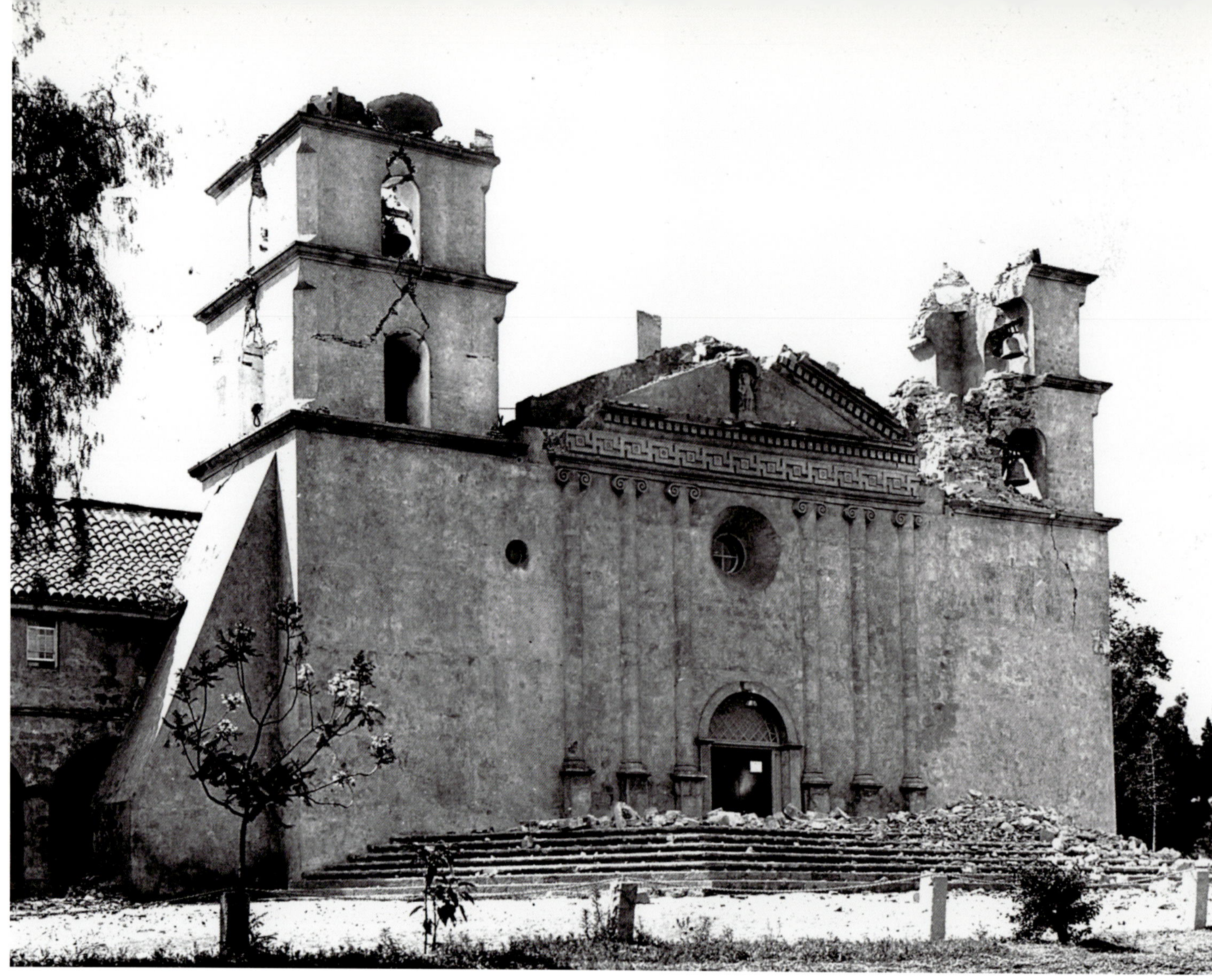

At Mission Santa Bárbara, the earthquake of 1925 destroyed bell towers, toppled the pediment, and felled the statues of Hope and Charity carved by the Chumash mason Paciano Guilajahichet. Courtesy of the Santa Bárbara Mission Archive-Library

Primm was also a regional inspector for the Civilian Conservation Corps (CCC), a program created by the federal government in the early days of the Great Depression to put unemployed young men to work. Over its nine-year span, about fifteen hundred CCC labor camps would be established across the country. Shortly after visiting La Purísima, Primm received a telegram from the National Park Service, asking him to help find locations for additional CCC camps in southern California, where, at the beginning of the great dust bowl migrations, there were already many unemployed workers. The ruined Mission La Purísima proved to be just what the federal government was looking for.

By the early 1930s the historic preservation movement in the United States had begun to come of age. On the East Coast, John D. Rockefeller Jr. was funding the restoration of Colonial Williamsburg, a monumental project that for the first time proposed to restore an entire historic town, with an emphasis on scrupulous architectural fidelity to original buildings. Williamsburg, which would be completed after World War II, exercised a major influence on the historic preservation movement nationwide. Preservation societies in New England and elsewhere were becoming increasingly active, and citizens' groups in cities such as Charleston and San Antonio were advocating for the preservation of historic

1919
First of Zorro stories is published, set at Mission San Juan Capistrano.

1920
Benefit ball in San Francisco raises $35,000 for restoration of Mission San Carlos Borromeo; first celebration of Old Spanish Days festival in Santa Barbara.

1922
Father St. John O'Sullivan begins restoration of the Serra Chapel at Mission San Juan Capistrano.

districts. In California several local preservation projects had elicited considerable interest. The Candle Day celebration at Mission San Fernando Rey had raised $3,500 in 1916; a benefit ball in San Francisco had raised $35,000 for the restoration of Mission San Carlos Borromeo in 1920. In 1922 Father St. John O'Sullivan began restoring the Serra Chapel at Mission San Juan Capistrano, and he soon became a forceful advocate for the funding and restoration of the rest of the site. Following the earthquake of 1925, a statewide fund-raising drive financed the repair of Santa Barbara's downtown as well restoration of the mission, also damaged in the quake.

Responding to pressure from local historical groups, states across the country were also becoming involved. In California the creation of the California State Park Commission in 1927 and passage of the State Park Bond the following year put the state firmly on the preservation path. Legislation passed in the early thirties initiated the State Landmarks program; by the end of 1932 78 sites had been registered, and by the end of the decade the number would rise to 376, making it the most ambitious and sophisticated such program in the nation.[2] Mission-related acquisitions included the remains of Mission San Francisco Solano (1926), the nearby rancho of Mariano Guadalupe Vallejo (1933), and much of the town surrounding Mission San Juan Bautista (1935). The coming decades, meanwhile, would see considerable activity in mission restoration and reconstruction. A number of new projects would be undertaken, their widely divergent approaches reflecting the differing circumstances of individual missions, different interpretations of the mission heritage, and varying philosophies of historic preservation.

One of the most important developments of the 1930s in historic preservation was the increasingly active role of the U.S. government. Much of this activity was part of the expanded federal programs of President Franklin D. Roosevelt's New Deal, which employed both skilled and unskilled workers to document and preserve the nation's rapidly vanishing

The east side of Mission La Purísima's *convento* building was still relatively intact when this photograph was taken in about 1892. By 1910 the tile roof was gone and the exposed walls were in ruins. Photograph by C. C. Pierce. Courtesy University of Southern California, on behalf of USC Special Collections

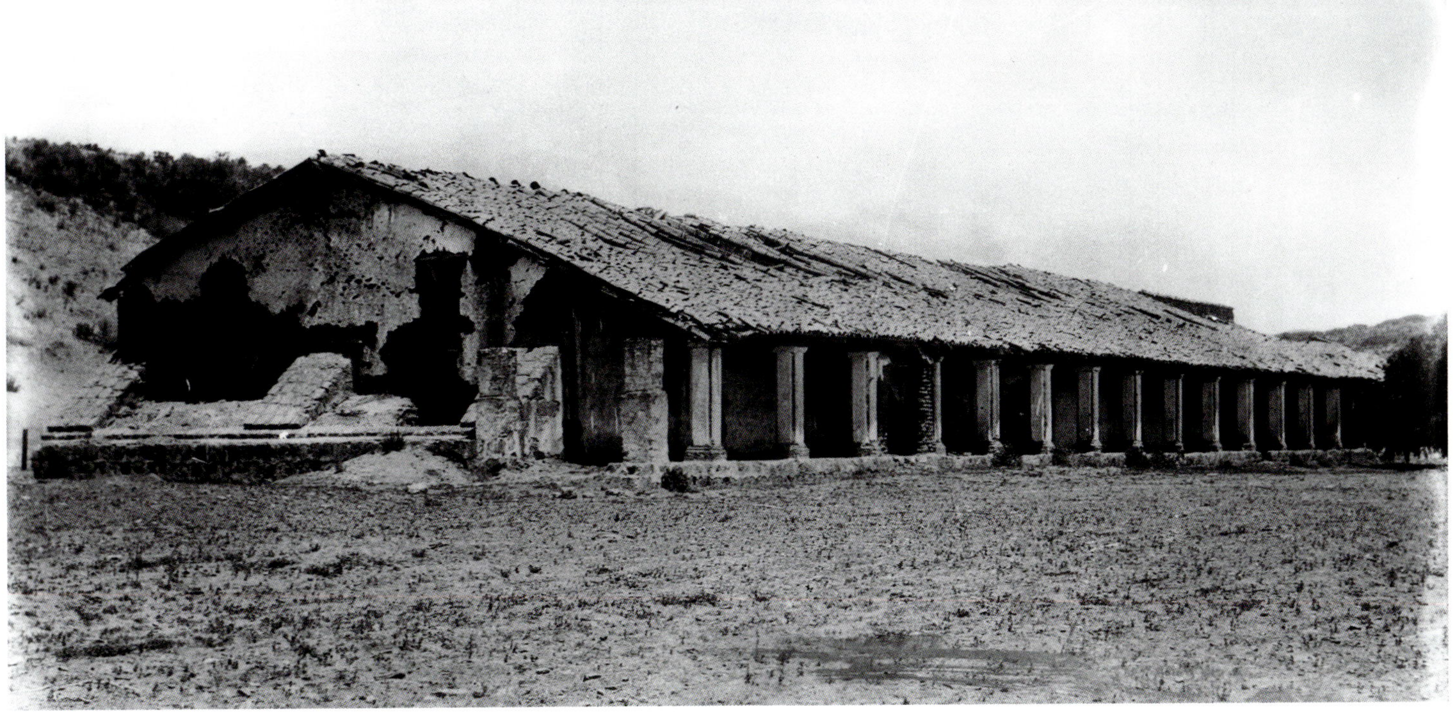

1923
Premiere of the *Ramona Pageant* in the desert town of Hemet.

1925
Earthquake damages Mission Santa Bárbara; restoration of Serra Chapel completed at Mission San Juan Capistrano.

1926
William A. R. Goodwin and John D. Rockefeller begin restoration of Colonial Williamsburg in Virginia.

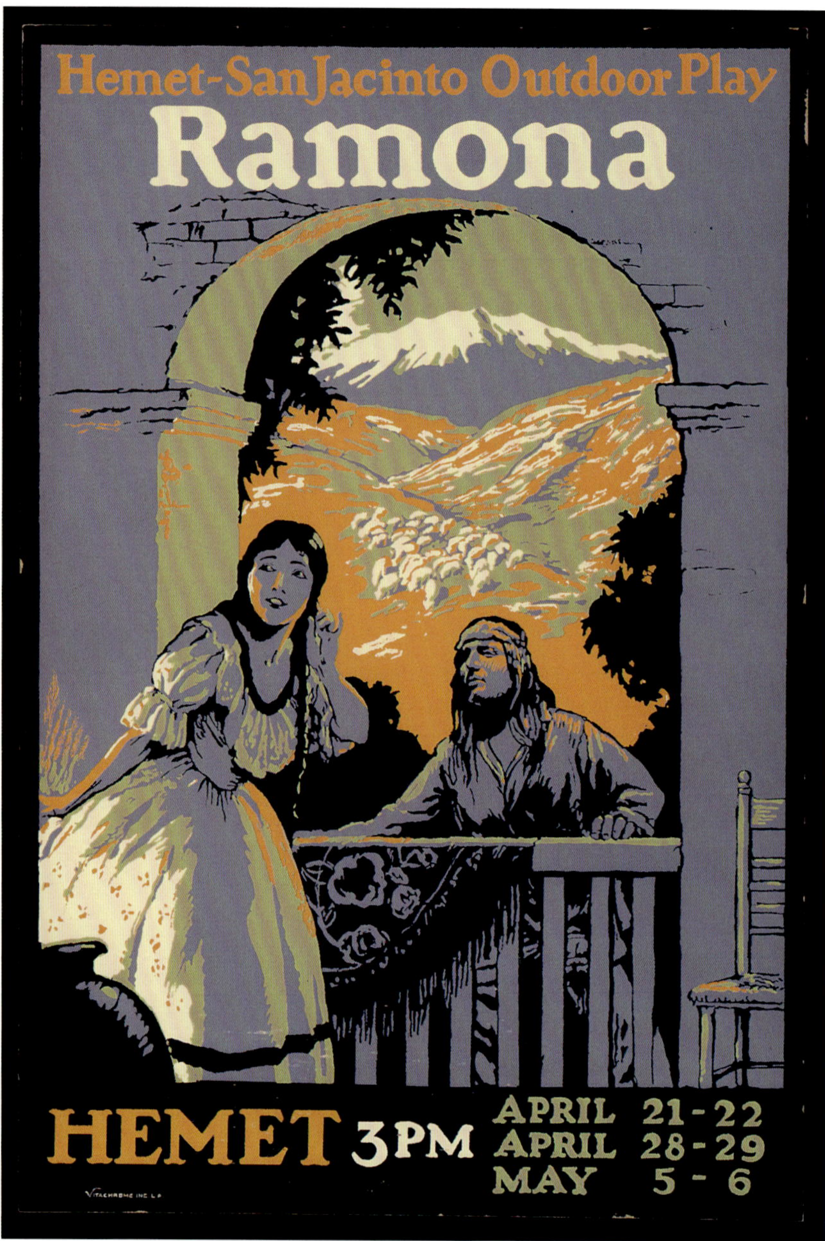

Poster for the 1928 Ramona Pageant in the high-desert California town of Hemet. The pageant, based on Helen Hunt Jackson's 1884 novel recounting the love between an Indian man and a mestizo woman, helped perpetuate the mission myth. This romantic view of California's Spanish and Mexican past influenced the restoration of the missions. Courtesy of the Ramona Pageant Association

historic fabric. The Preservation of Historic Sites Act of 1935 laid the legal foundation for a national program to identify, acquire, preserve, and interpret historic sites. All such sites were placed under the National Park Service, including those previously administered by the Forest Service and the Civil War battlefields then managed by the War Department. These steps laid the foundations for the country's present system of historic parks, the National Register of Historic Places, and the National Historic Landmarks program. Of particular importance for the California missions were the Historic American Buildings Surveys (HABS) and the Index of American Design (Index). The HABS documentation consists of original measured drawings and large-format black-and-white photographs, as well as copies of historic documents; the Index produced drawings, photographs, and descriptions of original art and historical objects. Emphasizing the importance of recording original buildings and architectural elements, as well as historic furnishings and crafts, these programs elevated standards for restoration and reconstruction projects by providing a baseline of documentary material. Their archives remain invaluable resources (see pp. 72–73).[3]

There had been local interest in rebuilding Mission La Purísima for a number of years. When in 1912 the town of Lompoc commemorated the one hundredth anniversary of the mission's destruction in the great 1812 earthquake, this possibility was raised in the press. "The people of a pueblo or town, which can boast of squatting on or near the site of an ancient mission, regard themselves favored above other mortals," a local reporter had observed. "It would be well for the people [of Lompoc] to cast their eyes on the ruins.... [T]he foundations are there still... [and] it would not cost very much to reproduce it."[4] Ironically, it was the smaller second mission, built north of the Santa Ynez River after the earthquake, which would be reconstructed. The older and larger original site disappeared under the growing town.

The opportunity to restore Mission La Purísima as one of the New Deal's work relief programs sparked immediate action. The project quickly garnered the support of the longtime preservationist and *Oakland Tribune* publisher, Joseph R. Knowland, a powerful member of the Park Commission. As the CCC could operate only on state-owned land, Santa Barbara County quickly deeded the property to the state of California. By late summer 1934 housing for 175 workers had been built at the site, which was designated La Purísima State Historic Monument.[5] Additional land was acquired around the mission, and the project became arguably the most famous CCC initiative in California.[6]

1927
California State Park Commission established; dedication ceremonies held for restored Mission Santa Bárbara.

1929
Stock market crash sets off Great Depression.

1930
Popular book *Capistrano Nights*, featuring story of the swallows' annual return to Mission San Juan Capistrano, promotes mission as a tourist destination.

Debate arose over whether the site should be preserved as a ruin or reconstructed for educational purposes. The early Landmarks Club had been dedicated to the conservation—but not the restoration—of mission ruins. "We will preserve not only the stones of these venerable monuments, but the atmosphere of sanctity," proclaimed the club's founder, Charles F. Lummis. "Let their noble, broken walls testify to the spirit that built them.... We will not put back a single block of stone more than is necessary to arrest destruction, and we will let no work of our hands deface the work of their builders nor belie the spirit that wrought them." Lummis subscribed to a tradition of historic preservation developed in the Southwest, where ancient adobe and stone dwellings were stabilized and conserved but not reconstructed, following the work of early American archaeologists that emphasized the importance of scientific research in seeking to provide information on the past.[7]

In California, however, early research on mission sites had taken place in a culture shaped by the mission myth, which since its birth in the late nineteenth century had come to dominate the interpretation of the state's early history. The mission Indians occupied a supporting role in the story, subordinated to a larger narrative in which the missions brought the benefits of Christianity and European civilization to native peoples eager to receive them. In the 1920s and 1930s the mission myth reached its apotheosis. A new hero of the mission era appeared in popular culture with the publication in 1919 of the first of Johnston McCulley's Zorro stories, the *Curse of Capistrano*, which was immediately adapted into the silent movie *The Mark of Zorro*, starring Douglas Fairbanks. The *Mission Play* and the new Ramona Pageant, which debuted in 1923 in the high-desert town of Hemet with its saga of romance and racial injustice, drew audiences in the thousands. Throughout southern California, Mexican cultural expressions such as the fiesta were refashioned to celebrate the region's Spanish, as opposed to Mexican, cultural roots, for popular and tourist consumption. Santa Barbara's Old Spanish Days festival, which began in 1920, became one of the country's leading regional festivals, with celebrities such as Charles Lindbergh and

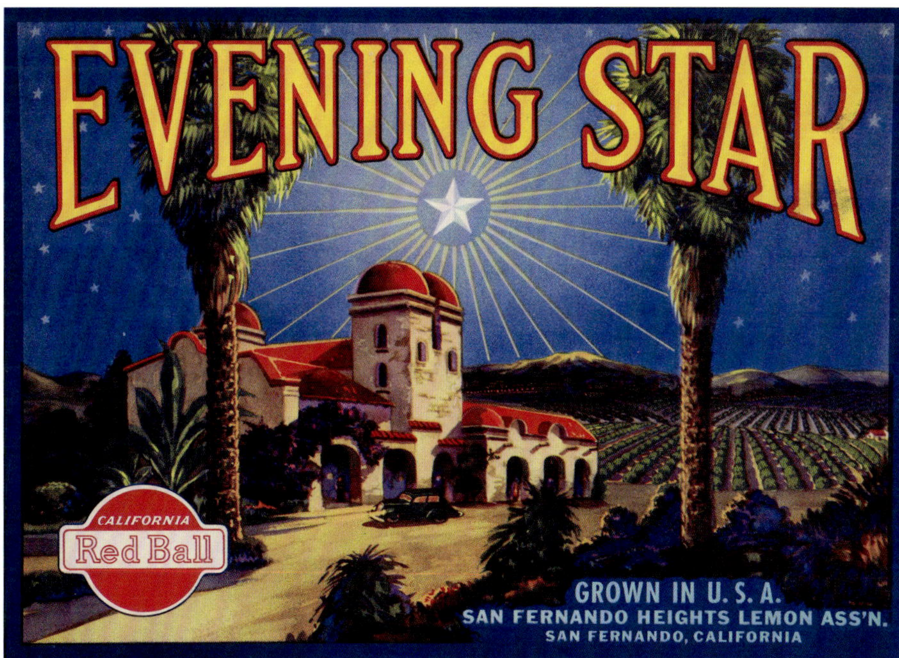

The missions continued to be used in commercial promotions well into the twentieth century. Seen here is a mythical mission, surrounded by abundant vineyards and illuminated from the heavens. Anonymous (American). *Evening Star, San Fernando Heights Lemon Assn., San Fernando, California*, ca. 1930–40. Color lithograph, 22.3 × 31.7 cm. Fine Arts Museums of San Francisco, Museum Purchase, Achenbach Foundation for Graphic Arts Endowment Fund, 1994.103.27

1931
California State Landmarks program established; ceremony celebrates reconstruction of Mission San Diego; a romantic Mexican marketplace opens at Olvera Street in Los Angeles.

1932
Half-scale replica of Mission Santa Cruz completed.

1932–55
Harry Downie restores Mission San Carlos Borromeo.

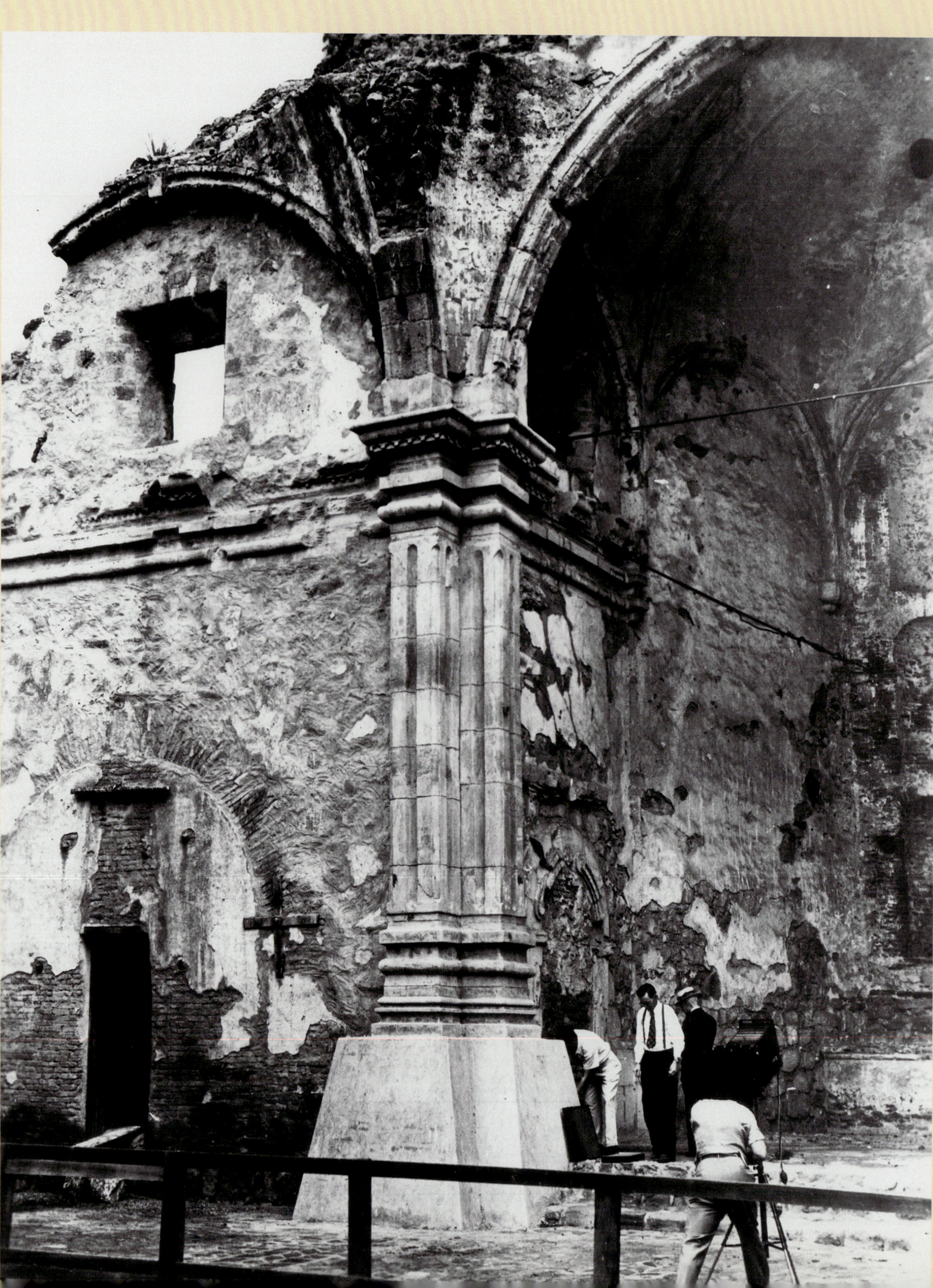

The Index of American Design

Among the New Deal's initiatives was the Federal Arts Project, which included a program called the Index of American Design. Brainchild of a New York textile designer and the head of the picture collection at the New York Public Library, the Index was a campaign to document the rise and development of American design in order to define the nation's cultural and aesthetic identity, thereby countering some contemporary perceptions that, compared to European nations, America lacked a rich historical artistic tradition. The purpose of the Index was not merely to create an antiquarian catalog but to provide inspiration for a new modern art that, rather than imitating European styles, would be truly American.

Hundreds of professional artists were carefully selected and trained to accurately yet sensitively document America's traditional folk, popular, and decorative arts. Between 1935 and 1942 Index artists traveled throughout the country, recording a wide range of objects, from Amish furniture to ships' figureheads, from dolls and duck decoys to pottery, textiles, and jewelry. For California, the missions provided the richest heritage, and the Index teams documented items of wood, copper, basketry, architectural elements, and religious items associated with both the Spanish and Mexican periods. Of particular value are the color renderings of wall paintings, often based on delicate, fading fragments still visible on peeling plaster. Virtually all of this original ornamentation, with the remarkable exception of the murals at Mission San Miguel and the sanctuary at Mission Santa Inés, has now been destroyed or overpainted, and the Index renderings provide the only surviving copy (see chapter 6).

In the years following World War II, as the United States became more open to influences from the rest of the world, the taste diminished for the kind of national folk art that had been popular in the 1930s, and American artists increasingly followed international styles. The Index's work, however, resulted in the most comprehensive pictorial survey ever produced of American folk, popular, and decorative art. Today the more than eighteen thousand watercolor renderings and a similar number of large-format black-and-white photographs produced by Index artists are housed at the National Gallery of Art in Washington, D.C.

OPPOSITE: Artists and photographers from the Index of American Design at work in the ruined sanctuary of Mission San Juan Capistrano in the 1930s. National Gallery of Art, Washington, D.C., Gallery Archives

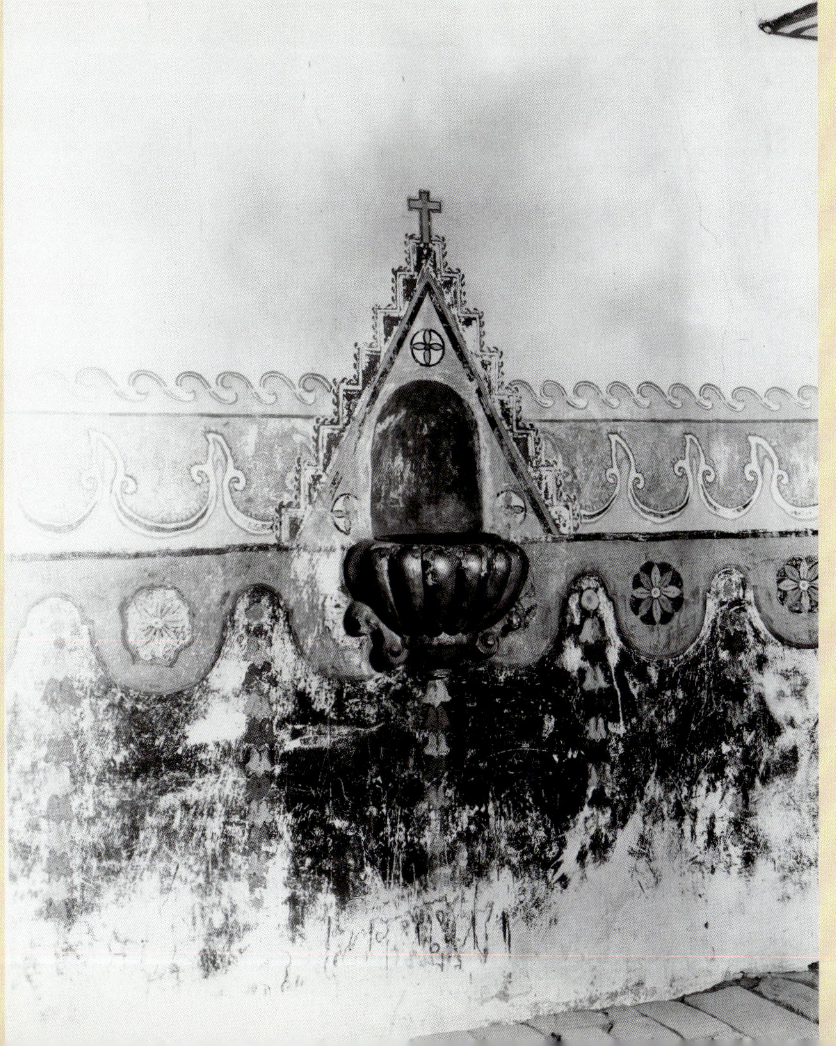

BELOW LEFT: Photograph from the Index of American Design project showing a carved stone holy water font and deteriorating wall decorations in the Serra Chapel, Mission San Juan Capistrano, ca. 1940. National Gallery of Art, Washington, D.C., Gallery Archives

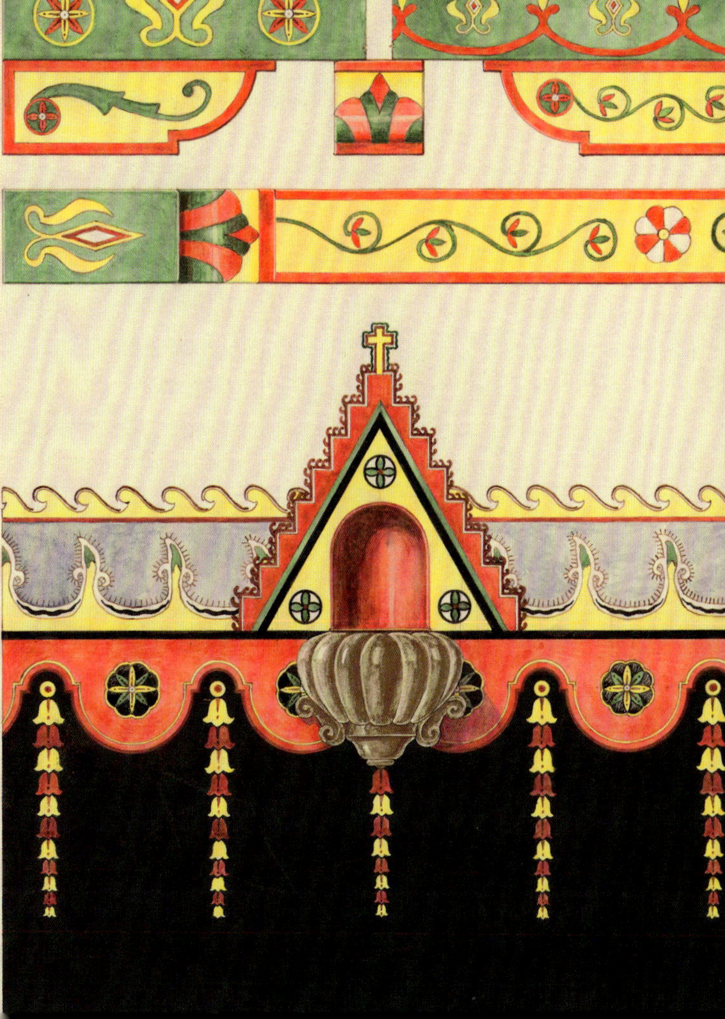

BELOW RIGHT: Artistic rendering of wall decorations as they were originally painted; above them are design elements from the Serra Chapel's ceiling beams and corbels. Randolf F. Miller, *Wall and Ceiling Decoration and Holy Water Font; Restoration Drawing.* Pencil and ink on paper, 1936. Image courtesy of the Board of Trustees, National Gallery of Art, Washington, D.C.

Will Rogers participating. The missions continued to be used for commercial promotion. Artists of the Plein Air and California Impressionist schools, meanwhile, were producing lovely, romantic depictions of the missions and their ruins. And part of the historic Pueblo de Los Angeles was restored and transformed into the Mexican marketplace at Olvera Street, which opened in 1931, with the aim of re-creating the romance of Old California.

While Lummis was able to separate preservation and promotion, other boosters and many restorationists who followed him, even those who could legitimately claim the best intentions, would often confuse the two. In the minds of many, David Hurst Thomas has noted, "the mission ruins, no matter how romantic, were too remote and confusing" for the general public. "If California was to eulogize a glorious pre-Anglo Hispanic past, then the missions must perforce be restored 'so that they could be read more easily by a popular audience.'"[8] The morally ambiguous complexities of historical mission life were not amenable to simple slogans and iconic images. "The flood of Anglos into California rapidly submerged all but selected, promotional aspects of Hispanic culture. Because the missions were integral to the search for a mythical identity, they were restored to appropriate heroic proportions."[9] This sentiment is reflected in the words of a federal official, an architect arguing for reconstruction of the La Purísima site during the depths of the Great Depression: "The Mission days were the days of contentment for which we hopelessly hope the future holds a return. To contribute toward preserving the spirit of this era is one of the finest things we can do."[10]

Questions of preservation versus restoration and reconstruction were debated in the late 1920s and early 1930s. Some missions, such as La Purísima, existed only as ruins and therefore required complete reconstruction; others, although severely damaged, still retained sufficient original features to allow for restoration. The approach favored by Lummis, which emphasized preservation only, and which in fact resembles in many ways modern preservation practice, fell into disfavor for decades.

By the time a renewed campaign began in the 1920s at Mission San Diego, where preservation activities by the Landmarks Club had begun in 1900, only the church facade, buttresses, and one room of the *convento* remained standing. Discussions of which path to take were eventually resolved in favor of a full restoration of the church, largely to promote the primacy of San Diego as California's "first city." Were the mission not to be fully restored, worried one booster, "there won't be enough to take tourists to see."[11] The new church, constructed in accordance with the original foundations, was primarily of reinforced concrete, although original materials such as locally made adobe bricks and tiles were used in places. Work was influenced by the Arts and Crafts movement, which—in emphasizing the nobility of traditional craftsmanship—unfortunately manifested in an exaggerated "handmade" unevenness in the adobe walls, producing an unrealistically lumpy surface.

On a Sunday morning in September 1931, the newly restored mission was rededicated. A crowd of some fifteen thousand attended the event, which included the celebration of a Pontifical High Mass, called by one observer "the most magnificent mass ever held in the city." Festivities also included a historical pageant, "The Restoration," celebrating the mission's history, as well as a fiesta in Balboa Park. The event overall, as one church official noted, was "not a dedication of the restored edifice as a church, but as a historic and civic shrine... dedicated to the city of San Diego [where] civilization and Christianity first took root" in California.[12]

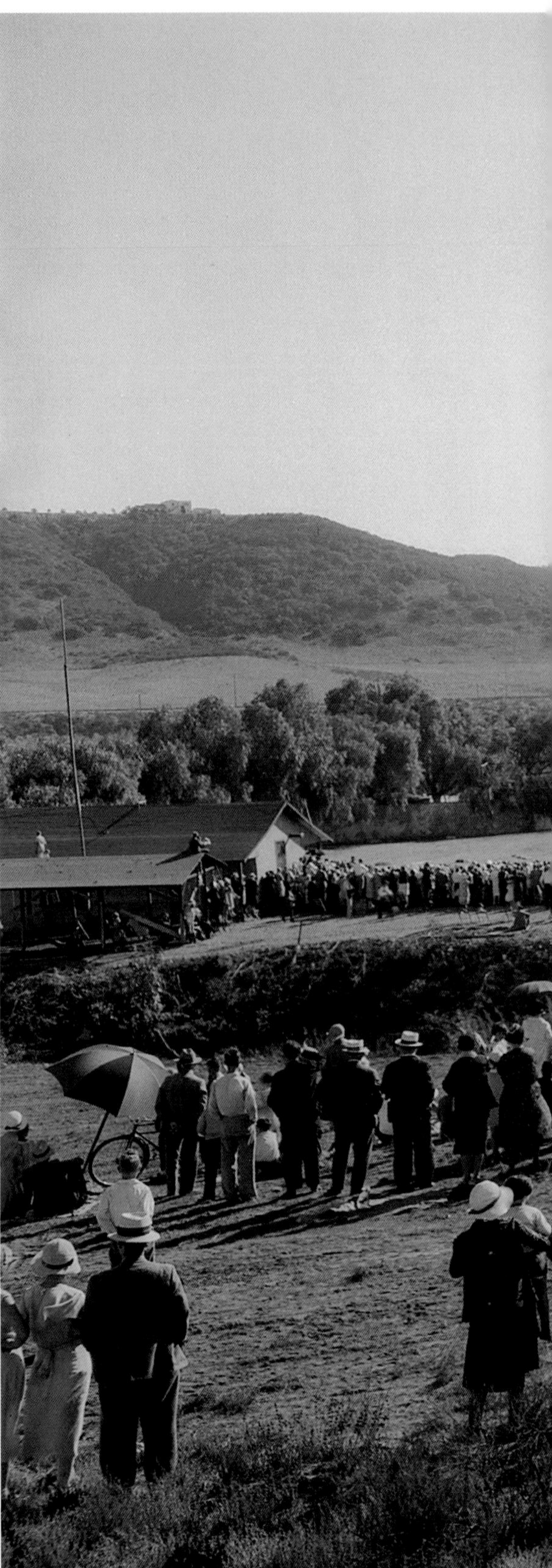

In the case of Mission La Purísima, however, arguments in favor of reconstruction were based predominantly not on romance or on the desire to promote a civic ideal. Noting that virtually no buildings remained of the original mission, groups such as the California State Historical Association put forth arguments based primarily on the potential educa-

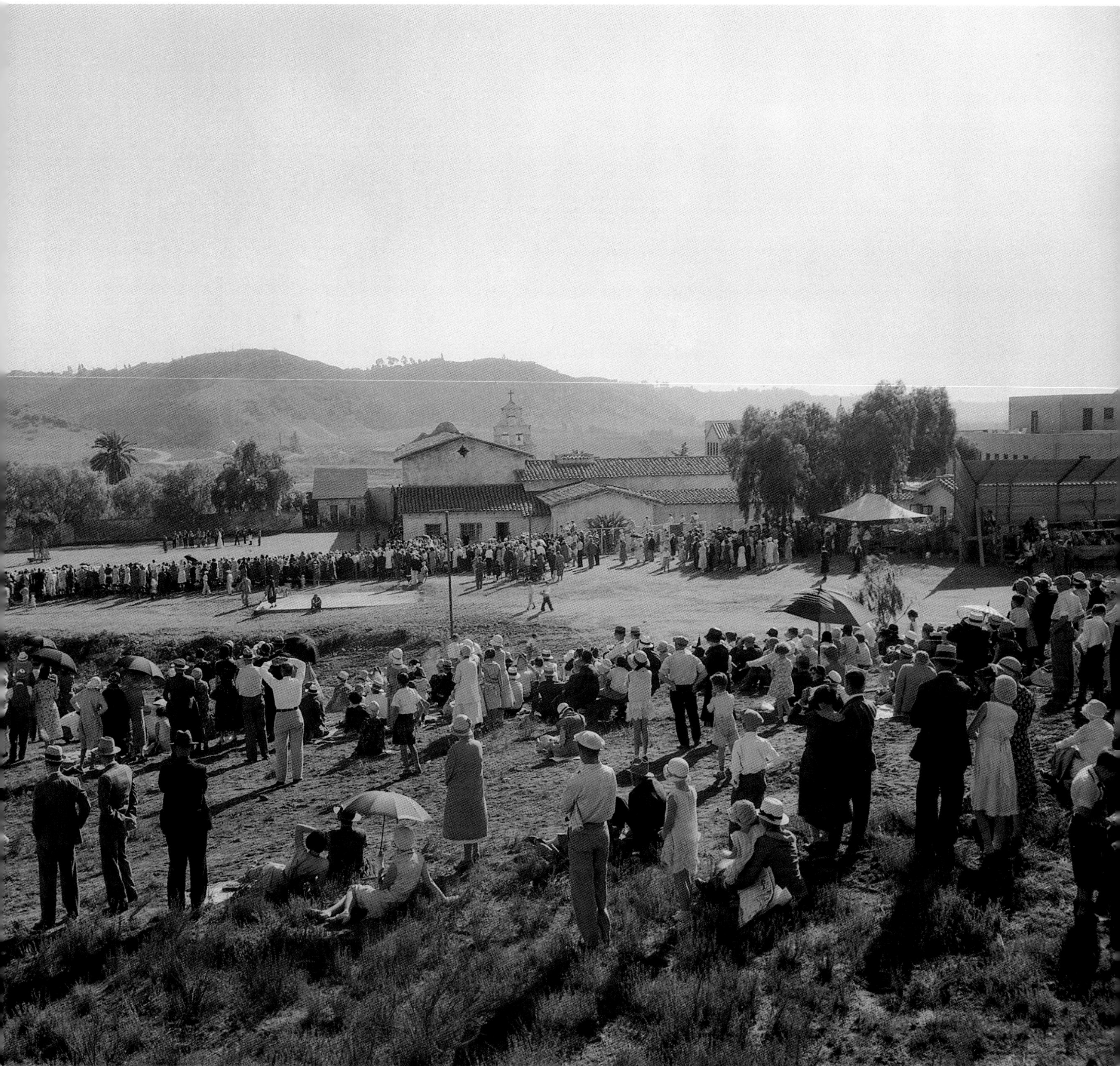

A crowd witnesses the rededication of Mission San Diego's restored church in September 1931. The event was marked by considerable ceremony, including a fiesta and a historical pageant commemorating the mission's history. The restored church was seen as an important civic and tourist attraction for California's "first city." © San Diego Historical Society

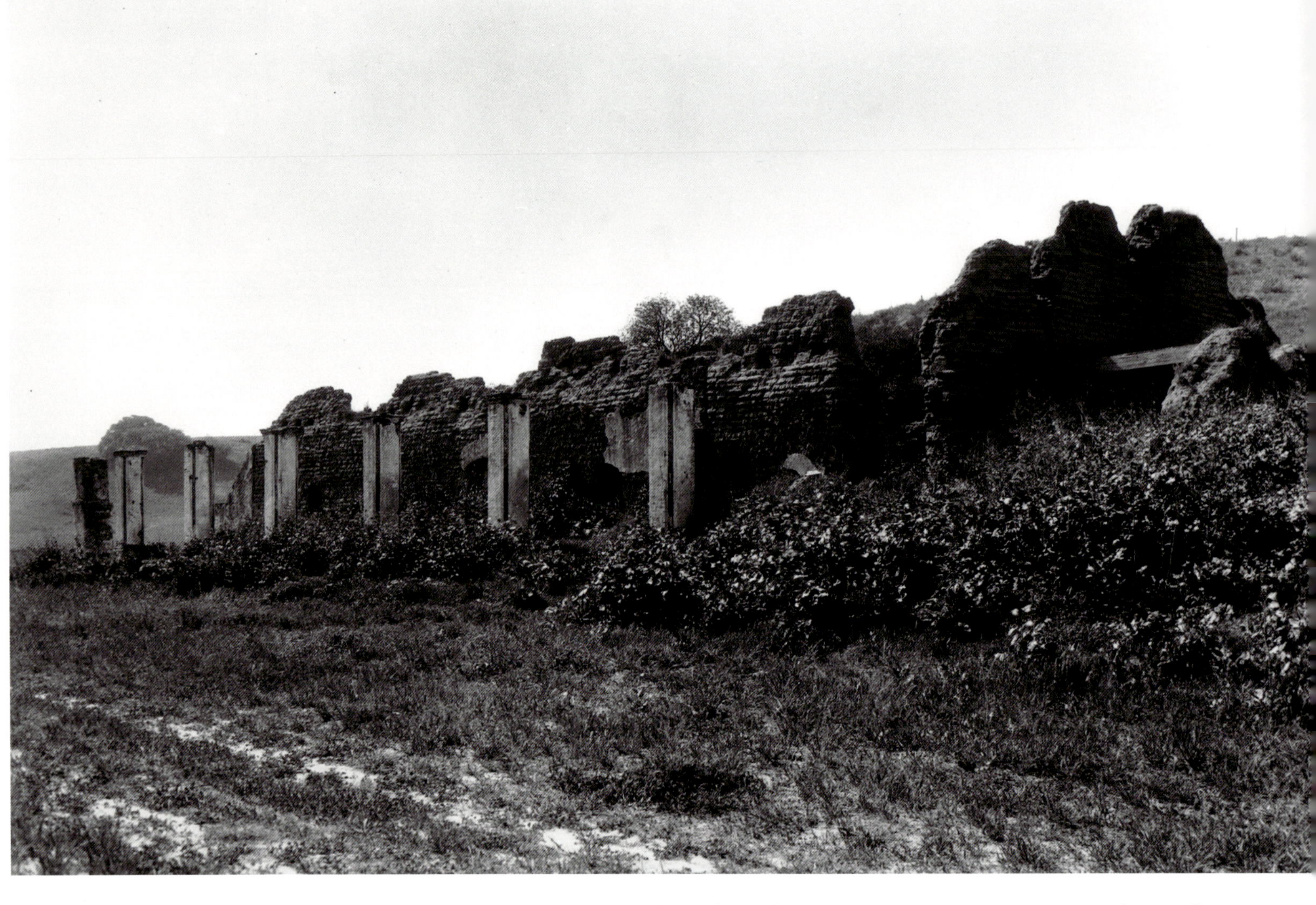

The ruins of the *convento* at Mission La Purísima, ca. 1934, just before the Civilian Conservation Corps began reconstruction of the mission. The lime-plastered tile columns contrast with the adobe walls, which had virtually melted away over the previous half century (see photo p. 69). Courtesy California State Parks

tional values "of the atmosphere of an authentic mission community in its natural setting."[13] In fact, the project brought objective methodologies to the reconstruction effort, in the process establishing high standards for the use of scientific archaeological research, for addressing a wide spectrum of mission life, and for producing historically accurate reconstructions.

The first phase of work, carried out in the manner of investigations in the Southwest, involved extensive studies of the ruins by archaeologists, including Mark R. Harrington, of the Southwest Museum in Los Angeles. Other restoration efforts of the time often focused on churches and *conventos* while neglecting buildings associated with the Native American populace, thereby inflating the "white, Catholic, European aspects of mission life."[14] At most missions, including the reconstructed Mission San Diego, the Native American presence was nowhere to be seen. But at La Purísima much of the entire mission establishment would be reconstructed, including shops and water systems, in addition to the church and *convento,* while extensive excavations were carried out in the Indians' dwellings. Experts consulted included Edith Webb, the renowned historian of neophyte mission life.[15]

1934–41
Workers of the Civilian Conservation Corps reconstruct Mission La Purísima.

1935–42
Artists of the Index of American Design document the country's folk and decorative art, including California mission murals.

Late 1930s
Restoration begins of church and *convento* at Mission San Fernando Rey.

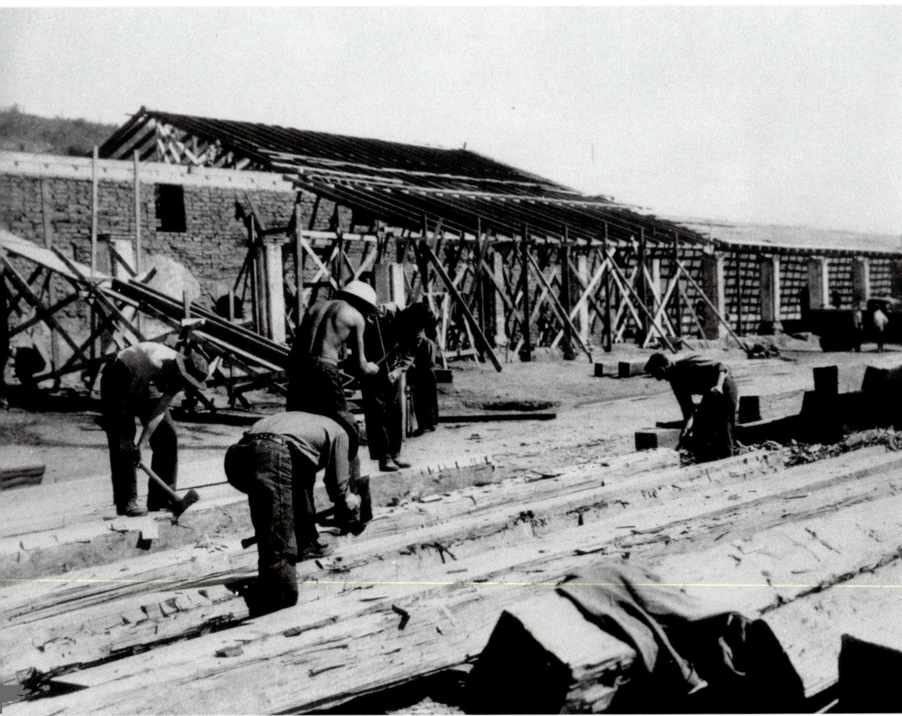

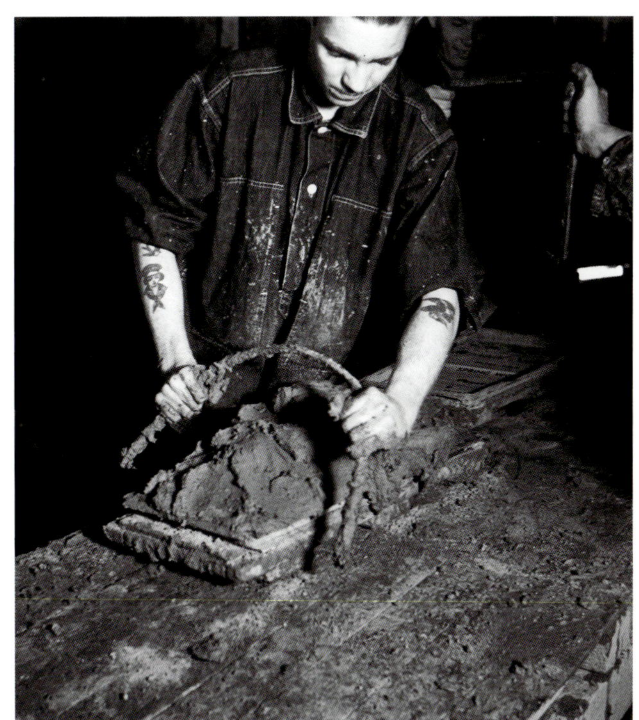

ABOVE LEFT: **Workers from the Civilian Conservation Corps using hand adzes to prepare beams for the reconstruction of Mission La Purísima. Some two hundred men, living in labor camps, toiled daily on the project, which took seven years to complete.** Courtesy California State Parks

ABOVE RIGHT: **After early experiments showed that modern methods could not produce authentic-looking products, workers were taught to use traditional techniques to make the hundreds of thousands of adobe bricks, roof tiles, and floor tiles needed for the mission's reconstruction. Here a worker forms tiles (*ladrillos*) in a mold; they will be sun-dried and then fired in a kiln.** Courtesy California State Parks

The reconstruction's architectural authenticity was championed by the project's indefatigable architect, Fred Hageman, who conducted detailed research in preparation for the project, searching out original mission documents, interviewing early residents, and visiting other missions to study their features and examine their HABS architectural drawings. Early experiments showed that old finishes could not be replicated with modern methods, so workmen were taught to mix adobe, fire tiles, and finish walls with simple tools, consistent with those used more than a century earlier. And as it had been decided to preserve as much of the original wall remains as possible, every effort was made to render the new material indistinguishable from the old.[16] "Had the old walls been torn down and cleared away, and construction started entirely new from the foundations, the size and appearance of the individual adobe bricks, floor tiles, and other structural elements would have had to be only relatively exact," Hageman recounts. "But since the new and the old had to be fitted in together, . . . it was . . . essential that reproduction of the original elements should be as exact as possible."[17] The paint used was from designs and colors gleaned from remnants found at the site, augmented by motifs recorded by Index artists at other missions. The only compromise was the installation of a modern, steel-reinforced concrete skeleton in the walls, to help minimize earthquake damage.

Once construction commenced, as many as two hundred men were involved daily in the massive job, which took more than seven years to complete. Workers typically stayed for ten months. They were housed and fed in military fashion and paid $25 per week, of which $20 was sent home to their families. For many, this was a marked improvement over the poverty they had known, and some recall the food as the best they had ever had.[18] Many also found satisfaction in the task itself. "At first I just thought it was all too much work," one worker recalled, "but then I saw the beauty of it coming up as the mission got built. We were doing something that would last. . . . Today I take my grandchildren there."[19]

1941
U.S. enters World War II; ceremonies mark completion of restoration projects at Missions La Purísima and San Fernando Rey.

1945
World War II ends.

1946
Carey McWilliams publishes revisionist history *Southern California: An Island on the Land*, challenging stereotypes of the mission myth.

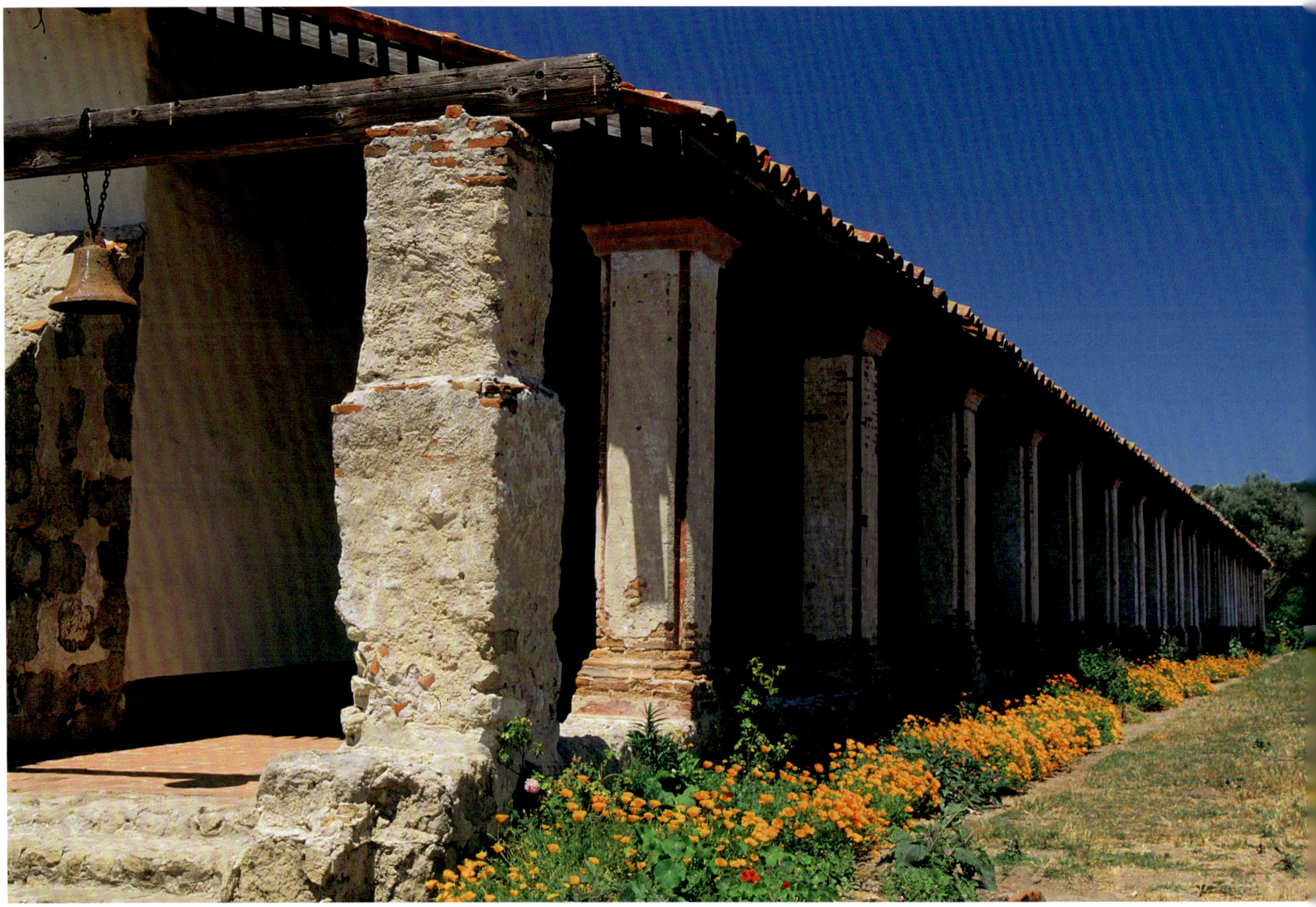

ABOVE: The reconstructed *convento* at Mission La Purísima, known as the Residence Building. The white arcade pillars, virtually all that had remained standing of this building, were incorporated into its reconstruction. Photograph by G. Aldana

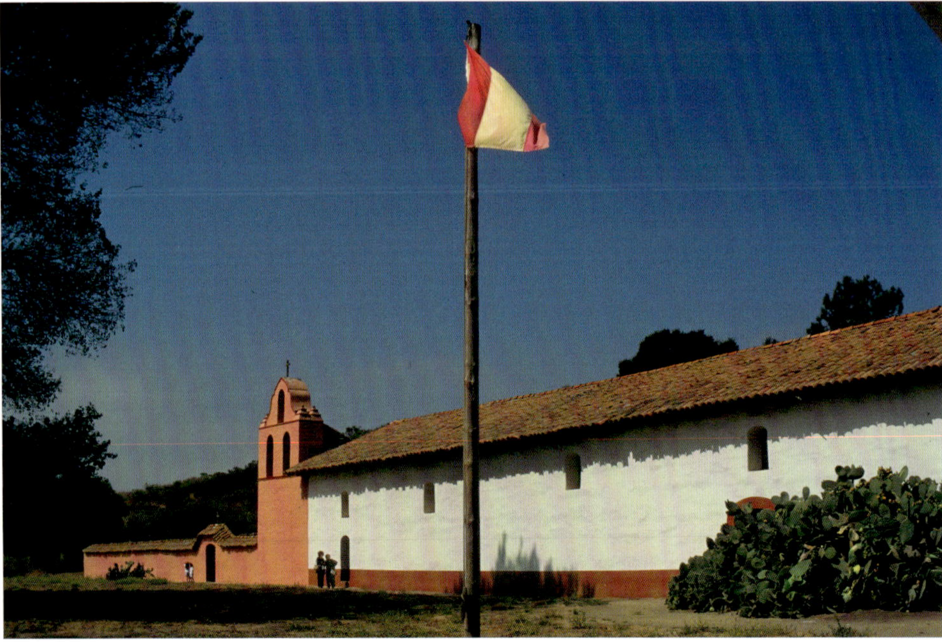

LEFT: View of the reconstructed church and *espadaña* at Mission La Purísima. In landscaping the grounds, efforts have been made to include types of plants that would have been present in mission days. Photograph by G. Aldana

It was a considerable task. The workers made by hand some 110,000 adobe bricks, 31,000 roof tiles, and 15,000 floor tiles just for the residence building, which was the first to be completed, in 1936. Two years later the water system, fountains, and cistern were finished. In 1939 the church exterior was completed; the shops and quarters building were finished in 1940, and work on the *convento* building and the church interior was wrapped up in 1941. "In some rooms tableaux were set up to represent the living conditions and industries at the mission," one scholar has written. "Other rooms were sparsely furnished to appear as they would have been found by a visitor in the first half of the nineteenth century."[20] Preservation issues were included in displays of rooms whose unfinished walls revealed restoration techniques. The mission garden, meanwhile, was populated with plants such as "pomegranates, figs, pears, pepper trees, grapes, and Castillian roses... from grafts, buds, and cuttings from original plants growing at different missions extending from Santa Clara to San Juan Capistrano."[21] The exemplary historical, archaeological, and architectural research had resulted in a restoration that would come to be known as the "Williamsburg of the West." The dedication ceremony was rather sparsely attended by the press, because on that day, Sunday, December 7, 1941, they had been called away by news of the Japanese attack on Pearl Harbor.

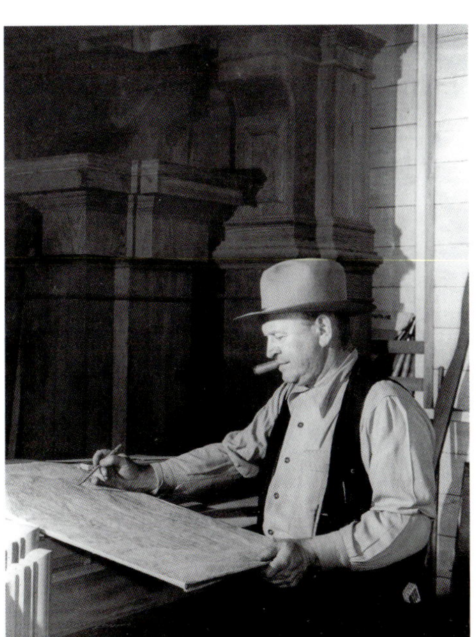

In the early days of the Great Depression, Harry Downie began restoring Mission San Carlos Borromeo as a labor of love, and his passion for mission restoration developed into a lifetime vocation. He became the leading authority on the subject and over the next twenty years would be involved in the restorations of nearly half of California's twenty-one missions. Courtesy Harry Downie Archive, Mission San Carlos Borromeo

While the reconstruction of La Purísima eventually involved the activities of thousands of workers, scores of experts, and $400,000 in federal funding, the restoration of the Mission San Carlos Borromeo church and the reconstruction of attendant buildings, which began at about the same time, were largely the work of a single man, Harry Downie. He first became interested in the subject when he was a child and would visit the missions with his father, an active member of the Native Sons of the Golden West. Trained in cabinetry and carpentry, Downie found himself out of work, like millions of others, in the early years of the depression. While visiting a friend on the Monterey peninsula in 1931, the young carpenter was asked by the monsignor of San Carlos chapel in Monterey to help repair some statues stored in the attic of the rectory. From there he moved to Mission San Carlos Borromeo. Downie, who came to be regarded as the state's premier mission restoration expert of his day, later fondly reminisced, "I came for one month, and I've been here thirty-five years."[22]

As an operating church, Mission San Carlos Borromeo had preservation needs quite different from those of La Purísima, a museum and state park. To address this, Downie combined a rigorous concern for historical accuracy with a practical adaptation of buildings to new uses, anticipating what has come to be widespread modern practice. Throughout the project he focused on creating a pleasing aura of authenticity. First he replaced the high-peaked roof of the chapel, inexpertly added some seventy years earlier, with a more accurately pitched roof covered with tiles, thereby restoring the mission's historical appearance. The walls were repainted and massive doors hung in time for the church's rededication in July 1936. Within a year, three rooms of the *convento*—thought to be the oldest surviving mission constructions and to include the residence of Father Serra—were reconstructed and dedicated as well. In the following years Downie excavated and rebuilt parts of the mission quadrangle to serve the modern functions of the religious facility. The remaining wings of the mission quadrangle were filled in between 1937 and 1955 with a portion of a school, a chapel, a rectory, and a museum.[23]

Downie also worked tirelessly to recover statuary, furniture, and other items that had disappeared from the church during its long period of abandonment. Vestments from the mission had been secured at the Royal Presidio Chapel in Monterey. Accepting dinner

1948
Centenary of Gold Rush reawakens interest in California history; William Randolph Hearst establishes fund to finance restoration projects at several missions.

1950s
Archaeological excavations at Sonoma Mission State Historic Park.

1955
Restoration completed of Mission San Antonio, under guidance of Harry Downie.

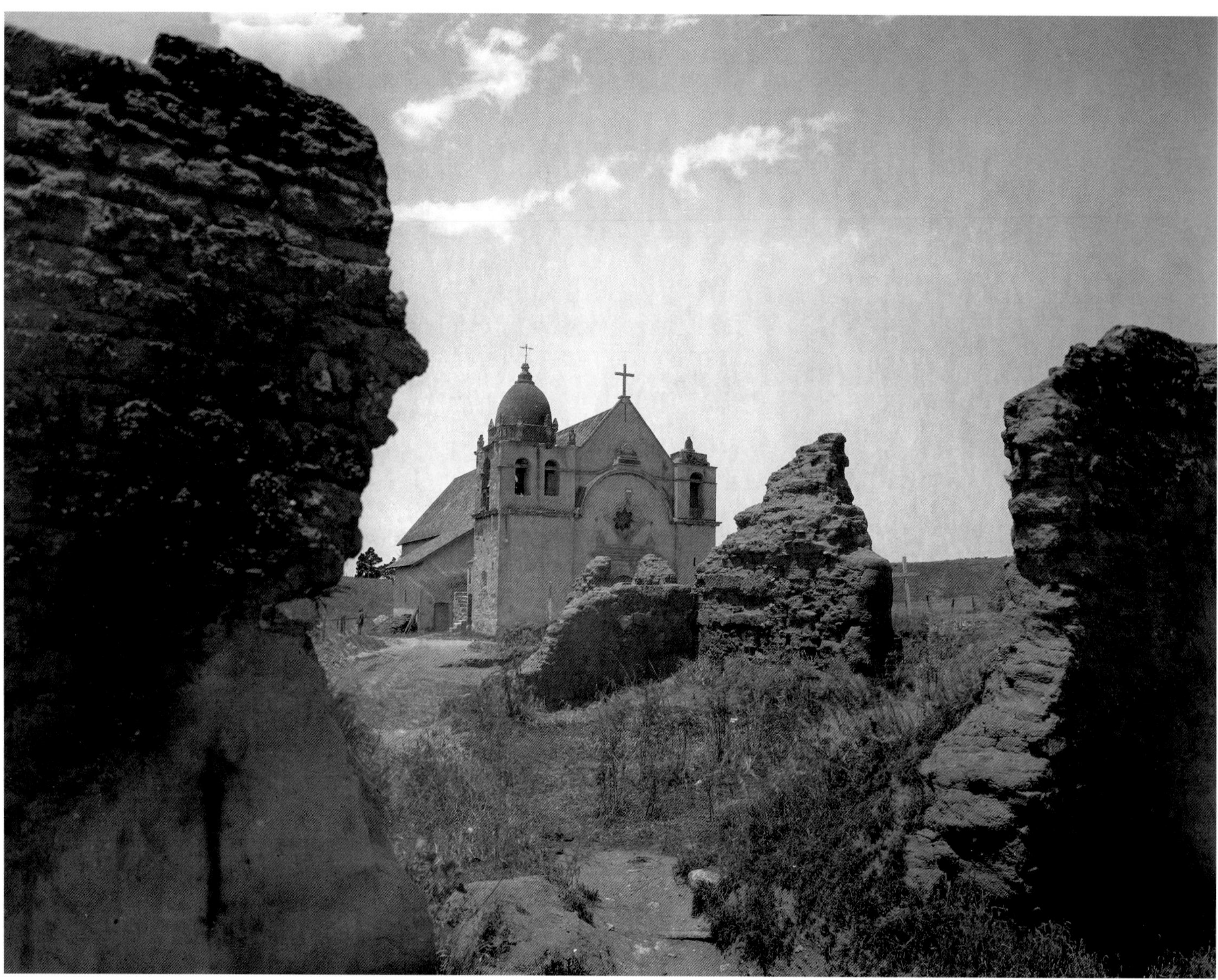

View of Mission San Carlos Borromeo's church, ca. 1890, preserved through the efforts of Father Casanova in the 1880s. Although the steeply pitched roof was not historically accurate, it served to prevent further deterioration of the building. Courtesy Harry Downie Archive, Mission San Carlos Borromeo

invitations at the rectory, Downie would steal several back on each occasion. He was caught when the vestments were displayed at Mission San Carlos Borromeo but convinced Church authorities to allow them to remain there.[24] Downie appreciated the theatrical aspects of his mission reconstructions and often donned a Franciscan habit when guiding tourists through the church, allowing himself to be addressed as "Father Downie."

In his work Downie favored architectural rather than archaeological traditions of restoration. Rather than serve as research tools, his excavations simply located historic building foundations by scraping off the overlying soils, allowing him to then align his modern constructions with these footings. He also had an eye for the final result and maintained some flexibility when re-creating a building's historical appearance, remarking that he carried out his restorations "the way they would have done it if they'd had a little money."[25] When footings were found indicating that a historic room and porch in the *convento* once obscured part of the church facade, he simply did not rebuild them.[26] Traditional building materials and techniques were used whenever possible, and old adobe clay from the mound ruins was sometimes used in the rebuilding. He was instructed in the techniques of adobe construction by Mexican workmen, and in restoring the graveyard he consulted

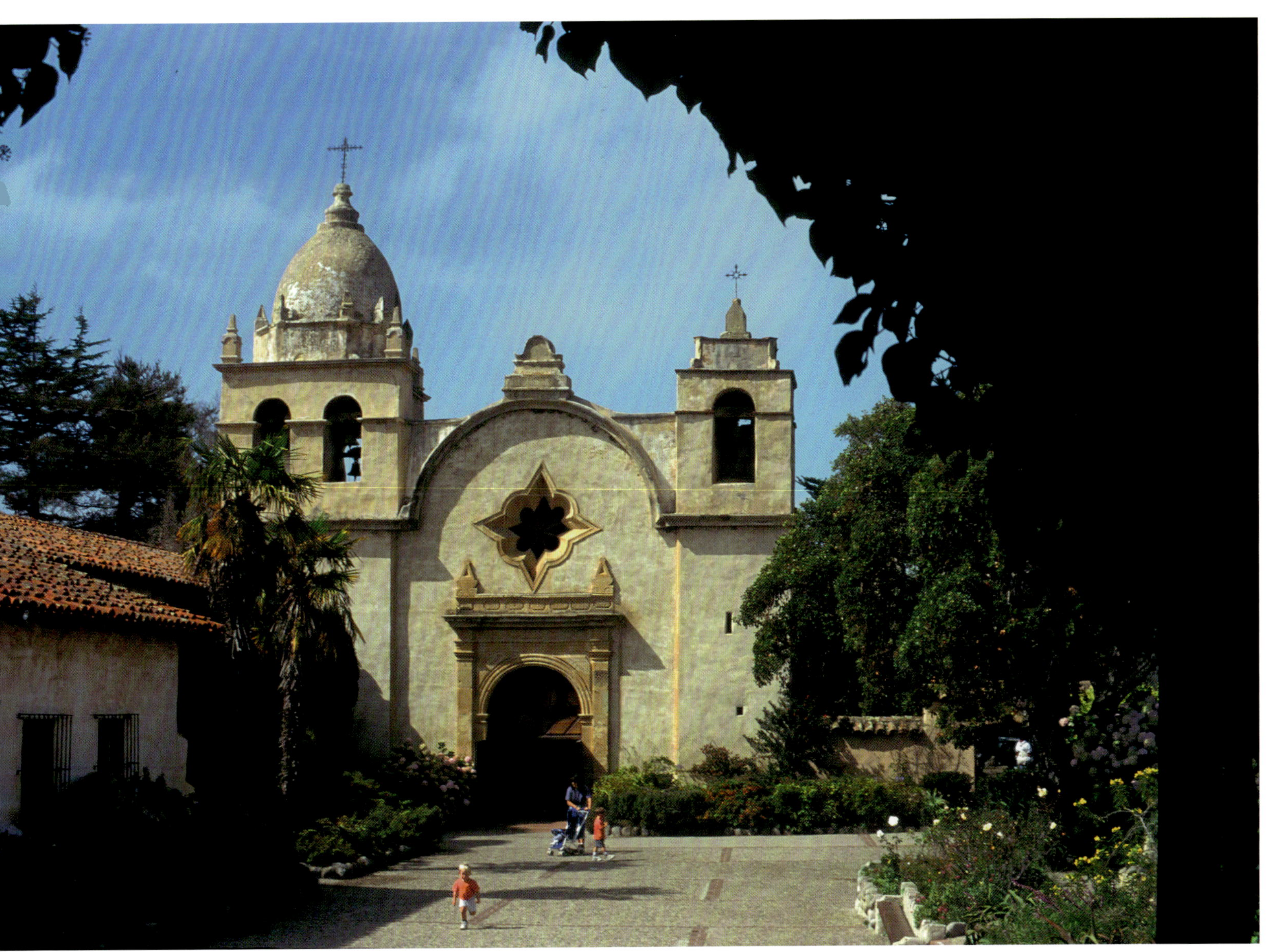

Recent view of Mission San Carlos Borromeo's church, with the reconstructed *convento* building on the left. The church's lower roofline and curved nave ceiling were reinstated by Harry Downie in his 1936 reconstruction. Lush modern landscaping now fills the old mission plaza. Photograph by G. Aldana

descendants of mission Indians.[27] When completed, walls and statuary were antiqued to lend a patina of age. Downie popularized authentic architectural reconstructions and the proper care of the missions' art and artifacts, concepts that would prove invaluable for all future projects. He grew to be considered the most accomplished restorer of his day, and over the next few decades he would be called on to advise in the restorations of nearly half of the California missions. Although future restorations and reconstructions would use more rigorous methods of research and execution, Harry Downie performed a critical role in introducing the public to the importance of historic research and authenticity.

As a living church with an active and engaged parish, Mission San Juan Capistrano faced some issues similar to those at San Carlos Borromeo, although for several reasons its restoration would follow a somewhat different approach. The large complex had gradually fallen to ruin after its sale in 1845 and subsequent abandonment. In the 1890s the Landmarks Club cleared tons of debris and rebuilt roofs to protect the remaining structures. When Father St. John O'Sullivan arrived in 1910, he began his lifelong work of gradually refurbishing and stabilizing the mission buildings. In 1922 he commenced restoration of the Serra Chapel, which was completed in 1925. It was furnished with items saved from

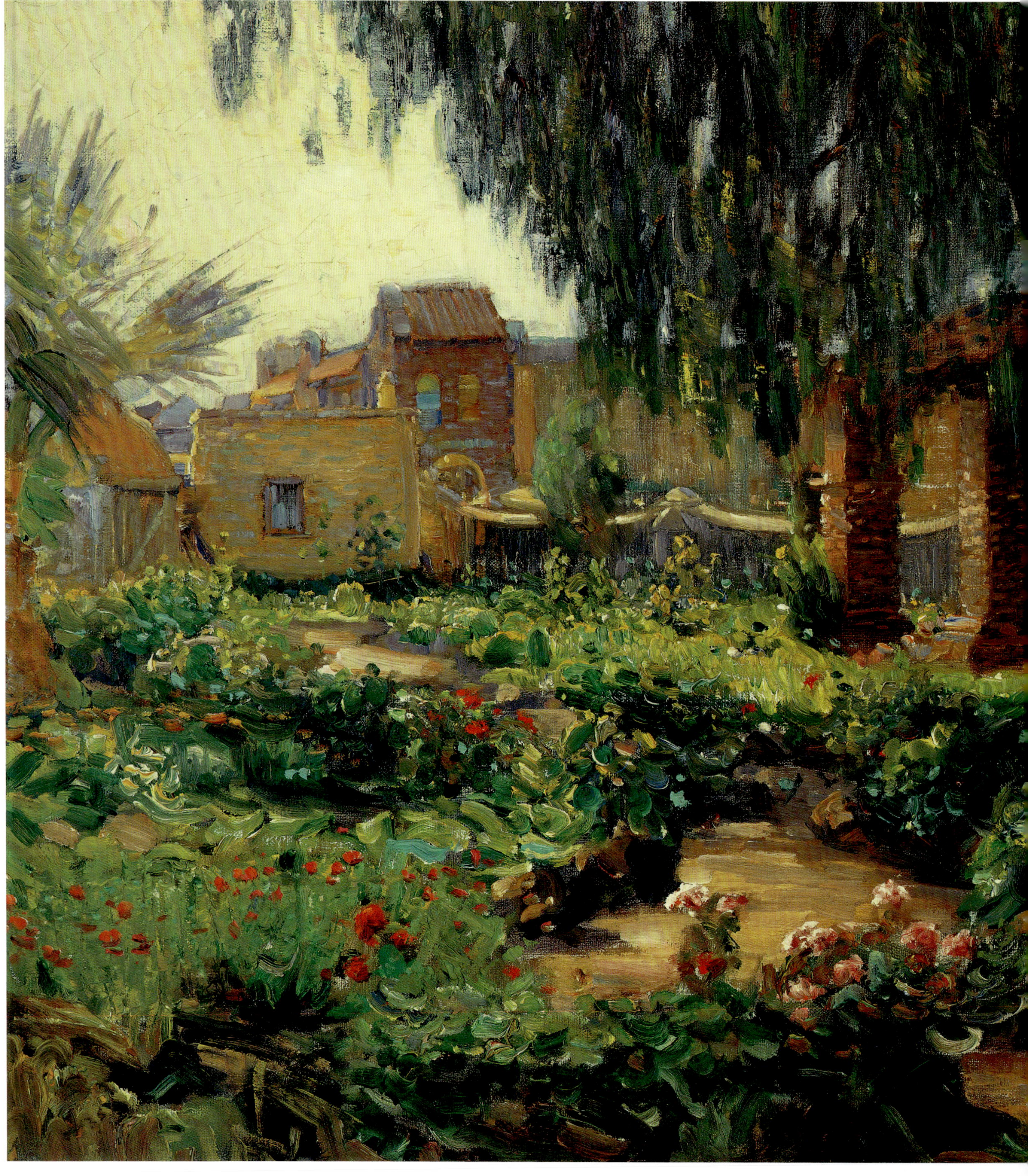

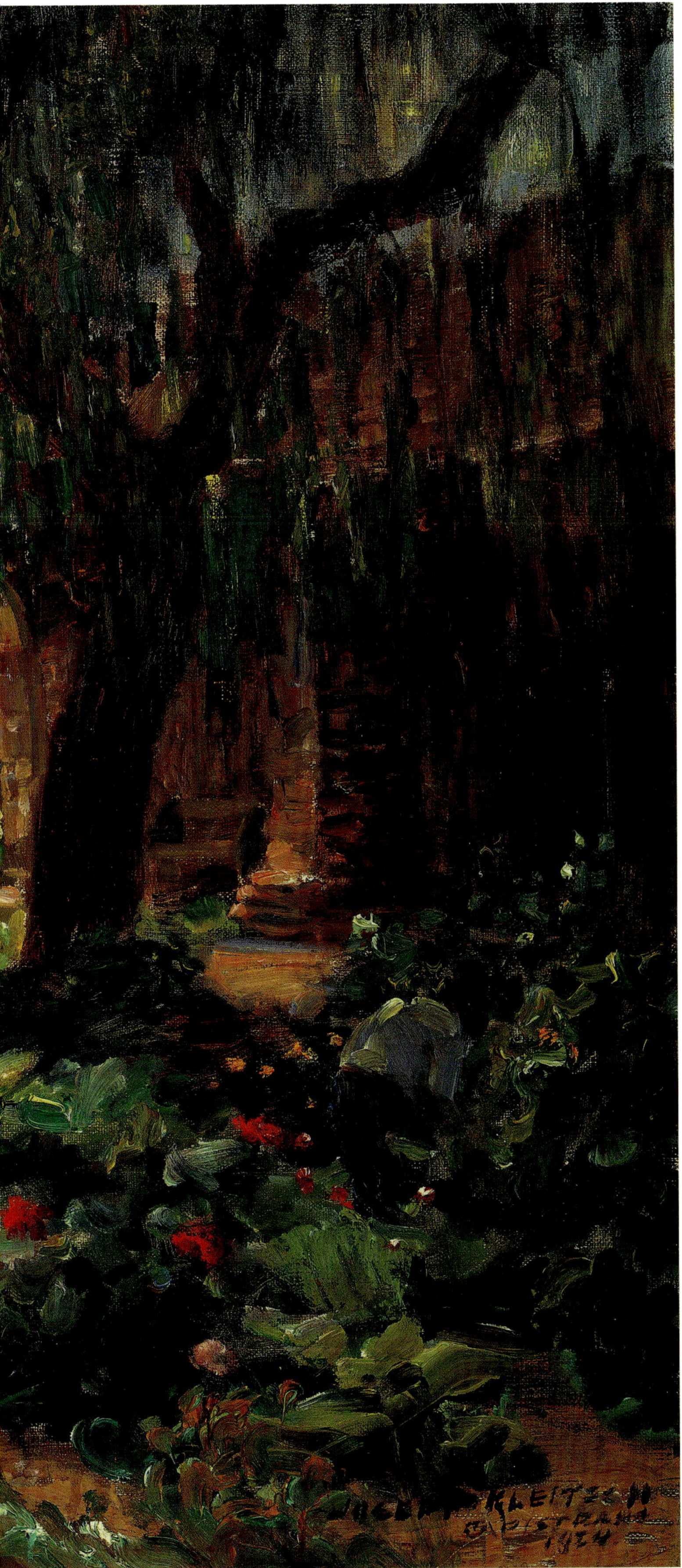

the original church and crowned with a four-hundred-year-old baroque cherrywood *retablo* from Barcelona (see pp. 194–97). Father O'Sullivan developed the quadrangle garden as a tourist attraction and actively promoted the mission, writing a short book for tourists and inviting artists to paint there. The many renderings of the mission and its new, lush gardens included some of the finest Impressionist paintings produced in California.

Father O'Sullivan also worked with writers to popularize and promote the mission's story. The book *Capistrano Nights*, by Charles Saunders, published in 1930, recounted legends and folklore and prominently featured the story of the swallows that depart from and return to the mission on about the same days every year. This story caught the imagination of a journalist from the *Los Angeles Times*, who dutifully began reporting it annually. During the depths of the depression, audiences nationwide found comfort in the reassuring narrative of the faithful birds.[28] San Juan Capistrano has become one of the most popular missions. It is visited by hundreds of thousands of tourists every year.

By the late 1930s mission ruins statewide were being subjected to various approaches to restoration and reconstruction. At Mission San Fernando, restoration of the church and *convento* was initiated in the late 1930s by the resident priest, assisted by the archaeologist Mark Harrington, who had previously been involved at La Purísima. Money was raised through local fund-raising efforts, adobe bricks were molded, and the HABS architectural drawings and Index artistic renderings were consulted to ensure accuracy. In 1941 five thousand people attended the rededication of the church after nearly seventy years of closure. Work continued after the war, when replicas of the historic west and south quadrangle wings were completed.[29]

During World War II, restoration activity slowed, but the centenary of the gold rush in 1948 stimulated interest in California's past. In 1948 the newspaper baron William Randolph Hearst established the Hearst Mission Restoration Fund with an initial grant of $500,000 to be divided among the nineteen missions owned by the Church.[30] Notably, Hearst funded rebuilding of the quadrangle at San Miguel and the workshop buildings at San Fernando Rey. He employed Harry Downie for restoration projects at San Juan Bautista and San Luis Obispo, where "modern elements were removed, some rebuilding was carried out, and both missions were restored to their historical appearance."[31]

Perhaps Hearst's most ambitious undertaking was that closest to his heart and home: the extensive reconstruction of Mission San Antonio, located within his vast ranch adjoining his lavish Mediterranean Revival estate at San Simeon. Hearst had earlier repeatedly tried to purchase the mission ruins, but the Church would not sell. As a consolation, in 1929 he had instructed his San Simeon architect, Julia Morgan, to construct a Mission Revival "hacienda" on a hill overlooking the historic site, where

In the early decades of the twentieth century, the landscaped gardens of Mission San Juan Capistrano became a popular subject for painters of the California Impressionist school. The flowers and luxuriant plantings adorning the quadrangle's enclosed interior courtyard contrast with its original spare, dusty appearance (see p. 48). Joseph Kleitsch, *San Juan Capistrano*, 1924 (detail). Oil on canvas. Courtesy of The Irvine Museum, Irvine, California

he could entertain guests. Hearst then generously funded the extensive rebuilding of the ruined mission. Carried out under the guidance of Harry Downie and completed in 1955, it included reconstruction of the church and *convento* wing and the addition of a modern Franciscan retreat center with an exterior sympathetic to mission-period design. Downie's influence is also evident in the heavy-handed bulldozing of the adobe ruins, which allowed him to accurately position the new wall footings but resulted in the loss of valuable historical and archaeological information.

By the mid-1950s La Soledad was the only mission still in ruins and without any reconstruction. In the next decade its chapel and *convento* were reconstructed through fund-raising carried out by the Native Daughters of the Golden West. The work was once again directed by Harry Downie. He ensured a historically accurate building and assisted in finding appropriate historic furnishings, but he again disregarded the site's archaeological potential, bulldozing adobe walls to their foundations in order to place the new structure. During these years the mission caretaker was also excavating the site, uncovering graves in the old chapel floor, massive grinding stones, and caches of artifacts. Some artifacts recovered during these endeavors are now on display in the mission's small museum, although there are virtually no notes or photographs documenting methods and findings. Subsequent archaeological excavations carried out during the 1980s demonstrated the wealth of artifacts and historical information still present in portions of the ruins that have not been destroyed.[32]

Since World War II the mission myth has been challenged by more egalitarian interpretations of mission history and heritage. Revisionist histories, beginning with Carey McWilliams's *Southern California: An Island on the Land* (1946), questioned the long-

View of the Mission San Fernando Rey *convento* in disrepair, ca. 1880. There are holes in the corridor roof where the tiles are missing, plaster has fallen from the lower colonnade and adobe walls, and the circular fountain in the foreground is overgrown with weeds. Photograph by C. C. Pierce. Courtesy University of Southern California, on behalf of the USC Special Collections

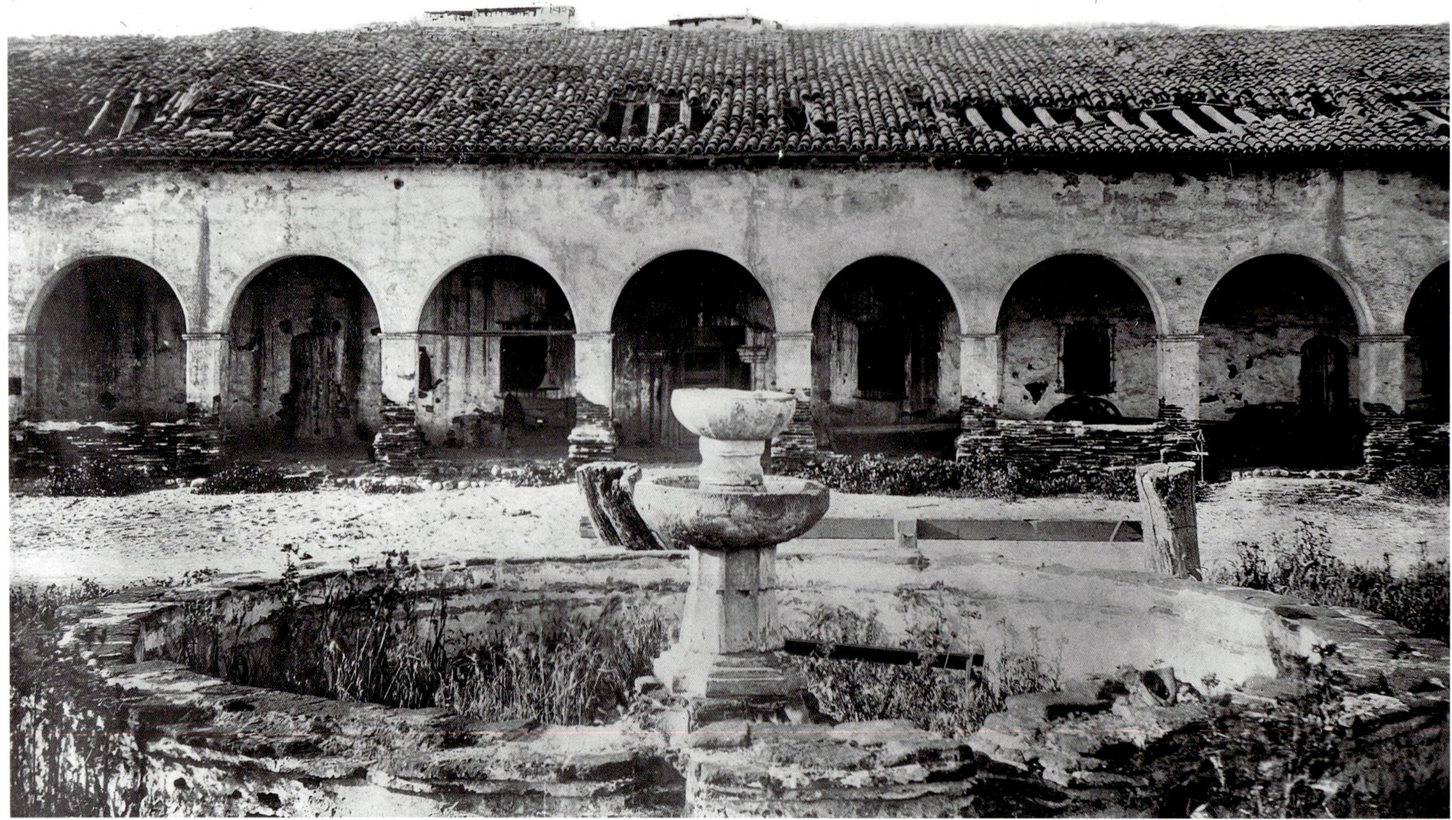

1955–65
Reconstruction of Mission Soledad by Native Daughters of the Golden West.

1958
Santa Cruz Mission State Historic Park established.

1966
National Historic Preservation Act of 1966 mandates increased state involvement in historic preservation.

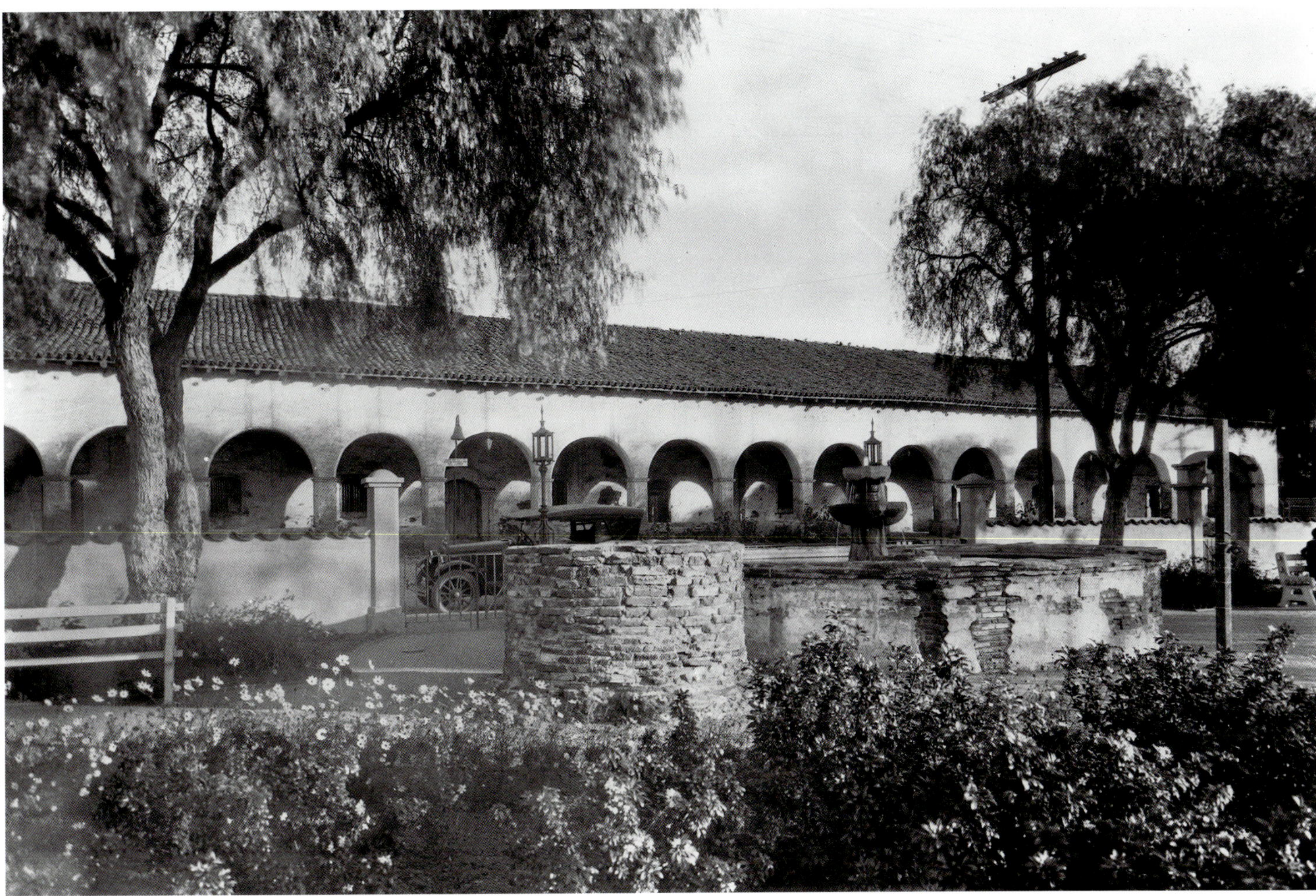

View of the Mission San Fernando *convento*, ca. 1926. The cloister's roof and walls have been restored, the fountain has been repaired, and the adjacent park has been landscaped with flowers and benches. These improvements underscore the success of early restoration efforts led by the Landmarks Club; the 1930s would bring additional restoration of the church and *convento*. Photograph by C. C. Pierce. Courtesy University of Southern California, on behalf of the USC Special Collections

held Eurocentric assumptions that had characterized much early writing and research. Sherburne F. Cook's *The Conflict between the California Indian and White Civilization* (1976) provided groundbreaking demographic studies on the devastating effects of Spanish colonization on indigenous populations. Whereas boosters and earlier writers had widely lauded the "civilizing effort" of the missions, the pendulum now swung in the other direction, as new scholars and Indian advocates excoriated the mission system for the destruction of Native American peoples and cultures. The fresh viewpoint gained momentum from the liberal politics of the 1960s and the rise of Native American political and social awareness, producing a wave of new scholarship that challenged the old mission myth and shed new light on the lives of Native Americans. This new scholarship brought to light the resistance and rebellion of the neophytes, as well as the lives of the Mexican artisans and others who resided and worked in Alta California. The debate about the mission heritage has continued, and although no general consensus has emerged, recent scholarship reflects a more measured and nuanced assessment of California's complex mission past.

Archaeologists added to this dialogue early on, by bringing new insights to the study of mission ruins. At Sonoma's Mission San Francisco Solano, explorations carried out in the 1950s by University of California archaeologists revealed additional *convento* rooms and other features that had been missed when the state razed and rebuilt the chapel and

1960s
Archaeological excavations begin at San Diego Mission and Presidio.

1970s
Archaeological excavations at Mission San Buenaventura.

1971
Sylmar earthquake damages Mission San Fernando Rey; church destroyed.

Archaeology: Window on the Past

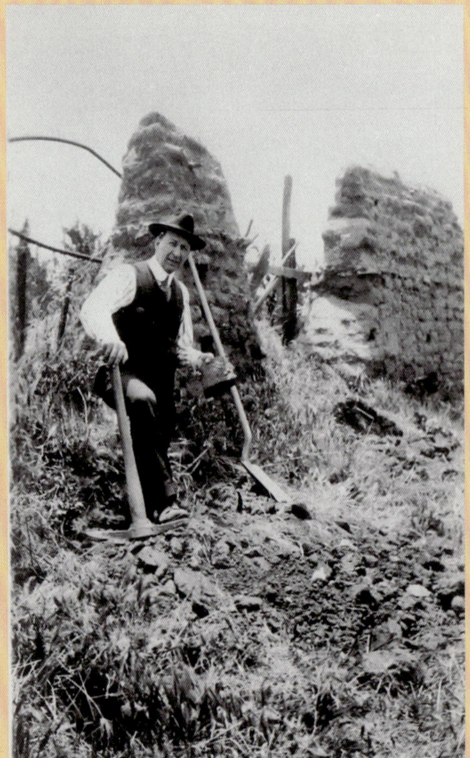

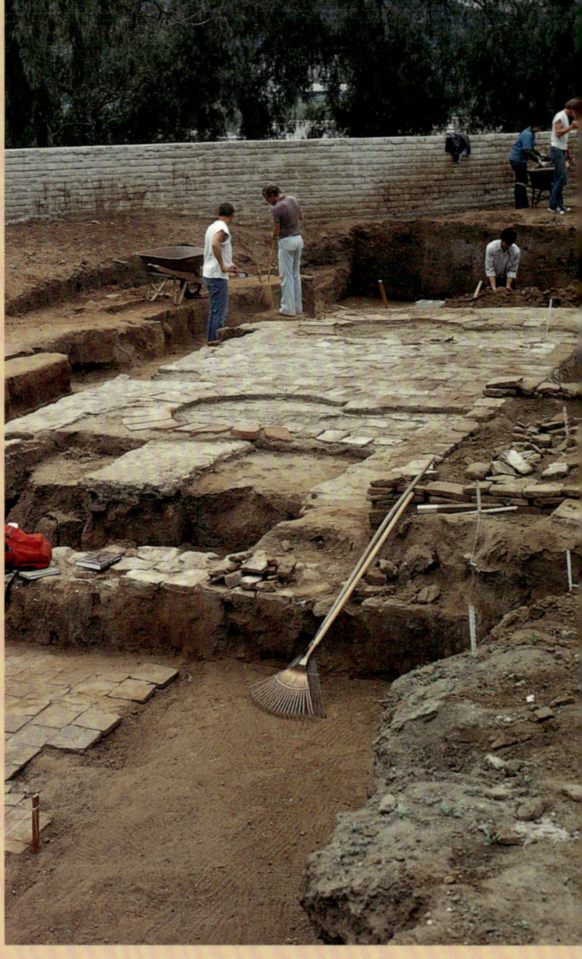

ABOVE: Some early mission enthusiasts used shovels to dig for "treasures" in the ruins of the old missions, unknowingly destroying sensitive archaeological information. Courtesy of The Bancroft Library, University of California, Berkeley

ABOVE RIGHT: Archaeological excavations at Mission San Diego began in the 1960s and continued for some four decades, involving university students, teachers, and the general public. Here a tiled floor is exposed in the east wing in 1977. Photograph by Julia Costello

In a state where ideology has played such an important role in defining the mission heritage, unique and valuable information is contained in archaeological remains. Researchers in the Southwest had long recognized the commonalities between prehistoric villages of adobe and stone and early Spanish communities and understood that careful excavation would reveal details of the occupants' lives. But in California the "story" of the missions seemed to have already been told in the mission myth, and for much of the twentieth century, "excavations" at most mission sites were conducted simply to identify the locations of footings for reconstructions.

Archaeological remains, however, are impartial records of what took place in the past. Although only the most durable cultural goods survive (such as stone, metal, ceramics, glass, shell, and bone) along with evidence of constructions (such as buildings, structures, fire hearths, terracing, pits, and privies), these remains are completely democratic. Rich and poor, women and men, natives and newcomers—all left their imprint on the land to be read by future scientists. Archaeology is especially important for revealing the realities of populations that traditionally were poorly documented in written records or subjected to biased chronicles.[33]

In California the study of archaeological remains on sites of the Spanish and Mexican periods has provided an unparalleled look into the lives of all who lived and worked on the missions, Spanish padres and Native Americans, soldiers and civilians. Seeds, bones, and cooking vessels reveal what people ate; tools and remains of industry, the crafts they practiced; ditches, dams, reservoirs, and fountains, how water was harnessed and distributed. Carvings, ornaments, beads, and talismans provide glimpses into personal lives; and imported ceramics, metal, and glass show how the California missions were connected to the rest of the world.

In recent years archaeological studies have deepened our understanding of many aspects of mission life. They show that native hunting and gathering practices continued, augmenting the new staples of corn, wheat, and beef. Traditional religious practices also continued, along with stone-tool making in this land where metal was rare and expensive. Study of artifacts from individual dwellings shows how the lives of the neophytes consisted of a mix of new and old traditions. Analysis of human skeletal remains reveals the often tragic effects on neophytes of changed diet, disease, and daily labor. The careful excavation of buildings' floors and walls, meanwhile, tells stories of renovations, modifications, decorations, and changes of use over time. Excavations have also revealed the locations of tanneries and orchards, neophytes' and soldiers' villages, and gardens, threshing floors, and baking ovens.

Archaeological remains, however, are a fragile and nonrenewable resource. Once the subtle layers of earthen floors, fire hearths, postholes, and artifacts are destroyed, they can never be reconstructed. Archaeological remains on mission sites can be likened to books that can be read only once: they must be either preserved for the future or carefully studied before they are destroyed.

convento some thirty years before.[34] More recently, this mission has emerged as an example of how reconstruction issues should be presented to the public. At the visitors' entrance, panels inform the public that "reconstruction of this mission and many others throughout the state was... often accomplished without the benefit of historical or archaeological research... [and] based on romanticized paintings and accounts of the 19th century."[35] Other exhibits describe in detail how modern research is carried out and discuss past and recent park constructions. One mission historian has observed, "Mission Solano explicitly owns up to what it is, a heavily reconstructed interpretation of the past."[36]

Innovative work was carried out at other missions as well. Until recently, the site of Mission Santa Cruz featured no original buildings; it was marked only by an 1899 brick church and an elegant, half-scale mission replica constructed in 1932. In 1958 Santa Cruz Mission State Historic Park was established when the California Department of Parks and Recreation purchased the sole building remaining from the historic mission, an adobe block of seven neophyte dwellings built in 1824. After secularization, this block of rooms was acquired by Californio families and modified into residences. Extensive archaeological studies carried out in the 1980s revealed the layers of history embedded in the building and its surrounding grounds.[37] Now restored, the Santa Cruz Mission Adobe is the state's best-preserved original mission neophyte dwelling. Its carefully documented interpretive presentations have made a significant step in "redressing the extraordinary invisibility of Indians at today's California missions."[38]

In 1970, with the passage of the California Environmental Quality Act (CEQA), which requires government agencies to address (along with other issues) the impact of proposed projects on sites of architectural and archaeological importance, projects at mission sites came under full public scrutiny. While the value of historically sympathetic reconstructions was by then largely accepted by the state, the Catholic Church, and the general public, the

Reconstruction of the church and quadrangle at Mission San Antonio began in 1948, funded by William Randolph Hearst and overseen by Harry Downie. The few extant original elements were incorporated into the reconstruction, including the mission's unique *ladrillo* facade and the *convento*'s colonnade of *ladrillo* arches, both seen here. Photograph by G. Aldana

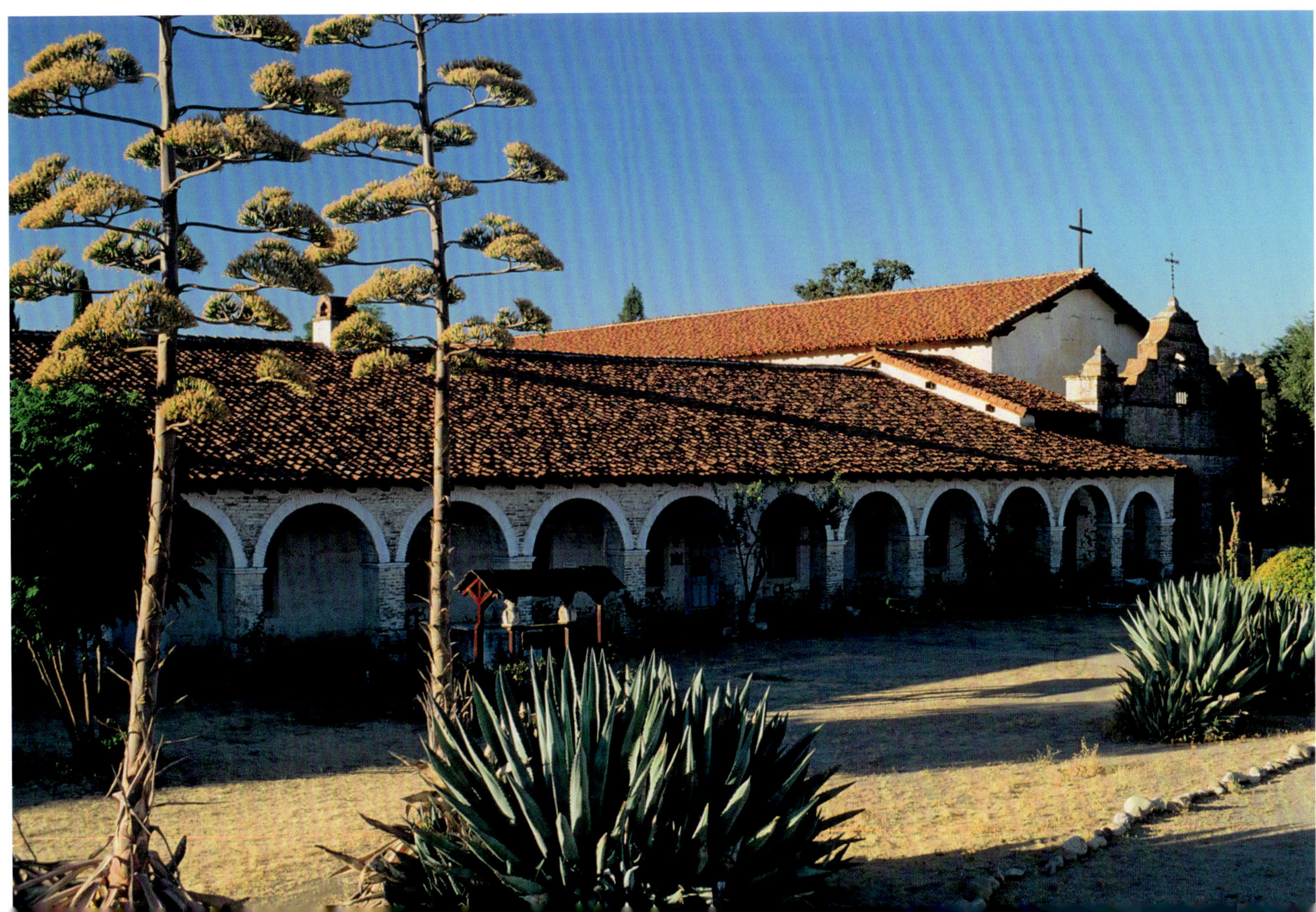

importance of archaeology for illuminating the mission past was still poorly understood. However, as interest in the Native American experience at the missions continued to grow and researchers sought new interpretations not filtered through Anglo-dominated histories, archaeological data has provided a wealth of information. One of the first large-scale investigations was initiated in the 1970s by the Ventura Redevelopment Agency on land adjacent to Mission San Buenaventura, producing such impressive finds that an archaeological park and museum were constructed.[39] In the 1980s reconstruction of a part of the *convento* wing at Santa Inés and the church at San José was preceded by mandated archaeological studies. At Mission San Diego, public protests resulted in relocating the site of the new parish hall away from the historic quadrangle area.

At Mission San Juan Capistrano, a new conservation philosophy was developed emphasizing minimal impact—conservation, not restoration—and regarding earlier restorations of the 1920s and 1930s as part of the mission's ongoing history. Many admirable accomplishments have been carried out, including the seismic retrofitting of the ruins of the Great Stone Church and, most recently, the preservation of the Serra Chapel.

An exemplary archaeological and historical study was launched in 1966 at the Santa Barbara Presidio State Historic Park by the Santa Barbara Trust for Historic Preservation. With only two adobe dwellings remaining from the original presidio quadrangle, a group of Santa Barbara visionaries worked methodically to reconstruct an accurate replica of the original Spanish fort. Archaeological excavations gleaned all that could be learned from the soils while documentary research guided authentic replication of architecture and furnishings. Adobe bricks were made locally, tules were laid under the fired tiles, and rawhide strips were cut from fresh hides to tie the rafter poles. The reconstruction did not succumb to the allure of Santa Barbara's luxurious and colorful garden foliage: the presidio plaza is bare and dusty, as it was in historic times.

The extensive and varied nature of California's mission-period heritage guarantees that preservation, restoration, and interpretation efforts will continue to be diverse. Many missions are beginning to address the role of Native Americans in their interpretive exhibits, although much more remains to be done. Today the missions still face myriad challenges. Of those still owned by the Roman Catholic Church, some, such as Santa Bárbara, are well-maintained icons, but others, such as San Miguel, teeter on the brink of ruin. Many maintain poorly conserved museum displays and outdated interpretations, inhibited by factors ranging from lack of funding or interest to a steadfast adherence to extolling the Franciscan endeavors. Others have found comfort in the mission myth, such as at Mission San Juan Capistrano, where verdant gardens of questionable historical accuracy grace the landscape and thousands of visitors each year enjoy its ambience of romance and cloistered solitude. The missions in the California State Parks system reflect the more recent scholarship in mission studies. The mission Indian experience is interpreted at the Santa Cruz Mission Adobe, and restoration problems are discussed at Mission San Francisco Solano. Visitors to Mission La Purísima enjoy period gardens and a well-developed facility where an active volunteer organization, well-trained docents, the local Chumash, and a living history program have worked together to provide active interpretation of the more favorable aspects of nineteenth-century mission life. All of these missions and their stories, historical and romantic, are part of today's California mission experience.

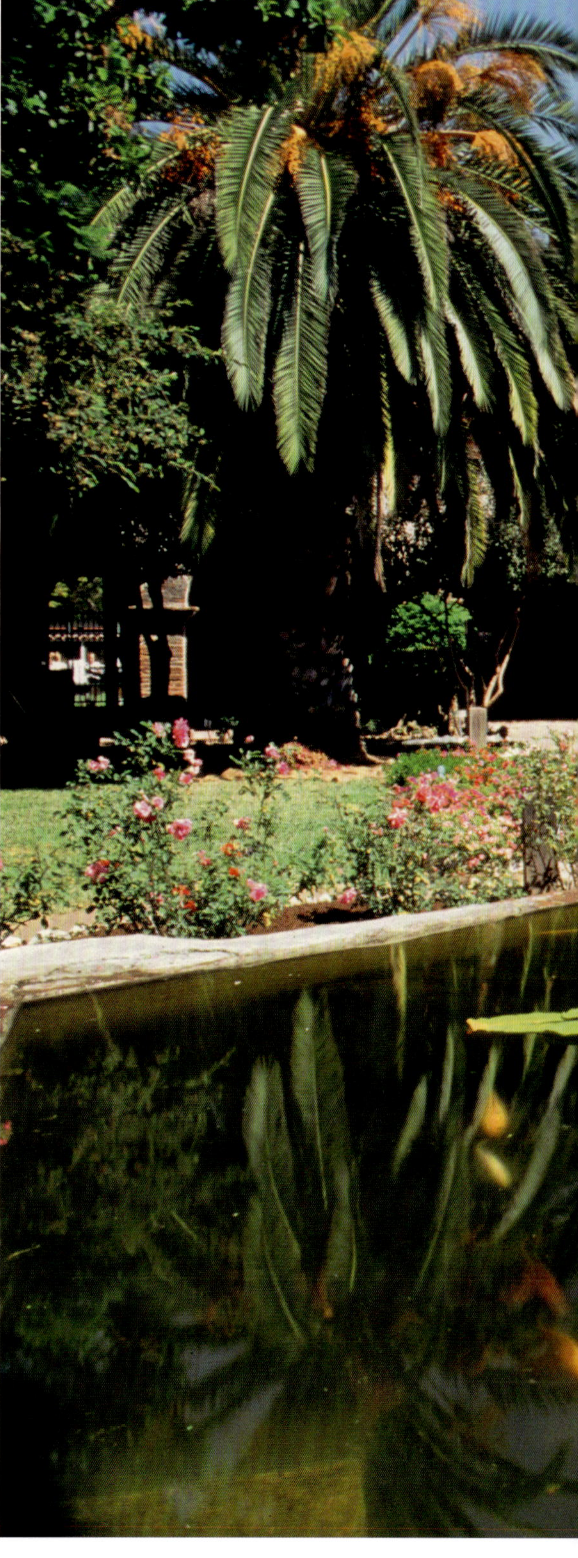

1971
National Trust for Historic Preservation opens western field office in San Francisco.

1990
Getty Seismic Adobe Project begins study of historic buildings in California.

2003
San Simeon Earthquake damages church, threatens structures and murals at Mission San Miguel.

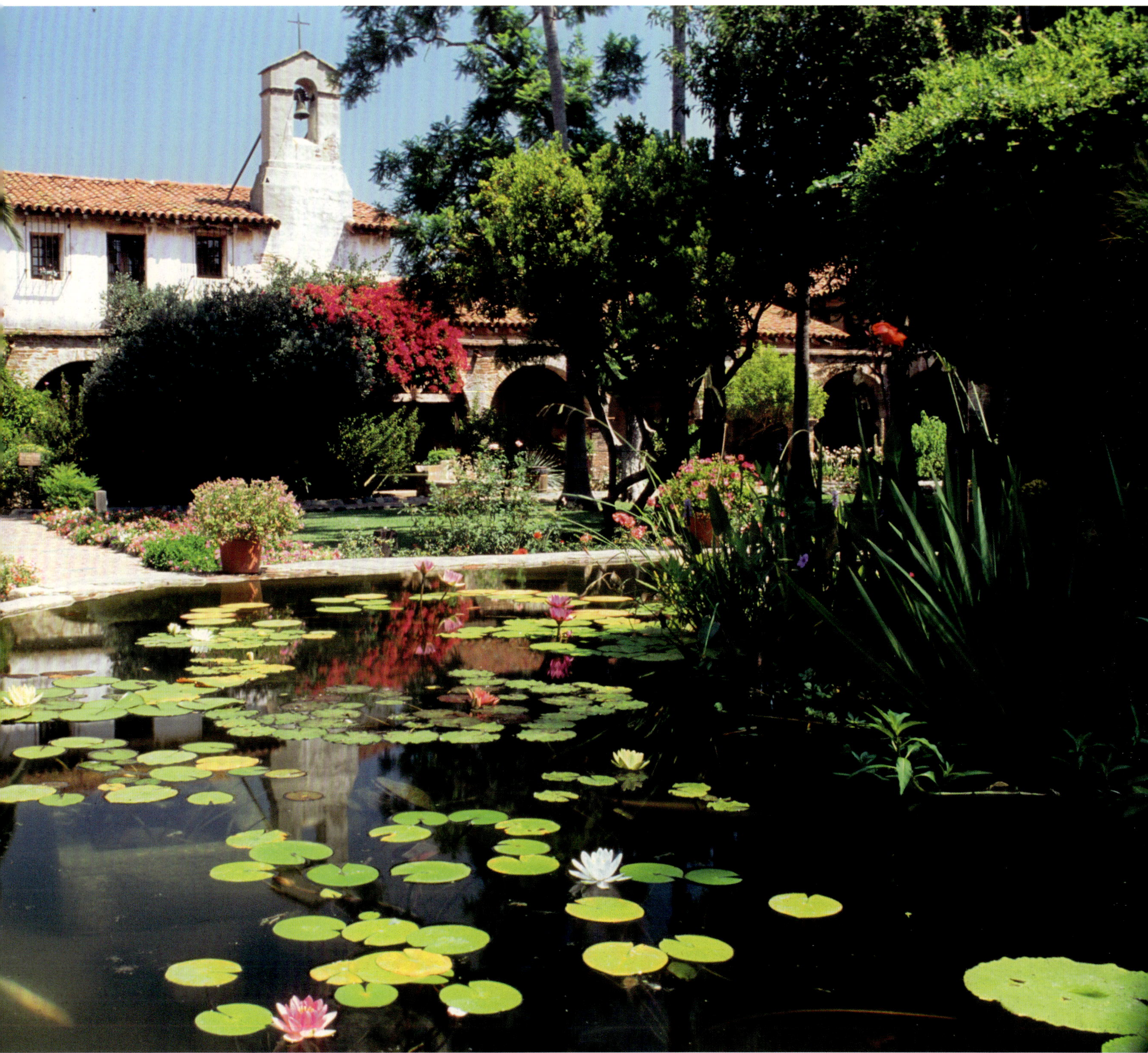

The beautiful landscaped gardens of Mission San Juan Capistrano, while not historically accurate, offer visitors a sense of romance and cloistered tranquility. Photograph by G. Aldana

2004
Federal government approves California Missions Preservation Act; after opposition on grounds that the act violates separation of church and state, funding is withheld.

2006
Conservation completed of ruins of the Great Stone Church at Mission San Juan Capistrano.

2009
Seismic stabilization completed on church at Mission San Miguel.

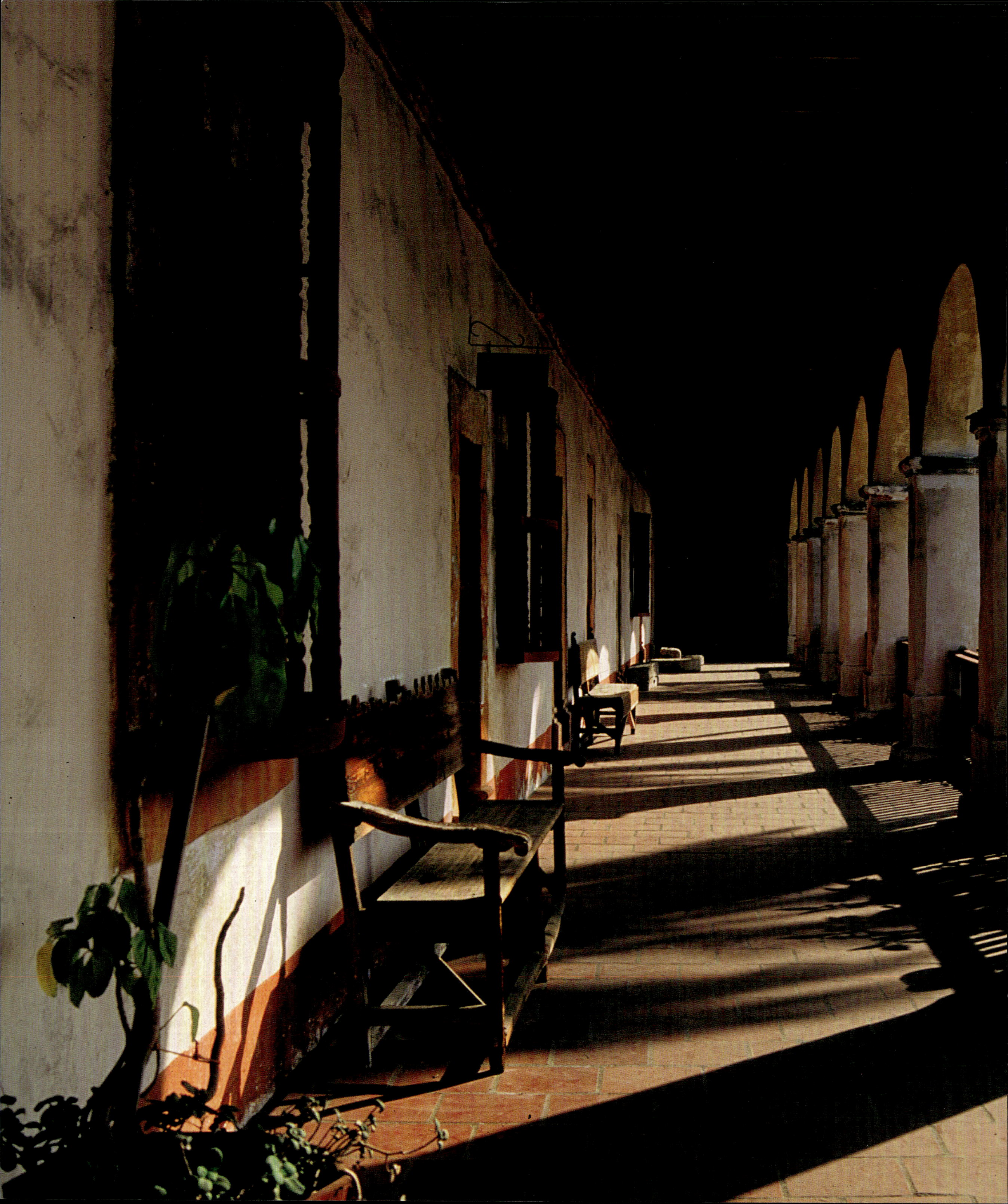

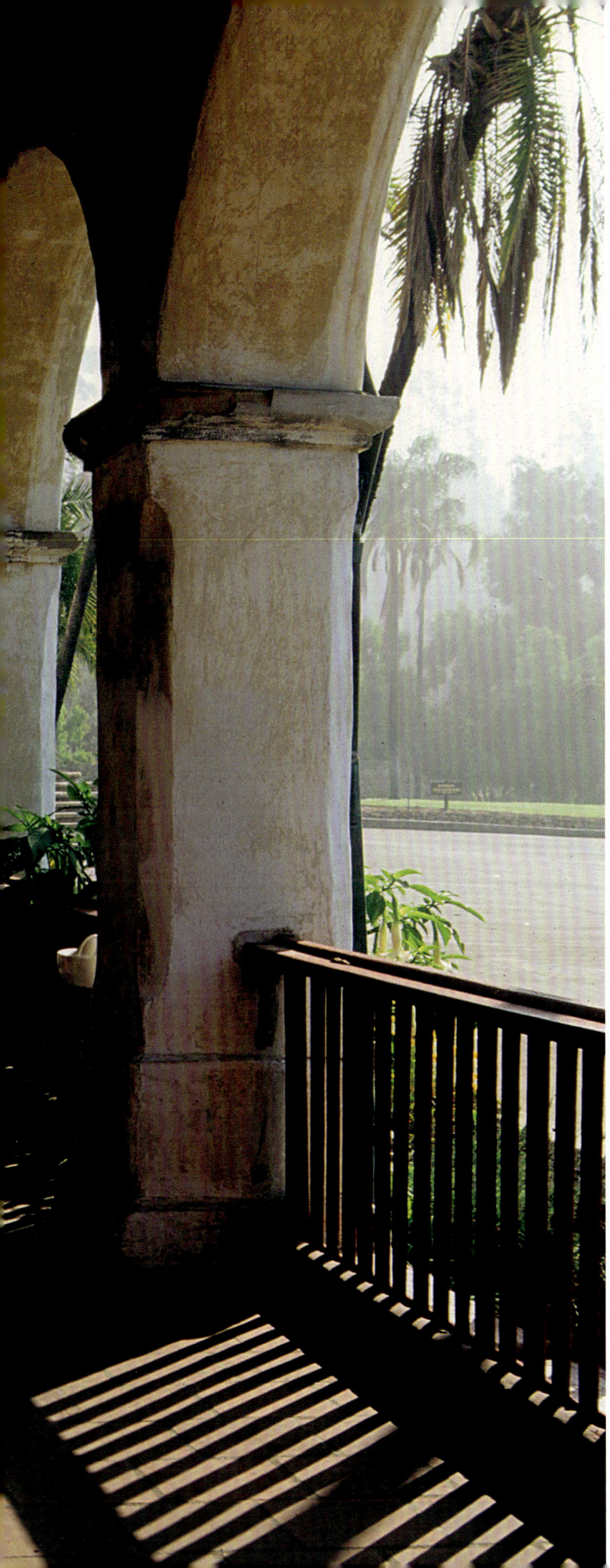

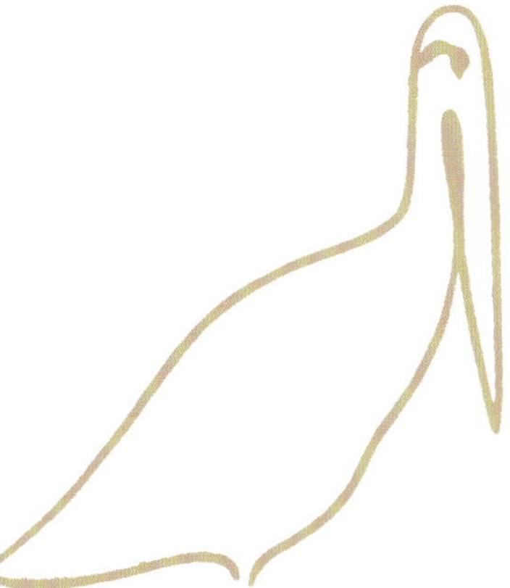

Chapter Four

ARTISANS AND ARCHITECTURE

In September 1790 Alta California's governor, Pedro Fages, petitioned the viceroy in Mexico for fifty-one skilled workers to assist in developing the missions and presidios in the province. Early the following year, the master mason and stonecutter Manuel Esteban Ruiz, accompanied by his journeymen, Joaquín and Salvador Rivera, boarded the frigate *Aránzazu* in San Blas, on the Pacific coast of New Spain. The three men arrived in March in the Alta California capital of Monterey, where much of the presidio compound, with its guard towers, barracks, storerooms, and chapel, had been repaired and rebuilt after a fire two years earlier.

LEFT: Wide, sweeping corridors at mission *conventos* provided shaded areas for rest and socializing. Here at Mission Santa Bárbara, the wooden benches and window grills evoke the feeling of mission days. Photograph by G. Aldana

ABOVE: Pelican drawn by a neophyte at Mission San Juan Capistrano.

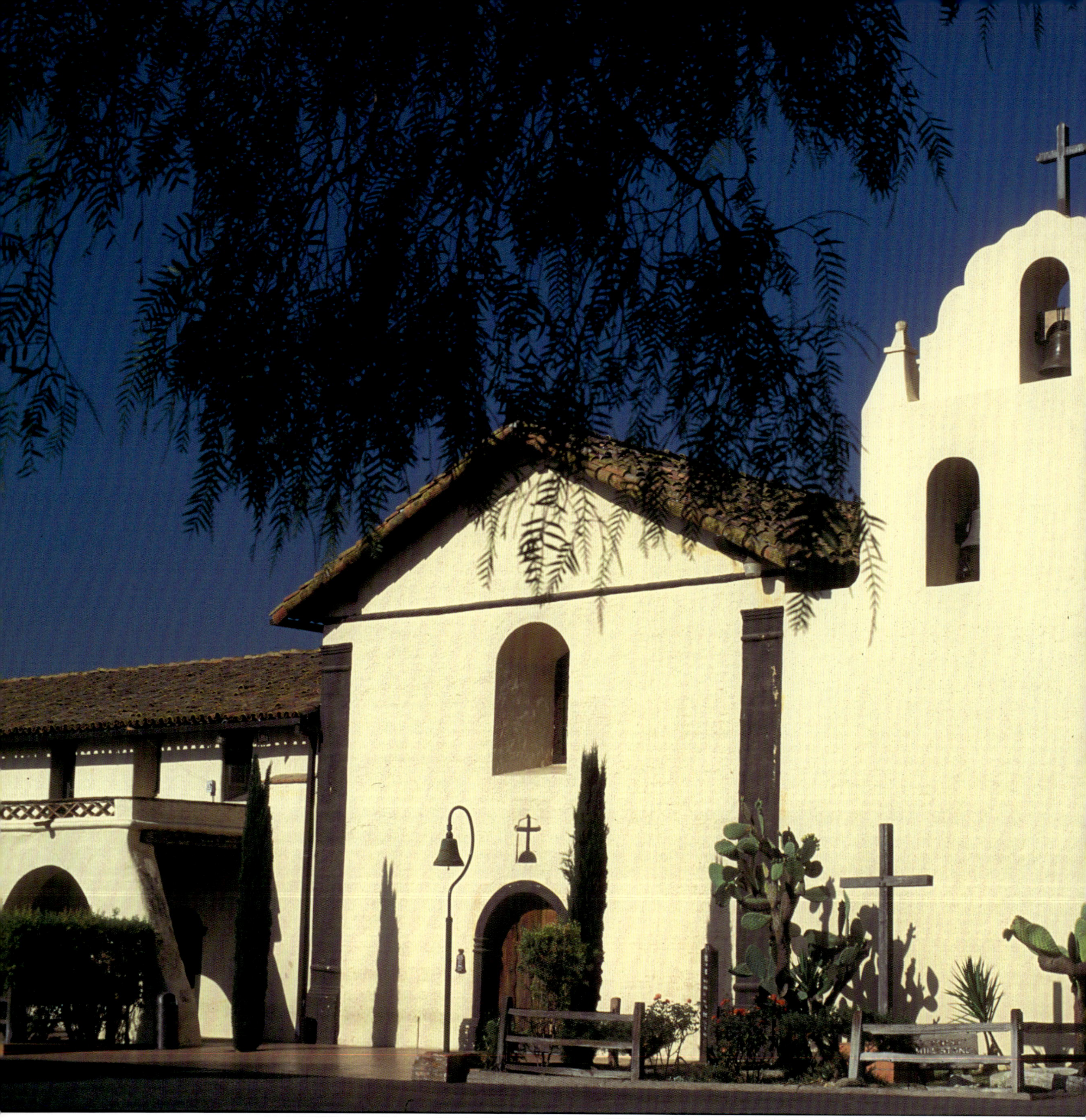

The church at Mission Santa Inés was constructed of adobe with a *ladrillo* facade in 1817; it features painted pilasters on the corners. The dramatic bell tower is an accurate reconstruction dating to 1947. Photograph by G. Aldana

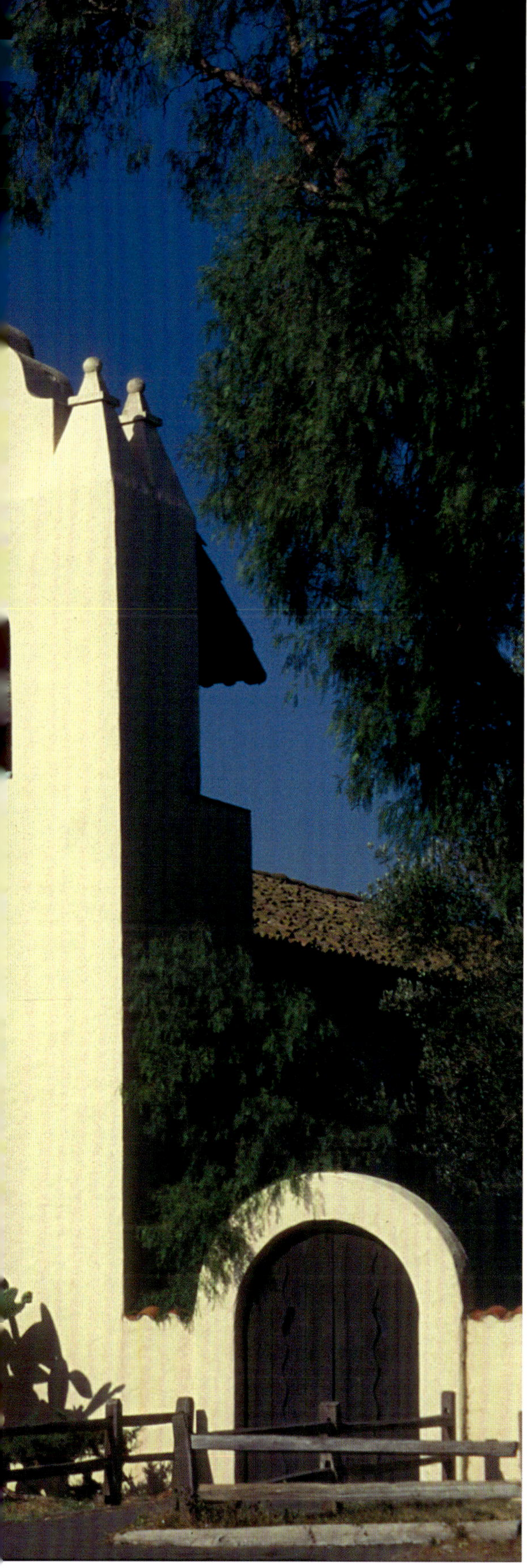

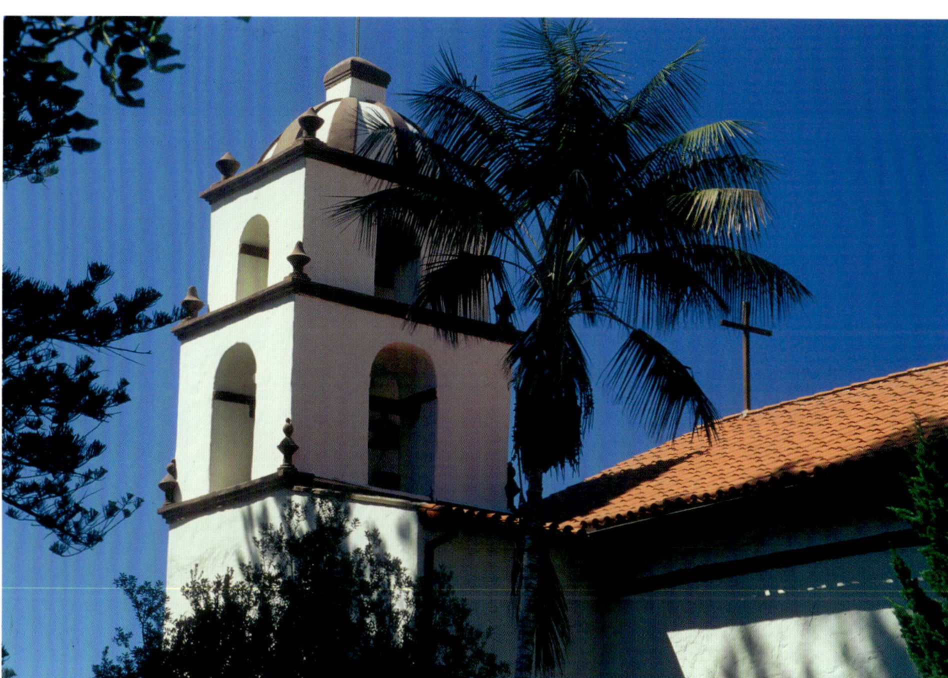

ABOVE RIGHT: The distinctive bell tower at Mission San Luis Rey, with its two-story stepped bell chambers. Photograph by G. Aldana

The shortage of skilled workers had been a problem in the province since the 1770s, when Serra had requested and received additional artisans. Especially important were skilled builders who could direct construction projects and train the growing neophyte populations in the building trades. Selected for their moral character as well as for their technical abilities, these skilled men and those who followed would play a crucial role in the development of Alta California.

In Alta California there were no architects, in the modern sense of the term. As had been true in the building of European cathedrals, the construction of the California missions was typically executed under the guidance of a master mason who performed various functions, including those of architect, stonemason, and general contractor. Priests at each mission certainly controlled decisions about the general styles of churches built under their direction, but only a few were actively involved in their design and construction. Professional artisans from New Spain, many of whom were mestizo, influenced the Franciscans' choices in varying degrees and were the ultimate architects and executors of the designs.[1] As for the actual construction of the missions, it was carried out by California's indigenous people, and the adobe and stone buildings they erected represent the largest and most visible products of their industry.

As the spiritual center of community life, mission churches, as well as churches at presidios and pueblos, received the vast majority of architectural embellishments and art (see chapters 5 and 6). They generally included some basic features of Spanish and Mexican churches, adapted to meet the social demands and building materials of the new land. The church presided over the mission plaza, generally adjoining one end of the *convento*, with its gable-end entrance facing this open public space.[2] The main portal was often fronted by a stepped platform, which could serve as a stage for religious events and performances. Ceremonies were also held in the inner patio of the quadrangle, in the *corredor*, and in the mission plaza.[3] Twice as tall as other buildings, churches featured a long nave for the congregation, a sanctuary at the far end for the holy rituals, and a choir loft over the entrance lighted by a small window opening to the facade. A baptistery room was typically attached to the side of the nave near the door.

Vitruvius: Building by the Book

In Vitruvius's *De architectura*, priests and artisans found guidance for everything from orienting and designing buildings to firing tiles and making lime plaster to laying out aqueducts. During the reign of the Roman emperor Augustus (44 B.C.E.–14 C.E.), the Roman engineer Vitruvius compiled construction and engineering knowledge of his day to serve as a handbook throughout the Roman Empire. The only surviving treatise on Classical architecture, the work defined the three key considerations of design: *firmitas, utilitas, venustias* (strong, useful, beautiful). His belief in the importance of proportion in the art of building led him to define the "Vitruvian Man"—drawn famously by Leonardo da Vinci—as a manifestation of a natural geometric order. *De architectura* was rediscovered in 1414 and published in Latin, Italian, French, English, German, Spanish, and other languages; it is still in print.[4] Vitruvius's work was certainly present in Alta California, as a 1787 Spanish edition, *Los diez libros de arquitectura*, has survived at Santa Barbara Mission Archive-Library, and in 1817 the clergy at San Miguel were requesting a copy of Vitruvius from the governor.[5]

Two other architectural books found in mission libraries were *Elementos de toda la arquitectura civil* by Cristiano Rieger (ca. 1750) and *Arte y uso de arquitectura* by Fray Lorenzo de San Nicolás (1639). The latter was enormously popular in New Spain and "provided builders with a method for determining not only the measurement of church naves, but also the depth of foundations and the thickness of walls."[6]

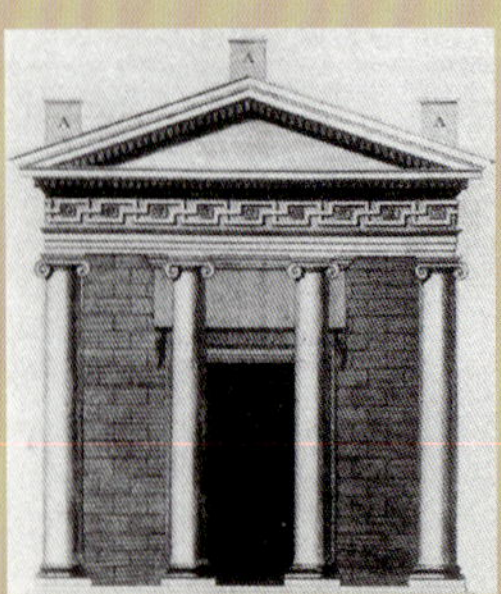

This drawing of a classic facade in the 1787 edition of Vitruvius's architectural guide inspired the design of Mission Santa Bárbara. Courtesy of the Santa Bárbara Mission Archive-Library

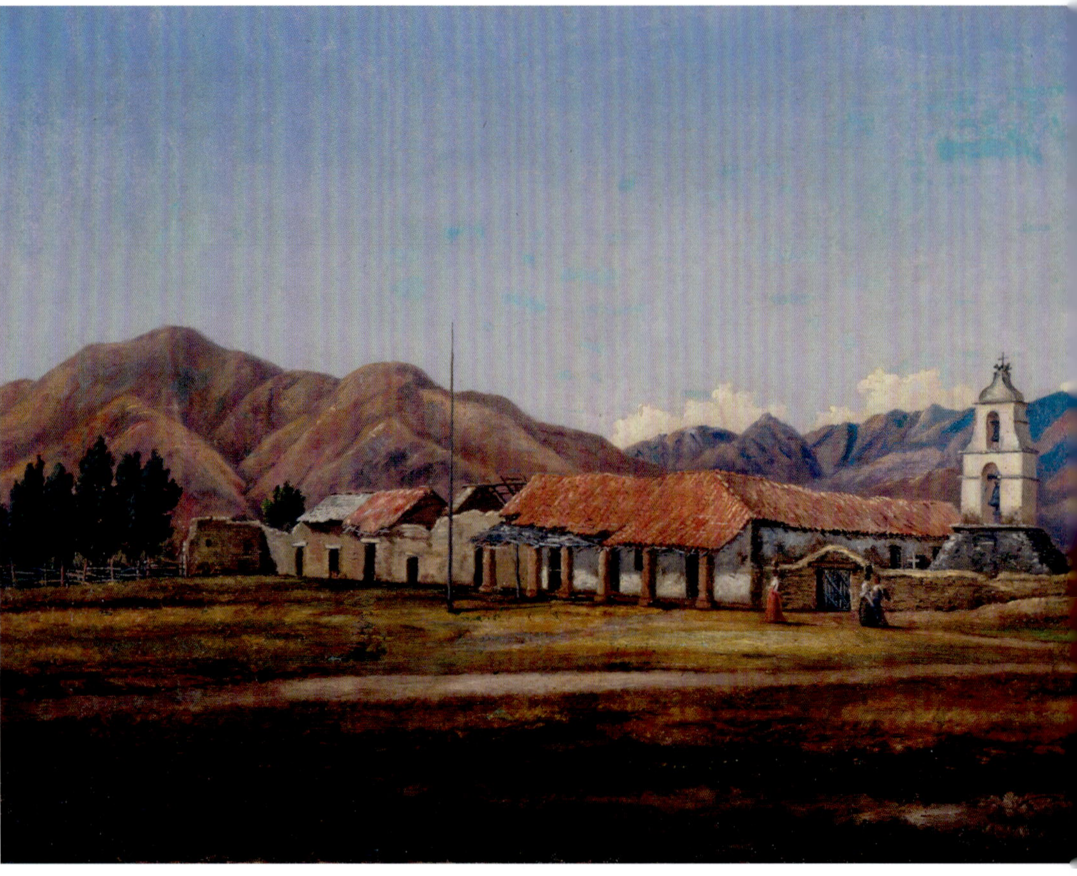

All mission churches had exterior plaster of lime-and-sand stucco, following the Roman formula of three parts clean washed sand to one part burned lime, slaked with water.[7] Doors were made of boards on wood frames with wrought iron bosses and clinched nails. The roof typical of California missions was settled on after a process of trial and error. A number of mission churches were originally constructed with ambitious barrel-vaulted and terraced flat roofs (both termed *azoteas*) with roof drains (*canales*).[8] These roofs were favored in the dry climate and geologically stable terrain of Mexico and New Mexico but proved ill suited to the winter rains and earthquakes of Alta California. They were abandoned in favor of gabled, red-tiled roofs, the tiles being produced as early as 1776, at Mission San Antonio.

One of the most prominent architectural features was the *campanario*, a general term for the construction where the bells (*campanas*) were hung. Most of the missions had their bells hung in *espadañas*, walls with windowlike openings where the bells could swing freely.[9] Sometimes *espadañas* were freestanding walls, as at Pala Asistencia; sometimes they were attached to the church facade, as at Mission Santa Inés. *Espadañas* were also incorporated into the facade itself, as at Missions San Luis Obispo, San Francisco de Asís, and San Antonio. Several of the missions, such as San Juan Bautista, San Francisco Solano, San Rafael, Soledad, and San Miguel, lacked *campanarios* altogether and hung the bells from a simple wood frame. Actual bell towers, or *torres*, graced several of the missions. In Alta California these were generally of solid construction—rubble or adobe filled—and were topped by short stepped terracing and a hemispherical dome.[10] Some contained baptisteries, and at Santa Bárbara one of the towers contains a narrow, winding, interior staircase.

Generally, mission exteriors were spare and clean, although facades, doors, and windows often featured some ornamentation. The missions' architectural styles have generally

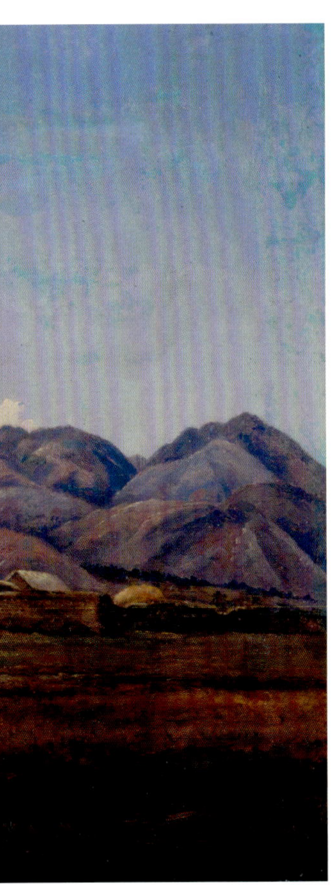

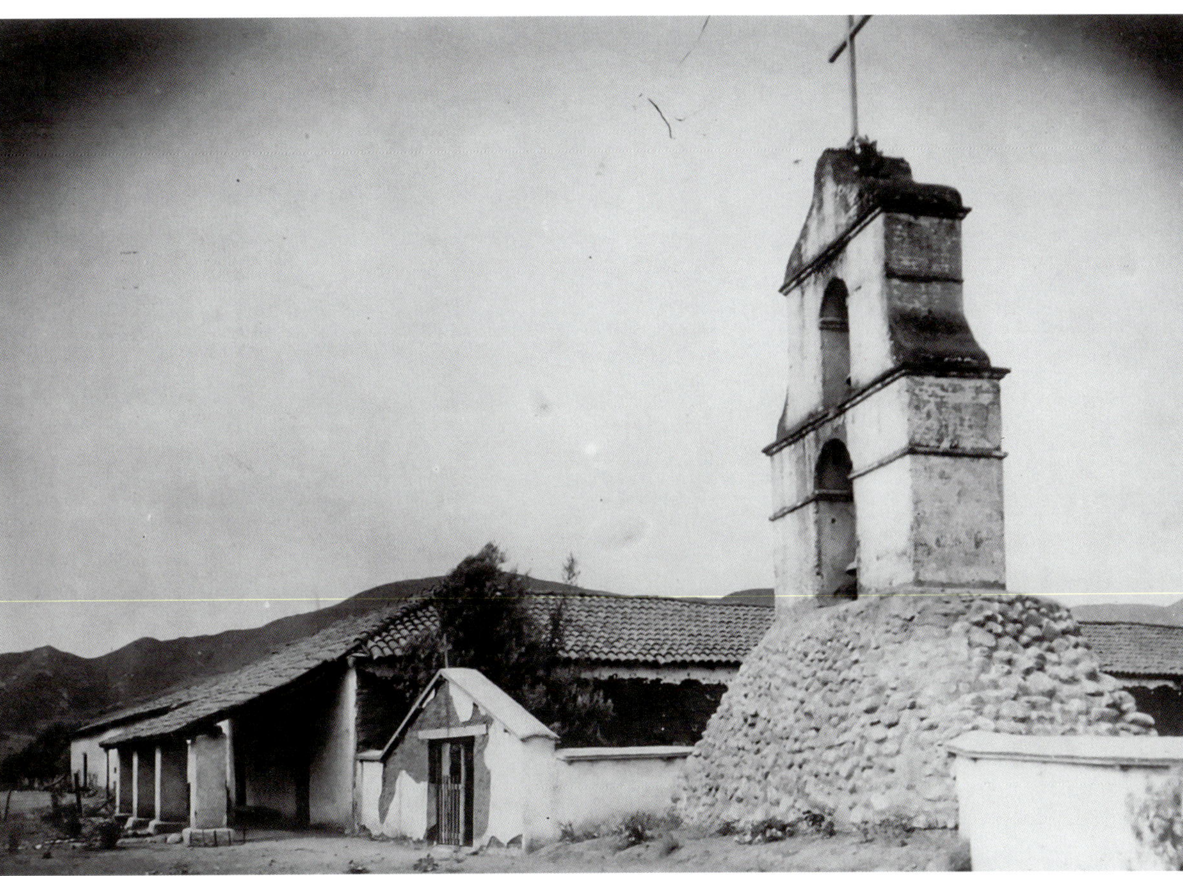

ABOVE LEFT: Rancho de Pala, an outstation of Mission San Luis Rey, became an *asistencia* when a chapel was dedicated there in 1816. At its height, some 1,300 Native Americans were associated with it. Here the front wing has fallen into disrepair, while the church and freestanding *espadaña* remain in good condition. Henry Chapman Ford, *San Antonio de Pala*, 1883. Oil on canvas. Courtesy of the Mission Inn Foundation and Museum, Riverside California. From the collection of The Historic Mission Inn Corporation

ABOVE RIGHT: The church, west wing, and *espadaña* of the asistencia San Antonio de Pala, after being restored by the Landmarks Club in 1903. Courtesy of The Bancroft Library, University of California, Berkeley

been identified by terms such as Classical, Baroque, and Neoclassical, and some scholars have argued that Alta California's Franciscan missions represent a unique style of their own. Kurt Baer, a noted architectural scholar, used formal style designations to categorize the mission churches: Roman or Classical, Baroque, Neoclassical, and Fortress. Although Baer believed the California mission churches were most akin to those of New Mexico based on the extensive use of adobe, he argued that they represent a unique California Franciscan mission style, with little similarity to the missions of Florida, Texas, or even Arizona.[11] The Fortress style is said to have originated at the cathedral of Córdoba, Spain, a former mosque.[12] The carved stone facade of Monterey's Royal Presidio Chapel simulates that of the earlier Mission San José, in San Antonio, Texas. Mission San Xavier del Bac outside Tucson is not dissimilar from Mission San Luis Rey and also compares with the ruins of the Great Stone Church at San Juan Capistrano with its domes, pendentives, arches, lanterns, and other embellishments.

Like all Spanish New World architecture, the California missions incorporated many Moorish (*mudéjar*) influences, traceable to the eight-hundred-year Moorish occupation of the southern Iberian Peninsula. Among these influences is an emphasis on interior rather than exterior decorations, leaving broad expanses of undecorated wall surface, as well as the use of interior patios.[13] Distinctively multilobed door and window arches are also traceable to *mudéjar* influences, as is *citarilla*, a latticework constructed of *ladrillos*, or fired bricks.

The builders of the mission churches worked with three locally available materials, adobe, *ladrillos*, and stone. All three were familiar to the immigrant artisans from New Spain, and each had advantages and drawbacks that directly influenced the degree of architectural sophistication possible for a given church; indeed, the architectural achievement

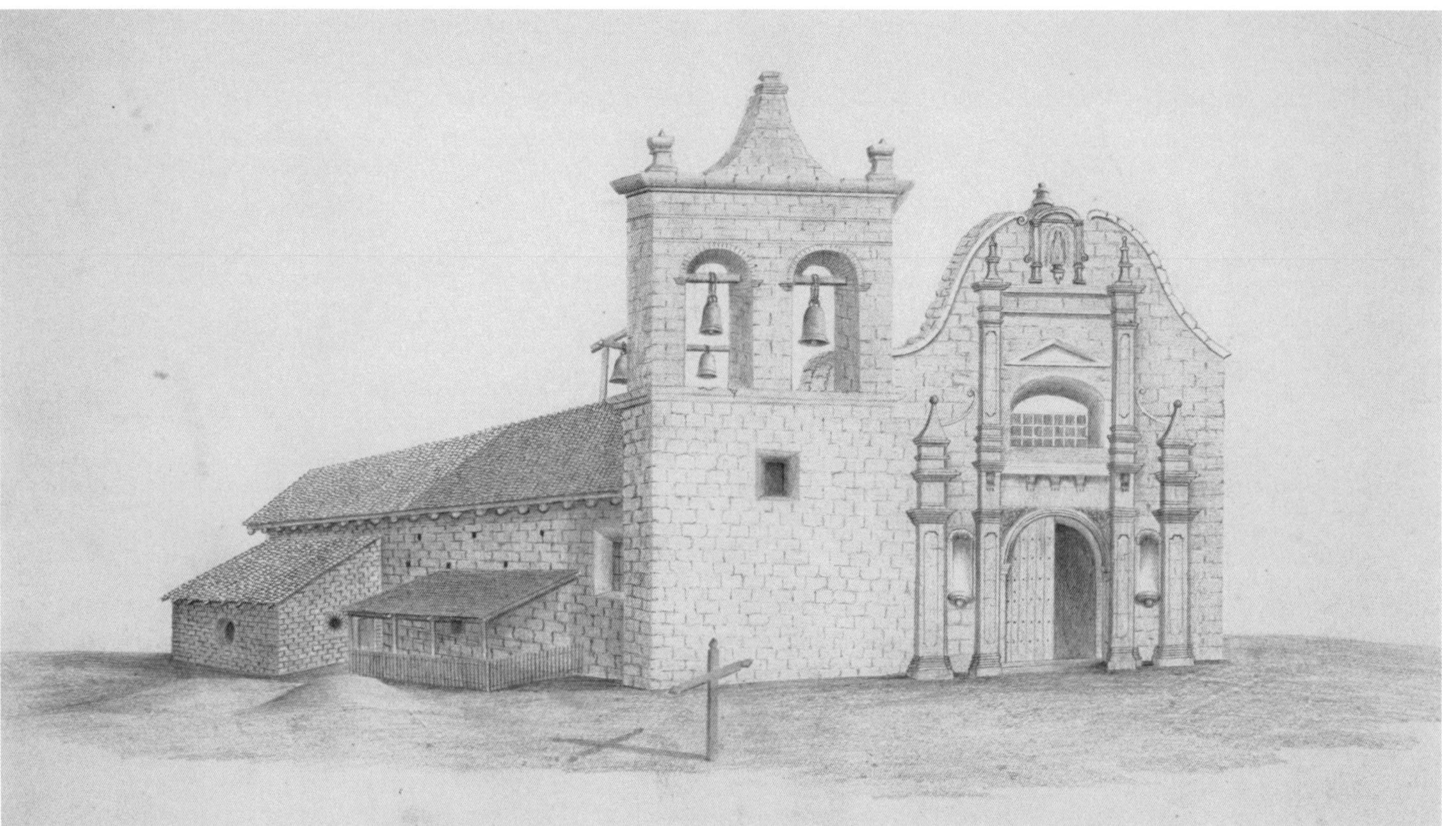

The elaborate stone chapel at the Monterey Royal Presidio was designed by the master mason Manuel Esteban Ruiz and completed in 1794. Its ornate facade, which incorporated Baroque and Neoclassical elements, was the most elaborate of any of the mission-period Alta California churches. Drawing by Henry Miller. Pencil sketch on paper. Courtesy of The Bancroft Library, University of California, Berkeley

of a church was largely dependent on the medium used. The most humble and frequently selected was adobe—earthen bricks fashioned out of local soils and dried in the sun. When roofed, plastered, and protected from groundwater, adobe walls are enormously durable and provide effective insulation, although their soft surface does not lend itself to decorative relief. Stone not only produces much stronger walls but also allows for complex architectural designs and embellishments. Stone masonry is a hard-mastered skill, however, and there were few stonemasons in Alta California. Adobe walls with a *ladrillo* facade provided a practical compromise between adobe and stone: the fired construction tiles permit finer architectural detailing, and they can be easily manufactured on building sites, provided the builders possess the requisite knowledge and fuel is available.

As a mission establishment developed, the construction of its churches followed a predictable sequence. “The first temporary quarters, hastily built, were little better than brush huts with grass-thatched roofs,” observed Eugène Duflot de Mofras during his visit to Alta California in 1840–42. “The second structure at most of the missions was of adobe. . . . As soon, however, as a mission was strong and prosperous, the pride of the padre usually extended to an ambition to build a church in more lasting material, hence stone or burned brick were employed.”[14]

The arrival of master stonemason Manuel Esteban Ruiz and his journeymen, Joaquín and Salvador Rivera, in 1791 coincided with the ambitious plan of Father Fermín Lasuén, who had succeeded Father Junípero Serra as president of the Alta California missions in 1784, to improve his domain by replacing adobe mission churches with superior ones in stone. In particular, Lasuén had in mind the church at Mission San Carlos Borromeo, where he presided. No sooner had Ruiz and his journeymen arrived, however, than Governor Fages, much to Lasuén’s annoyance, appropriated their services to design and build a stone chapel at the presidio.[15] Ruiz submitted his design of an elaborate Baroque facade

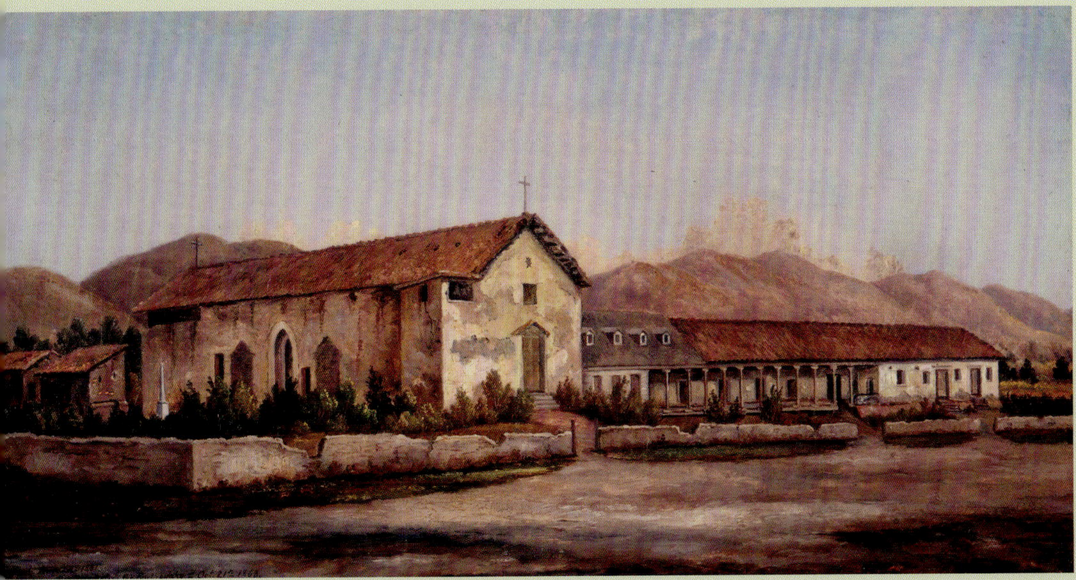

LEFT: This painting showing the adobe church and *convento* at Mission San José was based on photographs taken before the 1868 earthquake that destroyed the buildings. Henry Chapman Ford, *Mission San José*, 1882. Oil on canvas. Courtesy of the Mission Inn Foundation and Museum, Riverside, California. From the collection of The Historic Mission Inn Corporation

BELOW: Mission San Miguel's simple adobe facade belies the wealth of wall murals adorning its interior. Seen here ca. 1876–80, the church and *convento* remain standing, while the surrounding mission buildings have been abandoned. The ghost line of a former roof can be seen on the north wall of the church. Photograph by Carleton Watkins. Albumen print. Courtesy of The Bancroft Library, University of California, Berkeley

Churches of Adobe

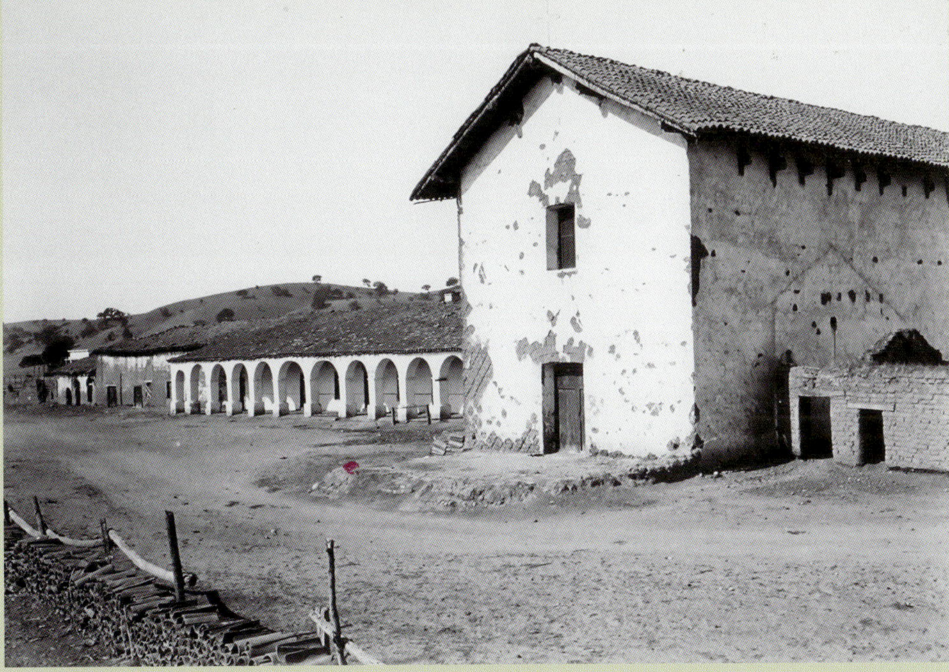

The basic adobe church was one of the first permanent buildings constructed at a mission. Bricks were made of local silty-loam soils augmented with sand to ensure even drying and with fibers such as straw to bind the mixture. The wet "mud" was mixed in pits and then pressed into molds generally measuring about 11 by 22 inches and 4 to 6 inches thick. Laid out in rows and turned to ensure even drying, they were manufactured by the thousands and stored until needed for construction. Adobe walls were laid on top of substantial stone foundations that elevated the earthen wall above ground level, preventing water from being drawn into the bricks. Foundations also carried the weight of the building, and large structures such as churches typically had stone footings at least 5 feet wide and 6 to 7 feet deep. The adobe bricks were laid with a mud mortar in an interlocking pattern of headers and stretchers. Finished walls were covered with a mud plaster made of a finer-grained mix than the bricks themselves that often included plant material or hair from hides as a binder. The exposed brick surfaces were prepared by *rejoneao*, a procedure in which the surface was scored with a sharp implement and small rocks or bits of roof tile inserted in the grooves, providing a mechanical key for the wet plaster. The final wall surface was whitewashed, as additional protection from the weather and also to provide a pleasing white surface. For important buildings such as the church and the *convento*, the final plaster would be made of lime, producing a hard and durable finish.

At secularization, nearly half the surviving California mission churches were these rectangular adobe buildings with walls spanned by wooden beams and roofs covered with fired tiles. Despite their simple designs, these adobe churches reveal a substantial range of architectural innovation on the part of the clergy, master craftsmen, and other artisans who designed and built them. The plain church facades were often embellished over the years as the mission matured, as at San Luis Obispo, where the distinctive *espadaña* was added in 1832.[16] Mission San Francisco de Asís displays a detailed Classical entablature on its facade (also an *espadaña*), which is unusual in that it was constructed of adobe, not *ladrillos*. Mission buildings also featured Roman and segmental arches constructed of adobe, such as those at the *convento* at La Purísima and the churches of San Miguel and San Antonio. The facade of Mission Santa Clara's church displayed a distinctive and elaborately painted design. Such painted facades may have been common, as traces of paint have also been found on those at Missions San Luis Rey, San Gabriel, San Buenaventura, Santa Bárbara, Santa Inés, and San Antonio.[17]

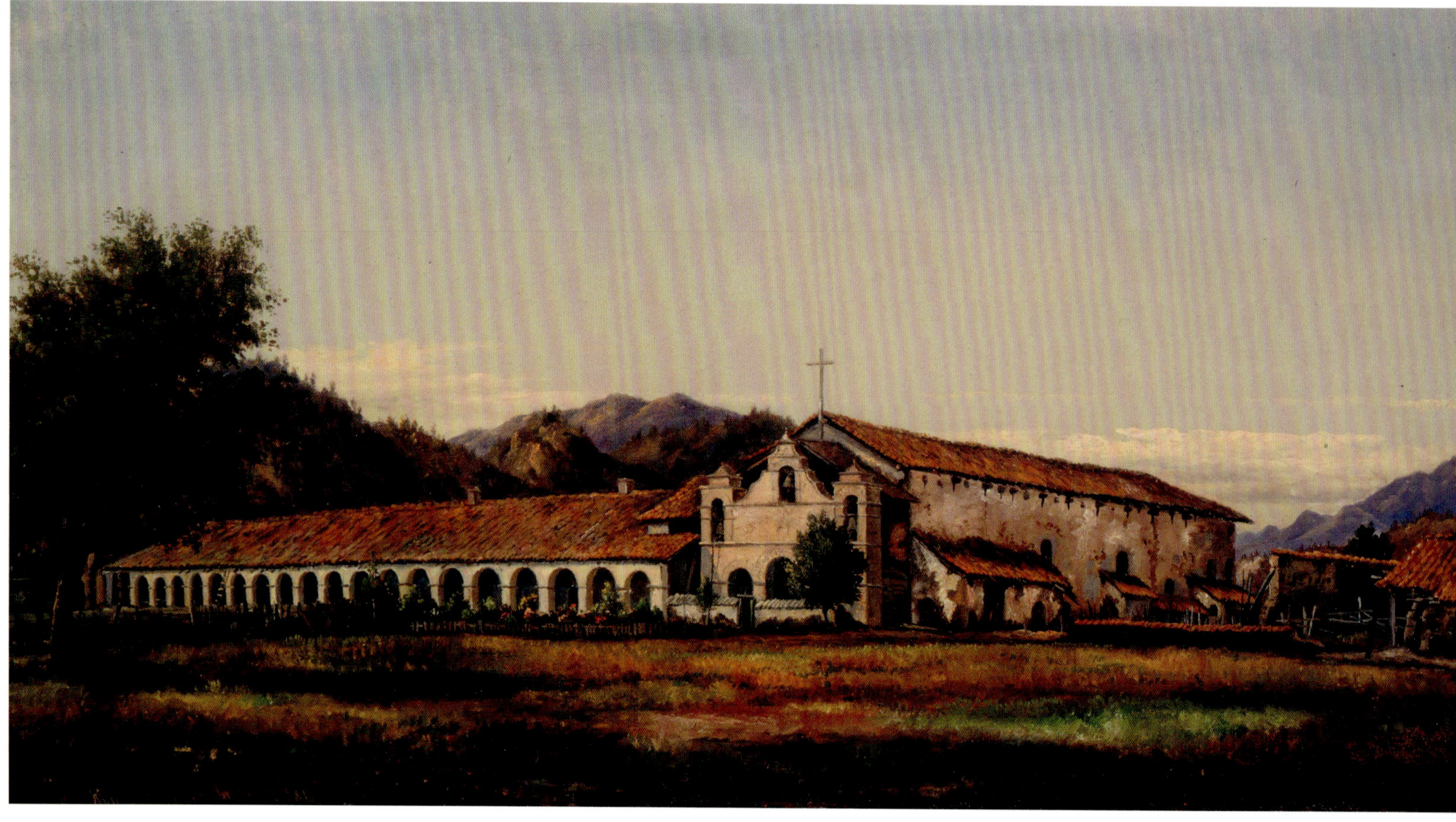

Mission San Antonio de Padua's simple adobe church building was fronted by an elaborate and distinctive *espadaña* of *ladrillos* and an atrium with a barrel roof. Completed in 1813, it was likely the work of the neophyte masons Pedro Antonio Mendoza, Matías Mendoza (Pedro's son), and Simeón Figuerola. Henry Chapman Ford, *Mission San Antonio de Padua*, ca. 1881. Oil on canvas. Courtesy of the Mission Inn Foundation and Museum, Riverside, California. From the collection of The Historic Mission Inn Corporation

to Antonio Velásquez, architectural director of the Royal Academy in Mexico City. Work was suspended briefly while the design was reviewed and modified, as Velásquez simplified the upper portion of the facade into a Neoclassical style that was not only more fashionable but also less costly to execute.[18] Even simplified, the result is the most elaborate and ornate facade of any of the California churches, incorporating numerous Classical elements.[19] At the curved, pedimented gable, above the Doric pilasters and entablature, is a carved statue of Our Lady of Guadalupe—the only such monumental statue made in California. This singularly important church was never abandoned but served the royal governors of Spain, the provincial officials of Mexico, and the Americans at their capital of Monterey. Although some changes were made over the years—the addition of a cruciform transept and main altar and alteration of the windows in 1858; the addition of a pyramidal roof on the bell tower in 1893—the Royal Presidio Chapel at Monterey is one of the finest survivors of California's mission era.

In December 1792 Lasuén finally obtained Manuel Ruiz to design and build the new church at Mission San Carlos Borromeo, although he continued oversight at the Royal Presidio Chapel until its completion in 1794. This transfer was likely made possible by the arrival of another master stonemason, Santiago Ruiz (possibly Manuel's brother), and his journeymen (likely his sons), who were assigned to assist at the Royal Presidio Chapel in November of that year.[20] By 1792 the mission, with its buildings set on a rise overlooking the sea, had begun to prosper, supporting eight hundred neophytes. There was a church, made of adobe with bells hung on a frame in front. Also of adobe was a *convento* for the fathers, residences for the soldiers, a storehouse, and a cookhouse where large kettles were used to prepare the daily fare of *atole* (a porridge of cooked, ground grain). All the buildings were roofed with poles and thatch, and the adjacent neophyte village consisted of some

Churches of Adobe and *Ladrillo*

Churches built of both adobe and *ladrillo* represent the most ambitious design undertakings available for locations that lacked suitable building stone. *Ladrillos*, like *tejas*, are fired in kilns and therefore require greater expertise in their manufacture than does the simple fabrication of adobe bricks. The square brick (measuring about 11 by 11 by 1.5 inches) was used for flooring, columns, walls, and veneers and as reinforcement around windows and doors. Prepared clay was pressed into molds, dried, and fired in kilns. *Ladrillos* provided improved resistance to weathering and facilitated the addition of crisp architectural details that could not be executed in adobe. Use of adobe with *ladrillo* facing was common in Mexico, in the Sonoran Desert, including Arizona, and in California. A wide array of tile shapes and sizes were manufactured at some missions to produce not only details on church facades but also decorative columns and arches.

Six of the surviving mission churches and the Plaza Church in Los Angeles were constructed of adobe and *ladrillo*.[21] The churches at San Buenaventura and San Luis Rey were erected by the master builder José Antonio Ramírez, who used a Classical facade with pilasters and detailed molding on both buildings. Two of the best-known mission profiles are distinguished by their unique *ladrillo* facades: the exuberant *espadaña* at Mission San Antonio de Padua, likely executed by neophyte masons Pedro Antonio Mendoza, his son Matías Mendoza, and Simeón Figuerola; and the undulating Baroque gable at Mission San Diego, erected by master mason Miguel Blanco.[22]

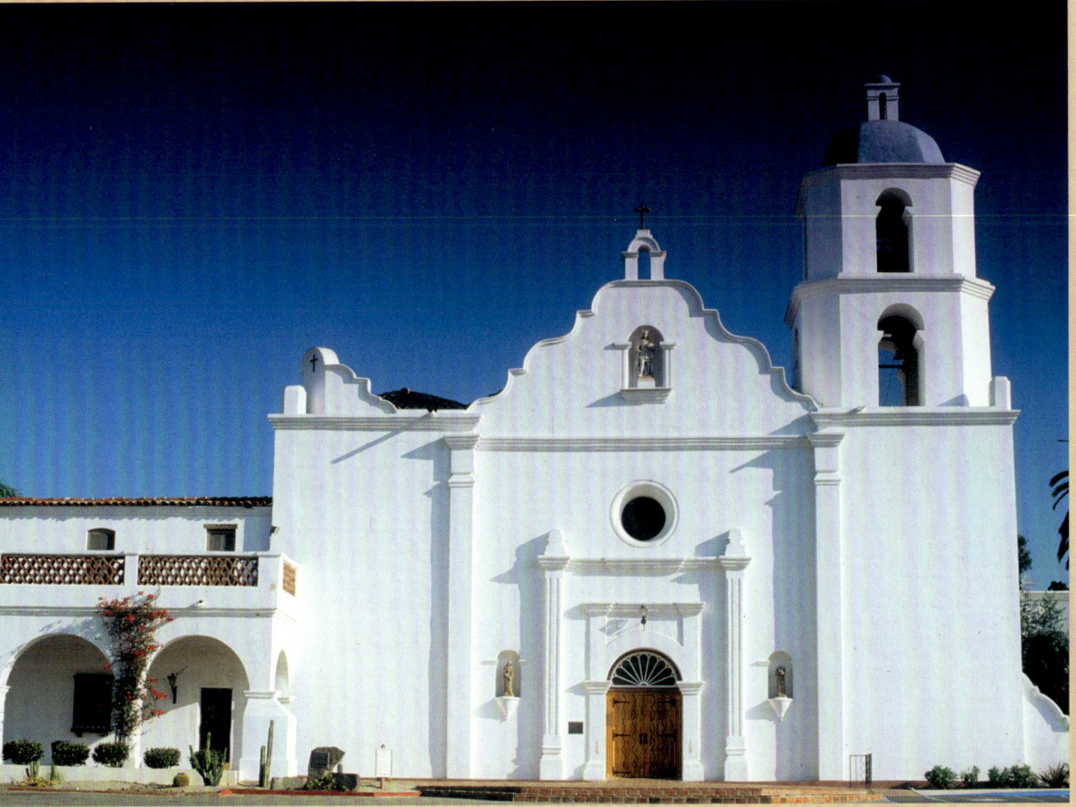

LEFT: The church at Mission San Luis Rey, designed by José Antonio Ramírez, features detailed molding and a two-story stepped bell tower. Photograph by G. Aldana

BELOW LEFT: The church and *convento* at Mission Santa Inés, completed in 1817, and shown here ca. 1876–80. Photograph by Carleton Watkins. Albumen print. Courtesy of The Bancroft Library, University of California, Berkeley

BELOW RIGHT: The church at Mission San Buenaventura, completed in 1809, designed by José Antonio Ramírez. Its façade, like that of Mission San Luis Rey, features pilasters and detailed molding. Henry Chapman Ford, *Mission San Buenaventura*, 1880. Oil on canvas. Courtesy of the Mission Inn Foundation and Museum, Riverside, California. From the collection of The Historic Mission Inn Corporation

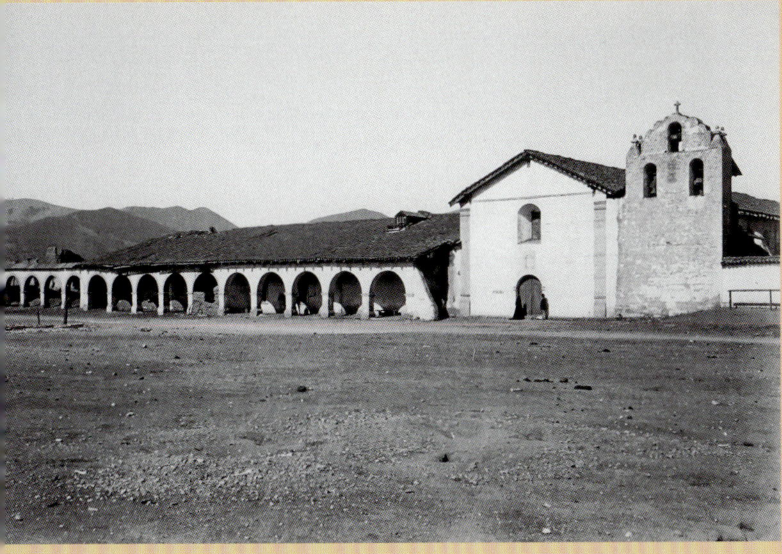

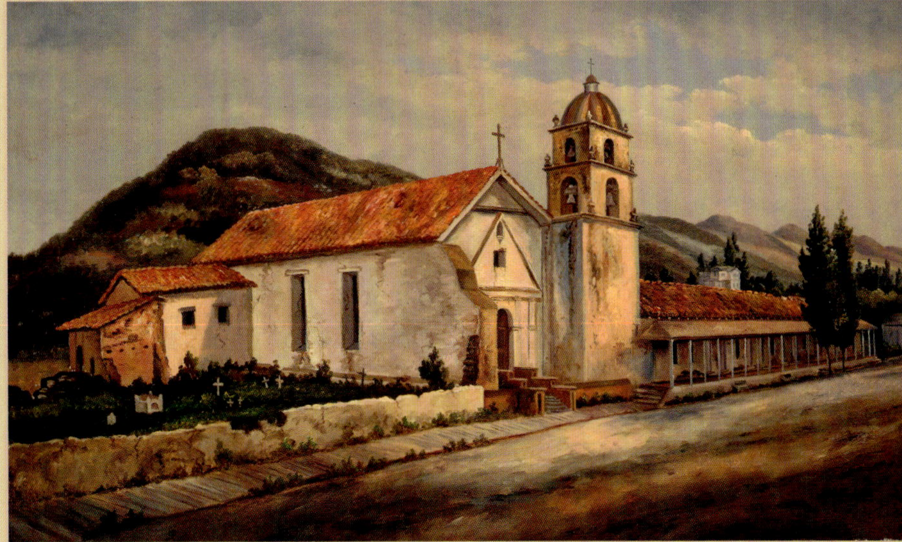

Churches of Stone

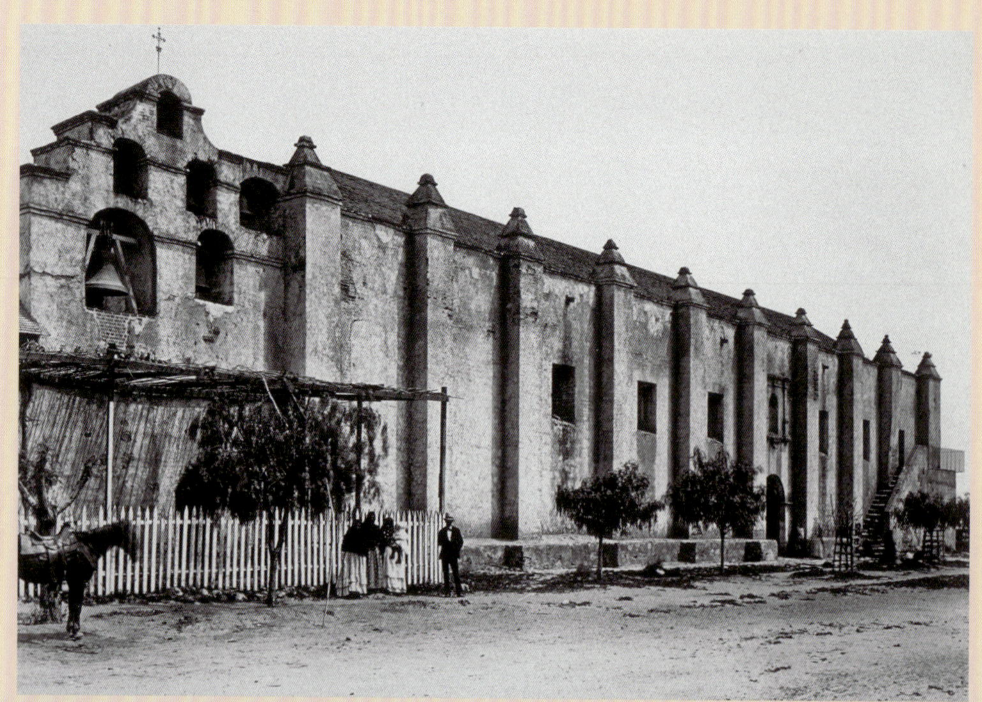

Stone churches represent some of the most architecturally ambitious and enduring structures of Spanish and Mexican California. Churches of stone could display intricate carvings and detailing not possible in adobe, and in this earthquake-prone country they were considered safer.[23] In Alta California, however, good building stone was not widely available. Stones used in foundations could be gathered from nearby streams and fields, but stone fit for forming into blocks for wall construction had to be quarried from geologic exposures. Quarries, when found at all, were often some distance from a mission, and their transport of the stone posed additional problems. The magnificence of the completed structures, however, compensated for the additional effort, as is seen

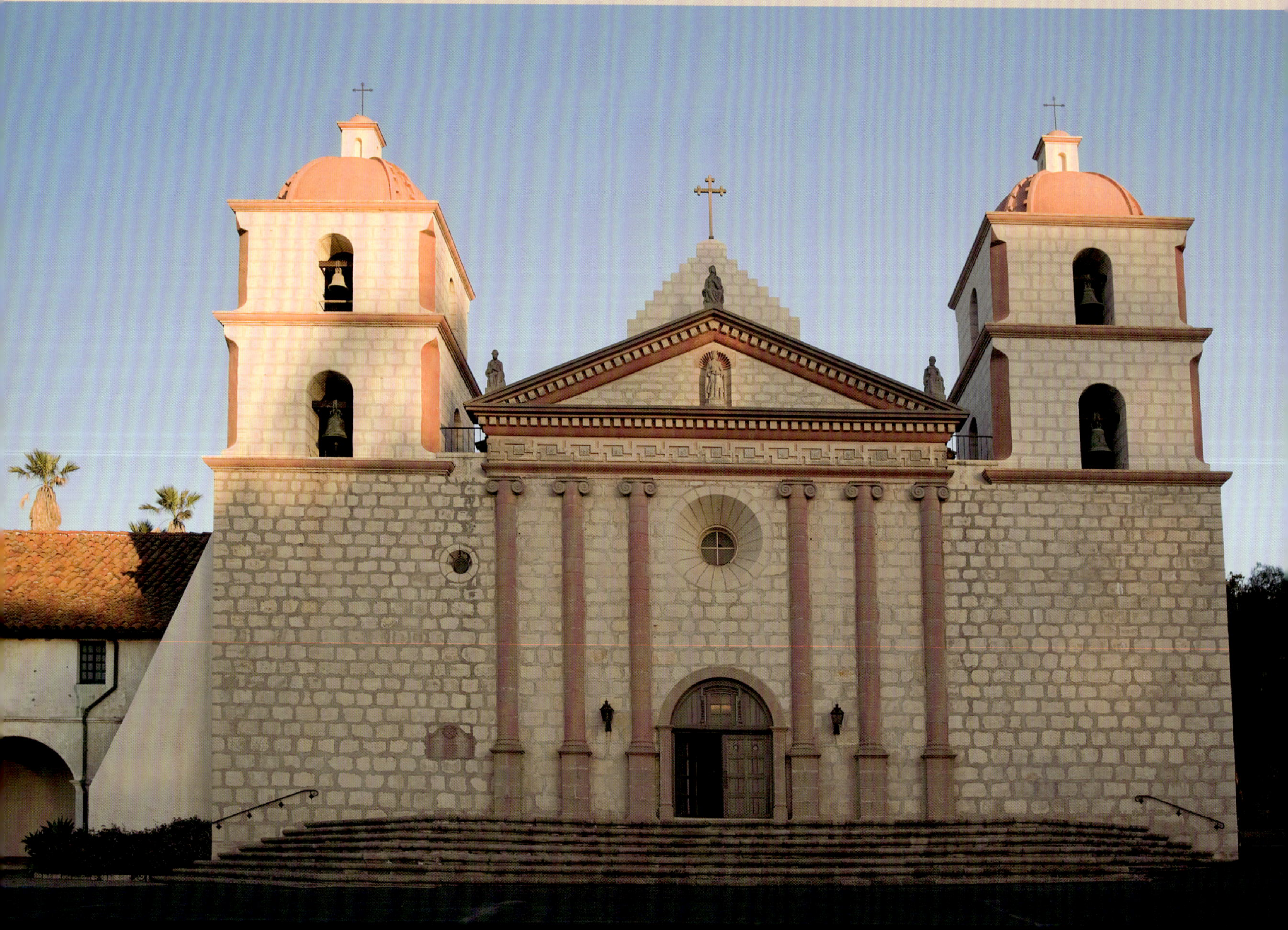

in the impressive stone churches that have survived: at the Royal Presidio Chapel in Monterey and at Missions San Carlos Borromeo, San Gabriel, and Santa Bárbara, as well as in the ruins of the Great Stone Church at Mission San Juan Capistrano.

For the mission padres, the completion of a church in stone was a crowning achievement. The stone churches designed by Manuel Esteban Ruiz at the Monterey Presidio and Mission San Carlos Borromeo were completed in 1794 and 1797, respectively. At Mission Santa Cruz the stone church was completed in 1794 by the master mason José María López, while the distinctive stone church at San Gabriel was likely designed by Father Antonio Cruzado. In 1796 Mission San Juan Capistrano had obtained a builder for its great stone church from Sinaloa, the master mason Isidro Aguilar, who died somewhat mysteriously three years before its completion in 1803. And at Mission Santa Bárbara, the stone church, the fourth church erected at the site, was begun nearly thirty years after the mission's founding, erected by the master mason José Antonio Ramírez. In 1820 Fathers Antonio Ripoll and Francisco Suñer proudly recorded the accomplishment. "The present church of this mission, begun in 1815, was finished this year," they wrote. "It is of hewn stone and mortar, with very strong walls, heavy buttresses, and towers two stories high, holding six bells, three of them hand bells. It has a plastered ceiling with paintings, and marble columns and altar tables in the Roman style, of which there are three.... The floor of the church is of burnished bitumen, which makes it very neatly finished. With this, and the various embellishments that have been placed thus in the church, as well as in the sacristy, it is very agreeable to the sight, strong, and elegant."[24]

ABOVE OPPOSITE: The distinctive stone church at Mission San Gabriel, with its pillar-like buttresses and distinctive *espadaña*, resembles the Moorish cathedral in Córdoba, the home of Father Antonio Cruzado, who may have influenced the design. Photograph by Carleton Watkins, ca. 1876–80. Albumen print. Courtesy of The Bancroft Library, University of California, Berkeley

BELOW OPPOSITE: Mission Santa Bárbara's stone church, completed in 1805 under the direction of the master mason José Antonio Ramírez, is the most Neoclassical of California's mission churches. Photograph © Bill Dewey

sixty thatched huts. A garden and an orchard were well established, and row crops were planted in irrigated fields, which produced corn, wheat, barley, peas, and beans. There were more than a thousand head of both cattle and sheep, along with herds of some three hundred horses and goats.

Several artisans and workers, including the master carpenter José Antonio Ramírez, were already living at the mission when Ruiz arrived to take control of the project. More would arrive in the next few years, including blacksmiths who would train a generation of neophytes in that trade. Ruiz set to work designing the church and stockpiling supplies. Construction of the stone church endured various delays, as there was a shortage of materials and tools, difficulties locating a good stone quarry, and inadequate harvests, which made it difficult to pay the laborers. When it was clear that the original completion date could not be attained, Ruiz's initial contract was extended. For this he requested a lower daily rate, only 14 reales rather than 18, if in return his family would be allowed to come from Guadalajara to join him. The governor endorsed this request, in the hope that the master craftsman might stay on in Alta California and build churches for Missions San Gabriel, San Buenaventura, and others. At this time there was one other master mason and three journeymen masons in Alta California, but none, the governor felt, had Ruiz's "ability of working, teaching, and setting good examples for the Indians."[25] Work on the mission, meanwhile, slowly progressed. A good sandstone quarry was finally located. Stone blocks were cut. The walls went up, roofed with tiles. The stone floor was laid. The Baroque stone church designed for Father President Fermín Lasuén was completed in 1797 (see pp. 174–77). Ruiz, however, decided not to stay in the new land. A few months later he returned to Guadalajara, joining his family and his journeymen, who had returned earlier. At this point they all disappear from the mission story.

Variations on Ruiz's story occurred many times over the decades. In all, nearly one hundred artisans of the building trades came to California from New Spain during the Spanish and Mexican eras. Many were recruited in San Blas, including twenty-eight soldier-artisans assigned to the presidios. Although most were identified as "Spanish," virtually all were born in the New World of mixed Spanish, Indian, or African ancestry, and all were literate. By the 1830s and 1840s this group had been augmented by another sixty or so foreigners from Europe and the United States. While many, like Ruiz, returned home after their tours, others signed on for additional contracts (ranging from one to five years in length), lured by such inducements as paid travel for family members and salaries that ranged well above those common in Mexico City and Guadalajara. Some convicts with skills received commuted sentences and were sent to California, and a few individual missions made independent contracts with artisans.[26] In addition to masons, there were carpenters, sawyers, tilemakers, millwrights, and wheelwrights. There were blacksmiths and armorers to make tools such as axes, stonecutters' picks, and trowels and to fashion items such as hinges, keys and locks, wagon parts, vessels, weapons, and window grills. Artisans of nonbuilding trades included tanners, tailors, potters, broadloom weavers, and cobblers.[27] While Agustín Dávila and Esteban Munras were recognized as distinguished painters, special talents were often inherent in various crafts. Manuel Ruiz, for example, carved the large statue of Our Lady of Guadalupe for the front of the Royal Presidio Chapel, and the master carpenter Vicente Valenzuela made violins. Other immigrants brought skills unrelated to their vocations; for example, the master carpenter Salvador Béjar (Véjar) made fireworks for celebrations, and Tomás Gonzales, a soldier from Sinaloa, was hired to decorate the Santa Bárbara Presidio chapel.[28]

On arriving in Alta California, artisans were distributed throughout the mission system for specific tasks or lengths of time. As the Spanish government paid their wages,

Objects of Daily Life

Often overlooked in surveys of mission art are works used in everyday life produced by both artisans and their trained neophyte apprentices.[29] The chance of survival for objects was directly related to their functions: those associated with the church and religious observances were more likely to be rescued and retained; mundane items of daily life were generally disregarded. In addition, the fragile and consumable nature of many items and the low value placed on objects of California Indian manufacture by nineteenth-century American society contributed to the poor survival rate of most mission products. What was not taken or destroyed during secularization was left to decay. Widespread interest in folk and Native American art awaited the Arts and Crafts movement beginning in the late 1880s, by which time most mission-made items had disappeared.

Furniture made in the mission workshops featured both carved ornament and lathe-turned features typical of styles in Mexico. Functional items such as tables, benches, cabinets, chairs, choir loft railings, confessionals, and dressers for storing vestments were not imported on supply ships but instead manufactured in mission workshops. Missions Santa Bárbara, Santa Inés, and La Purísima were well known for the high quality of their woodworking, a skill well developed by the Chumash in pre-mission times. In the post-mission period, furniture makers from La Purísima went to work in the furniture shop of William Goodwin Dana at Nipomo. Over the 175 years since secularization, the many hundreds of pieces of furniture made by mission carpenters have been reduced to several score, while examples of pottery, weaving, and other items of daily life are virtually nonexistent.

Basket weaving, a textile art, was highly developed by Native Californians before contact with Europeans. The practice was continued at the missions, producing functional vessels that often combined traditional and Spanish designs. Straw hats were also woven, as were *petates* (floor mats), and *sopladores*, fans used to ignite coals. Although use of the needle was known in prehistory, soldiers' and settlers' wives taught mission Indian women additional needle arts, such as crochet, drawn-work, tatting, and

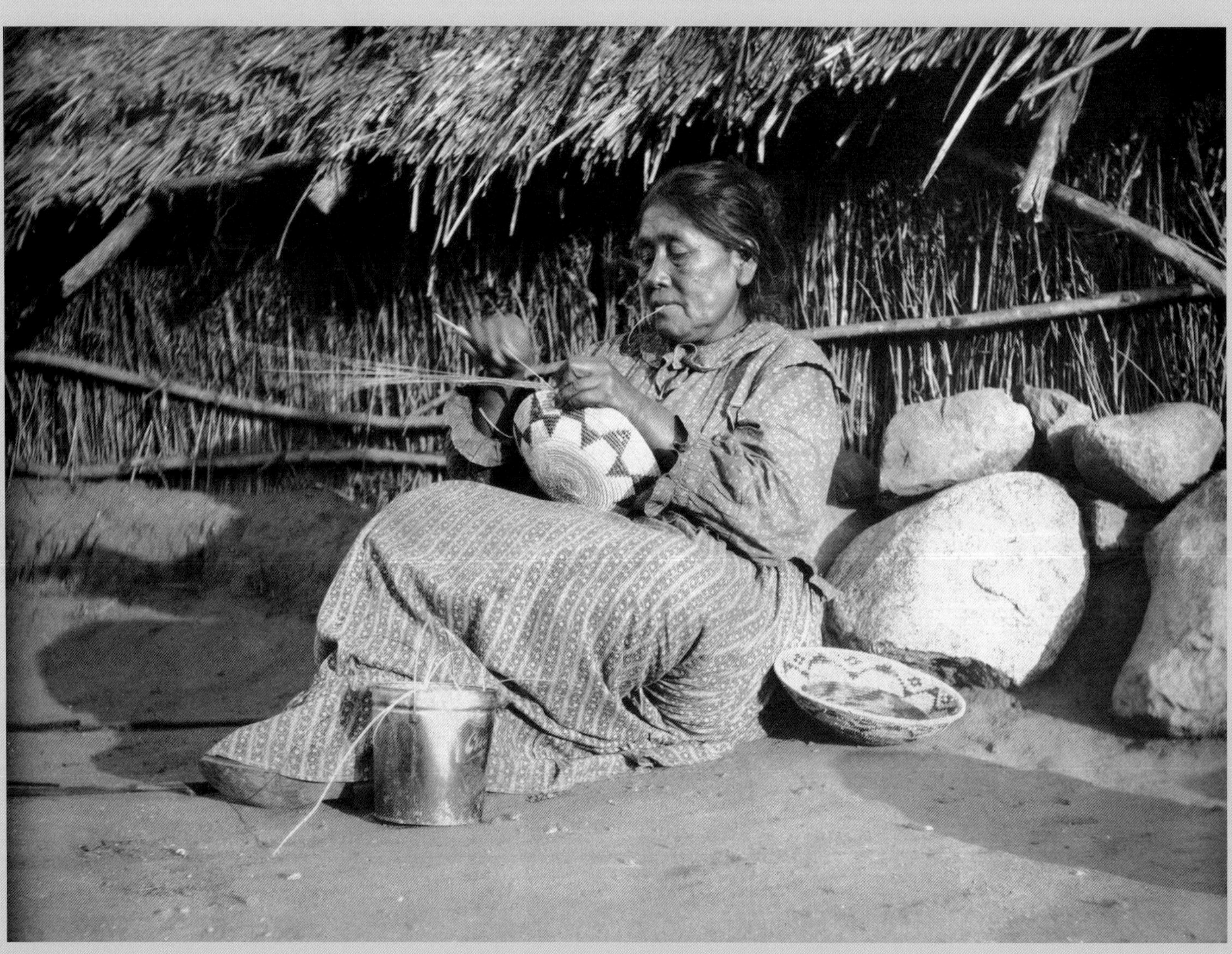

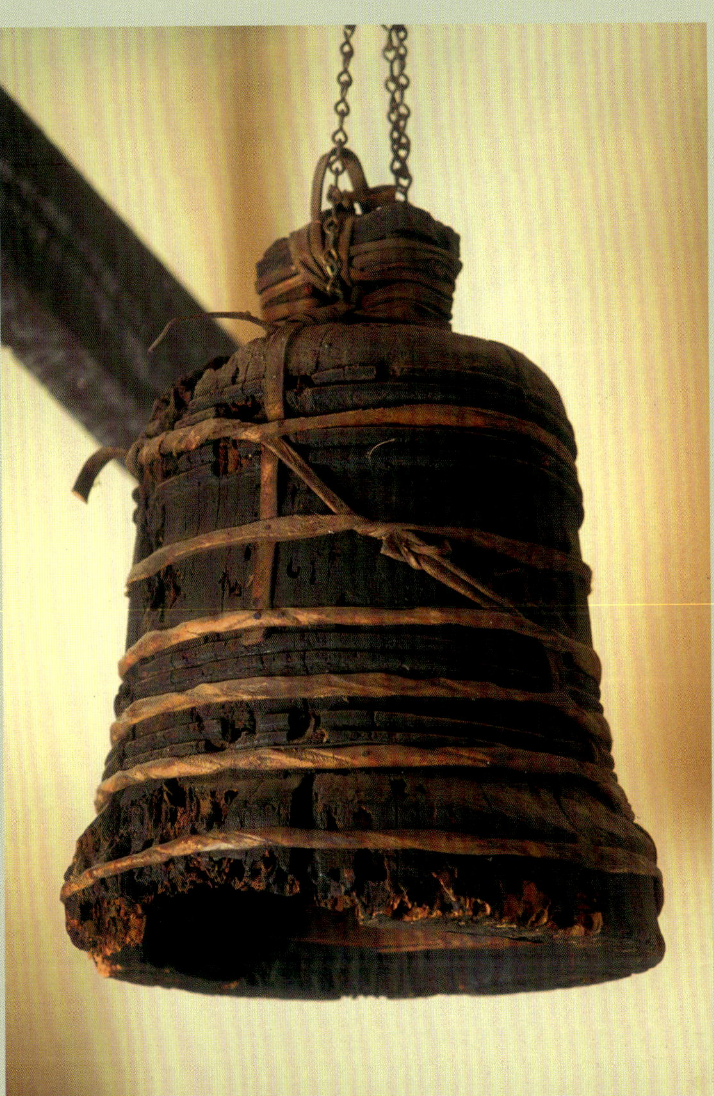

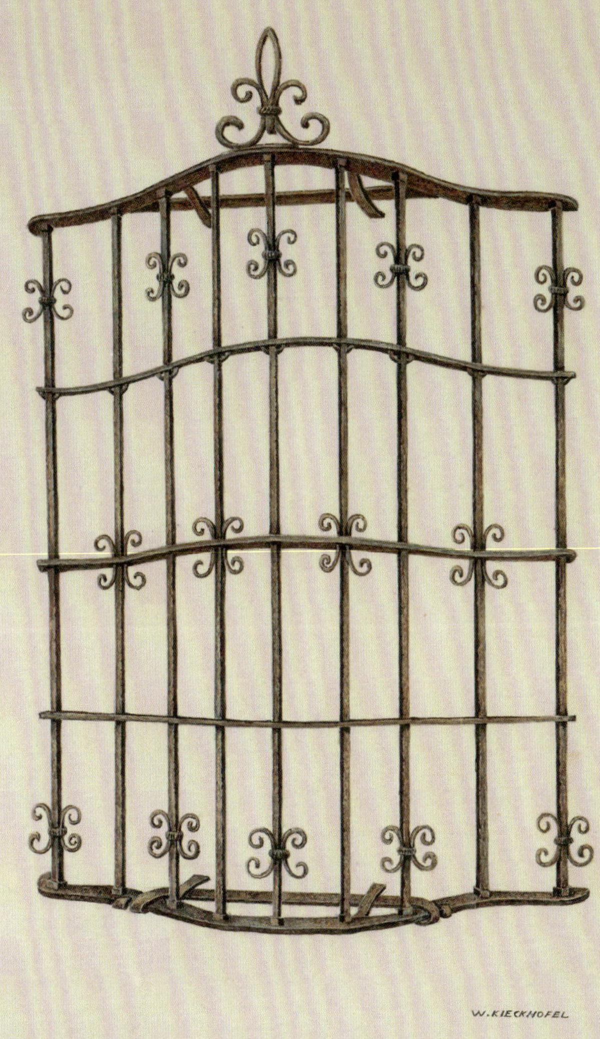

embroidery (similar to the *colcha* embroidery of New Mexico), as well as common sewing. The continuation of these arts after secularization is evidenced by Helen Hunt Jackson's purchase of Indian-made laces in the 1880s.[30]

Some neophyte stone carvings have survived, primarily those attached to architectural elements. Paciano Guilajahichet (Paisano), Chumash sculptor of the statues on the facade of Mission Santa Bárbara, is said to have also built the plaza *lavandería* and carved the animal heads there. Also at Santa Bárbara, the skull-and-bones relief above the door to the cemetery was similarly well sculpted, probably by a neophyte.[31] Animal head–shaped water spouts at Missions San Gabriel, San Buenaventura, and San Luis Rey are also the work of native converts.

The production and working of leather was an essential mission industry. It began with hide tanning and resulted in shoes, saddles, hats, leggings, *botas* (boots), and other useful items, virtually none of which have survived. Leatherworking tools were imported to carve and prick or punch designs in the saddles and the *botas*, which were often wholly covered with intricate designs on the exposed surfaces. Fortunately, a few beautifully worked seats for confessionals and a baptismal were preserved, undoubtedly because of their religious associations.

Ironworking was taught to the neophytes, and by the 1830s at least twenty-three neophytes were serving as master blacksmiths throughout Alta California. Their skills were invaluable in ensuring production and repair of necessary tools such as axes, chisels, knives, hoes, shovels, and plow points. Hinges and nails were also certainly produced in abundance. Some projects involved artistry, such as the making of decorative *rejas* (iron window bars), crosses, and weather vanes for church roofs, as well as altar railings and decorative split work for interior accessories such as candleholders and sconces.[32]

OPPOSITE: California's native people excelled at basketry, an art that was continued throughout and after the mission period. Here a Native American woman weaves a basket at the San Antonio de Pala *asistencia* in the late nineteenth or early twentieth century. © San Diego Historical Society

ABOVE LEFT: Cast bells were expensive in Alta California, and many missions made do with homemade wooden versions before they could attain ones of metal. This rare preserved example at Mission San Buenaventura is bound with rawhide strips and would have provided a serviceable resonance when struck with a clapper. Photograph by G. Aldana

ABOVE RIGHT: Rendering of an iron window grill at Mission San Fernando Rey, by an artist working with the Index of American Design; the grill was especially ornate and may have been fashioned by the master blacksmith Rafael Arriola, from Nayarit, who resided at the mission between 1811 and 1813. William Kieckhofel, *Iron Grille*, 1941. Watercolor, colored pencil, and graphite on paper. Image courtesy of the Board of Trustees, National Gallery of Art, Washington, D.C.

the workers were to be used not simply to build for the Franciscans but to teach skills to the neophytes; their moral character, therefore, was considered to be as important as their technical skill. Some craftsmen came with their families; two married neophyte women; and others wed local Californio daughters, or within the clannish artisan community. The government sometimes offered them enticements to stay, including the right to be granted land. Married artisans received a living allowance for their wives, and, after 1795, they were provided a neophyte couple to live with them as servants (but whom they were obligated to educate and maintain).

The artisans of New Spain were organized in guilds with strict membership guidelines, based on *mudéjar* tradition dating to the Middle Ages in Europe. Guild members were specialists in various specific crafts, and there were three levels of proficiency: apprentice, journeyman, and master. The Guild of Architects comprised carpenters, masons, and stonecutters. Masons were further certified as *de lo prieto* (of the dark) or *de lo blanco* (of the white). The former could erect adobe buildings and were not required to be literate; the latter could build in stone and conduct appraisals.[33] All certified *maestro* (master) builders, however, were required to demonstrate competency in applied geometry, algebra, the history of architecture, drawing, and stonecutting. *Maestros* were also allowed to work for themselves and to take on journeymen and apprentices.

Division of labor was clearly spelled out: appropriate masons directed construction of the stone foundations and walls, carpenters framed windows and the roof, and masons returned to lay floor and roof tiles. In frontiers like Alta California, however, as artisans were rare and greatly in demand, distinctions between the purviews of different guild specialties—adobe, stone, and wood—became increasingly blurred. The masons were generally occupied with construction of the few stone churches and those irrigation systems where their skills were most essential, while most of the adobe construction was carried out by carpenters. José Antonio Ramírez arrived in Alta California as a master carpenter, learned stone masonry from the Ruiz clan, and eventually became the premier mason in the province—all without official guild sanction.[34]

Life on the California frontier was demanding. Artisan families were large, with an average of nine children. Infant mortality and death of mothers in childbirth were high everywhere but were higher in remote Alta California due to the lack of doctors. Artisans whose California-raised children married into local families were bound to stay by the tight social bonds of Spanish society. It is interesting that not one of the children of the immigrant artisans took up their fathers' trade, in part because the mission building boom was over by the time of secularization and in part because of greater opportunities in ranching and in the military. After their contracts expired, the artisans rarely supported themselves solely with their craft but also were farmers or held public office or taught school.

The importance of the critical skills brought by these builder artisans cannot be overstated. The colony was constructed using their engineering and technical knowledge to dam streams and carry water to fields; to select timber and work wood for furniture, looms, mills, carts, and windows; and to raise walls and roofs to shelter the populace. The absence of a mason was dramatically chronicled at Mission La Purísima, where, in 1798, the padre writes, "As the primitive church is not spacious enough to gather in it all the Indians…, the missionaries here have seen themselves compelled to lay the foundations for the new church this year; but, owing to the entire ignorance of the Fathers, there is necessary a master or masters, who are experienced in this matter, otherwise the work will not be done with sufficient security for stability."[35] The misgivings of the fathers were warranted. The walls reached as high as thirty feet above the ground, but "instead of being six to seven feet thick… they were barely three feet thick," a visitor in 1883 noted on inspecting the ruins.

Master Builder José Antonio Ramírez

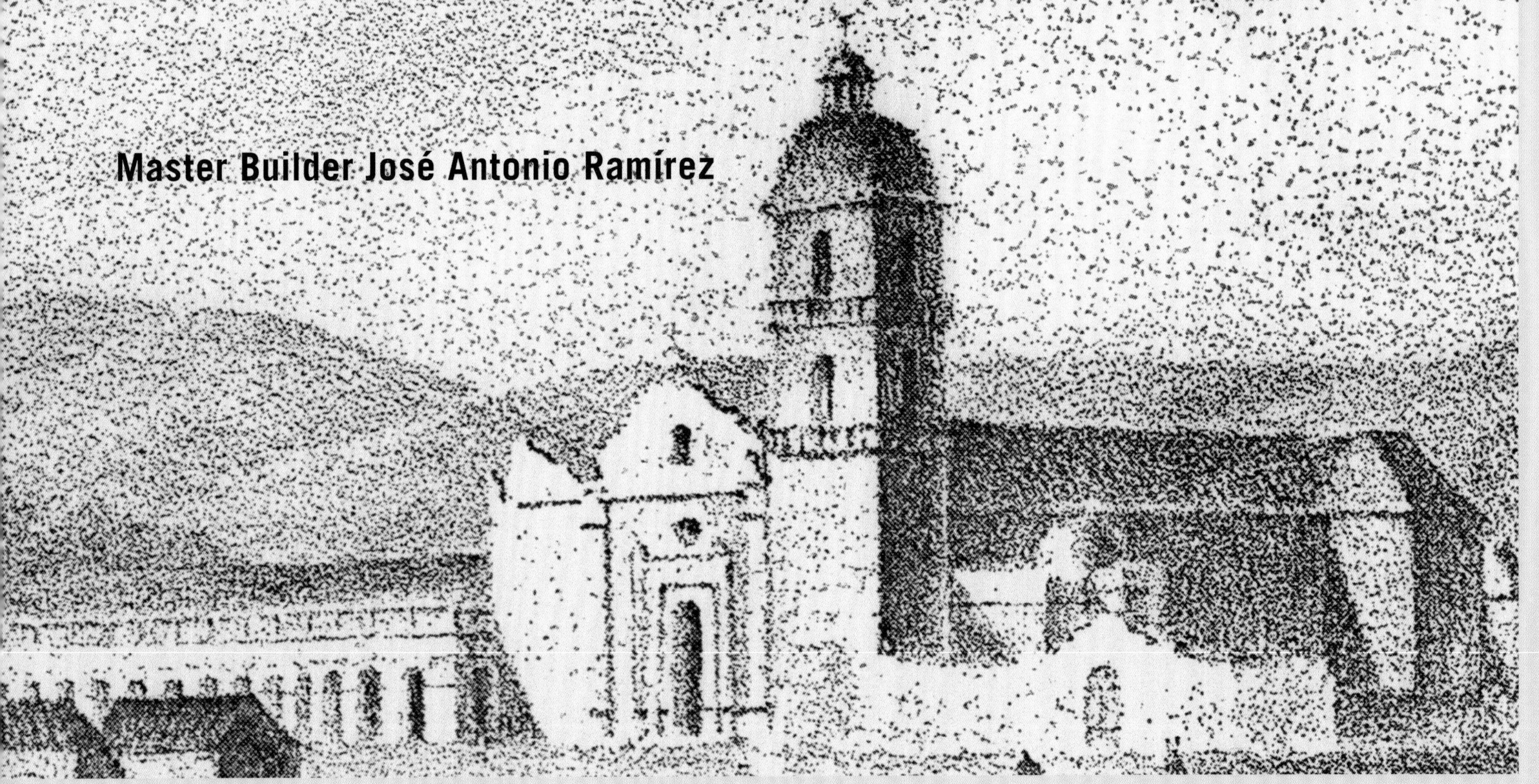

José Antonio Ramírez, a master carpenter from Jalisco, Mexico, was one of the most prolific builders in Spanish California.[36] In Monterey, Alta California, in January 1792, at the age of thirty, he signed a four-year contract to teach his trade to at least twelve individuals. Exceeding the purview of his guild, he spent his remaining thirty-five years employed in the province, playing an important role in the construction of a remarkable number of mission churches.

He was first assigned to Mission San Carlos Borromeo, serving as master carpenter and teaching resident neophytes the building trades. Ramírez arrived about the same time as master mason and stonecutter Manuel Esteban Ruiz and his assistants and apparently worked with them on the construction of both the stone church at Mission San Carlos Borromeo and that of the Royal Presidio Chapel. It was likely during this time that Ramírez acquired skills in stoneworking, attaining a proficiency that, in addition to his mastery of carpentry, in later years established him as the premier master builder of Alta California. Although his contract at Mission San Carlos Borromeo ended in 1796, he remained working there for some seven years, as evidenced by records indicating that he served as godfather for baptisms of Indians and Spaniards and witnessed marriages at the mission. Ramírez himself would never wed. He ran into some trouble with the authorities early in his stay, and the governor wrote that he should be docked pay for time lost as a result of his "voluntary defect or vice." This may have been a penchant for drinking. He also had an affection for chocolate, although this would not likely have elicited a reprimand.

Ramírez then traveled south to Santa Bárbara, where in 1800 he contracted to work for two years at the mission, for a salary of one peso and dinner per working day and two pounds of chocolate per month. In 1804 he is recorded at Mission San Juan Capistrano, identified as a "*criollo* from New Spain and artisan... in the capacity of carpenter," and subsequently appears at Missions San Fernando Rey, San Gabriel, and San Buenaventura. His contract at Mission La Purísima, dated April 29, 1811, states that he "binds himself to assist in making the stone basins, canals, and all the washing places and drinking trough after finishing the fountain, and besides to direct during the time the carpenter work, and the Mission is to pay him 200 pesos in silver, with board, 3 drinks a day, and 2 lbs. of chocolate monthly."[37]

His solid work brought him advancement, and in his later years he worked more as a designer and director than as a craftsman on a remarkable number of projects throughout the province. In 1811 he also signed on as architect and director of the new church at San Luis Rey, which was completed in 1812. Ramírez then settled in the Los Angeles area, working at Mission San Gabriel, where he also served some years as *mayordomo* (manager). Evidence strongly suggests that he traveled to Santa Bárbara during these years, directing construction of the new stone church at that mission, which was finished in 1820. This Neoclassical design, clearly taken from a Roman temple facade depicted in Vitruvius's book, shows that Ramírez was following current trends in moving away from the Baroque style.

While at Mission San Gabriel Ramírez directed construction of the adobe-and-*ladrillo* Plaza Church in Los Angeles, which was completed in 1822. On the church he employed facade pilaster-buttress elements with pyramidal caps borrowed from San Gabriel. Ramírez died in 1827 at the age of sixty-four and was buried in the Plaza Church cemetery. That year the French visitor Auguste Duhaut-Cilly commented on the church at San Luis Rey: "The buildings were planned on a grand scale after the ideas of the Father. He himself, and alone, could have superintended the construction, but he secured the cooperation of a very skillful man who had previously aided in the construction at Mission Santa Barbara. In fact, though the buildings at Santa Barbara are much more sumptuous, the hand of the same artist will be recognized here."[38]

ABOVE: The majestic appearance of Mission San Luis Rey was praised by Auguste Duhaut-Cilly, who made a sketch of the mission, a detail of which is seen here, when he visited in 1827. See p. 22. Courtesy University of Southern California, on behalf of the USC Special Collections

The Chumash Carpenter Pacomio

Pacomio Poqui was born at the Ranchería de Esniscue in about 1794 and was baptized at Mission La Purísima in 1803.[39] In August 1807, at the age of twelve or thirteen, he married the eleven-year-old neophyte Gordiana. The couple, childless, lived at La Purísima until Gordiana's death some twelve years later. During this time Pacomio trained as a carpenter, first under master carpenter Salvador Carabantes and, after 1811, with the noted José Antonio Ramírez. After the mission was destroyed by an earthquake in December 1812, the builders undertook the enormous task of constructing a new establishment some three miles to the north. In addition to Pacomio, the neophyte journeymen carpenters Mariano Francisco, Sebastián Tomás, and Juan Nepomuceno worked on this project. Following the death of Gordiana, Pacomio and Tomás traveled to Monterey, where they worked on the presidio for several months. In February 1820 Pacomio married the widow Eusebia María at La Purísima, and in December their daughter, María de Jesús, was born.

By this time Mission La Purísima was well established at its second location and experiencing the decline in population felt throughout the province, with 662 recorded residents in 1824. The local Chumash had complied with but not succumbed to Spanish and Mexican rule and responded to the beating of a La Purísima neophyte at Santa Inés with an uprising that lasted a month and encompassed three missions. Pacomio emerged as the leader of the La

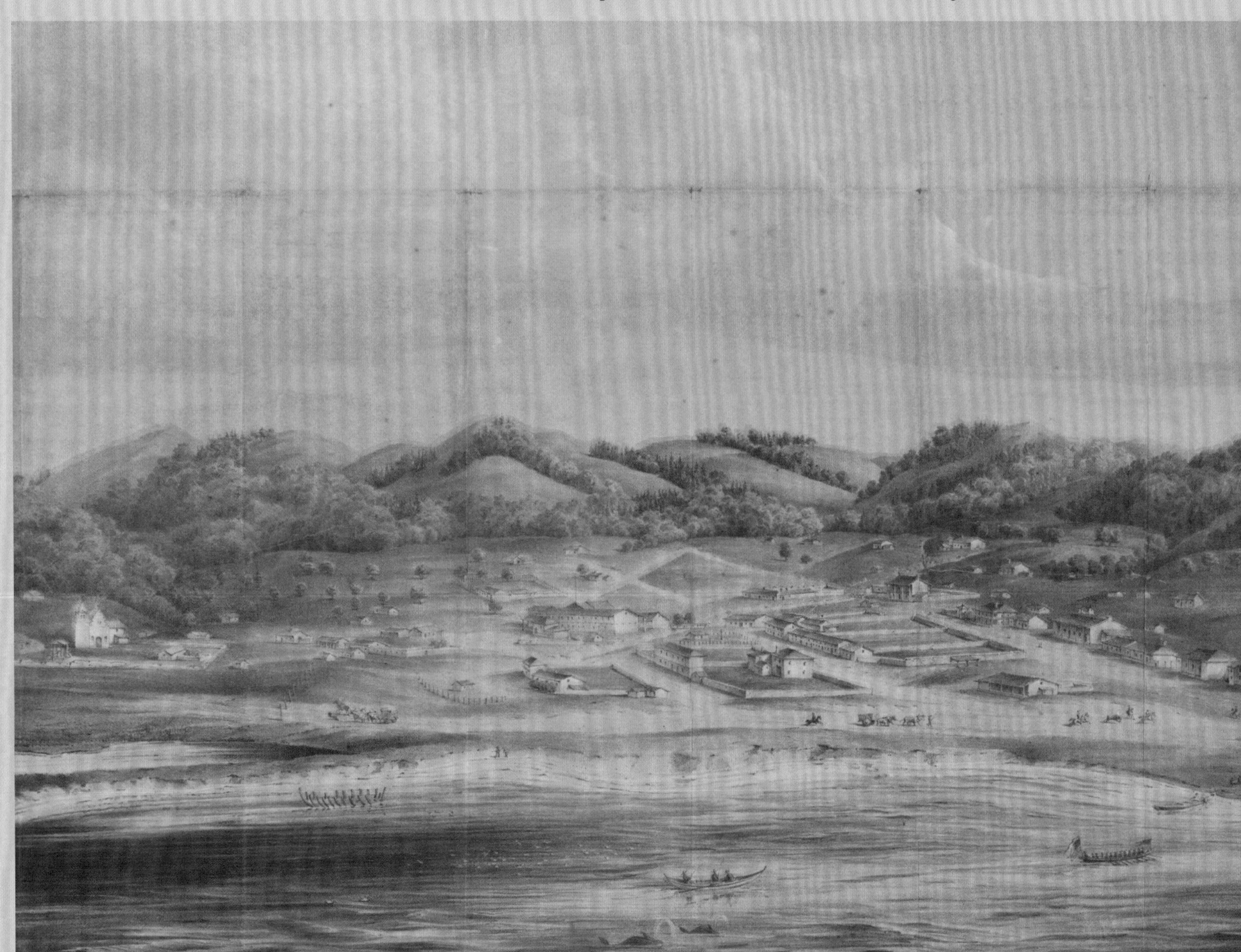

Purísima forces, the last to bow to military defeat. Although sentenced to ten years of hard labor at the presidio followed by exile, he apparently was allowed to move to Monterey with his wife and daughter, perhaps providing service to the presidio there. Pacomio became a well-known furniture maker, although, unfortunately, none of his pieces have been conclusively identified. When Mission La Purísima was secularized in 1833 and 1834, Pacomio petitioned for a share of the property but was denied, on the grounds that he had "voluntarily separated himself from the mission community."[40]

At this time Monterey was the booming capital of Mexican California, as foreign traders set up business in what was becoming a cosmopolitan port town. The population of 1,600 in 1830 swelled to nearly 2,000 by 1845. The close society of neophyte artisans likely formed a supportive clan in the burgeoning community. At the age of thirteen, Pacomio and Eusebia María's daughter, María de Jesús, married the mason Gregorio, who may have participated in the 1824 uprising. In 1836 both couples, along with the twenty-five-year-old carpenter Carlos Pacomio, were living in the same house. Pacomio Poqui was described by contemporaries as "a well-educated neophyte, skillful carpenter and cabinet-maker, patriotic in his ideas" and "an intelligent citizen and member of the *ayuntamiento* [town council] at Monterey."[41] As a measure of his acceptance in Californio society, in 1836 the former rebel leader served as a *comisario de policía* in Monterey.[42] María de Jesús died in 1836, perhaps in childbirth. Pacomio and his wife, Eusebia María, both succumbed in the smallpox epidemic of 1844.

In his years in Monterey, Pacomio adapted to his changed circumstances and succeeded not only in supporting his wife and family with skills learned as a journeyman but also in becoming an active member of his community. He also retained ties to his Indian heritage and on occasion was seen singing "Chumash songs while dancing, dressed only in a breech-clout, his body painted red, white, and black, and with feathers on his head."[43] Decades later, his songs, remembered and sung by an old Costanoan woman, were recorded by the anthropologist A. L. Kroeber. They are preserved today at the Phoebe A. Hearst Museum of Anthropology at the University of California, Berkeley.

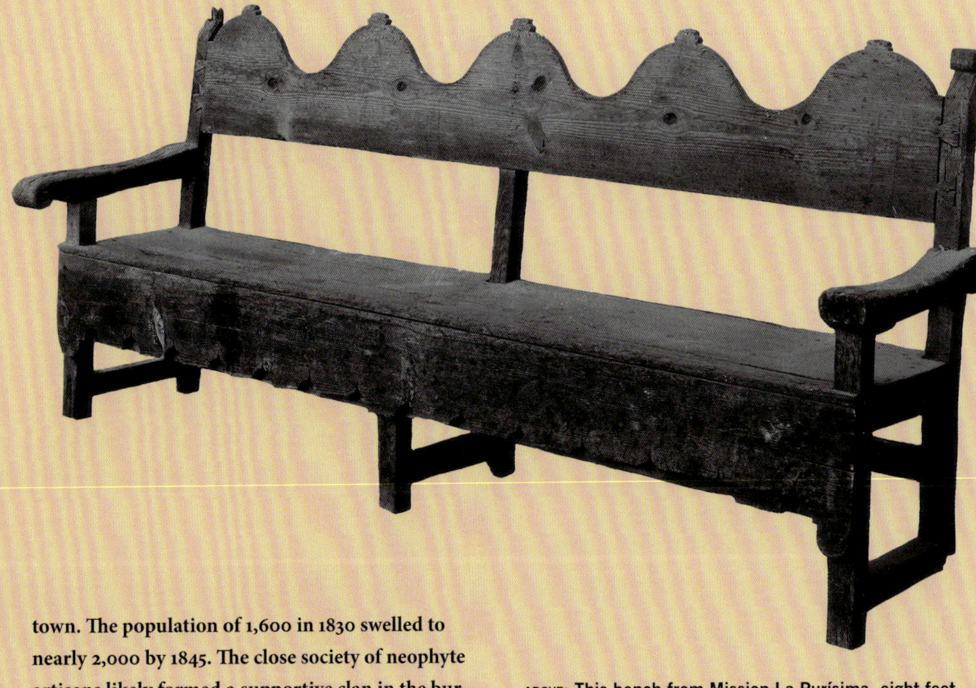

ABOVE: This bench from Mission La Purísima, eight feet long and nearly four feet high, may have been made by Pacomio. It was in the possession of a local family when it was documented by the Index of American design in 1940. Courtesy of the Board of Trustees, National Gallery of Art, Washington, D.C.

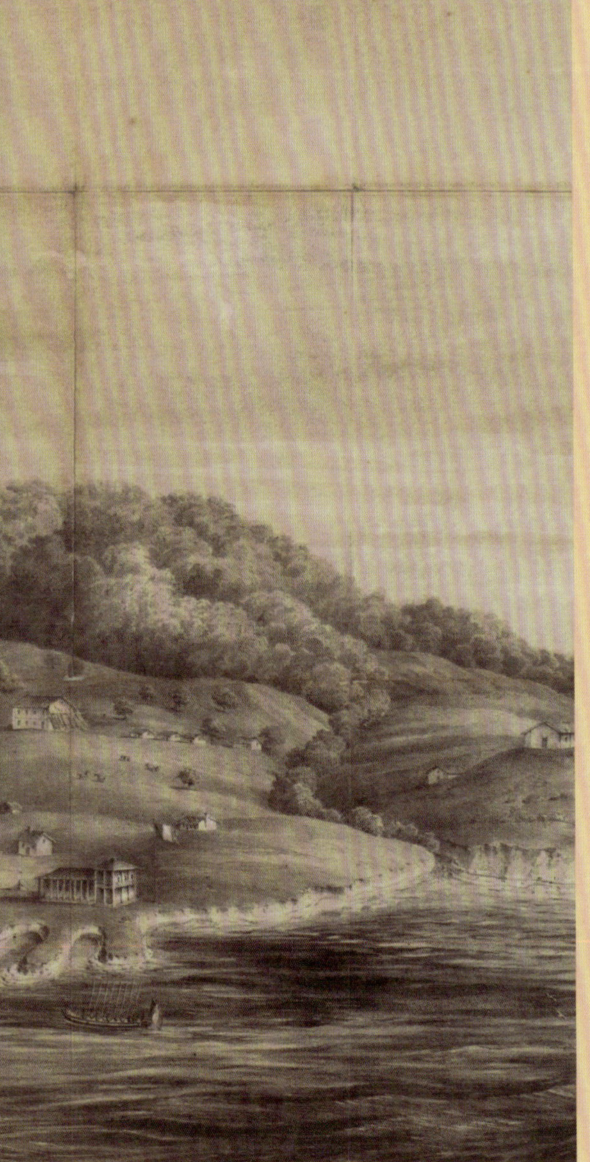

LEFT: Monterey, seen here in 1842, was the capital of California and its largest port. The Custom House can be seen down by the wharf, the Royal Presidio Chapel to the left. The Chumash rebel Pacomio moved here with his family in the late 1820s; he worked as a successful furniture maker and served both on the town council and as a police commissioner. Courtesy of The Bancroft Library, University of California, Berkeley

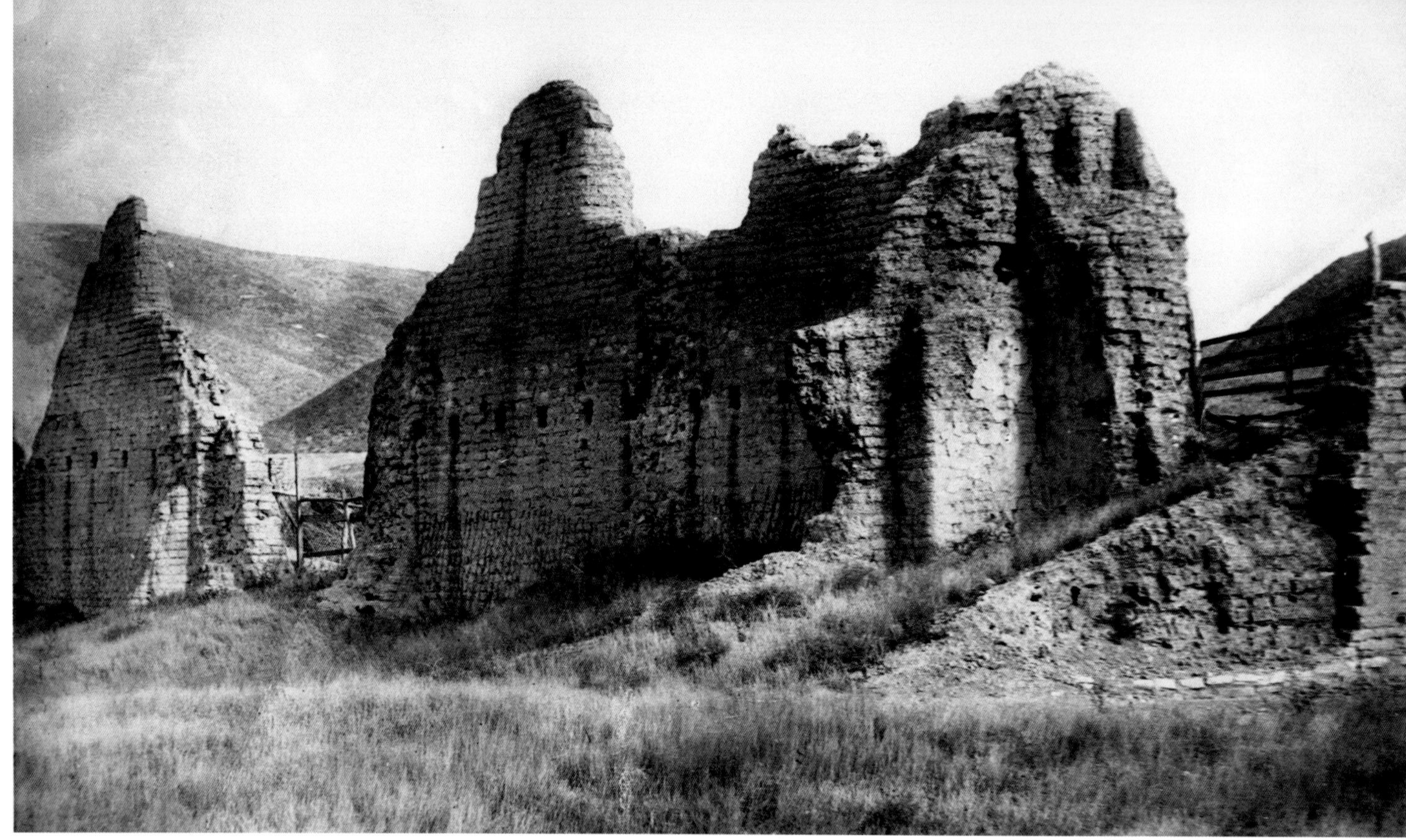

These ruins of the church at the first site of Mission La Purísima were photographed in 1905, when portions of the south wall were still standing. Inexpertly constructed without a master mason to guide the work, the initial walls were too thin, and a veneer of unbonded adobe was added in an unsuccessful attempt to strengthen the building. Courtesy of the Santa Bárbara Mission Archive-Library

They "were subsequently strengthened with extra walls" that "were not in bond with the first, and were sometimes laid up against a wall that had previously been plastered and painted."[44] The earthquake of December 1812 completely destroyed this church, as well as the adobe kitchen and garden walls and one hundred neophyte dwellings, prompting the abandonment of this location.

Throughout the mission era, the missions and presidios relied heavily on Indian labor, both skilled and unskilled, and one of the artisans' principal responsibilities was the training of Indian neophytes. Local mastery of trades by trained neophytes reduced the colony's dependency upon Mexico for blankets, clothing, soap, and other imports.[45] Presidio soldiers posted at the missions and their wives also provided practical instruction to the neophytes in such tasks as carpentry, blacksmithing, and needlework. Indian craftsmen were trained either at the presidios or at the missions, which the padres preferred because of what they regarded as the corrupting influence of the presidio soldiers and the likelihood that the Indians would simply be used as laborers. Over the years, increasing numbers of trained neophytes became accomplished masons, carpenters, blacksmiths, and painters. Available records, which certainly underrepresent the numbers of neophyte craftsmen, name 103 who became trained builders, including 50 carpenters, 25 masons, 23 blacksmiths, and 3 painters. Four neophytes are identified as *maestros*.[46]

The lives of mission Indians are not as thoroughly documented as those of the padres, soldiers, and other *gente de razón*. While the careers of many *criollo* (creole) artisans can be partially reconstructed through church and government records, the names of neophyte builders rarely appear in these chronicles. In recent years, however, diligent scholarship by Mardith Schuetz-Miller has resulted in an indispensable reference, *Building and Builders in Hispanic California, 1769–1850*. Added to the biographies of Spanish, Mexican, and foreign-born workers are those of native artisans, providing enticing snapshots of some of the many skilled Native Americans who served as journeymen and master builders, constructing the California colony.[47]

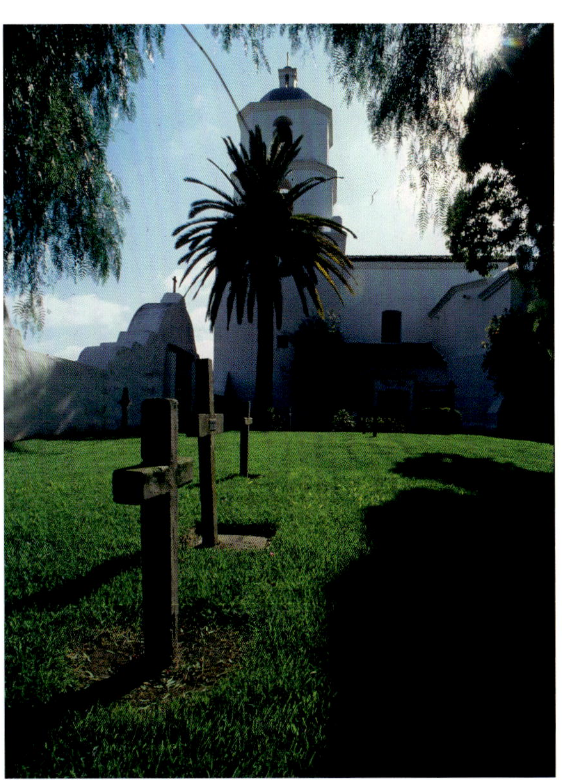

The bell tower at Mission San Luis Rey rises above the cemetery, where thousands of neophytes who lived and worked at the mission are buried anonymously. Photograph by G. Aldana

The Indian mason Honorio Matgesh participated in the construction of Mission San Carlos Borromeo's stone church, and he continued his work at this mission until his death some twenty-five years later. The carpenters Pacomio Poqui, Mariano Francisco, Sebastián Tomás, and Juan Nepomuceno worked on the 1813 church at La Purísima, which featured a unique linear design with side entrances. Mission San Rafael, originally a mission *asistencia* of Mission San Francisco de Asís, was constructed with the considerable toil of three accomplished neophytes from that institution: the mason Januario and the carpenters Ygnacio and Gudelio.[48] At Mission Santa Clara, the 1825 church and many of the buildings are attributed to the skills of the former soldier Juan Ignacio Alviso and his Indian assistant, Vicente.[49] The mason Juan Pedro Timiyahaut, born in about 1795 to neophytes at Mission San Buenaventura, directed the laying of adobe bricks during the construction of the mission's new church around 1813–15. And at Santa Bárbara, a Chumash mason named Paciano Guilajahichet, who was also a canoe builder and bear dancer, carved the statues adorning the facade, as well as animal-head statues on the plaza *lavandería*. He was so interested in the project, a report states, that "during all the time he was busy with this work, [Paciano] seldom went to dinner."[50]

Those Indians who became trained artisans experienced an elevated status at the missions. They are frequently noted as witnesses at marriages and baptisms, a role generally accorded to socially important community members. There is evidence of a social network of journeymen in brothers entering a trade together or sons and godsons following in the footsteps of their elders. Friendships also developed between masters and these journeymen, evidenced by their names appearing on wedding and christening documents. A policy of self-determination for selected Indians, instituted by Governor Pablo de Solá after 1815, served neophyte builders well. With their advanced Spanish-language skills and artisan talents, many lived and worked at various missions. Donato, a blacksmith from Soledad, was at San Francisco in 1820 and San Juan Bautista in 1823, and in 1828 he requested emancipation.[51] Particularly ambitious and talented neophytes appear to have applied to train as artisans, as is indicated by the multiple talents of many artisans: at Mission San Rafael, the carpenter Elzeario was also a singer and musician, and the mason Januario was an interpreter. The Mission San Fernando blacksmith Rogerio was also noted as a flutist and singer, spoke Spanish, and could conduct services in Latin.[52] Others also distinguished themselves in leading rebellions, such as the carpenter Pacomio Poqui, one of the ringleaders of the Chumash Revolt of 1824.

The churches of the California missions, built in difficult circumstances on an isolated frontier, owe their existence to the determined plans and diligent labor of many different people. "The construction of this edifice would have been nothing to excite surprise, had it been built by Europeans," noted the Frenchman Duhaut-Cilly, when he visited Mission Santa Bárbara in 1827. "But if one considers that it is the work of poor Indians, guided by an ecclesiastic; that it is erected in a country which, though it contain all the materials required, at least supplies them to the hand using them only in the rough state in which nature produces them; one cannot tire in admiration."[53]

In general, the names of the master builders of the churches constructed in stone, considered the most "noble" of materials, are known to posterity. This is also true for most of those who constructed churches of *ladrillo* and adobe.[54] However, of the basic adobe churches, only one of the architects has been identified: the master carpenter Manuel Gutiérrez, who completed the third and final church at Mission San Fernando Rey, in 1806.[55] As for the master artisans who designed and built the other adobe churches, and the many other unknown artisans who assisted in their construction, the buildings themselves are the only enduring testament.

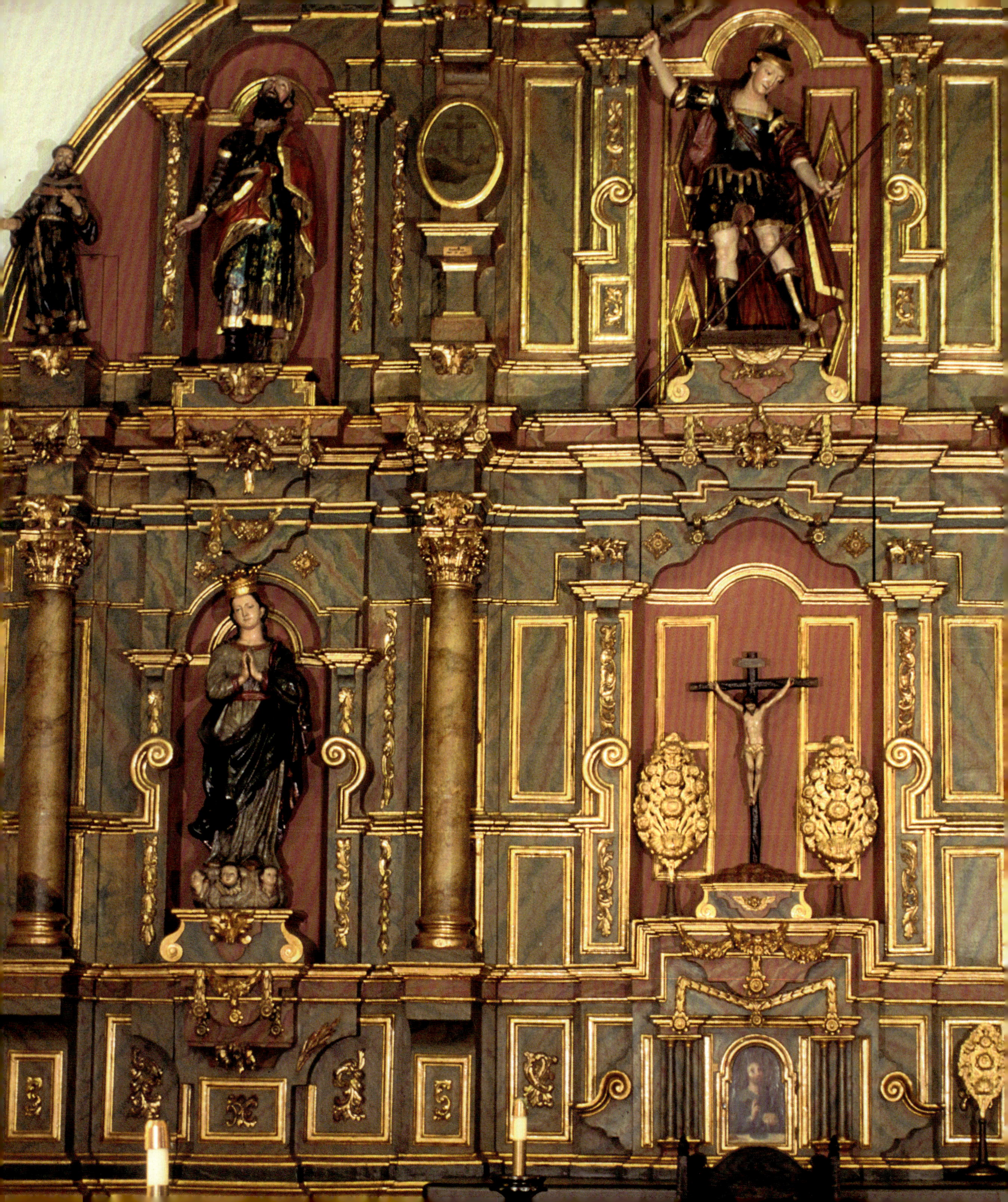

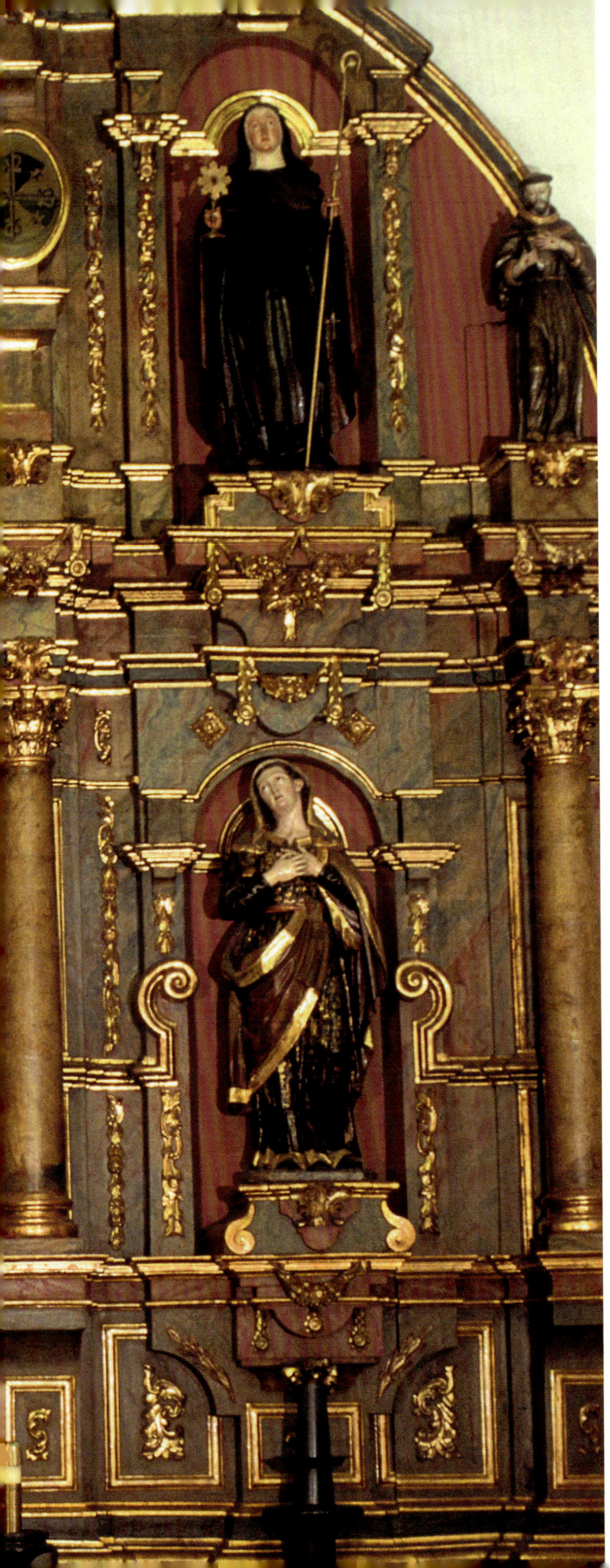

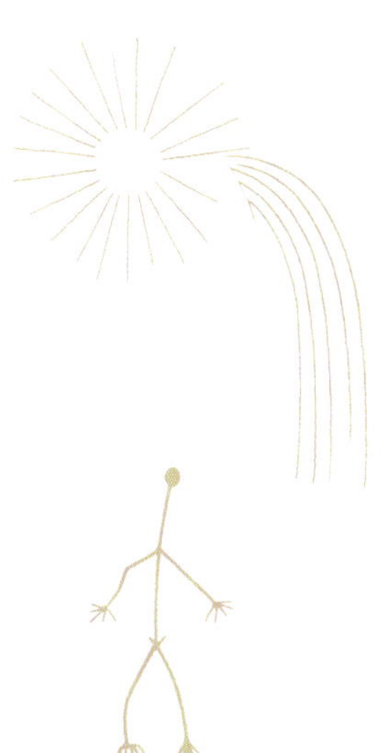

Chapter Five

ADORNING THE THEATERS OF CONVERSION

Visitors to the California missions often commented on the richness of their interior decor. "The church is a large, stone edifice, whose exterior is not without some considerable ornament and tasteful finish," noted the American Alfred Robinson when he visited Mission San Luis Rey in 1829, "but the interior is richer, and the walls are adorned with a variety of pictures of saints and Scripture subjects, glaringly colored, and attractive to the eye. Around the altar are many images of the saints."[1] Similarly, at Mission Santa Bárbara, Robinson noted, "From [the vestry], a door led into the church, where we beheld a gorgeous display of banners, paintings, images, and crucifixes of gold and silver."[2] Alexander Forbes made similar comments in 1835. "The church is, of course, the main object of attraction at all the missions, and is often gaudily decorated," he wrote. "In some of the missions where there is good building-stone in the vicinity, the external appearance of the sacred building is not unseemly; on other missions the exterior is very rude. In all of them the interior is richer than the outside promises."[3]

LEFT: Mexican *retablo,* or altarpiece, installed in 1796 at Mission San Francisco de Asís. Photograph by G. Aldana

ABOVE: Neophyte drawing from the nave of Mission San Miguel church.

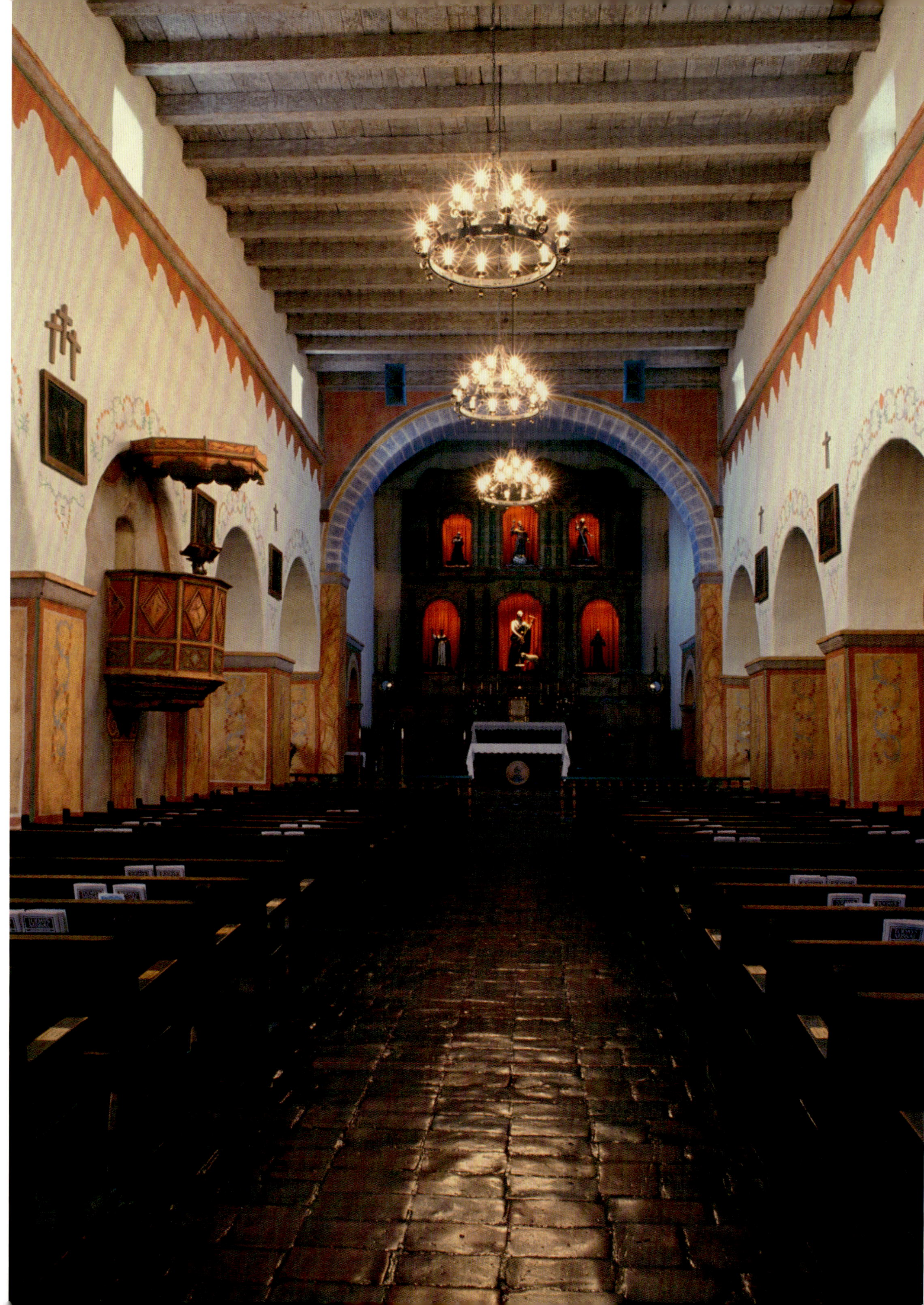

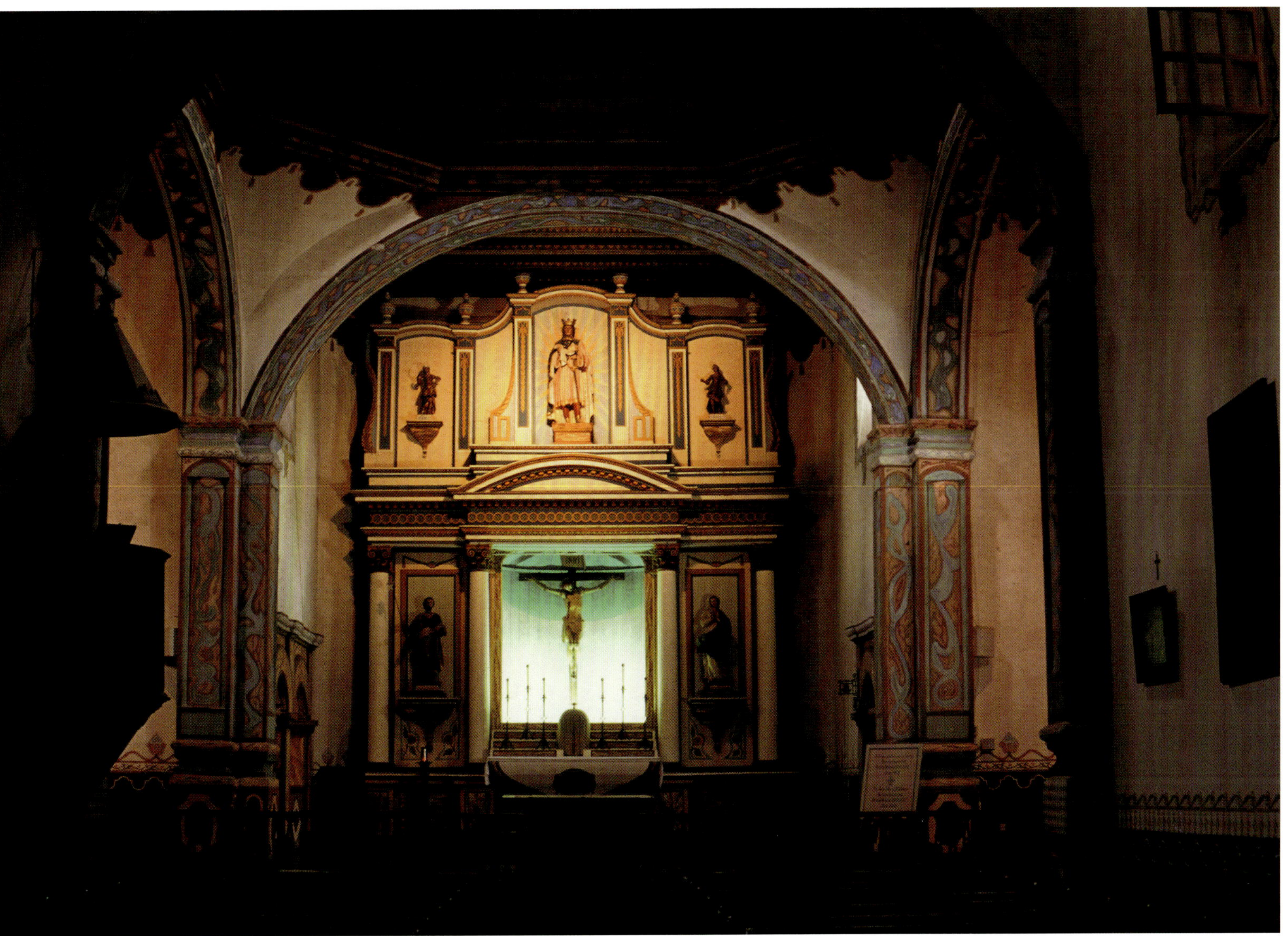

ABOVE: Ornate interiors helped make the mission church a "theater of conversion," where the Franciscans sought to impress neophytes with the dramatic pageantry of the service. The church at Mission San Luis Rey features a cruciform-like plan (with side transepts) and a unique central dome supported by eight columns added in 1829. Photograph by G. Aldana

OPPOSITE: The original *retablo* at Mission San Juan Bautista dramatically showcases the statues of saints with a bright cloth backdrop. *Retablos* and statuary played an important role in setting the stage for the performance of Roman Catholic rituals. Photograph by G. Aldana

This wealth of adornment was part of a carefully conceived plan, as the Franciscans, a mendicant order whose priests took a vow of poverty, sought to impart the splendor, majesty, and rich narrative of their faith. All the techniques used in California had been developed and refined elsewhere in the New World. "It was usually the interior of the mission that received the most decoration," one scholar has written. "It has been said that the Franciscans made their churches literal 'theaters of conversion' wherein religious dramas, processions, tableaux, pageants, dances, music and rites played to the spiritual needs of the neophytes."[4] The primary goal of the Franciscans was to bring *gentiles* (non-Christian Indians) into their fold to save their souls. The church was the staged setting in which these conversions took place. Although the California churches were not as sumptuous as those in New Spain, they were undoubtedly opulent in the eyes of their native congregations.

How the Native American audience received these staged presentations certainly varied considerably and changed over time. As attendance at services was mandatory, the size of the congregation could not be used as a measure of devotion. For some neophytes, the attraction of Catholicism was likely its apparent access to power symbolized in ritual glitter, music, and costumes. For others, these trappings lost their appeal and became symbols of oppression. And some may have been spiritually moved by the message of the Franciscans.

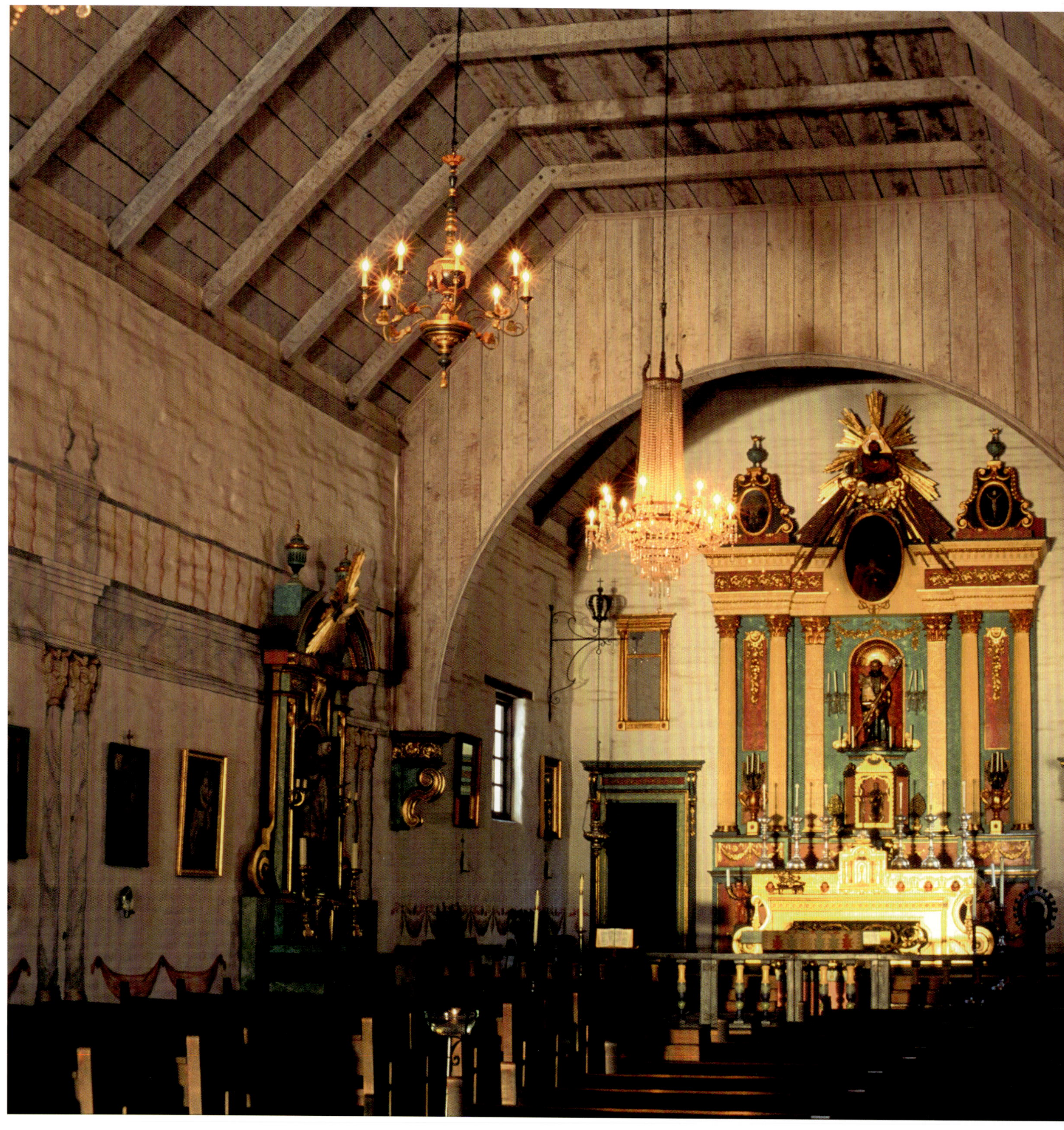

The reconstructed church at Mission San José displays statues and artifacts saved from the destruction of the original church in an earthquake in 1868. The walls and ceilings of the original church were covered by the fresco paintings of the artist Agustín Dávila, creating a sumptuous interior decor. Photograph by G. Aldana

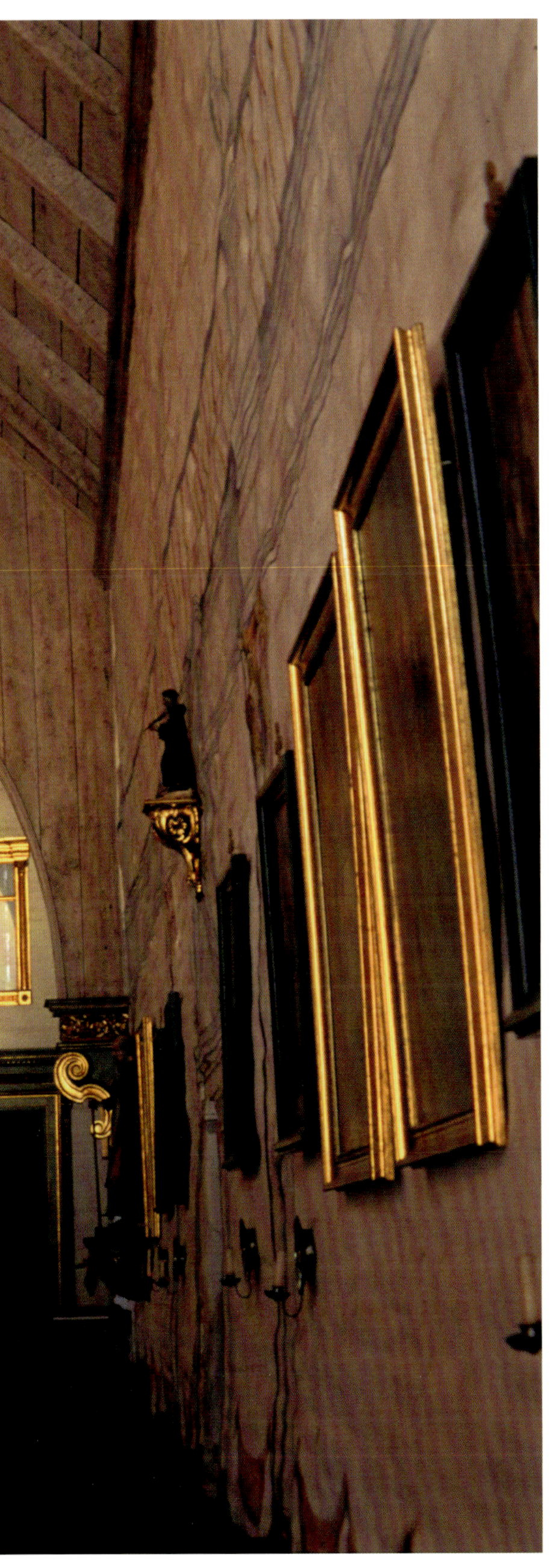

There is also considerable evidence that syncretism was actively at work, a process whereby indigenous people appropriate symbols and meanings of a new religion and recombine them with elements of their own belief system. As one scholar reports, this process "allowed neophytes to adopt various teachings and symbols of the Catholic faith [and] then transform these into Indian cultural practices in form and meaning."[5] With the concurrent practice of both Catholic and indigenous customs at the missions, it would be difficult to determine which were heartfelt religious observances and which were rote rituals.

In these "theaters of conversion," an abundance of adornments, such as altar screens (*retablos* or *reredos*), paintings, statuary, and other accoutrements set the stage for the performance of Roman Catholic rituals. Religious art was understood to be artifice by the artists in Mexico and by the priests who ordered the pieces. The images were intended not as idols to be prayed to but as symbols for religious ideas, displayed to give form to characters in the sacred narratives being taught, to serve as prompts to the imagination, and to visualize the events recounted. The statuary was idealized, sometimes emotionalized to evoke passion and stir religious fervor. It is impossible to imagine the didactic process of catechizing without the visual aid of paintings and statuary and the dissemination of religious prints. There were no books to read to engage the missions' neophytes, only oral instruction, rote learning, music practice, and contemplation of visual art.

In the early years, all the art and religious items were imported from New Spain, brought in small lots for new establishments and then on request from the fathers—a process that took months at best. Furnishings and decorations were supplied from sources in Mexico, and shipments frequently included items rotated in from older establishments.[6] As a result, some of the art displayed at the California missions is older than the missions themselves, reflecting earlier Baroque aesthetic traditions, not the new wave of Neoclassicism seen in the design of some altarpieces and mission architecture. Because of this selection process and also because this religious art tended to be rescued and cared for, "in [the California] missions, as in those of Arizona and New Mexico, are the oldest collections of seventeenth- and eighteenth-century art, and particularly religious art, in this country."[7]

The most important single item was the *retablo*, the painted or constructed backdrop behind the altar. Often covering the entire wall of the sanctuary at the head of the nave, the *retablo* served to hold and display sacred and decorative religious art. If a *retablo* was not yet available when construction of a mission's church was completed, the wall at the head of the nave behind the altar was painted in designs imitating architectural elements, such as faux marble columns and defined niches. These were covered over when the wooden *retablo* was eventually installed.[8] The gilt-accented altarpieces and statues, with their sumptuous multilayered carved, gilded, and painted draperies, shone in the candlelit penumbra of the stolid masonry churches. Whether the *retablos* were painted directly on the wall, made of painted canvas (*lienzo*), fashioned of painted and gilded wood, or formed of brick, stone, and plaster, they were designed to focus the attention of the congregation on the imagery and inspire awe and piety.[9]

The styles of the *retablos* reflected current fashion and the taste of a mission's padres. Alta California's earliest years coincided with the exuberant Baroque style then popular in Mexico, which was challenged in 1785 by the new Academy of San Carlos in Mexico City. This Neoclassical revolution in the design and furnishings of churches eventually reached Alta California. The 1796 altarpiece of Mission San Francisco de Asís was a transitional piece featuring both Baroque and Classical elements. The *retablos* installed subsequently at Missions San Miguel, San Gabriel, San Buenaventura, and San Luis Rey and at the Mission San Francisco de Asís side altars were Neoclassical and served to popularize the style throughout the colony. Elaborate side pulpits with overhanging sounding boards to amplify the orator's voice often accompanied the *retablo*.[10]

Printed Images

Prints—lithographs, woodcuts, and engravings—were popularly circulated in the New World to inspire individual devotion. Inexpensive and easy to ship, they often sufficed until paintings could be obtained. For example, in April 1774 Junípero Serra arrived at Mission San Gabriel, founded three years earlier, with "a painting of the Archangel Gabriel that [he] commissioned in Mexico. They retire[d] the previous image, a missal-page print, and h[u]ng the new painting above the altar."[11]

Prints also served as models for New World artists to follow in depicting the various saints accurately, with their appropriate attributes. Some prints were framed and decorated the walls of the *conventos*, or priests' residences, as well as the church proper, as is indicated by extant inventories, orders, and invoices. Since individual missions are known to have imported hundreds of prints, it is clear that the missionaries also distributed them to the neophytes. Although once ubiquitous, prints were later considered of such little historic, religious, or artistic value that regrettably few have survived to the present.[12]

An engraving of the Tenth Station of the Cross by Pellegrino de Colle, published in Venice in 1778 and preserved in the archives at Mission Santa Inés.
Courtesy of The Santa Bárbara Mission Archive-Library

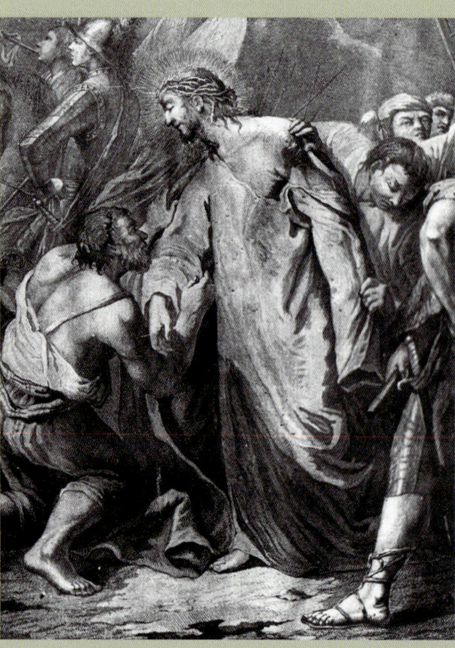

The ordering, construction, and installation of a *retablo* was one of the most important steps in the creation of the theater of conversion, and great care went into its selection. In 1808, for example, Fathers José Senan and Marco de Vitoria requested for Mission San Buenaventura "a main altar *reredos* for the new church, marbleized, and with the moldings, gables, and other ornaments gilded; completely carved." "The niches, and which saints should be included, the dimensions of the *reredos*, and other things which the artisan will know how to carry out, are put down in enough detail, in the drawing which we are sending," they wrote.[13]

The artisan who completed this order was José María Uriarte, likely of Mexico City. He apparently built *retablos* for nine other Alta California missions.[14] The San Buenaventura work, made of cedar and pine and "in modern taste," cost 4,505 pesos; it measured the specified 10 by 7 *varas* (about 30 by 21 feet) and arrived packed in forty-five boxes.[15]

Retablos were complemented by a wide range of other elements, which heightened the effect on the potential convert. The mission churches, although illuminated only by candles and whatever natural light the small window openings afforded, were radiant during the celebration of Mass through artful use of gilt and mirrors. Altar vessels and utensils were silver, gold-washed silver, or gessoed and gilded with gold or silver leaf to present a shiny reflective surface. Wall-hung candle sconces were backed with polished metal or multiple mirrored concave reflectors called, appropriately, *reverberos.* Candelabras suspended from the ceilings were generally painted and gilded or made of polished metal; prosperous mission churches boasted imported crystal chandeliers, the ultimate in light-show effects.[16] Mirrors in gilded frames to reflect light were used in abundance, hung directly on the altarpiece and walls of the sanctuary.[17] The glass doors in *vidrios* (glass-covered *nichos* for statues) had similar reflective effects, and *nichos* (recesses in walls or freestanding containers) were sometimes lined with gold or silver paper and decorated with artificial flowers of foil.

The vessels used in the celebration of Mass were generally fashioned of gold, silver, or silver gilt. The incense burners, altar card holders, missal stands, chalices, ciboriums (for holding the host), and monstrances (used for the elevation and display of the host during benediction) were usually of intricate designs and precious metals, sometimes enhanced with jewels. All were imported from Mexico, where the precious metals were mined and exceptional Spanish Colonial metalwork was produced.

Native neophytes likely crafted many items for the altar and for use in religious rituals, only a few of which have survived. At Mission Santa Bárbara the Chumash neophytes, skilled at abalone-shell inlay from their precontact culture, crafted a remarkable tabernacle. In addition to the *enconchado* work (decorative use of opalescent shell, popular in Central and South America), the whole is painted in bright colors and gilded and of a shape and size totally unlike imported examples from New Spain and Mexico. Also surviving at Mission Santa Bárbara is a picture frame similarly inlaid with shell and undoubtedly also executed by a Chumash.[18] Another venerated neophyte creation is a unique reliquary at Mission San Carlos Borromeo said to have belonged to Father Junípero Serra. It is brightly painted in red and yellow and decorated with carved motifs of wheat and grapes symbolizing bread and wine, the body and blood of Christ. Also crafted by neophytes at San Carlos Borromeo—and on display there—is a bas relief roundel of the Lamb of God (Agnus Dei) intended for the front of the altar.[19] As Henry Chapman Ford observed there

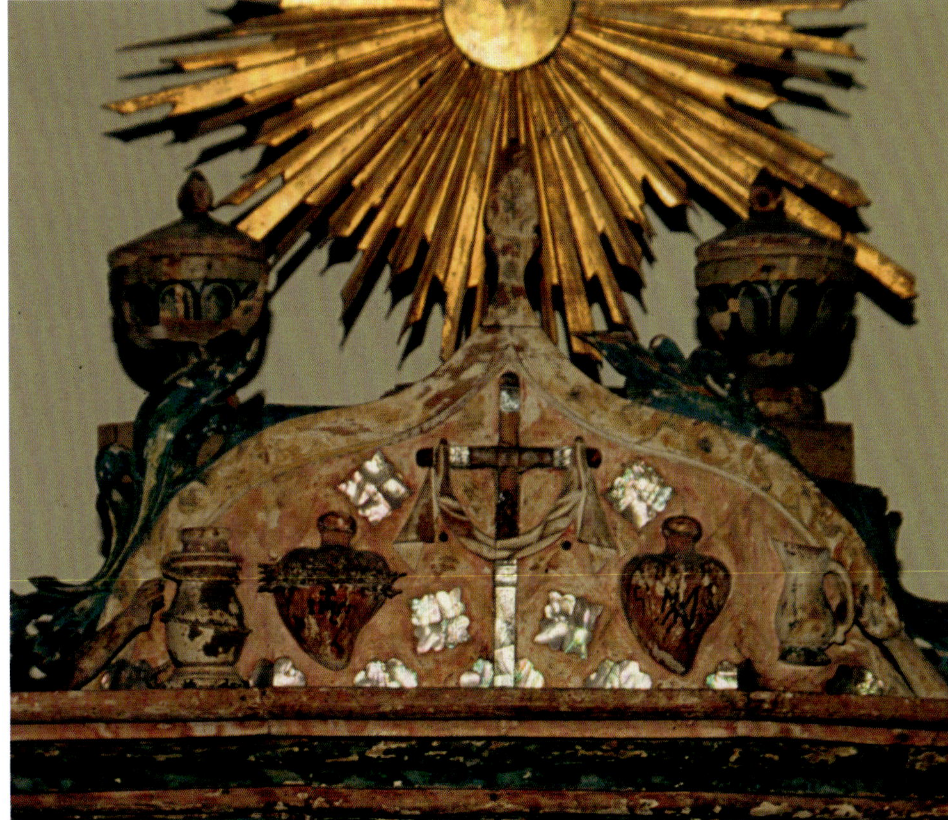

The extraordinary tabernacle at Mission Santa Bárbara, made by Chumash artisans for the main altar of the church. It is faced with mirrors and traditional abalone inlay work. The top of the tabernacle, pictured here, combines local abalone shell with a mother-of-pearl cross imported from Jerusalem. Photograph by G. Aldana

in 1881, "The altar, pulpit, confessional, and missal-holder wrought from cedar of the Sierra de Santa Lucía, and the baptismal font and polished receptacles for holy water fashioned by native hands; all remained as silent monitors to connect us with the early mission days."[20]

The vestments worn by the clergy when celebrating the rites were similarly splendid. Fashioned of the finest silk damasks, crepes, and brocades from China, they featured metallic gold and silver threads, with borders and embroidery of the same. "Adjoining the [vestry] was a small but convenient dressing-room," noted Robinson, "where were arranged the numerous dresses and ornaments used in the church services, some of them rich and of the most costly description."[21] Many of the California missions have fine collections of vestments, some of which are believed to have been brought by Serra to Upper California from Lower California when the missions were first founded. Missions San Luis Rey, Santa Inés, San Carlos Borromeo, San Juan Bautista, and Santa Clara have large collections,[22] although most mission museums display some examples.

A wall plaque carving of the Lamb of God at Mission San Carlos Borromeo, made by mission neophytes. Photograph by Julia Costello

Mission churches also dramatically featured depictions of saints reflecting Franciscan Catholic iconography practiced in the New World that was well established by the eighteenth century. Certain central figures appear repeatedly in mission collections, for example, the Virgin Mary as the Immaculate Conception and Our Lady of Solitude (Nuestra Señora de la Soledad); San José holding the Christ child and a lily staff; San Antonio holding the Christ child; San Francisco with a crucifix; and the Virgin Mary as the Sorrowing Mother (Madre Dolorosa). Groupings of statues on the altarpieces were arranged hierarchically in tiers, with the patron saint generally at the pinnacle, the Virgin as the Immaculate Conception at the center above the tabernacle, and saints on either side in one or two tiers. Popular combinations include San Francisco or Santo Domingo to the left and San José or San Antonio on the right.

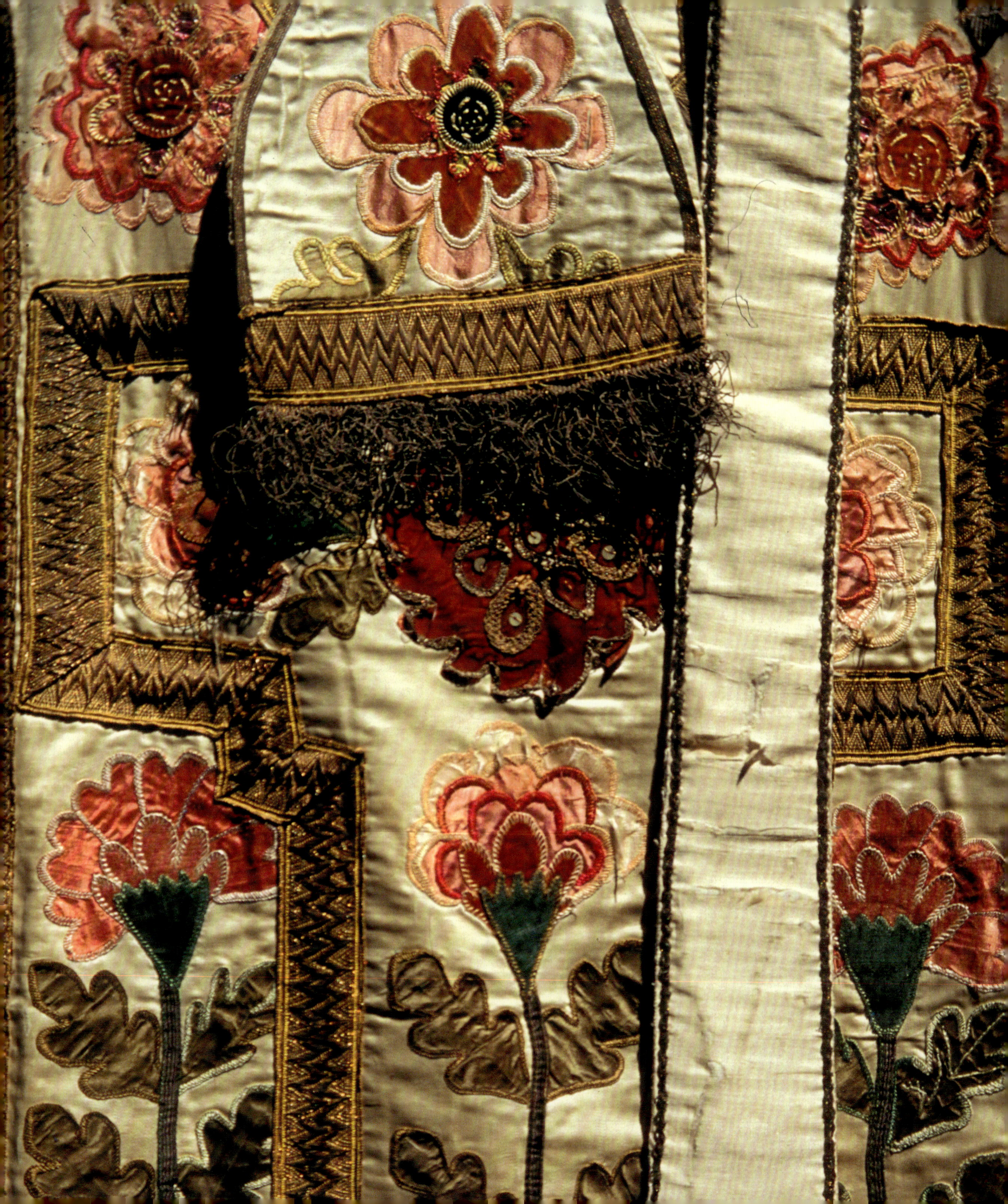

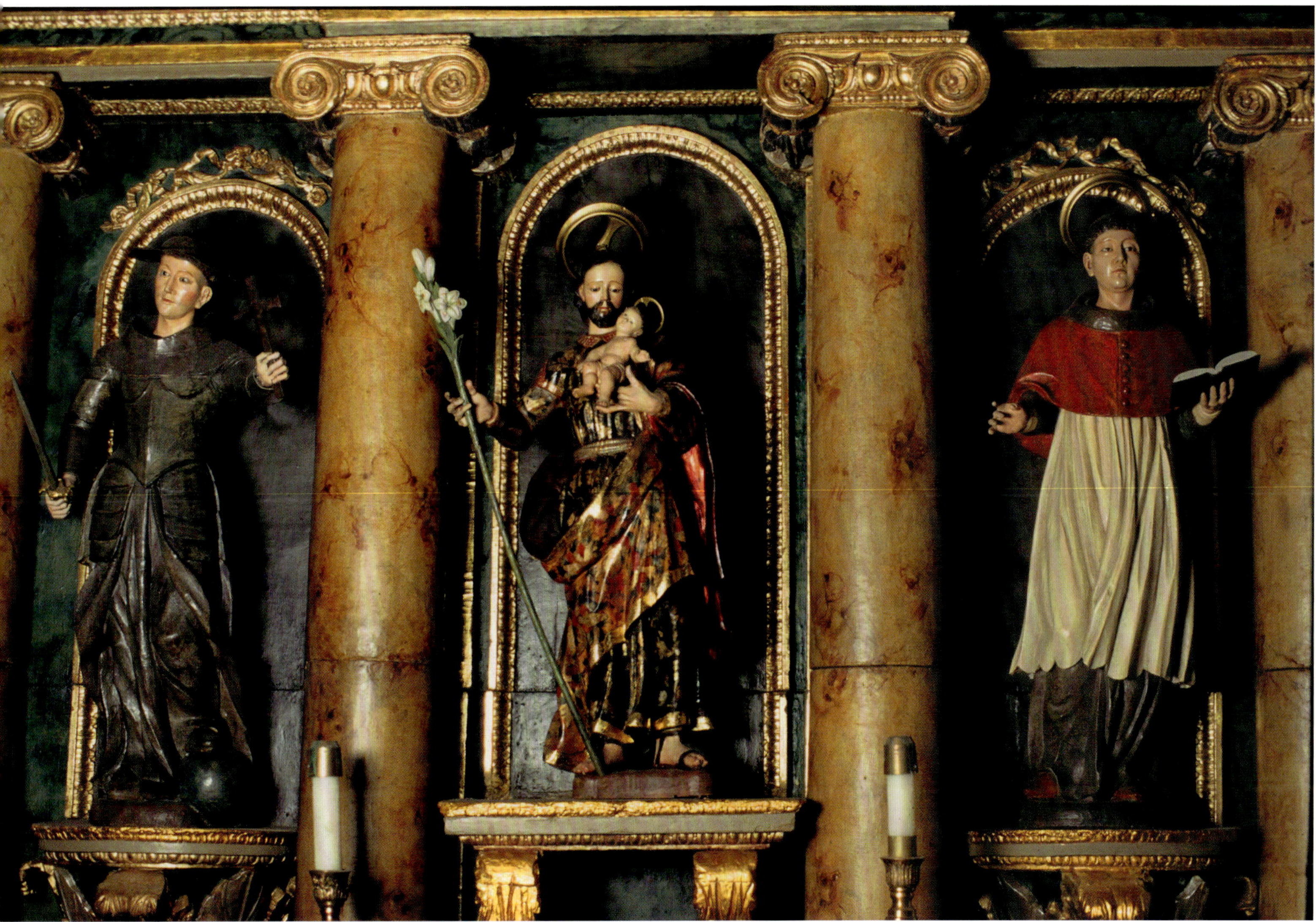

ABOVE: Three saints adorn the side altar at Mission San Francisco de Asís: San Juan Capistrano is on the left, San Antonio de Padua in the middle, and San Buenaventura on the right. Photograph by G. Aldana

OPPOSITE: Vestments for the clergy were of fine embroidered silk damasks, crepes, and brocades from China. Glittering threads of gold and silver added to the splendor of church ceremonies. Seen here is a detail of a vestment at Mission San Buenaventura. Photograph by G. Aldana

During the time of the missions, the left, or "cross," side of the church was generally where the men were seated during Mass, while the women were seated on the right, or "birth," side.[23] Images of San Francisco holding the crucifix and founders of other religious orders were assigned to the cross (male) side of both the church and the main altar. Side altars to the Virgin were on the right (female) side along with birth-associated statues such as those of San José and San Antonio holding the Christ child. The patron saints of the missions—those for whom the establishments were named—were always represented by a statue or painting or both, and effort was made to have an image of the patron saint present at the founding ceremony. San José was invariably represented in all the churches since he was the patron of all the California missions.

Some of the works imported from Mexico appear to have been ordered as much for the benefit of the Franciscan priests and the soldiers as for the edification of the Indian neophytes. These include images of saints who were members of the Franciscan and other religious orders, such as San Francisco, San Antonio, San Buenaventura, and Santo Domingo. The lives and martyrdoms of these saints were probably not part of the catechism taught the Indians but served to inspire and lift the spirits of the priests on the remote frontier. The large number of images of the Virgin as the Immaculate Conception reflected the Marianism, or devotion to the Blessed Virgin Mary, of the Franciscans.

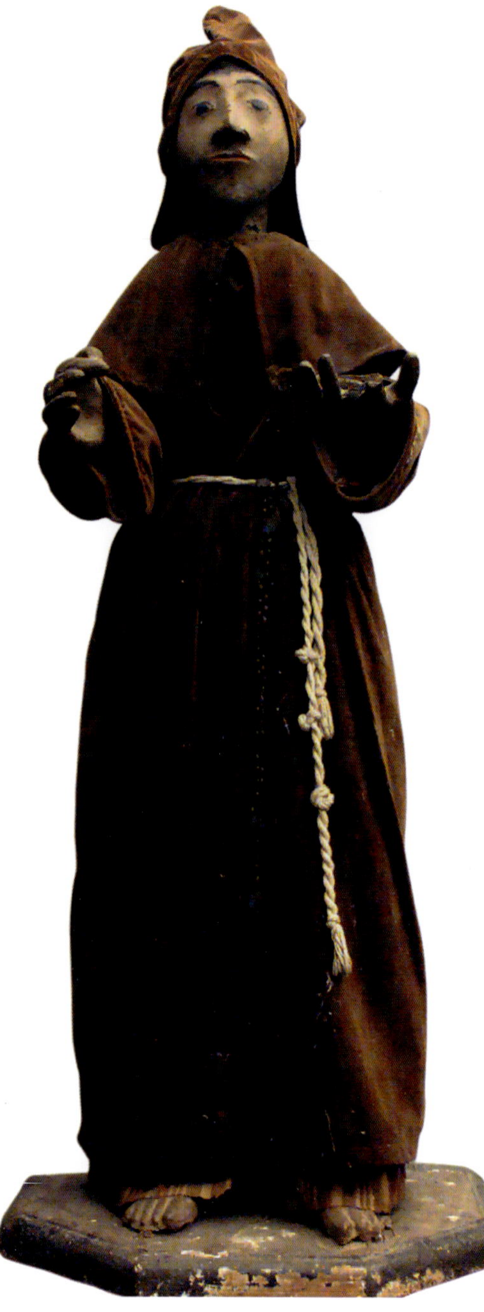

A wooden statue (*bulto*) of San Antonio, made by neophytes of the San Antonio de Pala *asistencia* to adorn the main altar. Recently restored, it now rests in the museum adjacent to the church. Photograph courtesy South Coast Fine Arts Conservation Center

The statues in the California missions represent the central players in the life of Christ, the Virgin, and saints of Church history. These eighteenth-century statues were realistic in the glowing flesh tones of the face and hands and the use of human hair and glass eyes and teeth, and fantastic in their attire rendered in *estofado*—a technique of layered surface decoration that represents fine brocade cloth. A gesso base is applied over carved wood, followed by a layer of burnished gold leaf, which is covered in turn with painted designs. Pricking and incising the surface creates additional motifs, exposing the gilding beneath. The rich effect often surpasses the textiles it simulates.

Some life-sized statues with movable joints were imported. These *imágenes para vestir* were dressed and arranged in various poses when they were carried in processions, often seated on chairs mounted on litters. At Mission Santa Cruz, a life-sized Virgin Mary as Nuestra Señora de la Candelaria (Virgin of the Purification) was the object of considerable devotion starting in 1822. Her earrings and necklaces were imported from Mexico, as was fine raiment for numerous holidays, and all were kept in a trunk in the mission sacristy. Later moved to Mission San Carlos Borromeo, Nuestra Señora de la Candelaria was for a long time displayed in a glass *nicho*, re-dressed as Nuestra Señora del Carmelo. She now resides in storage at the mission, brought out at Christmas in the role of a kneeling Mary.

Religious statuary was also produced by Native American converts in Alta California. Perhaps the most famous is the *bulto* (carved wooden religious figure) of San Antonio from Mission San Luis Rey's Asistencia San Antonio at Pala. Tradition identifies the artist as a Luiseño Indian from Pala, and records show that the patron saint presided over the main altar from the founding in 1818 until recent times. Now restored, the *bulto* is displayed in the Asistencia's museum with its historic companion statues of the Blessed Virgin and Santo Domingo.

Mission San Carlos Borromeo also displays in its Convento Museum several important examples of Native American religious carvings. Among these is a small carved wood statue of San Benito with an embracing snake, in poor condition. Harry Downie carved its likeness in stone for the *nicho* over the belfry stairway.[24] Also on display is a fine painting of a soul in purgatory above painted flames, intended for the gate of the *campo santo* (cemetery). Elsewhere, Native American carvings of religious figures include a rendering of the Virgin of Guadalupe at Mission San Luis Rey and a small limestone bas relief carving of a saint in a *nicho* at Mission Santa Bárbara. The *nicho*'s design is similar to that painted on the mission's original cloth altar screen, or *lienzo*.[25]

At Mission Santa Bárbara, the pedimental stone sculpture of Santa Bárbara and its companion sculptures of Faith, Hope, and Charity were commissioned in 1818–20 from the Chumash canoe builder, mason, and carpenter Paciano Guilajahichet (Paisano).[26] Traces of color indicate they were originally painted before being mounted on the tympanum of the church facade. Faith, occupying the apex of the pediment, had disappeared by the 1850s, and the other two statues were damaged in the 1925 earthquake. The latter are now restored and displayed in the mission museum; replicas of all three stand in their original places. These are the sole extant examples of monumental stone sculpture executed by California Indians during the mission era.[27]

Although today altar screens in the California missions feature only statues, during the mission period they displayed paintings as well. Like statues, devotional paintings of the principal religious figures functioned as symbols and instructional aids. Paintings, however, played an expanded role in the conversion process, because they illustrated scenes in greater detail and more realistically. Large paintings of heaven and hell, intended as deterrents to sin, featured suffering souls and placed considerable emphasis on flames and other tortures. "The parish church is very clean . . . and ornamented with rather good paintings,

La Conquistadora

The most remarkable *imágen para vestir* in California, the life-sized Our Lady of Bethlehem (Nuestra Señora de Belén) at Mission San Carlos Borromeo, can claim a long and adventurous history. In 1769 Archbishop Francisco Antonio de Lorenzana y Butrón of Mexico City gave the statue to Inspector General José de Gálvez to accompany the first settlers to Alta California, so that it might bear the title "La Conquistadora," conqueror of the souls of the Native Americans of Upper California. The statue was present in San Diego in 1769 for the founding of the first mission. As Serra noted, "For almost a year it... [was on] the altar.... It was there during all Masses, high or low, that were celebrated there; also during the daily prayers, both morning and evening."[28]

The following year Father Junípero Serra accompanied the statue on the ship *San Antonio* and presented it at the founding of Monterey on June 3, 1770: "The... beautiful statue of Mary, Most Holy (belonging to Your Most Illustrious Lordship), occupied the middle space directly above the monstrance of her Most Holy Son. And there Our Lady stood on guard over the church."[29]

Although Serra, as promised, returned La Conquistadora to Gálvez in La Paz in 1770, the inspector general apparently reconsidered its disposition, as Serra next took the statue to Mission San Carlos Borromeo, where it was installed on the main altar by 1775. A silver crown, decorated and partially gilded, commissioned by Capitan Juan Bautista Matute, presumably in gratitude for saving his ship at sea, was placed on the statue in 1802.

After the secularization and abandonment of Mission San Carlos Borromeo, La Conquistadora was preserved by members of the Cantúa family, the last resident Indians at this mission. La Conquistadora's adventures during subsequent years typify the complex destinies of many mission statues. As the statue was not on display, La Conquistadora's infant was removed and placed in the empty arms of a statue of San José at the Royal Presidio Chapel in Monterey. In 1876 María Ignacia Cantúa de Dutra moved the statue with her to Monterey. Here it was garbed in María's wedding dress and was the subject of devotional visits representing Nuestra Señora de Belén.

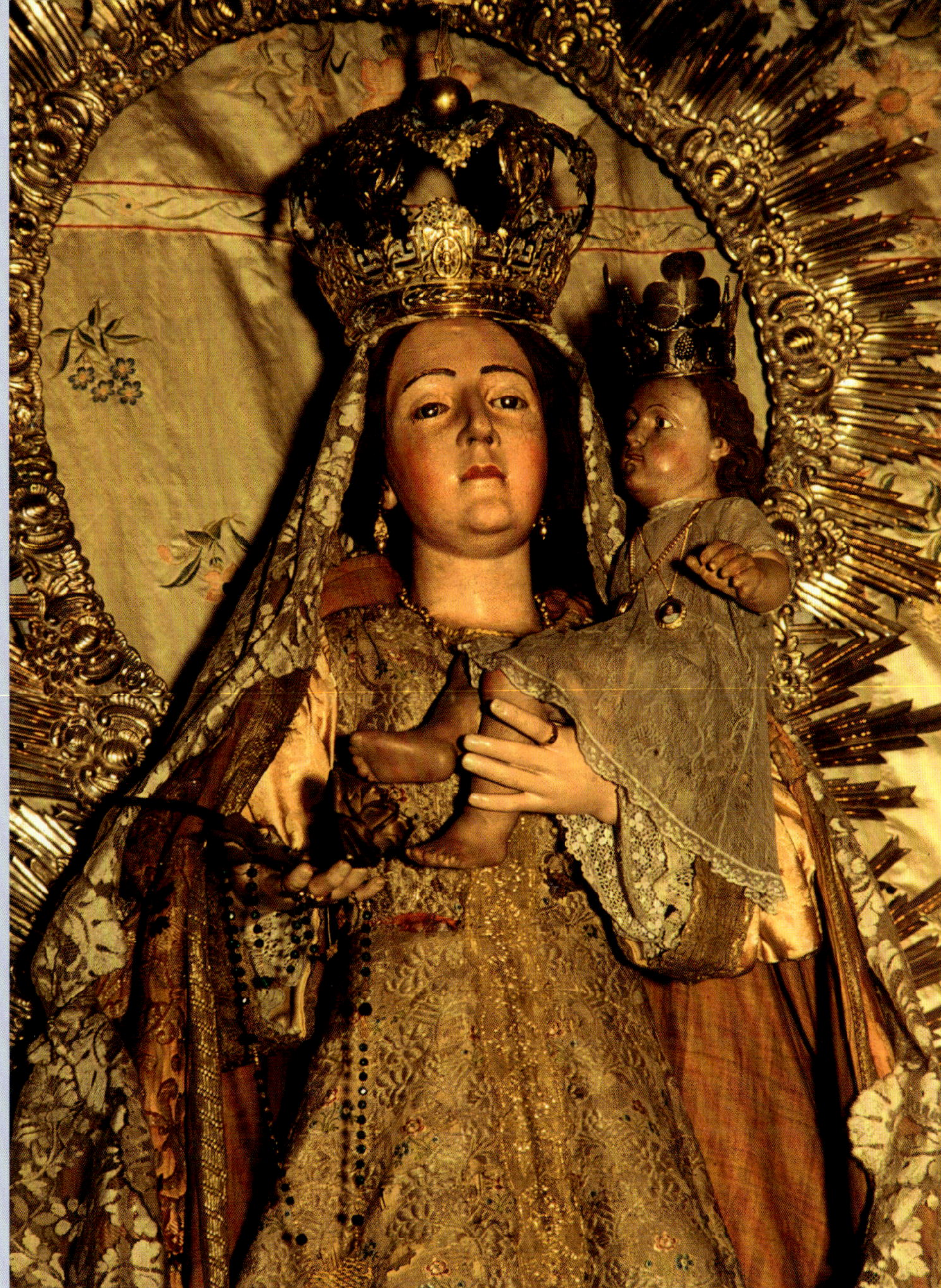

In 1925 the statue was inherited by the artist Tulita Westfall, descendant of the pioneering Boronda family, and in 1945 she returned it to Mission San Carlos Borromeo, now adorned with gold acorn earrings. Here La Conquistadora was gratefully received by Harry Downie, who carefully replaced the insect-damaged portions of her wooden torso (maintaining the statue's original 5-foot, 2-inch height), dressed her in Mexican silk and brocade, and reunited her with both her silver crown and Christ child.

As a side effect, when Downie removed La Conquistadora's Christ child from its foster location in the arms of San José at the Royal Presidio Chapel, he had to provide a substitute. So he went to Mission Santa Cruz and took the Christ child from that statue of San José, replacing it with a replica that he made himself.

Historically, La Conquistadora occupied the central *nicho* of the altarpiece at Mission San Carlos Borromeo, just below the statue of that mission's patron saint. During the restoration Downie redesigned the altar to feature a large central crucifixion scene, similar to the one he made for the Royal Presidio Chapel. Today, exquisitely dressed, La Conquistadora occupies the Mortuary Chapel on the cross side of the church.

The statue of La Conquistadora, photographed here in 1995, resides in a glass case at Mission San Carlos Borromeo. Photograph by G. Aldana

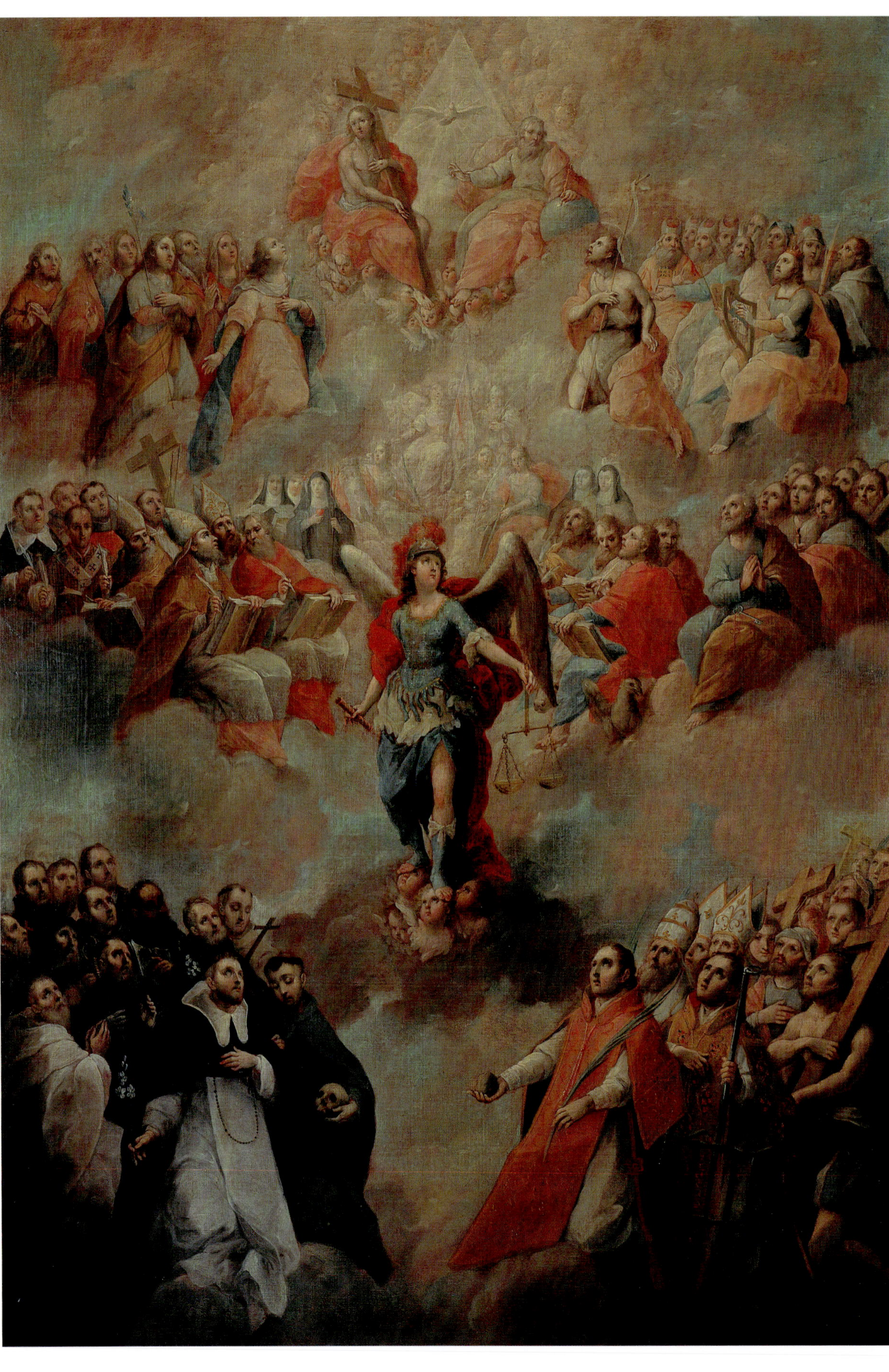

copied from originals in Italy," noted the famous world traveler Jean-François La Pérouse, at Mission San Carlos Borromeo in 1786, in comments that reflected prejudices common at the time. "One sees there a picture of hell . . . as it is absolutely necessary to impress vividly the senses of the new converts. . . . I have my doubts that the picture of Paradise, which is placed opposite . . . , produces on them as good an effect; the state of quietism which it represents . . . [constitutes] ideas too sublime for rude, coarse men, but it was necessary to place rewards by the side of the punishments.[30]

For the most part, the paintings that hung in the California missions date from the latter part of the eighteenth century and were executed by artists in Mexico and in New Spain. (See chapter 6 for discussion of paintings executed by individuals in California.) Judging from the number of signed paintings and canvases attributed to him, José de Páez was the painter most often featured in the California missions. Serra himself specifically requested that the Colegio de San Fernando purchase paintings for the California missions from Páez's atelier. In August 1775, for example, Serra ordered a painting of San Juan Capistrano, directing that "they should find a good engraving and have Páez paint it or some other good artist."[31] In 1777 he requested two specific paintings, suggesting that the college "get together with the painter Páez and arrange for both."[32] Every mission baptistery required an image of Christ being baptized by John the Baptist, and several of these came from the Páez studio.[33]

Rivaling the importance of Christ's baptismal scene for the Franciscans was a set of the Vía Crucis (Stations of the Cross), fourteen images that chronicle the story of Christ's final suffering and death. All the California mission churches displayed the fourteen stations along the walls of their naves, although initially some missions and presidio chapels had to make do with prints.[34]

OPPOSITE: This fine eighteenth-century Mexican painting would have served to reinforce the religious teachings of the Franciscans. In the center, San Miguel, Arcángel, carries scales to weigh the worth of souls at death; above him, the deceased petition for entry into paradise. The painting was sent to Mission San Antonio in 1786 and now hangs at Mission San Miguel. Photograph © Bill Dewey

BELOW: Paintings such as this depiction of hell at Mission Santa Bárbara and its companion piece depicting purgatory were intended to discourage sinning among the neophytes. Photograph by G. Aldana

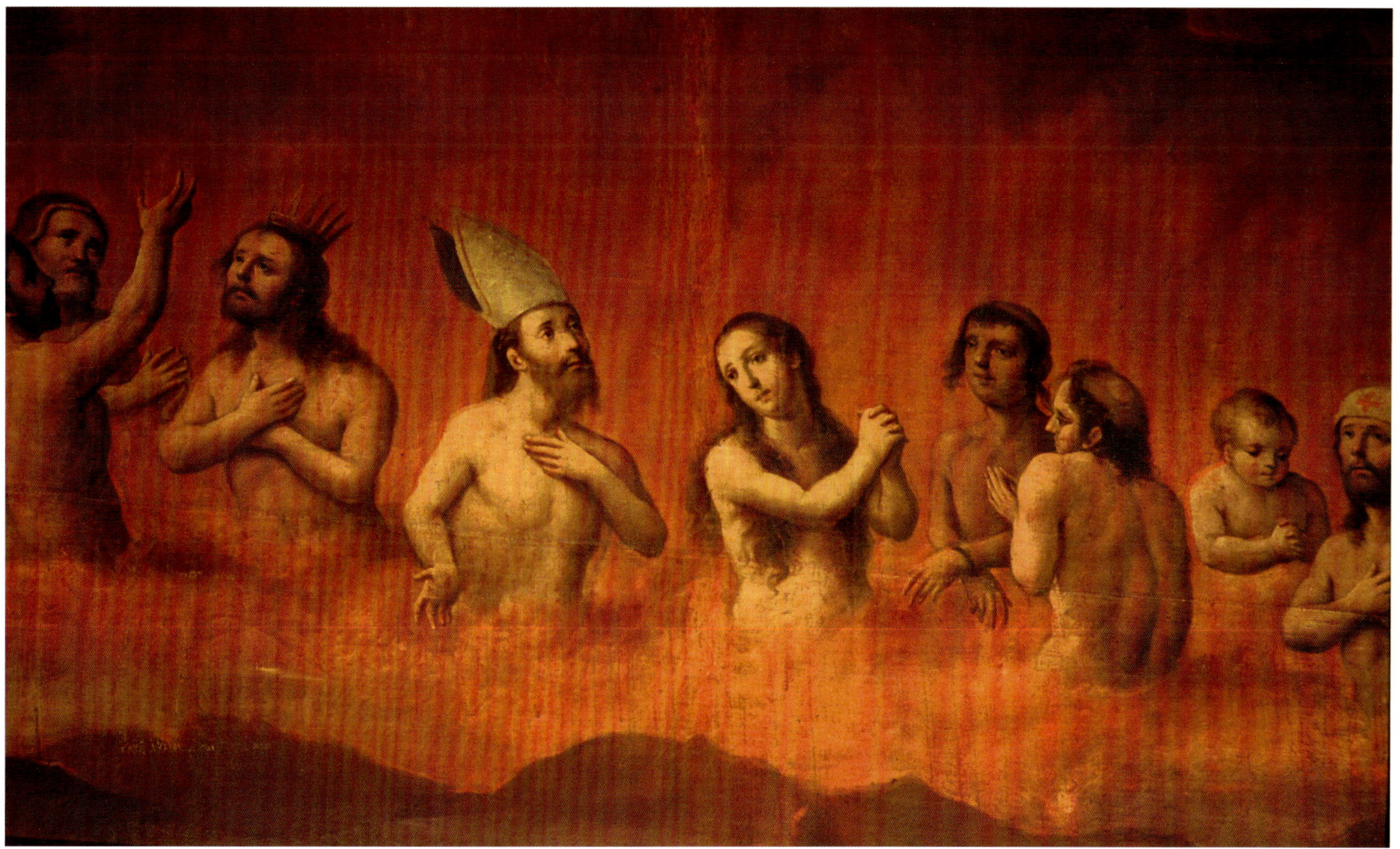

An unusual type of painting found in mission collections is described as *enrollado,* a roll-up canvas. These portable oil paintings were rolled up in a leather carrying tube. Perhaps because they were imported for presidio chapels, some art historians contend that these paintings were intended for use on military campaigns.[35] However, their presence in mission collections suggests that their portability was also useful in field visits to outlying Indian villages and ranchos. Priests used traveling communion cases for the field; why not paintings? An *enrollado* painting of John the Baptist would be especially useful as priests frequently baptized new Indian converts in remote village locations.

No discussion of the paintings of the California missions should omit reference to copies of the painting of Nuestra Señora de Guadalupe, whose image was widespread. Nuestra Señora de Guadalupe is the indigenous New World manifestation of the Virgin Mary who revealed herself to Juan Diego, a Mexican Indian. Speaking in Náhuatl, she asked that a church be built in her honor on the place of her revelation, but the bishop required confirmation of this manifestation. She provided blooming roses in the midst of winter and arranged them in Juan Diego's cloak. When these were presented to the bishop her miraculous image appeared imprinted on the cloth.[36] The message of La Virgen Morena (the Brown-Skinned Virgin) of faith, hope, and consolation to the economically and politically

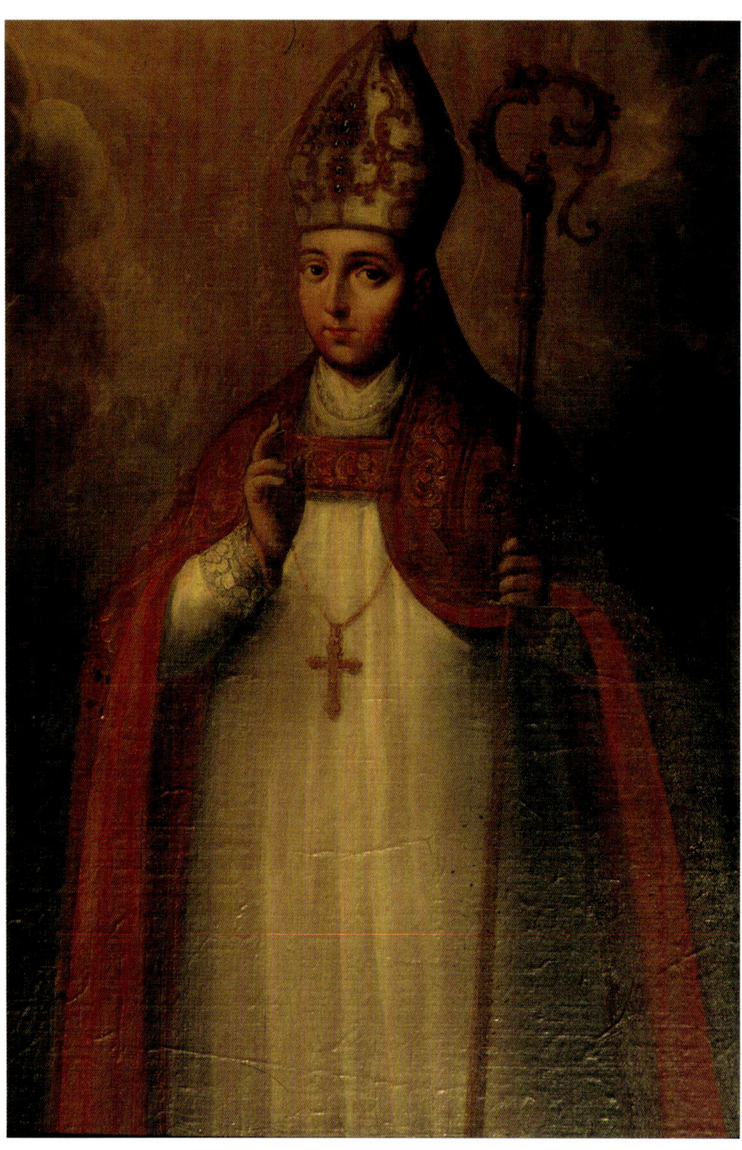

BELOW LEFT: **Portrait of San Luis Obispo by the artist José de Páez of Mexico City. Paintings by Páez, who was a favorite of Father Serra, founder of the California missions, adorned a number of missions. This work has been hanging in Mission San Luis Obispo since 1774. Oil on canvas.** Photograph by G. Aldana

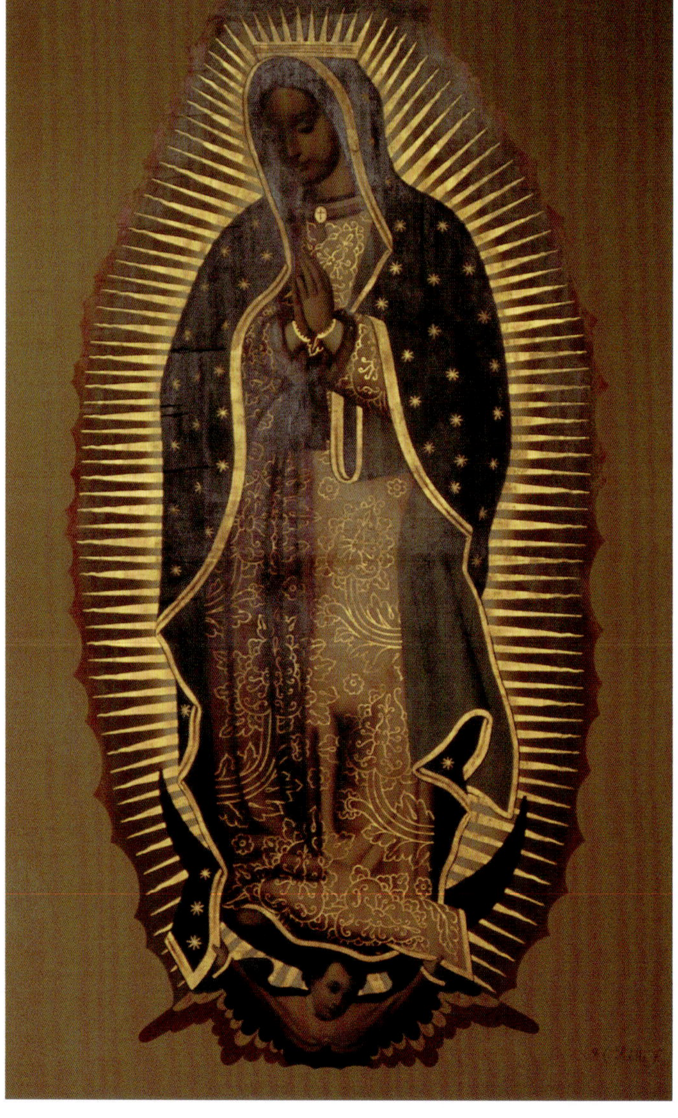

BELOW RIGHT: **Nuestra Señora de Guadalupe, the indigenous New World manifestation of the Virgin Mary, believed to have revealed herself to a Mexican Indian, was widely venerated in California. This painting of the revered figure has been at Mission Santa Bárbara since between 1872 and 1885. J. C. Padilla, *Nuestra Señora de Guadalupe*. Oil on canvas.** Photograph by Julia Costello

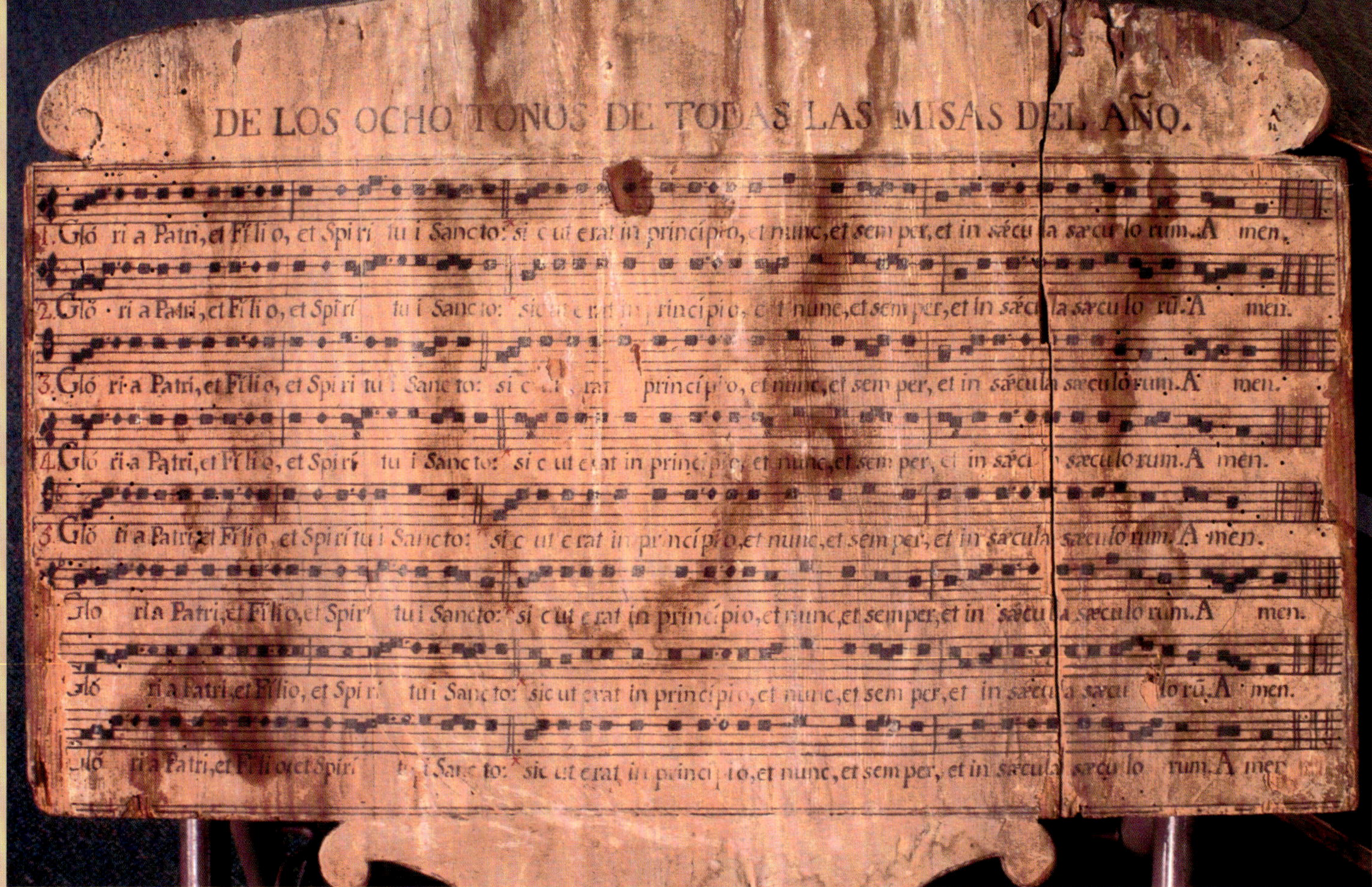

Music at the Missions

The importance of music was noted by Alfred Robinson when he attended Mass at Mission Santa Clara in 1832. "The music was well executed, for it had been practiced daily for more than two months under the particular supervision of Father Narcisco Durán," he wrote. "The number of musicians was about thirty; the instruments performed upon were violins, flutes, trumpets, and drums; and so acute was the ear of the priest that he would detect a wrong note on the part of either instantly, and chide the erring performer."[37] The integral role of music in the religious rites of the Church has often been overlooked. Production of music involved active participation and engagement of the neophytes to a greater degree than did memorizing prayers and catechism.[38]

Music was taught at all the missions, and neophytes participated in singing Mass and in other rituals with chanted Latin responses. Mission choirs and bands were made up of select groups of neophytes who received intensive musical training and enjoyed high status in the community. Among the missions, songs always had the same words, although melodies varied depending on the choir director, producing some interesting results. Robinson observed, "The musicians attached to the choir were practicing, and played some very fine airs; rather unsuitable, however, to the place.... It was not unusual, both there and at the churches of other missions, to hear during the mass the lively dancing tunes."[39]

Mission Santa Clara was especially well known for its music. A drum, twelve flutes, a bass violin, a violin, and violin primers were ordered for the mission's orchestra in 1808. Eventually added to these were bugles, cellos, clarinets, brass cymbals, double basses, horns, oboes, triangles, trumpets, and an organ.[40] Sometimes the performances had a strange, almost surreal quality. "One of the Fathers purchased from a French whaler thirty complete uniforms and organized a band," noted a visitor. "It was not without keen surprise that we heard [these] musicians... sing the Marseillaise, as the congregation rose, and escorted the procession singing 'Vive Henri IV.' After Mass, upon asking one of the fathers how these Indians happened to know these airs, I was informed that one of his predecessors had bought a small organ from France and that the Indians, after hearing the airs, had instinctively arranged the songs for use by the various instruments."[41] The anthem of the French Revolution was undoubtedly chosen for its melody, not its message.

Among the most important musical items in mission collections was the violin made by José Carbajal, a Mission San Antonio neophyte, in 1798. Carbajal ingeniously copied his violin from an imported instrument, fashioning it from local bay laurel and other woods, and played it for many years in the mission orchestra. His great-great-grandson Leonard Lane eventually donated the violin to Mission San Antonio. In 2000 the instrument was restored and featured in several concerts of period music. Sadly, in summer 2003 it was stolen from Mission San Antonio's museum. It is irreplaceable.

This music board made at Mission Santa Inés was affixed to the top of a lectern box on a pedestal, reaching to a height of over six feet. Photograph by G. Aldana

oppressed natives of Mexico drew widespread devotion. The original image was copied by painters and printers and revered throughout the New World and beyond. Missions San Carlos Borromeo and San Juan Bautista have large examples of the image with figures in the corners illustrating the story of Juan Diego, the Virgin, and the roses.[42] Mission Santa Cruz has a fine small painting of Nuestra Señora de Guadalupe that was brought to the mission in 1797, according to its annual report of that year. This image may have been especially important to the mestizo soldiers and settlers of Alta California.

After Mexico won its independence from Spain in 1821, the northern California missions were turned over to Mexican Franciscans from the Colegio de Nuestra Señora de Guadalupe in Zacatecas, and many of the original Franciscans (also known as Fernandinos) retired to their headquarters, the Colegio de San Fernando in Mexico City. The Zacatecan priests' devotion to the Blessed Virgin Mary as Nuestra Señora del Refugio (Our Lady of Refuge) resulted in the addition of a number of paintings of that subject to California mission collections. In 1843 Nuestra Señora del Refugio was declared the patroness of the diocese of both Californias. Still later in the nineteenth century, Victorian-style paintings of Santa Vibiana gained popularity and were disseminated to those missions still functioning, including Santa Inés, San Juan Bautista, and Santa Cruz.

During the period of secularization and abandonment, much of the fine and decorative art of the missions was rescued and moved to different locations, often to an active parish. Santa Inés, with its remarkably large collection of original art and other church items, likely received objects not only from Mission San Miguel but also from neighboring Mission La Purísima when it fell into ruins. Mission San Luis Rey retains many items from the Mission San Diego and San Diego Royal Presidio Chapel collections. Sets of the Vía Crucis were also moved around between missions, so the ones on display today at a particular mission may not have originated there. Unfortunately, many pieces of art at the missions were not saved. When Henry Miller visited Mission San Carlos Borromeo in 1856 he noted that the church was partly fallen in and that "some saints, as large as life, cut in wood and painted, are still to be seen; they are riddled with bullets, having served as a target."[43]

In the twentieth century, when restoration of the missions began, those whose restoration was completed first were often given church furnishings of still-decrepit missions. Many artworks originally from Mission San Antonio, for example, are now displayed in Mission San Miguel, and many objects originally belonging to Mission Soledad can be seen at the Royal Presidio Chapel in Monterey. Similarly, when Mission San Carlos Borromeo was restored, the vestments and silver vessels of both Soledad and the Monterey Royal Presidio Chapel were transferred to its museum. Improved understanding of early Baroque mission decoration and its precedents in Mexico led to a revival of the Baroque in mission architecture in the latter part of the twentieth century. Following this new fashion, a sumptuous sixteenth-century gilt *retablo* from Ezcaray, Spain, was installed at San Fernando Rey in 1991.

The altar arrangements in the restored missions of today also reflect changes in liturgy, now featuring large crucifixes on the altars, often with Nuestra Señora de Dolores (Sorrowing Mother) on the left and San Juan on the right, as at Mission San Carlos Borromeo and the Royal Presidio Chapel. Over time, images of the Immaculate Conception have been moved from the main altars, perhaps because of changes in doctrine, iconographic preference, or emphasis in the religious orders administering the churches. Although many original paintings and statues may be removed from missions' main altars and naves for display in museums and side chapels, these venerable items, ever vulnerable to the vicissitudes of time and climate, are still regarded with devotion and respect. It is heartening to see that they are increasingly being conserved and restored.

OPPOSITE: **Nuestra Señora del Refugio (Our Lady of Refuge) was widely venerated by the Zacatecan priests who administered many of the Alta California missions after 1821. This striking painting resides at Mission San Francisco de Asís.** Photograph by G. Aldana

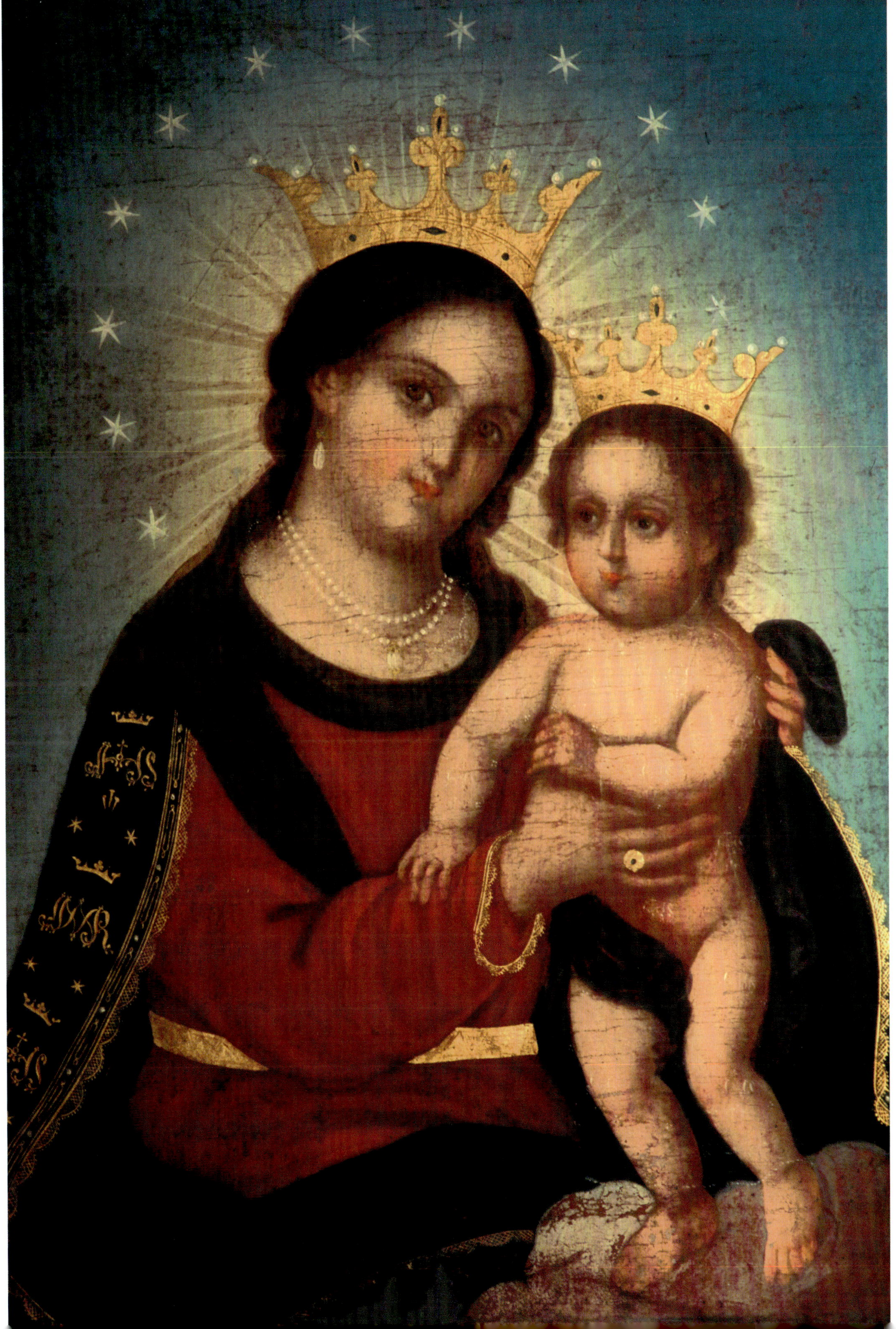

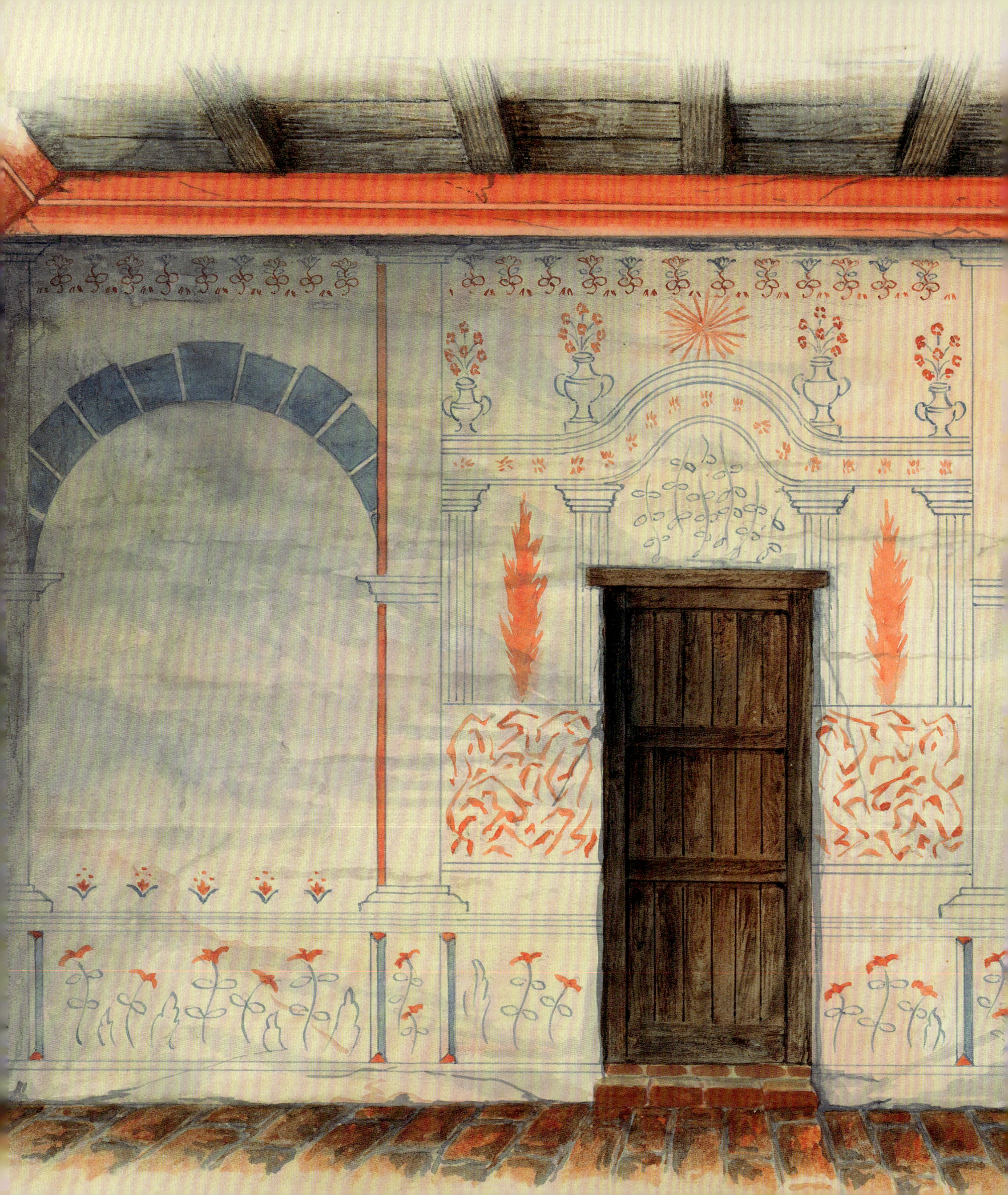

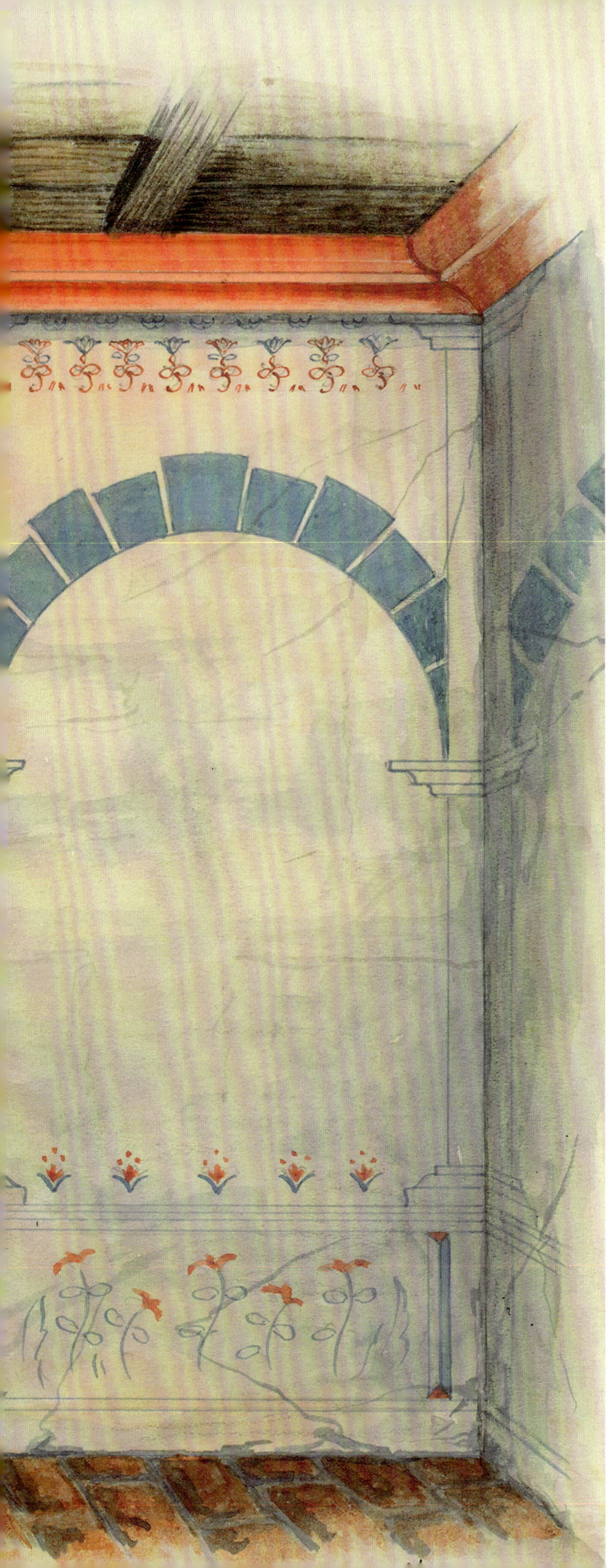

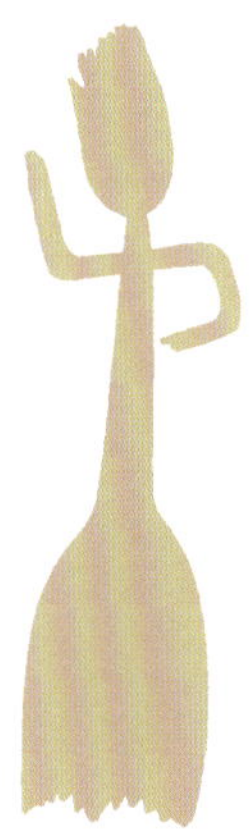

Chapter Six

PAINTING AND PAINTERS IN EARLY CALIFORNIA

Preparing for a fiesta at Mission San Fernando Rey in 1936, celebrants were hanging decorations in rooms in the *convento* when a large piece of plaster fell off a wall. The plaster split open, revealing colorful painted designs that had long been hidden under layers of whitewash. The timing of this discovery could not have been more fortuitous, for it coincided with the work being done by the artists of the Index of American Design, the program established in the early days of the New Deal to record the nation's artistic treasures. Index artists who visited the mission soon after the discovery "were quick to recognize [the] possibilities. They examined the fallen plaster and looked to the doorways and other locations for any slight traces of decoration. On the standing walls, careful lest they might break further large areas of plaster from the adobe walls, a gentle tapping and flaking process was evolved to loosen the whitewash and plaster, layer by layer."[1]

LEFT: Artists from the Index of American Design, studying fragments of faded plaster, reconstituted this wall design in the "Governor's Room" at Mission San Fernando Rey's *convento* in 1937. Geoffrey Holt and Harry Mann Waddell, *Restoration Drawing: Wall Painting and Door.* Watercolor, colored pencil, pen and ink, and graphite on paper. Image courtesy of the Board of Trustees, National Gallery of Art, Washington, D.C.

ABOVE: Native American painting of the traditional deity Tobet, venerated by the Tongva, Acjachemem, and Luiseño peoples, on a wall of the Serra Chapel at Mission San Juan Capistrano.

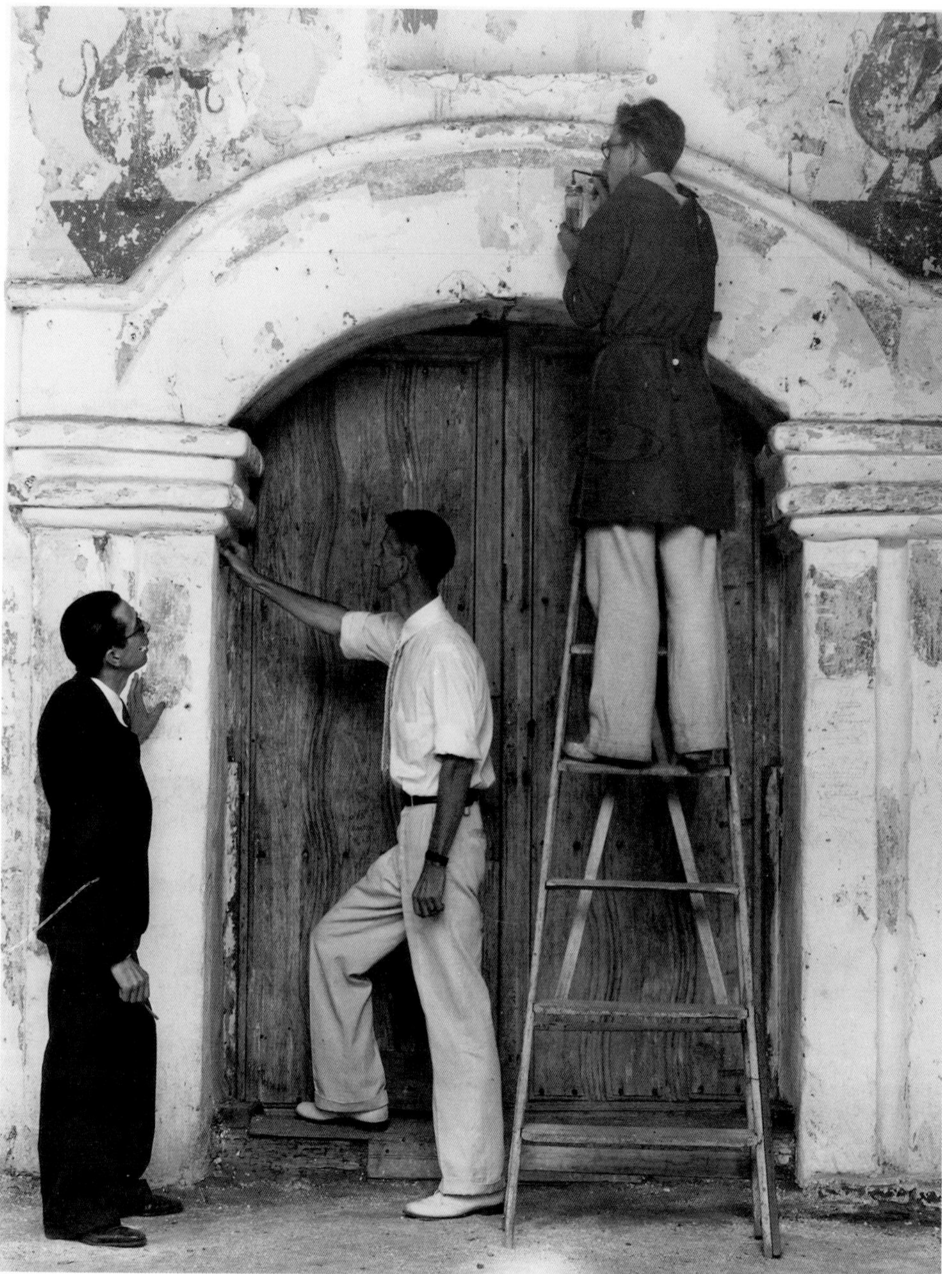

Artists from the Index of American Design examine the entryway to the *convento*'s *sala* at Mission San Fernando Rey, ca. 1937. The artists were trained to duplicate precisely the wall decorations. In most cases, their artistic renderings are all that survive of these historic murals. Courtesy of the Board of Trustees, National Gallery of Art, Washington, D.C., Gallery Archives

Once the layers of plaster and whitewash were removed from the *convento* walls, the artists found brightly painted designs, with colorful dados (bands of decoration on lower walls), cornices, and embellishments around openings. Some of these design elements appeared to be of Native American rather than European origin. The *convento*'s extensive decoration was carefully documented with photography, drawings, and stunningly detailed watercolors, which have come to provide the only available record of these now-vanished original murals.[2] In the nearby mission church, which was nearly in ruins, fragments of plaster suggested salmon-colored murals and doorways adorned with simulated stone arches in black and blue. Although the extensive decoration of Mission San Miguel was well known, the San Fernando Rey discovery suggested that such murals might be much more common than previously believed. Index artists were inspired to continue their research under surface plaster at several other missions, where additional original wall decorations were indeed found.[3] Over the years, the fragile nature of these murals—susceptible to

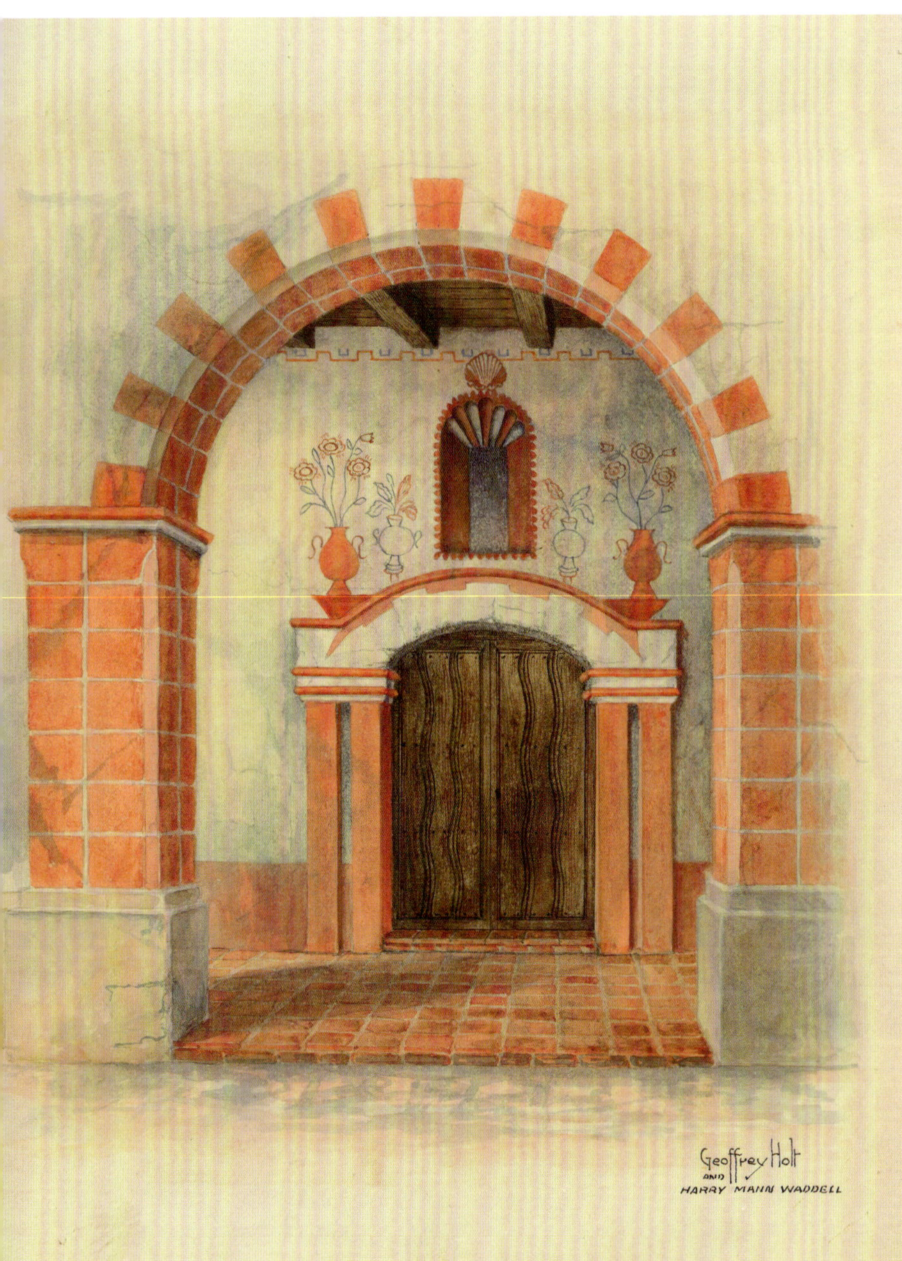

both deterioration and renovations—had resulted in tragic losses. The once lively and evocative walls conveying the mood and atmosphere of California's mission world had been whitewashed or plastered over and were largely forgotten for almost a century.

The art of painting in the California missions dates to the first establishments. In 1771, within months of the mission's founding, the resident fathers at Mission San Gabriel wrote back to Mexico, requesting, among other items, a dozen artists' paintbrushes and a book about "*Pintar sin Maestro, o algo semejante*" (Painting without a Teacher, or something similar).[4] Over the next few decades, with the difficulties of transporting goods from San Blas to Alta California and the growing numbers of converts, priests throughout the mission system sought to develop artists among their congregations. Judging by travelers' accounts, a fair number of canvas paintings must have been produced. "The nave, the altar, and the vestry are decorated with paintings, the best ones of which came from Mexico," noted the French captain Auguste Bernard Duhaut-Cilly, visiting Mission Santa Bárbara in 1827–28. "The rest are from the hand of the Indians themselves."[5] Generally of simple execution, these native works were not preserved as often as was art imported from Mexico and New Spain.

Of these easel paintings on canvas, perhaps the most enthralling of neophyte art, only two examples survive: a cycle of the Vía Crucis executed at Mission San Fernando in the 1820s and a rare painting of the archangel San Rafael at Mission Santa Inés (see pp. 132–33 and p. 137). Stylistically similar in their linearity, lack of perspective, and directness of expression, these paintings are deeply moving as tangible cross-cultural communications from the past.

By far the most widespread form of painting was mural art. European wall painting has ancient roots, and in Spain it included both figurative Romanesque murals in the north and purely decorative Moorish designs in the south. In New Spain these elements were integrated with a lively and rich indigenous mural tradition to produce ornamental painting that was both more colorful and more intricate than its European antecedents. When California was colonized, it was this hybrid style that was carried into frontier areas.[6] Mission wall decoration bore some similarity to the rock art practiced for millennia by some native California groups, with the Chumash efforts being especially outstanding. Native California pictographs are generally believed to have been spiritual in nature and executed primarily by male shamans. Subjects appear to include mythological beings, cosmology, visions, ceremonial events, and prayers and offerings. Many sacred concepts were likely hidden in geometric motifs that bear only symbolic relationships to the meanings behind them. Elaborate body painting was also popular among precontact tribes. The Chumash also colorfully decorated their canoes, grave markers, and other amenable items. It is likely that the local affinity for painted decorations encouraged the neophytes' appreciation for colorful mission murals.

Artistic rendering, ca. 1937, of the wall decorations at Mission San Fernando Rey seen on the facing page, as well as the entry's corridor arch. The faded colors are shown in their original hues, and vases of flowers on top of the lintel are brought back to life. The exterior of the colonnade was decorated with a faux stone-and-tile design. Geoffrey Holt and Harry Mann Waddell, *Restoration Drawing: Main Doorway and Arch to Mission House*. Watercolor, colored pencil, and graphite on paper. Image courtesy of the Board of Trustees, National Gallery of Art, Washington, D.C.

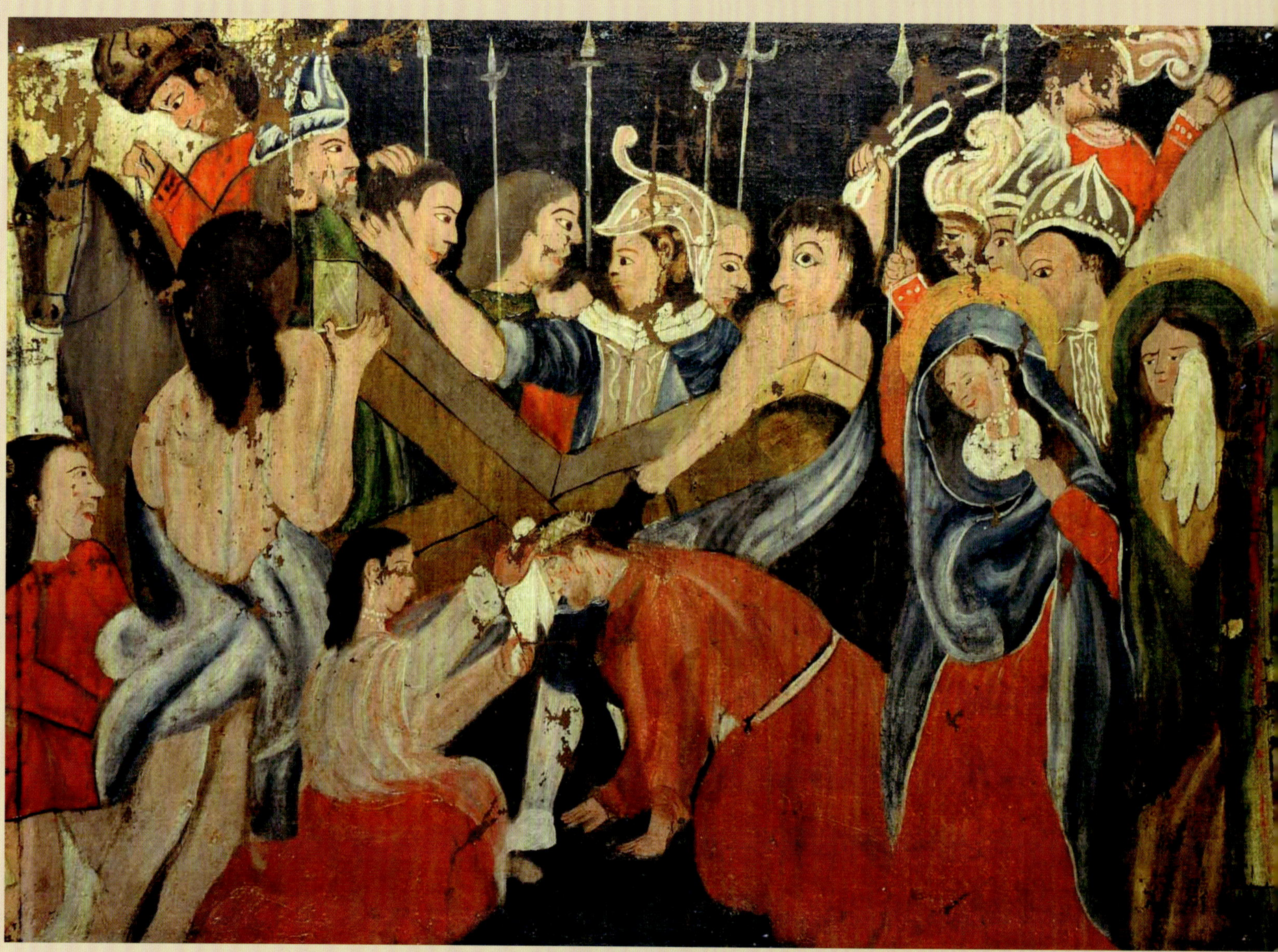

A Native American Vía Crucis

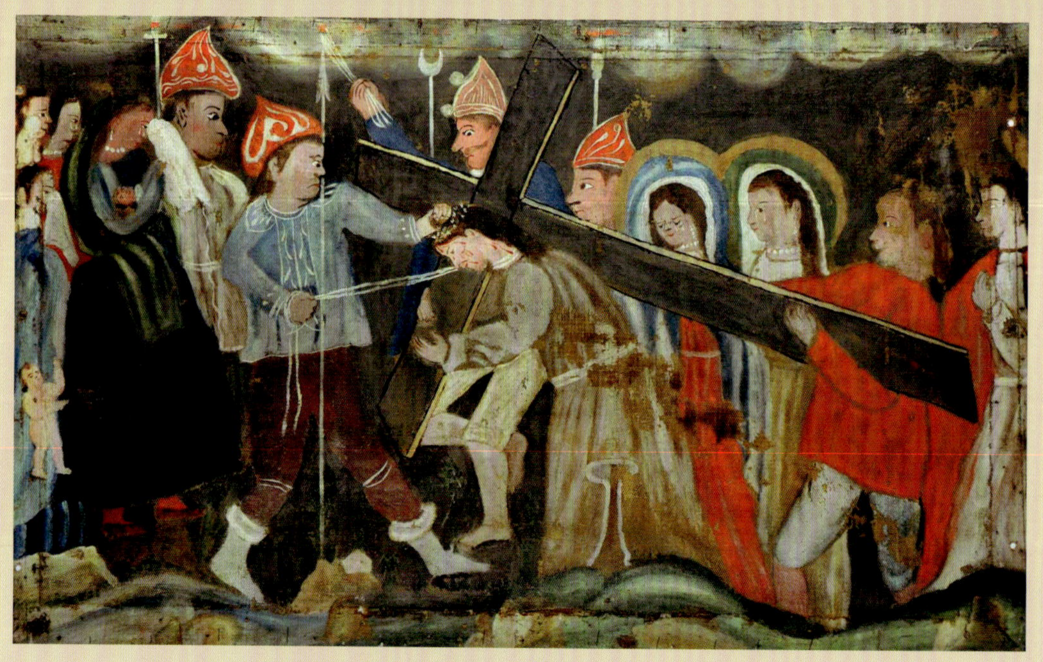

The most famous Native American paintings of the mission era are certainly the fourteen Stations of the Cross (Vía Crucis) produced at Mission San Fernando and now residing at Mission San Gabriel. The fourteen stations of Jesus' progress along the road to Calvary had been standardized into iconic scenes that often lined the nave walls of a mission church. For newly founded missions, these images were typically displayed on small prints until canvas paintings could be obtained. At Mission San Fernando, instead of ordering a set of Vía Crucis paintings from Mexico, the neophytes painted their own versions.

The first reference to the completed works is in the 1849 inventory at San Fernando, which lists "*la Via Sacra 14 cuadros muy ordinarios*" (a set of Stations of the Cross, 14 very ordinary pictures). The paintings remained at San Fernando until the 1870s, when they were removed and stored at the Plaza Church in Los Angeles. Rediscovered during the Mission Revival era,they were sent on tour: to the State Fair in Sacramento in 1892, and to the World's Columbian Exposition in Chicago in 1893, and then to the Los Angeles Chamber of Commerce. The works were finally transferred to Mission San Gabriel, where for a time they decorated an outside corridor before being hung in the museum, where they now rest. The Indian Vía Crucis is now protected as a famous asset of Mission San Gabriel and has been professionally restored; reproductions hang in their place in the San Gabriel nave.

A large body of literature exists about these works, much of which is inaccurate and has been countered by recent scholarly research.[7] They were thought to be the work of a single neophyte painter, Juan Antonio,[8] from the Ranchería de Topanga, but internal differences in technique and style reveal the hands of several Native American artists working in concert. Legends that the pigments were derived from flower petals and that the canvases were made from ships' sails have also been disproved.[9]

Sadly, the nineteenth-century prints that served as the models for these paintings have not been identified, except for one, an engraving of Station IV from a press in Mexico City. It is clear that the San Fernando Indians inserted variations on its figures and setting, a license presumably taken with the other images as well.

What is most intriguing is that these innovations by the Indian painters may provide a glimpse into the minds of the artists themselves. Are they creating a faithful Catholic rendering of the story of the Crucifixion, or is there encoded in the works a statement of Native American defiance of the Spanish colonial occupation? The art historian Norman Neuerburg and the historian George Harwood Phillips differ in their interpretations of many of the images, although both agree that the man holding the base of the cross in Station IV appears to be a neophyte. Neuerburg further suggests that it may be a self-portrait of the artist. Phillips sees other depictions of neophytes, distinguished variously by their features, skin color, and clothing. Most persuasive is Station VI, where Veronica (wiping Christ's face) and the two men holding the cross appear to be Indians.[10] Phillips goes on to suggest that the native artists "turned some of Christ's Roman persecutors into Spaniards . . . with huge, unintelligent eyes and sinister grotesque expressions."[11] Two of Christ's civilian tormentors in Station VII, Phillips thought earlier, might depict neophyte *alcaldes*, many of whom abused their powers. Reconsidering this first assessment some thirty years later, Phillips has concluded, "This now seems a bit of a stretch, but who knows?" Indeed, modern scholarship has exposed evidence of native defiance of government and church laws through careful examination of primary documents. Why not also through art?

Disparities between possible print models for the Vía Crucis scenes and the Mission San Fernando paintings continue to provide fodder for speculation. Much of this debate might be settled if a full set of the original print models were found. The true meaning of these remarkable works, however, will likely forever remain a mystery—emblematic, perhaps, of the complex and layered history of the missions themselves.

Three paintings from the Vía Crucis (Stations of the Cross) painted by Juan Antonio and other neophyte artists at Mission San Fernando Rey. OPPOSITE ABOVE: Station 6, *Veronica Wipes the Face of Jesus*. OPPOSITE BELOW: Station 8, *Jesus Meets the Daughters of Jerusalem*. BELOW: Station 9, *Jesus Falls for the Third Time*. In the view of some scholars, several figures in the paintings are depicted as Native American or Spanish; Veronica and the two men holding the cross in Station 6, for example, appear Indian in features and dress. Oil on canvas, ca. 1808–1820s. Photographs by Bill Dewey

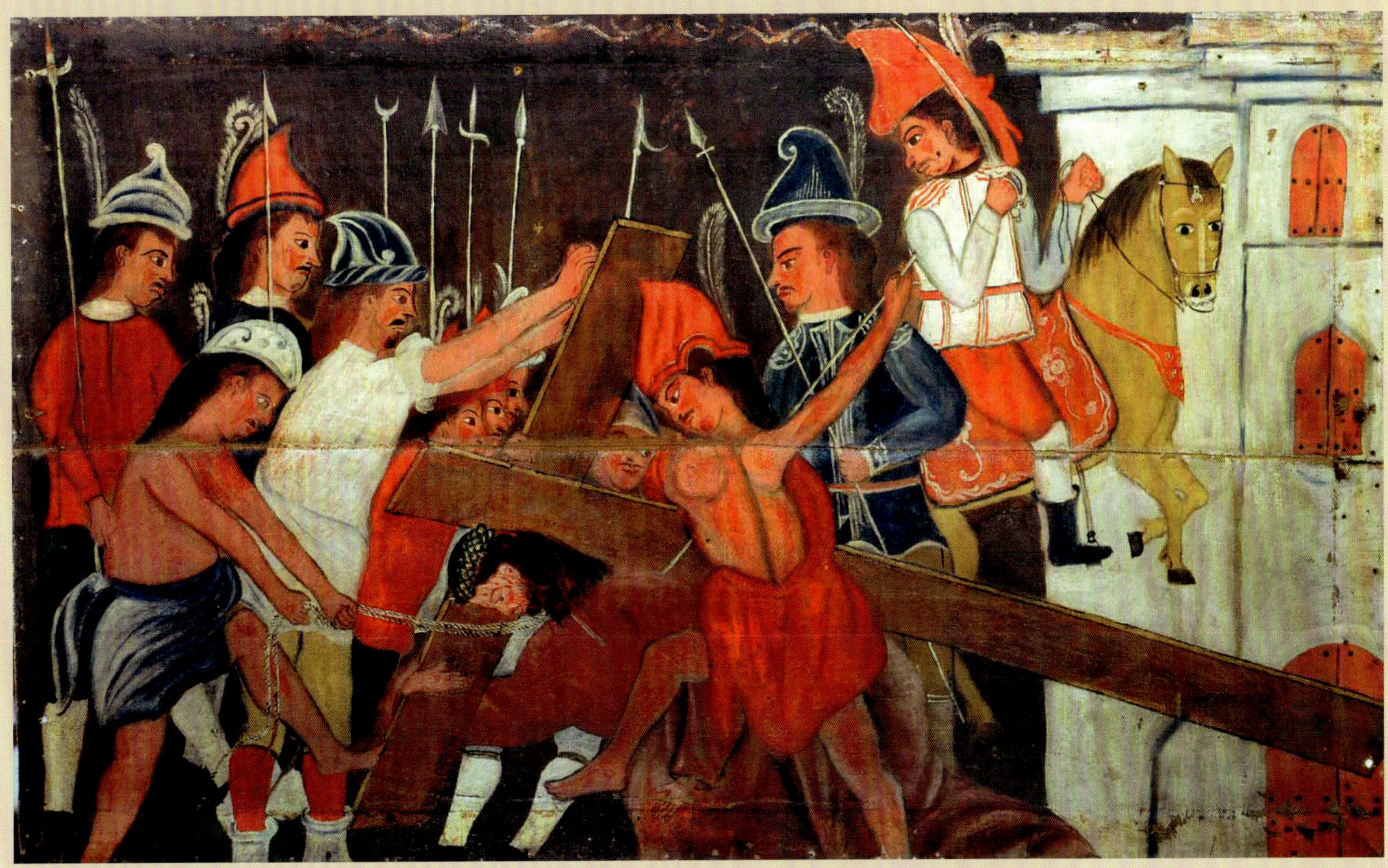

Both Indians and Spaniards were adept at making paints and pigments from local clays and minerals. Red was made from hematite (red ochre) and cinnabar, white from diatomaceous earth (chalklike fossil rock), and black from charcoal, burned graphite, and asphaltum. To these sources the Spanish added pigments imported from Mexico. Requisition lists from Mission Santa Bárbara in 1797 and 1800, for example, include three pounds of *cardenillo* (verdigris, for green); three pounds of *almagre* (red ochre); two pounds each of *bermellón* (vermilion), orange color, purple ochre, and yellow ochre; and three bottles of linseed oil, used as a binder.[12] Paintbrushes were requisitioned, as well as made of local materials.

The painted zones on mission walls followed period styles in Europe. One of the most prominent features comprised carefully executed designs that mimicked architectural embellishments unavailable in this frontier outpost. As cut stone for pilasters, window surrounds, and corner quoins was not easily available—and marble was unattainable—these architectural elements were reproduced in painted designs, some realistic and some fanciful. The painted dado running around the base of the walls could consist of simple bands of color or repetitive geometric or vinelike floral designs. The cornice or frieze at the top of the walls could be marbleized or display a geometric pattern, as with the Greek design at Mission Santa Bárbara; a simulated lambrequín (valance) or cloth swag, as at San Luis Rey and San Buenaventura; rows of flowers, as at San Fernando Rey; a balustrade, as at San Miguel; or a Doric frieze, as at San Carlos Borromeo.[13] Side wall fill patterns were reminiscent of both traditional cloth hangings in European churches and wallpaper, which "arrived in California at least as early as 1795 when hand-painted Chinese wallpaper was used to cover the walls of the baptistery at Mission Santa Clara."[14] Wallpaper rolls on the invento-

Exploratory work by the artists from the Index of American Design included removal of overpainted surfaces to reveal the designs still present on earlier layers. These walls of the Governor's Room at Mission San Fernando Rey shows the results of that exposure in 1936. Courtesy of the Board of Trustees, National Gallery of Art, Washington, D.C.

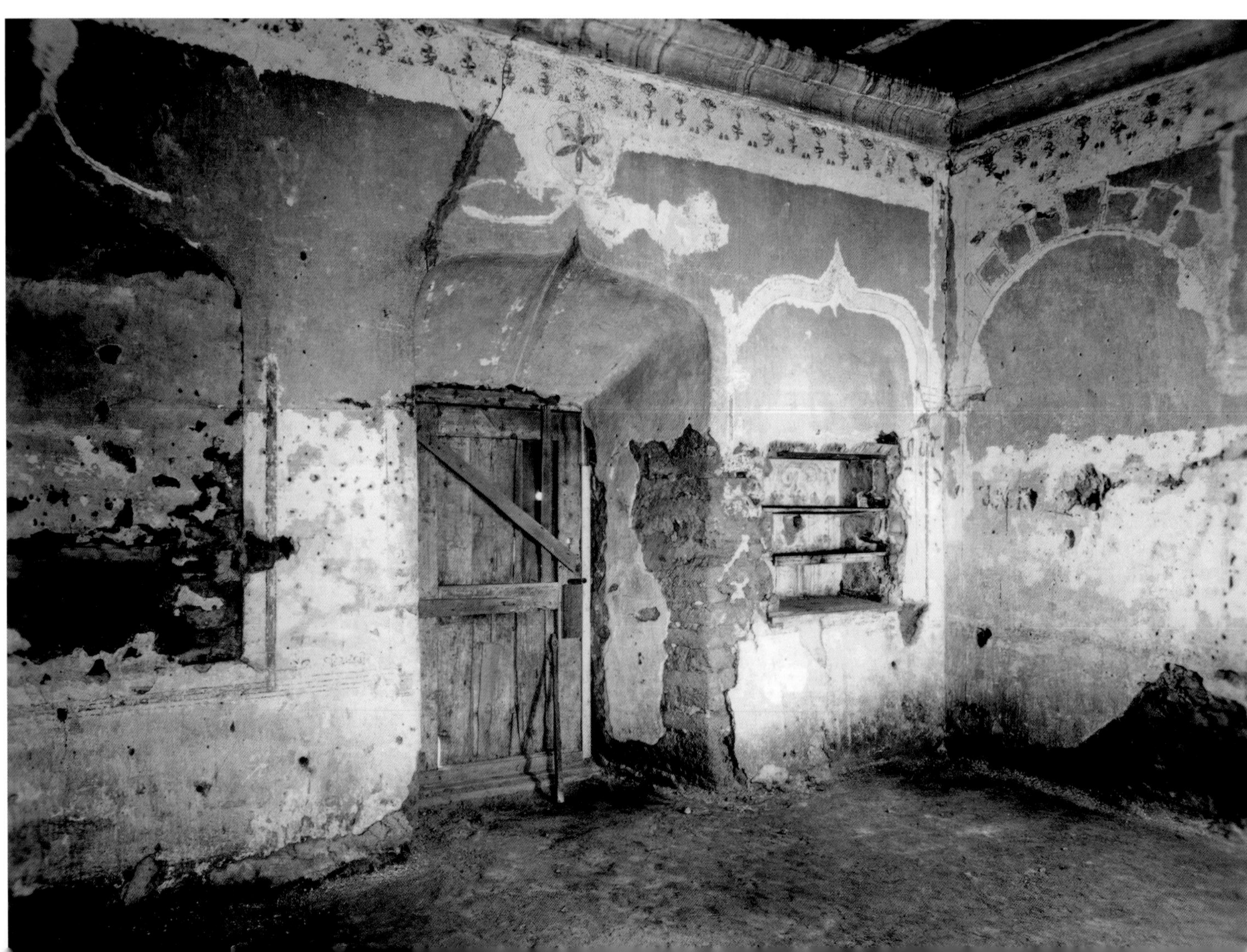

ries of Missions Santa Bárbara and San José had geometric, floral, and religious motifs that enlivened the broad whitewashed surfaces. Windows and door openings were frequently embellished, and ceiling rafters and corbels were usually brightly decorated.[15] With the possible exception of San Rafael, painted decorations adorned the interior walls of virtually all the mission churches and many rooms in *conventos*, most famously at San Fernando Rey. As for other mission buildings, although our knowledge is limited by the few such structures that have survived, painted decoration has been found on the doorway to a water filter house at La Purísima, and a leading scholar has stated that "decoration was probably the norm rather than the exception throughout the missions."[16] The earliest mission-era wall painting may be that in the Santa Bárbara Presidio chapel, said to have been produced by the soldier Tomás González in 1784. Unfortunately, the mural no longer exists. Most of the surviving original mission wall decoration was likely executed between 1810 and the early 1820s, although painting was being done at Santa Clara and San José in the mid-1830s.[17]

Painted decorations could be executed as soon as a mission had whitewashed the walls of its adobe buildings, and painting was probably the final stage of a building's construction. Planning the mural began with the selection of motifs, which were readily available from drawings, prints, ornamented books, and fabrics.[18] Some artisans may well have brought pattern books with them to California. The designs were commonly laid out over the surface of a whitewashed wall by etching their contours into the dry plaster. True "fresco" painting was rare in Alta California, identified only recently at the Royal Presidio Chapel in Monterey (see p. 162). This technique is executed on wet plaster, allowing the paint to bond with the wall surface and resulting in a more durable finish.[19]

Artistic rendering, ca. 1939, of the original wall decoration at Mission San Fernando Rey seen on the facing page. A decorative frieze runs around the top of the wall, and a floral dado of flowers enlivens the wall's base. Three painted Moorish arches define the doorway and two side spaces, one of which contains a niche with shelves. Geoffrey Holt and Harry Mann Waddell, *Restoration Drawing: Wall Painting.* Watercolor, colored pencil, pen and ink, and graphite on paper. Image courtesy of the Board of Trustees, National Gallery of Art, Washington, D.C.

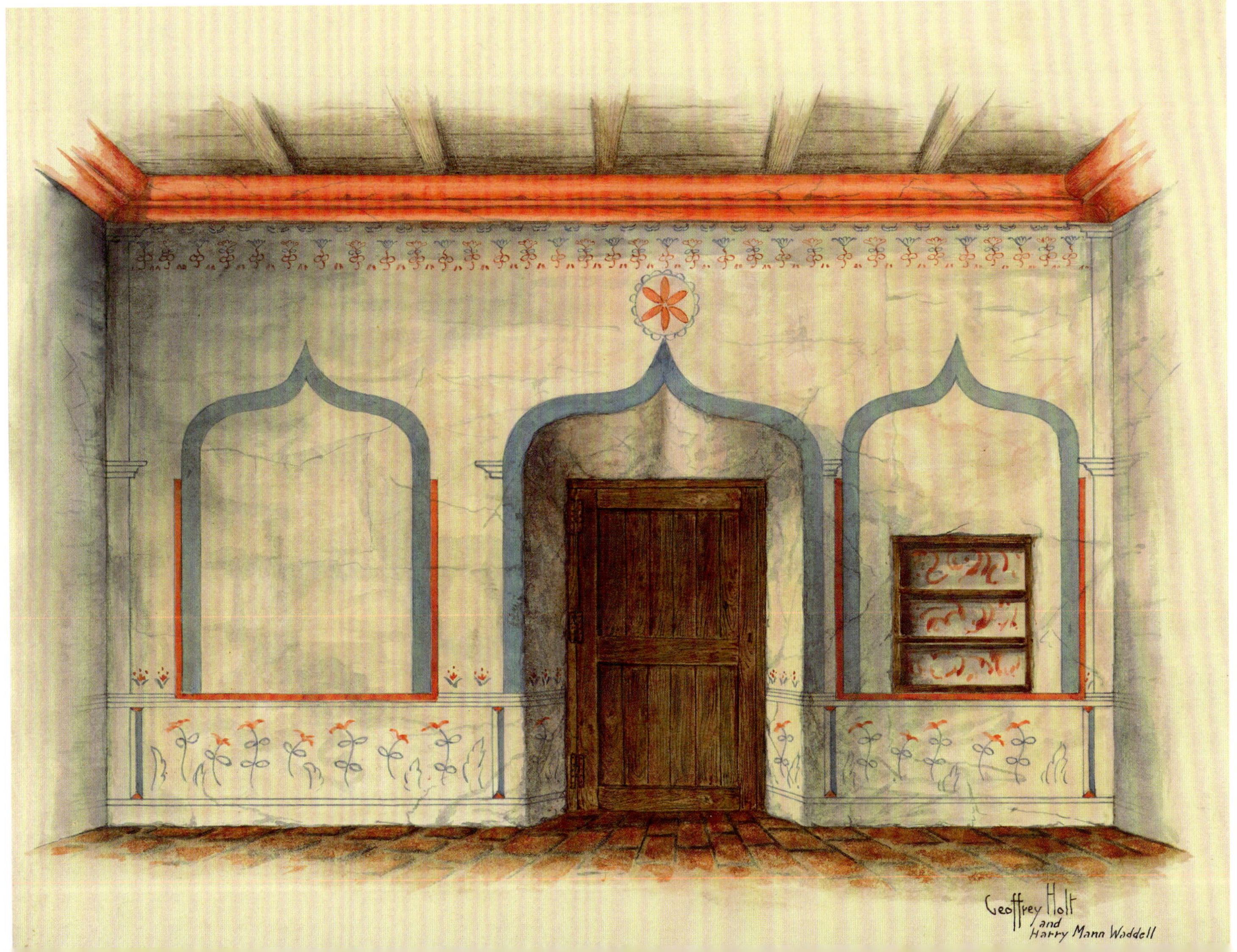

Straight lines were established by the use of a pigmented string stretched taut and snapped, similar to chalk snap lines of today. Evidence of both etching and snap lines has been identified on mission walls. Pigments would be prepared with an oil binder, and the designs would then be infilled, with the individual painters perhaps holding their colors in seashells, such as those preserved at Mission San Miguel. A single artisan would have directed each project, assisted on large undertakings by a number of trained neophytes. During the life of a mission original designs could be modified or changed, a process that began in the Spanish period and continues to the present day. The old wall surface was overpainted with a new coat of whitewash or, in some cases, a new layer of lime plaster, before the new design was executed.[20] Some of these mural designs can be attributed to specific artisans, but most were created by anonymous individuals—artisans and neophytes, foreign visitors, presidio soldiers and clergy.

One of the most important known artists was the Catalan merchant and painter Esteban Munras, who came from Barcelona and settled in Monterey around 1820. He is largely

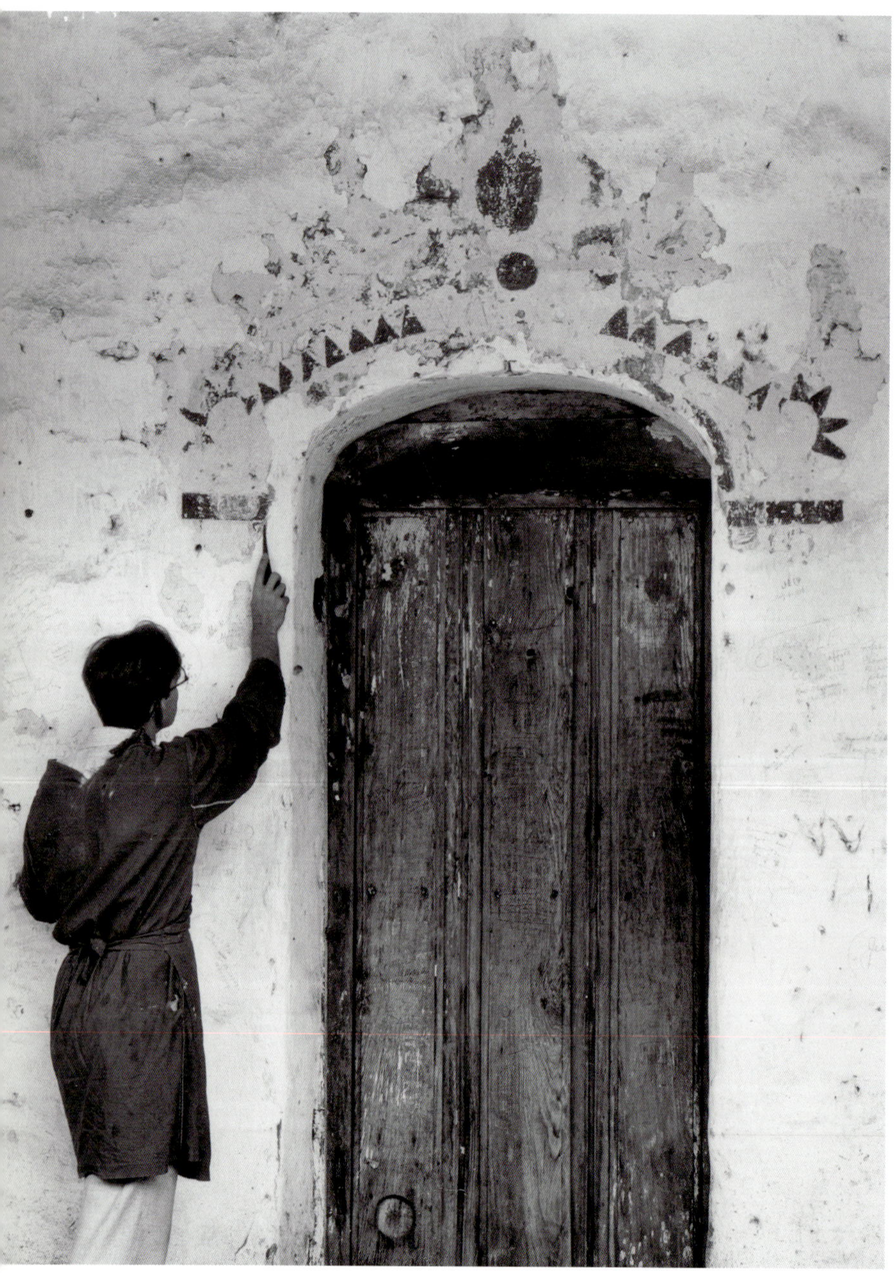

BELOW LEFT: This artist from the Index of American Design is shown gently removing a more recent layer of plaster, exposing the underlying painted designs over an exterior door on the *convento* at Mission San Fernando Rey, ca. 1939. National Gallery of Art, Washington, D.C., Gallery Archives

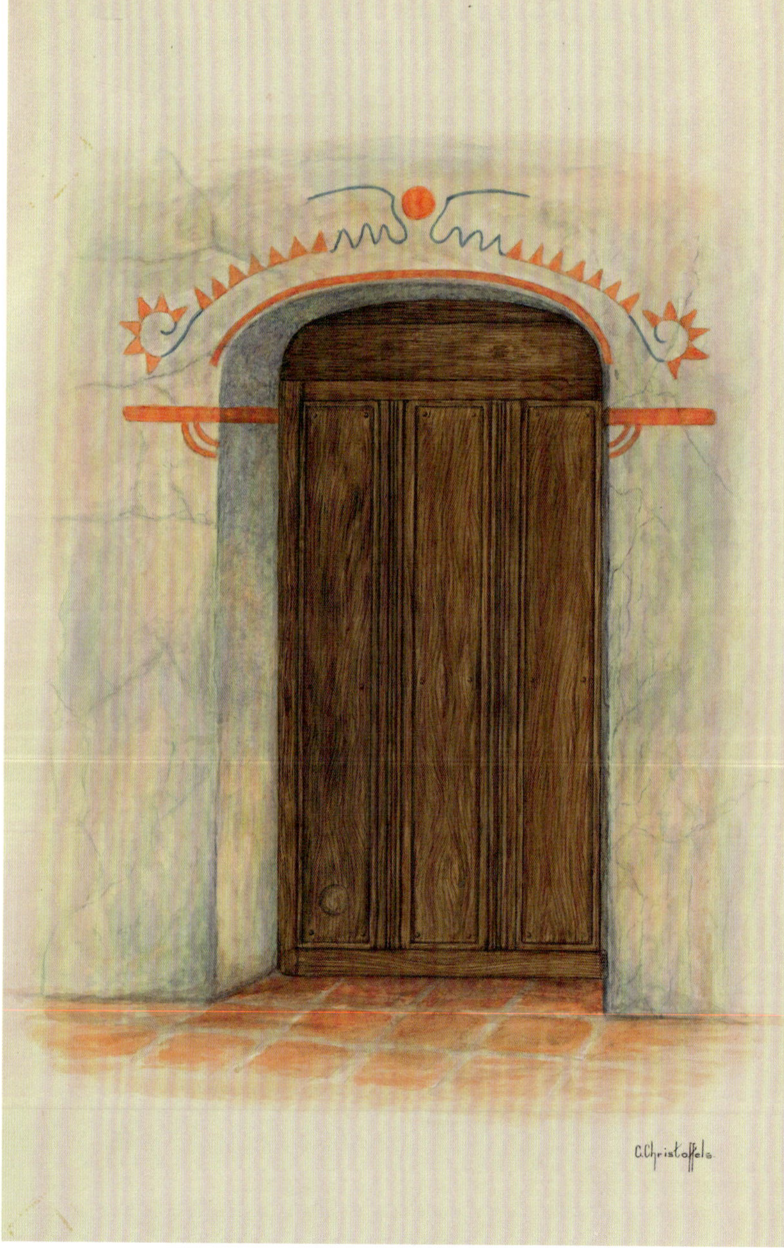

BELOW RIGHT: Artistic rendering of the original decoration on the wall of the Mission San Fernando *convento,* 1941. Cornelius Christoffois, *Restoration Drawing: Wall Painting and Door, Façade of Mission House.* Watercolor, colored pencil, and graphite on paper. Image courtesy of the Board of Trustees, National Gallery of Art, Washington, D.C.

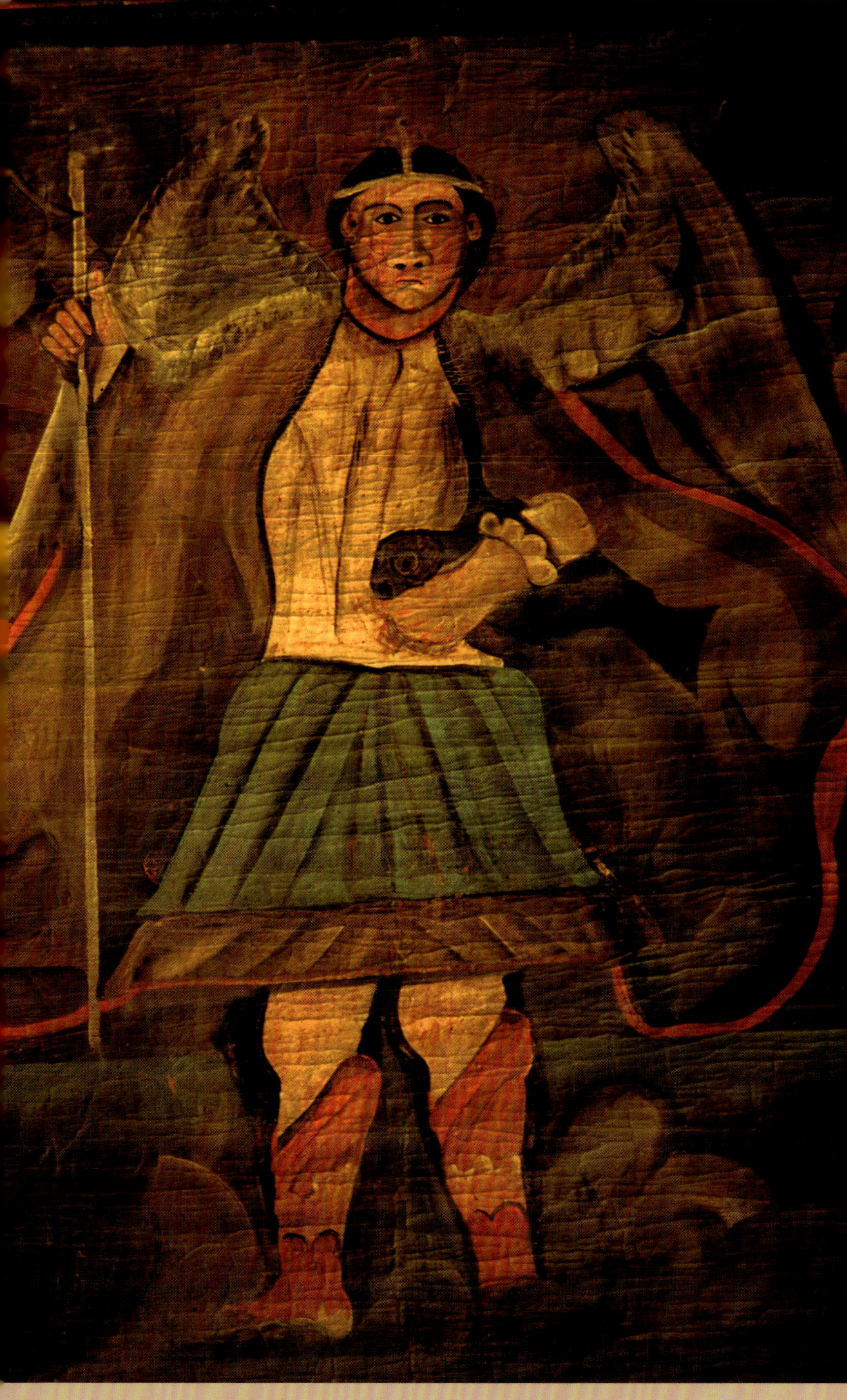

A Chumash San Rafael

Along with the Stations of the Cross, the only known surviving Indian canvas painting from the mission period is a depiction of the archangel San Rafael by a Chumash artist at Mission Santa Inés. It poses an intriguing question: Why does it portray San Rafael, when San Miguel was one of the most popular saints of the California missions and represented much more frequently in mission art? The answer may in the attribute always associated with San Rafael: a fish.

The Chumash were the most accomplished mariners in pre-Spanish Alta California, colonizing the Channel Islands in oceangoing canoes and regularly harvesting fish with both nets and lines. During the mission period they continued their deepwater fishing, encouraged by the fathers to supplement the food supply. Since the Chumash traditionally carved effigies of wildlife, it seems reasonable to suppose that this image might possess several levels of meaning. Whereas the European saint always carries a slim fish suspended from a line, this fish is quite robust; and the Chumash San Rafael hugs it close to his body, as if it were a familiar companion. Also, the fish in the Chumash painting is larger than is usually the case, and therefore thematically more important. Rather than being a conventional depiction of the saint, is this a portrait of a distinguished Chumash leader, depicted as San Rafael and carrying an actual fish?

Portrait of San Rafael, Arcángel, by an anonymous Chumash artist at Mission Santa Inés. The saint is depicted with Native American features. Oil on canvas, ca. 1820. Photograph by G. Aldana

responsible for the incomparable decoration of the Mission San Miguel church, the only surviving, truly original church interior in California.[21] Munras is said to have carried out the artwork for his friend and fellow Catalonian Father Juan Martín, the mission's resident priest. The altar and pulpit may have been constructed by the Irish carpenter John Bones, who was at the mission in 1821 when Munras was working there.[22] Certainly these constructions and the wall designs were conceived as a unified whole. While Munras designed the unique coloration and extensive patterns, the painting was undoubtedly carried out with the assistance of trained neophytes living at San Miguel. The use of stencils can be identified in the precise repetition of the designs, which "are typically neoclassical but rather more colorful than would be found in non-frontier areas."[23]

The San Miguel church decoration is unequaled in color, diversity, and scope in Alta California. It is divided into three major areas: the entrance and choir, the nave, and the sanctuary. The entrance walls are a pale green framed with borders of a Greek key motif over a deep dusty pink dado with marbleizing, and the ceiling, the bottom of the choir loft, is blue with brown accent lines suggesting panels. The nave is lined with blue-painted

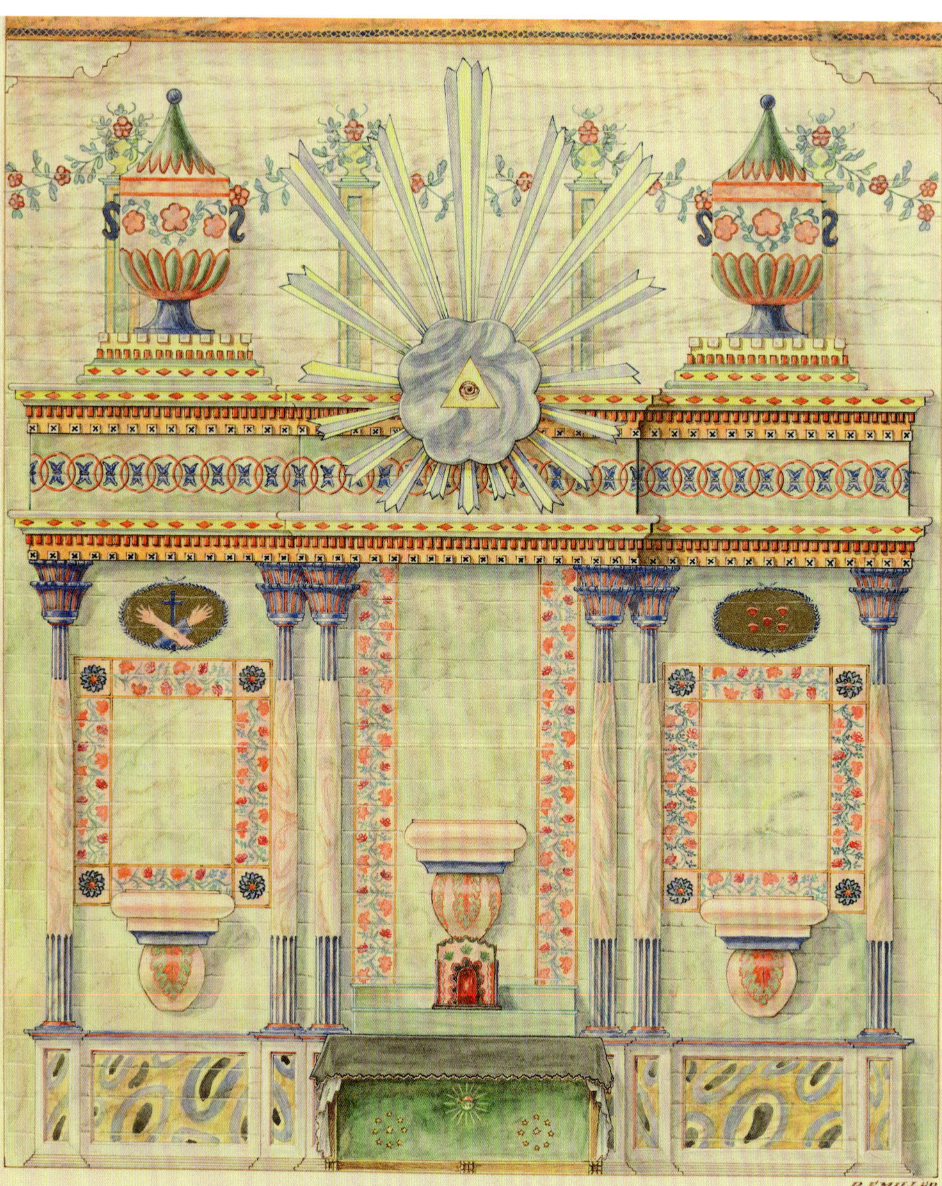

RIGHT: The rendering of wall decorations in the sanctuary of Mission San Miguel, Arcángel, completed by artists from the Index of American Design in 1937. Randall F. Miller, *Reredos and Wall Paintings.* Watercolor, colored pencil, pen and ink, gold ink and graphite on paper. Image courtesy of the Board of Trustees, National Gallery of Art, Washington, D.C.

OPPOSITE: The wall murals and *retablo* of the Mission San Miguel sanctuary in 1995, prior to the earthquake in 2003. The murals were conceived by the artist Esteban Munras and executed with the help of mission neophytes in 1821. As is evident from comparison with the rendering from some sixty years earlier (at right), the magnificent adornment has survived completely intact. Photograph by G. Aldana

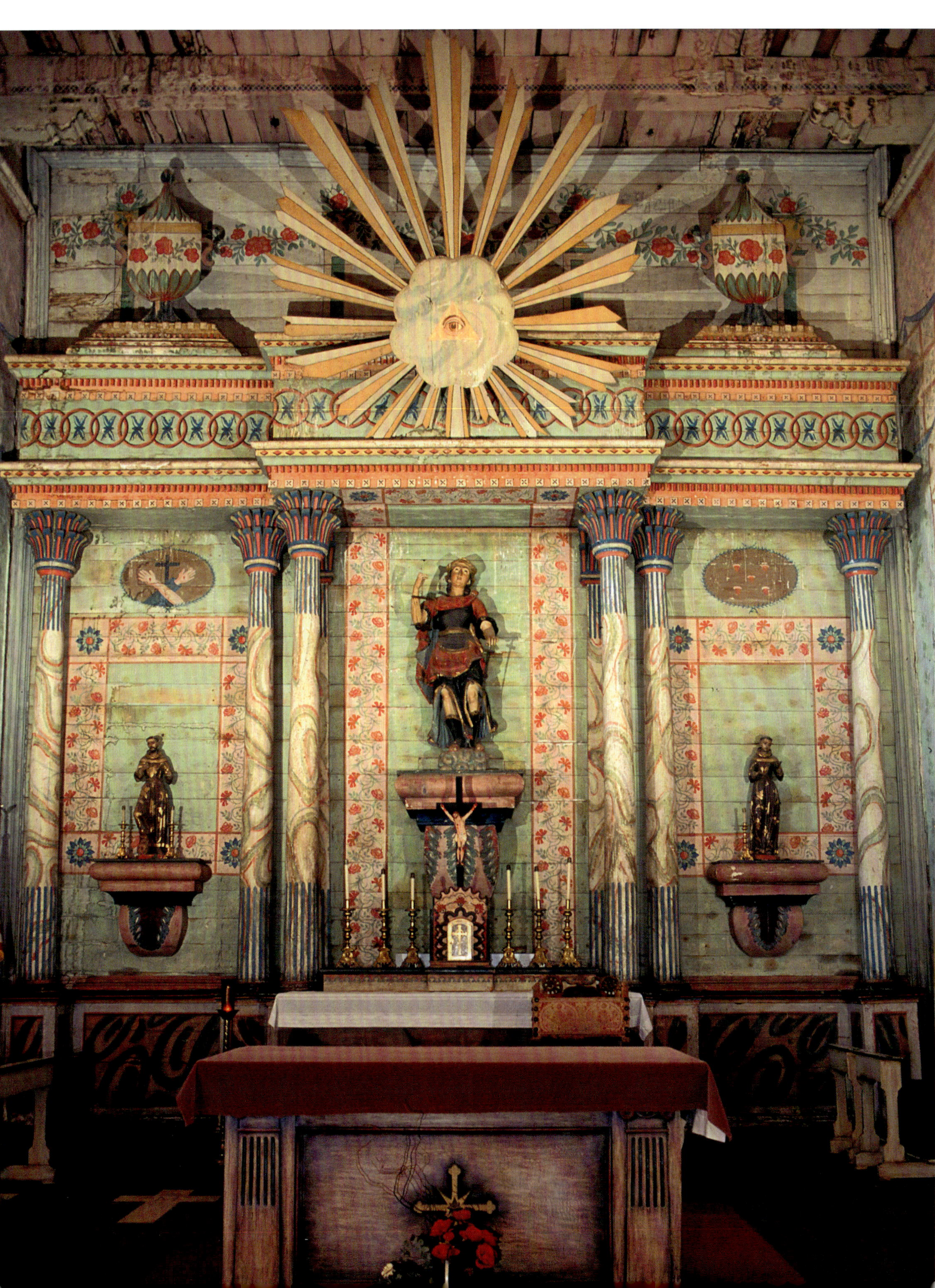

images of Roman Doric columns that, somewhat oddly, do not align with each other across the room. Between the columns are panels of pale green, suggesting sheets of cloth pulled tight, with stenciled leaf patterns resembling embroidery on their borders (see photos pp. 3 and 231). The nave ceiling is decorated similarly to that of the choir. The frieze is a painted balustrade suggesting a balcony encircling the room; the dado along the base of the walls simulates marble. The windows (with one exception) simply break through the wall patterns with no framing and "in total disregard to the designs on the walls."[24] The sanctuary walls are also painted to simulate hanging cloth, but here in tones of green, lavender, and pink, and side altars are rendered on the side panels. The sanctuary ceiling is exuberant with "designs stenciled in blue on pale pink: rosettes on the beams with a 'rattlesnake' band

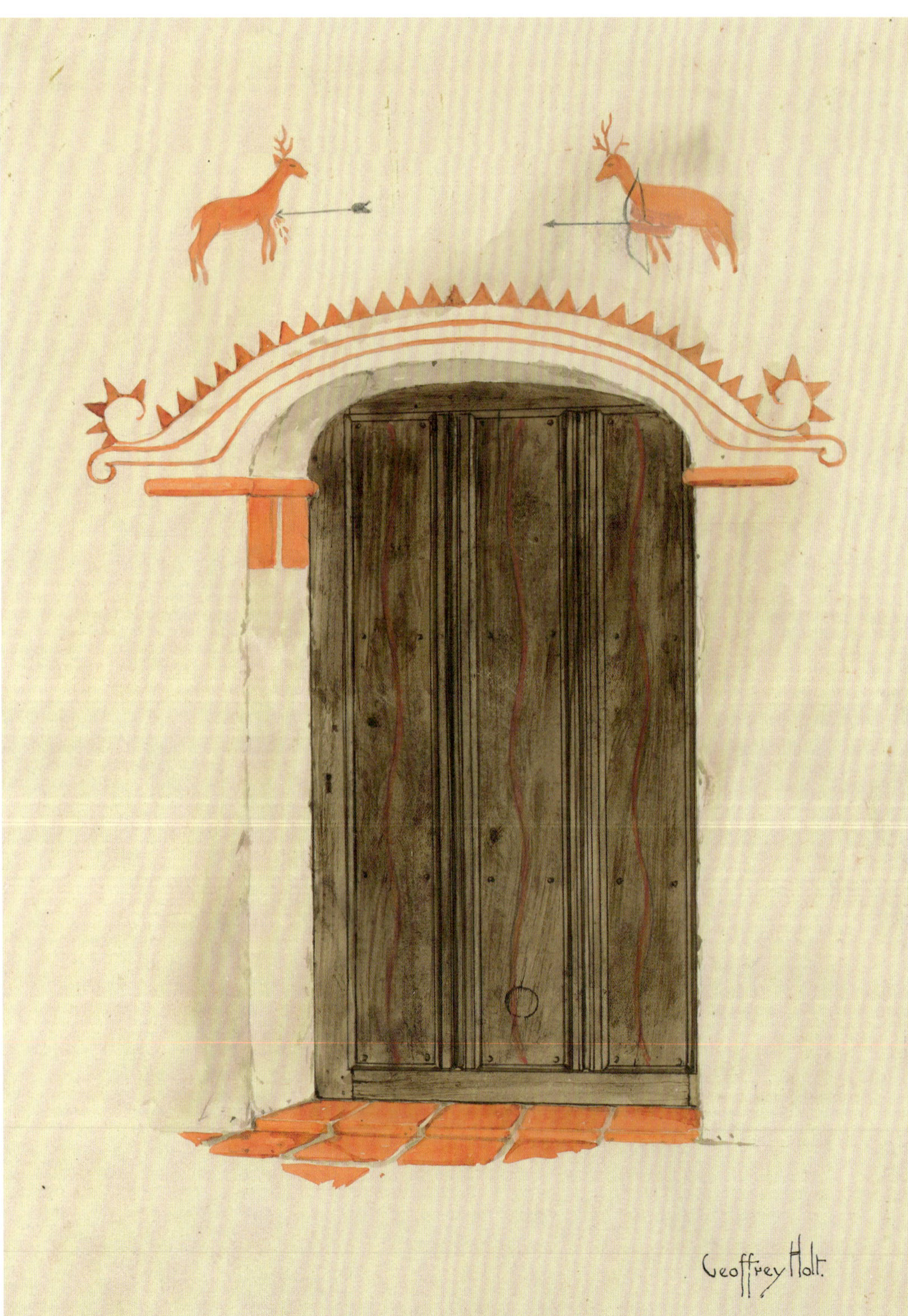

Artistic rendering of original wall decoration at Mission San Fernando Rey, 1937. This scene is perhaps the most famous of the San Fernando Rey murals. Placed over an exterior door in the *convento*, it depicts a deer (at left) being stalked by a Native American hunter wearing a deerskin camouflage. The depiction of this activity suggests that the neophytes continued some traditional practices. Geoffrey Holt, *Restoration Drawing: Wall Decoration over Doorway, Facade of Mission House.* Watercolor, colored pencil, pen and ink, and graphite on paper. Image courtesy of the Board of Trustees, National Gallery of Art, Washington, D.C.

along the side; larger motifs made up of oak leaves and small quatrefoils between wide bands of small dots on the panels between."[25] The adjoining sacristy is entirely covered with a wallpaper-type design of stenciled flowers topped with a wide frieze of grape tendrils on a pale yellow ground.[26]

Although European styles dominate at all missions, Native American motifs are also to be found. At the Mission San Fernando *convento*, for example, among the murals that the Index artists recorded were a vineyard scene and an Indian deer-hunting motif. Geometric forms could have come from either European or native traditions. Although generally ascribed to the former, they may have held a totally different significance to the Indians as symbols of their own traditions.[27]

Artistic rendering of Native American wall painting at Mission San Fernando Rey, 1937. This well-known vineyard scene from the *sala* in the *convento* shows four workers under tall, stout vines. When this mural was repainted during restorations in 1941, it was significantly altered, and much of its authenticity was lost. Geoffrey Holt, ***Restoration Drawing: Wall Decoration over Doorway in Mission House.*** Watercolor, colored pencil, pen and ink, and graphite on paper. Image courtesy of the Board of Trustees, National Gallery of Art, Washington, D.C.

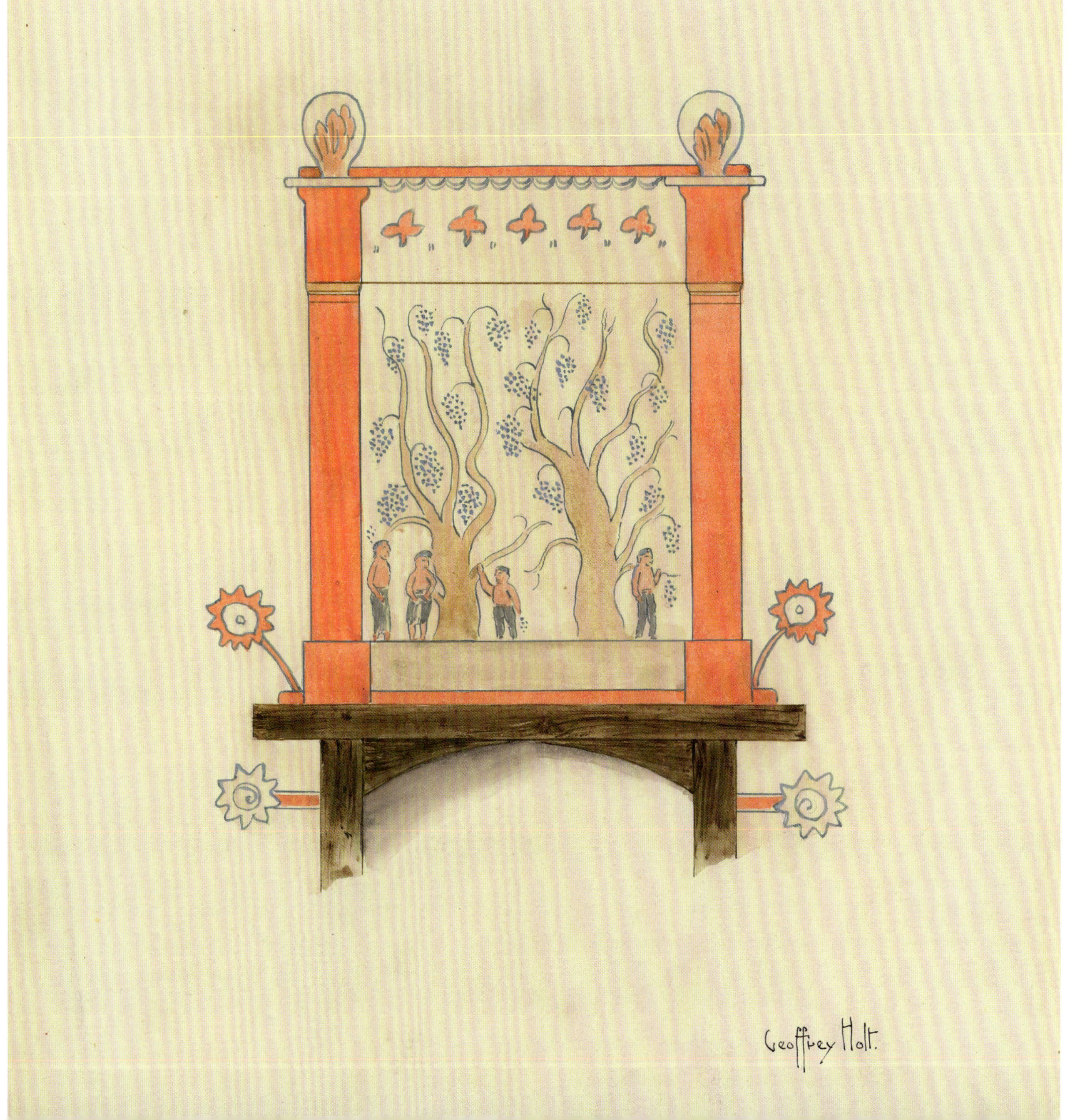

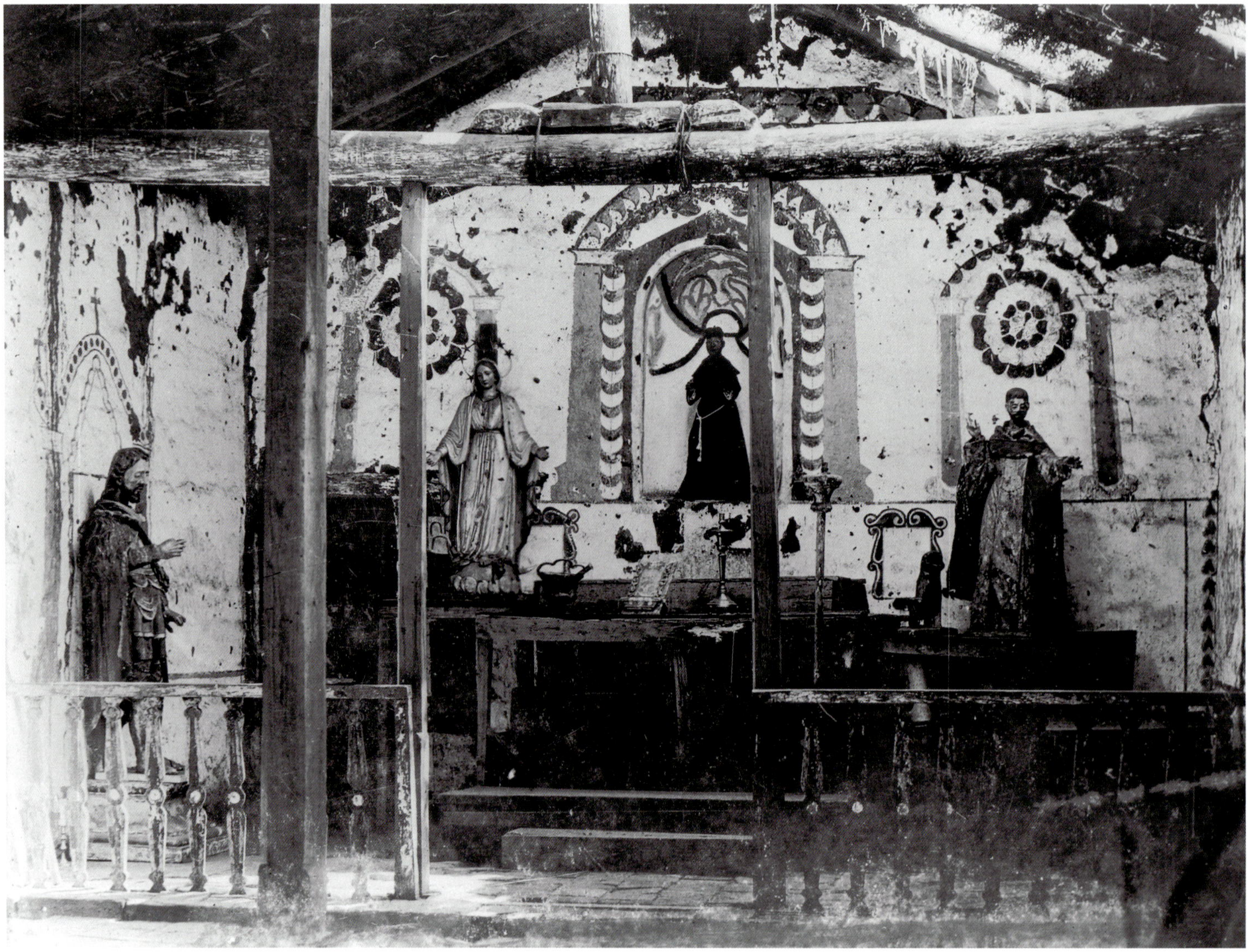

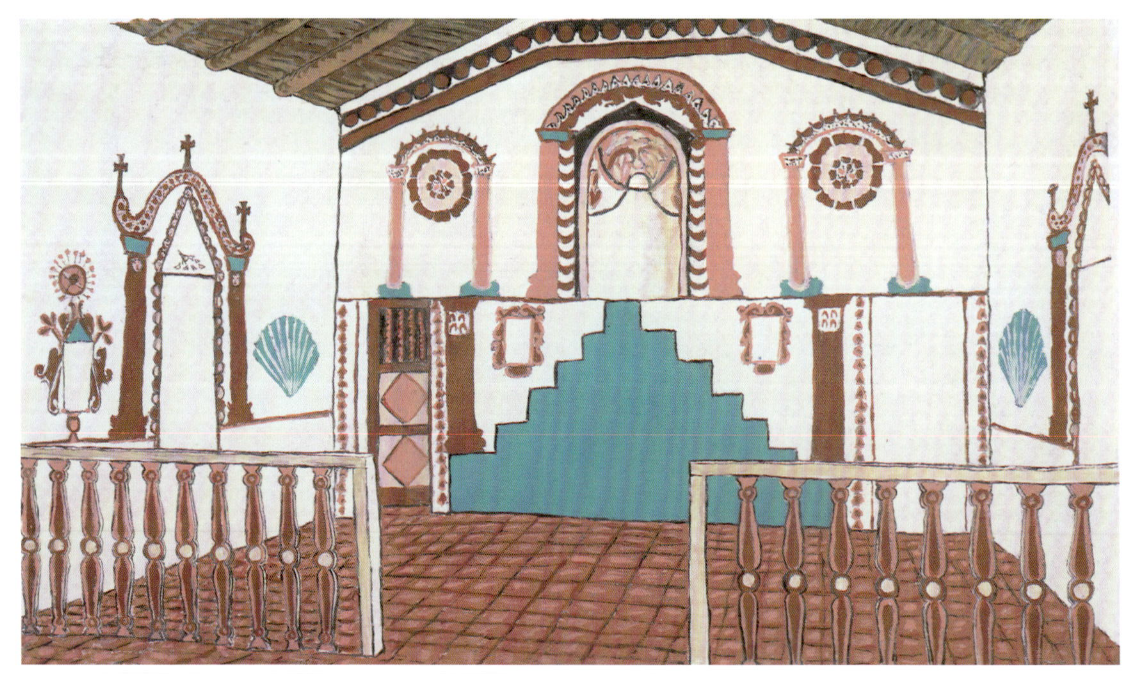

ABOVE: The sacristy at the *asistencia* San Antonio de Pala, ca. 1898. The abundant murals executed by resident neophytes associated with Mission San Luis Rey can be seen. The walls were whitewashed shortly after this photograph was taken, reportedly by a priest unaware of their importance to the native congregation. In the center is a wooden statue of San Antonio, also made by neophytes. Photograph by C. C. Pierce. Courtesy University of Southern California, on behalf of the USC Special Collections

RIGHT: Rendering by Norman Neuerburg depicting the murals in the sacristy at Pala Asistencia, without the wooden altar and statues, as they would have appeared when first completed in the 1820s. Courtesy of the Santa Bárbara Mission Archive-Library

Among the most extensive examples of neophyte art in California are the murals at the chapel at the Pala Asistencia, almost certainly designed and executed by the Luiseño neophytes working under only minimal supervision from the fathers at distant Mission San Luis Rey. They contain some of the most abundant Indian motifs, including birds, plants, and other elements similar to those found on baskets. All four walls were painted, with separate designs for the nave and sacristy. Columns connected by arches lined the body of the church, linked by a distinctive dado featuring crosses set into bases with curved tops. These designs, unfortunately, were among those whitewashed near the turn of the twentieth century, reportedly by a priest unaware of their importance to the native congregation. Fortunately, the walls had been extensively photographed in the 1880s and 1890s, providing documentation of the original motifs. When he visited the mission around that time, the painter Henry Chapman Ford remarked that the colors were red, green, and black, although these cannot be reliably correlated with the black-and-white photographs. The nave features a central niche, where the *bulto* of San Antonio resided, with painted columns supporting a crownlike arch. On each side are painted arches enclosing large rosettes, simulating niches but probably empty until statues were moved here from Mission San Fernando Rey after secularization. Side altars are defined by columns topped by arches with crosses. Other motifs in the church include a mother quail and her young, cherubim, a large shell, and "a picture frame of exuberant form topped with a disk of probable Indian significance."[28] The designs have been replicated and creatively repainted many times using historical photographs, in a manner inspired by, but not exactly reproducing, the originals. The original designs may still lie underneath the layers of subsequent plastering and could potentially be uncovered and in-painted to more accurately replicate the first, mission-era murals.

It is unfortunate that few of the artists who designed and executed the California mission murals are known today by name. Some, however, such as Esteban Munras, are identified in documents and oral sources. Others include the Chumash artist Juan Pacífico, who is credited with participating in the work at Missions Santa Bárbara and San Buenaventura. An Indian named Teófilo (baptized Lucas) is associated with the painted designs on the Great Stone Church at San Juan Capistrano, which was destroyed in the 1812 earthquake. The artist Agustín Dávila, from New Spain, produced the elaborate ceiling and wall designs at Mission Santa Clara. At Mission Santa Bárbara, Father Esteban Tapis is recorded as the designer of the original church decorations, which Father Fermín Lasuén described as having been done "with great skill, especially in the area around the altar." This work was damaged in the 1812 earthquake and lost in the subsequent rebuilding of 1815–20, replaced by designs likely influenced by then master builder José Antonio Ramírez. Tapis also designed the painted *retablo* for Mission San Juan Bautista, executed by the Boston sailor-turned-carpenter Thomas Doak, who bested the proposal of Californio Mateo Chávez (75 cents per day) by offering to work for room and board. The military also had talented artists, including Tomás González, who painted the Santa Bárbara Presidio Chapel, and the commandant of the Presidio of San Diego, don José de Zúñiga, who "wrote a letter to his mother . . . [stating] that he executed the decoration in the chapel there himself."[29]

Once the mission period ended, the murals at the California missions were exposed to a wide range of risks. In the years after secularization, as the mission roof tiles were taken and the walls crumbled and melted into the soil, much of

Graffiti: Etched in Plaster

A fascinating variety of incised graffiti can be found in the dado areas near where the neophytes sat and knelt during Mass. Graffiti was apparently tolerated by the mission authorities, and many such expressions have been recorded by Norman Neuerburg at San Miguel, San Juan Capistrano, and Santa Cruz, among other missions.[30] Notable design elements are animals, insects, and human figures. At San Miguel the graffiti includes an image of a sailboat, perhaps seen from the landing at San Simeon, the mission's beach rancho. A similar vessel was found incised on the walls of the Cooper-Molera Adobe's kitchen in Monterey, a room that was used by Indian cooks. There is clearly much room for further investigations, particularly when old flaking paint is removed or falls away from earlier surfaces. One has but to look.

Man on horseback, etched into an arch in front of the main *convento* entrance at Mission San Luis Rey.

The Artist Agustín Dávila

Agustín Dávila arrived in Alta California in 1834 at the age of twenty-nine with the Híjar-Padrés expedition. The next year he settled at Mission Santa Clara, where he began his California painting career by producing the most elaborate of all California mission ceilings. For this he covered the wooden boards of the church sanctuary with a heavenly vision that evoked the decorated domes of European churches: the monogram of Jesus in a circle of cherubim surrounded by angels playing instruments. In the four corners were images of the four Doctors of the Church, while the Virgin as the Immaculate Conception and Saint Joseph were positioned above the altar with the Trinity. Dávila, who was from Mexico City, was certainly familiar with the painted dome of that city's cathedral, a descendant of the great painted domes of Europe.[31] The painted facade of the church was also Dávila's creation. Inspired by Mexican neoclassical altarpieces, it featured paired columns with cornices flanking the main portal, along with painted statues in simulated niches.

The following year Dávila was engaged at Mission San José to paint "three new altars, doors, balustrades, the baptistery, the sacristy with a landscape (*perspective*), a niche (*template*), a pediment (*sotobanco*), and the sanctuary."[32] On completion of the project he moved to San Francisco and married thirteen-year-old María de Jesús Félix, and the couple welcomed a daughter a year later. They resided in Branciforte and then relocated to Santa Barbara in 1842, where two more children were born. In 1845 Dávila received the grant to Rancho Corral de Quati near Mission Santa Inés. Another child was born there. In March 1848 the master painter was killed near the mission by a neighbor, reportedly for killing chickens. Of all his artistic works, the only remaining piece is a baptismal font and stand at Mission San José that is still in use.[33]

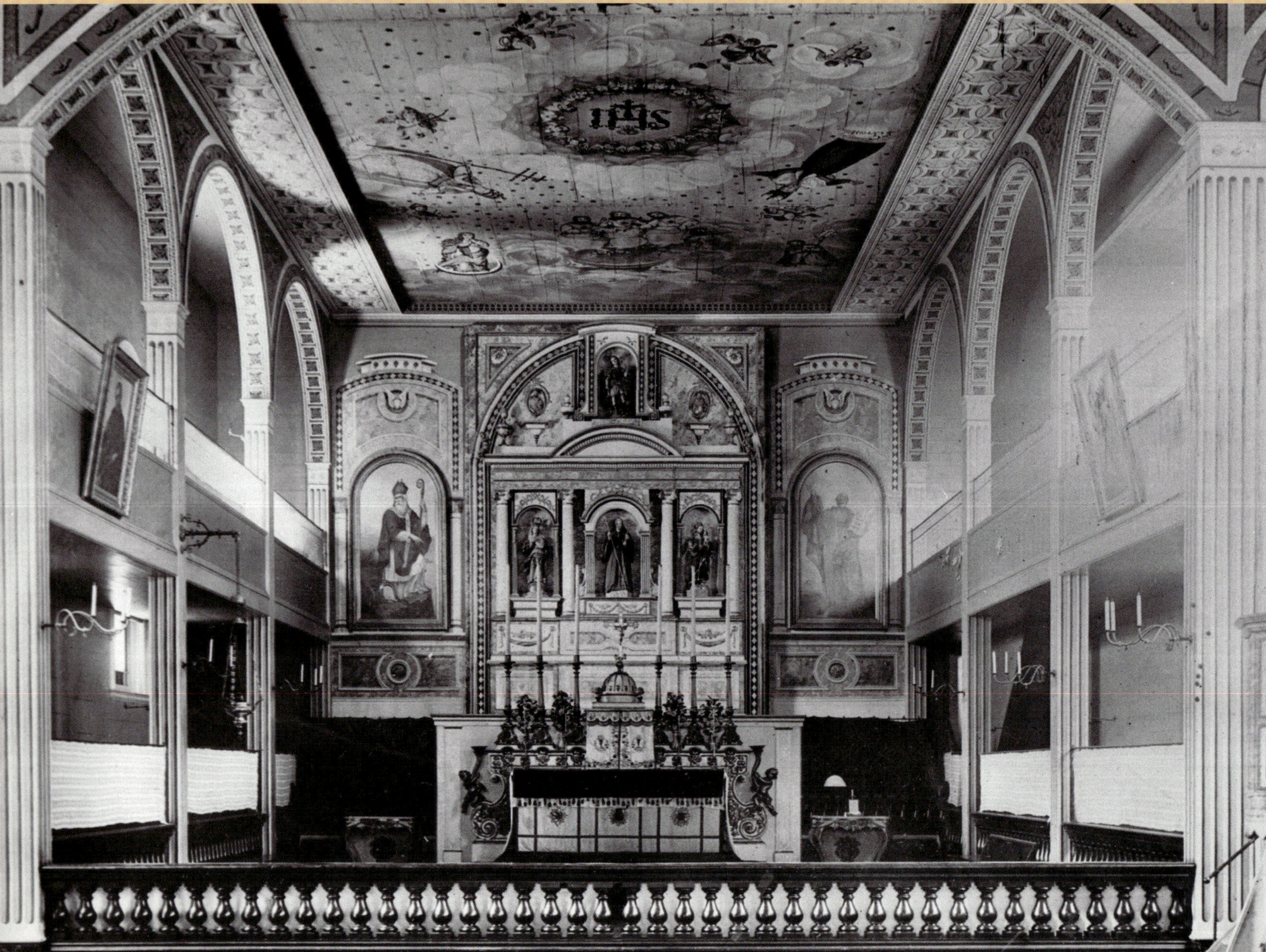

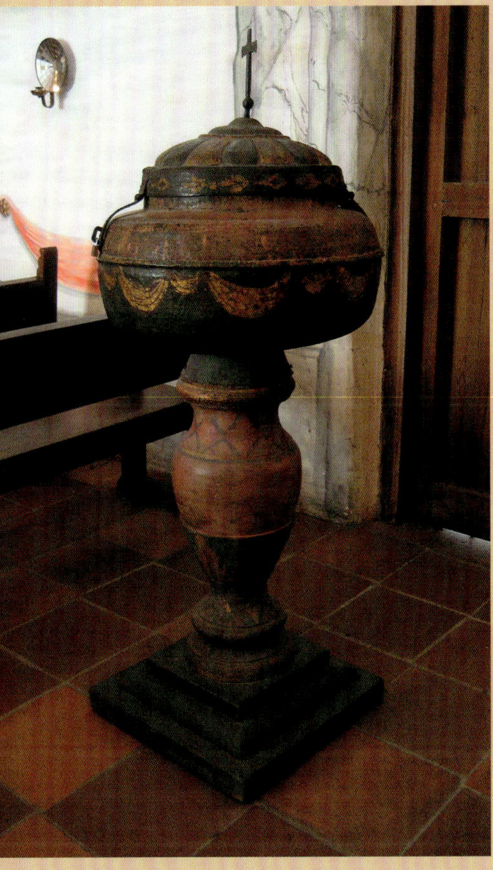

LEFT: Hand-decorated wooden baptismal font at Mission San José, the only known surviving work by Dávila. Photograph by Julia Costello

BELOW: A rendering of the facade at Mission Santa Clara de Asís as it would have appeared when Dávila painted it in 1835. Lost in the fire of 1926, the facade's design elements have been re-created in relief on the modern reconstruction. Painting by Roger Arno (detail). Courtesy of Bellerophon Books, Santa Barbara

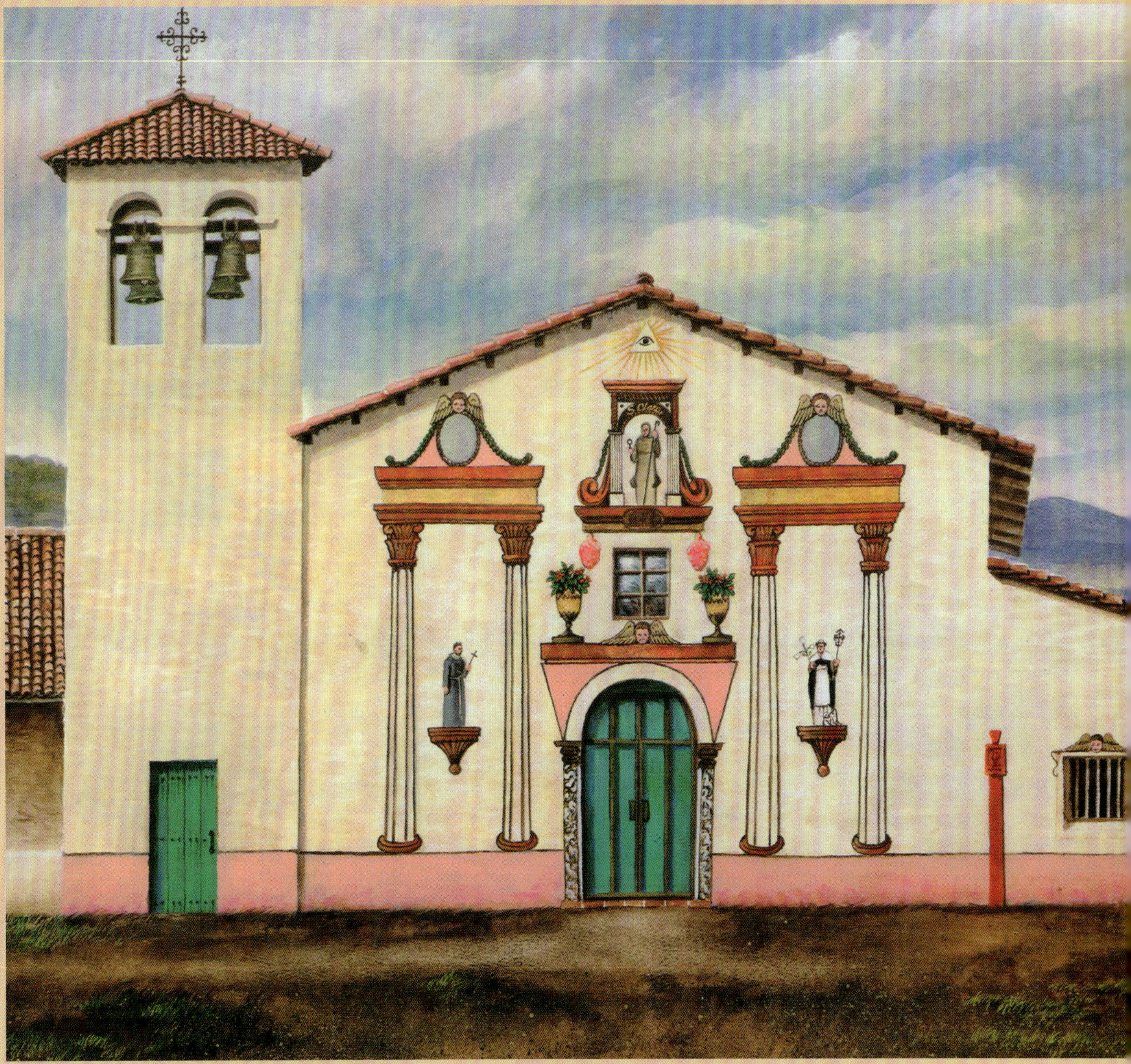

OPPOSITE: The interior of Mission Santa Clara de Asís, ca. 1885. The ceiling mural, painted by the artist Agustín Dávila in 1835, was lost when the church burned down in 1926. Dávila's wall paintings had been lost earlier when the church was widened in 1884. Photograph by C.C. Pierce. Courtesy University of Southern California, on behalf of the USC Special Collections

the wall decoration disappeared or was seriously damaged. During the early years of the American period, when the Catholic and Hispanic heritage of the missions was widely unpopular, some mission interiors were redecorated according to British Victorian taste or whitewashed to modernize and dim their Hispanic origins. Dávila's facade at Mission Santa Clara was covered with a twin-towered Italianate facade in 1861, and the adobe walls, which were said to have been decorated on the interior with images of the apostles, were removed and replaced by ones of wood when the nave was widened that year. Only the elaborate painting on the sanctuary ceiling survived into modern times, and this was consumed in a fire in 1926. Victorian renovations were also undertaken at Mission San Luis Obispo in 1880. The church portico and campanile, as well as the *convento*'s front colonnade, were removed; the adobe walls were clad in wooden siding, and an incongruous New England steeple was added. The nave ceiling of Mission San Gabriel was covered in wooden boards and the decorative walls overpainted; the lively murals in San Juan Capistrano's Serra Chapel were whitewashed; and a Victorian-style altarpiece was installed over the painted wall decorations at Mission San Buenaventura. Later, on the wave of the Mission Revival style, at some missions, such as Santa Inés and San Fernando, all the exposed lintels and woodwork were painted dark brown.

Other changes in the churches also took place. Canvas paintings of the Vía Crucis were replaced by plain wood crosses and the gilt and colorful ornamentation suppressed in favor of the straightforward Arts and Crafts style or the simple Protestant tastes of the early twentieth century. Replica missions such as those at Santa Cruz and San Rafael, and to some extent San Francisco Solano, followed this trend as well.

Very few of the missions that survived into the twentieth century had not had their mission-period wall decorations overpainted. Most of the original murals had been lost to well-intentioned efforts to modernize the churches or to refurbish fading painted motifs with a "fresher" look. The historic importance of this decorative art designed and executed during the mission period was not fully appreciated.

The secrets of the old walls began to be rediscovered as a fortuitous result of a fire in 1920 at Mission San Luis Obispo. The wooden paneling that had been installed in the sanctuary and over the nave ceiling protected the original beams from the flames, and once it was removed, the underlying decorations were revealed: scrolls in light blue and rose on the wooden lintels, as well as a painted frame around the front door, surmounted by the papal crown with cardinal's staff and bishop's crozier.[34]

Then, in 1936, came the discoveries at Mission San Fernando and the demonstration by the Index artists that complete original painted designs, not just fragments of color, could be uncovered through careful excavation of overlying layers of paint and plaster. Few people appreciated this revelation, however. Even today, the magnificent historical documentation produced by the Index artists remains largely unknown, both to historians and to the general public.

Our current appreciation for mission wall decoration is a direct result of the research and restoration work of the scholar and artist Norman Neuerburg.[35] Neuerburg lamented in 1977 that while Spanish and Mexican California have "furnished the subject matter for a vast number of writings," most of this work pays "little or no attention ... to the artistic history of the province." Architectural accomplishments have received some attention, he acknowledged, but "the figurative arts and crafts have been ... neglected. ... The fact that one is faced with a provincial art [California] of a provincial art (Mexico) of a provincial art (Spain in relation to Italy), and the

The Chumash Artist Juan Pacífico

The painter known as Pacífico (Sunicamiol), or Juan Pacífico, was born on December 4, 1797, to Chumash parents at Mission San Buenaventura. At that time the mission was one of the finer ones, as many of its buildings had been rebuilt after a fire several years earlier. Building continued—tanneries, granaries, and adobe houses for some of the nearly one thousand neophytes—during the years of Pacífico's childhood. The Indians also built a seven-mile-long aqueduct that brought water from the Ventura River to irrigate the mission's orchards and gardens.

The art of painting was not unknown to the Chumash, who had traditions of painting on their canoes and other wooden items, on rock surfaces, and on their bodies using native pigments. The new mission church was completed in 1809, and interior decorations were applied between 1810 and 1811, when it is recorded that "the altars were gilded and the ceiling painted."[36] For this effort, it is likely that thirteen-year-old Juan Pacífico was selected as one of the apprentices to work with the chief artisan, as when, in 1817 and 1818, twenty-year-old Pacífico participated in the work of applying additional decorations to the church. The neophyte journeyman helped produce "marbleized pilasters and cornices, painted side altars, urns, terraced dado borders, swags with pendant bouquets, leaf, and window surrounds." He also is reported as taking part in decorating the nearby chapel of San Miguel, which was completed at this time.[37]

Pacífico married three times. He wed the widow Emerenciana at San Buenaventura in September 1824. Six years later, in June 1830, following Emerenciana's death, he married another widow, Luisa Gonzaga. She, like Emerenciana, also died childless. In May 1839 the forty-two-year-old Pacífico wed Cirianca, and the couple had two children: Desiderio in 1840 and Manuel María de Alta Gracia in 1842.[38]

The church at Mission San Buenaventura has continued to be the center of an active congregation through secularization and into the present. The early community included not only Californio settlers and new American arrivals but also a remarkable number of former neophytes who received small land grants for gardens along the Ventura River.[39] Pacífico continued to work as a painter and report-

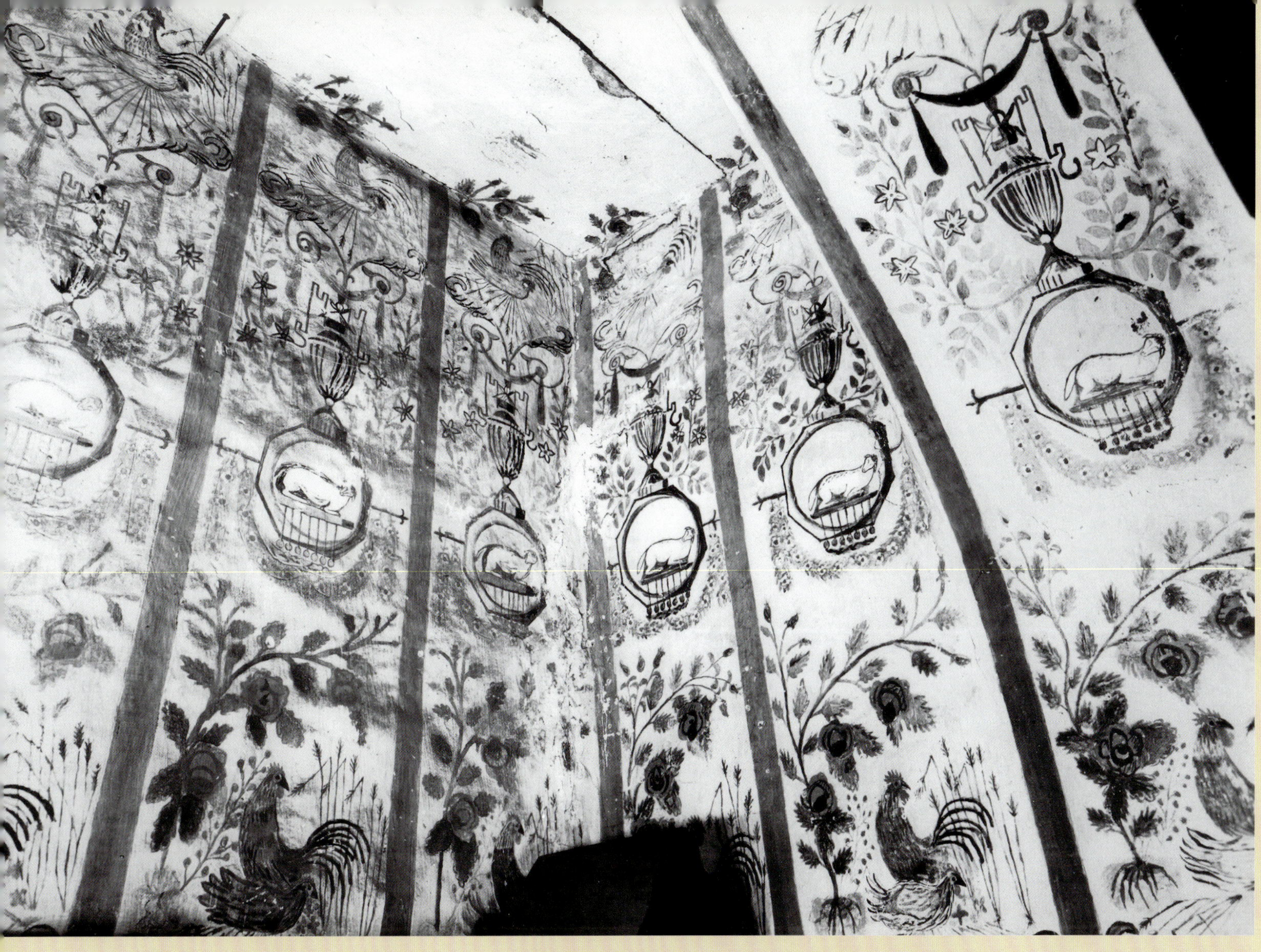

edly made his paints in an adobe row house south of the mission. Oral histories specify that he added meat of the red tuna, egg whites, and pitch to the pigments. He also used urine, which he collected in clay pots, as a mordant for the paint.[40] In addition to being a painter, he was a singer and a musician and, like other talented artisans in Alta California, likely enjoyed respect and high status within his community. Pacífico died in May 1843. He was buried in the cemetery at Mission San Buenaventura.

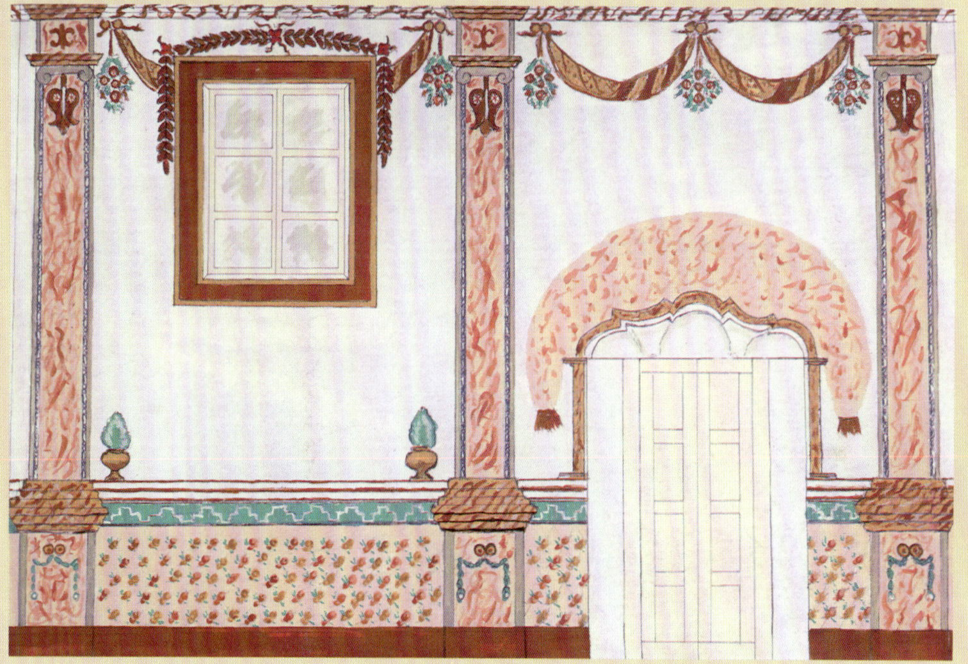

ABOVE: The abundant wall decoration in the baptistery at Mission San Buenaventura, were likely worked on by Juan Pacífico. Since this photograph was taken in 1937, these decorations have been covered with a new surface. National Gallery of Art, Washington, D.C., Gallery Archives

RIGHT: Rendering by Norman Neuerburg depicting the decorative scheme of the side walls of the San Buenaventura church, likely executed by Juan Pacífico. Courtesy of Bellerophon Books, Santa Barbara

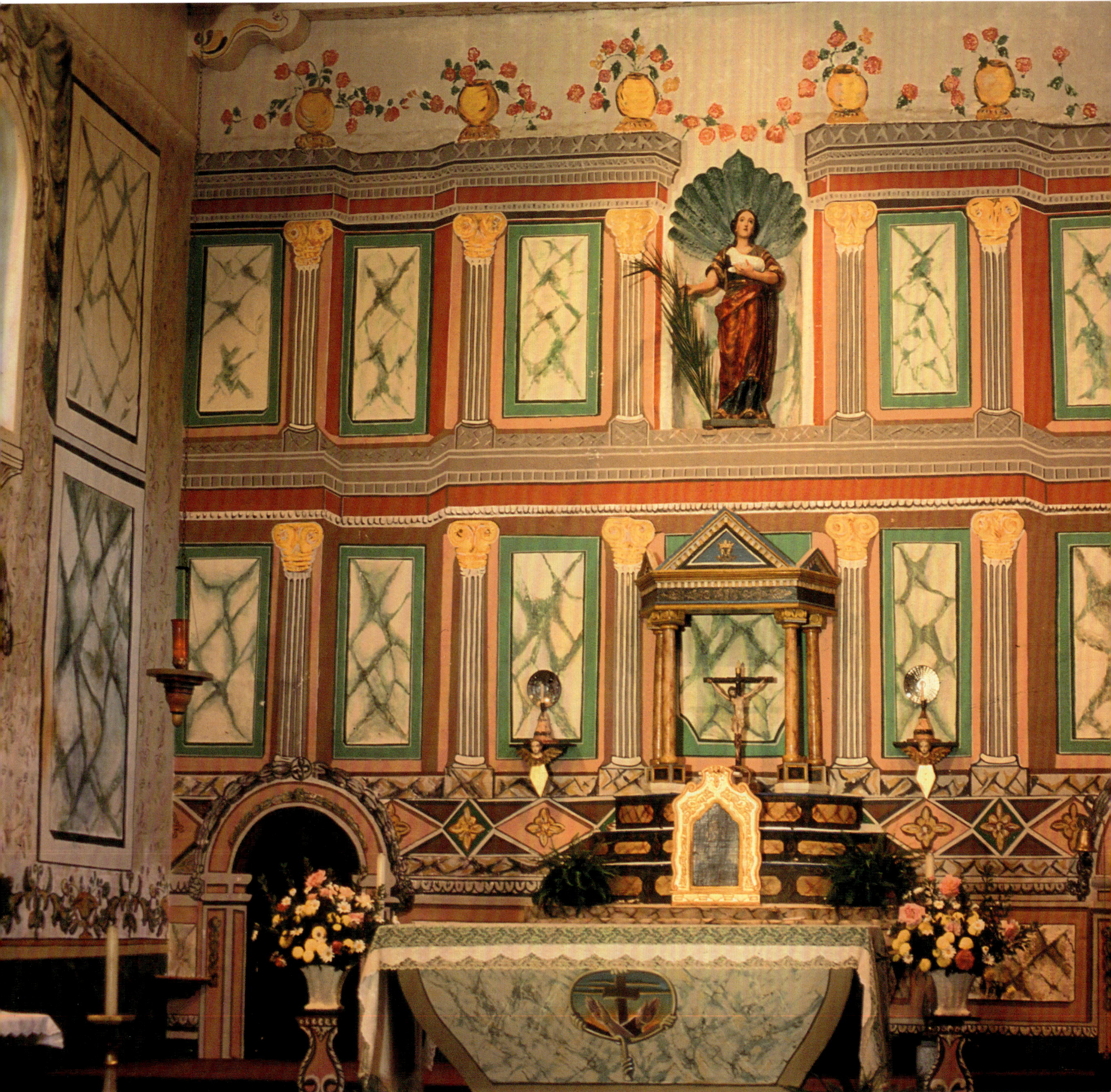

A magnificent original painted *retablo* of faux columns and marble panels adorns the sanctuary of the church at Mission Santa Inés. The statue of Santa Bárbara in the central shell niche has recently been restored. Photograph by G. Aldana

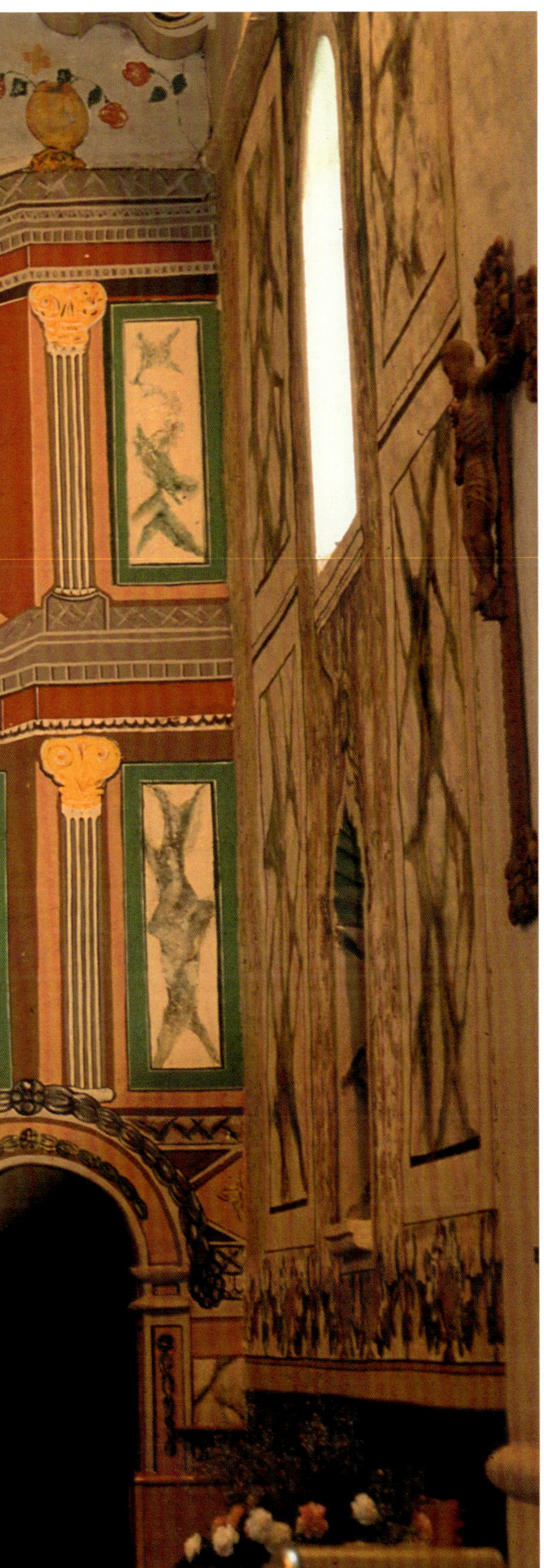

strong European bias of art historians in this country," have discouraged serious study of Alta California's artistic contributions.[41]

In the upsurge in interest in American heritage and its ethnic roots following the country's bicentennial celebrations, Neuerburg finally found a willing audience for his message. His advocacy for mission arts included identifying and restoring original wall paintings, most famously at Mission San Fernando Rey, where he did much of the initial repainting himself. Neuerburg also conducted extensive study at San Juan Bautista, discovering several overlying schemes of mission-period decoration. He climbed down behind the wooden *retablo* at Mission San Francisco de Asís to study the pre-1796 paintings on the wall (which are still intact) and crawled into the attic of Mission San Gabriel to observe early layers of red painted designs. There was not a mission that did not receive his scrutiny. His knowledge of and enthusiasm for his subject inspired many of the missions to investigate and re-create their former decorative schemes or add appropriate alternatives if the originals had been destroyed without being recorded. This interest has resulted in the creation of interpretive displays at a number of missions tracing the history of their wall murals. Restorers throughout California—at Missions San José, San Juan Capistrano, San Luis Rey, Santa Inés, and Santa Cruz and the Santa Bárbara Presidio—sought his advice.

Interest in authentic historic mission decoration was revitalized in spirit, if not always in faithful reproduction. While original mission art is rare, it does survive. Mission Santa Inés still preserves an impressive amount of early mission wall decoration in its sanctuary and sacristy. Here the overall architectural plan for the sanctuary was derived from an engraving of a Roman theater pictured in an architectural manual at Mission Santa Bárbara. A bold Greek key Neoclassical border with flowers remains in the sacristy, whereas the sanctuary bespeaks the Baroque enthusiasm for faux painted marble finishes. These motifs apparently date to repairs made after the 1824 Chumash rebellion, as other designs underlay them.[42] The nave decorations have been overpainted with a modern floral design pattern.

In a region prone to earthquakes, however, murals are only as safe as their supporting walls are strong. Earthquakes are the greatest threat not only to mission buildings but also to the treasures they enclose. Sadly, it was at the Mission San Fernando *convento*, where Native American motifs proliferated, that the greatest recent losses of Native American art occurred. Although the building survived the 1971 Sylmar earthquake, subsequent repairs left the original painted walls permanently compromised. Fortunately, the designs had been recorded by the Index of American Design, and many of these original motifs have been refashioned atop the new plaster, including the vineyard scene and the famous Indian deer-hunting motif. Other rooms have been redecorated with less accurate renderings lacking the delicacy and grace of the originals.

San Fernando would not be the only mission whose murals would be threatened by earthquakes. In recent years San Miguel has had to confront similar issues. With problems such as these awaiting resolution, the preservation of the few surviving original painted mission decorations remains a significant challenge. In the past, countless works were lost when the buildings they adhered to collapsed. In buildings that survived, renovations often destroyed original wall fabric during the long decades when attention was not paid to the stories embedded in their plaster surfaces. So, too, with churches that continued to serve active congregations, where modernizing of old designs often replaced authentic paintings with convenient facsimiles. More encouraging, however, is the likelihood that under the layers of new plaster and paint still more murals executed during mission days are preserved, awaiting discovery.

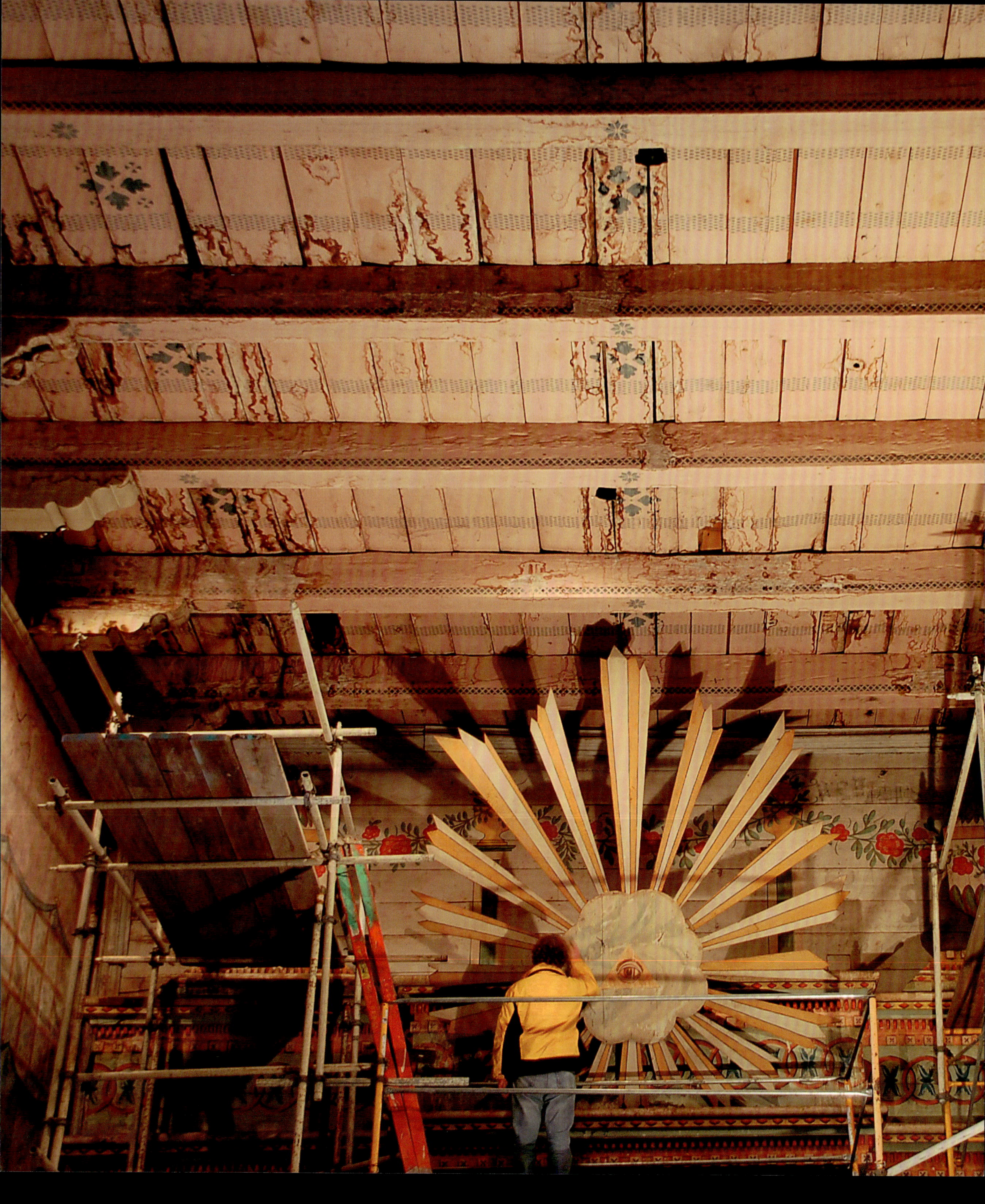

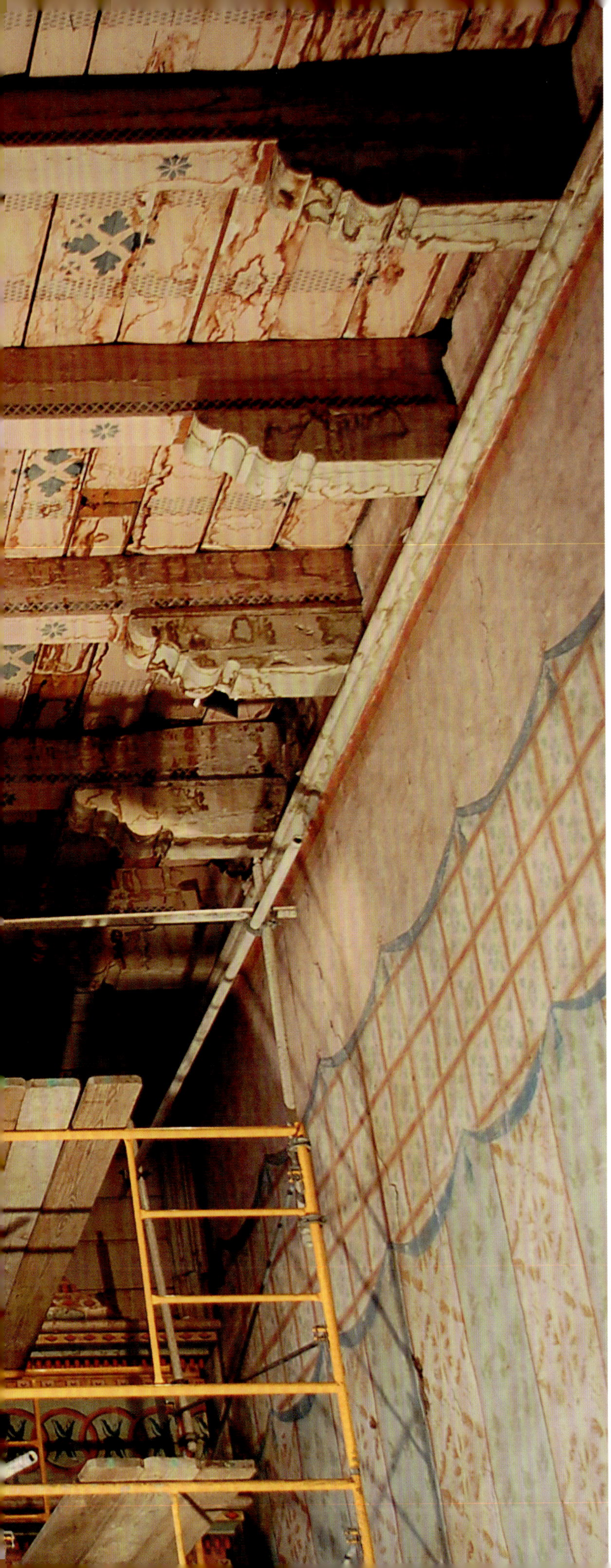

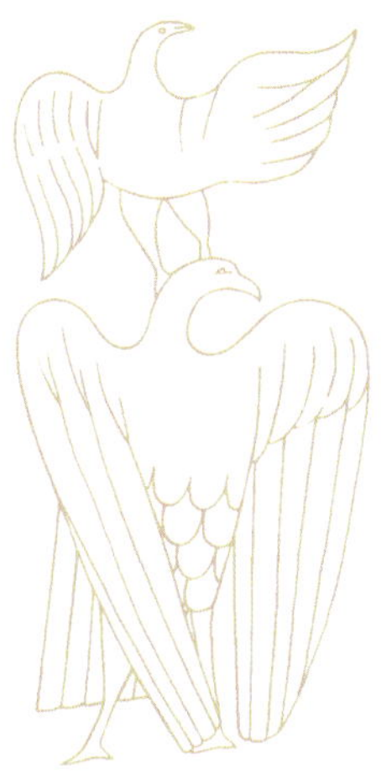

Chapter Seven

PRESERVING CALIFORNIA'S MISSIONS

Shortly after 11:00 A.M. on December 22, 2003, the central California coast was rocked by an earthquake measuring 6.5 on the Richter scale, the largest to strike the region in fifty years. At Mission San Miguel, Arcángel, the only surviving wing of the original *convento* was badly damaged. The church, too, suffered serious harm: walls cracked, plaster fragments fell, statues tumbled and broke. Of particular concern was the extensive hand-painted decoration adorning the walls. These magnificent murals, designed by the Catalan painter Esteban Munras and executed in the 1820s with the assistance of Native American neophytes, constitute the only complete surviving mission-period church interior in California. The future of these delicate murals was now threatened by the possible collapse of the walls on which they were painted.

LEFT: A wood conservator examines the wall decorations at Mission San Miguel, Arcángel, after they were endangered by the 2003 earthquake. Photograph by Anthony Crosby

ABOVE: Native American design scratched inside the doorway of the priests' residence at Mission San Fernando.

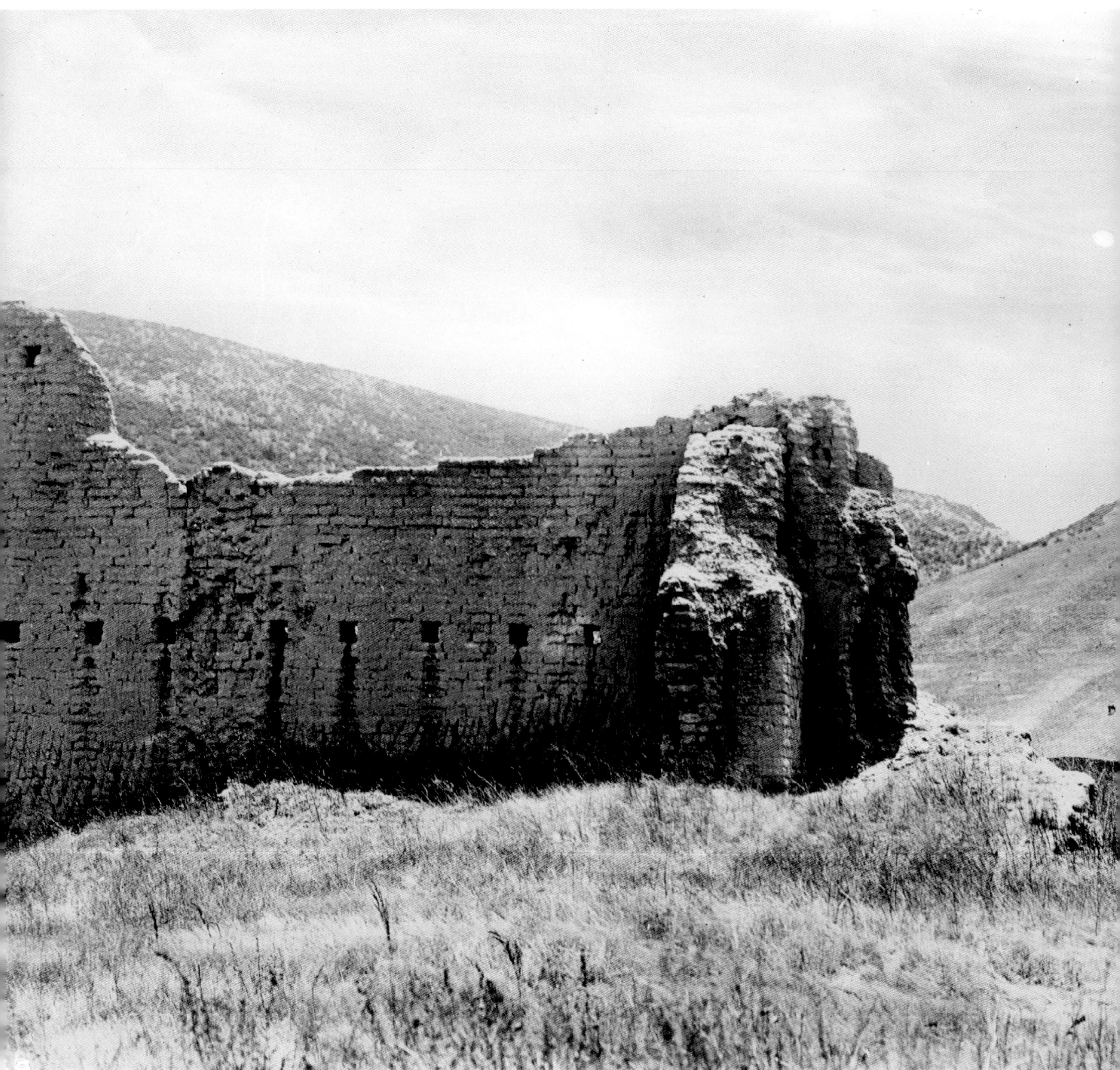

Ruined adobe walls of the first site of Mission La Purísima, ca. 1890. The mission was destroyed in the earthquake of 1812. To the right, a crevass appears to threaten the remaining ruins. Photograph by C. C. Pierce. Courtesy University of Southern California, on behalf of the USC Special Collections

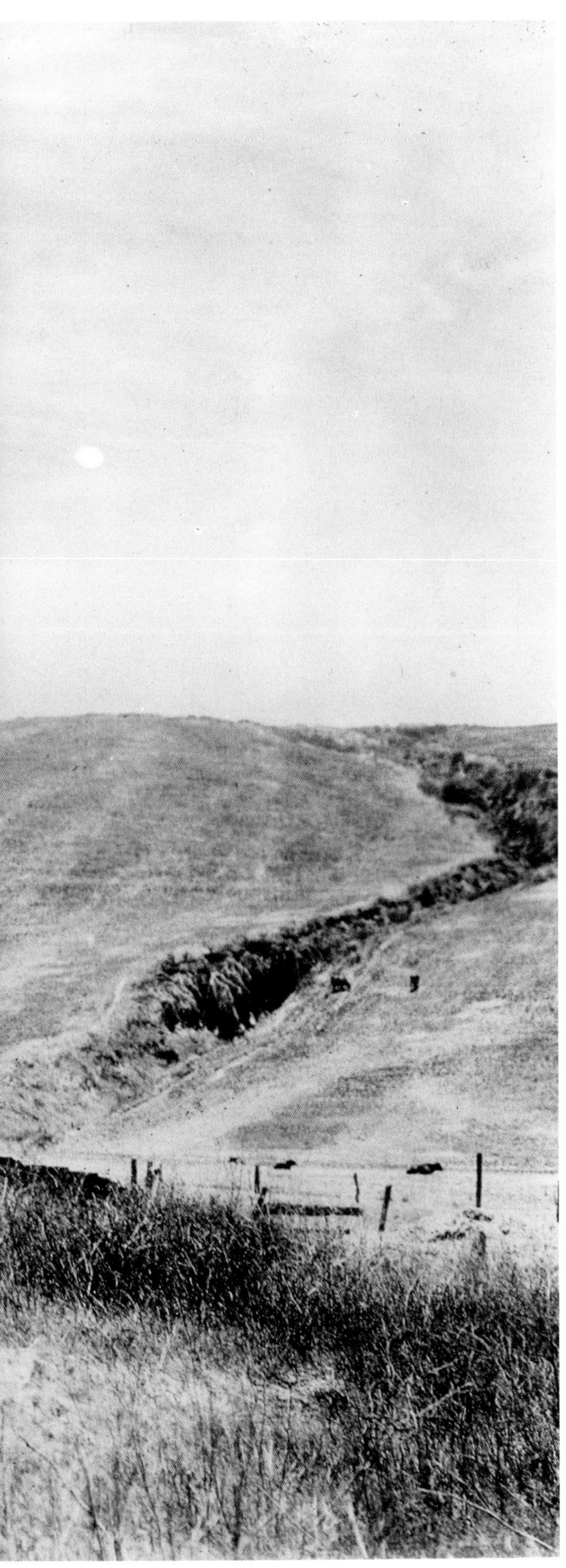

Earthquakes have bedeviled the California missions since their founding. Virtually all have suffered significant damage, and many of their structures have been completely destroyed. The Great Stone Church at San Juan Capistrano was felled in the earthquake of 1812; thirty-eight adults and two children inside the church were killed. Mission La Purísima was so devastated by the same earthquake that the entire mission *casco* was abandoned for a new site some three miles distant. "The extraordinary and horrible earthquake, which this Mission suffered on the memorable day of the glorious Apostle St. Thomas," Father Mariano Payeras recounted, "entirely destroyed the church and vestry, buried . . . various images and paintings, and ruined the greater part of the furniture. . . . We shall . . . go to work constructing from poles and grass what is indispensable until the earth becomes quiet."[1]

Earthquakes are not the only threat facing these venerable structures and the irreplaceable treasures they contain. Buildings are endangered by lack of maintenance, rain and weather, and inexpert earlier repairs, while their paintings, sculpture, books, and other artifacts may be damaged by inappropriate display or storage conditions, or may be lost as a result of inattention or theft. Funding for even modest conservation measures is difficult to obtain. While the missions' central place in the California experience has been widely recognized for more than a century and much has been done to preserve them, they still face serious challenges. Recent advances in historic preservation techniques are being brought to bear on these challenges, however, with significant promise for the future.

As the triumphal narrative of the mission myth has given way to a more balanced and complex understanding of California's mission heritage, so, too, have the practices of historic preservation evolved considerably from the well-meaning but heavy-handed and often speculative restorations and reconstructions that took place during the first half of the twentieth century. Preservationists today generally favor an approach of minimal intervention, which seeks to arrest deterioration and preserve a mission in its current state rather than return it to some past glory. The conservation of any cultural heritage site begins with an assessment of why it is important, using the concept of cultural significance to articulate the meanings and values of the place. Cultural significance includes historical, architectural, artistic, spiritual, and religious values, as well as a place's symbolic meanings to the various segments of the community. For example, many of the state's Native Americans view the missions as an important part of their heritage. Members of the local Salinan tribes know that their ancestors built Mission San Miguel's church and painted the interior, and they feel a close connection with the historic building and its art. Understanding the values of cultural heritage sites and collections is fundamental to making decisions about their care and conservation.

In view of the missions' complex history, it is not surprising that today this heritage possesses a remarkable richness of meanings. Most missions continue to have active parishes and therefore possess considerable religious value to their congregations as places of worship. Some missions generate significant economic benefits derived from their role as popular tourist destinations. One such case is Mission San Juan Capistrano, whose development as a public attraction has benefited the entire town. Missions may also be important educational resources, as at Mission La Purísima State Historic Park, where the reconstructed complex displays perhaps the state's most historically accurate vision of mission life.

Mission Landscapes

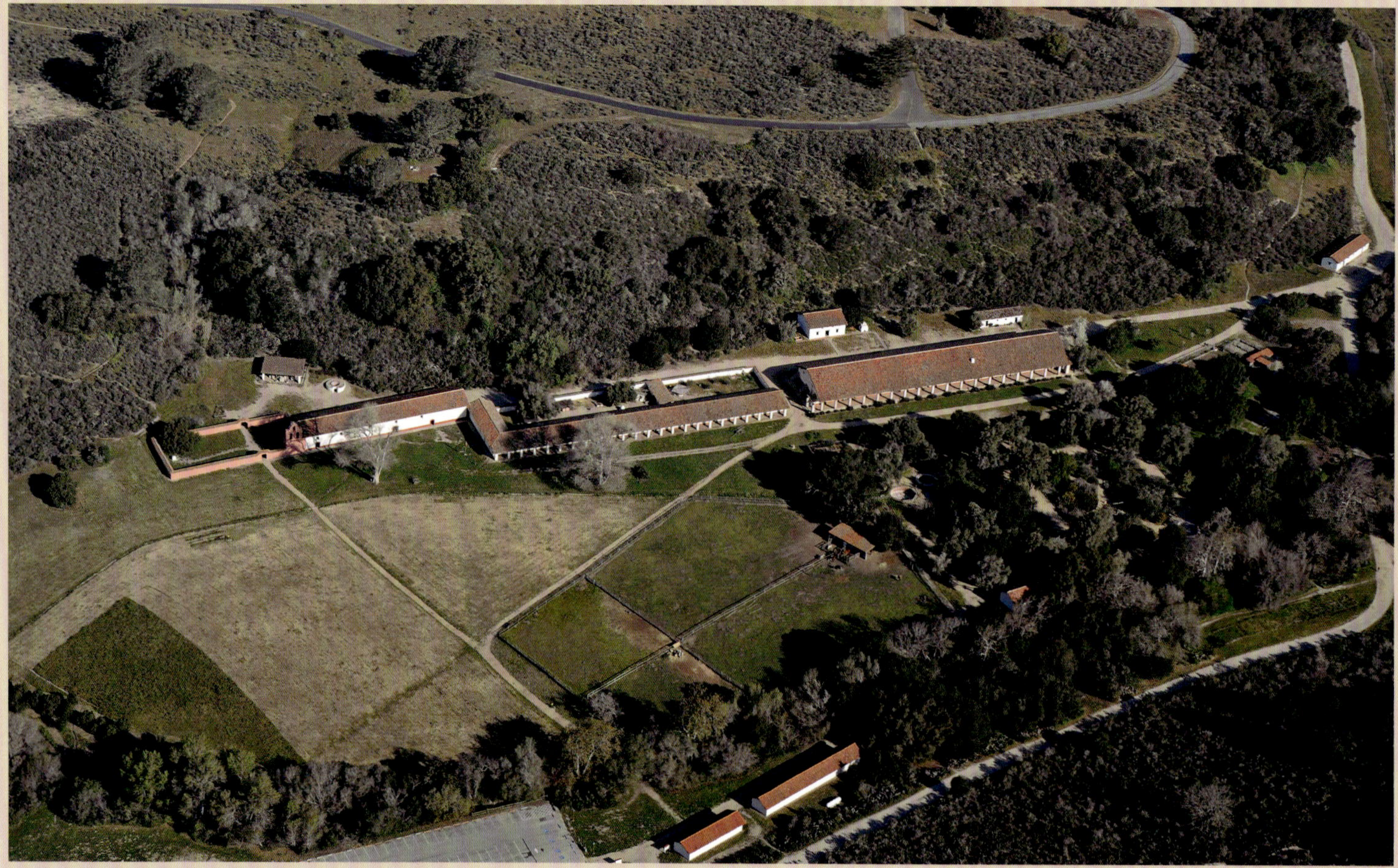

From their inception, the California missions transformed the pre-European landscape to one ordered around a village community surrounded by agricultural and ranching lands. Over the past two centuries, with the relentless progression of historical events—secularization, the granting of rancho lands, the gold rush, statehood, and, most recently, urbanization—the mission landscapes of early California largely disappeared. A few missions located off the beaten track, however, to some extent escaped that fate and still convey a sense of an authentic historic landscape.

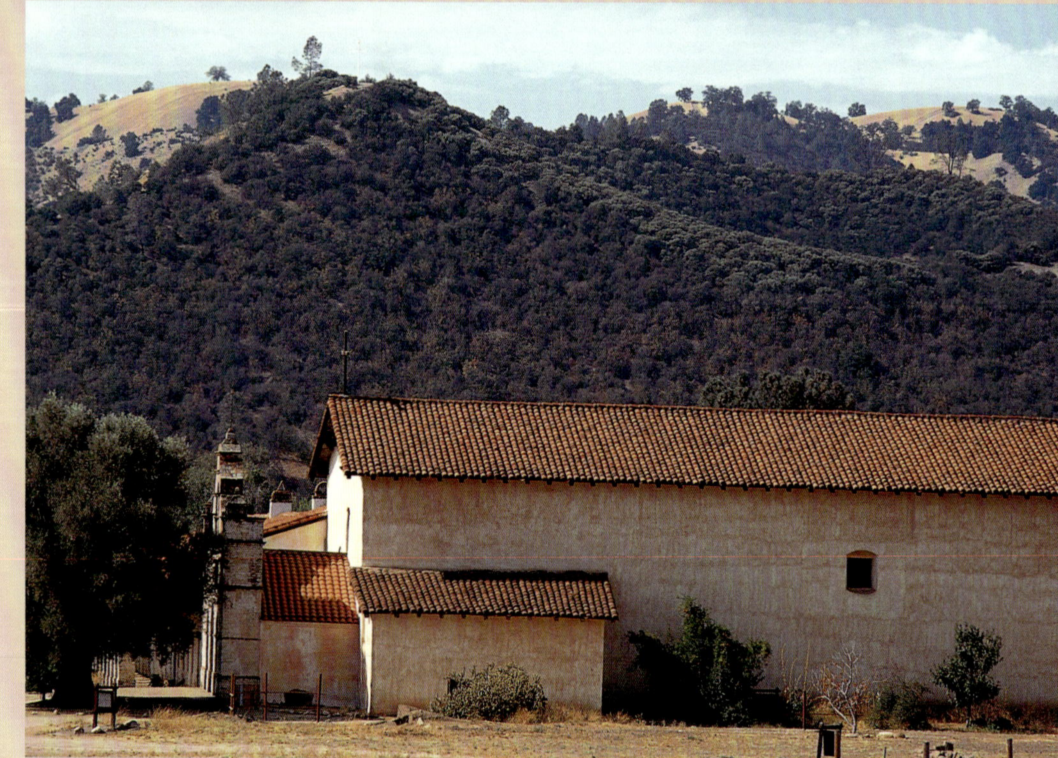

Justifiably, the most famous extant mission landscape is that of the reconstructed complex at La Purísima Mission State Historic Park. The mission's location in a small side canyon of the Santa Ynez River now protects the park visually from modern development along that watercourse. With the reconstruction of a complex of mission buildings, water systems, and gardens, visitors can fully experience the historic setting. The continued acquisition of land by California State Parks has not only protected the mission setting from encroaching residential development but also added about 1,800 acres of surrounding mesa land where trails lead to natural landscapes.

An important component of any historic landscape is its significant viewshed, an identifiable scenic or historic view that contributes to the landscape's character and helps us to understand its historic context. Managing these landscapes is another challenge facing conservators, in California and around the world, as they attempt to balance preservation with often-conflicting land-use and development interests.

In the case of the California missions, significant viewsheds convey the isolation of these outposts and the relationships between the site and natural or man-made features. For instance, Mission Santa Inés sits high on a bluff overlooking Alamo Pintado Creek, with the Santa Ynez Mountains as a backdrop. Although the mission is flanked on the north by the tourist town of Solvang, the vista south from the church and *convento* overlooks its water system, mills complex, agricultural fields, and the Coast Range and is virtually devoid of modern intrusions, providing an authentic glimpse into the mission complex with all its constituent parts.[2]

Mission San Antonio, although less known, undoubtedly enjoys the largest unaltered authentic mission setting in California. Some 156,000 acres of mission lands were preserved from development, first by William Randolph Hearst and then by Fort Hunter Liggett, providing an unparalleled expanse of grazing lands and mission facilities. The mission complex commands a view of the Valley of the Oaks, with the Santa Lucia Mountains rising behind and Mission Creek meandering by on the west. Efforts to restrain expansion of the adjacent Fort Hunter Liggett headquarters into the mission viewshed have been relatively successful. Today, the vast scale of this oak savannah landscape is little compromised, and the long drive on rural roads necessary to reach this mission affords a sense of temporal as well as physical remoteness, as if one were truly journeying into the past.

ABOVE OPPOSITE: The setting of Mission La Purísima, protected by nearly two thousand acres of state park, retains its historic ambience.

BELOW OPPOSITE: Mission San Antonio de Padua is surrounded by a vast oak savannah; this setting has changed little since mission days, affording visitors the opportunity to experience an authentic mission setting. Photographs © Bill Dewey

Today each mission faces its own set of preservation-related challenges. Although comprehensive conservation plans have been developed for a few missions, the condition of most reflects the much less controllable forces of history and nature, as well as the predominance of some historic and cultural values over others. Some missions have fallen to ruin; some have been lovingly restored or rebuilt, with varying degrees of historical accuracy. In addition to the buildings themselves—the venerable structures of adobe, *ladrillo*, and stone that endure an often-perilous existence—the mission heritage also resides in art, artifacts, and furnishings. There are the rare remaining wall paintings, whose existence, as at San Miguel, is entirely dependent on the health of the structure that supports them. There are canvas paintings and religious statues, textiles and manuscripts, and objects of daily life that have survived from a distant past. Finally, there are archaeological remains, preserved as ruins or lying underground and as yet unstudied. There are the larger settings of the missions themselves, landscapes that in some cases still evoke the missions' authentic historical settings. Each of these tells a different part of the mission story.

The task of confronting these challenges requires considerable expertise. Architects, engineers, and conservators work to preserve the buildings; planners and landscape architects work to preserve the historic landscapes; historians strive to record the authentic stories; museum curators inventory and track historic objects; archaeologists excavate, reveal, and interpret rare fragments of mission life; and specialists ranging from conservators to curators care for the various treasures the missions contain.

Modern conservation practice is guided by a number of well-articulated principles. Fundamental to these is an understanding of the significance of the place, building, or object—the cultural resource—so that change is managed in a way that minimizes the impact on the values that constitute its significance. A cardinal feature of this principle is the tenet of minimal intervention: do only as much as necessary to safeguard the place, building, or object in question. Whenever possible, changes undertaken that affect its cultural values aim to be reversible—capable of being easily removed or re-treated. Such factors as an owner's particular needs, the extent of available resources, and other unique conditions are also considered.

The mission buildings constitute in themselves one of the great treasures of California's heritage. Over the years, the once-vast mission establishments have been diminished, and today few original structures—primarily churches and *conventos* of the central quadrangle—remain. Of the twenty-one mission churches extant in 1832, only ten original church buildings survive. Of these, four are built of adobe (San Luis Obispo, San Francisco de Asís, San Miguel, and the Serra Chapel at San Juan Capistrano); four of adobe and *ladrillo* (San Buenaventura, San Luis Rey, San Juan Bautista, and Santa Inés); and two of stone (San Gabriel and Santa Bárbara). Augmented by the chapels at the Los Angeles plaza, the San Antonio de Pala *asistencia*, and the Monterey Presidio, this small group provides the rare opportunity for today's visitors to enter into sacred spaces created in the forge of history and preserved by nearly two centuries of devotion. Original missions are imbued with an atmosphere that replicas and reconstructions, no matter how accurate, can never truly capture. In these spaces, planned by Spanish priests and constructed by Native Americans, was played out the complex intercultural drama, uplifting or tragic, that created California. Here mission populations gathered for daily morning prayers before the neophytes went to labor in the fields and industries, as priests chanted the Mass and images of saints looked down from the walls. Here were held baptisms, confessions, and marriages, as well as services commemorating the countless deaths of neophytes from the diseases that

Moisture Damage

Water damage, although not as dramatic as earthquakes, can prove pervasive and insidious and is a major threat to the integrity of all historic buildings, including those made of adobe and stone. This longstanding problem was responsible for the ruin of many mission buildings in the decades of abandonment after secularization in the 1830s. Adobe bricks are made from soil mixed with water, sand, and an organic material as a binder. Pressed into molds and sun dried, these bricks are remarkably strong—until moisture is reintroduced. Lack of maintenance and resulting water seepage from faulty roofs, rain gutters, and downspouts is the main culprit. Poorly sealed windows are another. Poor drainage at the base of buildings can trigger rising damp, resulting in salt deposits on the walls. The subsequent process of wetting and drying erodes wall surfaces.

"Soft" lime mortars and plasters, developed by the Romans and used by the Spanish, are porous and "breathe," allowing modest dampness to evaporate. Traditional lime- or earth-based renders (exterior plaster) and finishes protected adobe bricks from direct contact with the weather, providing an easily replaceable sacrificial layer. The widespread "repair" technique of the 1940s through 1960s, using portland cement, turned out to have a very damaging effect. When cement was applied to adobe walls, often over chicken wire, its hard, water-repellent surface proved so impermeable that when moisture did occur in the walls it remained trapped behind the cement veneer, slowly eroding the adobe wall from within. Modern conservation practice recommends that cement coverings, including renders, plasters, and "aprons" (surface coverings placed along the lower portions of walls), be replaced with renders and mortars similar to the original material, allowing the walls to breathe.[3]

Ladrillos have also suffered from similarly ill-informed restorations. In some cases, impervious stucco was applied over a metal lath frame that was secured with galvanized nails to *ladrillo* columns in a mission's arcade. These nails expanded when oxidized in the presence of moisture and air, damaging the historic tiles. In other cases, a cement mortar was added to *ladrillo* constructions; over time, the stronger mortar pulled away the surface of the tiles. Now mission *ladrillo* arcades are remortared and restuccoed using soft lime mortars.

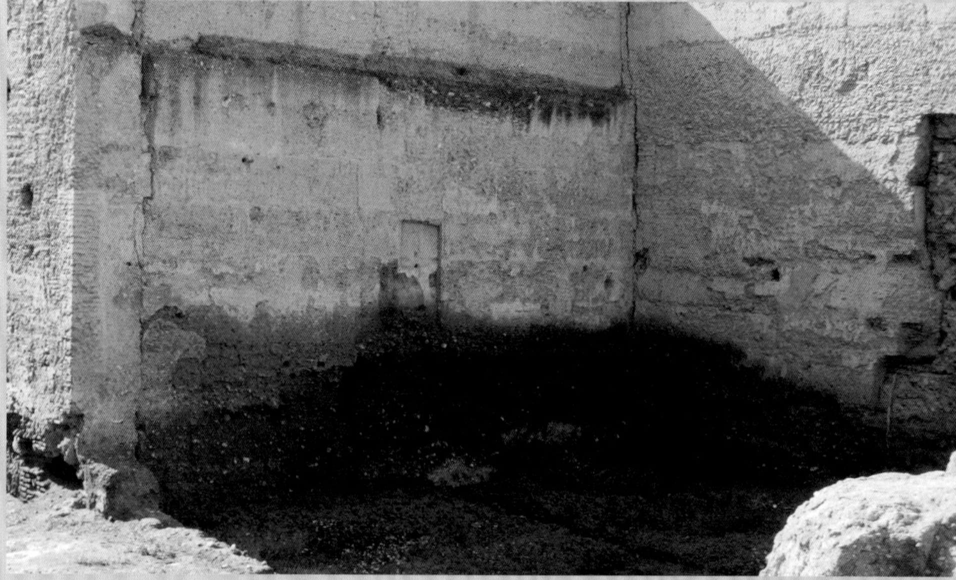

ABOVE: Earthen buildings worldwide frequently suffer problems of rising damp along the lower portion of walls. Absence of a protective roof and poor drainage of groundwater are among the most common causes for this type of damage. Seen here is an earthen building in Morocco. Photograph by Claudia Cancino. © J. Paul Getty Trust

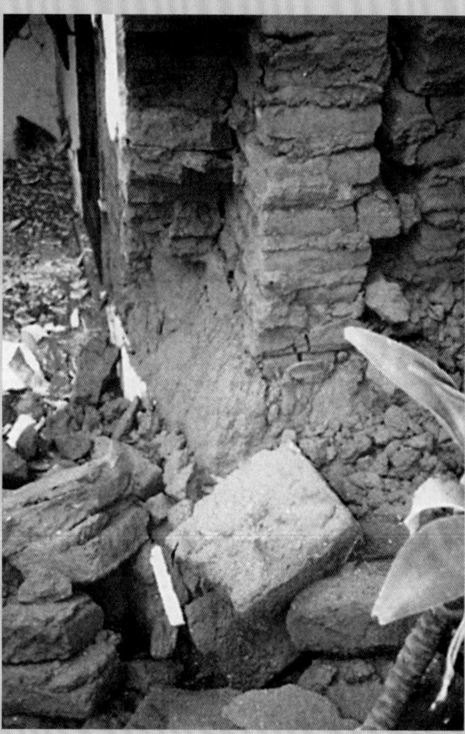

RIGHT: Moisture damage contributed to the collapse of these walls in the del Valle adobe. Getty Conservation Institute

Water damage can best be prevented by keeping adobe and stone walls dry, performing regular maintenance with fairly simple and inexpensive measures. These measures include ensuring that the roof and rainwater gutters and downspouts are in working order; that grading and underground drainage systems carry water away from buildings; that covered corridors and extended roof overhangs, where appropriate, shield walls from the weather; and that the external ground level is below the interior floor level. Lush plantings near mission buildings, in addition to being historically inaccurate, can be dangerous because the irrigation they require is often the principal source of moisture damage to the building. Landscaping near adobe walls should be kept to a minimum and limited to drought-tolerant plants.

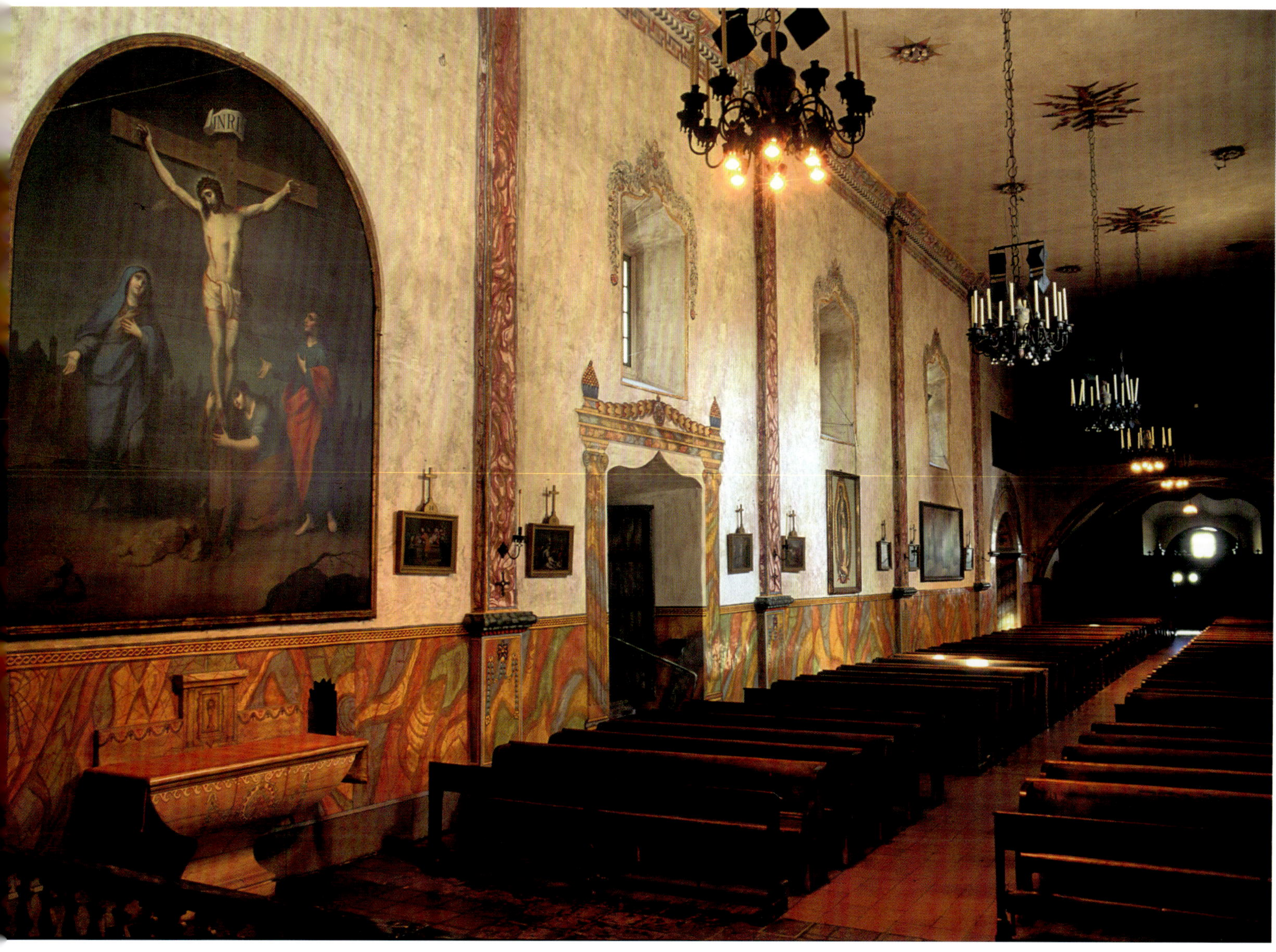

Original mission buildings are suffused with an atmosphere that replicas and reconstructions can never duplicate. Seen here is the interior of the stone church at Mission Santa Bárbara. Photograph by G. Aldana

swept through the mission establishments. It is in these places of power and mystery that the missions' complex legacy becomes most fully present.

Because the Alta California missions were constructed along the most active earthquake area of North America, the seismic retrofitting of these unreinforced masonry buildings is of particular importance for the preservation of California's mission heritage. The success of this work underpins all other efforts, for it is of little use to protect murals, paintings, and sculptures when all may be lost in a devastating earthquake.

Of the three materials used in mission construction—stone, *ladrillo*, and adobe—adobe is the most susceptible to earthquake damage. Efforts to stabilize historic adobe buildings, some 350 of which remain statewide, began in the late nineteenth century with the Landmarks Club. Early efforts were aimed primarily at arresting decay and not at dealing with problems associated with earthquakes. Reconstructions, such as those at Mission San Antonio in 1907, were done with new adobe bricks, with no apparent consideration of seismic risks. These early efforts at San Antonio and elsewhere often ended in collapse of the buildings.

In the 1920s traditional building materials such as adobe and lime plasters were replaced with concrete and portland cement mortars, which were widely used in reconstructions

OVERLEAF: A team of conservators at Mission San Miguel, following the 2003 earthquake that endangered the church's incomparable murals. Between the painted blue columns are panels of pale green; a painted balustrade, or balcony, runs along the top of the walls; the dado along the base of the walls simulates marble. Photograph by Anthony Crosby

because they were strong and inexpensive. At San Diego, the new church of 1931 was largely concrete, with some infilling using adobe bricks. At Mission San Carlos Borromeo, in 1936, Harry Downie also used portland cement concrete to reconstruct the stone church and, later, to build new wings for the mission quadrangle. It was commonly believed that adobe walls were not strong enough to withstand seismic events; therefore, concrete columns and wall-top beams were used as a support frame, with adobe bricks serving as mere infill. This technique was used in the 1930s for construction of the buildings at Mission La Purísima, as well as at Mission San Antonio de Padua in 1948. In later years, steel reinforcing rods were inserted through adobe walls to increase stabilization in the event of an earthquake. This method was used for reconstruction of the new church at Mission San José in the 1980s. When the church at San Fernando Rey was reconstructed after the 1971 Sylmar earthquake, it was built entirely out of reinforced concrete, in accordance with current thinking.

While these approaches may have served well for reconstructions, the insertion of massive concrete posts and beams in historic adobe buildings required removal of large amounts of the original adobe wall and introduced an incompatible building material to the structure. (The Serra Chapel at Mission San Juan Capistrano was subjected to this type of retrofit in the 1950s.) New, economical methods were needed that would preserve a maximum amount of historic fabric. This was a challenge not only in California but also in many other parts of the world where adobe is a principal building material. To address these needs, in 1990 the Getty Conservation Institute initiated the Getty Seismic Adobe Project (GSAP) to investigate alternatives to existing methods of seismic retrofitting (see pp. 160–61).[4]

Stone churches, considered by the Spanish to be more resistant to earthquakes, are still dependent on solid construction techniques to withstand temblors. However, the domed roof and ceilings of the Great Stone Church at San Juan Capistrano were not strong enough to withstand the 1812 earthquake, and the enormous bell tower, said to have stood 125 feet high, reportedly toppled sideways, scattering stones throughout the surrounding village. The church at Mission Santa Bárbara suffered damage to its facade and towers in the 1925 earthquake; the subsequent repairs were carried out with portland cement mortar. Problems with the material caused severe cracking in the facade, prompting its reconstruction in the 1950s using a reinforced concrete core with a stone veneer.

The seismic strengthening of mission buildings, if not carefully executed, can pose hazards as well as benefits. Although current seismic stabilization techniques seek to minimize the destruction of a building's historic fabric, they still involve a certain amount of intervention and risk to the original materials. For example, the fixing of upper-wall compression bands and stabilizing diaphragms, as well as the scaffolding, drilling, and general construction activities, may damage delicate wall decorations.

The effects of the 2003 San Simeon earthquake at Mission San Miguel provide an example of this conservation dilemma. While major structural damage was inflicted on the church building itself, the decorated plaster surfaces survived largely intact. Before plans could be developed or action taken to seismically strengthen the building, long-term protection of the original decorations needed to be assured. Planning began with extensive documentation of conditions and removal of statuary, paintings, and church furnishings. This was followed by the evaluation of the original decorative wall plaster, the original windows and doors and ceilings, and the altar *retablo*. A range of issues have had to be addressed, from major challenges such as designing a seismic retrofit that does not disturb the wall paintings to preventing the protective sheeting laid over the walls from abrading some of the fragile paint. Conservators have been able to stabilize the walls, and the seismic retrofit and conservation of the mission church and sacristy are to be completed in 2009.

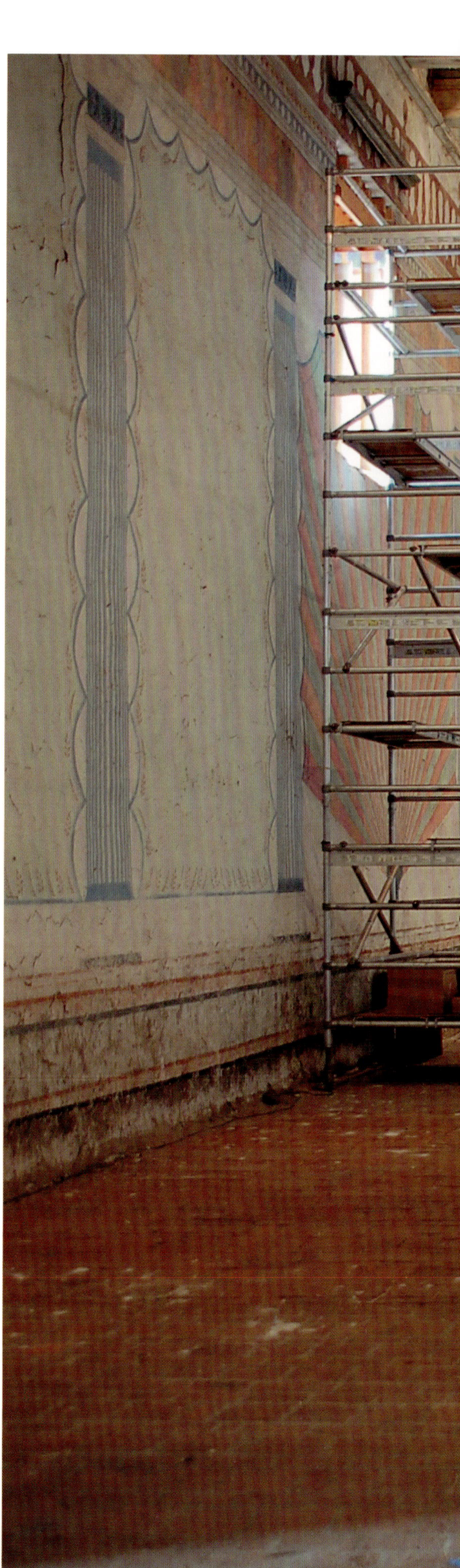

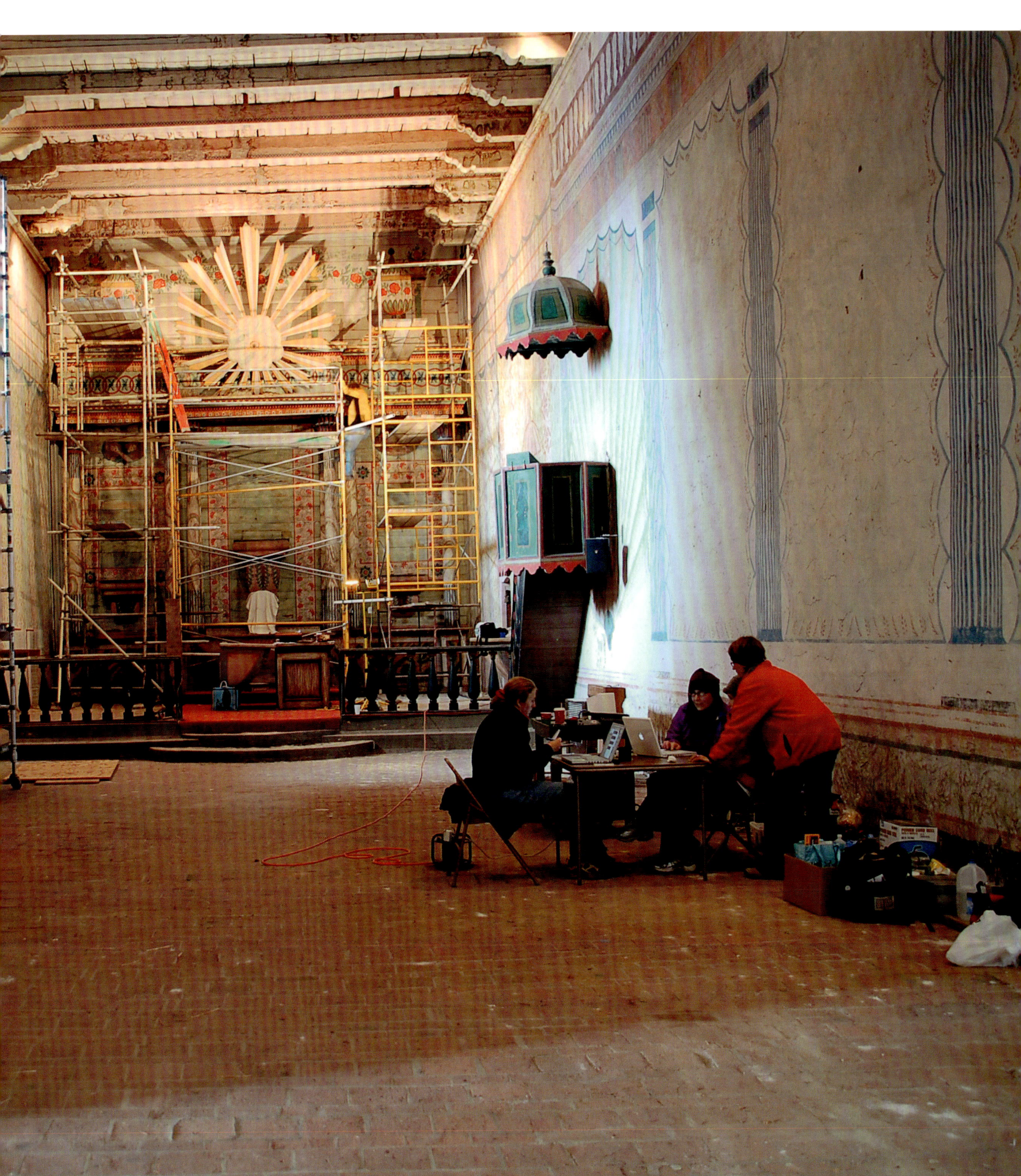

The Getty Seismic Adobe Project

The Getty Seismic Adobe Project, initiated in 1990, brought together a multidisciplinary team of engineers, architects, architectural historians, and architectural conservators to study dozens of historic adobe buildings in California and develop a minimally invasive and economical means of seismically retrofitting these structures. Early on, the group agreed that any work must begin by acknowledging that each building is unique and that any interventions or structural work must be guided by a thorough understanding of the historical methods used in the original construction and a recognition of significant remaining fabric. It was found that while adobe walls can actually bear a surprising amount of vertical weight, they are susceptible to the shaking of earthquakes, which produces fractures around windows and doors, eventually resulting in isolated wall segments that will fail. As a prominent seismic structural engineer remarked, "The common belief that a building is strong because it has already survived several earthquakes is as mistaken as assuming that a patient is healthy because he has survived several heart attacks."[5]

After developing and testing new retrofitting techniques, the project team developed ways to provide seismic protection at a reasonable cost while substantially preserving the integrity of the original historic structure. These techniques include simple compression banding around the upper walls to hold fragmented sections together and the use of a flexible interior diaphragm (similar to an attic floor) to prevent the structure from twisting. The bands themselves are of flexible woven plastic; they run in tandem around the interior and exterior, pinned to each other by through-wall anchors. Steel rods are then inserted vertically through the walls in predrilled holes to enhance stability. These techniques have been applied at the *convento* and church at Mission San Miguel and at the Royal Presidio Chapel in Monterey, as well as to other historic adobe buildings in California.[6]

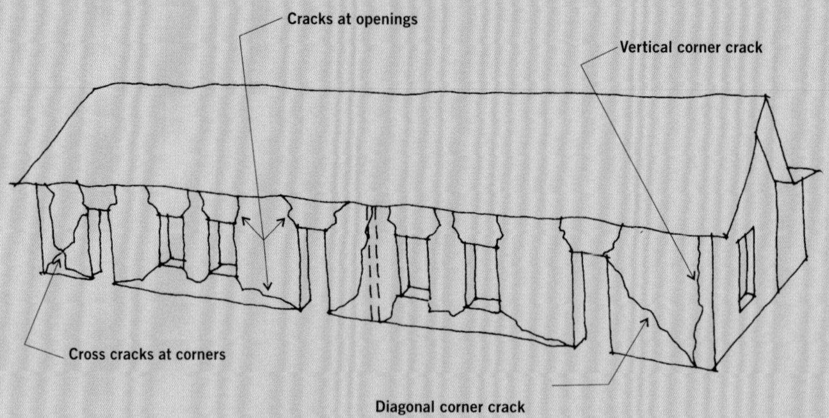

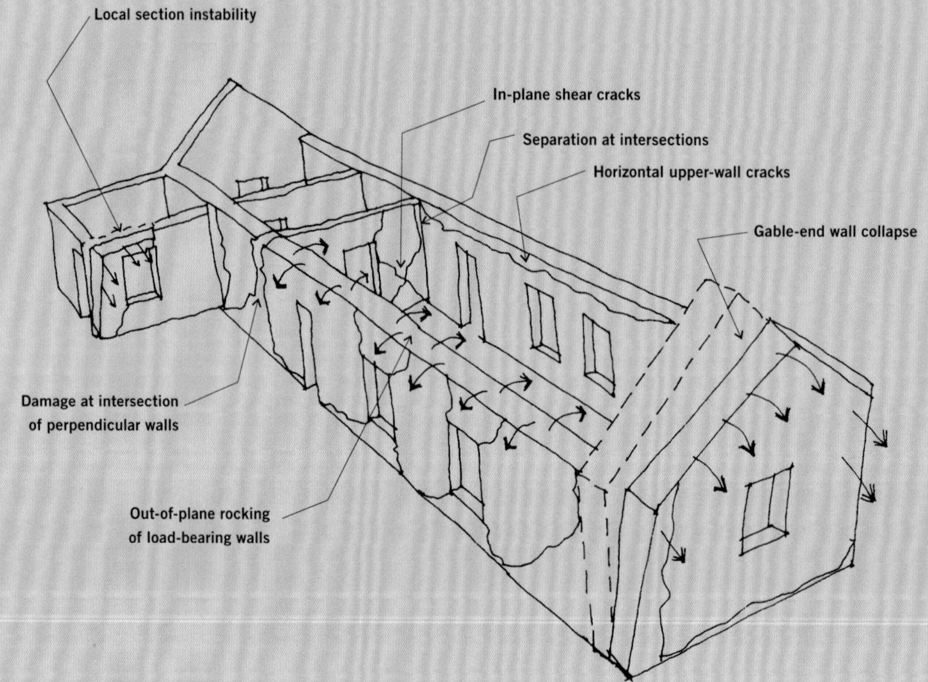

Diagrams illustrating the principal kinds of damage observed in historic adobe buildings after the 1994 Northridge earthquake. Of particular concern both for issues of safety and for potential loss of historic fabric were gable-end walls, which are generally tall and poorly attached and have large height-to-thickness ratios. They suffered severe cracking, causing instability, even collapse. Getty Conservation Institute

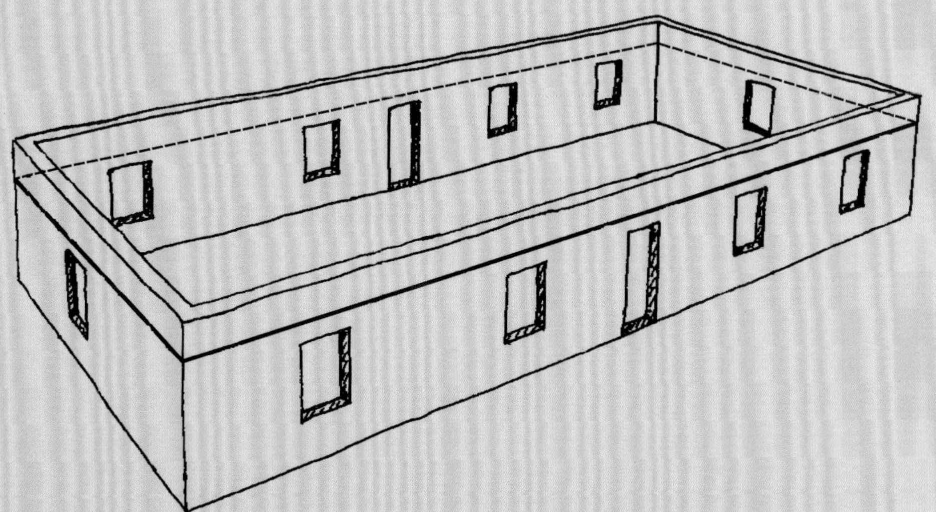

A diagram showing upper-wall horizontal reinforcement used to stabilize adobe walls. This reinforcement can be a bond beam, straps in conjunction with the floor or roof system, or a partial diaphragm. Getty Conservation Institute

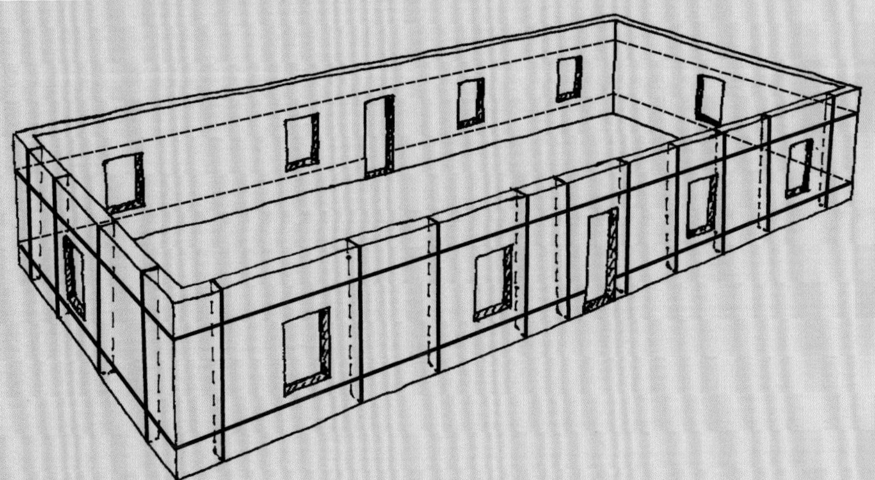

Diagrams showing how vertical reinforcements such as surface straps or internal center-core rods can be combined with upper and lower horizontal reinforcements to stabilize adobe walls (left) and how horizontal cable end connections were used in the retrofit of the historic del Valle adobe (below). Getty Conservation Institute

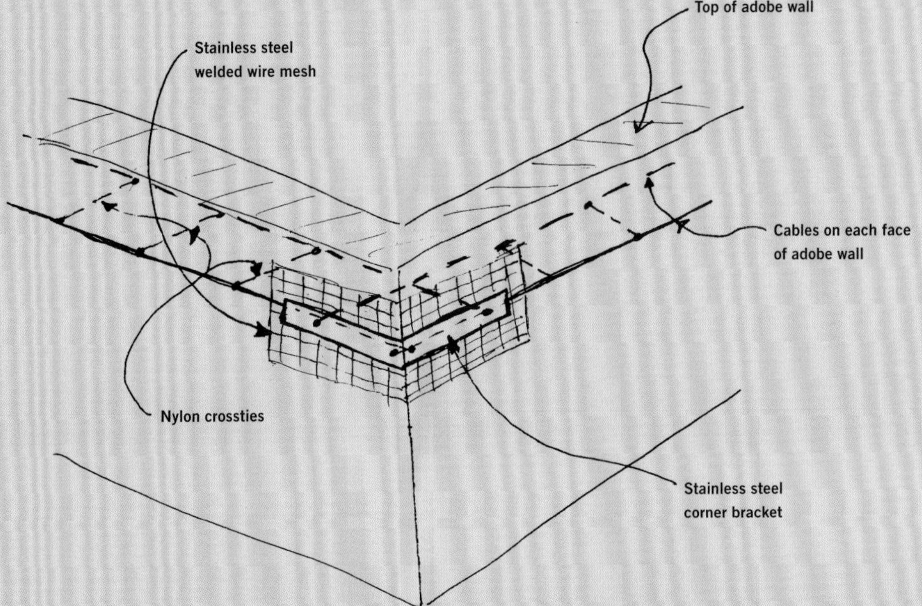

Conservation and Discovery: Murals

Conservation work can sometimes reveal hidden secrets. When seismic work began in 2007 at the Royal Presidio Chapel at Monterey, no evidence of early wall decoration had yet been discovered. The 1942 stucco wall surface was decorated only with a simple dado band. During the recent seismic stabilization work, however, exposure of the window sills revealed an underlying faux stone pattern that inspired the workers to investigate further for original wall surface finishes. The results were stunning. In total, four historic dado designs were identified, all dating to before 1855; the earliest may have been painted in the 1790s, when the chapel was constructed. In addition, the original functions of nave doors were established through their decorative motifs, and long-plastered-over confessionals and a holy water font were revealed. Most extraordinary, the earliest decorative scheme—featuring red geometric elements and renderings of Corinthian capitals—appears to have been executed on wet plaster, perhaps the first evidence of true fresco work in California.[7]

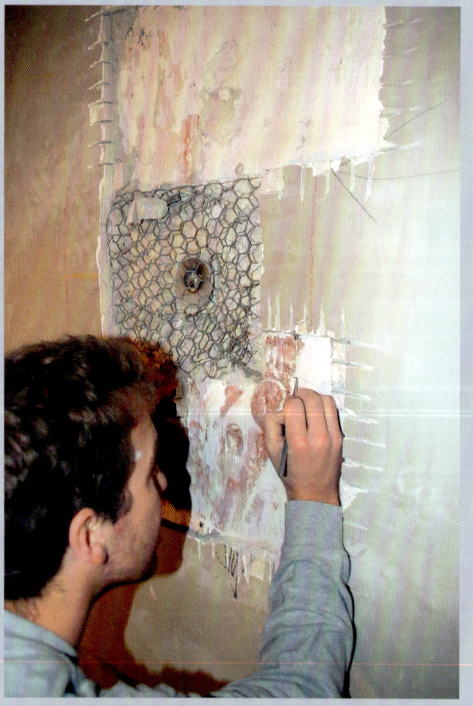

A conservator at the Royal Presidio chapel carefully removes more recent plaster layers to reveal part of an early paint scheme depicting a Corinthian column. The wire lathe and steel through-bolt seen here are part of the seismic strengthening system. Photograph by Anthony Crosby

The multitude of treasures inside the historic buildings of the California missions—paintings, sculpture, rare manuscripts, furniture, vestments, objects of daily life—face myriad dangers too. Poor inventory systems can pose problems when liturgical changes prompt the removal or reordering of original fixtures such as tabernacles, altars, and baptismal fonts, some of which may then be lost or stolen.

From the periods of secularization and abandonment through modern times, the lack of security at mission grounds and buildings has led to theft and vandalism of artworks and artifacts (a problem facing churches worldwide that are seeking a balance between protecting precious artifacts and providing public access for worshippers and tourists). In 1999, for example, a painting of San Vicente Ferrer by the artist José de Páez was stolen from Mission San Miguel, and in 2003 a violin made by the neophyte Carbajal was taken from the museum walls at Mission San Antonio de Padua.

More than half a century ago, the art historian Kurt Baer wrote about the poor condition of paintings in mission collections. "The larger pieces," he noted, "had been removed from their stretchers and folded several times to facilitate transportation, probably in chests for ship or donkey freight. Along the fold lines the paint has cracked badly. Others have been buffeted about and are bruised, torn, or dented. The majority have years of accumulated grime that has dulled some colors almost beyond recognition. Still further damage to the paintings has resulted from rigorous washing."[8] Many such dangers persist today. Rapid changes in temperature and humidity can cause a canvas to expand and contract, cracking the paint layer. Whereas the massive stone or adobe walls in some mission churches provide effective climate control, attics and other facilities are not appropriate for storing paintings, and they may rapidly deteriorate.

Awareness of the importance of these artworks has improved considerably in recent decades, however, and missions are now increasingly allocating scarce funds to the conservation of selected works. In general, it is best to keep paintings in a controlled environment in which damaging light and heat are minimized. Cleaning, which may alleviate the effects of accumulated dust and soot, needs to be carried out by a trained conservator, as even wiping the surface of a painting with a feather duster can dislodge small fragments of paint.[9]

The process of cleaning paintings long clouded by soot from candle smoke and dust from centuries of exposure often reveals their histories. In 2002 Mission San Gabriel commissioned conservators to restore its famous set of Stations of the Cross, painted by neophytes at Mission San Fernando Rey. When the Eleventh Station of the Cross arrived at the studio, it was found to have been damaged by previous restorations. "Most edges of the painting were missing," the conservator recalled. "The canvas [had] deteriorated and developed holes, so someone [had] glued the painting to masonite to give it better support. Then the surface [had been] totally overpainted. In fact, during one restorer's restoration, a beard was added to Mary's face and she became a he."[10] In this instance, the recent conservation work clarified the painting's original meaning.

Like paintings, sculptures can be easily relocated. Usually placed within *nichos*, on *retablos*, or on small stands affixed to church walls, they can fall and break during earthquakes. Statues are generally made of wooden parts, often with gesso or cloth garments, and therefore are susceptible to all the threats facing these materials: rot, mold, and insect infestations. Other painted wooden items such as *retablos*, pulpits, altar railings, and furnishings are subject to similar problems.

Conservation and Discovery: Sculpture

The conservation of sculptures can sometimes have unexpected consequences. The true nature of one sculpture, for example, was discovered during conservation. "When the statue from San Juan Capistrano arrived at our studio, he was masquerading as San Antonio . . . complete with a baby Jesus on his arm," the conservator recalls. "The entire surface was heavily overpainted with glossy enamel paint. Imagine our surprise when, after testing, we discovered a silver and gold leaf suit of armor beneath the overpaint. This was not San Antonio. Hiding under his coat of enamel was the patron saint of Mission San Juan Capistrano."[11] Similarly reconfigured, the life-sized statue of San Luis Obispo from Mission San Luis Obispo went through three versions of vestment design, layered one over the other, the most recent painted by Harry Downie in 1948. Restoration work reestablished the 1800 *estofado* design of flowers and also dressed the saint's hands in their original black gloves.[12]

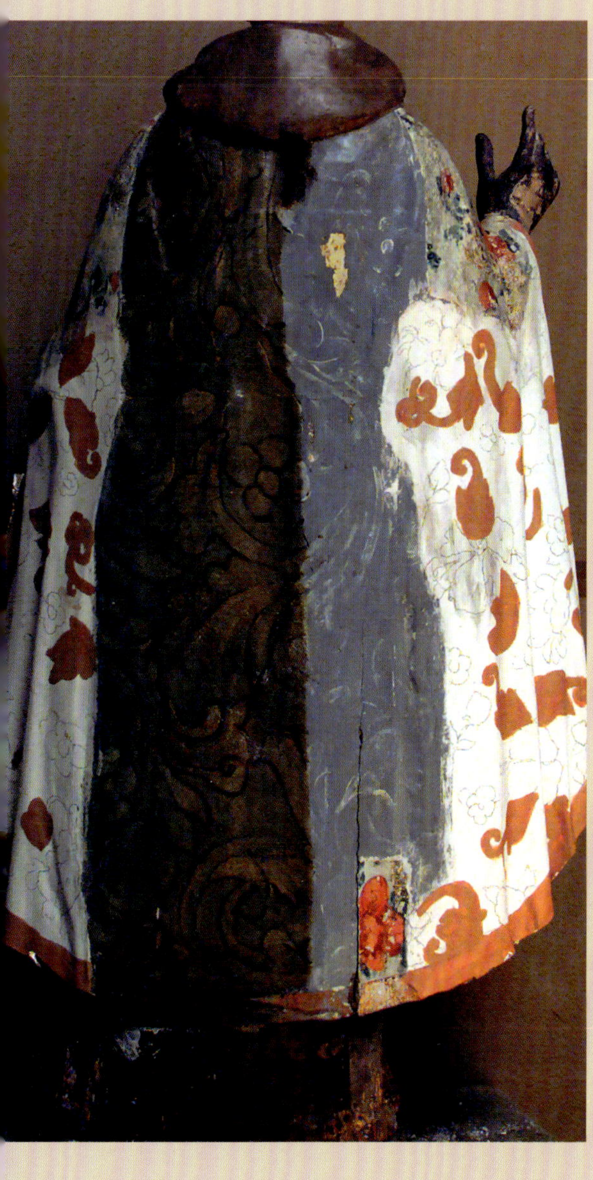

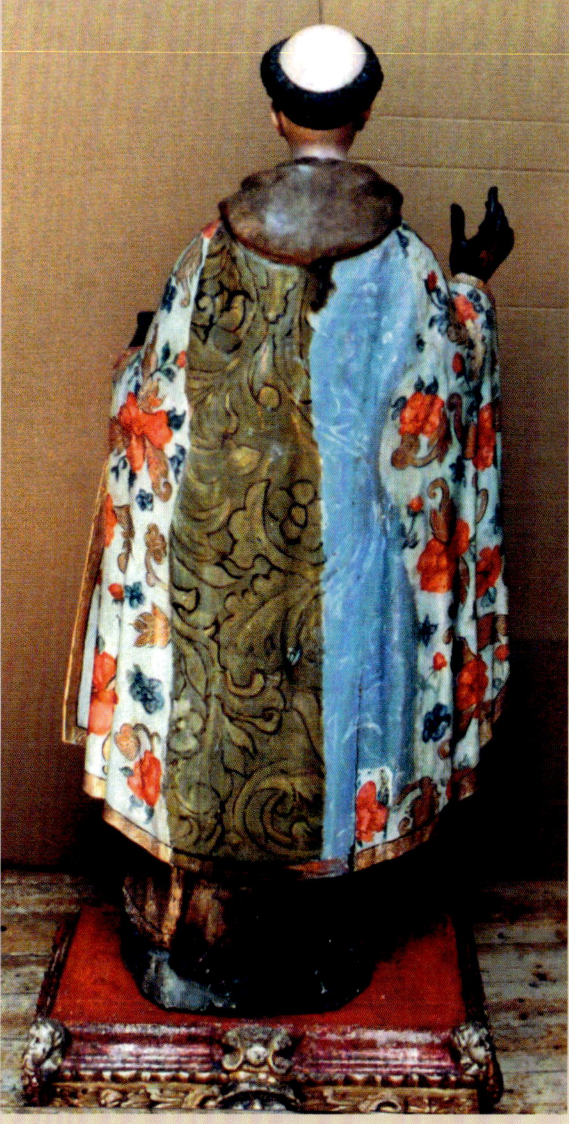

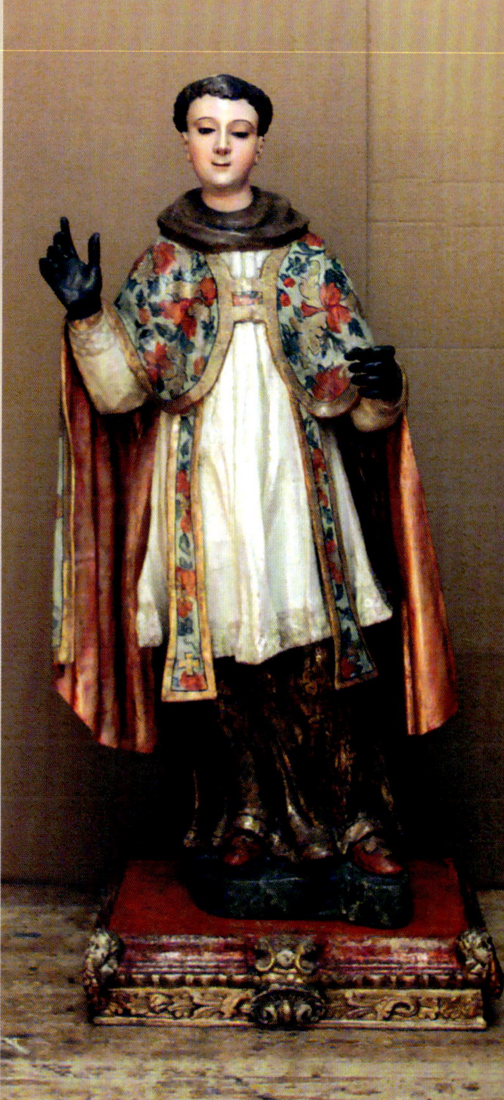

During restoration of this life-sized statue of San Luis Obispo, later layers of overpaint, seen at left, were removed, exposing the original 1800 *estofado* design of bright flowers, seen at center and at right. Photograph courtesy South Coast Fine Art Conservation Center, Santa Barbara

The Santa Bárbara Mission Archive-Library

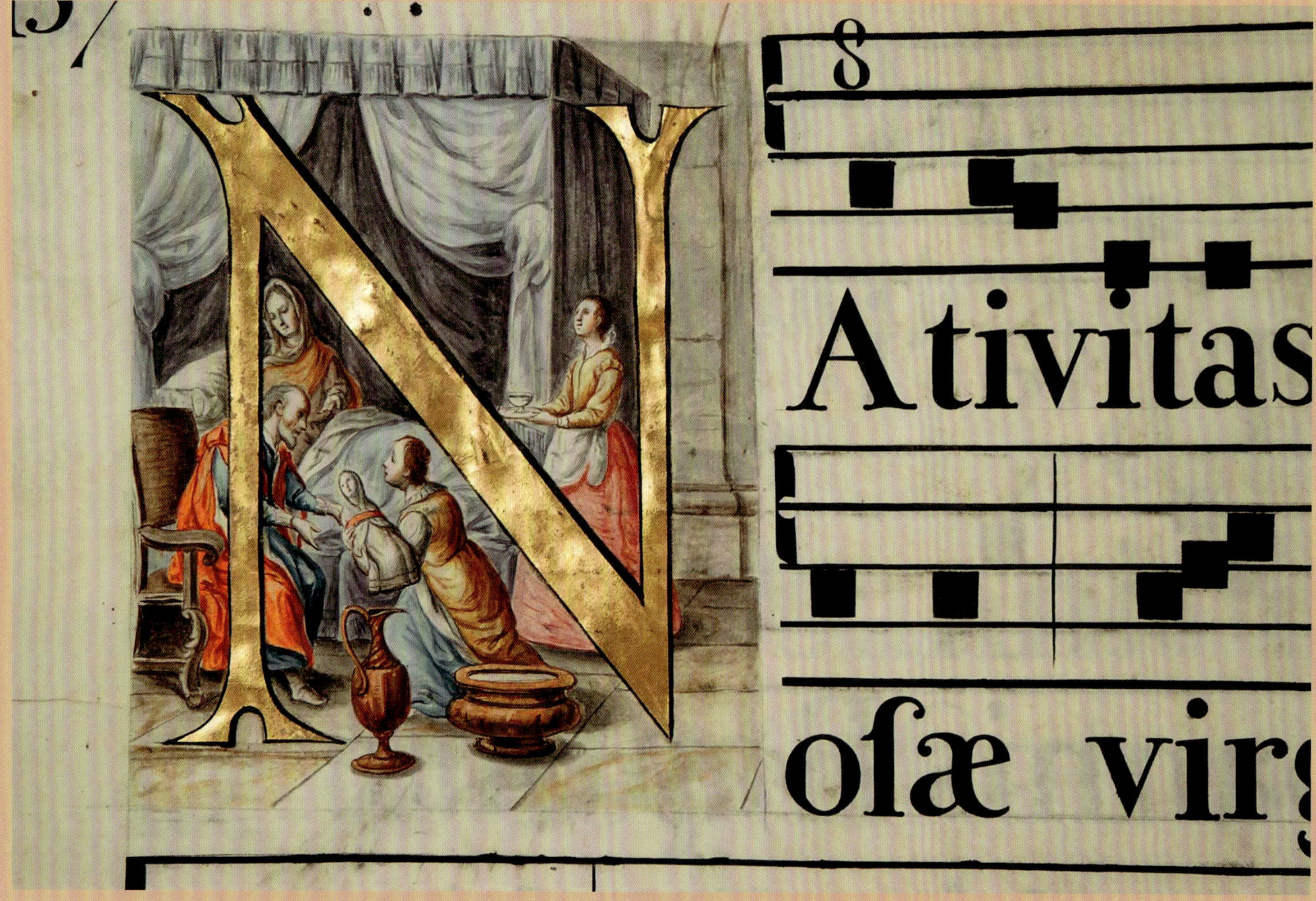

Illumination from *Antiphonarium Romanum*, Colegio Apostólico de San Fernando, Mexico, 1774. Courtesy of the Santa Bárbara Mission Archive-Library. Photograph by Bill Dewey

The Santa Bárbara Mission Archive-Library is one of the most significant repositories of mission-related documents in California. Since its founding in 1786, Mission Santa Bárbara has functioned as a Franciscan-administered church. From the 1830s through the 1850s, when many of California's mission complexes were suffering serious physical decline, a large number of mission records were transferred to Santa Bárbara, which replaced Mission San Carlos Borremeo in Carmel as the principal Franciscan church in California.

Today notable holdings of the Archive-Library include the Junípero Serra Collection, a group of over one thousand documents relating to the California missions' founder, and the California Mission Documents Collection, which contains over four thousand documents. The Archive-Library also houses California's largest collection of mission sacramental registers, which are an invaluable resource for historians and genealogists. Other notable holdings include the papers of one of Spanish and Mexican California's most important families, the de la Guerra family of Santa Barbara, as well as a complete set of Edwin Deakin's oil paintings of the California missions.

In addition to the centuries-old documents at the core of its collection, the Archive-Library contains a large number of photographic negatives from the nineteenth and early twentieth centuries, which present additional conservation concerns. Like many privately funded archives, it faces significant challenges in attempting to preserve its invaluable collections and continuing to make them available to researchers. Information about visiting and using the Archive-Library may be found on its Web site, www.sbmal.org.

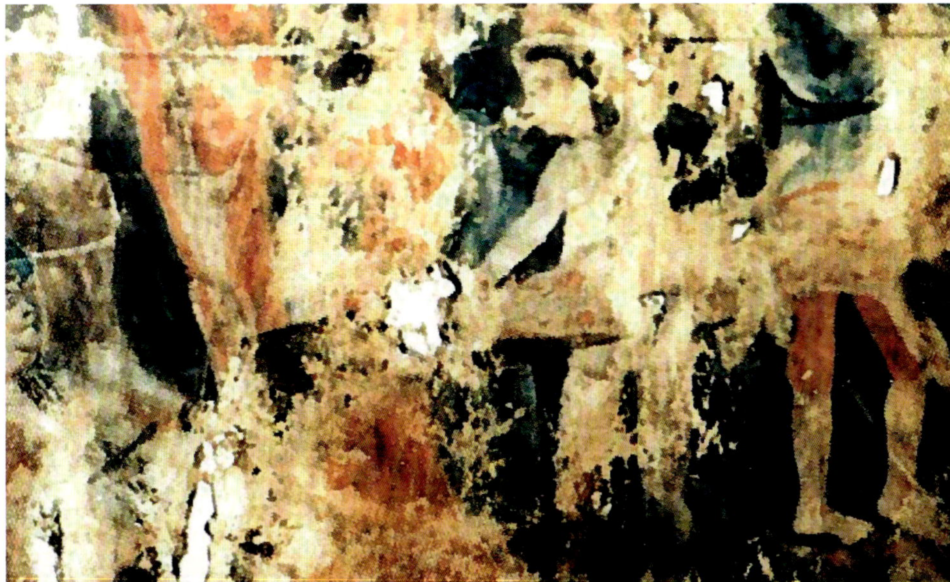

The painting of the Eleventh Station of the Cross, before restoration. During an earlier, ill-advised treatment, the badly damaged canvas had been glued to a masonite surface and then overpainted. Photograph courtesy South Coast Fine Art Conservation Center, Santa Barbara

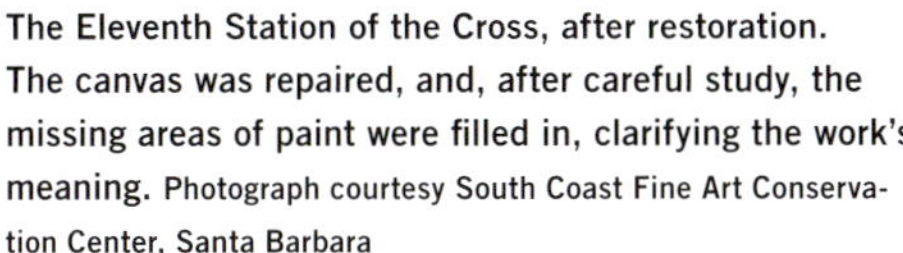

The Eleventh Station of the Cross, after restoration. The canvas was repaired, and, after careful study, the missing areas of paint were filled in, clarifying the work's meaning. Photograph courtesy South Coast Fine Art Conservation Center, Santa Barbara

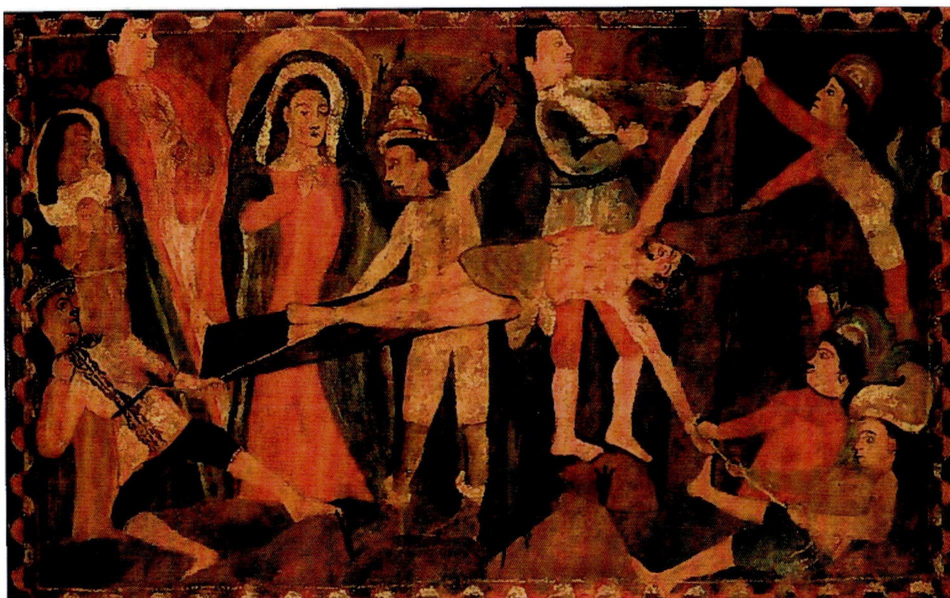

The display of textiles is also fraught with conservation problems. Cloth takes up and releases humidity, causing deterioration, and when exposed to light during display, suffers degradation of its colors. Vestments are often hung vertically, becoming stressed over the years by the pull of gravity, especially at the shoulders. Condensation in closed glass cases promotes mildew, which can go undetected on the rear and interior of fabrics. Conservators look for the presence of insect debris, cobwebs, and small holes as clear signs of pests. In addition, a regular part of collections maintenance is detection of microbes that produce mildew and fungus.

Historic collections of books in the California missions, including handwritten ledgers, hand-painted musical scores, and imported printed volumes, are among the cultural treasures of the mission period. By far the most extensive collection is housed at the Santa Bárbara Mission Archive-Library, where the volumes are available to scholars for research. Other notable collections reside at Missions San Carlos Borromeo and San Fernando Rey. Among the dangers to such collections are deterioration from light exposure, the corrosive effects of dust, and changes in humidity. In addition, books that are shelved in a vertical

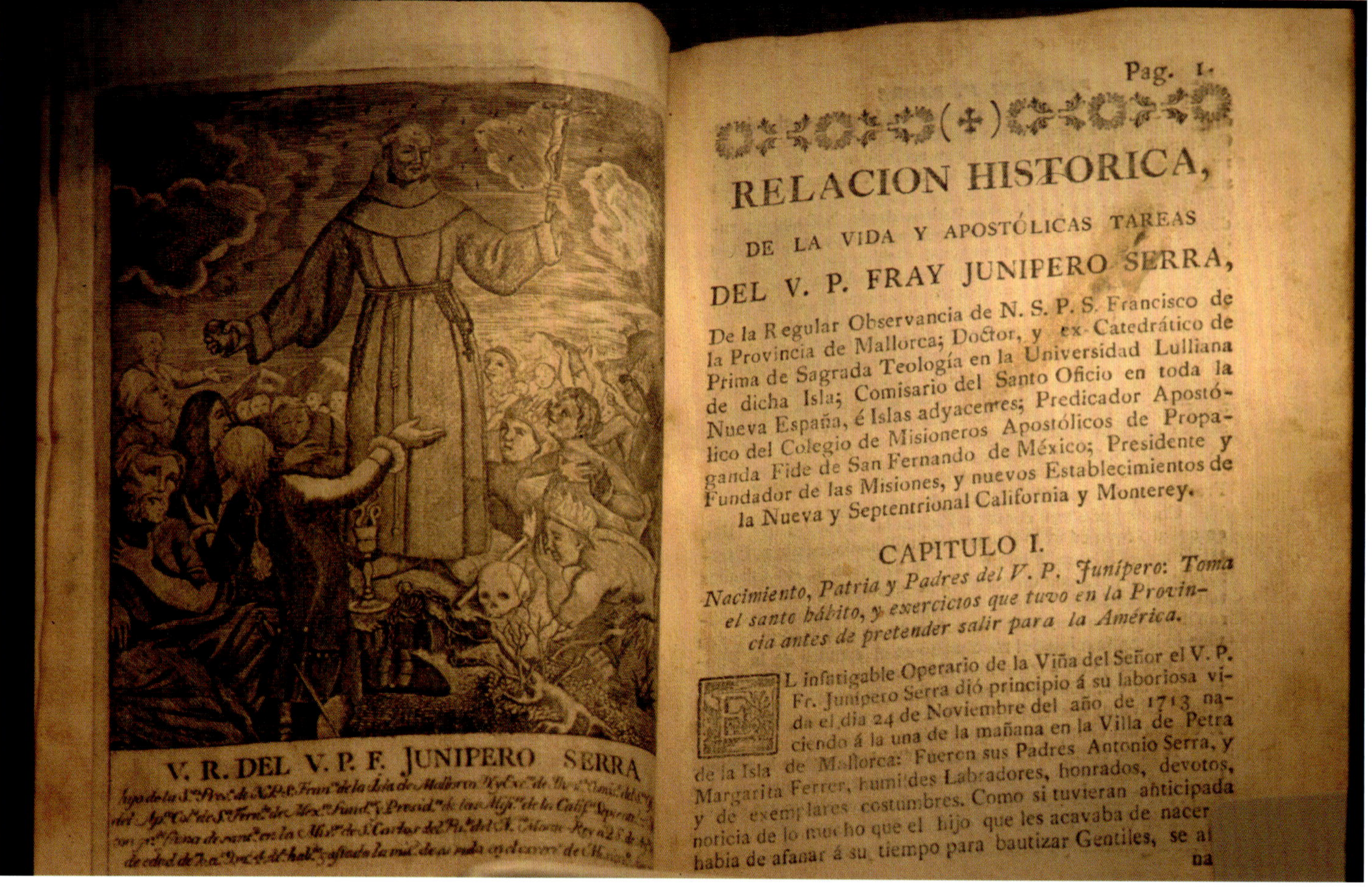

A rare original edition of Francisco Palóu's 1787 biography of Father Serra is among the treasures in the archive at Mission San Carlos Borromeo. Photograph by G. Aldana

position are subject to stress on their bindings. Also, many insects, including silverfish, bookworms, and the common fly, pose a threat to paper products. Conservators recommend that when books and other manuscripts are not on display, they should be encased in protective, acid-free archival files or boxes; wooden bookshelves, which contain destructive acids, are not appropriate.

Archaeological remains are still to be found near many mission churches and *conventos.* Workshops, neophyte residences, water systems, and cemeteries may lie under adjacent fields, gardens, and parking lots. Trenching for electrical lines or grading of parking areas has frequently revealed such remains. Even modern buildings have been found to overlie intact mission foundations. For these reasons, careful study and planning precedes any earth-moving projects taking place in areas surrounding mission *cascos.* Archaeological remains hold unique information about the past, and their exposure and interpretation have proved popular with visitors at Missions Santa Bárbara, San Luis Rey, San Juan Capistrano, and San Buenaventura. These irreplaceable and nonrenewable assets can be excavated only one time, however, and the analysis of archaeological findings can be time-consuming and expensive. And once ruins are exposed to the air, they begin to deteriorate, posing complex and costly conservation problems for the future. Archaeologists now advocate preservation, not excavation, of archaeological remains, unless these resources are threatened by imminent destruction.

One of the greatest challenges to all the missions is securing sufficient funds to meet conservation and maintenance needs. Since the nineteenth century, many individuals and organizations have attempted to preserve them. Today individual missions often

Case Study: San Juan Capistrano

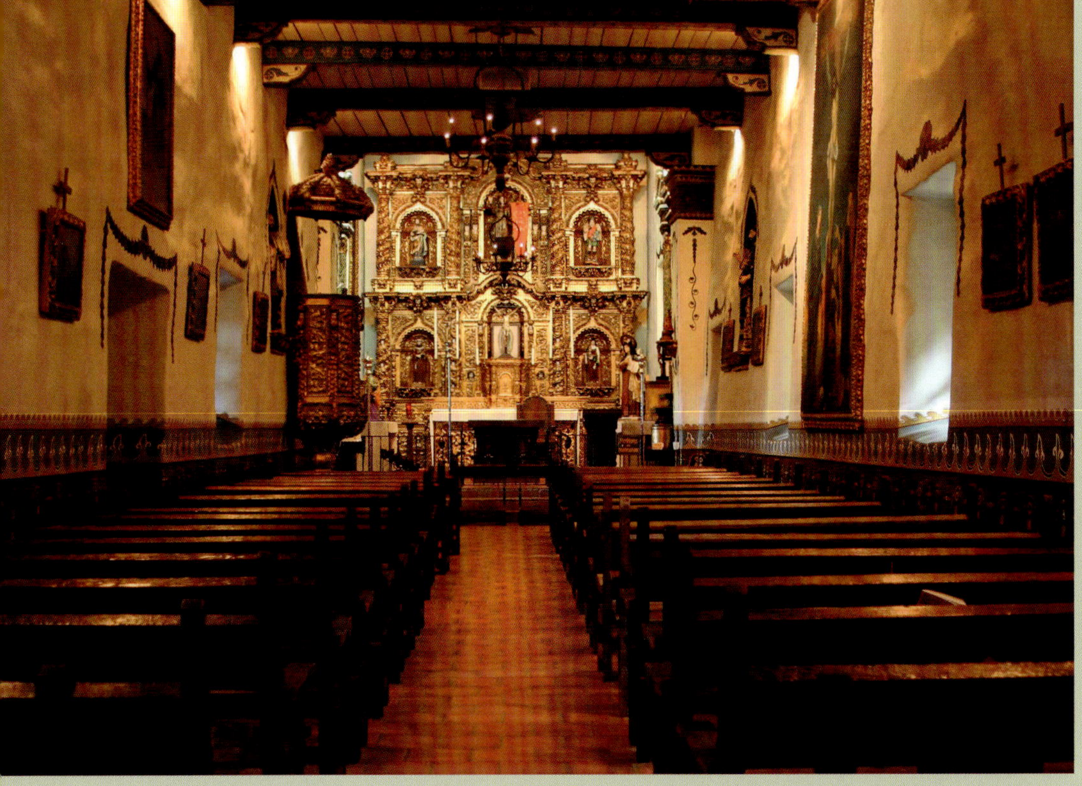

LEFT: A recent conservation program at the Serra Chapel stabilized the adobe wall plasters and repaired the outside of the building. It also featured the cleaning and conservation of the Baroque gilded *retablo*. Conservators removed heavy metal leaf added in an earlier restoration, returning the altarpiece to its historical appearance. Courtesy Mission San Juan Capistrano

BELOW: The conservation of the ruins of the Great Stone Church, seen at right, was completed in 2006. Courtesy Mission San Juan Capistrano

Mission San Juan Capistrano is unique among the California missions by virtue of its long-term interest in and commitment to conservation, its successful fund-raising and organizational capacity, and its wide-ranging and comprehensive approach to historic preservation. The mission's Great Stone Church was destroyed in an earthquake in 1812, and in the late nineteenth and early twentieth centuries the Landmarks Club helped to stabilize the structure and prevent the entire mission from falling into irreparable ruin. In the 1920s, Father St. John O'Sullivan initiated restoration activities, which continued over subsequent decades. A number of these restorations, however, created new problems, and in the late 1990s the mission developed a comprehensive master plan aimed at reversing prior conservation efforts and preserving the historic mission's many assets.

There are a number of projects recently completed or currently under way. Following the preservation of the ruins of the Great Stone Church, completed in 2006, perhaps most important is the conservation of the Serra Chapel, built by Acjachemen (Juaneño) neophytes in 1782 where Father Serra, the founder of the California missions, is known to have conducted services. This project comprises a wide range of activities, such as stabilization of original wall plasters and repairs of the badly damaged adobe exterior, including removal of cement wainscoting from an earlier restoration, which has resulted in damage to the walls. It also includes the cleaning and conservation of the Baroque *retablo*, installed in 1924, which had also suffered from a misguided restoration, when it was covered with heavy metal leaf. Conservators have determined, however, that underneath almost all surfaces the *retablo* appeared to retain the original seventeenth-century burnished water gilding. The recently added overleaf is being removed, and the *retablo* is being restored to its historical appearance. Also under way is the conservation, cleaning, and reframing of the seventeenth-century Stations of the Cross paintings, as well as the conservation of the chapel's interior wall decorations and the installation of improved humidity and temperature monitoring systems.

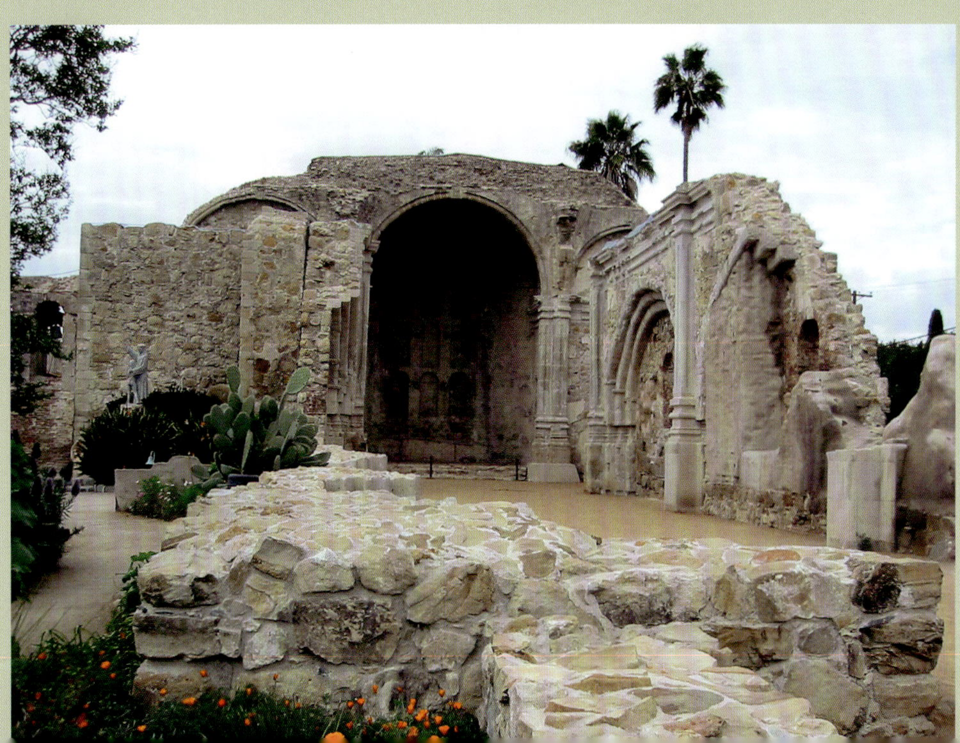

have support groups that work to raise funds for their study, restoration, and maintenance. Dioceses of the Roman Catholic Church and individual parishes must often weigh the spiritual needs of their communities against the conservation needs of their historic buildings and artifacts. This is a problem encountered by other spiritual sites and places of worship around the world, where shifting liturgical or religious practices conflict with the heritage values.

The California Missions Foundation, the only statewide organization dedicated to funding preservation of the California missions, has engaged in a number of initiatives, including a recent campaign in collaboration with the National Trust for Historic Preservation (NTHP) to preserve Mission San Miguel, designated one of America's "11 Most Endangered Historical Places" in 2006 by the NTHP. Sometimes preservation initiatives have encountered problems, stemming in part from conflicting interpretations of the missions' many values. In 2004, for example, the federal government approved the California Missions Preservation Act, which was to provide $10 million in federal funds, to be matched by the Foundation, for the repair and conservation of the missions and their art and artifacts. Because most of the mission churches are owned by the Catholic Church and are still used for religious services, a lawsuit was filed challenging the act's constitutionality on the grounds that it violated the separation of church and state. Opposition to the act was based largely on emphasizing the missions' religious value, virtually to the exclusion of all others—historical, cultural, artistic, and symbolic. When no money was allocated by Congress to fund the act, the lawsuit was dropped. The legal question and debate, however, have yet to be resolved. A solution no doubt lies in recognizing the missions' full range of values and in developing conservation programs that take them all into account.

Fortunately, efforts to secure recognition for historic places of worship through public/private partnerships, such as Save America's Treasures, have met with more success. Missions San Juan Capistrano, San Luis Rey, and San Miguel have been designated as official projects of this program.[13] It is clear that support for the California missions must go forward with a broad base of support from the state's present population. These historic buildings, artworks, artifacts, ruins, and landscapes—sacred and secular alike—that have managed to survive to the present deserve our utmost efforts to ensure they will be with us for centuries to come.

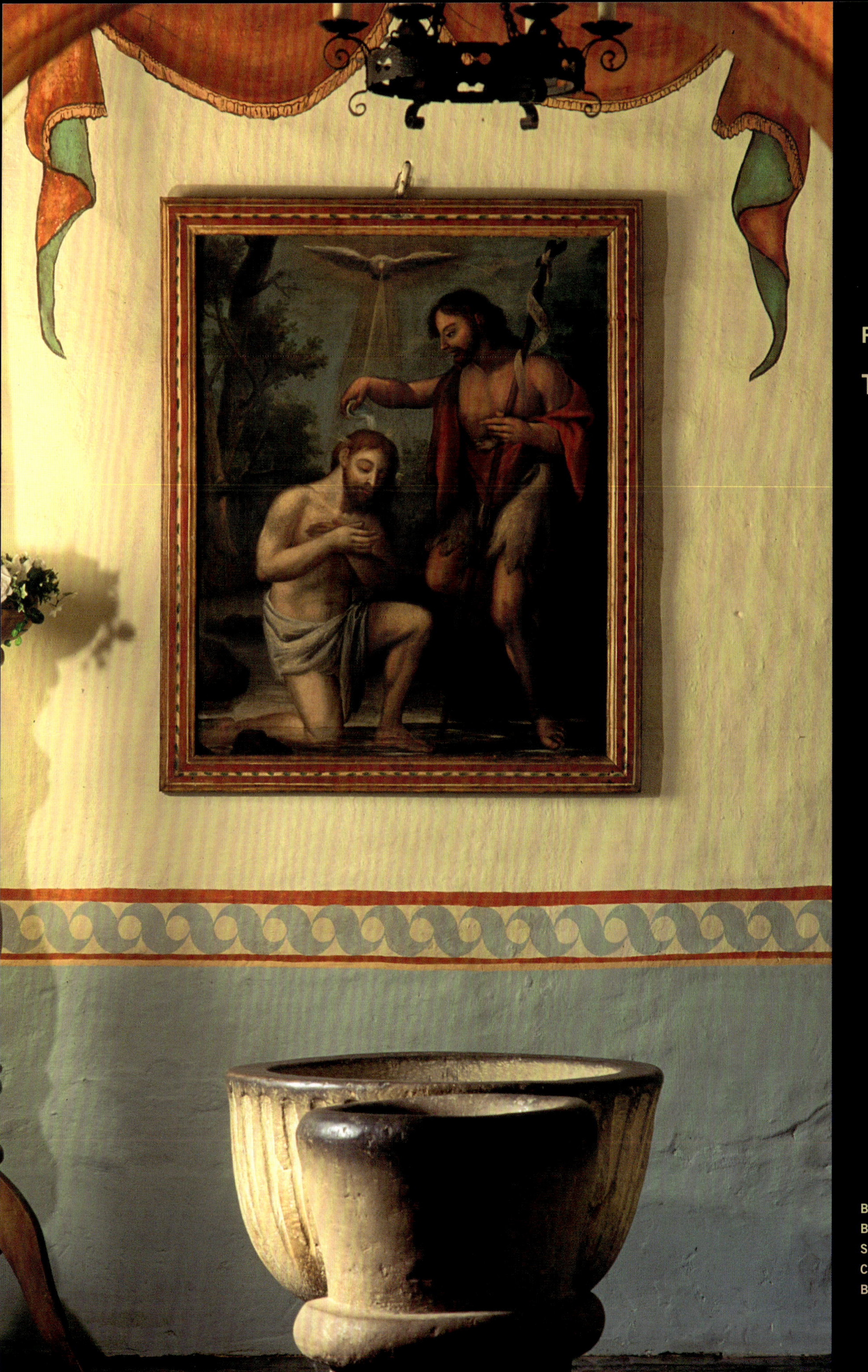

Part Two

The Missions

Baptismal fonts at Mission Santa Bárbara, in front of a painting by the Spanish artist José de Páez; it depicts Christ being baptized by John the Baptist. Photograph by G. Aldana

San Diego de Alcalá

FOUNDED JULY 16, 1769

Location: *San Diego*

Founder: *Father Junípero Serra*

Presidio District: *San Diego*

Peak Mission Population: *1,829 (1824)*

Major Native Groups: *Ipai, Tipai, Luiseño, Pai Pai, Kiliwa*

Historical Assets: *Baptistery, church facade, front wing buttresses, one room of* convento, *cemetery ruins, museum*

Existing Church: *Reconstructed 1931, of modern concrete with adobe infill*

Ownership: *Roman Catholic Church, Diocese of San Diego*

Historical Status: *California Historical Landmark (No. 242); National Historic Landmark*

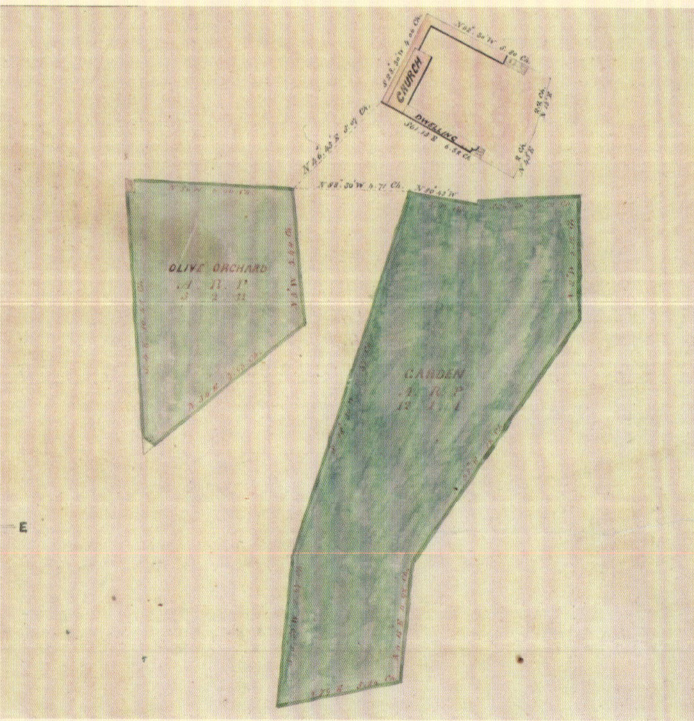

Map of the *casco* by the surveyor John G. Cleal, 1854 (detail). Courtesy of The Bancroft Library, University of California, Berkeley

Mission San Diego, the "mother" mission of California, was the first of twenty-one missions scattered along some 650 miles of the Alta California coast.[1] Originally located adjacent to the presidio near the sea, it was moved in 1774 about six miles up the San Diego River to gain access to more favorable agricultural lands and also to distance converts from abuses by the soldiers. The local Tipai resisted colonization, and skirmishes weeks after the mission's founding left three dead on each side. In 1775 as many as eight hundred warriors joined to attack both the mission and the presidio, resulting in the death of Father Luis Jayme along with a blacksmith and a carpenter who were asleep in their beds. Another Tipai rebellion a few months later concluded with the trial, imprisonment, torture, and ultimate release of three village captains, with one having died in captivity.[2]

San Diego, like other early missions, grew slowly, with tule-and-pole structures gradually replaced by those of adobe and tile. As at other missions in this region, herds of livestock rapidly increased in number and crops prospered. By 1808 the population had reached fifteen hundred, requiring a larger church. To direct construction, the Franciscans likely employed the master mason Miguel Blanco, who executed a design considered old-fashioned even at the time of its execution.[3] The *ladrillo* facade featured a Moorish *alfiz* (decorative door bracketing), as well as a distinctive undulating Baroque *espadaña.* Massive front buttresses were added in 1811 when the roof cracked, fortuitously allowing the nearly completed building to survive the 1812 earthquake. The decorative facade was soon covered with a tiled portico supported by three arches. Other notable constructions at Mission San Diego included an extensive water system, which brought water six miles downriver and outlasted the mission by several decades.

The mission was abandoned soon after secularization. Its buildings were occupied by the U.S. Army from 1849 to 1857, during which time the church was reconfigured as both barracks and stable and roofed with shingles. The original roof's tiles were salvaged by San Diego's town residents, and the mission's extensive adobe buildings melted rapidly back into the earth. In 1900 the Landmarks Club initiated preservation of the ruins, but by the 1920s, when serious restoration efforts began, only one room of the *convento* remained standing, along with the church's facade and buttresses, which were all that could be saved.[4] The reconstruction of the church in 1931 adhered to contemporary standards of historical accuracy, and where possible

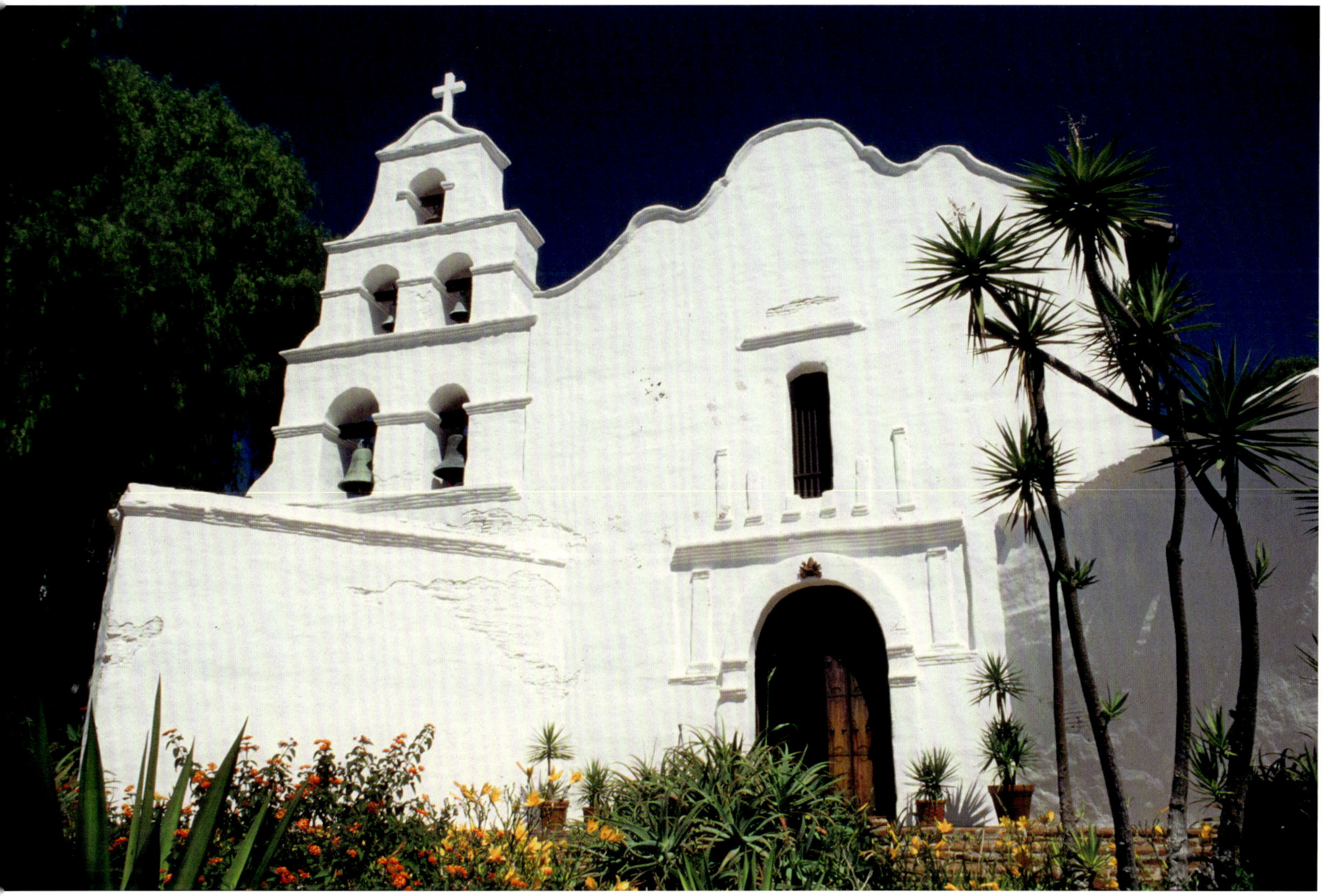

Modern view of Mission San Diego, with its distinctive front buttresses, facade, and *espadaña*. Photograph by G. Aldana

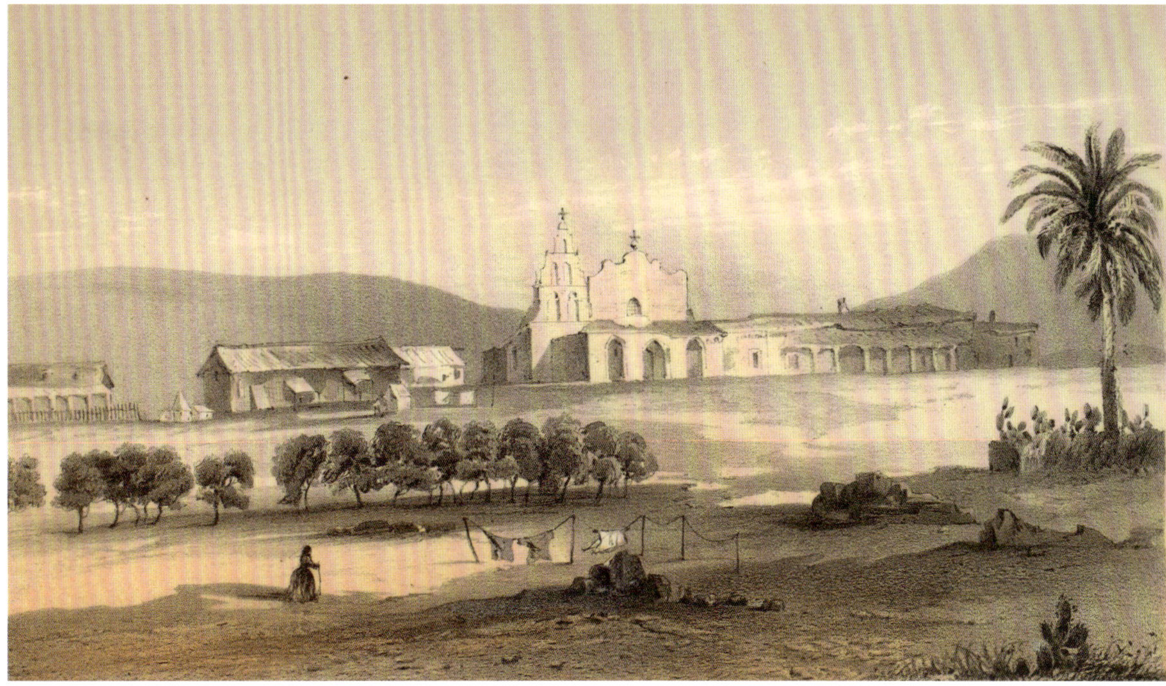

View of Mission San Diego, ca. 1854, showing the *espadaña* intact; the roofs and the buildings are beginning to decay. Artist unknown, color lithograph. Courtesy of The Bancroft Library, University of California, Berkeley

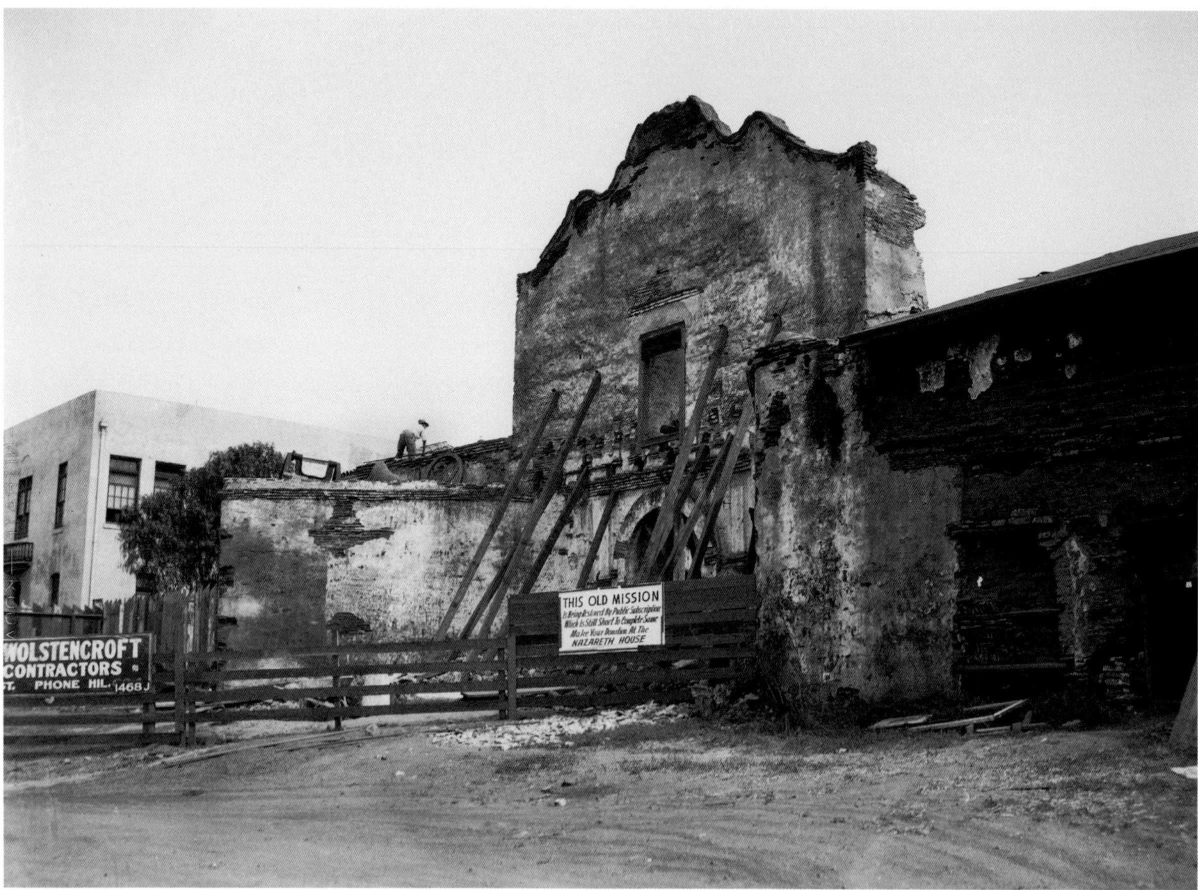

View of the mission in 1930, as reconstruction begins. Only the facade, buttresses, and one *convento* room remain from the original buildings. Courtesy of the San Diego Historical Society

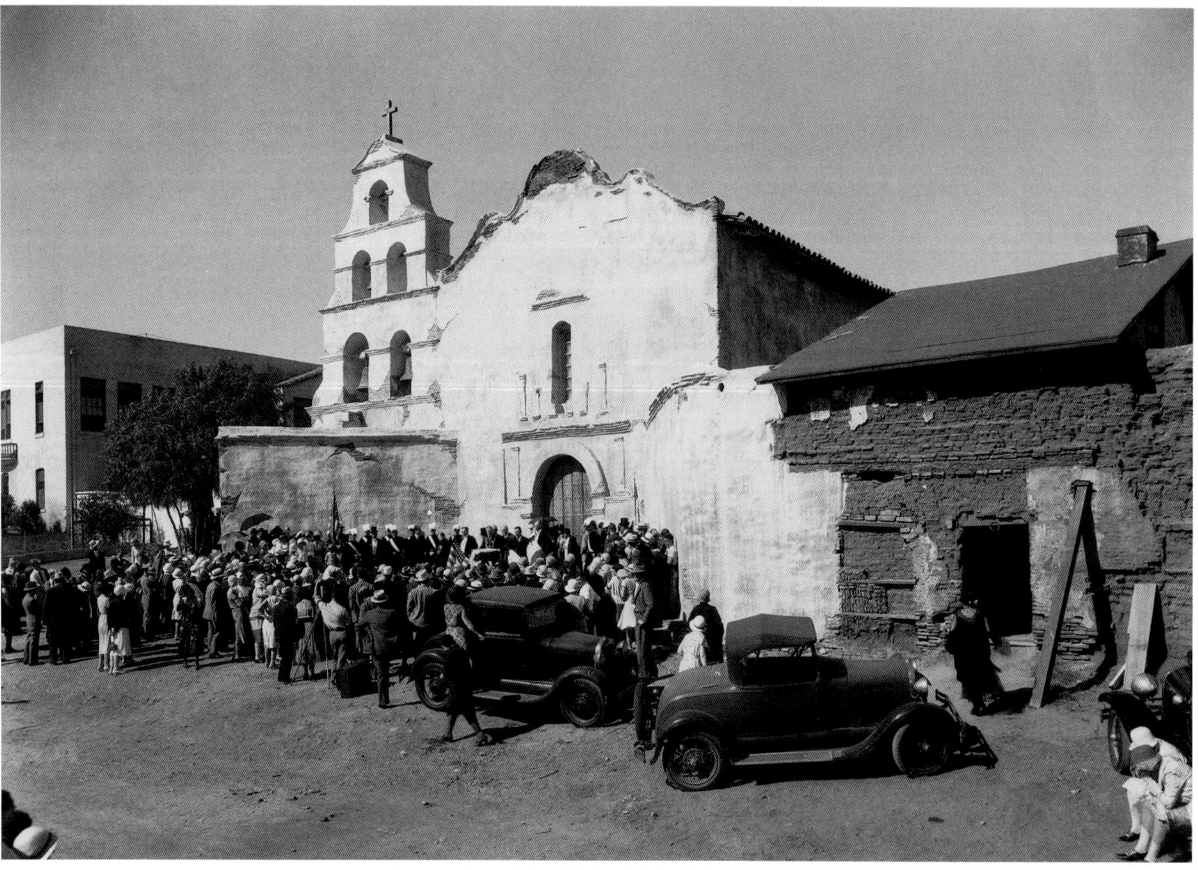

A crowd celebrates the rededication of Mission San Diego's reconstructed church in 1931. Courtesy of the San Diego Historical Society

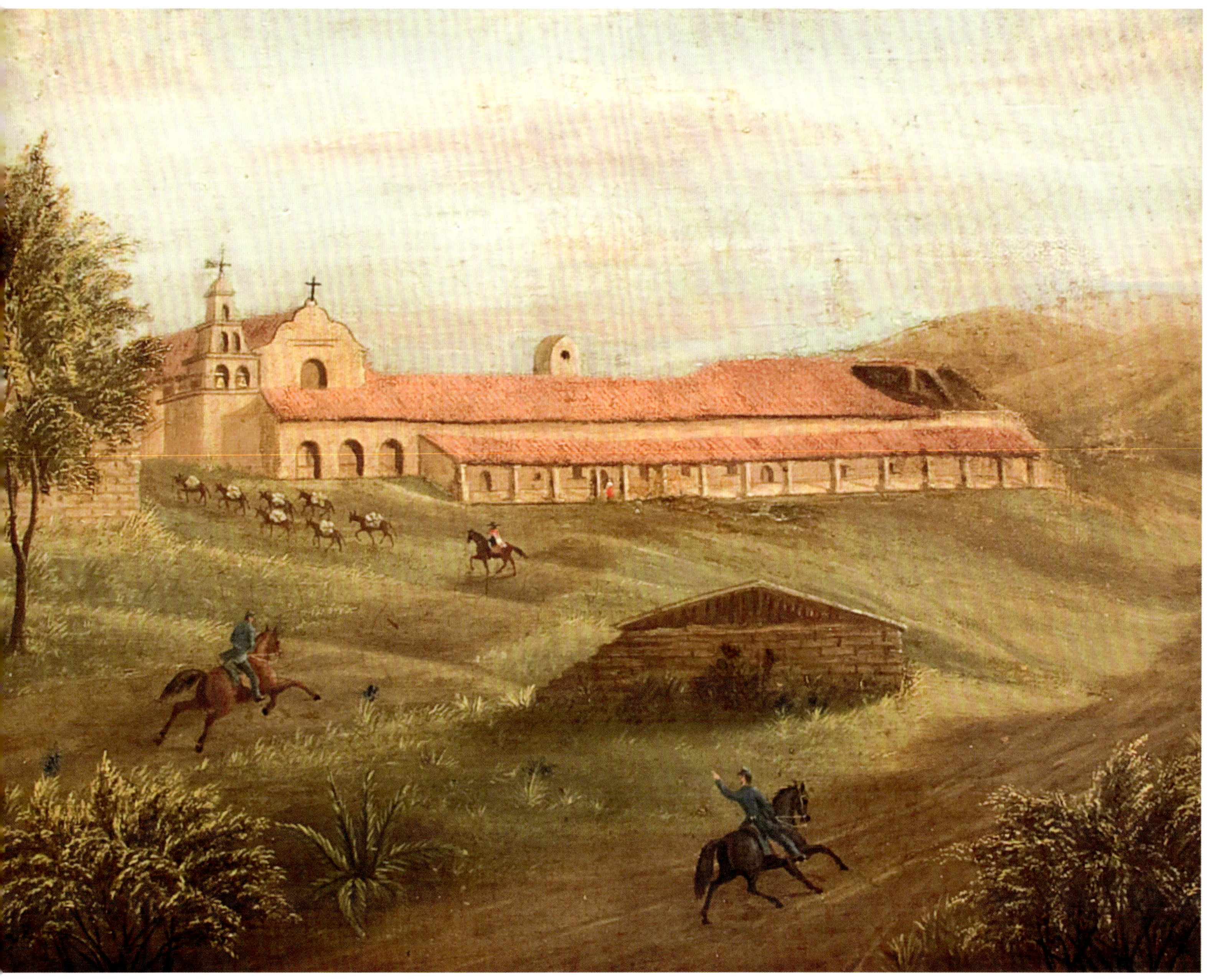

original materials were replaced in kind: locally made adobe brick and tiles and hand-hewn wood were used, although the walls were largely constructed of reinforced concrete.[5] A misguided attempt to replicate the soft unevenness of adobe surfaces resulted in a lumpy finish on the nave walls. Two decades of archaeological excavations of the mission quadrangle began in the late 1960s; however, most of the findings from this work have remained unpublished.[6] During preliminary construction of a parish hall in 1989, the early mission and U.S. Dragoon cemeteries were discovered on the east side of the quadrangle and are now preserved under a grassy park. Original mission art and religious items are displayed in a small museum, documenting the history of modern Mission San Diego's large and active parish.

Artistic portrayal of the mission and its landscape setting, ca. 1850. The original covered portico can be seen in front of the church, as well as the colonnade fronting the *convento*. H. M. T. Powell, *Mission San Diego*. Oil on canvas. Carl Dentzel and Elisabeth Waldo Dentzel Collection, Elizabeth Waldo-Dentzel Studios, Northridge, California

San Carlos Borromeo del Río Carmelo

FOUNDED JUNE 3, 1770

Location: *Carmel*

Founder: *Father Junípero Serra*

Presidio District: *Monterey*

Peak Mission Population: *876 (1795)*

Major Native Groups: *Costanoan, Esselen*

Historical Assets: *Original stone church walls; fine collections of books, art, and liturgical artifacts on display*

Existing Church: *Constructed of stone, completed in 1797; restoration in 1936 with a reinforcing concrete collar around the top of walls*

Ownership: *Roman Catholic Church, Diocese of Monterey*

Historical Status: *California Historical Landmark (No. 135); National Historic Landmark*

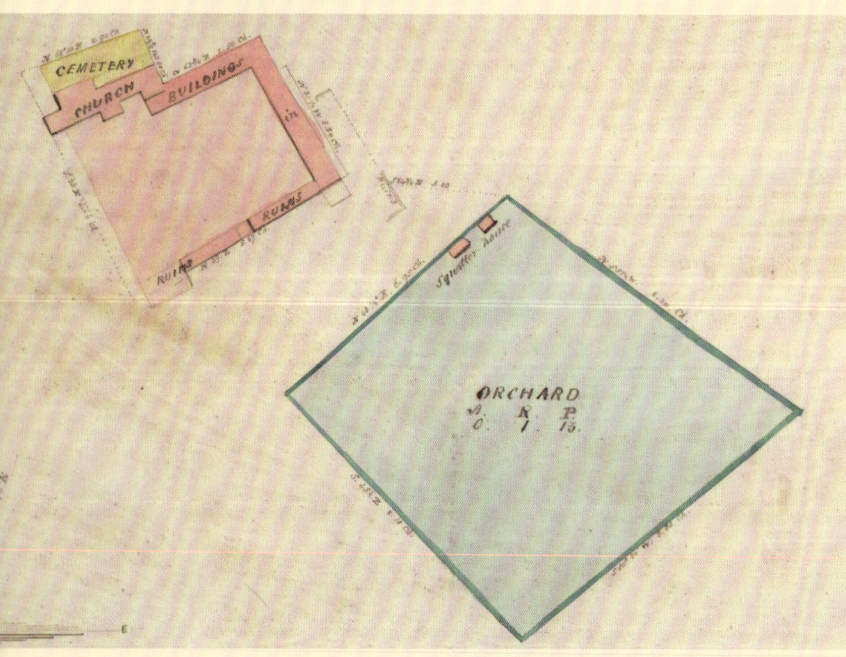

Map of the *casco* by the surveyor George Black, 1854 (detail). Courtesy of The Bancroft Library, University of California, Berkeley

OPPOSITE: The bell tower of Mission San Carlos Borromeo, a survivor from mission days. Photograph by G. Aldana

Mission San Carlos Borromeo del Puerto de Monterey was established alongside the presidio on Monterey Bay, a location chosen by Governor Portolá for its strategic naval advantages. However, the prevalent fog, paucity of native villages, lack of water for irrigation, and proximity to ill-behaved soldiers made this location unsuitable for a mission. In 1771 Father Serra moved the establishment four miles to the favorable south-facing coast of the peninsula and the mouth of the sunny and fertile Carmel River valley. Here the renamed Mission San Carlos Borromeo del Río Carmelo was very successful in crop production but did not develop the large livestock herds typical of other missions in this district. After 1808 no new recruitments were carried out, and the population steadily declined. By 1832 only 185 neophytes were identified on the church rolls.[1] The mission achieved historical prominence, however, by serving as the Franciscan headquarters in Alta California for more than thirty years.

When Fermín Lasuén succeeded Junípero Serra as father president of the Alta California missions in 1784, he launched the ambitious objective of replacing adobe churches with superior ones in stone. In particular, he sought to elevate the architectural character of the church at San Carlos Borromeo, where he presided. This goal was well served by the master stonecutter and mason Manuel Esteban Ruiz, who arrived in California in 1791. In 1793, after designing and initiating construction of the stone chapel at the Monterey Royal Presidio, Ruiz began work on the distinctive San Carlos Borromeo church, joined by the journeymen Joaquín Rivera and Pedro de Alcántara Ruiz and the neophyte trainee Honorio Matgesh. Ruiz oversaw all aspects of construction, from quarrying stone in the nearby Santa Lucia Mountains to laying foundations and raising the shiplike inwardly curving nave walls. When the construction was finished in 1797, Ruiz returned with his family to Guadalajara but not before he had instructed numerous neophytes in the arts of stonecutting and masonry.[2] The church at Mission San Carlos Borromeo is the most *mudéjar,* or Moorish inspired, of all the California mission churches, featuring asymmetrical towers, a unique star window, and a vaulted baptistery with influences of Spanish Gothic.[3]

After secularization of the mission in 1834, its buildings fell gradually to ruin as adobe walls melted into the earth and the roof of the stone church collapsed. Exhumation of the remains of Fathers Serra, Crespí, Lasuén, and López in 1882, and their reinterment in 1884, galvanized Father Angelo Casanova's efforts to save the stone church;

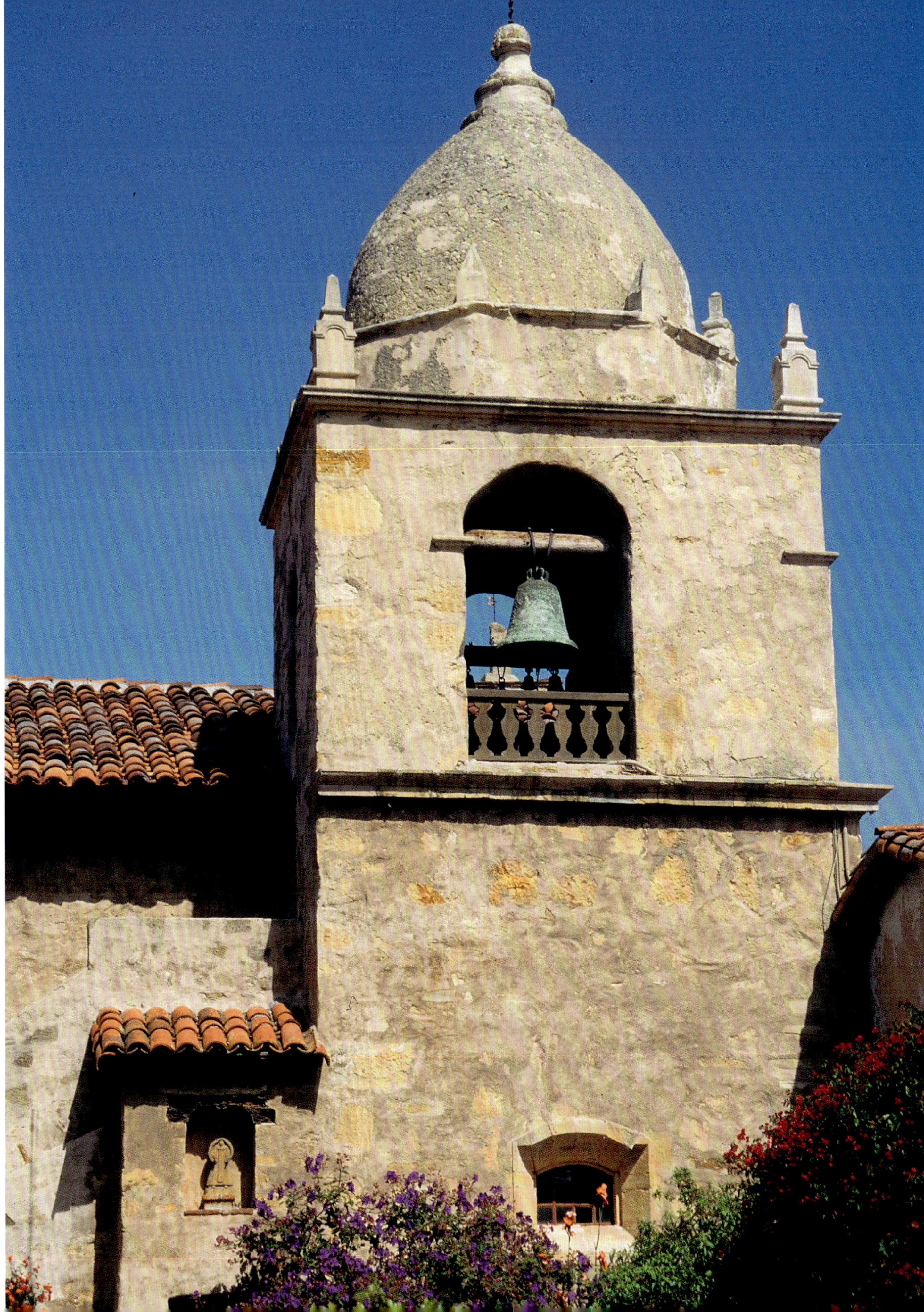

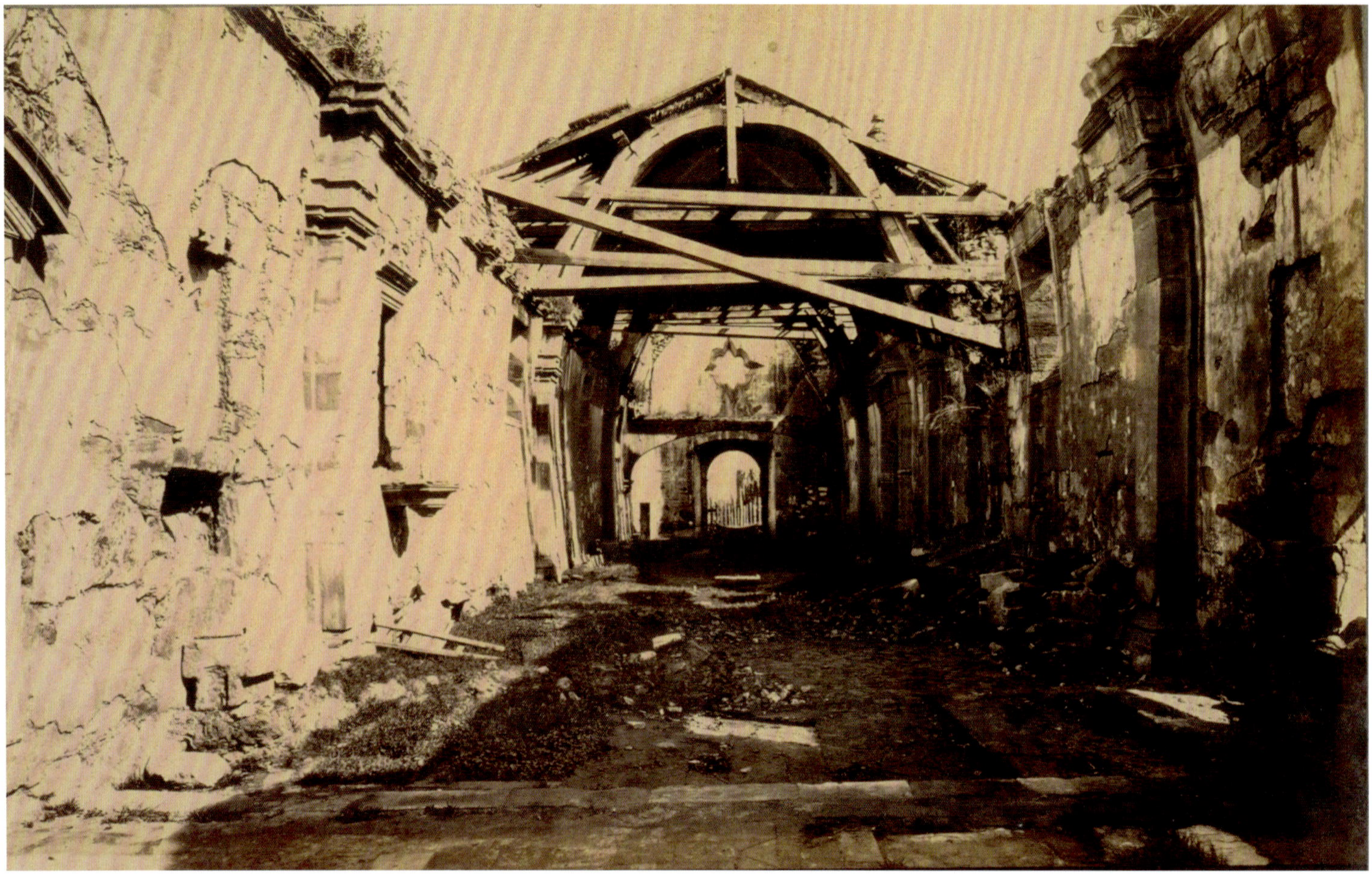

The ruined interior of the mission, ca. 1880, showing remains of the distinctive arched ceiling over the nave. Library of Congress

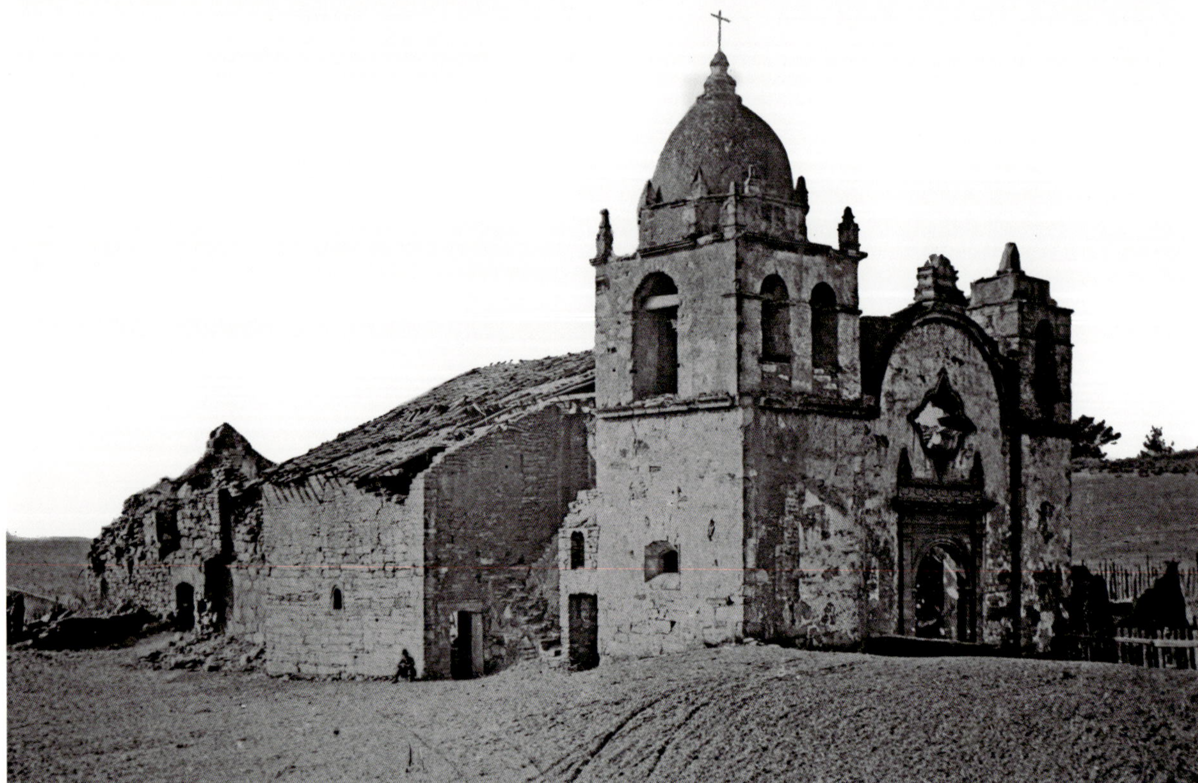

View of the mission, ca. 1876–80, before it was restored by Father Casanova; the stone walls are falling to ruin. Photograph by Carleton Watkins. Courtesy Mission San Carlos Borromeo

a sturdy, if inaccurate, roof succeeded in this for over half a century. The eventual restoration of the church under the hands of Harry Downie provided additional renown for this mission. Downie also turned his efforts to collecting original art and artifacts to furnish the expanding mission complex, frequently acquiring objects from nearby churches. The mission's growing fame attracted additional donations, with the result that San Carlos Borromeo has one of the most extensive collections of mission-period items in California. Many of the statues and paintings have been restored, and efforts are being made to conserve the large library and a number of rare artifacts. In 1961 Mission San Carlos Borromeo was honored by being designated a Minor Basilica by Pope John XXIII.

View of Mission San Carlos, ca. 1890–97, showing the church as it appeared after being restored by Father Angelo Casanova in 1884. Adobe ruins can also be seen; in the background are the Carmel River and Carmel Bay and, in the distance, the Point Lobos hills. Photograph by C.C. Pierce. Courtesy University of Southern California, on behalf of the USC Special Collections

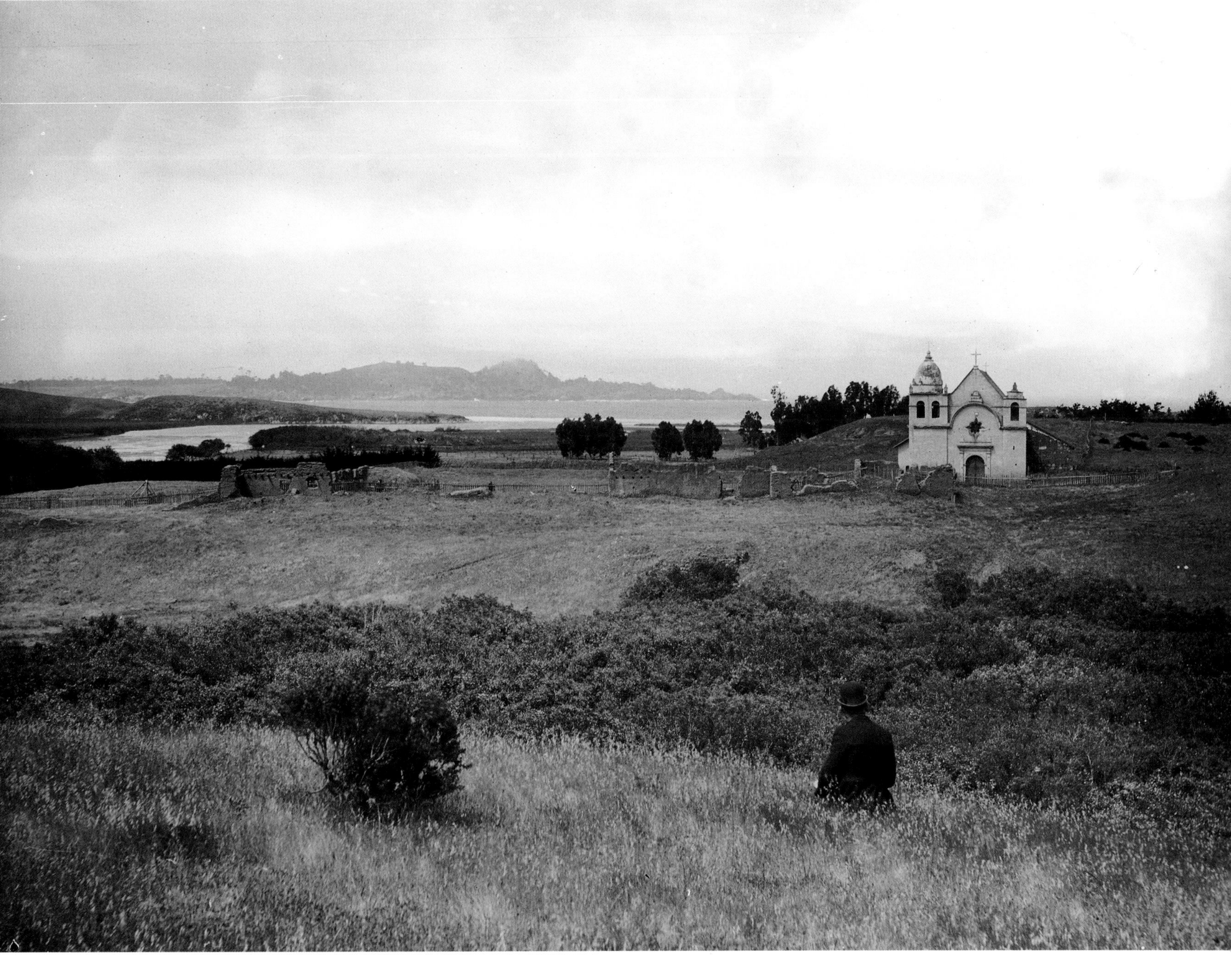

San Antonio de Padua

FOUNDED JULY 14, 1771

LOCATION: *Jolon*

FOUNDER: *Father Junípero Serra*

PRESIDIO DISTRICT: *Monterey*

PEAK MISSION POPULATION: *1,952 (1802)*

MAJOR NATIVE GROUPS: *Salinan, Esselen, Yokuts*

HISTORICAL ASSETS: *Base of adobe church walls and* ladrillo *atrium,* convento *colonnade; wine vats, ruins of grist mill, threshing floor, tanning vats, cemetery, and extensive water system; archaeological remains of Indian residences, shops and storage rooms and other facilities; extensive historical landscape setting; museum with artifacts*

EXISTING CHURCH: *Reconstructed with reinforcing concrete and steel, 1948–55*

OWNERSHIP: *Roman Catholic Church, Diocese of Monterey*

HISTORICAL STATUS: *California Historical Landmark (No. 232)*

Mission San Antonio de Padua was sited in an open oak valley in the Santa Lucia Mountains southeast of Monterey. Although it was the most populous of the missions in its district, it was a poor producer of crops and livestock, perhaps because of its high elevation. In compensation, the mission developed its lands with at least seven ranches, located between the Salinas River and the Pacific Ocean, which were occupied and managed by the neophytes. Four of the ranches had permanent adobe dwellings. These lands were favorable for raising sheep and fowl, bean and wheat production, and vineyards.[1]

The building program at Mission San Antonio was ambitious and, in 1776, claims the first recorded manufacture of fired tiles in Alta California, which were used on the new church. It is likely this technology was introduced by Eugenio Rosalío, a soldier and mason stationed at the mission as a member of the guard. The present church was completed in 1813, its plain facade embellished with the addition of a barrel-vaulted portico and a ladrillo *espadaña*, features that were

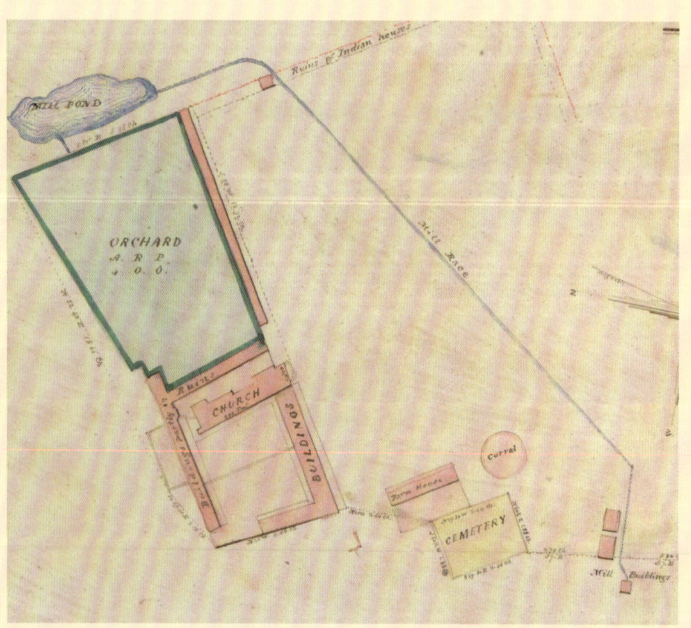

Map of the *casco* by the surveyor George Black, 1854 (detail). Courtesy of The Bancroft Library, University of California, Berkeley

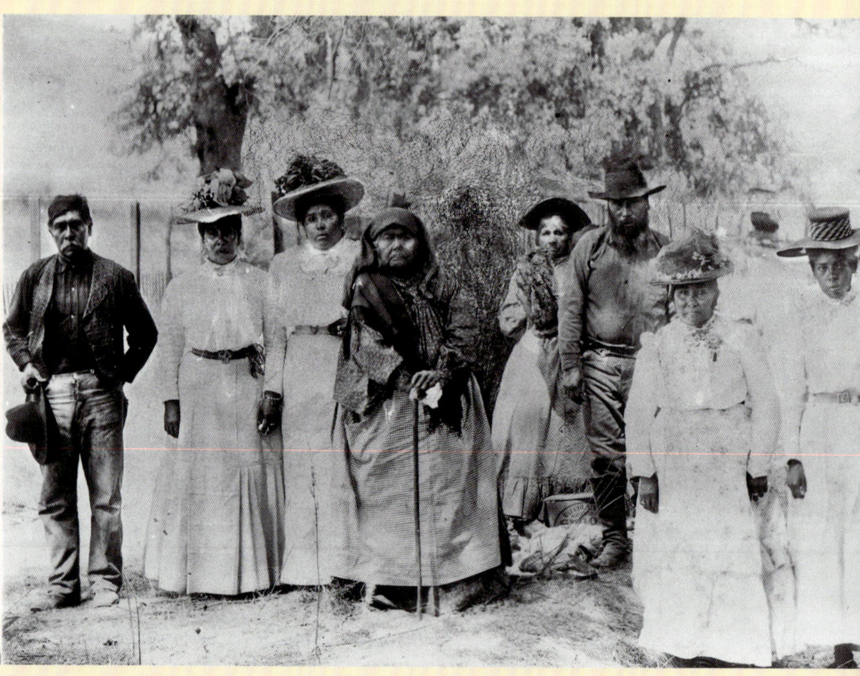

Salinan neophyte Perfecta Encinal (center with shawl-covered head) and members of her family in the late nineteenth century. They continued to live near Mission San Antonio after its abandonment and advocated restoration of the church. Courtesy University of Southern California, on behalf of the USC Special Collections

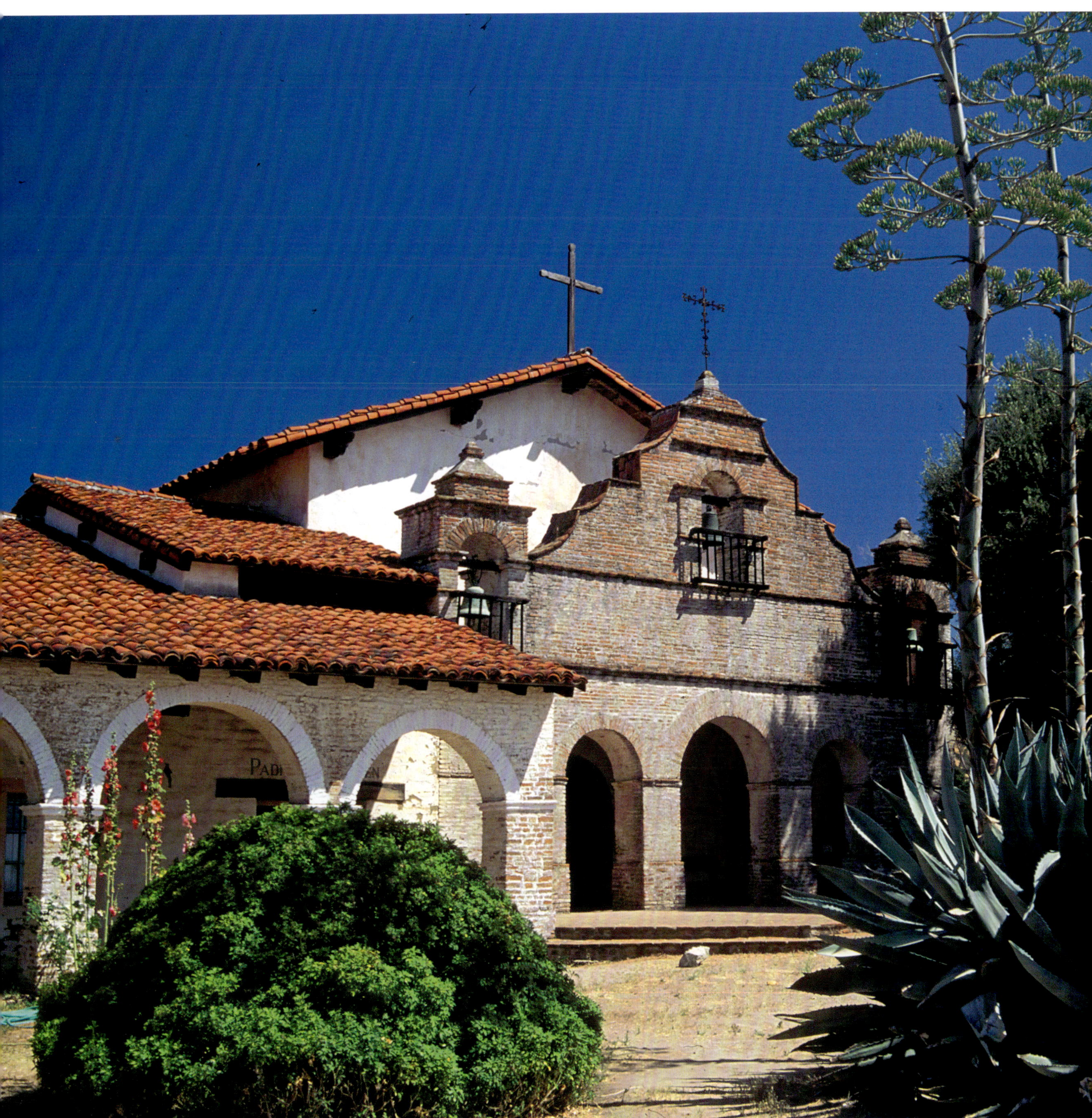

The *espadaña* and *convento* columns at Mission San Antonio, built of *ladrillos*, are among the few surviving portions of the original buildings. Photograph by G. Aldana

much imitated during the Mission Revival period. The master mason who designed the building is unknown, but the neophyte masons Pedro Antonio Mendoza, his son Matías Mendoza, and Simeón Figuerola were probably involved in its construction.[2]

Due to the mission's location in the isolated Santa Lucía Mountains, after secularization in 1835 several of the mission ranches granted to former neophytes were retained by them for many years. Eusebio and Perfecta Encinal, for example, worked some five hundred acres a few miles above the old mission, irrigating a vineyard and orchard and raising sheep, hogs, and cattle. Eventually, however, the Indians were displaced from these claims, although many remained in the vicinity, and the faithful safeguarded the church's religious items.

The remarkable preservation of much of the mission's lands is a result of two events: consolidation of land by William Randolph Hearst into a 250,000-acre ranch during the 1920s and 1930s and the transference of 165,000 acres of this estate into Fort Hunter Liggett in 1940. As a result, Mission San Antonio is unique in having its history preserved in the surrounding landscape: sites of prehistoric native villages and rock art; outlying mission ranch stations, vineyard, and extensive water systems; sites of neophyte and immigrant settlements after secularization; and many other associated archaeological remains. Since 1858 the 33-acre mission *casco* has remained the property of the Roman Catholic Church.

Mission San Antonio was chosen as the first preservation project by the newly formed California Historic Landmarks League, which overcame substantial difficulties—including the effects of the 1906 San Francisco earthquake—to complete restoration of the church in 1907. This accomplishment stood until 1948, when a more extensive reconstruction of the mission *casco* was undertaken with funding from the Hearst Foundation and the Franciscan Fathers of California, under the guidance of Monterey's Harry Downie. The quadrangle ruins were stripped to their foundations and the new adobe buildings strengthened with steel and concrete. Preserved original elements include the base of the church's walls, the *ladrillo* portico, the columns of the front colonnade, and the massive wine vats within the *convento*. Since 1976 some three decades of archaeological studies have been carried out adjacent to the reconstructed mission quadrangle, reports on which are being prepared.[3] Despite the presence of the adjacent Fort Hunter Liggett headquarters complex, San Antonio retains the most extensive historic landscape setting of all the missions.

Interior view of the church at Mission San Antonio in 1891, showing the vaulted ceiling and decorative star motif. Photograph by C. C. Pierce. Courtesy University of Southern California, on behalf of the USC Special Collections

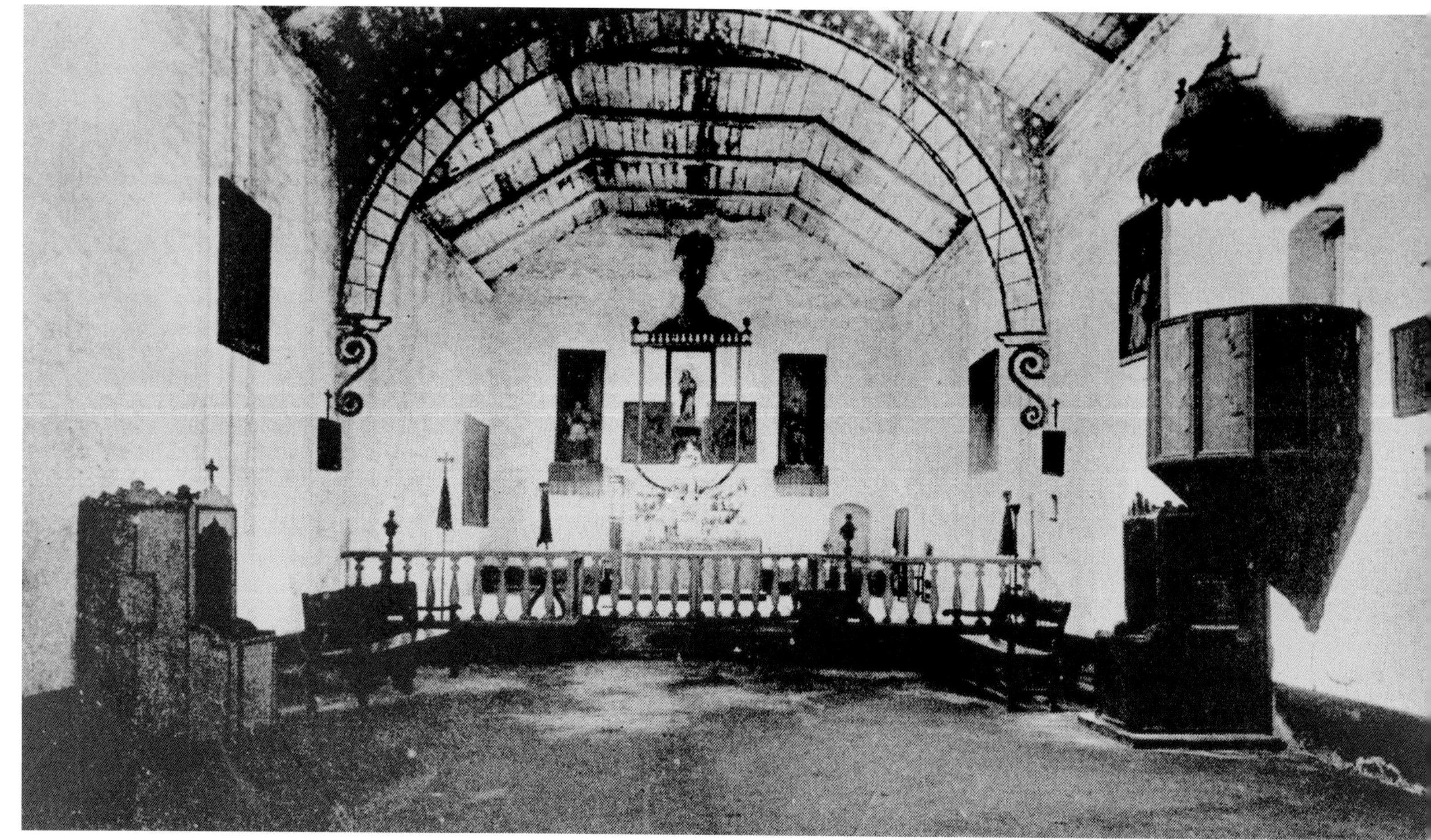

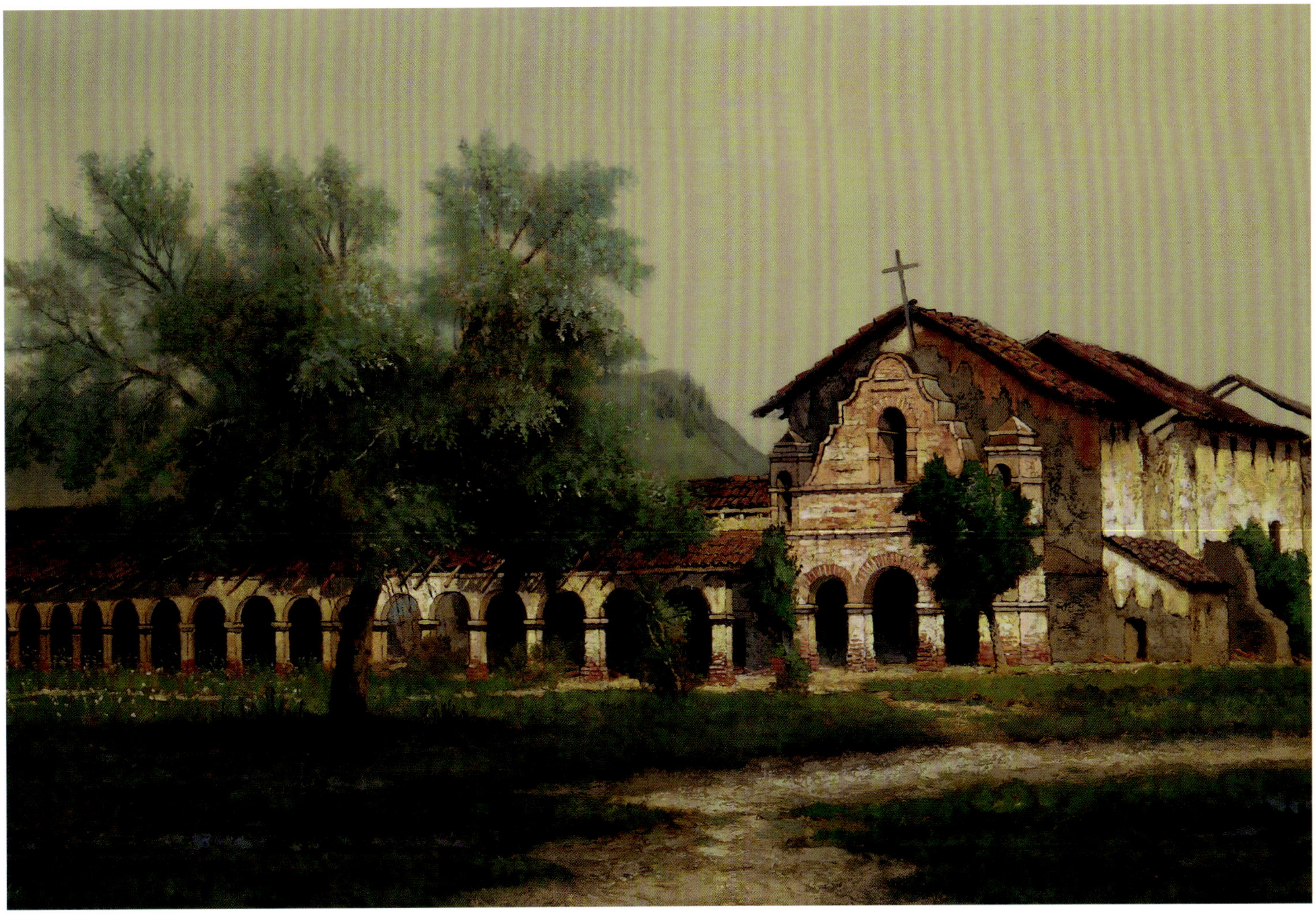

View of the deteriorating church and *convento* at Mission San Antonio, ca. 1899. Edwin Deakin, ***Mission San Antonio de Padua.*** Oil on canvas. Courtesy of the Santa Bárbara Mission Archive-Library

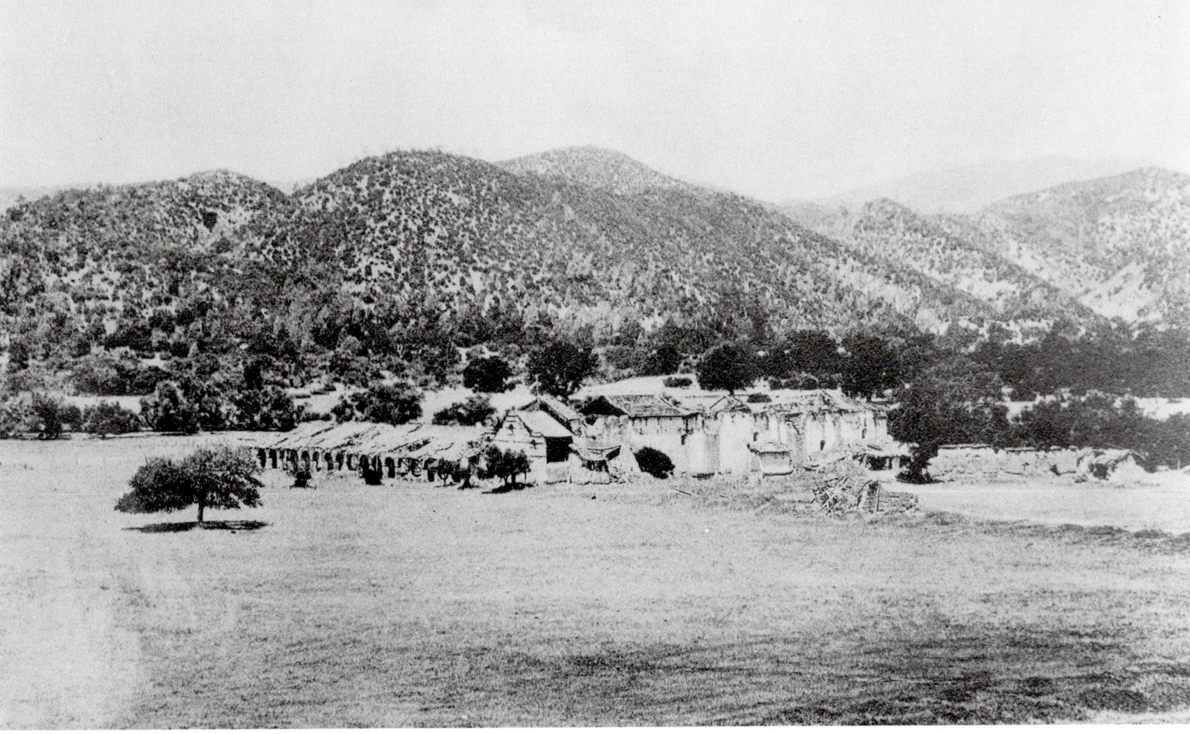

View of the mission and surrounding landscape in 1885; the setting has changed little in the past 120 years. Library of Congress

San Gabriel, Arcángel

FOUNDED SEPTEMBER 8, 1771

LOCATION: *San Gabriel*

FOUNDER: *Fathers Pedro Cambón and Angel Somera*

PRESIDIO DISTRICT: *San Diego*

PEAK MISSION POPULATION: *1,701 (1817)*

MAJOR NATIVE GROUPS: *Gabrielino (Tongva), Serrano, Cahuilla*

HISTORICAL ASSETS: *Original church with interior somewhat altered; intact sacristy; original adobe* convento *wing housing the museum and its extensive holdings; original winery, olive press, and tanning vats in garden*

EXISTING CHURCH: *Constructed of stone and* ladrillo*; completed in 1805*

OWNERSHIP: *Roman Catholic Church, Diocese of Los Angeles*

HISTORICAL STATUS: *California Historical Landmark (No. 158)*

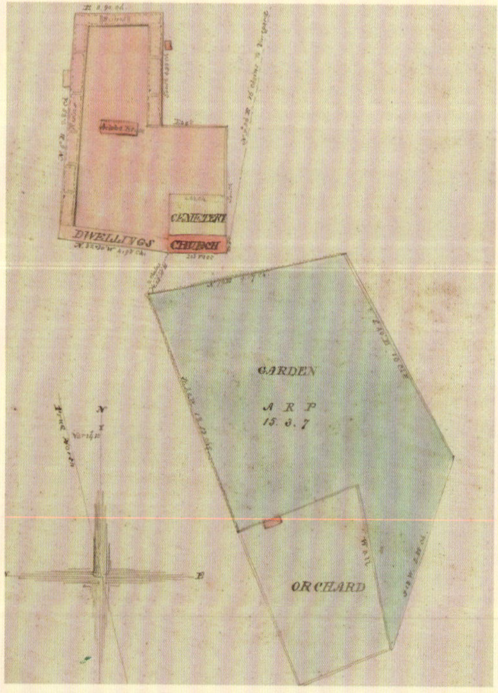

Map of the *casco* by the surveyor John G. Cleal, 1854 (detail). Courtesy of The Bancroft Library, University of California, Berkeley

Mission San Gabriel, Arcángel, pioneered the Spanish presence in what would later become Los Angeles and Orange counties. It was strategically located on rich agricultural lands, among populous native groups, and along major trail routes into Alta California from the east. With the exception of the Chumash, the Tongva were the wealthiest, most populous, and most powerful native group in Alta California.[1] One of the largest of the California missions, San Gabriel sustained a population of between 1,000 and 1,700 neophytes in the period 1788–1832. Crops were abundant, and in 1832 an extraordinary sixteen thousand head of cattle were grazing on mission lands. The economic success of San Gabriel allowed its energetic Father José Zalvidea to sponsor completion of the Plaza Church in the Pueblo of Los Angeles in 1822.

The church at Mission San Gabriel is one of the most distinctive in California. With the main entryway on the south side of the nave—and a smaller portal at the eastern end—it is described as being of the "Fortress style," typical of Mexican churches erected on street corners. In designing this church, Father Antonio Cruzado lined the exterior with pillar-like buttresses surmounted by *almenas* (pyramidal finials) that mimic his homeland's Moorish cathedral in Córdoba. The building is constructed of stone to the window level, with *ladrillos* above.[2]

A great deal is known about the builders of this church. Construction was under the direction of the Indian master mason Miguel Blanco from Baja California, who later built the final church at Mission San Diego de Alcalá (completed 1813). He was assisted by the San Gabriel neophyte mason Remigio. The master carpenter Salvador Carabantes, of Tepic, Nayarit, who had also worked in Baja California, was hired to install the doors and windows. The church roof was reconfigured from a vaulted form to a flat design due to cracking. The 1812 earthquake caused the closure of the church for fifteen years, and in the restoration of 1827 the new roof was a low gable design. This earthquake also felled the original bell wall, which was replaced during renovations by the distinctive *espadaña* located at the west end of the church.[3]

Although Mission San Gabriel was secularized with all the missions in California and its wealth absorbed by avaricious Californios, it was never abandoned by its congregation. While outbuildings fell into ruin, the church, along with its furnishings and altarpieces, was maintained. The *retablo* and statues are original, the ornate wooden pulpit

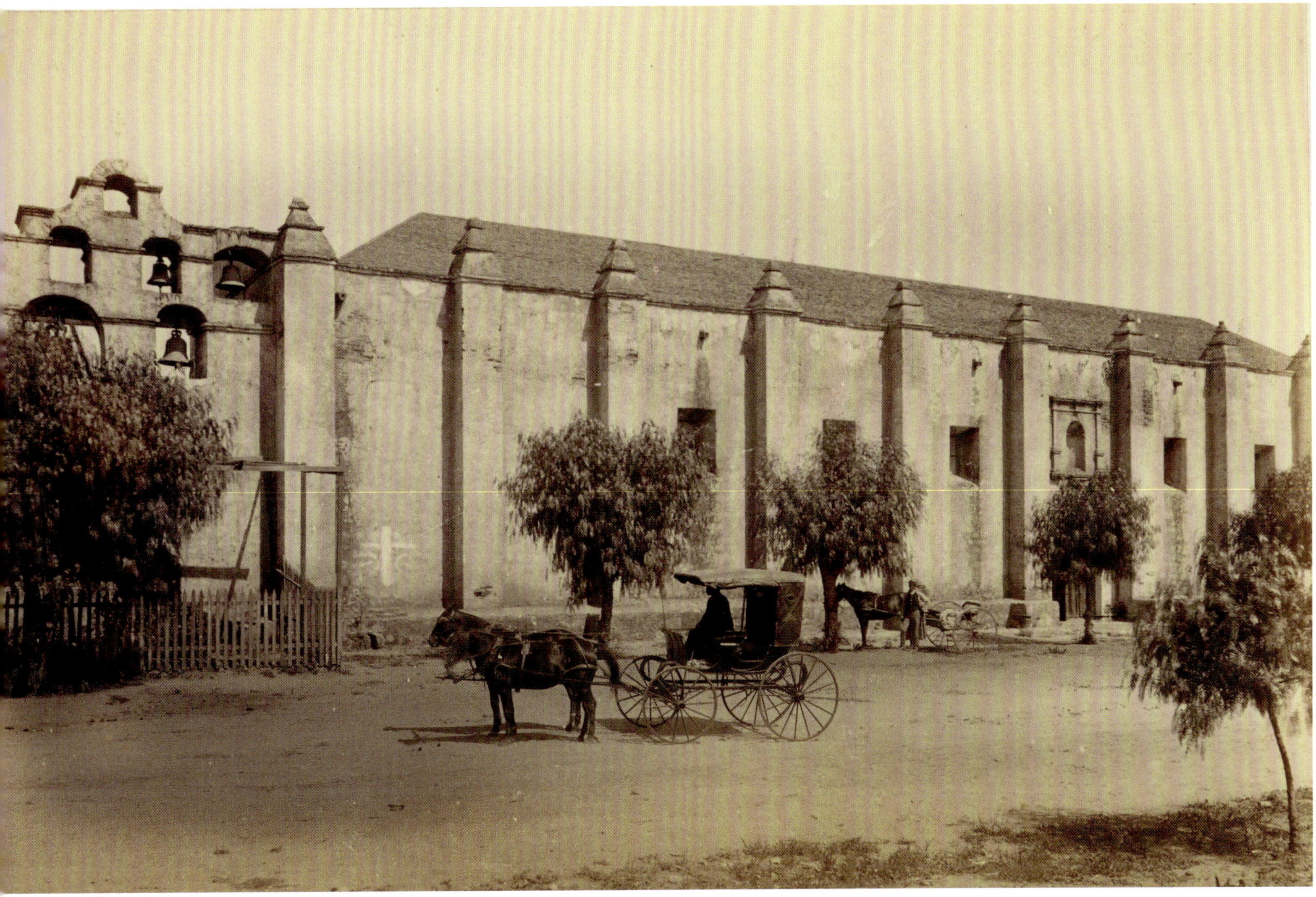

View of the mission, ca. 1876–80, showing its distinctive, pillar-like buttresses capped with pyramid-shaped finials. Photograph by Carleton Watkins. Albumen silver print. J. Paul Getty Museum. 88.XA.98.44

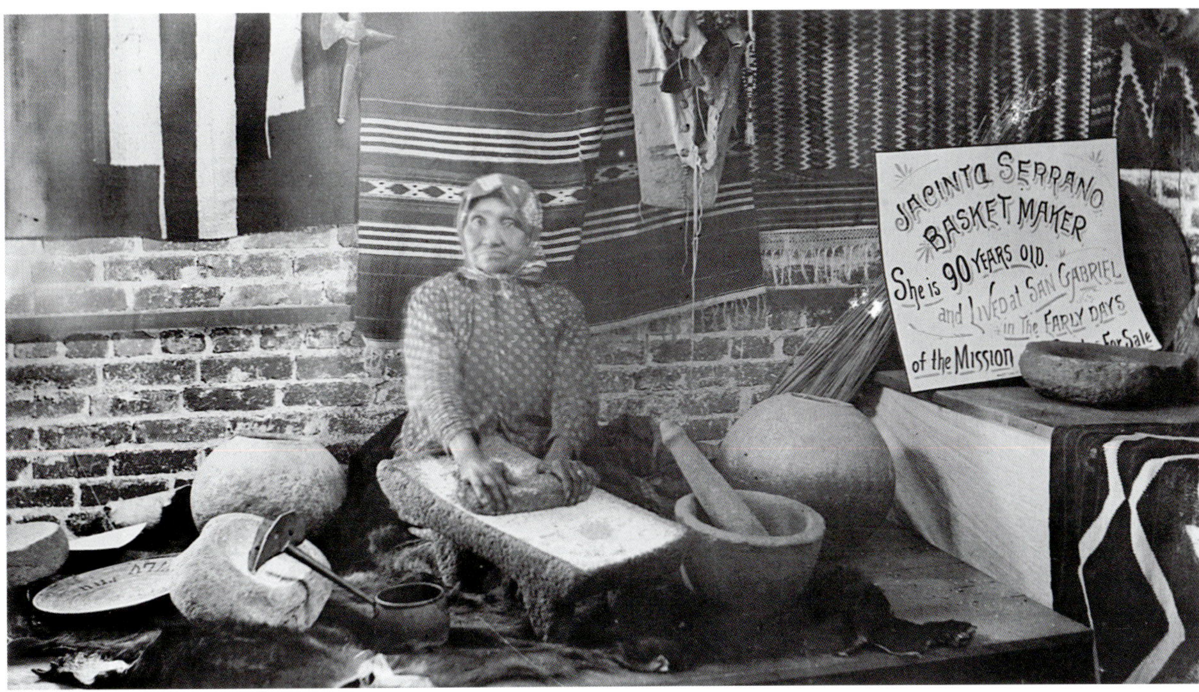

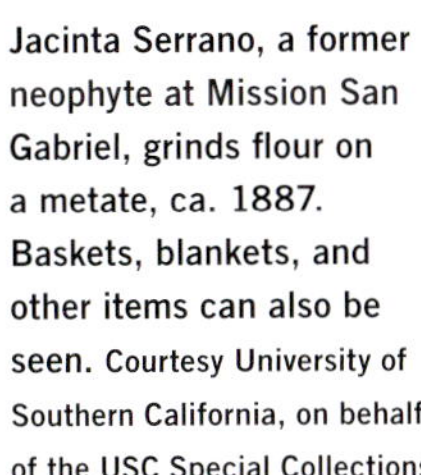

Jacinta Serrano, a former neophyte at Mission San Gabriel, grinds flour on a metate, ca. 1887. Baskets, blankets, and other items can also be seen. Courtesy University of Southern California, on behalf of the USC Special Collections

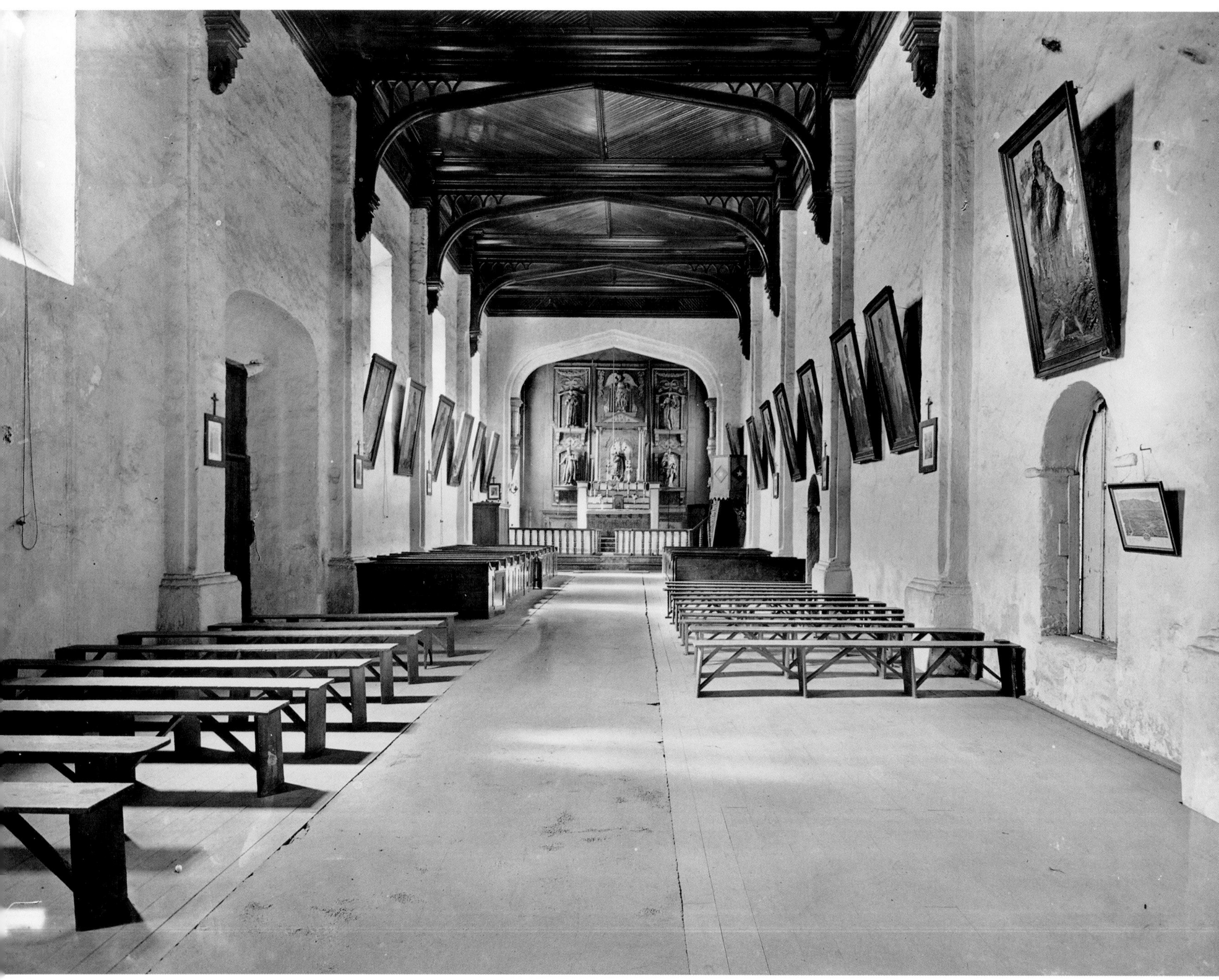

is still in place, and the baptismal font in the baptistery continues in use for baptisms. The museum contains a remarkable collection of art and furnishings, including the famous Vía Crucis (Stations of the Cross), painted by neophytes at Mission San Fernando Rey; replicas hang in the nave. The church has not been frozen in time, however: Victorian renovations include a wooden ceiling, and the overpainted walls probably hide original native paintings. San Gabriel still serves an active local community, a factor that enhances its atmosphere of historical authenticity.

Interior of the Mission San Gabriel church, ca. 1900. Paintings of saints hang from the walls, under the newly installed Victorian ceiling. Photograph by C.C. Pierce. Courtesy University of Southern California, on behalf of the USC Special Collections

OPPOSITE: The *espadaña* today. Photograph by Kurt Hauser

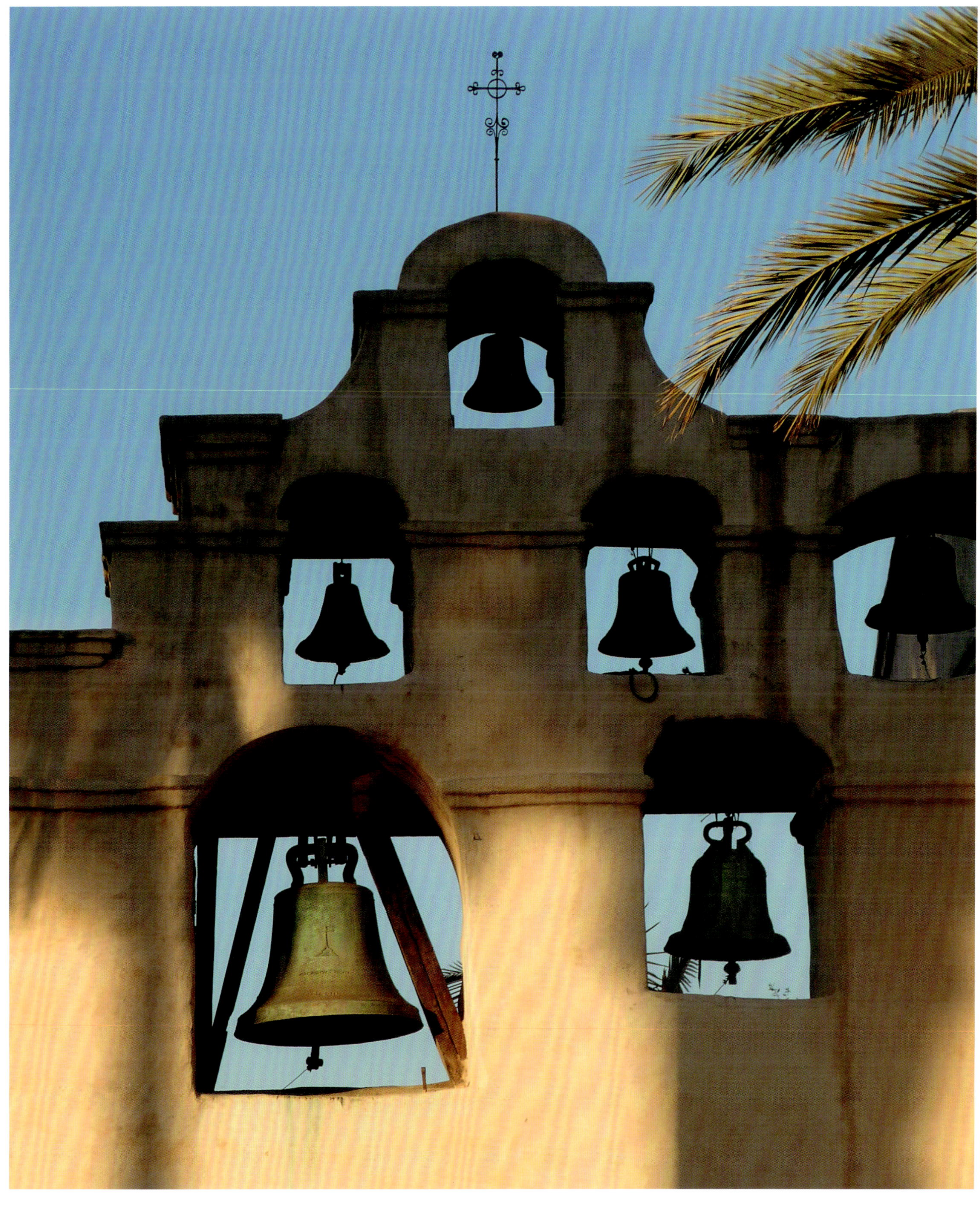

San Luis Obispo de Tolosa

FOUNDED SEPTEMBER 1, 1772

LOCATION: *San Luis Obispo*

FOUNDER: *Father Junípero Serra*

PRESIDIO DISTRICT: *Monterey*

PEAK MISSION POPULATION: *961 (1805)*

MAJOR NATIVE GROUPS: *Northern Chumash, Yokuts*

HISTORICAL ASSETS: *Adobe church (*campanario *and portico reconstructed in 1936),* convento, *stone kitchen walls, museum*

EXISTING CHURCH: *Constructed of adobe, completed in 1790*

OWNERSHIP: *Roman Catholic Church, Diocese of Monterey*

HISTORICAL STATUS: *California Historical Landmark (No. 325)*

Mission San Luis Obispo de Tolosa was one of the most successful agricultural producers in the Monterey Presidio District. Founded among the northern Chumash in the fertile Cañada de los Osos (noted for its abundance of grizzlies), it had the advantage of both coastal resources and rich river bottomlands. Animosities between local Indian groups resulted in the burning of the mission buildings soon after the mission was established. Much of San Luis Obispo's financial success is attributed to Father Luis Antonio Martínez, who managed its affairs from 1798 until his politically driven departure in 1830. The mission enthusiastically participated in the illegal hide-and-tallow trade during the Mexican War of Independence and continued this practice under Mexican rule.

Mission San Luis Obispo as portrayed by the American artist Henry Miller, 1856. There is an unusual enclosed patio in front of the church. Pencil sketch on paper. Courtesy of The Bancroft Library, University of California, Berkeley

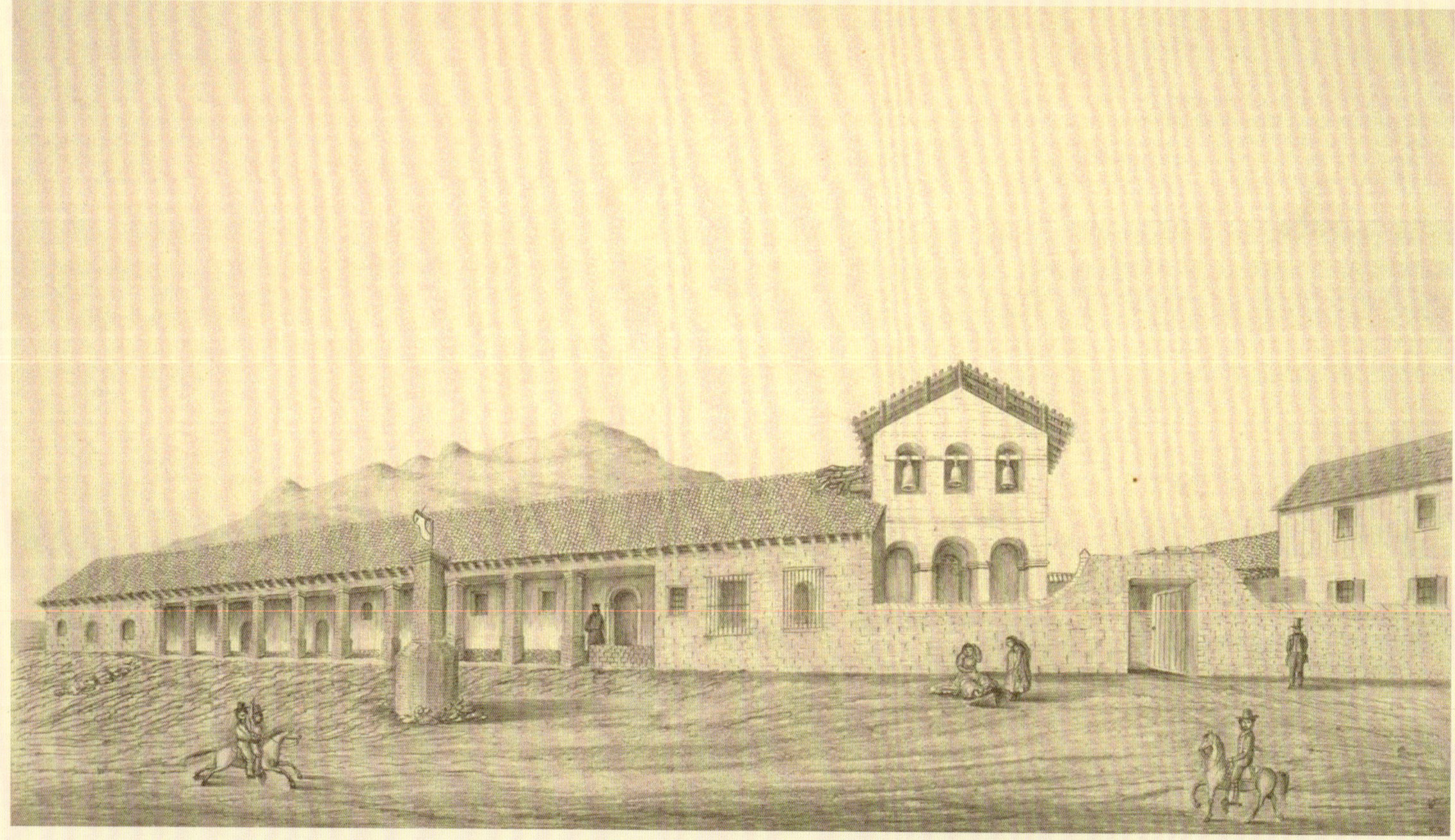

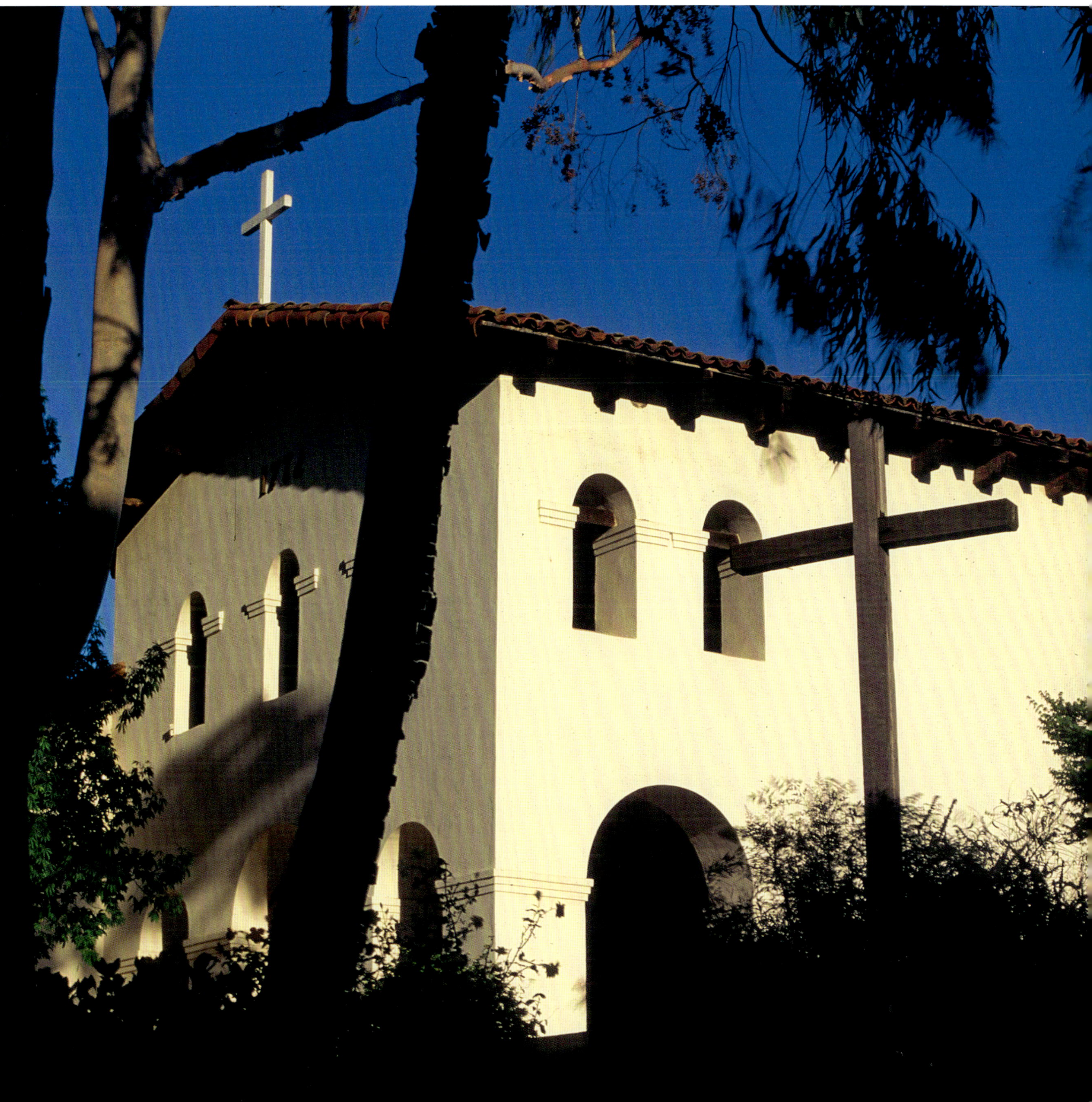

A view of the mission's *campanario* and portico, reconstructed in 1936. Photograph by G. Aldana

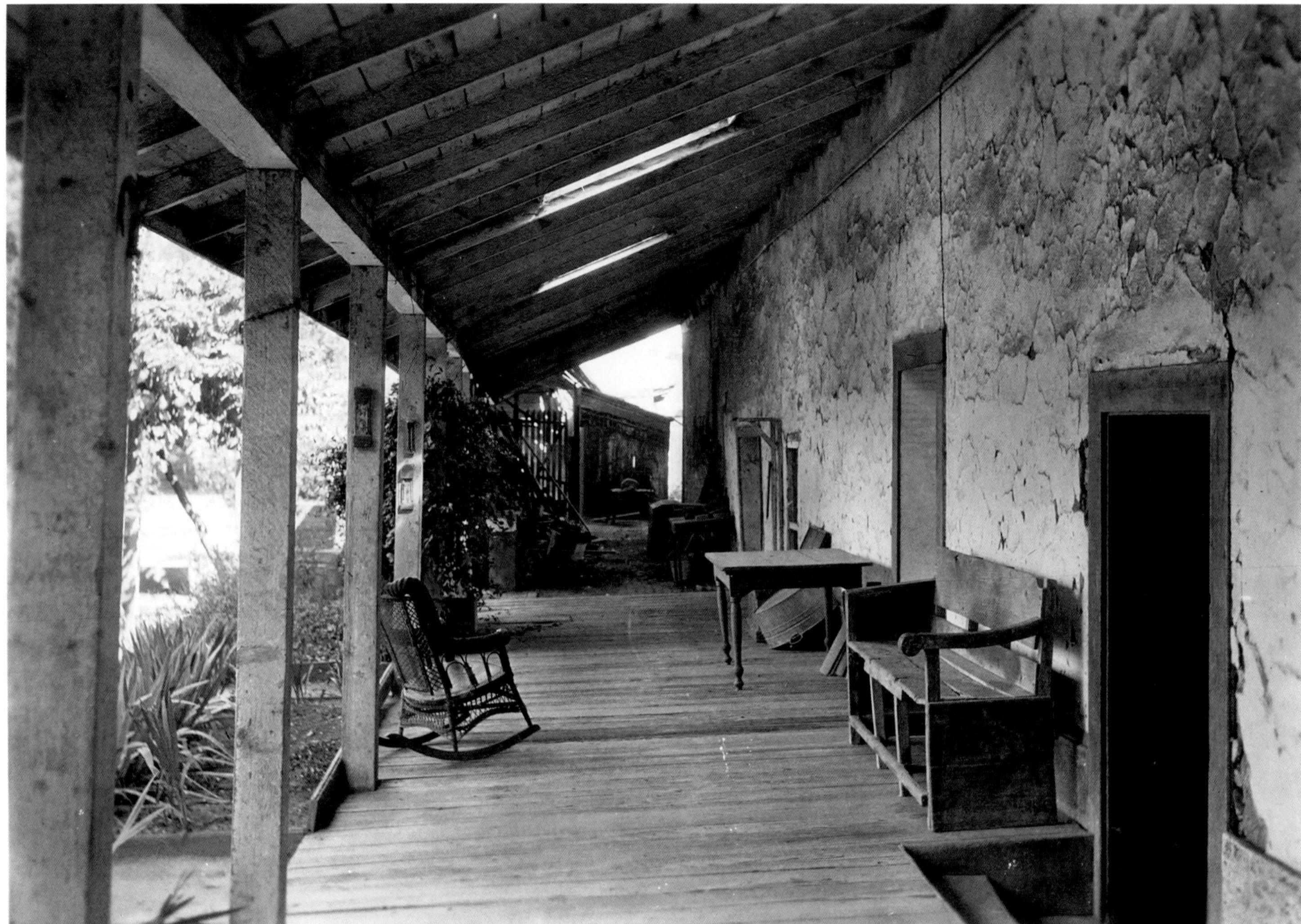

San Luis Obispo was one of the California missions that gave birth to a town, as Mexicans and then Americans settled around the establishment. Most of the mission's buildings were abandoned after secularization, but the church and *convento* wing were maintained by an active congregation. Following earthquake damage in 1868, the tile roof was replaced with shingles to reduce the weight on the old building. Additional renovations in 1880 included removal of the church portico, the *companario*, and the *convento*'s front colonnade; cladding of the adobe walls in wooden siding; and erection of an incongruous New England steeple. Although renovations were intended to "Americanize" the Spanish buildings, ironically they served to preserve much of the historic adobe structure. Wooden paneling in the sanctuary and over the nave ceiling protected the original beams from fire damage in the 1920s. Restoration of the buildings was effected in 1936, with removal of the exterior wooden sheathing and rebuilding of the *convento* colonnade and church portico. A remnant of the stone *cocina* (kitchen), once part of the west quadrangle wing, survives at the edge of the mission parking lot.

During restoration of the interior of the church in 1947, removal of the obscuring wooden paneling exposed original painted beams and the ceiling's unusual star design. A side transept, added to the north side of the altar in the 1890s, was extended in 1947–48. Recent overpainting of the walls has imposed a new flora and fauna schema on the stately building, although portions of the original design may still be preserved under subsequent layers of decorative efforts.[1] Conservation of religious art and historic items is under way, and seismic retrofitting of the church and *convento* was initiated in 2008.

North of Mission San Luis Obispo, the fathers established the *asistencia* Santa Margarita de Cortona in about 1787. It served a populous Chumash area rendered remote by the formidable Cuesta grade and became a prodigious producer of grain. The remarkable stone building here, completed in 1822, measures almost 140 feet long by 40 feet wide and originally contained a chapel, dwellings, and storage rooms. The unusual narrow slit windows—defensive in design—may represent a response to the corsair Hypolite Bouchard's attacks in 1818. The building ruins, on private property, have been preserved by being roofed and used as a ranch barn.

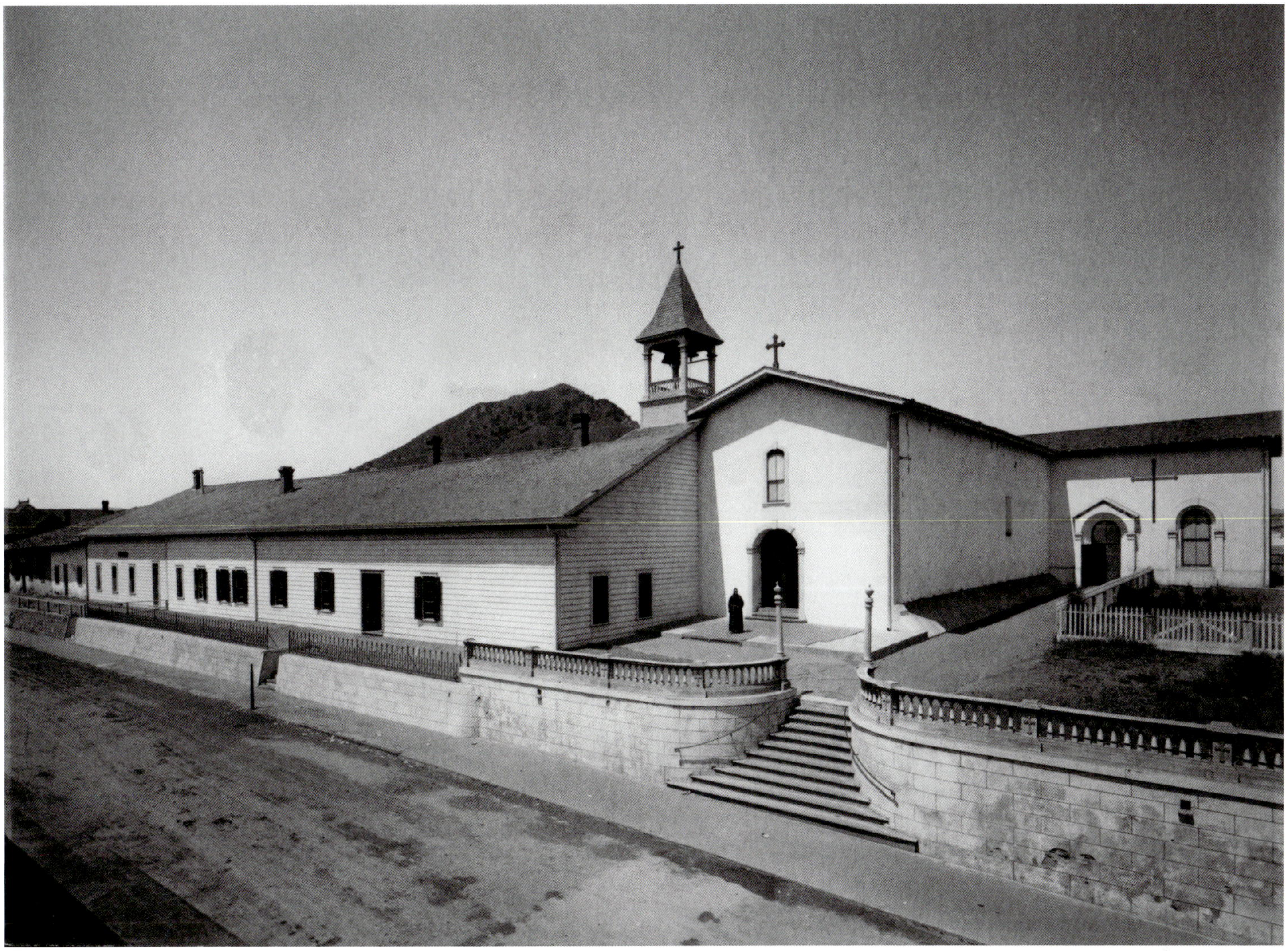

OPPOSITE: The rear of the *convento*, ca. 1900, with a hospitable porch used by the resident priests. Photograph by C.C. Pierce. Courtesy University of Southern California, on behalf of the USC Special Collections

ABOVE: The refurbished mission in 1905, with its adobe walls covered in wooden siding, the *convento* corridor enclosed, and the portico *campanario* replaced with a New England–style bell tower. Photograph by C.C. Pierce. Courtesy University of Southern California, on behalf of the USC Special Collections

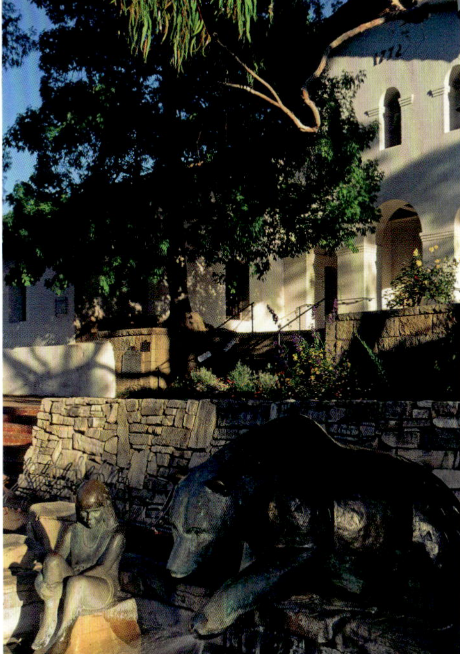

RIGHT: The historic mission is located in the bustling downtown area and plays an active role in the modern community. Photograph by G. Aldana

San Francisco de Asís

FOUNDED JUNE 26, 1776

LOCATION: *San Francisco*

FOUNDER: *Father Francisco Palóu*

PRESIDIO DISTRICT: *San Francisco*

PEAK MISSION POPULATION: *1,228 (1821)*

MAJOR NATIVE GROUPS: *Ohlone/Costanoan, Coast Miwok, Bay Miwok, Patwin, Wappo*

HISTORICAL ASSETS: *Church and cemetery, museum*

EXISTING CHURCH: *Built of adobe, completed in 1791*

OWNERSHIP: *Roman Catholic Church, Diocese of San Francisco*

HISTORICAL STATUS: *California Historical Landmark (No. 327)*

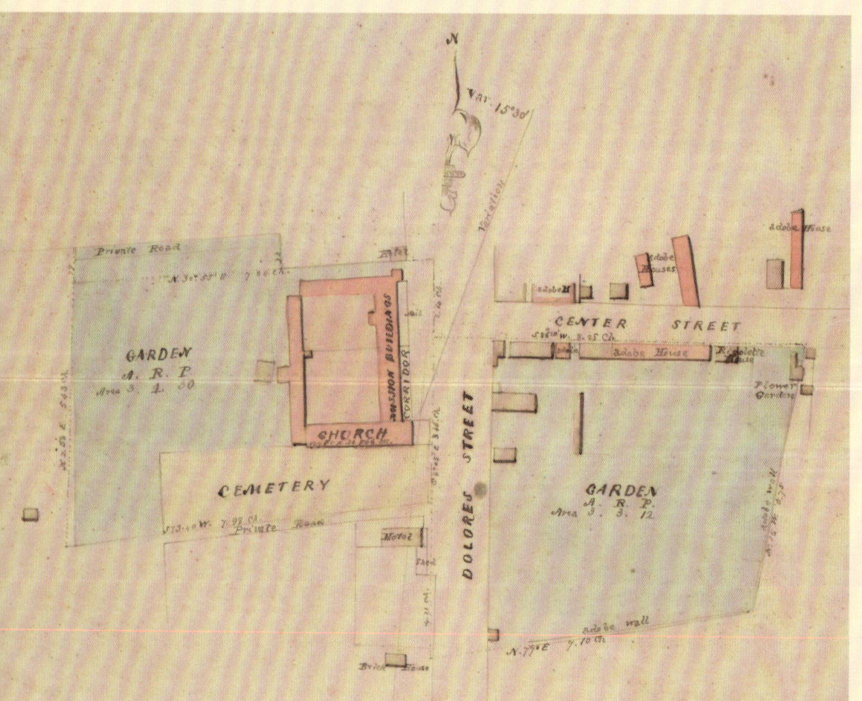

Map of the *casco* by the surveyor George Black, 1854 (detail). Courtesy of The Bancroft Library, University of California, Berkeley

OPPOSITE: The historic Mission San Francisco de Asís sits next to the 1918 parish church, designed in a Mexican Baroque–Moorish style and built of concrete and steel. Photograph by G. Aldana

The sites for both the presidio and mission of San Francisco de Asís (Mission Dolores) were chosen in 1776 by Lt. Col. Juan Bautista de Anza as part of the strategic colonization of California. The mission was established next to the Arroyo de Dolores, hence the popular name soon attached to the institution. This sixth mission, envisioned as the cornerstone of conversion for the northern tribes, struggled with the handicaps of inclement climate and poor agricultural lands. Converts were initially slow in coming, and it was ten years before the population exceeded five hundred. First to join were tribes from the peninsula, followed by East Bay Ohlone/Costanoans and then Miwok from both the northern bay and the Marin peninsula. After 1808 the annual population exceeded one thousand neophytes. Intermarriage between tribal groups was common as the high death rate of the neophytes, in particular of young women and children, encouraged remarriage.

The fathers recognized that illnesses common to all the missions were exacerbated at Mission San Francisco de Asís by the cool, overcast, and windy climate that prevailed year-round. To alleviate this suffering, the *asistencia* San Rafael, Arcángel, was established on the Marin peninsula in 1817 with 253 Coast Miwok transferred from the mission. Recruitment then shifted to the Wappo in the Napa and Sonoma areas and to the Patwin of the lower Sacramento Valley. The same conditions promoting ill health prevailed, however, and in 1823 Mission San Francisco de Asís's newly arrived Father José Altimira decided that his mission and San Rafael should be consolidated and moved north to the Sonoma area. Although backed by Governor Argüello and passed by the Territorial Assembly, the plan was declared illegal by Father President José Señán. As a compromise, San Francisco de Asís was retained, San Rafael obtained mission status, and a new mission, San Francisco Solano, was founded in the Sonoma valley. Father Altimira immediately transferred more than 500 neophytes to San Francisco Solano, primarily individuals and families who had initially come from this area. Only 208 neophytes remained at Mission San Francisco de Asís at the end of 1823. From this year until secularization in 1834, the population remained small, and the mission was characterized by visitors as poor and ill kept, as its former structures fell to ruin.[1]

During the years after secularization, the church was without a priest, the adherents served by clergy from Mission Santa Clara. The small landing three miles away at Yerba Buena was rechristened San

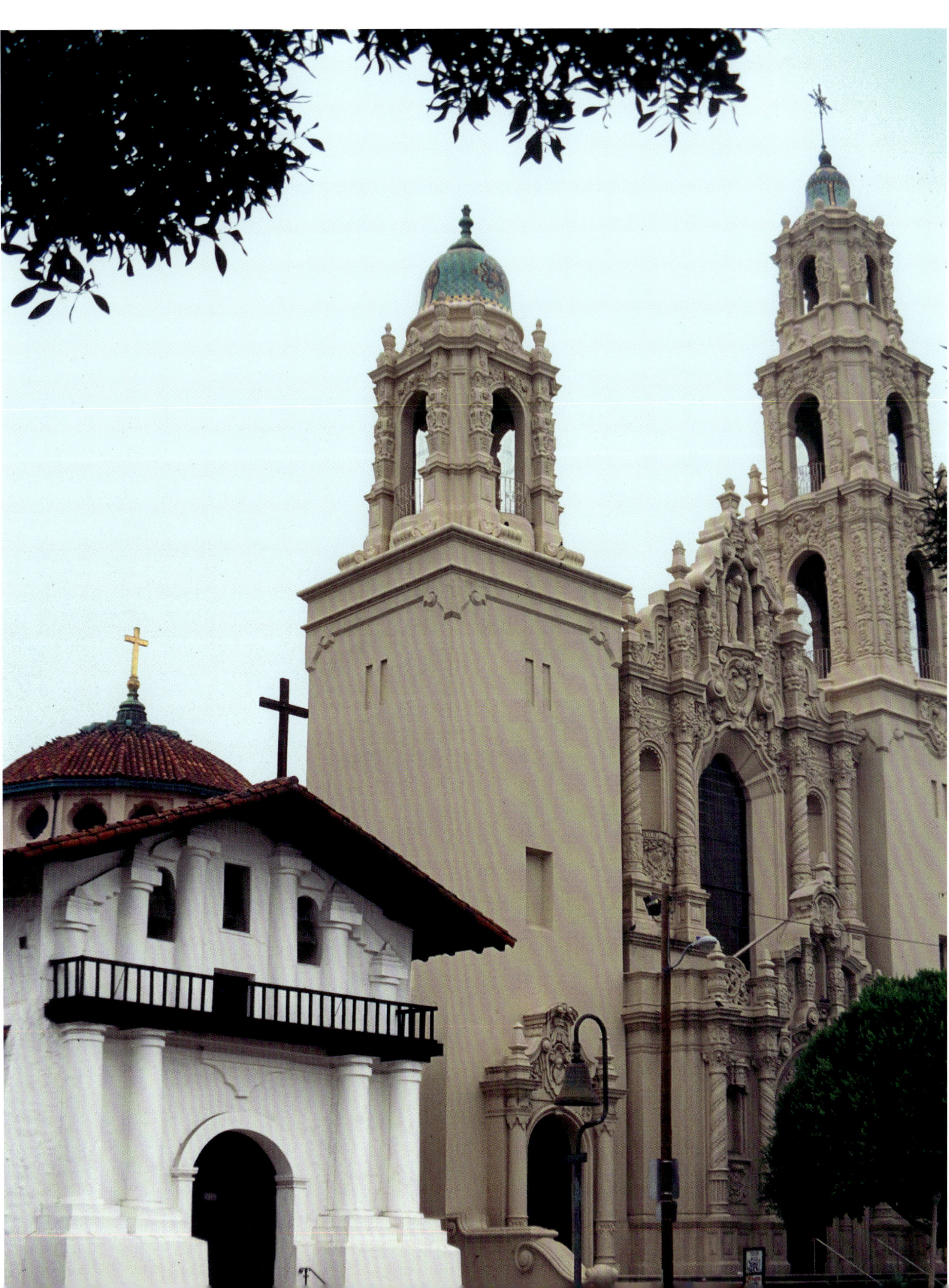

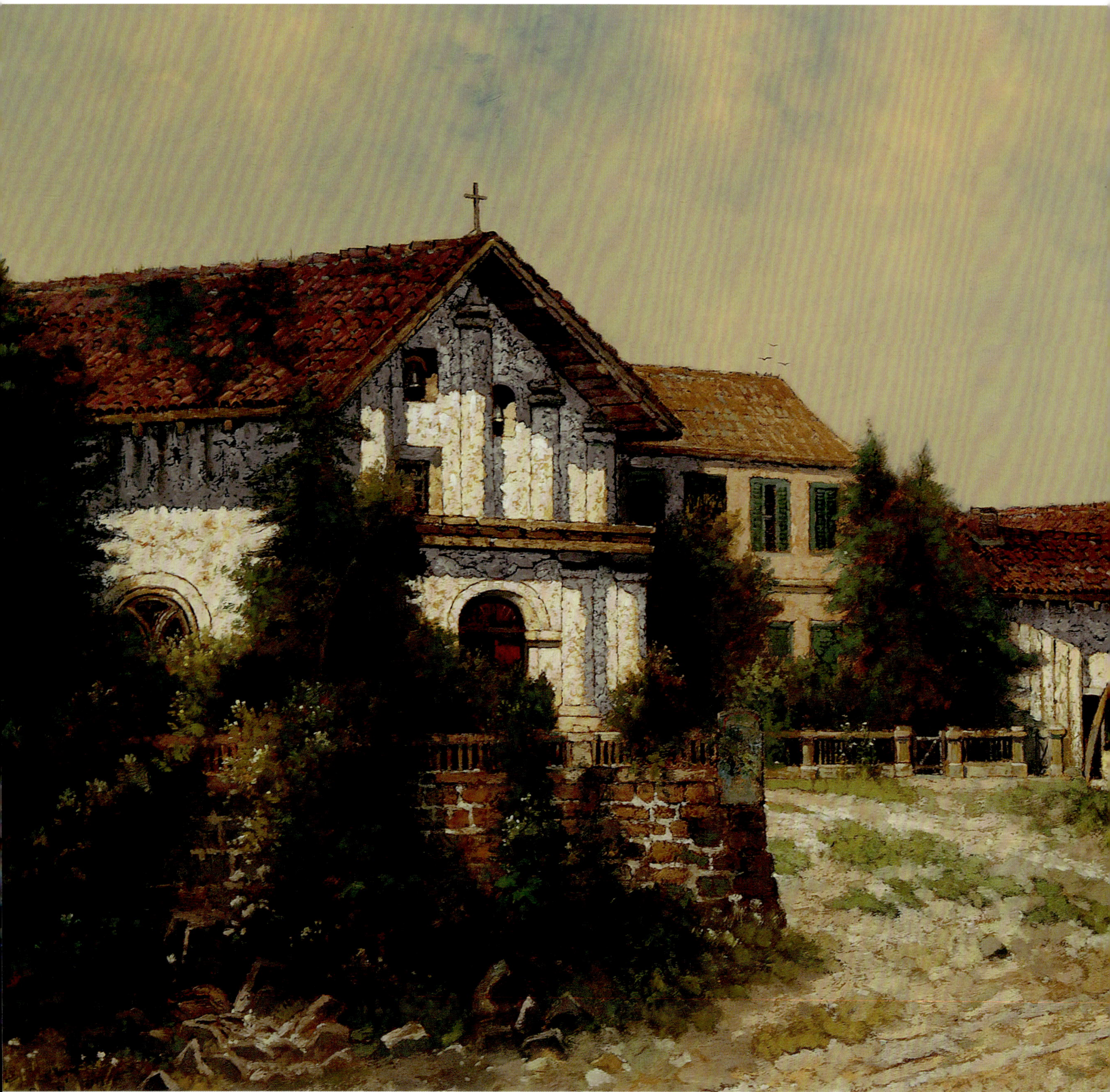

A somewhat romanticized artistic depiction of the mission, ca. 1899. Edwin Deakin, *Mission San Francisco de Asís.* Oil on canvas. Courtesy of the Santa Bárbara Mission Archive-Library

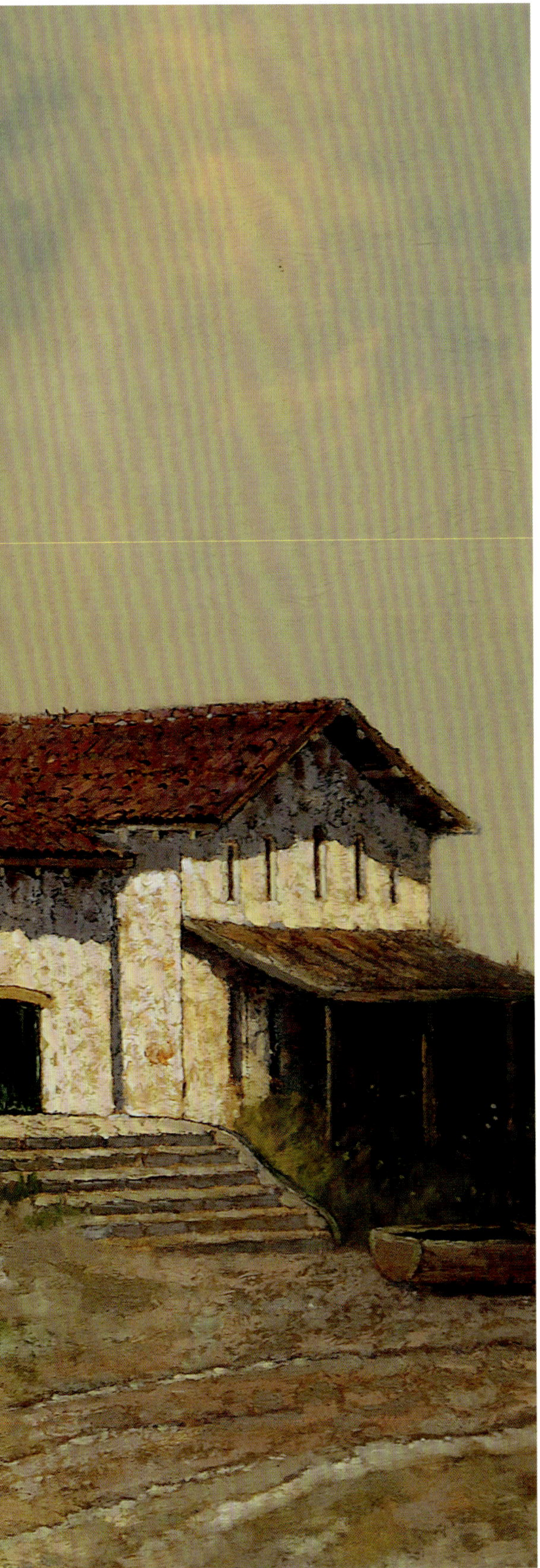

Francisco in 1847, just in time for the discovery of gold in the Sierra Nevada the next year. As the portal to the mines, the city spread rapidly southward and engulfed the old mission community. In 1849, although the mission church was still maintained as a sacred place of worship, its adjacent buildings housed a brewery, two taverns, a dancing room, a saloon, private lodgings, and a hospital.[2] In later years the imposed grid of streets truncated the mission cemetery, destroyed the north quadrangle rooms, and ran nearly at the doorstep of the church. In 1871 the growing congregation added a large Victorian church on the north side of the old adobe one. Ironically, the century-old structure weathered the 1906 earthquake, while the newer building was damaged beyond repair and replaced in 1918. Still a vital component of modern San Francisco, Mission San Francisco de Asís was granted basilica status in 1952 on the basis of its historical importance.

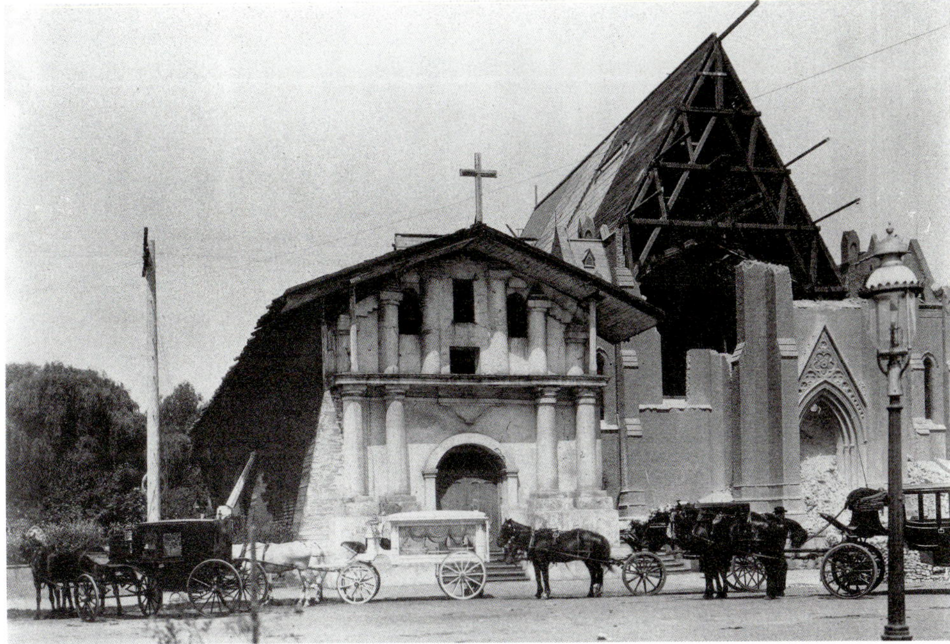

BELOW: View of the mission after the 1906 San Francisco earthquake; the historic church remained standing, but the brick church next door, built in 1876, lay in ruins. A funeral procession waits at the curb. Photograph by C.C. Pierce. Courtesy University of Southern California, on behalf of the USC Special Collections

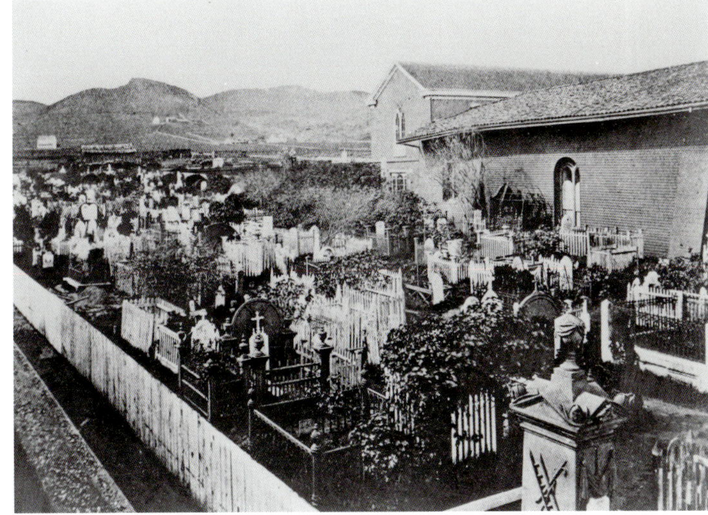

RIGHT: The original cemetery next to the church, ca. 1880, where the unmarked remains of hundreds of neophytes were interred. San Francisco notables continued to be buried in the cemetery well into the 1890s; their tombstones can be seen. Courtesy University of Southern California, on behalf of the USC Special Collections

San Juan Capistrano

NOVEMBER 1, 1776

Location: *San Juan Capistrano*

Founder: *Father Junípero Serra*

Presidio District: *San Diego*

Peak Mission Population: *1,361 (1812)*

Major Native Groups: *Acjachemen (Juaneño), Luiseño, Gabrielino (Tongva)*

Historical Assets: *Ruins of the 1806 stone church, 1782 adobe Serra Chapel, restored adobe* convento *and soldiers' quarters; remains of tanning vats, tallow processing, forge, olive press, winery, kitchen stoves, and unique metal smelter; museum*

Existing Church: *Constructed of stone in 1806; turned to ruins in 1812 earthquake; adobe Serra Chapel, built in 1782, reoccupied after 1812*

Ownership: *Roman Catholic Church, Diocese of Orange*

Historical Status: *California Historical Landmark (No. 200)*

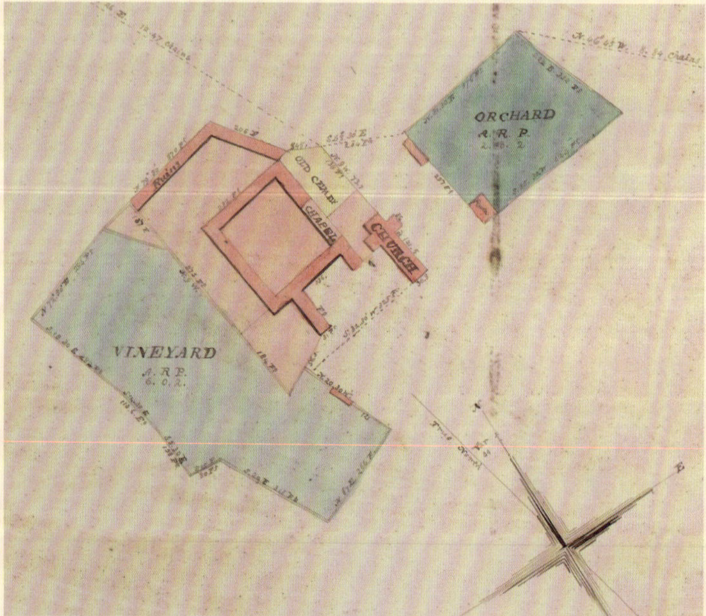

Map of the *casco* by the surveyor John G. Cleal, 1854 (detail). Courtesy of The Bancroft Library, University of California, Berkeley

Mission San Juan Capistrano was located on the fertile coastal lands of southern California and grew into a large and prosperous establishment. Its history, however, was not without difficult periods. First founded in 1775 by Father Lasuén, the temporary buildings were quickly abandoned when the community received reports of the Tipai attack on neighboring Mission San Diego. The second founding by Father Serra in 1776 was followed by steady growth. In 1811 mission accounts record a total harvest of over fifteen thousand bushels of wheat, corn, barley, and beans.

The Great Stone Church of Mission San Juan Capistrano, begun in 1797 and completed in 1806, was the most elaborate undertaking of all the California missions. One hundred eighty feet long and forty feet wide, it featured a Baroque vaulted ceiling surmounted by seven domes and a cruciform transept. The tiered bell tower was said to have stood 125 feet high and to have been visible for a distance of ten miles.[1] The building was designed in Mexico, and the work was executed by the master mason Isidro Aguilar, of Culiacan, who died in 1803, three years before its completion.[2] In use for only six years, the church was destroyed in the earthquake of 1812: the domed roof cracked, releasing stone and tiles on the congregation and killing forty, thirty-eight adults and two children. The enormous bell tower fell, scattering stones throughout the surrounding village. The bells were retrieved and hung in an *espadaña*, from where they ring today. Three fallen stones were salvaged and reused in later building projects. The ruined walls were left standing by the mission fathers and now provide an iconic image of this ambitious undertaking. The old adobe church was reoccupied for worship, and the mission continued to prosper.

With secularization in 1833, the mission population dispersed and adjacent villagers removed roof tiles from abandoned buildings for new construction. The old adobe walls melted into great mounds over former foundations. Interest in restoring Mission San Juan Capistrano began in 1895, when the Landmarks Club chose this site as one of its first projects. Among the surviving adobe buildings was the 1782 Serra Chapel, claimed to be the only remaining building in California where Father Serra administered the sacraments. During the years of abandonment, the chapel had fortunately been leased to a farmer for grain storage, retained its roof, and therefore survived. Mission restoration continued through the tireless efforts of Father St. John O'Sullivan, who patched and mended the adobe buildings over the

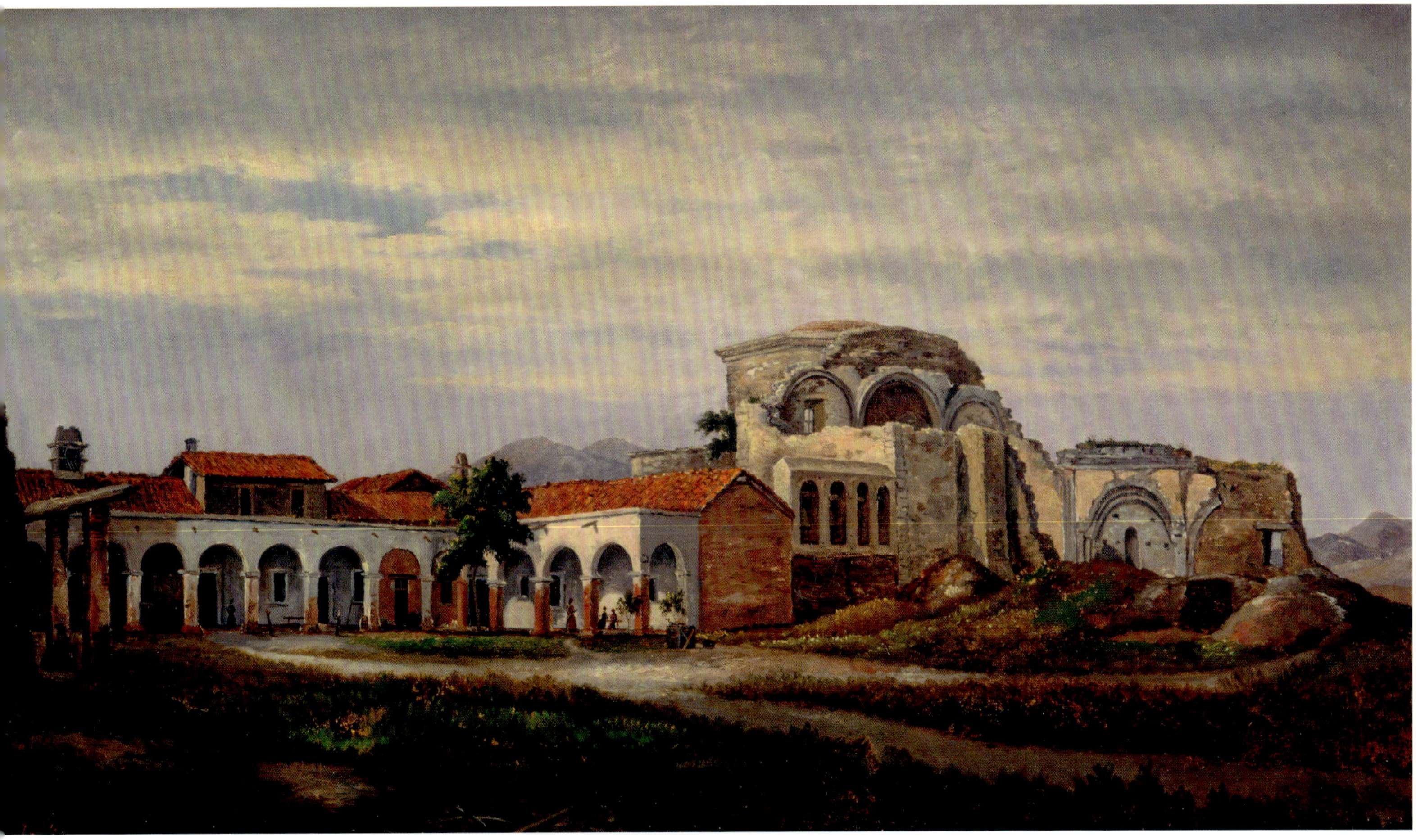

In this painting, the artist captured the grandeur of the church, turned to ruins by the 1812 earthquake. Henry Chapman Ford, *Mission San Juan Capistrano*, 1880. Oil on canvas. Courtesy of the Mission Inn Foundation and Museum, Riverside, California. From the collection of The Historic Mission Inn Corporation

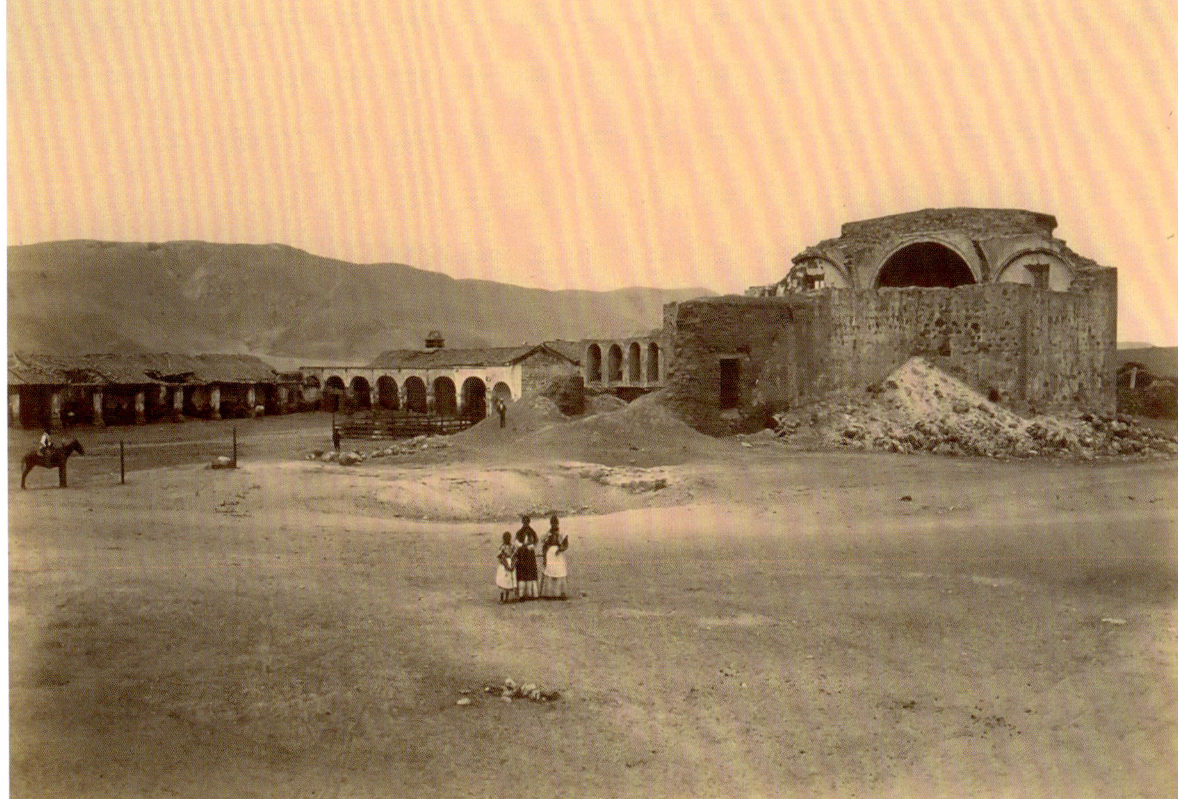

View of the mission, ca. 1877, showing the ruins of the Great Stone Church, seen at right. Several people posed for the photographer can be seen in front of the desolate, abandoned buildings. Photograph by Carlton Watkins. Albumen silver print. Bancroft Library, University of California, Berkeley

course of more than thirty years, adhering to historical accuracy in both form and materials. In 1924 he oversaw installation of a magnificent gilded Baroque *retablo* from Barcelona—estimated to be three hundred years old—in the newly restored Serra Chapel.

Restoration and preservation work has continued as an important element of mission activities, along with a program of archaeological investigations during the 1980s. Seismic stabilization of the Serra Chapel and south wing was carried out in the early 1990s, using concrete bond beams and buttresses. Seismic retrofit of the ruins of the Great Stone Church began in 1989 and was completed in 2004, at a cost of nearly $10 million. As a measure of its commitment to restoration, Mission San Juan Capistrano maintains an ongoing conservation program, with recent efforts directed to the Serra Chapel, including conservation of statues and artwork, stabilization of wall plaster and paintings, repair of the Baroque *retablo*, removal of destructive modern concrete plaster, and repair of deteriorating wood elements. These exemplary efforts ensure that Mission San Juan Capistrano's historical assets will be enjoyed by generations to come.

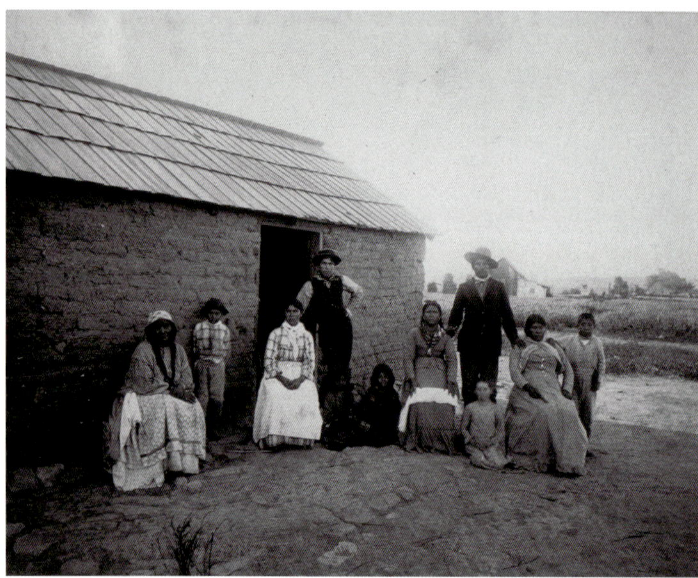

ABOVE: One of several neophyte families that remained in the vicinity of the mission after secularization. Descendants of these families remain part of the community today. Photograph by I. W. Taber, ca. 1895. Courtesy of The Bancroft Library, University of California, Berkeley

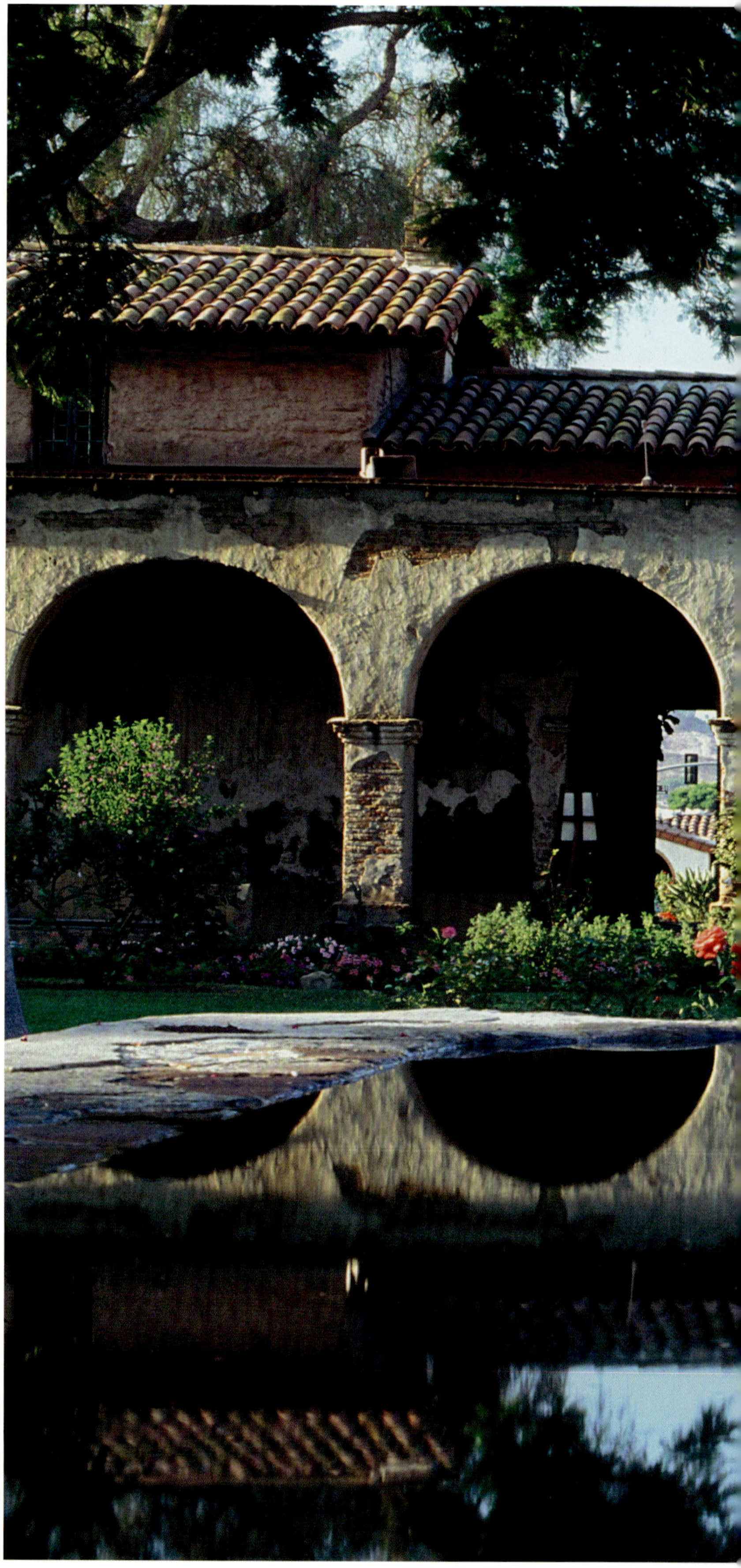

RIGHT: The restored mission buildings and their verdant gardens attract tourists and visitors to this romantic setting. Photograph by G. Aldana

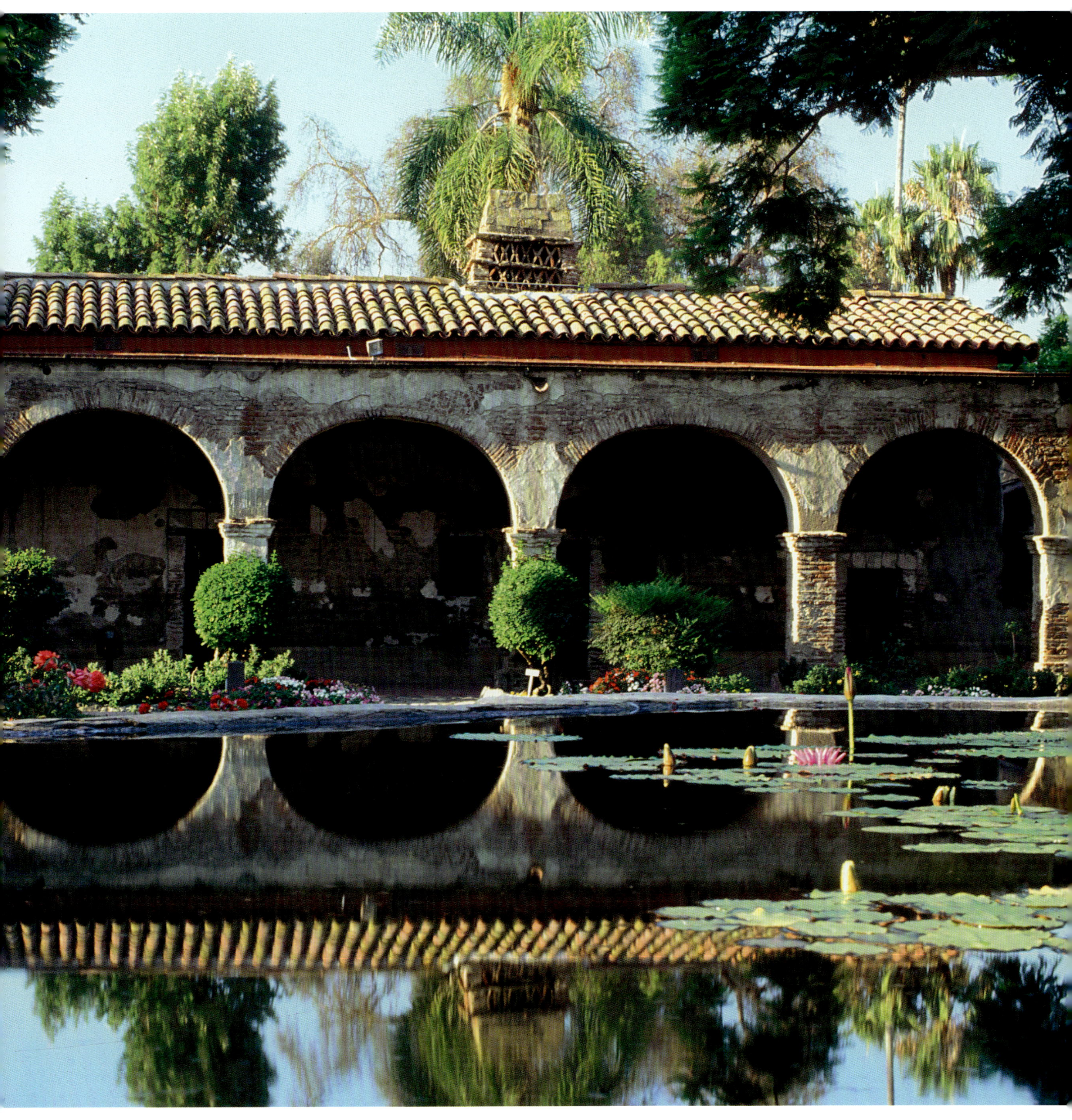

Santa Clara de Asís

FOUNDED JANUARY 12, 1777

LOCATION: *Santa Clara*

FOUNDER: *Father Thomás de la Peña*

PRESIDIO DISTRICT: *San Francisco*

PEAK MISSION POPULATION: *1,541 (1795)*[1]

MAJOR NATIVE GROUPS: *Ohlone/Costanoan, Yokuts, Sierra Mowok*

HISTORICAL ASSETS: *One adobe room (the Faculty Club) and remnant of an adobe wall, both once part of the mission quadrangle; Peña Adobe, neophyte residence*

EXISTING CHURCH: *Modern interpretation of reinforced concrete, completed 1929*

OWNERSHIP: *Santa Clara University (Roman Catholic Church, Society of Jesus)*

HISTORICAL STATUS: *California Historical Landmark (No. 338)*

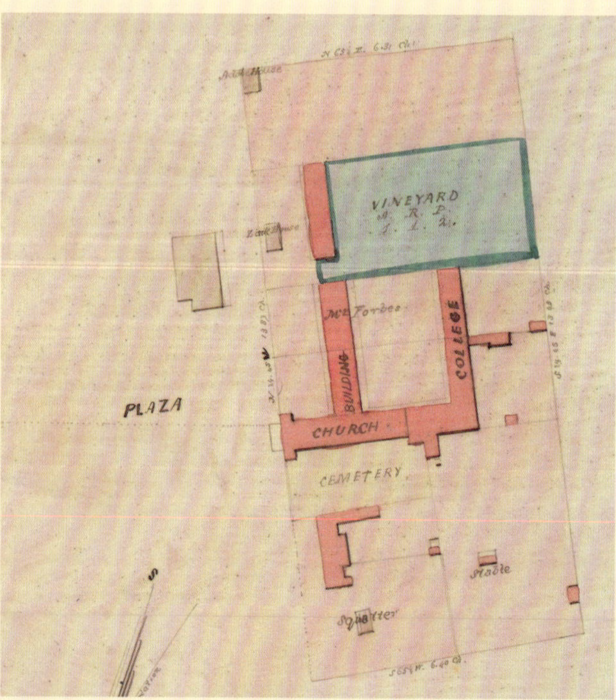

Map of the *casco* by the surveyor George Black, 1854 (detail). Courtesy of The Bancroft Library, University of California, Berkeley

Mission Santa Clara de Asís was the second mission established on San Francisco Bay, following Mission San Francisco de Asís by one year.[2] Its location was changed three times in response to flooding and earthquakes; it was established on its final site in 1818. The mission was located near an abundance of farmland, pasture, and water, producing ample provisions for its residents. Its population grew steadily as the missionaries recruited among the populous Ohlone/Costanoan villages. A social shift occurred in 1793, when entire villages appeared for baptism, adding more than 400 neophytes to the mission rolls within one year. The fathers then turned their efforts to the untapped villages of the San Joaquin Valley and the Sierra Nevada foothills, from which the mission brought in more than 1,400 Yokuts and some 450 Sierra Miwok. By secularization about forty years later, the 1,100 Clareños in residence exhibited a mixture of Native American languages, customs, and parentage.[3]

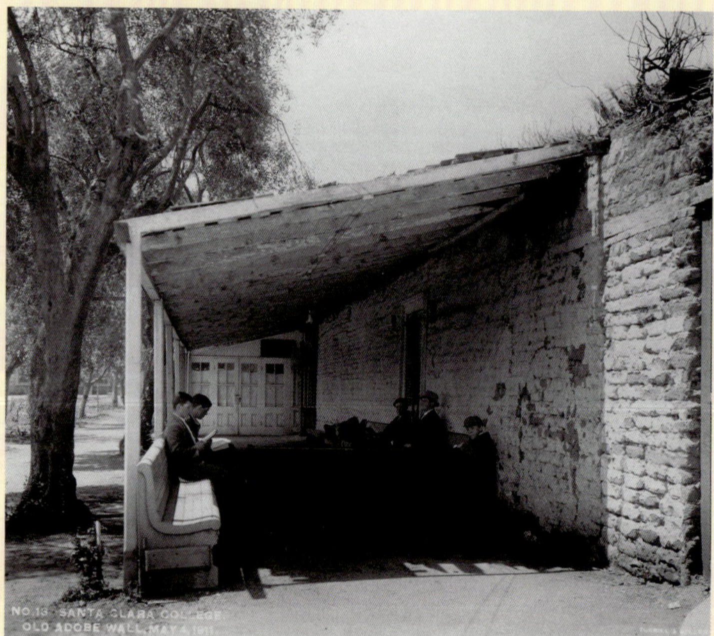

ABOVE: The largest remaining wall of the mission quadrangle, photographed in 1911; it was preserved by Santa Clara College as part of a shaded sitting area. Turrill-Miller Photographers, Santa Clara University Archives and Special Collections

OPPOSITE: View of the reconstructed church; the original painted decorative motif on the facade was re-created in relief when the church was rebuilt in 1929. Photograph by G. Aldana

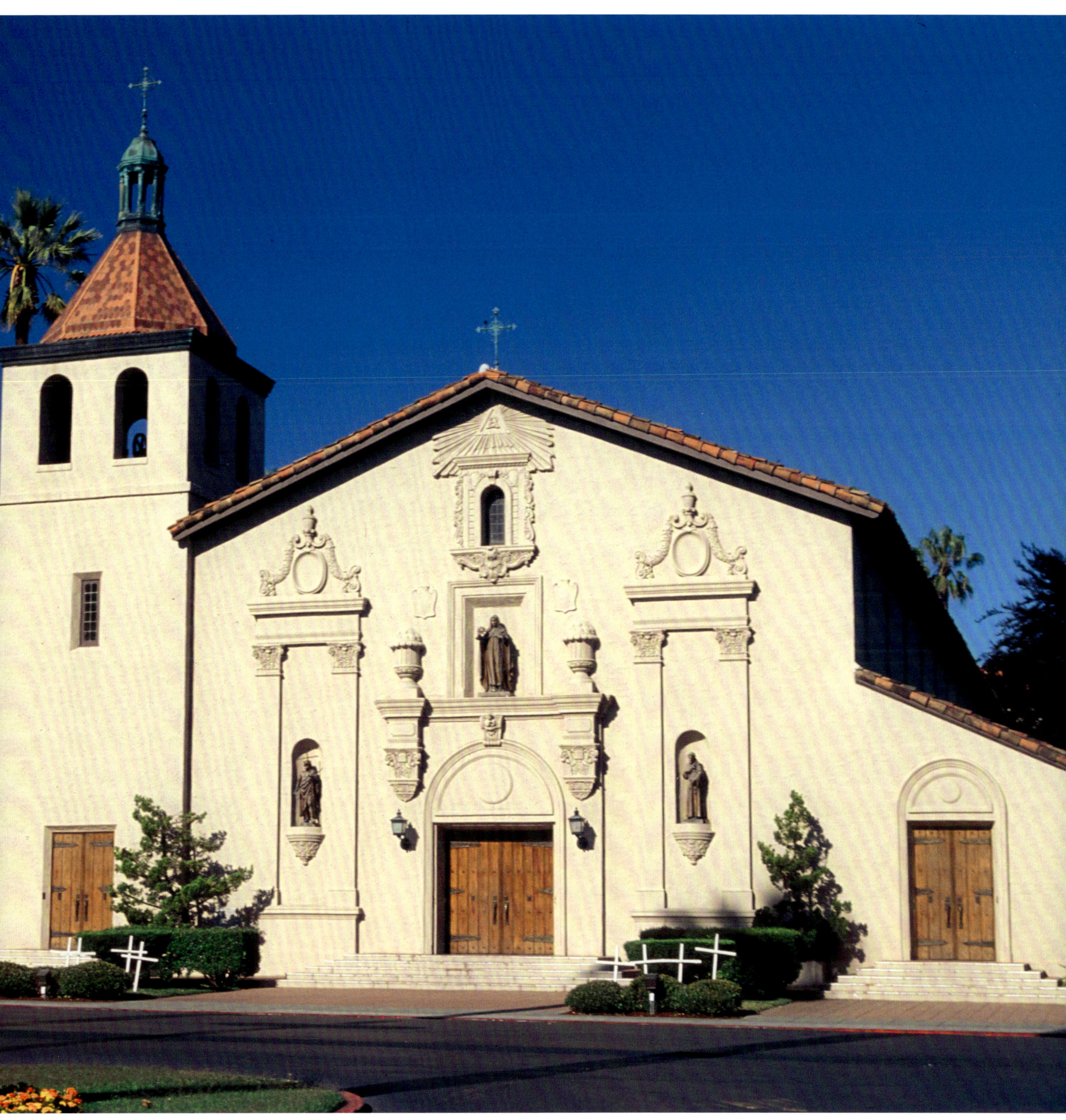

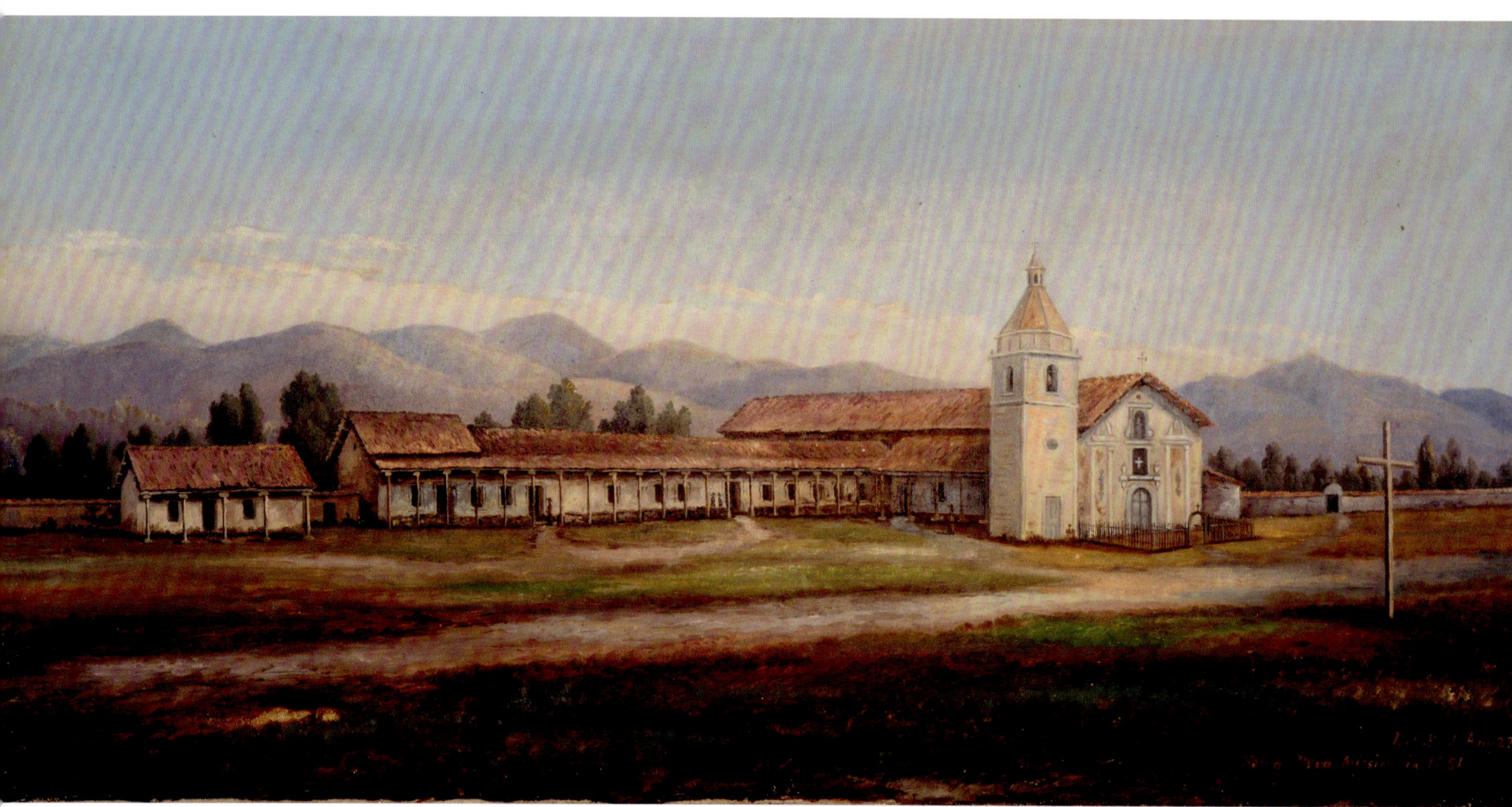

Construction activities were nearly continuous at Mission Santa Clara as the site was relocated, rebuilt, and repaired many times. A total of five churches were constructed. The third, completed in 1784, was acclaimed as the most elaborate in California. Its Neoclassical altarpiece, shipped from Mexico in 1802, cost 1,000 pesos. With relocation of the mission to its final site, however, first a temporary and then a final, fifth church was constructed, the latter completed in 1825. This last edifice had a simple adobe facade that was enhanced in 1835 by the exquisite Neoclassical paintings of the Mexican artist Agustín Dávila. Dávila also covered the wooden nave ceiling with a heavenly scene featuring musical cherubs and liturgical eminences that resembled the great painted domes of European churches.[4]

In December 1836 Santa Clara was the last mission to be secularized, its community of more than one thousand neophytes soon dispersing over the countryside. Some fifteen years later, Bishop Joseph Alemany turned the abandoned mission buildings over to the Jesuits to establish a school that was to become Santa Clara University. Before signing over the papers, however, Santa Clara's last Franciscan priest, Father José María del Refugio Suárez del Real, deeded a large adobe building—the former fourth mission church and later a boys' dormitory—to Candelaria, his mistress and the mother of his children. Suárez del Real also transferred the mission vineyard to Andrés Pico and provided a house for Antonio María Osio, where he penned his important treatise, *Historia de Alta California*.[5]

After 1851 the former mission was converted into a center for higher education. Over time, surviving mission structures served as administration building, Jesuit residence, library, laundry, and student residence. The church continued to serve as the heart of the community. The building's adobe belfry had been destroyed by heavy rains and replaced by a wooden one in 1841, and the Jesuits now further "modernized" the exterior in 1861 with a covering of clapboard. To accommodate its student and community congregation, the building was widened in 1884 by removal of the adobe nave walls. After surviving for 101 years, the mission was subjected to the ultimate disaster in 1926, when an accidental fire consumed the historic building. The current church, completed in 1929, is a concrete replica of the widened church of 1884, with the original painted designs on the facade now reproduced in relief plasterwork and the celestial ceiling replicated from photographs.[6] Only one adobe room and a partial wall ruin survive from the mission-period establishment, although recent documentary and archaeological studies have contributed much to an understanding of Mission Santa Clara's buried past.[7]

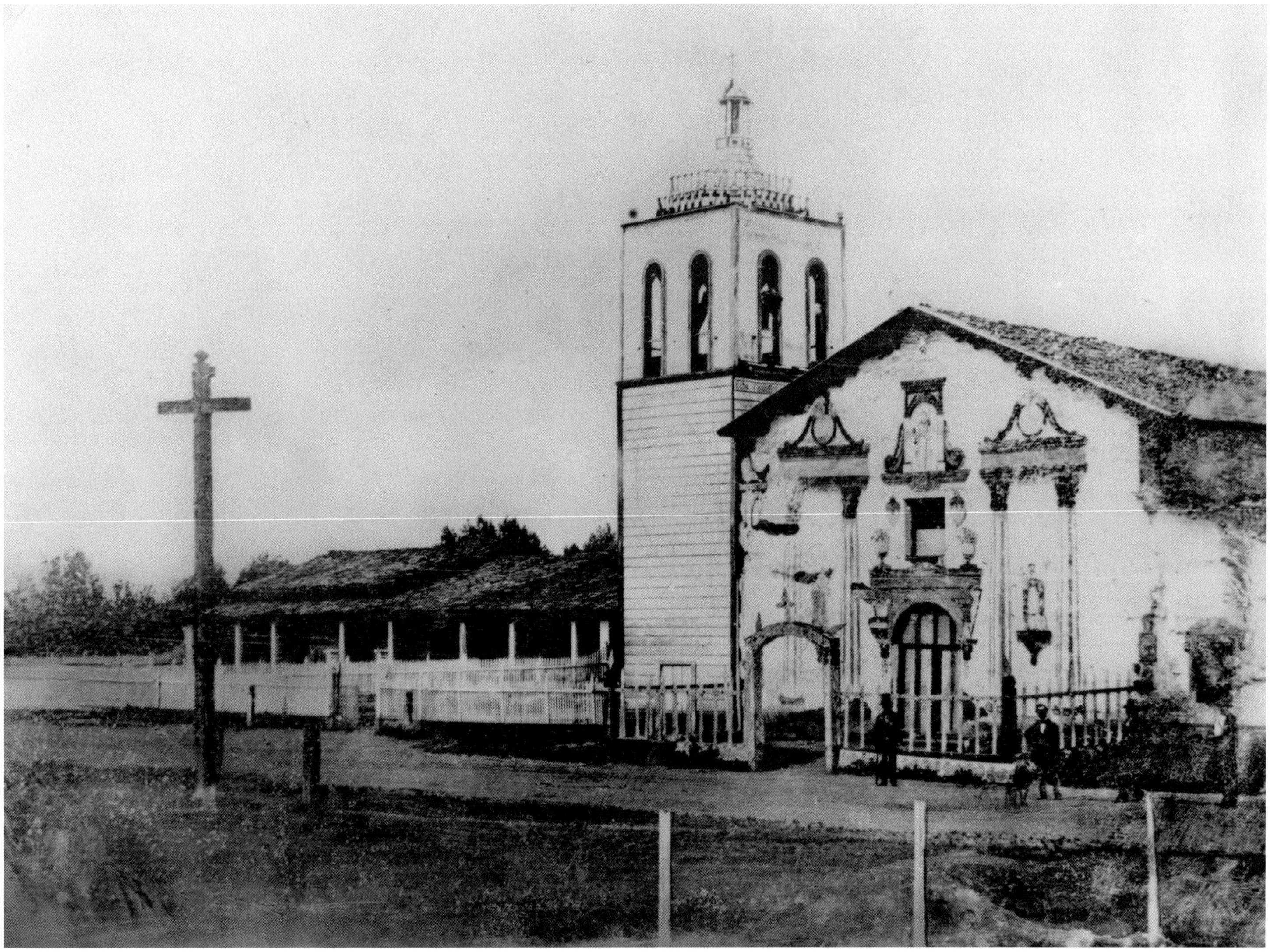

OPPOSITE: Artistic depiction of the mission church and *convento*, ca. 1883. Henry Chapman Ford, Mission Santa Clara. Oil on canvas. Courtesy of the Mission Inn Foundation and Museum, Riverside, California. From the collection of The Historic Mission Inn Corporation

ABOVE: View of the mission in 1854; the decorations on the facade, painted by Agustín Dávila in 1835, can be clearly seen. Photograph by James P. Ford. Daguerreotype. Santa Clara University Archives and Special Collections

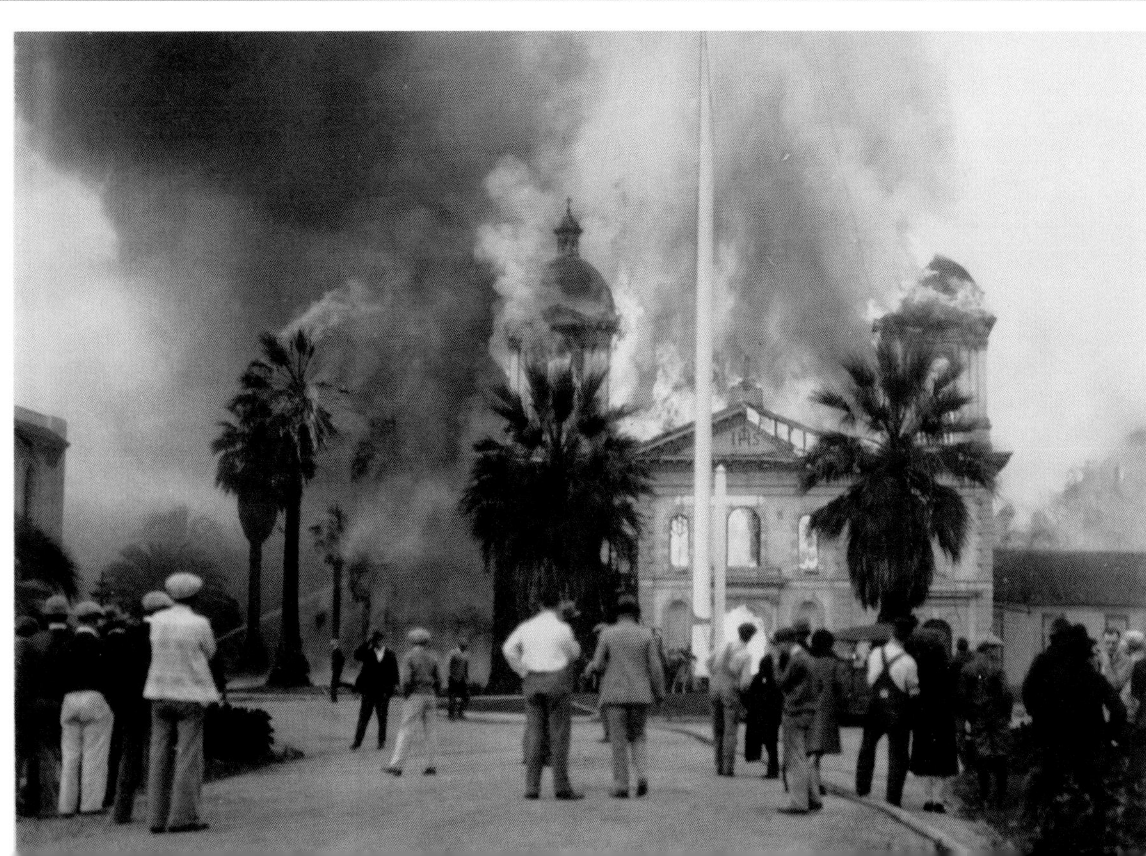

RIGHT: The mission burning in the catastrophic fire of 1926; the blaze destroyed the mission church, including its incomparable ceiling and wall murals. Photographer unknown. Santa Clara University Archives and Special Collections

San Buenaventura

FOUNDED MARCH 31, 1782

LOCATION: *Ventura*

FOUNDER: *Father Junípero Serra*

PRESIDIO DISTRICT: *Santa Bárbara*

PEAK MISSION POPULATION: *1,328 (1816)*

MAJOR NATIVE GROUPS: *Ventureño and Island Chumash*

HISTORICAL ASSETS: *Church; museum; archaeological findings in adjacent park with museum; segments of the water system*

EXISTING CHURCH: *Of adobe and* ladrillo, *completed in 1809; interior renovations of the 1890s reversed in the 1950s*

OWNERSHIP: *Roman Catholic Church, Archdiocese of Los Angeles*

HISTORICAL STATUS: *California Historical Landmark (No. 309)*

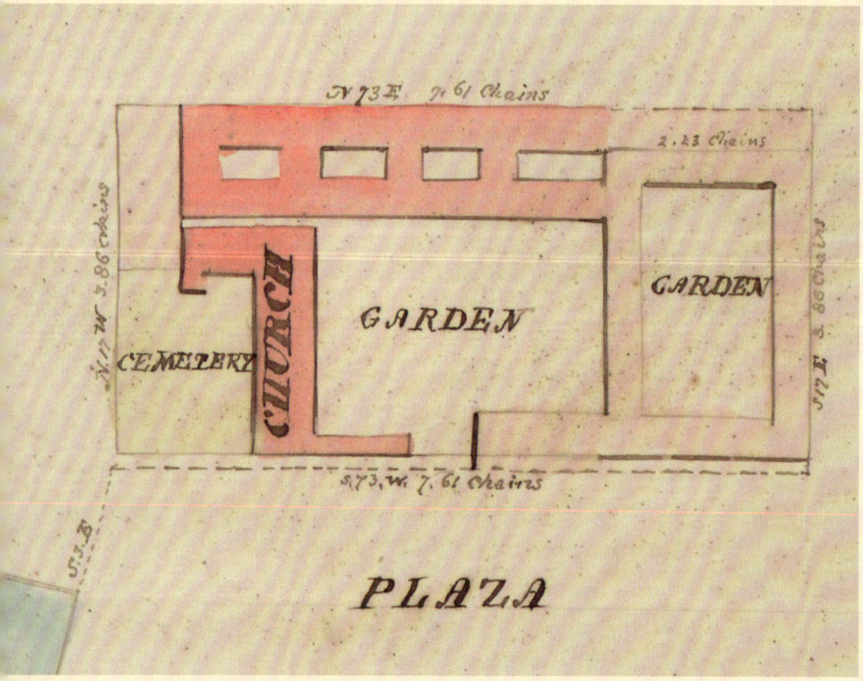

Map of the *casco* by the surveyor John G. Cleal, 1854 (detail). Courtesy of The Bancroft Library, University of California, Berkeley

Mission San Buenaventura was founded among the Chumash Indians, well known for their densely populated coastline, sturdy oceangoing canoes, and accomplished basketry. The Chumash, occupying a coastal exposure protected by the Channel Islands, developed an oceangoing culture in large wood-planked canoes, or *tomals*. The Chumash were arguably the most politically and socially complex group in California and extended from San Luis Obispo to Los Angeles. More than native groups in other parts of California, they continued traditional fishing and gathering practices and maintained tribal hierarchies well into the mission period.

This mission and Mission Santa Inés were the best agricultural provisioners in Alta California, far outproducing the other missions in per capita ratios of crops and livestock. The fathers here also participated early and prominantly in the illicit hide-and-tallow trade with English and American companies, in advance of Mexican independence in 1821. Portions of the extensive water system survive, including the filter house above the archaeological park adjacent to the church. The buttressed stone piers of the extraordinary siphon that carried water across the mouth of Cañada Largo have only recently slipped into the adjacent creek bed.

The handsome adobe church fronts Main Street, still asserting an important presence in this growing coastal town. The building is constructed of *ladrillos* and adobe, originally with a Classical facade featuring pilasters across the front topped by a pedimented gable. The architect was the master mason José Antonio Ramírez, famous for his work on at least six other churches in California. The appearance of the facade was altered after the 1812 earthquake: the height was reduced, and a buttress and buttressing bell tower were added to the front.[1] The building features strong Moorish elements with mixtilinear (decoratively shaped) door and window openings. The church was never abandoned. Enthusiastic efforts at modernization in the 1890s covered the ceiling and floors with milled lumber and enlarged the nave windows to receive darkening panels of stained glass. These changes were reversed in the 1950s, and the current building is little changed from the mission era. A museum occupies a nearby historic building, displaying rare church statuary, paintings, furnishings, and mission-period items; many of these are in need of conservation.

OPPOSITE: The mission church and *convento*, ca. 1899. Edwin Deakin, *Mission San Buenaventura.* Oil on canvas. Courtesy of the Santa Bárbara Mission Archive-Library

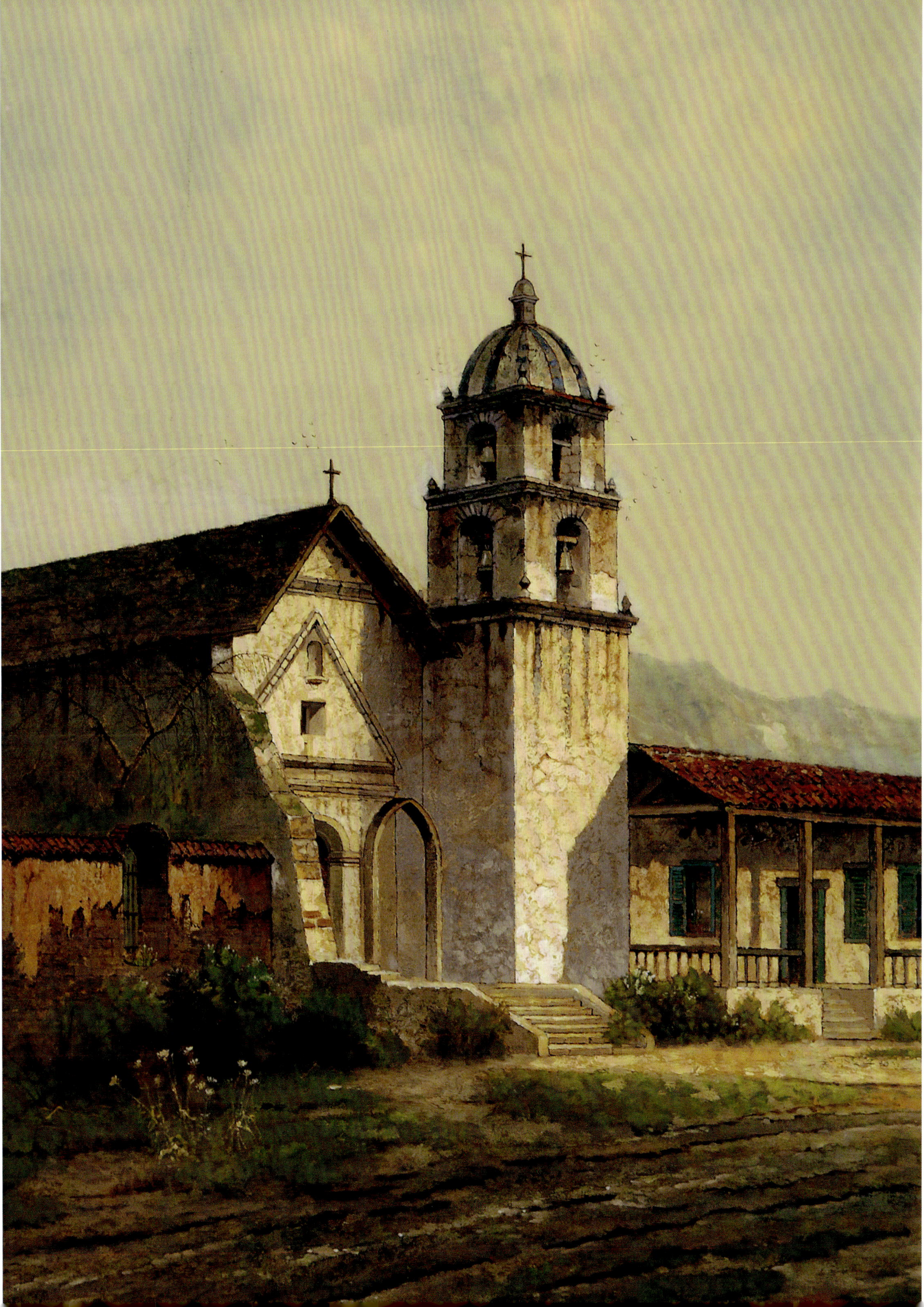

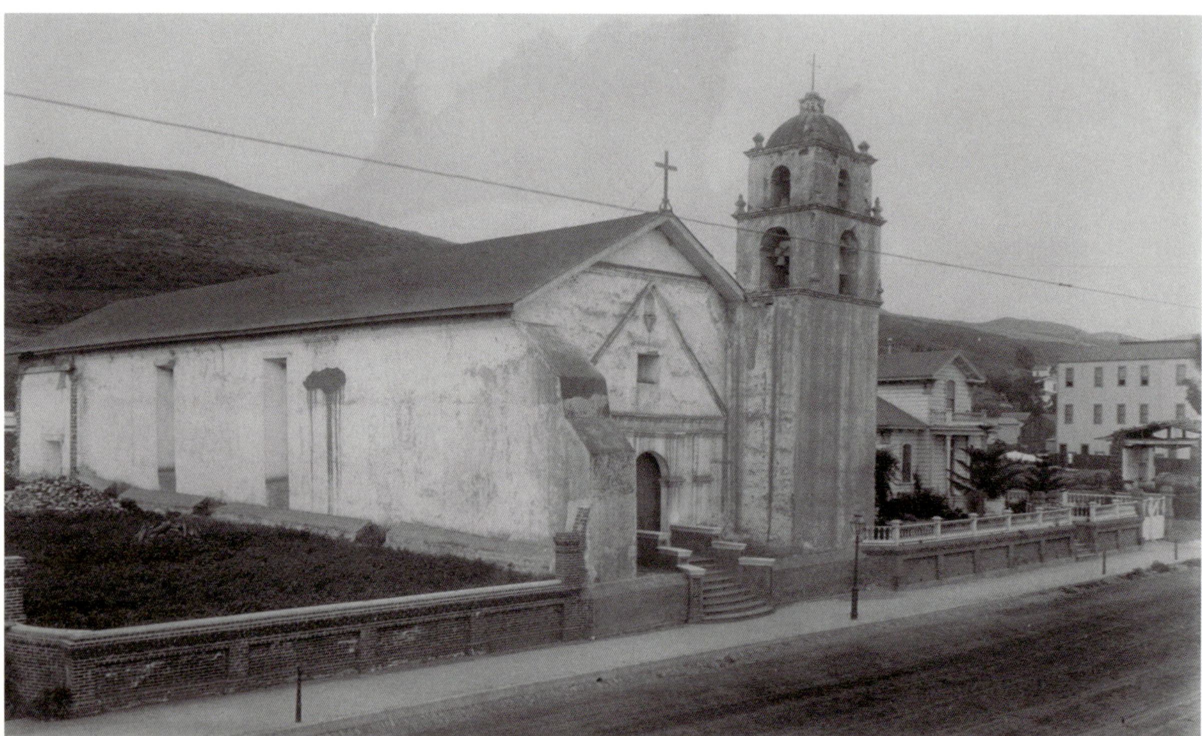

RIGHT: Mission San Buenaventura, ca. 1888. The church fronts the growing town's busy Main Street. Courtesy of The Bancroft Library, University of California, Berkeley

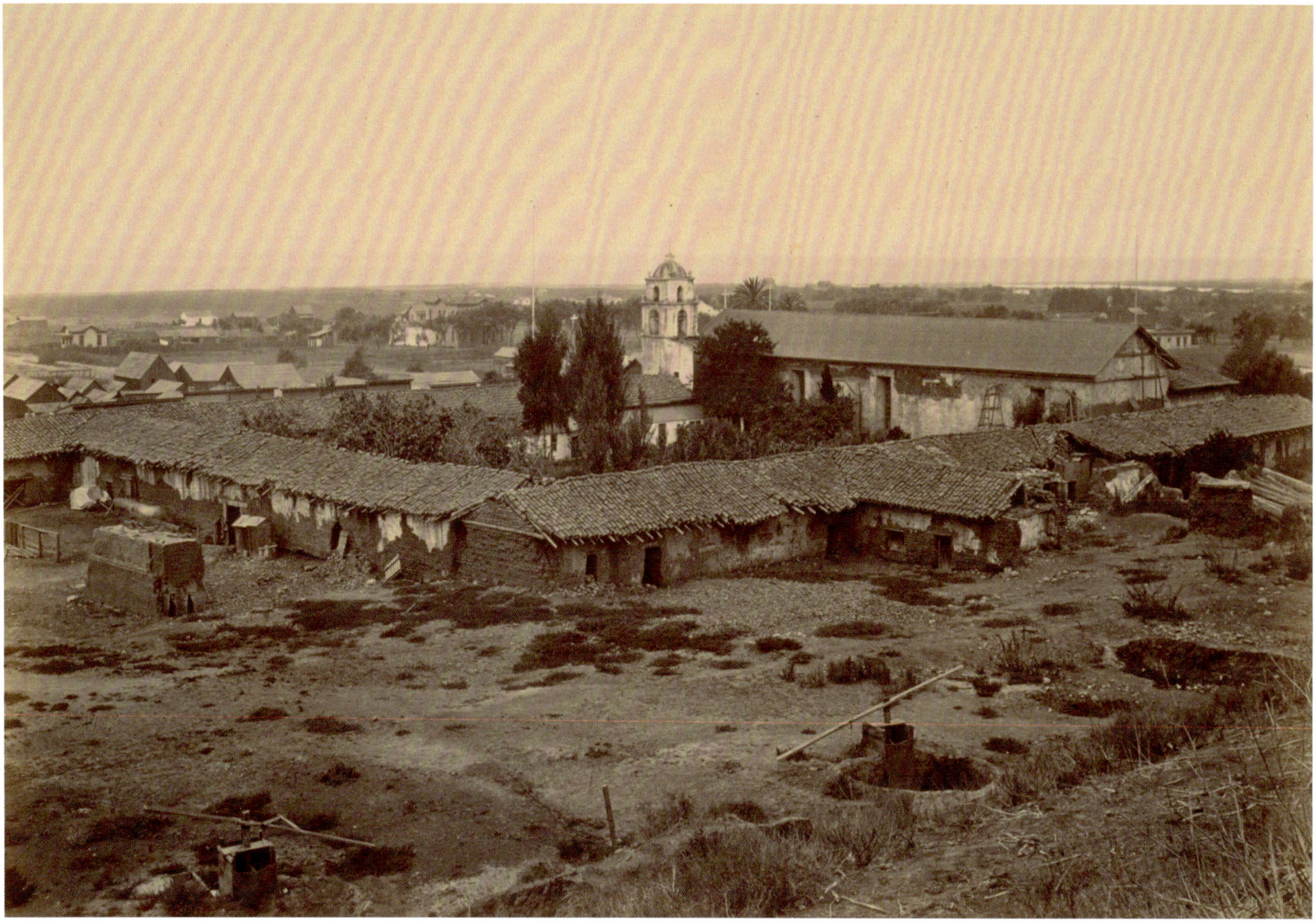

BELOW: Rear view of the tile-roofed mission quadrangle, which was still standing as late as the mid-1870s, when this photograph was taken. Photograph by Carleton Watkins. Albumen silver print. Courtesy of The Bancroft Library, University of California, Berkeley

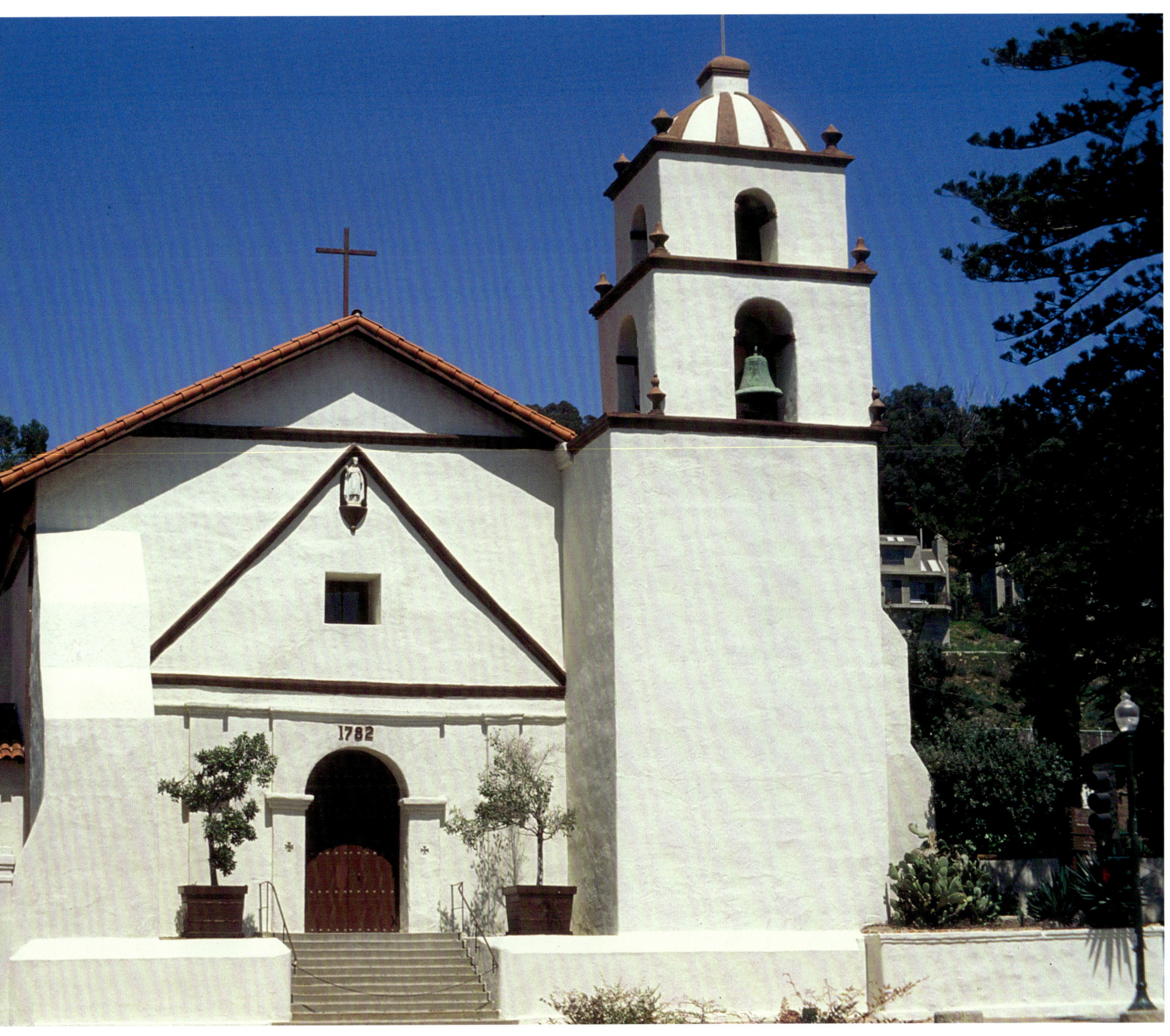

Recent view of the church, which has survived virtually intact. Photograph by G. Aldana

Mission San Buenaventura was the focus of one of the earliest professional archaeological excavations of a mission site in California.[2] In the 1970s archaeologists excavated a large area west of the church, uncovering the remains of a 3,500-year-old Native American village; foundations for the earliest church; remains of mission rooms, neophyte residences, aqueduct systems, and artifact deposits; and evidence of a later Chinese community. These well-studied and published finds led to the establishment of the Albinger Archaeological Park and Museum by the city of San Buenaventura. Mission foundations are interpreted on the landscaped grounds, and the recovered artifacts are effectively interpreted in the museum.

Santa Bárbara, Virgen y Mártir

FOUNDED DECEMBER 4, 1786

LOCATION: *Santa Barbara*

FOUNDER: *Father Fermín Lasuén*

PRESIDIO DISTRICT: *Santa Bárbara*

PEAK MISSION POPULATION: *1,792 (1802)*

MAJOR NATIVE GROUPS: *Barbareño, Ineseño, and Island Chumash*

HISTORICAL ASSETS: *Original church (reconstructed facade), remodeled* convento *buildings, fountain and* lavandería; *remains of reservoirs, mill, filter house, and tanning vat on nearby grounds; museum and extensive art and artifact collections; Archive-Library*

EXISTING CHURCH: *Of stone, completed in 1820; various repairs and bell tower restorations; rebuilt concrete facade with stone veneer*

OWNERSHIP: *Roman Catholic Church, Archdiocese of Los Angeles*

HISTORICAL STATUS: *California Historical Landmark (No. 309); National Historic Landmark*

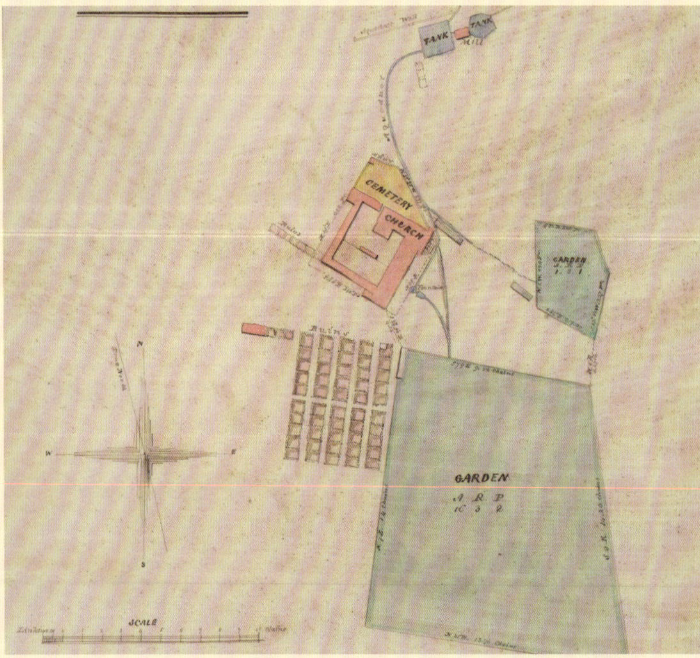

Map of the *casco* by the surveyor John G. Cleal, 1854 (detail). Courtesy of The Bancroft Library, University of California, Berkeley

Mission Santa Bárbara, Virgen y Mártir, was established about one and a half miles upslope from the Santa Bárbara presidio, whose foundations had been laid some four years earlier. Here the fathers erected one of the most long-lived and visually arresting of the California missions. With a population of close to 1,800 at its peak, Santa Bárbara was the largest mission in this presidio district. It was also, however, the poorest producer of crops and livestock, lacking the rich valley soils and rolling grazing lands of neighboring institutions. But the mission was favored with a skilled Chumash population, a mild climate, and access to ocean resources. At the mission the Chumash continued to make *tomals* (oceangoing canoes) and supplied the mission's tables with catches made in the deep waters of the channel. Neophytes from villages on Santa Cruz Island fled to this off-shore refuge during the 1824 Chumash revolt, stealing the mission's two *tomals.*

The stone church of Mission Santa Bárbara was constructed by California's well-known master carpenter and stonecutter José Antonio Ramírez between 1815 and 1820. It is the most Neoclassical of all the California missions, with a facade design based on an illustration in a Roman design book found in the mission library.[1] The bell towers were reconstructed using modern concrete following the 1925 earthquake, replicating their historic appearance but causing further structural failures. In the early 1950s the entire facade was rebuilt using steel-reinforced concrete clad in a stone veneer.

Mission Santa Bárbara is the only California mission never to have been deserted by the Franciscans.[2] In 1842 California's first Roman Catholic bishop established his see at the mission to administer the affairs of his diocese, which included all of Upper and Lower California. With stability assured, the mission became the repository for many documents, artifacts, and pieces of art from abandoned missions. The historic adobe buildings were also home to an apostolic college training novice Franciscans (1856–85), the Colegio Franciscano, a boys' school (1868–77), and St. Anthony's Seminary (1896–1901). In 1901 St. Anthony's moved to a handsome new complex of buildings north of the mission, where it remained until 1987.[3] While Mission Santa Bárbara's church and *convento* wing have splendidly survived—along with the picturesque fountain and *lavandería* (washing area)—other original buildings and archaeological remains

OPPOSITE: The classical façade and bell towers of Mission Santa Bárbara, reconstructed in the 1950s. Photograph © Bill Dewey

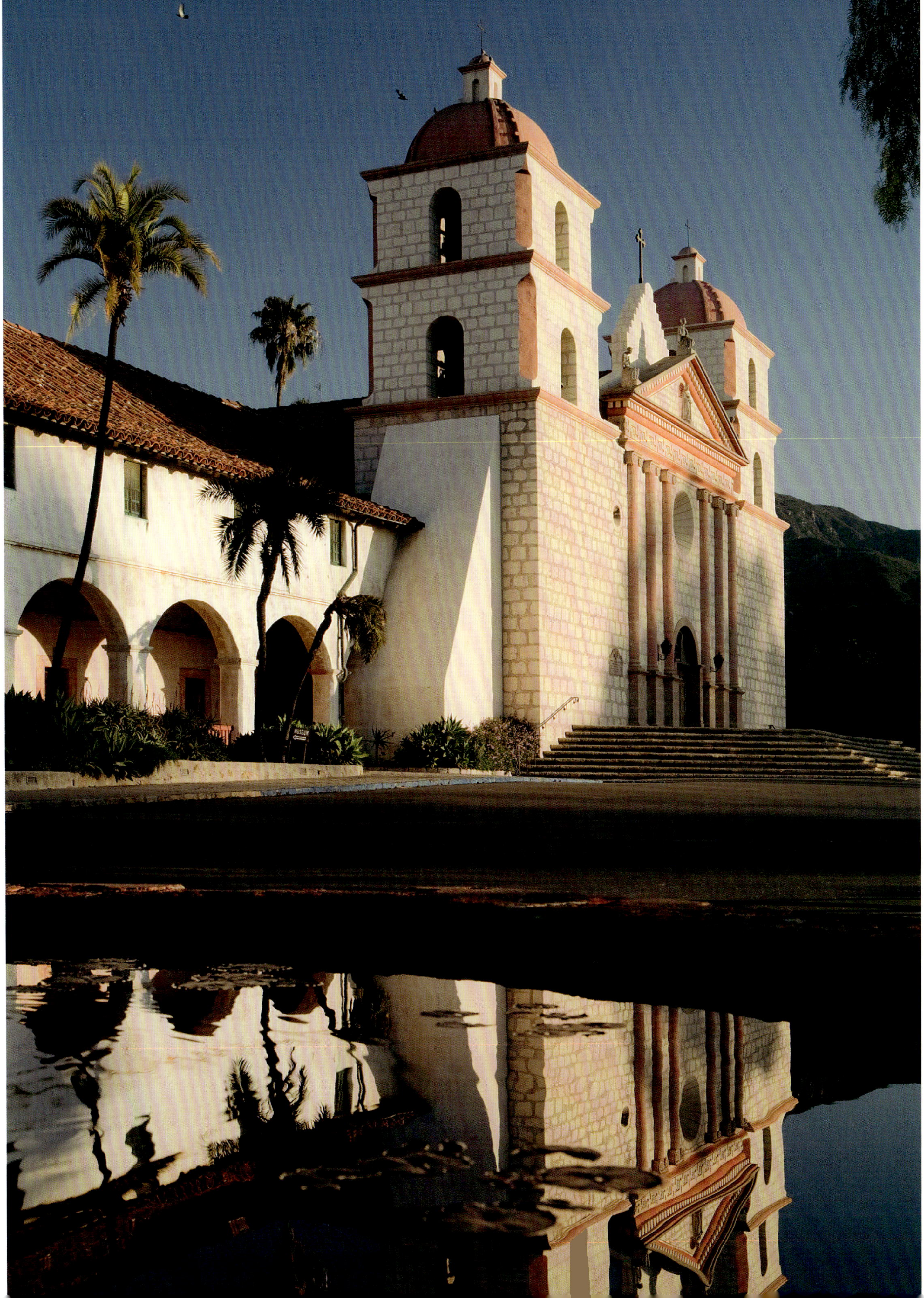

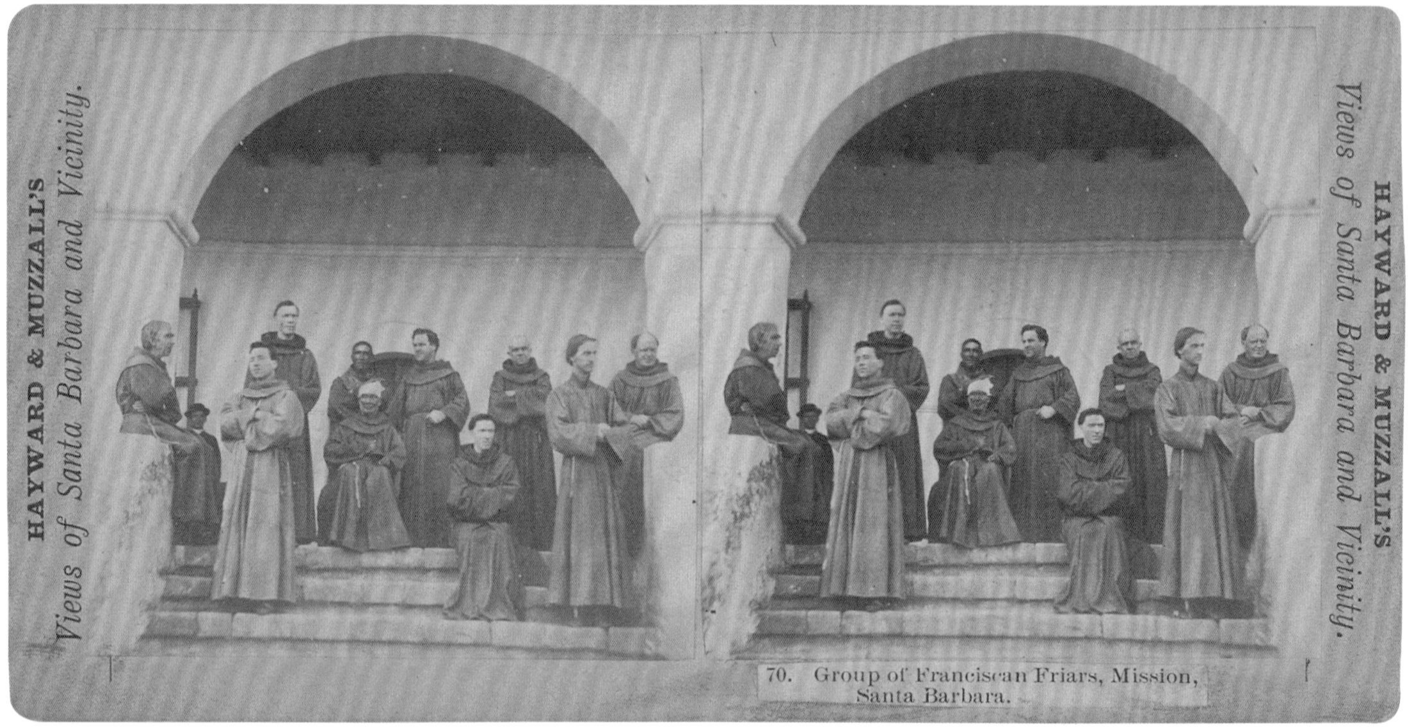
HAYWARD & MUZZALL'S
Views of Santa Barbara and Vicinity.
HAYWARD & MUZZALL'S
Views of Santa Barbara and Vicinity.
70. Group of Franciscan Friars, Mission, Santa Barbara.

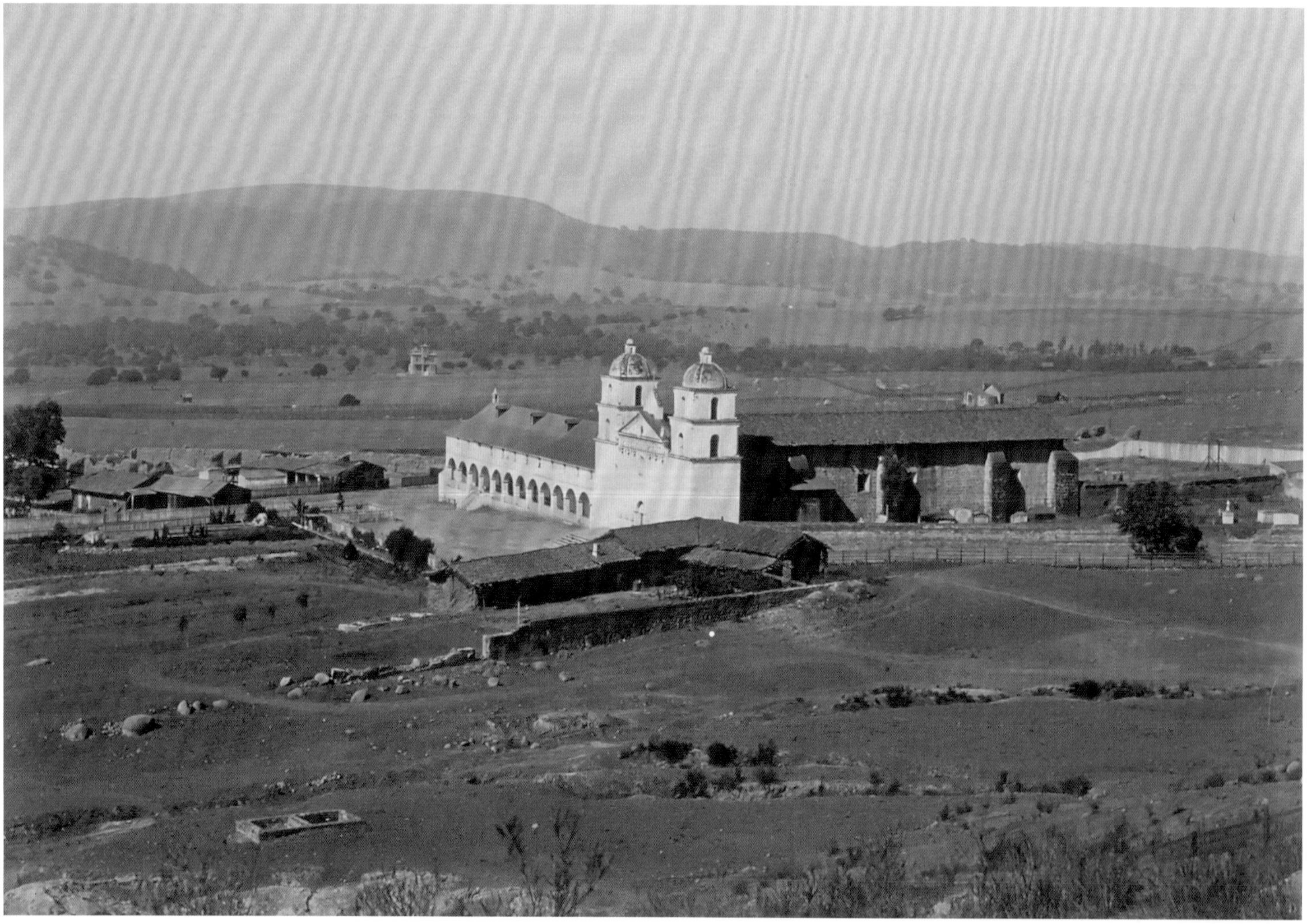

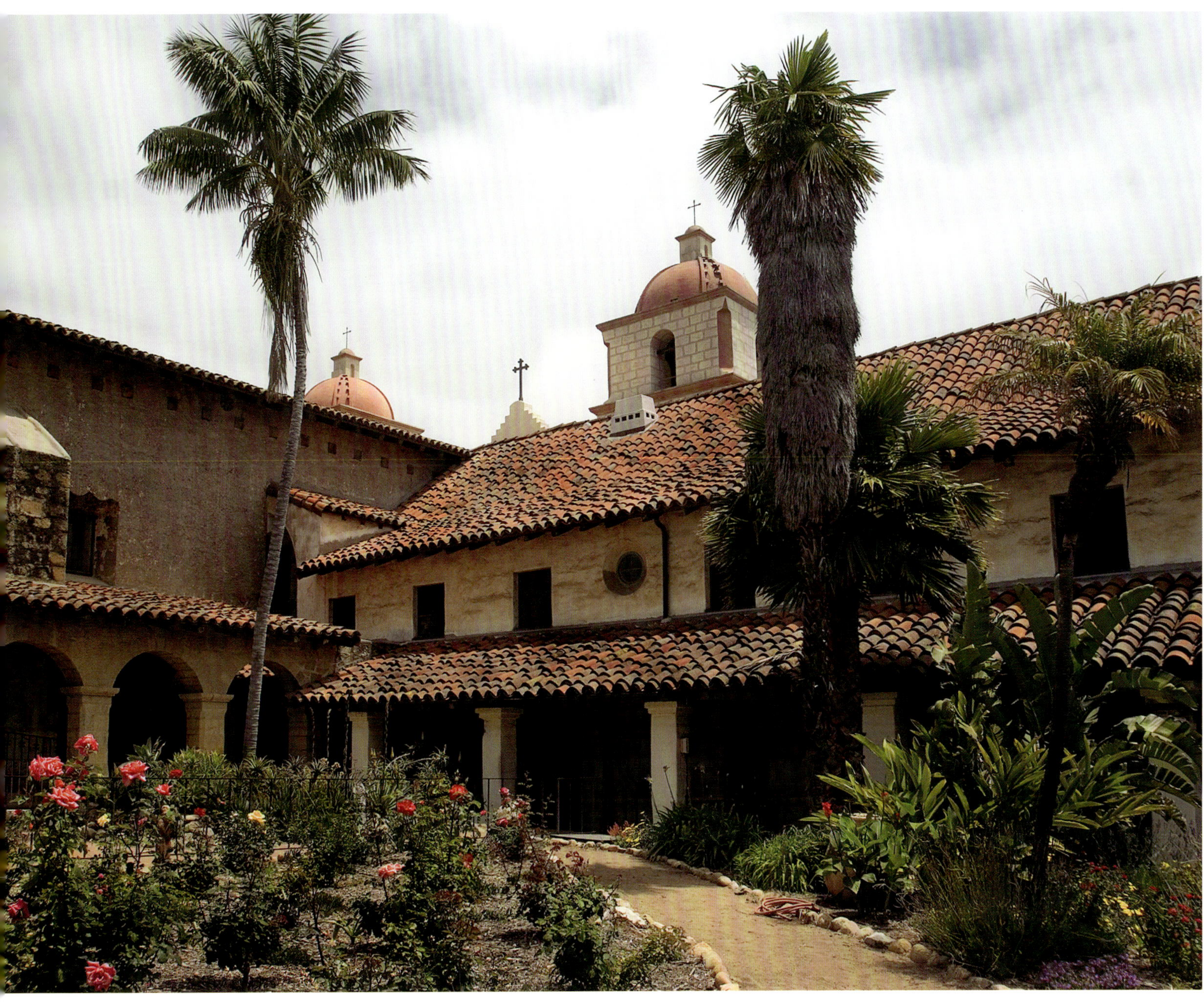

have disappeared under new construction, parking lots, and surrounding residential development.

Mission Santa Bárbara is still vitally engaged in both its historic past and the modern world. Although earthquakes repeatedly caused damage to the buildings, they were always carefully restored. Its Archive-Library houses one of California's most extensive collections of primary historical documents on the state's Spanish and Mexican periods. The mission's impressive collection of religious art, furnishings, and secular items has made its museum one of the best among the missions. Also preserved by the city of Santa Bárbara are remnants of the mission's extensive water system of dams, aqueducts, reservoirs, mills, and a filter house.[4] Santa Bárbara's title, Queen of the Missions, is aptly bestowed.

OPPOSITE ABOVE: Franciscan friars in front of the mission *convento*, ca. 1875–80. The Franciscans never abandoned the mission, and as a result it served as a repository for art and historical documents from other establishments. Photographs by Hayward and Muzzall. Stereograph. Courtesy of The Bancroft Library, University of California, Berkeley

OPPOSITE BELOW: View of the mission and surrounding landscape, ca. 1876–80. The majordomo's quarters and several neophyte dwellings are still intact. Photograph by Carleton Watkins. Albumen print. Courtesy of The Bancroft Library, University of California, Berkeley

ABOVE: The mission's inner courtyard, with its modern, floral landscaping, affords visitors and residents a sense of cloistered tranquility. Photograph courtesy of the Santa Barbara Conference and Visitors Bureau and Film Commission/Melissa Fargo

La Purísima Concepción de María Santísima

FOUNDED DECEMBER 8, 1787

LOCATION: *Original site: near intersection of Locust and F Streets, Lompoc. Second site: State Park three miles east of Lompoc*

FOUNDER: *Father Fermín Lasuén*

PRESIDIO DISTRICT: *Santa Bárbara*

PEAK MISSION POPULATION: *1,520 (1804)*

MAJOR NATIVE GROUPS: *Purisimeño, Ineseño, and Island Chumash; Yokuts*

HISTORICAL ASSETS: *First site, Lompoc: ruins of the church's stone doorway and plaza* lavandería, *archaeological remains. Second site: reconstructed in the 1930s by CCC and in the 1940s and 1980s by California State Parks; original portions of walls, columns, and buttresses in the Residence building; water features; reconstructed and preserved landscape setting; interpretive exhibits and museum*

EXISTING CHURCH: *Reconstruction completed between 1935 and 1937; made of adobe reinforced with concrete supports*

OWNERSHIP: *Original site: city of Lompoc and private landowners. Second site: State of California*

HISTORICAL STATUS: *Original site: California Historical Landmark (No. 928). Second site: California Historical Landmark (No. 340); National Historic Landmark*

Mission La Purísima was founded amid the populous Chumash villages of the western Santa Ynez Valley. Sited where the modern town of Lompoc now stands, it grew to a community of over fifteen hundred housed within a large complex of adobe buildings and a village of traditional native houses. Surrounding the church, residences, shops, and storage rooms were kilns for tiles and pottery, a threshing floor, tanning vats, corrals, aqueducts, reservoirs, orchards, and gardens. But the location of this establishment was not ideal. The Santa Ynez River ran between El Camino Real on the north and the mission on the south, resulting in isolation of the community, especially during winter's high waters.

In December 1812 a devastating earthquake, combined with torrential rains and flooding, destroyed the twenty-five-year-old establishment. Deeming the damage beyond repair, the priests appealed to the father president and the governor for permission to relocate the mission three miles to the north, to Los Berros (Watercress) Canyon. This would place La Purísima on El Camino Real and closer to more abundant water sources and more extensive lands for cultivation. Approval was received, and in 1813 construction of a new complex began. Differences in design and execution testified to experience gained at the original site: building walls were dramatically thickened and heavy buttresses added to withstand earthquakes. The traditional enclosed quadrangle was also abandoned in favor of one long line of buildings, a design unique in California.[1] The move proved advantageous as agricultural production increased in subsequent years.

After only twenty years at its new location, La Purísima—along with all the other California missions—was turned over to secular authorities. The remnant Chumash population, counted at 242 in 1839, was decimated by a smallpox epidemic in 1844. With the mission finally abandoned, the massive adobe walls began their slow decay. Although portions of the site were returned to the Catholic Church in 1874, the land with its ruins was soon sold and eventually acquired by private parties.

The resurrection of the second site as La Purísima Mission State Historic Park began in 1933 with the purchase of the site by Santa Barbara County. Although the Landmarks Club had been deeded the site in 1905, anticipated preservation work had not been carried out. The county saw the potential of Civilian Conservation Corps (CCC) crews as a restoration labor force and successfully petitioned the Department of the Interior to establish a camp for this purpose. In a

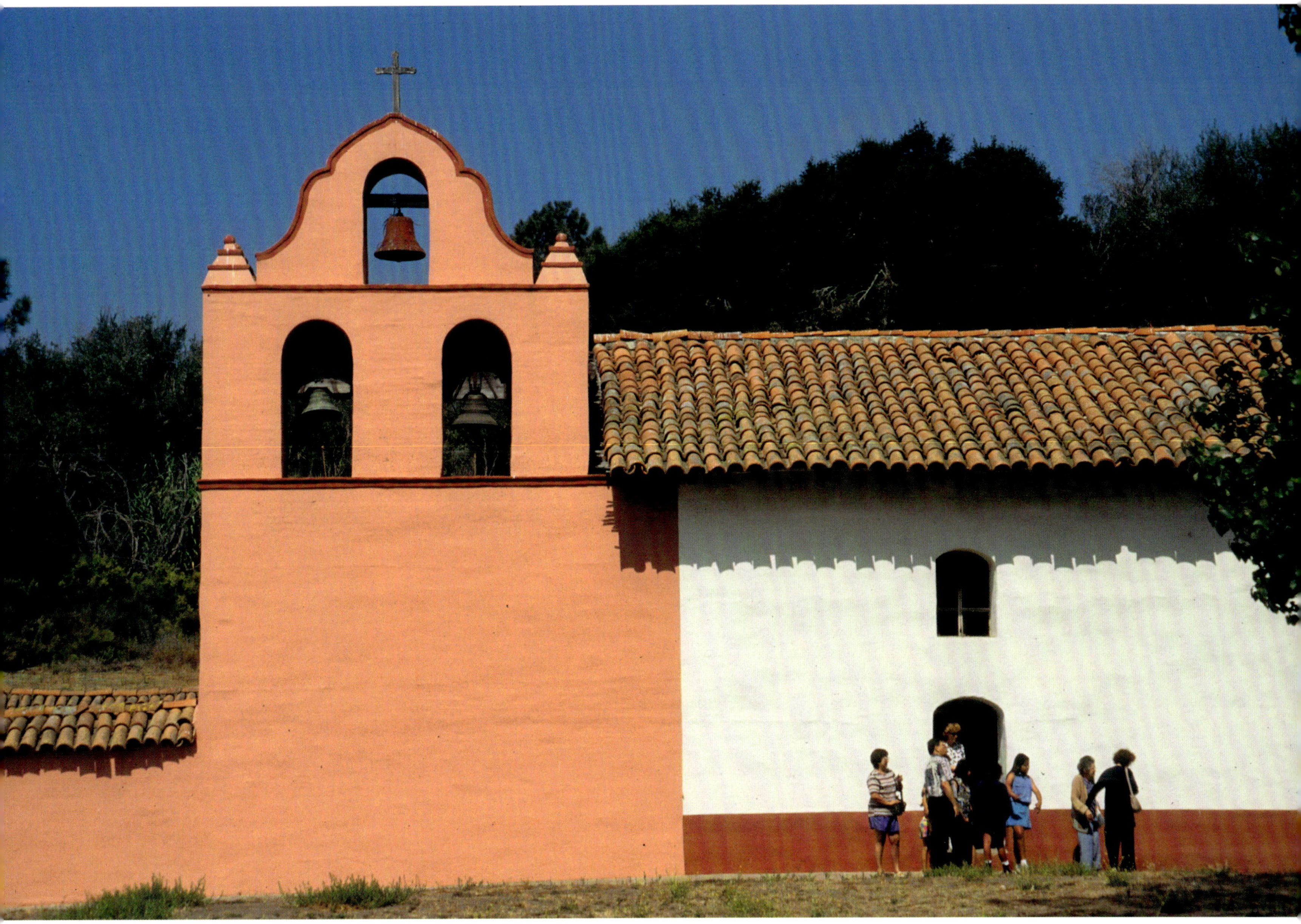

ABOVE: View of the church and *espadaña*, reconstructed between 1935 and 1937 by the Civilian Conservation Corps; the *espadana*'s design was borrowed from Mission Santa Inés. Photograph by G. Aldana

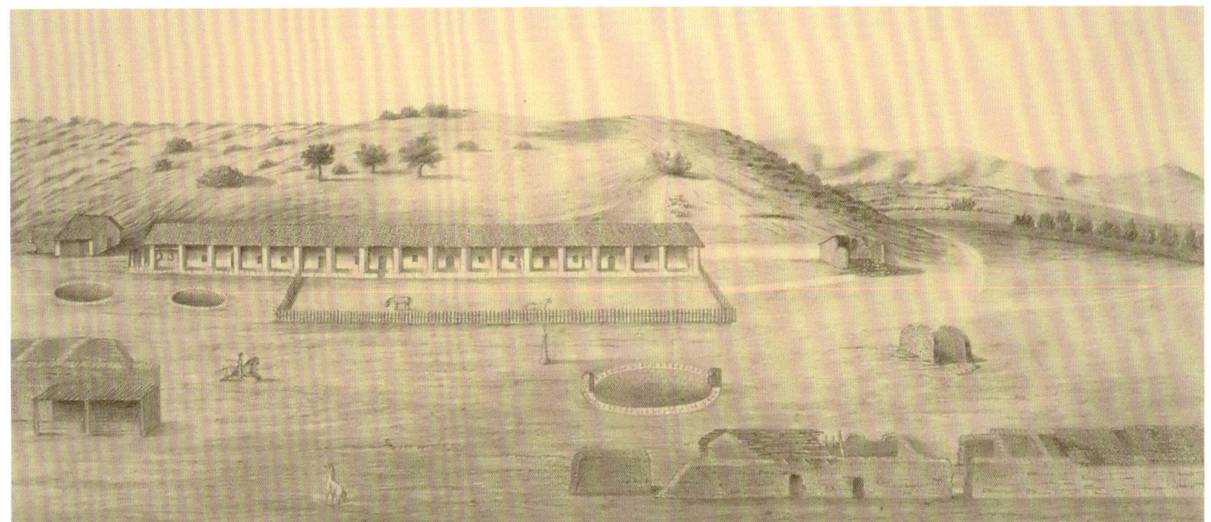

RIGHT: Mission La Purísima as portrayed by the artist Henry Miller when he visited on his tour of California in 1856; the unusual linear arrangement of the buildings is evident. Pencil sketch on paper. Courtesy of The Bancroft Library, University of California, Berkeley

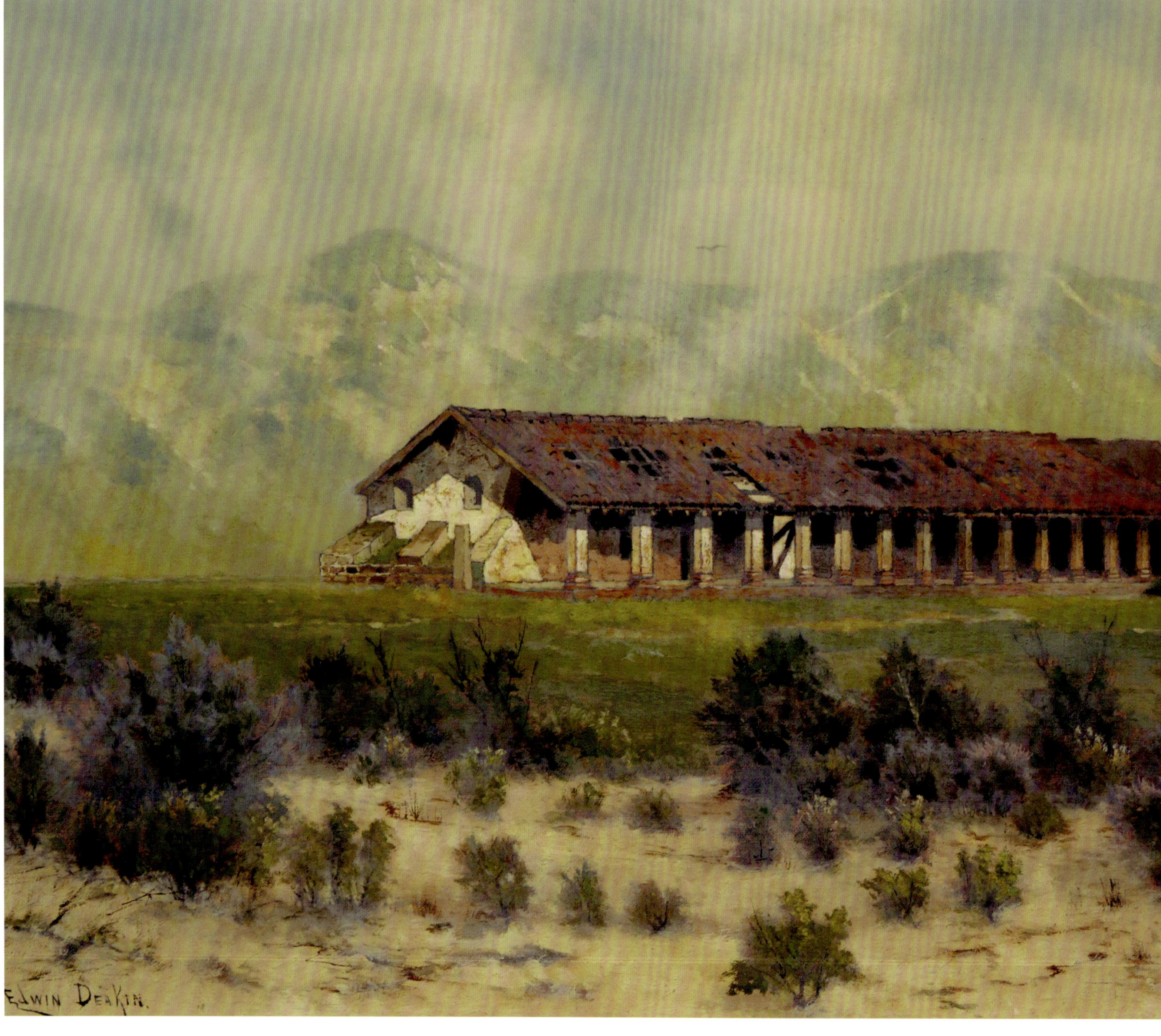

remarkable county-state-federal partnership, ownership of various purchased and donated parcels of land was transferred to the State of California, and La Purísima State Historical Monument was born in 1935. Three massive buildings were reconstructed of adobe reinforced with concrete and steel: the *convento* (Residence), the shops and quarters, and the church, along with the plaza fountain and portions of the aqueduct system. Where possible, original wall portions, columns, and buttresses were integrated into new construction. The extraordinary work of the CCC crews in discovering and then replicating many of the tools and methods used by the original builders has resulted in the designation of the site as a National Historic Landmark. Subsequent archaeological studies have maintained a high standard for accurate historical interpretations.[2] California State Parks has added to the complex by reconstructing the infirmary and *monjerio* buildings in the 1940s and the blacksmith shop in 1983.

Mission La Purísima's relocation to Los Berros Canyon has proved advantageous not only to its original residents but also to modern visitors. The isolated valley provides an ideal landscape setting for the building reconstructions and cultural reenactments that have made La Purísima one of California's most popular mission destinations.

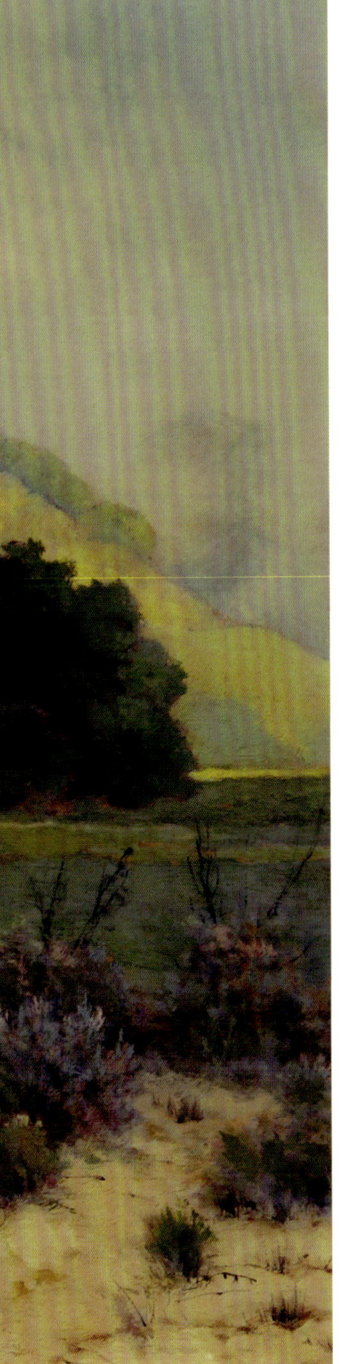

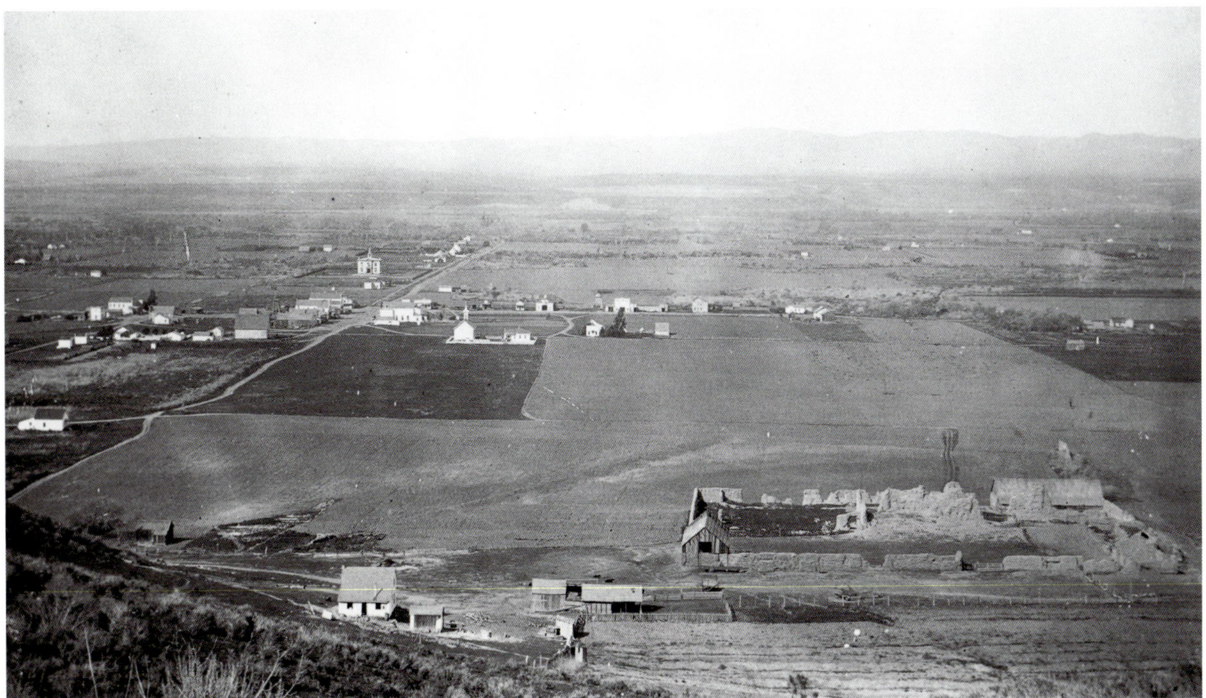

ABOVE: The ruins of the first site are seen here in 1885 on the outskirts of the town of Lompoc, which is beginning to encroach. Courtesy of the Santa Bárbara Mission Archive-Library

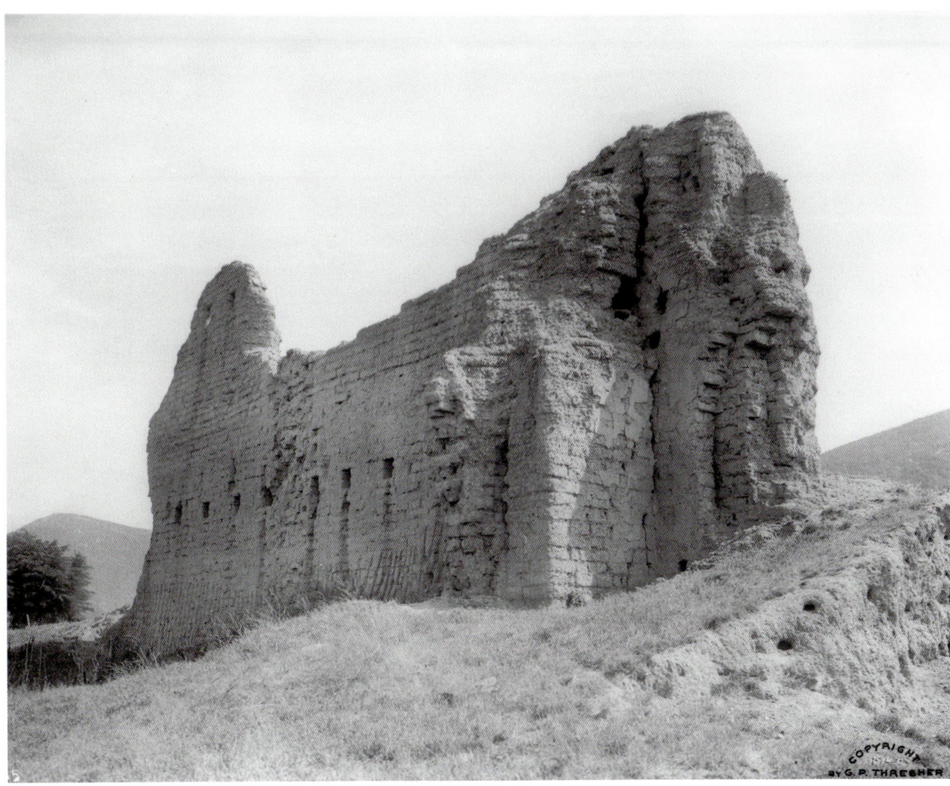

RIGHT: View of the ruins of the south wall of the first site's church, 1905. It was constructed in 1803 and collapsed in the 1812 earthquake. Photograph by George P. Thresher. Courtesy University of Southern California, on behalf of the USC Special Collections

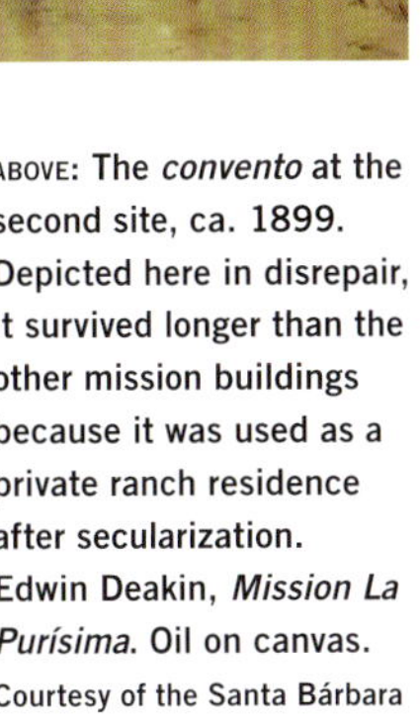

ABOVE: The *convento* at the second site, ca. 1899. Depicted here in disrepair, it survived longer than the other mission buildings because it was used as a private ranch residence after secularization. Edwin Deakin, *Mission La Purísima.* Oil on canvas. Courtesy of the Santa Bárbara Mission Archive-Library

La Exaltación de la Santa Cruz

FOUNDED AUGUST 28, 1791

LOCATION: *Santa Cruz*

FOUNDER: *Father Fermín Lasuén*

PRESIDIO DISTRICT: *San Francisco*

PEAK MISSION POPULATION: *523 (1796)*

MAJOR NATIVE GROUPS: *Ohlone/Costanoan, Yokuts*

HISTORICAL ASSETS: *Adobe neophyte residence of 1871 (Neary-Rodríguez Adobe) restored with interpretive exhibits*

EXISTING CHURCH: *1889 brick church on site of original church; 1932 mission replica on adjacent block*

OWNERSHIP: *Church site: Roman Catholic Church, Diocese of Monterey; Neary-Rodríguez Adobe part of Santa Cruz Mission State Historic Park*

HISTORICAL STATUS: *California Historical Landmark (No. 342)*

Mission Santa Cruz was founded on the northern coast of Monterey Bay. With the smallest population of all the missions, it struggled during much of its tenure. Reaching a population of about five hundred only a few years after its founding, mission numbers declined steadily after 1821. Santa Cruz had a high rate of neophytes escaping the mission and was the location of the famous murder of Father Andrés Quintana in 1812 by a group of neophyte conspirators. It also suffered from loss of agricultural lands to the civilian community of Villa de Branciforte, secular demands on its resources, and ill treatment of neophytes by Branciforte residents. Tensions between the two communities were increased by the unequal division of resources: the mission, located on the west side of the San Lorenzo River, held the best cropland; Villa de Branciforte's lands east of the river were fit only for livestock pasturage.[1]

Founded in 1797, Branciforte was uniquely supported financially by the government and colonized largely by unprepared and ill-equipped artisans and retired soldiers, along with petty criminals from central Mexico. The community never prospered or took on the established character of the other civilian settlements of San José and

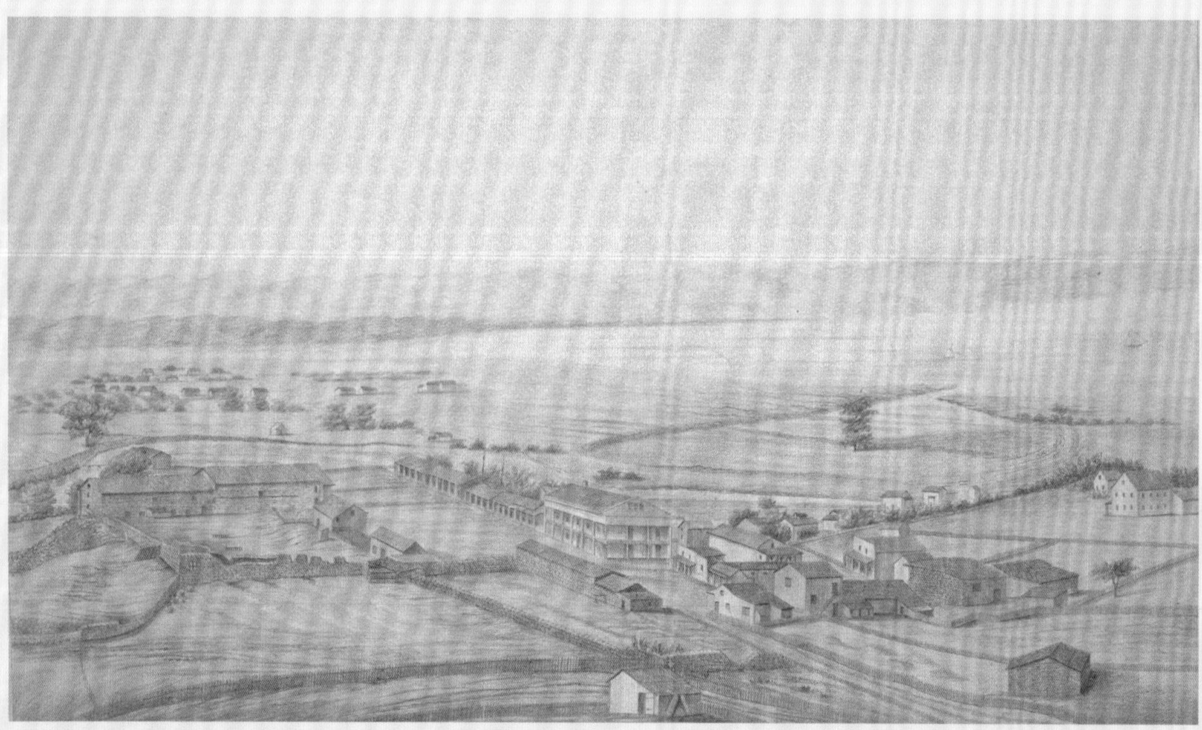

LEFT: In this 1856 drawing by Henry Miller, the Mission Santa Cruz church, the long building at the left, overlooks the growing town of Santa Cruz on the plain below. The large building in the center is the Eagle Hotel, an adobe that briefly served as the American town's first courthouse. Pencil sketch on paper. Courtesy of The Bancroft Library, University of California, Berkeley

OPPOSITE: A half-size replica of Mission Santa Cruz's church and *convento*, constructed near the original site in 1932. Photograph by G. Aldana

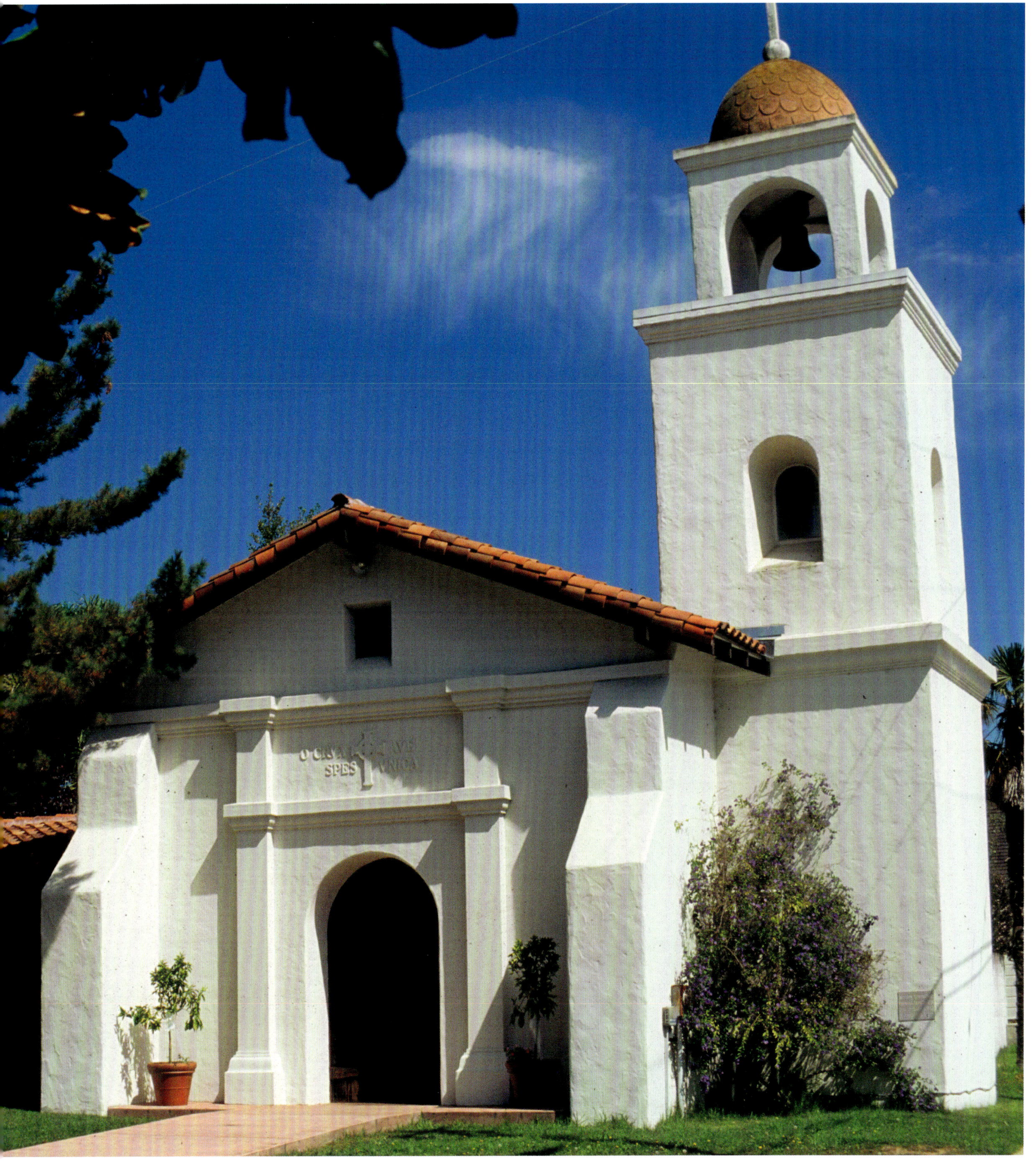
SPES

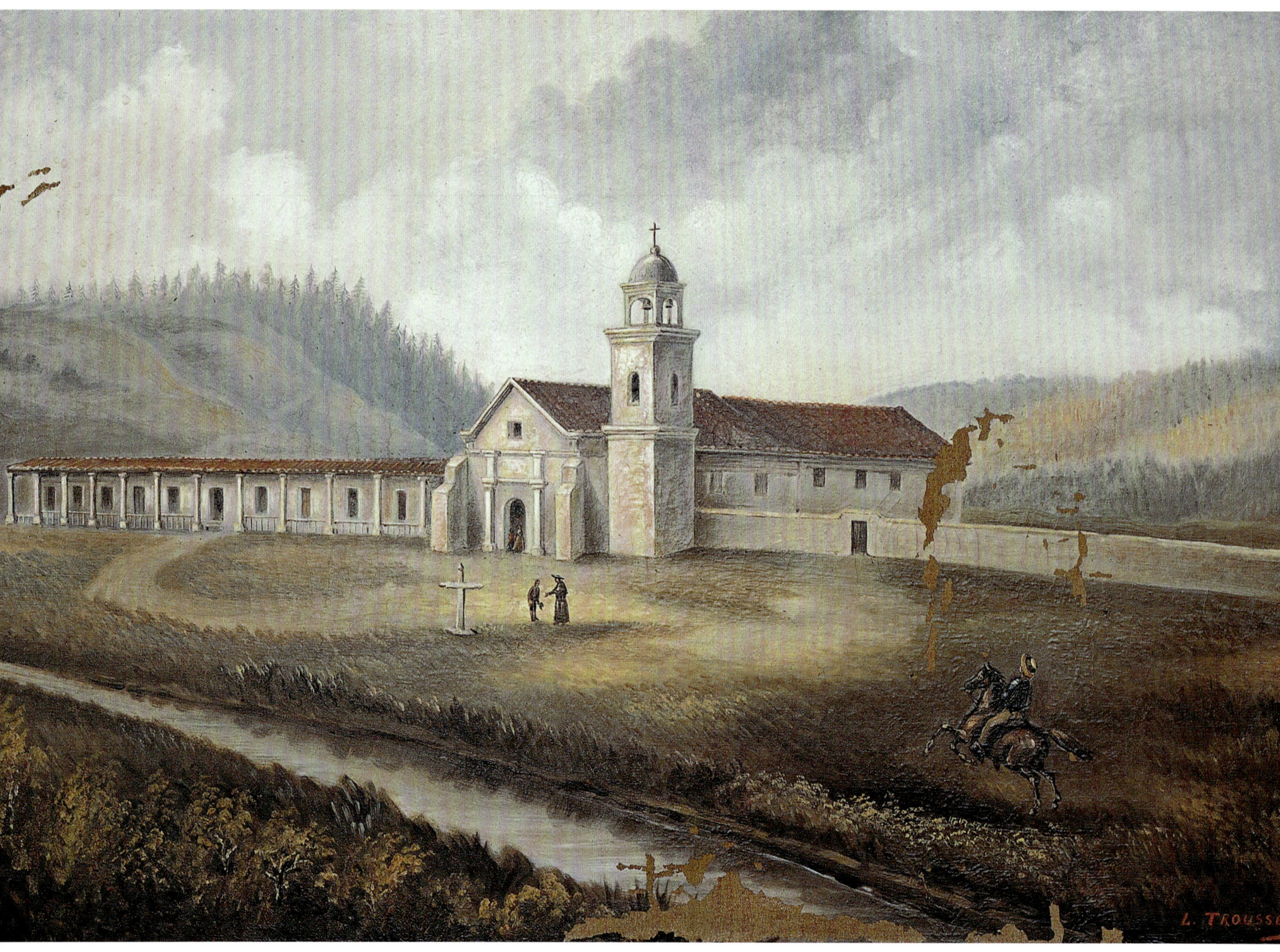

Los Angeles, which featured regular streets lined with adobe homes. While anticipating an attack of the corsair Bouchard in 1818, Mission Santa Cruz's population retreated to the hills for safety, and the Branciforte townsfolk looted the abandoned mission buildings. Eventually, a mutually beneficial relationship between the mission and the town emerged. Fortunes quickly improved for the settlers after 1821 when they began harvesting the rich stands of redwood and increasing their trade with foreign ships. The dispersal of mission lands to private ranchos after 1832 benefited many of the old Branciforte families, and their sons and daughters established prosperous households.

The church at Mission Santa Cruz is the only one in Alta California whose architectural appearance is not known. Church records detail its adobe nave, carved stone facade with added portico, *espadaña*, buttresses, and tiled roof. Dual arches led from the rear of the sanctuary into an office and sacristy, the baptistery sat underneath the exterior stairway leading to the choir loft, and a sequence of bell towers was erected in the 1830s. Despite the extraordinary numbers of skilled artisans involved in its construction,[2] the building was plagued with structural problems from water seepage and earthquakes. The bell tower collapsed in 1840, and an earthquake in 1857 brought down the front of the church. The only historic depictions of the structure are a series of watercolors documenting the destroyed building and providing a glimpse of its interior painted designs. The rear remaining portion was renovated for use as a girls' school in 1861 and may have served as a stable as late as the early 1880s. In 1889 a brick church of English Gothic design was completed on the site of the original mission church, and in 1932 an elegant, reduced-scale replica was constructed nearby.[3]

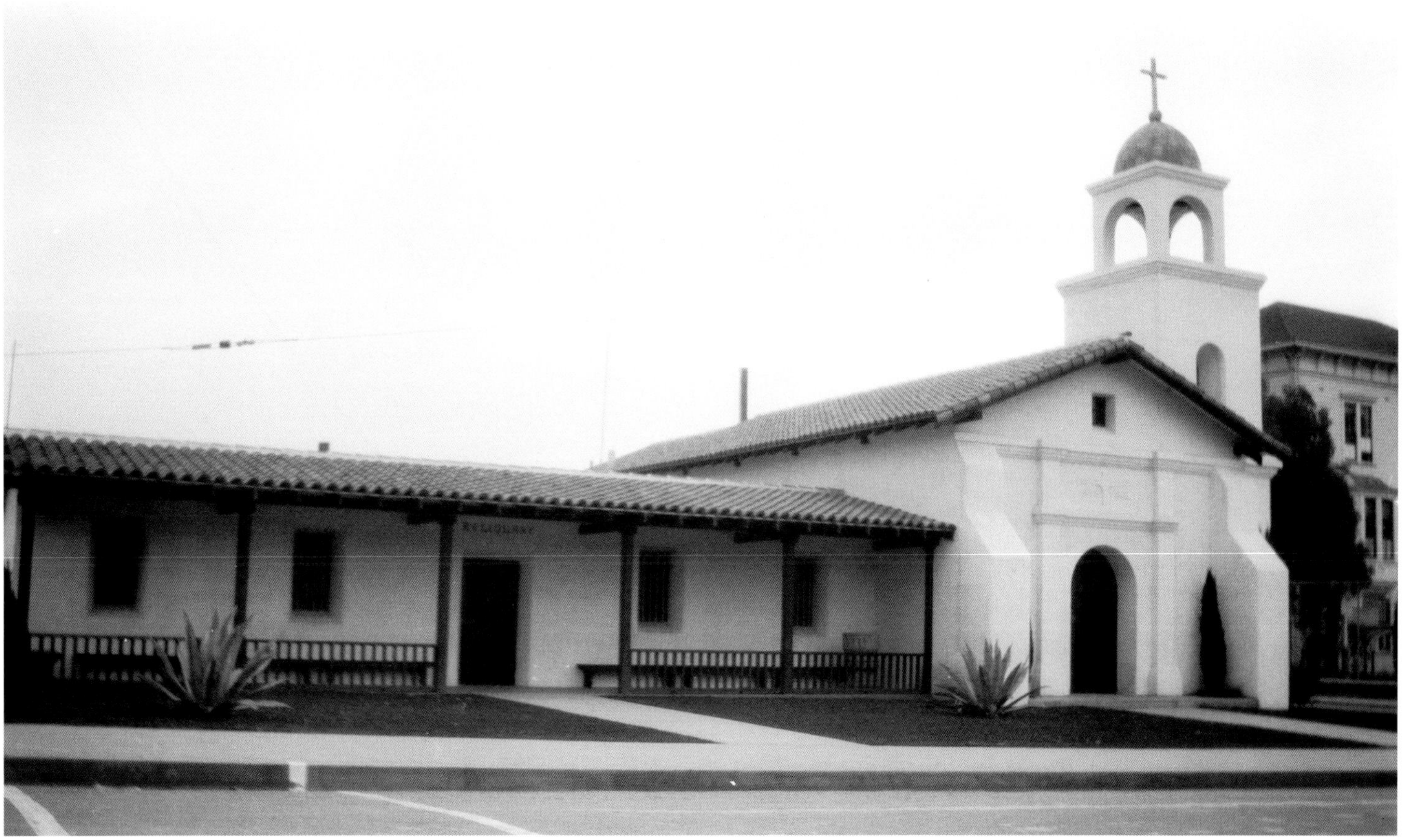

OPPOSITE: Mission Santa Cruz, as painted by the French artist Leon Trousset, ca. 1876. In his research for the painting, Trousset interviewed local residents to complement his inspection of the remaining ruins. Oil on canvas. Courtesy Holy Cross Church, Santa Cruz

ABOVE: Exterior view of the replica mission church and *convento*, 1934. Courtesy University of Southern California, on behalf of the USC Special Collections

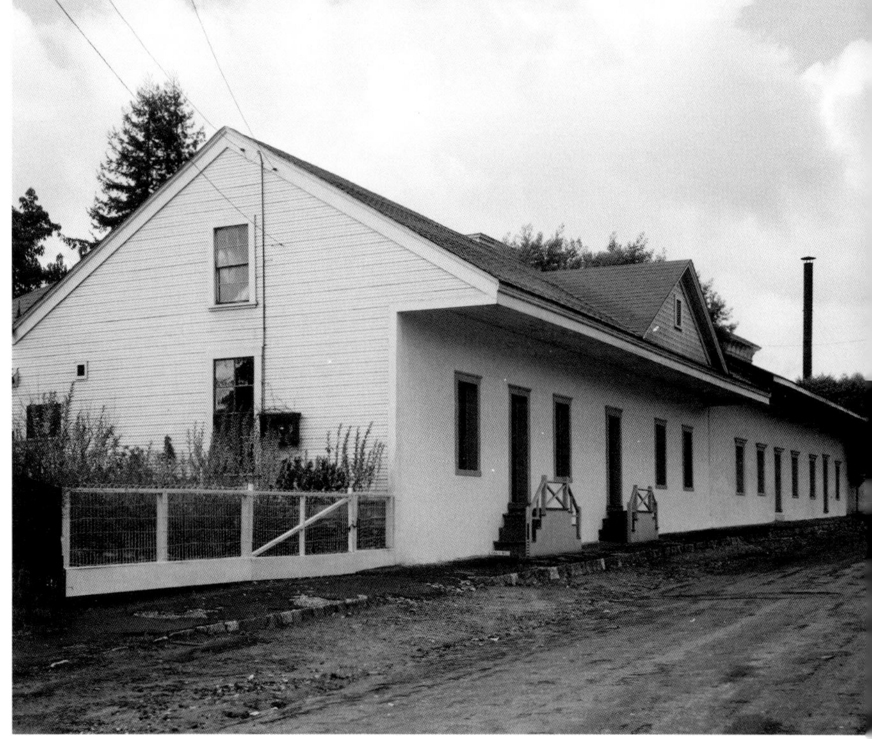

RIGHT: A row of neophyte residences, the only remaining original building at Mission Santa Cruz and one of the only surviving original neophyte dwellings at a California mission, ca. 1936. Library of Congress

The only surviving building from the mission period was constructed in 1824 as part of an adobe residence consisting of seventeen individual apartments for neophyte families. Although mission Indians continued to live in the rooms after secularization in 1834, the eastern seven rooms were converted into homes for the Rodríguez and Armas families by 1848. This sole remaining Mission Santa Cruz building was purchased by the California Department of Parks and Recreation in 1958, and extensive archaeological studies were carried out on both the building and the grounds in 1984–85.[4] Now restored, the building is one of the only original mission neophyte dwellings among the California missions.

Nuestra Señora de la Soledad

FOUNDED OCTOBER 9, 1791

LOCATION: *About 2 miles southwest of Soledad*

FOUNDER: *Father Fermín Lasuén*

PRESIDIO DISTRICT: *Monterey*

PEAK MISSION POPULATION: *688 (1805)*

MAJOR NATIVE GROUPS: *Esselen, Ohlone/Costanoan, Yokuts*

HISTORICAL ASSETS: *Archaeological remains of portions of the quadrangle, associated structures and features, and the neophyte village; museum*

EXISTING CHURCH: *Reconstruction completed in 1955; local adobe stabilized with bitumen*

OWNERSHIP: *Roman Catholic Church, Diocese of Monterey*

HISTORICAL STATUS: *California Historical Landmark (No. 233)*

Mission Soledad was founded along the lower reaches of the Salinas Valley, between the prosperous missions of San Antonio to the south and San Carlos Borromeo at Monterey. Although the mission grew to support a population of nearly seven hundred neophytes, it seemed plagued with ill fortune. A respiratory epidemic in February 1802, causing five or six deaths every day, was accompanied by the murder of three neophytes, demoralizing the residents. The river itself rose up and devastated the adobe community in 1824, 1828, and 1832, and the persistent fog produced rooms filled with damp and chill. There was high turnover in clergy as complaints of ill health were common, and the neophytes themselves were frequently reported as leaving the mission. The governor of Alta California, don José Joaquín de Arrillaga, died at Soledad in 1814 at the age of sixty-four and was buried beneath a chapel later destroyed by floods. Perhaps the most poignant tragedy was the death of Father Vicente Sarría, former father president and the first *comisario prefecto* of the California missions. Father Sarría served as the only friar at this struggling outpost from 1828 until his deteriorating health failed in 1835. His destitute congregation carried his body to Mission San Antonio for absolution and burial.

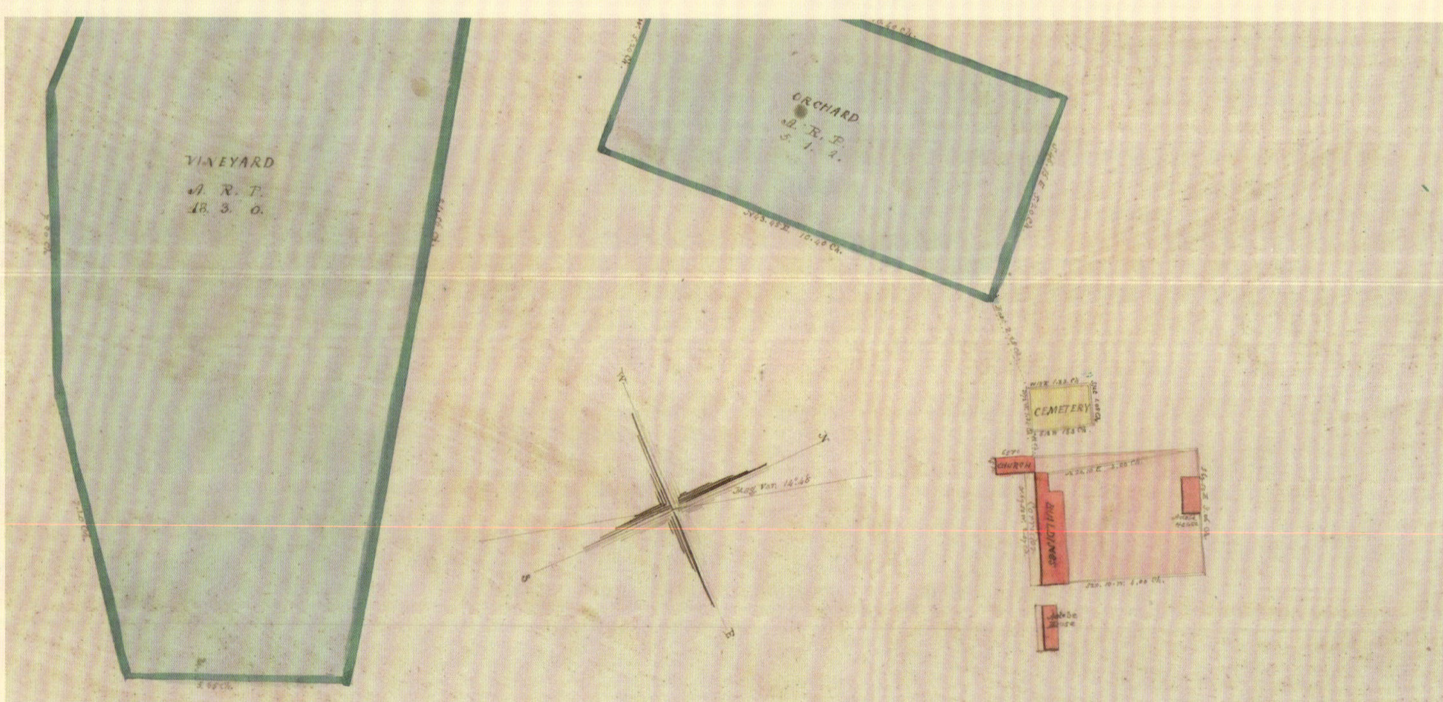

Map of the *casco* by the surveyor George Black, 1854 (detail). Courtesy of The Bancroft Library, University of California, Berkeley

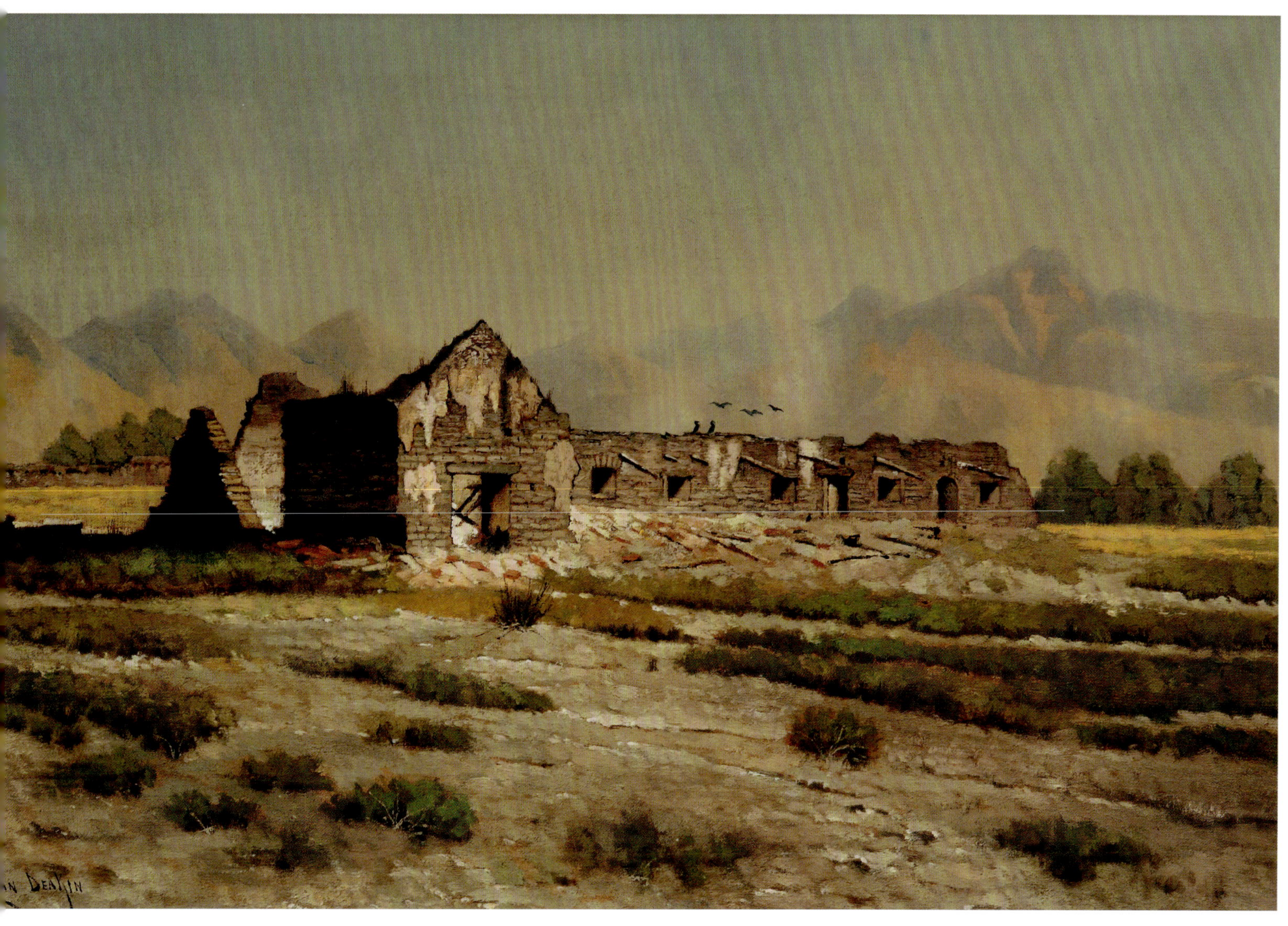

The desolate ruins of the church and *convento*, ca. 1899. Edwin Deakin, *Mission Soledad*. Oil on canvas. Courtesy of the Santa Bárbara Mission Archive-Library

The mission supported three outlying ranchos for running cattle and sheep: San Lorenzo, San Vicente, and San Fernando. Even with these, Soledad's lands were lacking many of the advantages of other California missions. Father Francisco Xavier Uría described the bleak mission landscape in 1827:

> The two sierras that form the *cañada* or *cañón* are very barren and unsuitable. The Mission has but a few patches visited by some herds of cattle toward the *tulares* northeastward. The Río de Monterey [Salinas] runs through the whole *cañón*, but this water serves only for the livestock because it is too low for irrigation. . . . In this way the groves and forests of the Mission have only some poplar, alder and willow trees along the river valley, and on the brow of the hills some very crooked live oak and similar crooked trees.[1]

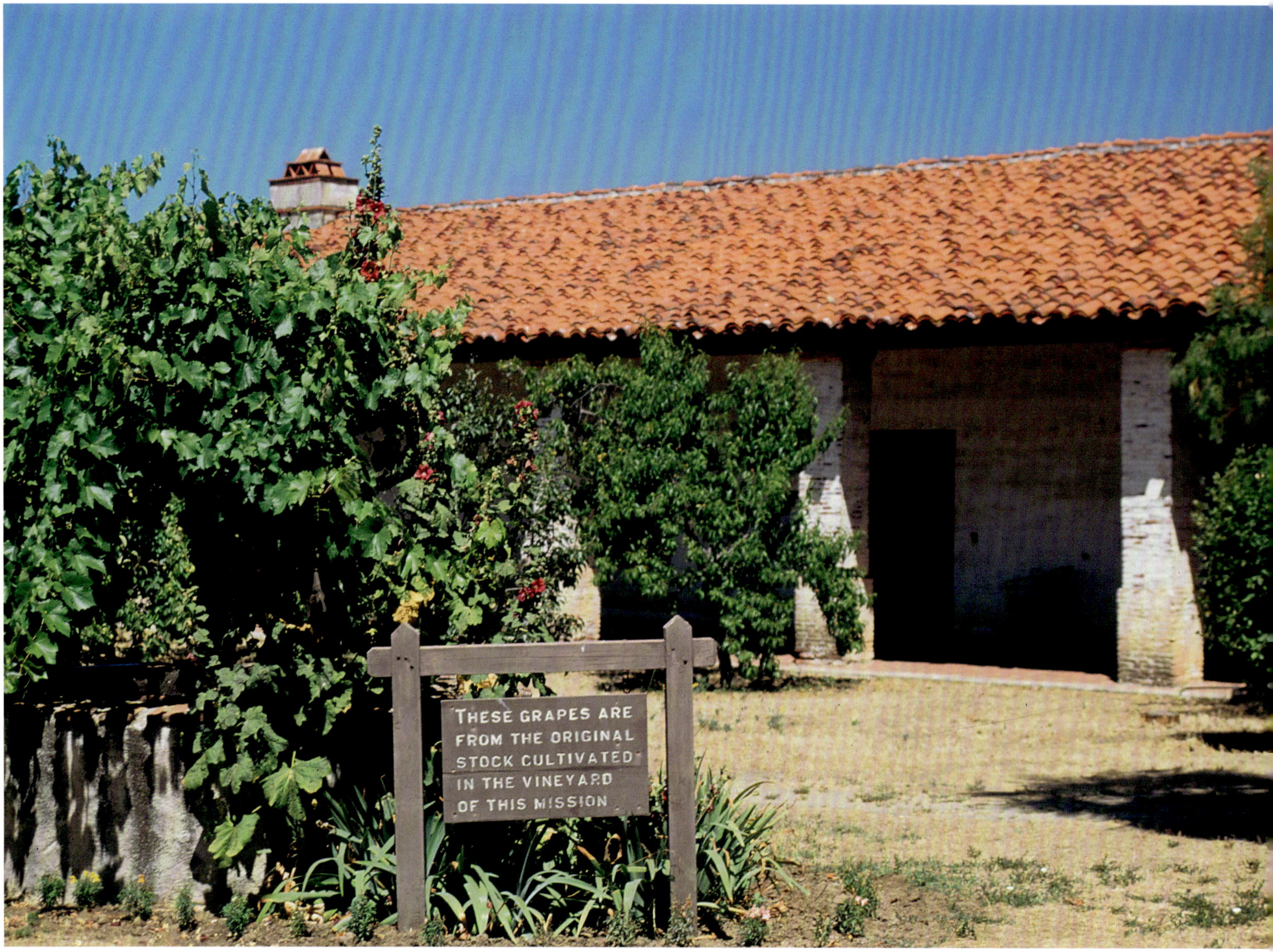

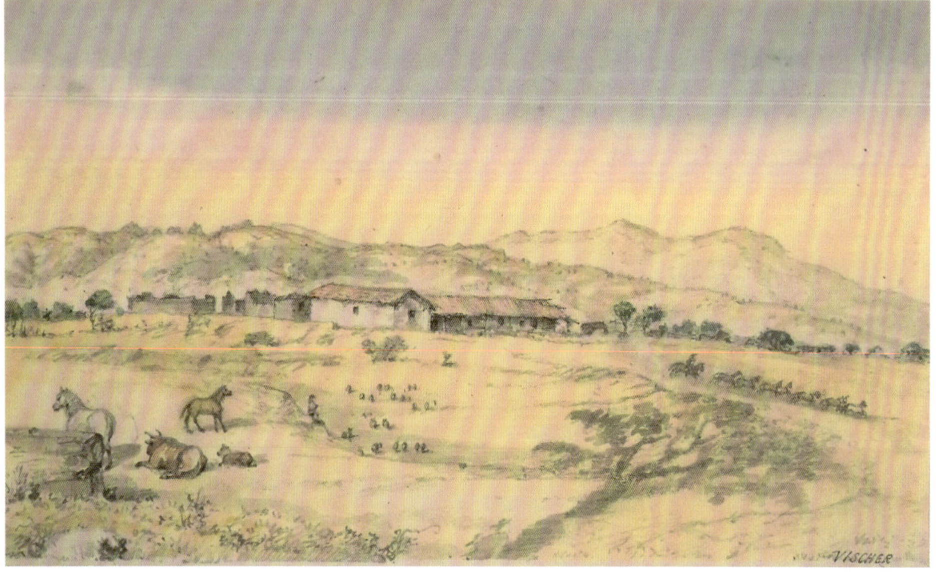

ABOVE: The *convento* at Mission Soledad (seen here) was reconstructed in 1963, following the church reconstruction in 1954. Photograph by G. Aldana

OPPOSITE: Ruins of Mission Soledad's *convento* and church, photographed by A.C. Vroman in 1898. After the buildings' roof tiles were sold to pay debts, the walls rapidly crumbled. Library of Congress

LEFT: The ruins of Mission Soledad, as depicted by Edward Vischer in 1873. The roof tiles are still in place, and the adobe walls of the church and *convento* are still standing. Watercolor on paper. Courtesy of The Bancroft Library, University of California, Berkeley

Abandoned after Father Sarría's death, the melting adobe ruins were neglected for more than a century. In 1939 the Native Daughters of the Golden West began raising money to reconstruct the chapel, an endeavor completed in 1955. Work was directed by Harry Downie, of Carmel, who bulldozed the church walls down to their foundations to guide the rebuilding. Downie also explored the adjacent *convento* ruins and oversaw the completion of its reconstruction in 1962. The mission caretaker, Oliver Pesch, was also actively digging at the site during the 1950s and early 1960s, uncovering graves in the old chapel floor, massive grinding stones, and caches of artifacts. His primary tools were picks, shovels, and backhoes, a heavy-handed assault on the fragile archaeological remains. It is estimated that he removed as much as three feet of earth from both the north and west quadrangle wing foundations. Some artifacts recovered during these endeavors are now on display in the mission's small museum, although there are virtually no notes or photographs documenting the methods and findings of either Downie or Pesch. In the 1980s professional archaeological excavations were carried out in a portion of the west wing, not only demonstrating the wealth of artifacts and historical information still present in undisturbed portions of the ruins but also documenting the extensive destruction that had taken place in the preceding decades by misguided enthusiasts.[2]

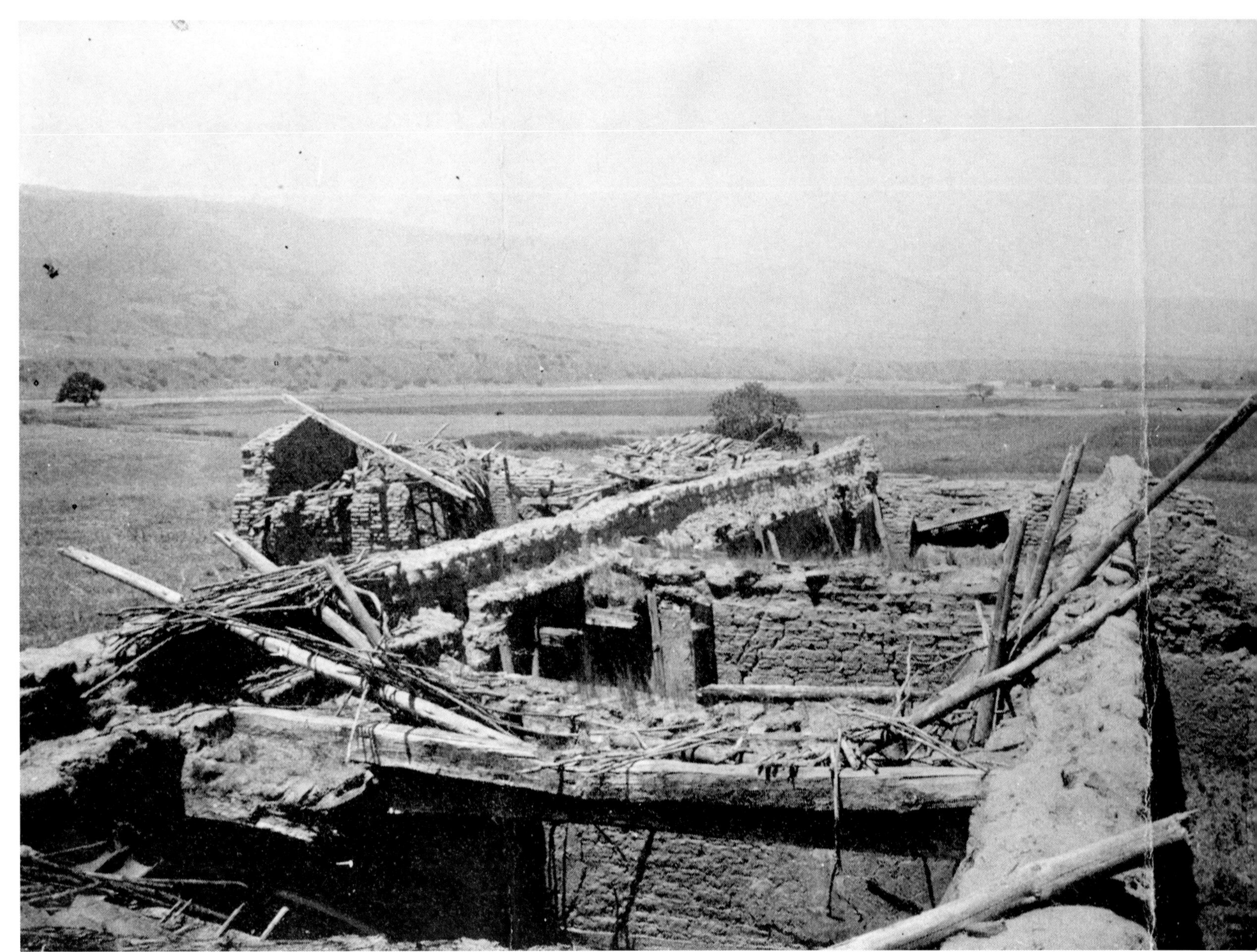

Mission del Gloriosísimo Patriarca San José

FOUNDED JUNE 11, 1797

LOCATION: *Fremont*

FOUNDER: *Father Fermín Lasuén*

PRESIDIO DISTRICT: *San Francisco*

PEAK MISSION POPULATION: *1,886 (1831)*

MAJOR NATIVE GROUPS: *Ohlone/Costanoan, Bay Miwok, Coast Miwok, Patwin, Plains Miwok, Yokuts, Sierra Miwok*

HISTORICAL ASSETS: *Portion of* convento *wing; museum*

EXISTING CHURCH: *1985 reconstruction in adobe with steel reinforcing rods*

OWNERSHIP: *Roman Catholic Church, Diocese of San Jose*

HISTORICAL STATUS: *California Historical Landmark (No. 334)*

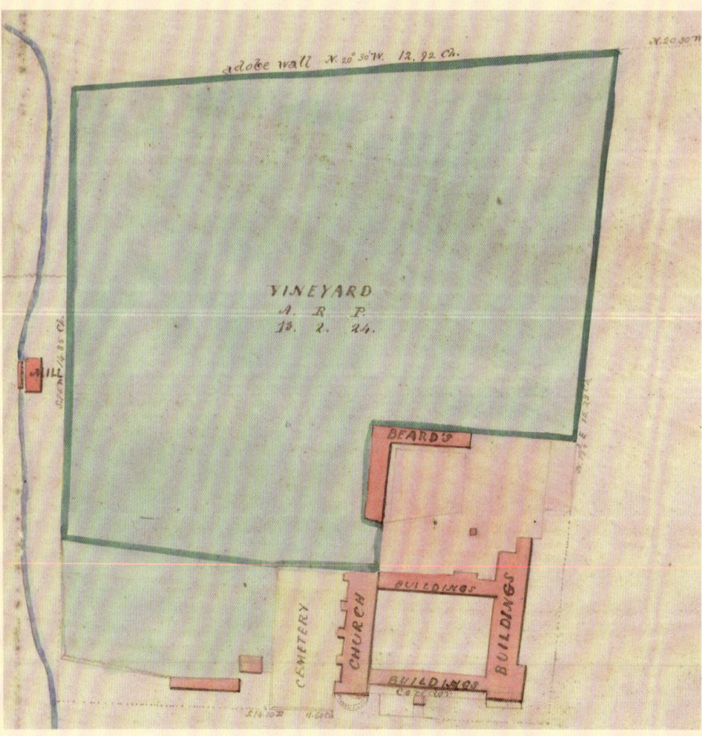

Map of the *casco* by the surveyor George Black, 1854 (detail). Courtesy of The Bancroft Library, University of California, Berkeley

Mission del Gloriosísimo Patriarca San José was the fourteenth mission founded and the first in a group of five approved as a major expansion of Alta California's colonization efforts. Its location on the east side of San Francisco Bay had already been missionized by Santa Clara, only twelve miles away, and most of the native peoples had moved to that establishment. The territory had become a haven for rebellious neophytes, however, and the military conducted several campaigns before San José began to gain converts. A virulent measles outbreak in 1806 caused many deaths, and within a few years the mission began to bring in Yokuts from the San Joaquin Valley, as well as Miwok speakers from Diablo Valley and the western Sacramento–San Joaquin River delta.

Around 1815 the population of the mission began to shift from coastal groups to interior Yokuts as large numbers of converts arrived from the Stockton and Lodi areas. By 1822 half of the San José neophytes were Yokuts, among which was Estanislao Cucunuchi, age twenty-eight, of the Lower Stanislaus River Laquisamne group. In 1828 he led other Laquisamne in a revolt against the Spanish by refusing to return from a holiday in their homeland. The horse-stealing rebels—joined by Yokut neophytes from Santa Clara—eluded military pursuers led by Mariano Guadalupe Vallejo. Estanislao Cucunuchi turned himself in to Father Narciso Durán the next year and was pardoned. His name survives on both a river and county in the region.[1]

After the mid-1820s San José ceded the Yokut territory to Mission Santa Clara and concentrated on recruiting among the Plains Miwok of the San Joaquin–Sacramento River delta. The mission's population became one of the largest in California, supported by fertile lands and pastures. The steady arrival of new recruits, however, was tempered by the high death rate of young women and children, which anguished the community. By secularization in 1834, nearly 60 percent of the mission population were Miwok speakers; the remainder represented the most diverse language mix of any northern California mission community. Known as the Chocheños, this population, as at other missions, had developed a unique identity that replaced former tribal-homeland affiliations. In 1834 more than 1,700 Chocheños still lived at the mission.[2]

The adobe church at San José was modified when an earthquake occurred during its construction in 1808: the walls were lowered, and the bell tower was shortened. Within the completed church the

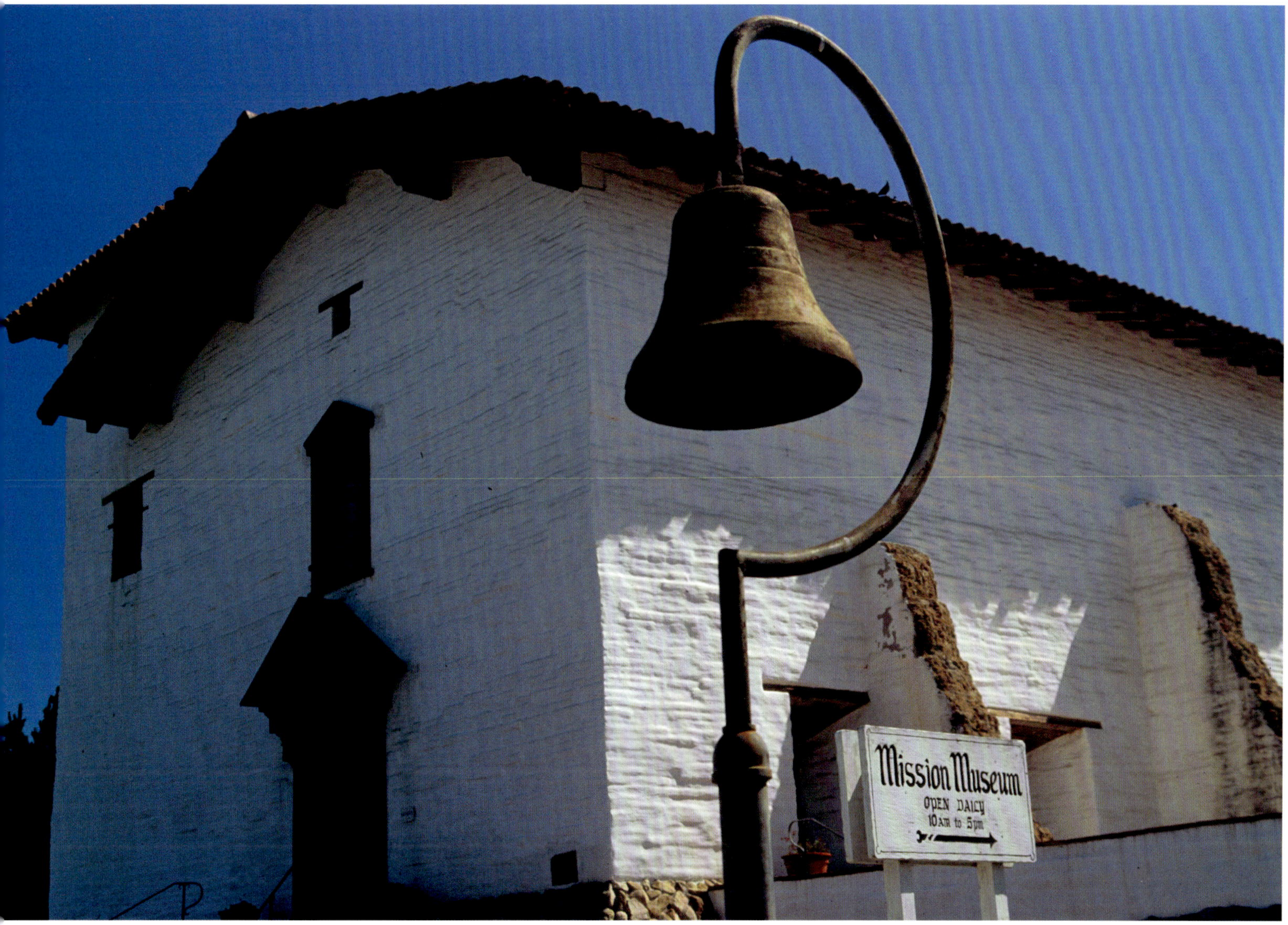

View of the 1985 replica of the church of Mission San José; the original was destroyed in an earthquake in 1868. Photograph by G. Aldana

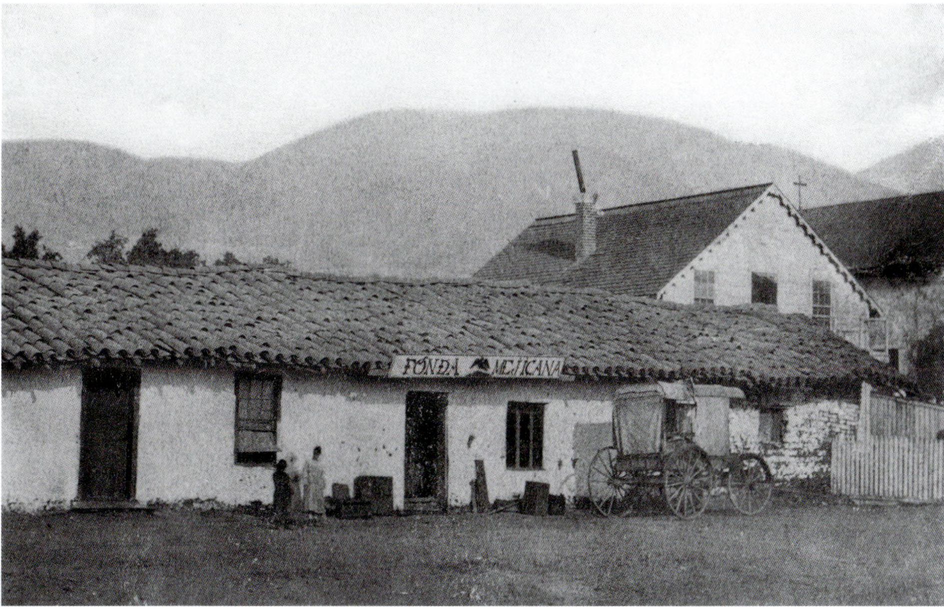

View of mission buildings, ca. 1867. As with other missions along busy roads, a commercial enterprise—in this case the Fonda Mexicana restaurant—now occupies formerly abandoned rooms. Courtesy University of Southern California, on behalf of the USC Special Collections

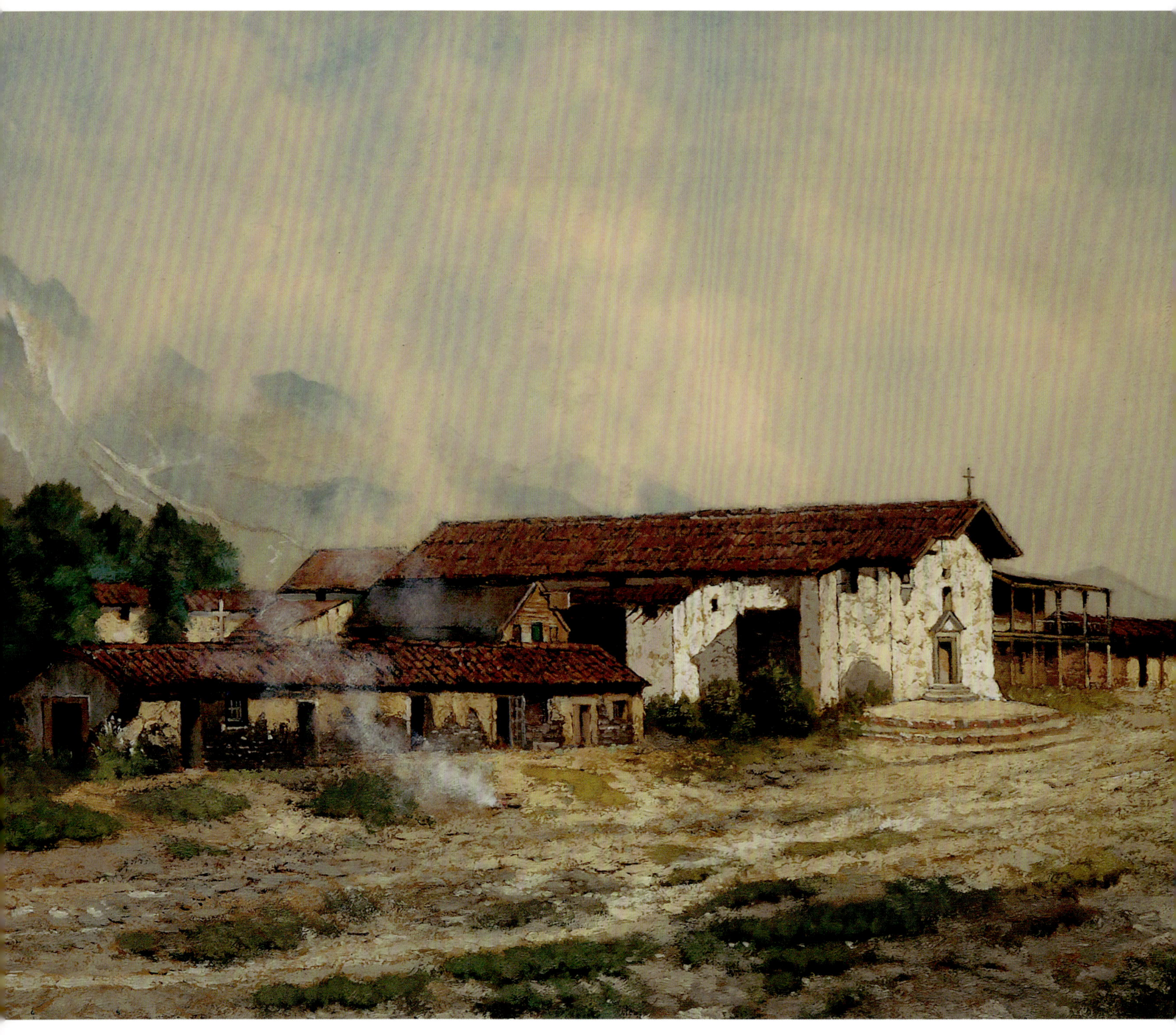

An artistic depiction of the mission, ca. 1899, likely based on the early photograph at right. Edwin Deakin, *Mission San José*. Oil on canvas. Courtesy of the Santa Bárbara Mission Archive-Library

mission band consisting of thirty neophyte musicians—dressed in uniforms obtained from a French ship—played both popular and secular music under the direction of the talented Father Durán. When Father Durán became father president of the missions in 1824, San José served as his headquarters. In 1835 the church interior was embellished when the noted artist Agustín Dávila was hired by Father José María González Rubio to decorate the establishment. Inventories reveal that the nave walls and ceiling were entirely covered with designs, as were the baptistery walls, and a dado was added to the sacristy. The details of the work are unknown, however, as in 1868 the church was brought down by a strong earthquake. Of Dávila's work at this and other missions, only the baptismal font survives.[3] San José's church was replaced by a wooden building that remained until 1985, when an adobe replica of the original was constructed using stabilized adobe bricks and steel reinforcing rods for strength. Archaeological excavations preceding this contributed to a faithful architectural rendering of the original.[4] A handsome portion of the adobe *convento* survived and now holds a museum with numerous artifacts from the mission period.

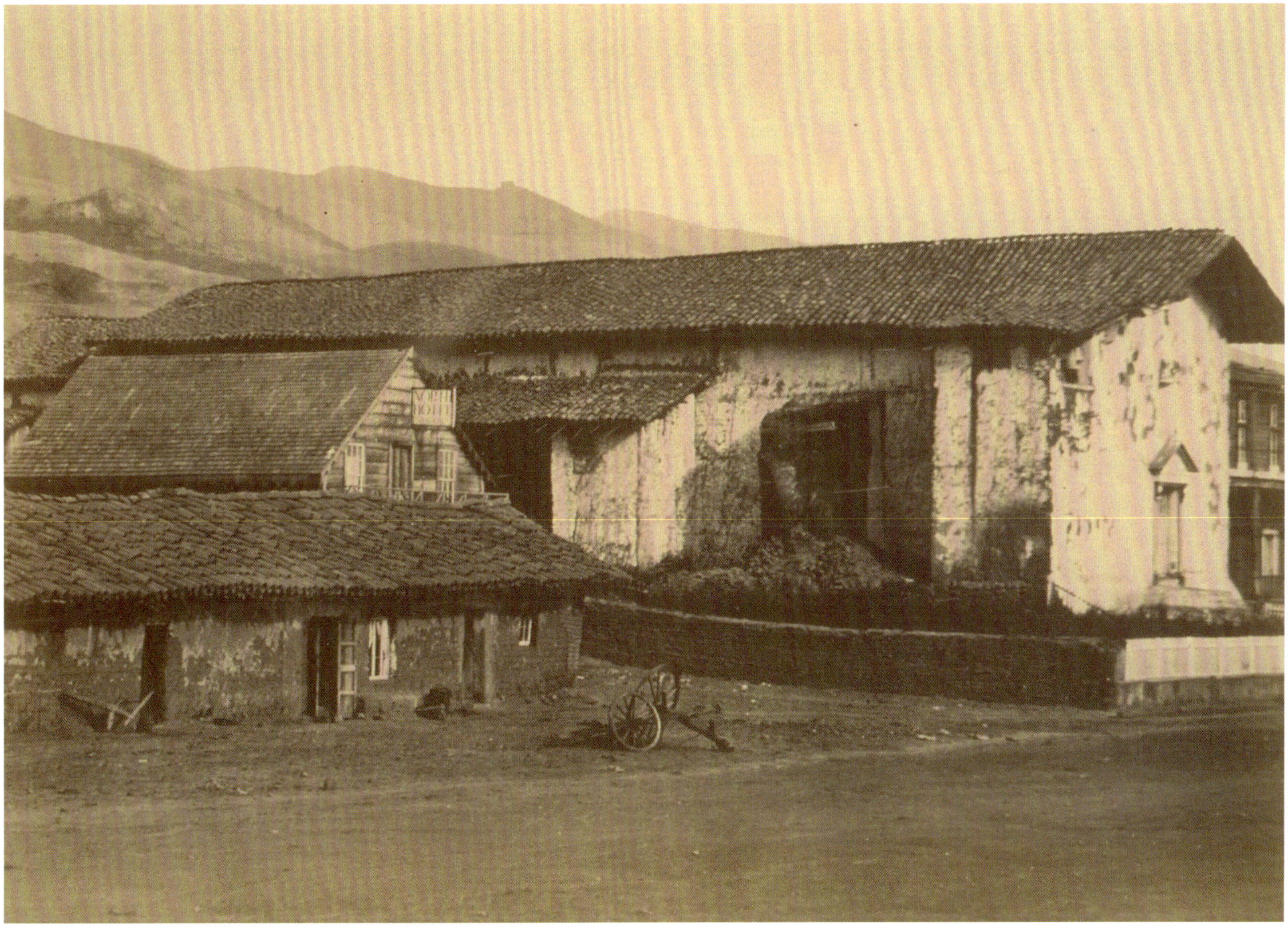

An early view of the mission, ca. 1852, showing the cemetery wall and adjacent buildings. Courtesy University of Southern California, on behalf of the USC Special Collections

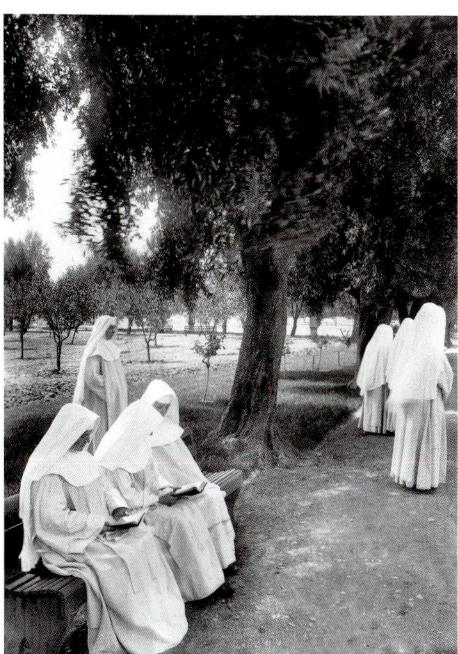

Dominican nuns in the mission's gardens, ca. 1906. The order Dominican Sisters of Mission San José arrived at Mission San José in 1891. Photograph by C. C. Pierce. Courtesy University of Southern California, on behalf of the USC Special Collections

San Juan Bautista

FOUNDED JUNE 24, 1797

LOCATION: *San Juan Bautista*

FOUNDER: *Father Fermín Lasuén*

PRESIDIO DISTRICT: *Monterey*

PEAK MISSION POPULATION: *1,248 (1823)*

MAJOR NATIVE GROUPS: *Ohlone/Costanoan, Yokuts, Sierra Miwok*

HISTORICAL ASSETS: *Central portion of the church,* convento *with tiled corridor; museum displays and collection of vestments; plaza landscape with Mexican- and early-American-period buildings, part of the San Juan Bautista State Historic Park; archaeological remains of the neophyte village*

EXISTING CHURCH: *Constructed of adobe with a* ladrillo *facade, completed in 1812; side walls and aisles rebuilt in 1949–50 with reinforced concrete*

OWNERSHIP: *Roman Catholic Church, Diocese of Monterey*

HISTORICAL STATUS: *California Historical Landmark (No. 195), National Historic Landmark District*

San Juan Bautista was founded on the fertile plain of the San Benito River, one of four missions established in 1797 by the ambitious father president Fermín Lasuén. The mission was quickly successful, with its population reaching nearly one thousand within six years and its livestock herds exceeding all others in the district. Unfortunately, it was sited astride the San Andreas fault, a misfortune that was to haunt the mission community.

As at other missions, Native American populations suffered high death rates once they were brought into the close quarters of mission villages. At San Juan Bautista declining numbers of neophytes made it necessary to extend recruitment eastward into the San Joaquin Valley and into the Miwok territory of the Sierra Nevada foothills. The difficulties that this mix of tribal groups presented was ameliorated in later years by the presence of Father Felipe del Arroyo de la Cuesta, a skilled linguist who is reported to have spoken dozens of languages and whose invaluable *Grammar of the Mutsun Language* was completed in 1815 and published in 1862.

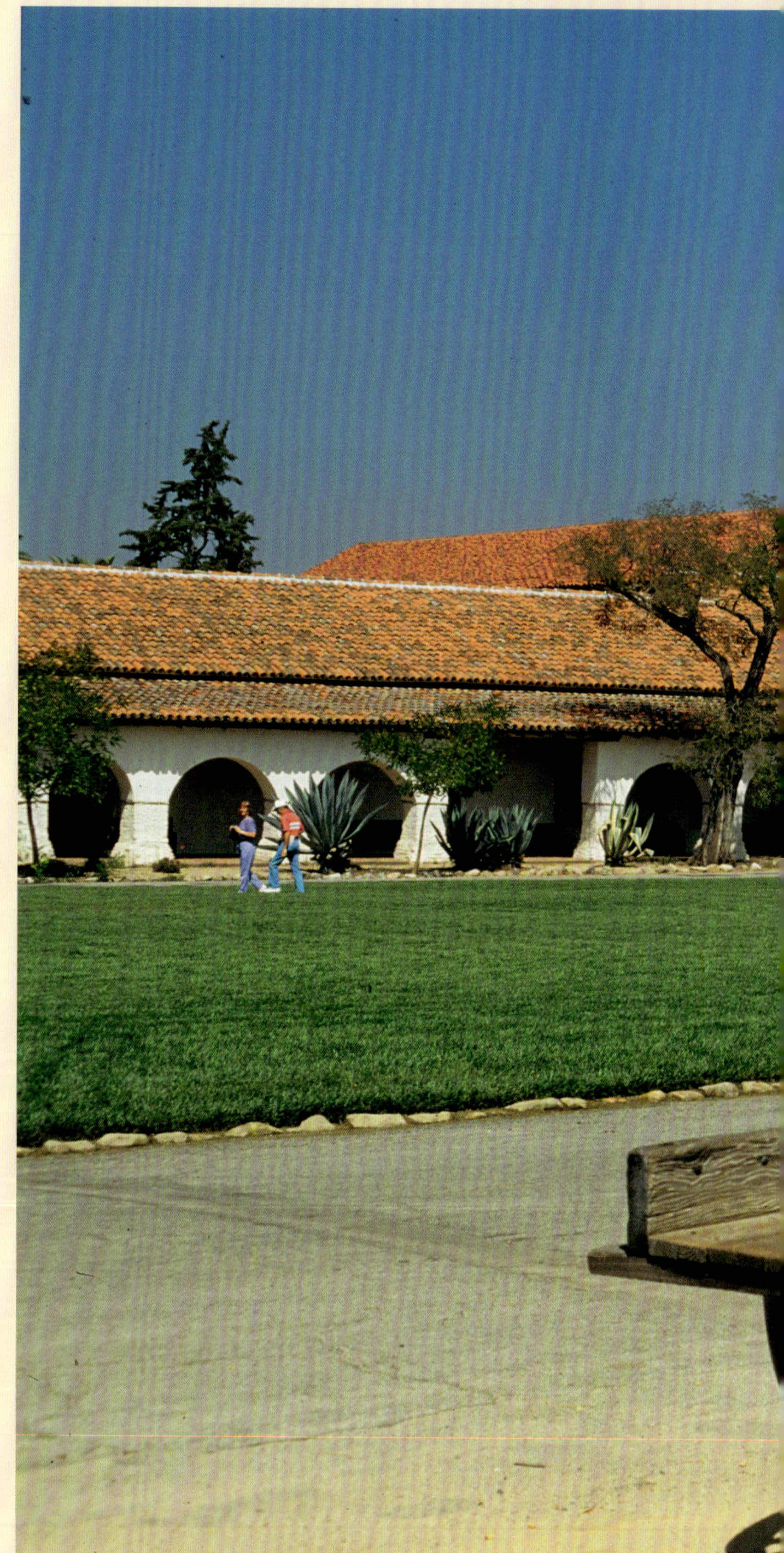

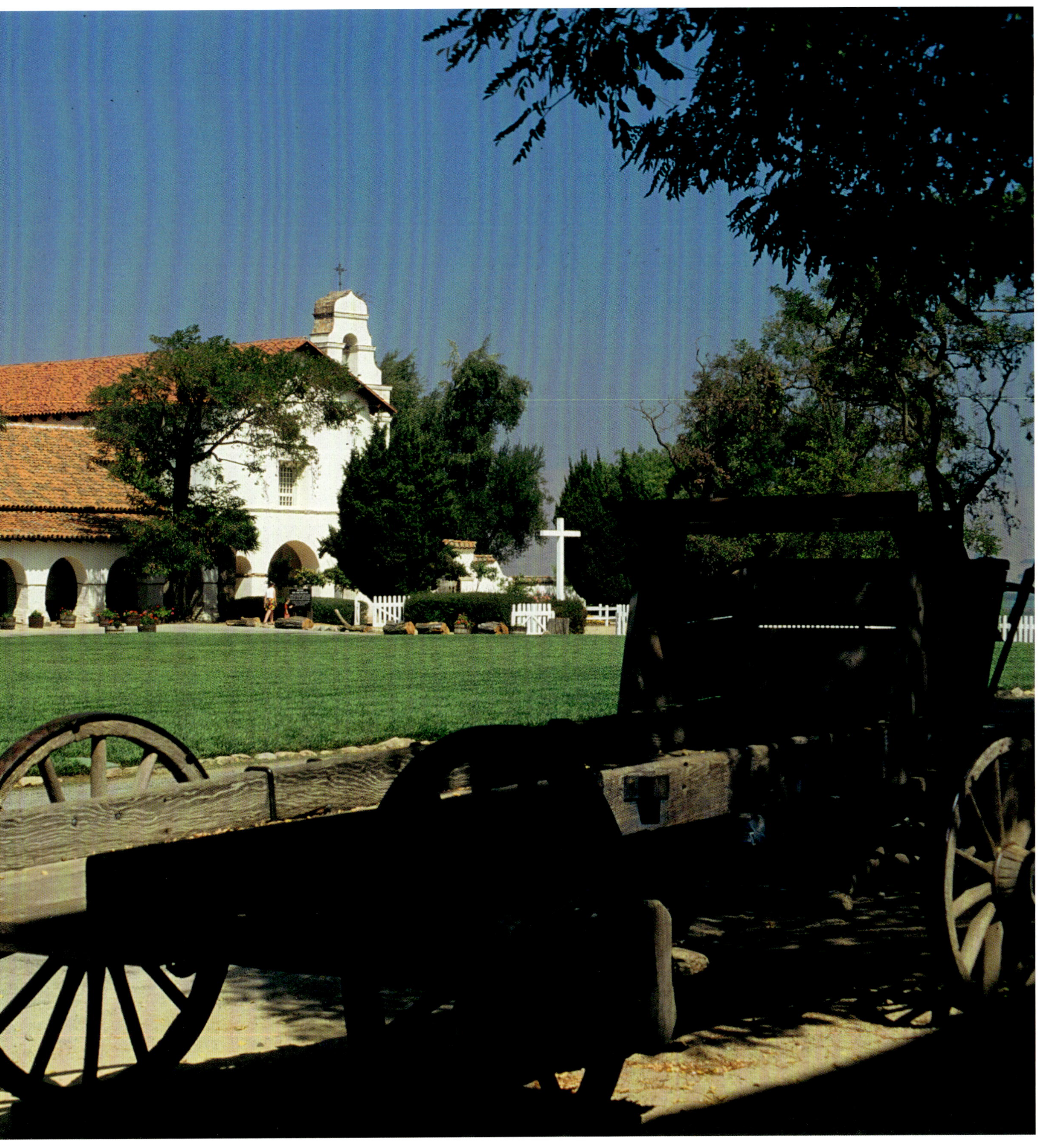

View of Mission San Juan Bautista; its church and *convento* still front the town's plaza. To the right of the church is the modern *espadaña* designed by Harry Downie as part of the extensive renovations of 1975–76. Photograph by G. Aldana

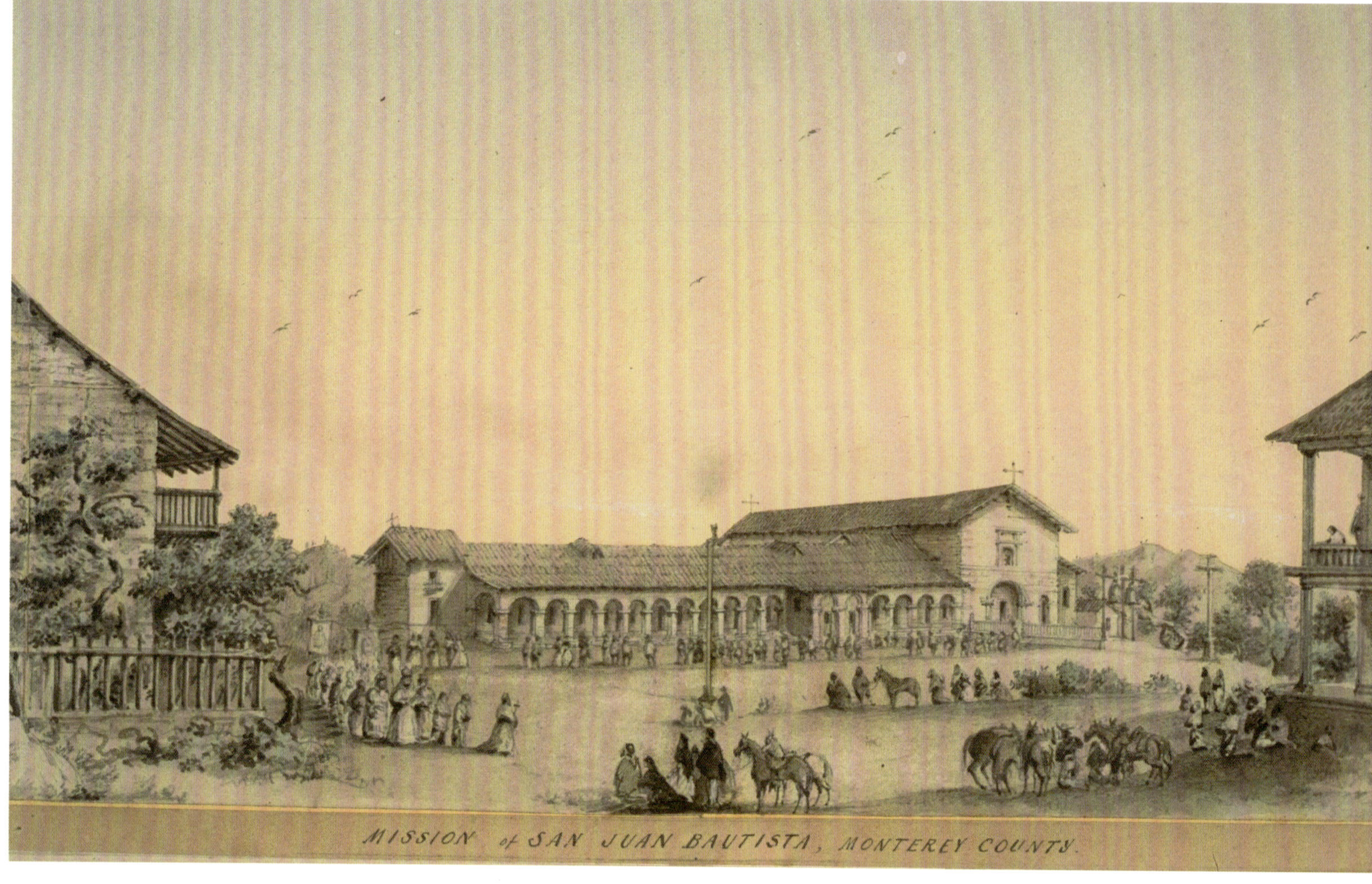

To accommodate the large congregation at San Juan Bautista, a new adobe church was begun in 1803, likely constructed by the master carpenter Manuel Rodríguez, corporal of the escort of solders stationed there. In 1808, following the arrival from Spain of Father Arroyo de la Cuesta, the church was grandly expanded, tripling the size of the nave with the addition of side aisles separated by arches of brick. This ambitious design was unique in Alta California. The church's walls, at forty feet, were among the highest constructed. Father Arroyo de la Cuesta had not been present in October 1800 when earthquakes shook the mission for twenty straight days, causing extensive damage. And as construction on the church progressed, more experienced voices apparently prevailed: the design was modified again, this time to increase stability rather than grandeur. The interior arches were filled in with adobes, except for the openings nearest the altar, which allow for side transepts.

This final design was completed in 1812 by the carpenter Leocadio Martínez, who apparently took over the project in 1809 after Rodríguez's departure. The church features a plain facade accented with a *ladrillo* portico and buttresses. Although bell tower foundations were laid, this structure was never built, and bells were hung on a wooden rack in front of the door. The altar was painted in winter 1818–19 by Thomas Doak, a carpenter from Boston, who continued to live near the mission until 1831 and probably helped to build the secular pueblo that began to grow around the plaza as early as 1814.[1] These Mexican- and then American-period buildings have been preserved as San Juan Bautista State Historic Park, making this setting the only authentic mission plaza landscape in the state.

Although San Juan Bautista was never without resident priests, the church continued to suffer from renovations and earthquakes. In the 1860s misguided modernizers covered the walls and ceiling with boards and built a New England bell tower alongside the adobe facade. The 1906 earthquake brought down the exterior walls of the church but left the nave intact. It was not until 1950 that the exterior walls were rebuilt—reinforced with concrete buttressing—and the wooden sheathing on the interior was removed. In 1975–76 additional renovations opened the long-filled arches leading to the side aisles, now presenting the church interior in a form never seen in mission days. A modern *espadaña* was added to the north side of the church at this time. A conservation program is preserving valuable historic collections at the mission, and archaeological studies in both the church and State Parks portions of the site provide additional historical information on life at San Juan Bautista.

OPPOSITE: In this 1862 painting by Edward Vischer, the mission church and *convento* front the plaza of the growing American town, where a religious procession is taking place. Watercolor on paper. Courtesy of The Bancroft Library, University of California, Berkeley

RIGHT: View of the mission, before 1875. It appears well kept; a white picket fence and young trees have been added in front of the church. Courtesy University of Southern California, on behalf of the USC Special Collections

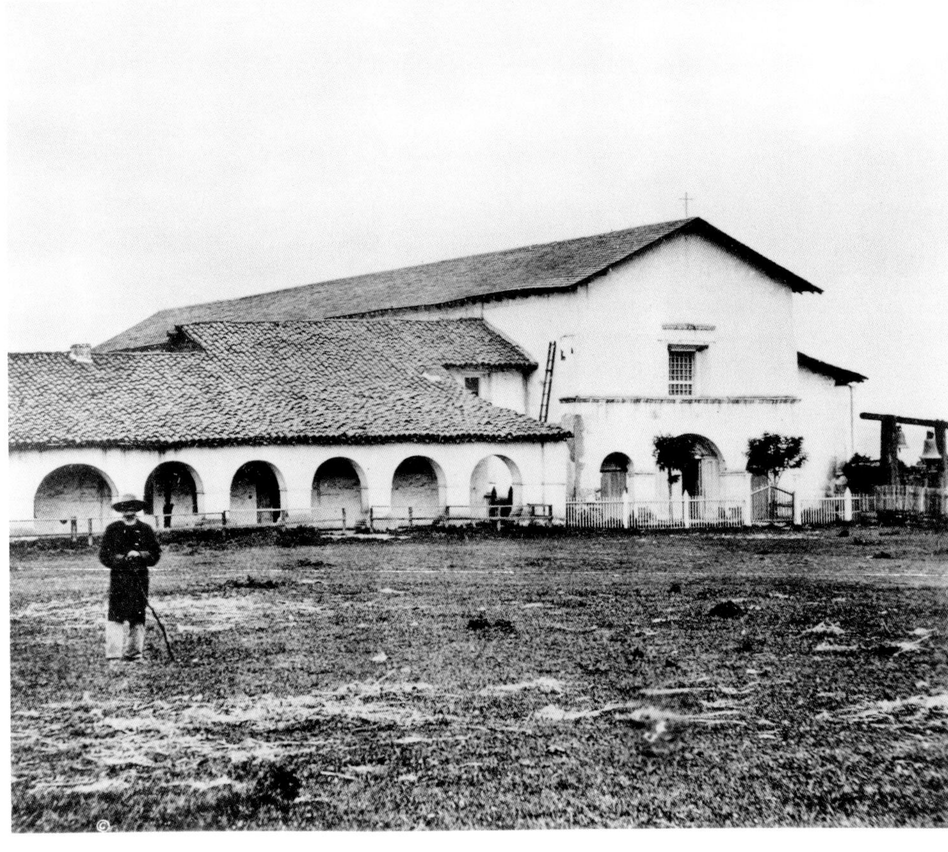

BELOW LEFT: View of the church nave, ca. 1893; the side arches have been filled in with adobe bricks, a modification made during initial construction. Paintings hang from the walls. Photograph by A.C. Vroman. Courtesy University of Southern California, on behalf of the USC Special Collections

BELOW RIGHT: Barbara Salosano, identified in this photograph as the last surviving neophyte from Mission San Juan Bautista, ca. 1902. Courtesy of The Bancroft Library, University of California, Berkeley

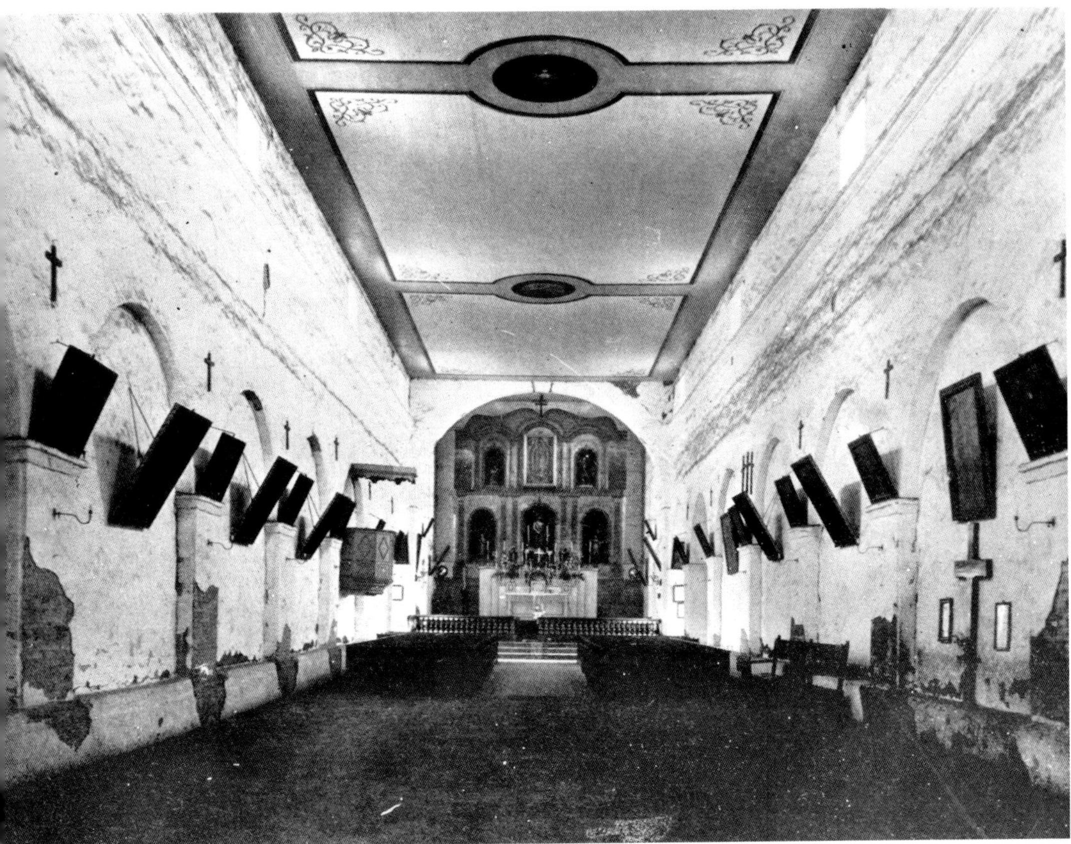

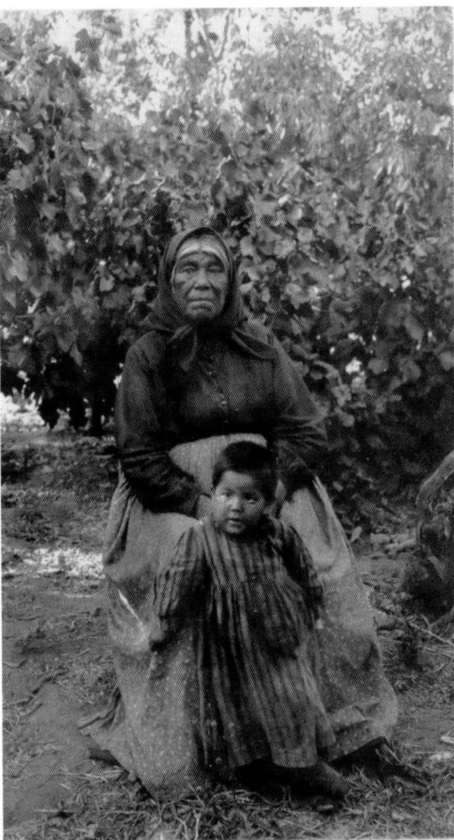

San Miguel, Arcángel

FOUNDED JULY 25, 1797

LOCATION: *San Miguel*

FOUNDER: *Father Fermín Lasuén*

PRESIDIO DISTRICT: *Monterey*

PEAK MISSION POPULATION: *1,076 (1814)*

MAJOR NATIVE GROUPS: *Salinan, Yokuts*

HISTORICAL ASSETS: *Adobe church and sacristy with extraordinary wall paintings; portion of adobe* convento, *archaeological remains of neophyte adobe dwellings; museum*

EXISTING CHURCH: *Constructed of adobe, completed in 1818*

OWNERSHIP: *Roman Catholic Church, Diocese of Montery*

HISTORICAL STATUS: *California Historical Landmark (No. 326); National Historic Landmark*

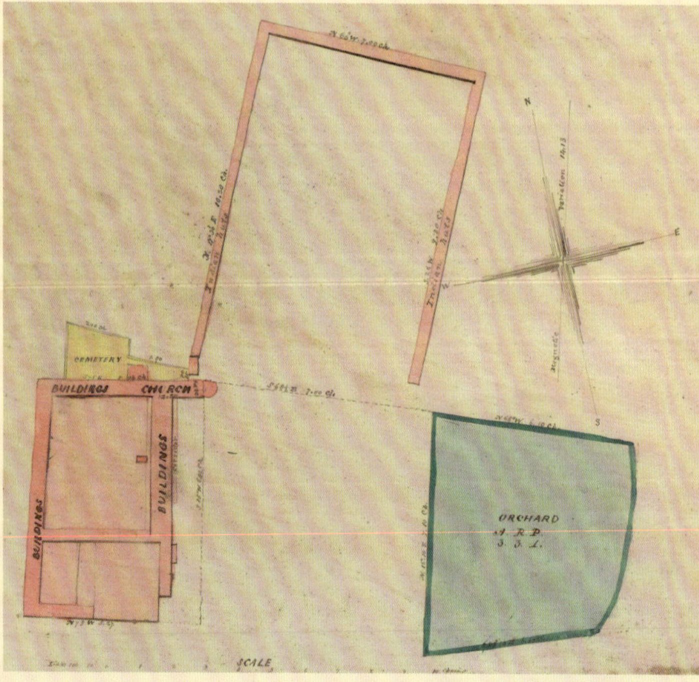

Map of the *casco* by the surveyor George Black, 1854 (detail). Courtesy of The Bancroft Library, University of California, Berkeley

Mission San Miguel, Arcángel, was founded on the upper reaches of the Monterey (Salinas) River, among the Salinan people. Its lands extended east some sixty-six miles to the *tulares* of the Central Valley and west thirty-five miles to the Pacific Ocean. Never an abundant producer of crops and livestock, the mission attained some economic success in the hide-and-tallow trade after 1821. Following native footpaths, a cart trail led to the sandy beaches at San Simeon, where ships offloaded purchased goods and took aboard dried cattle hides. Secularization brought about the disenfranchisement of the neophytes and the carving up of mission assets among Californio rancheros.

When Father Ramón Abella left San Miguel in 1841, the church remained without a resident priest for thirty-eight years. Over the succeeding decades, the *convento* variously housed a meat and vegetable market, a hotel and tavern, a shoe shop, and the local Howe Sewing Machine offices. It also saw the murder of eleven citizens, the resident Reid family and their visitors, by rogue travelers in 1848. After 1879, when a succession of priests also took up residence, repairs to the *convento* were initiated. Subsequent festivals and fund-raisers provided money for continued maintenance. Beginning in 1934, the quadrangle was reconstructed for use as a seminary and part of the *convento* was rebuilt. This work, completed in the 1950s, involved the manufacture of hundreds of thousands of adobe bricks, new foundations, and roofs covered with traditional tiles.[1]

Certainly the most extraordinary asset of Mission San Miguel is the extensively painted walls of the 1818 church, the only surviving original mission-period church interior in California. While it is fortuitous that the church was cared for by its congregation over almost four decades without a priest, it is nearly miraculous that enthusiastic restorers did not paint over the original motifs, a common practice at other missions. The artwork was designed and carried out by the Monterey merchant Esteban Munras for his friend and fellow Catalonian Father Juan Martín of San Miguel.[2] The execution of the painting was undoubtedly assisted by San Miguel neophytes.

The church has been kept roofed and dry, but it is now in imminent danger from seismic events. Shaken for more than a century by vibrations from passing railway trains, the mission was closed when the 2003 San Simeon earthquake caused major structural damage to its buildings. Seismic retrofitting was completed on the *convento*

BELOW: The only surviving original church interior from the mission era, pictured here before the 2003 earthquake. The walls are adorned with murals designed by the Catalan artist Esteban Munras and executed in the early 1820s with the assistance of neophytes living at the mission. Pale green panels, mimicking cloth coverings, are set among blue Doric columns; a painted balcony runs under the ceiling. Photograph by G. Aldana

RIGHT: Salinian descendants of neophytes from Mission San Miguel, 1934. Courtesy of The Bancroft Library, University of California, Berkeley

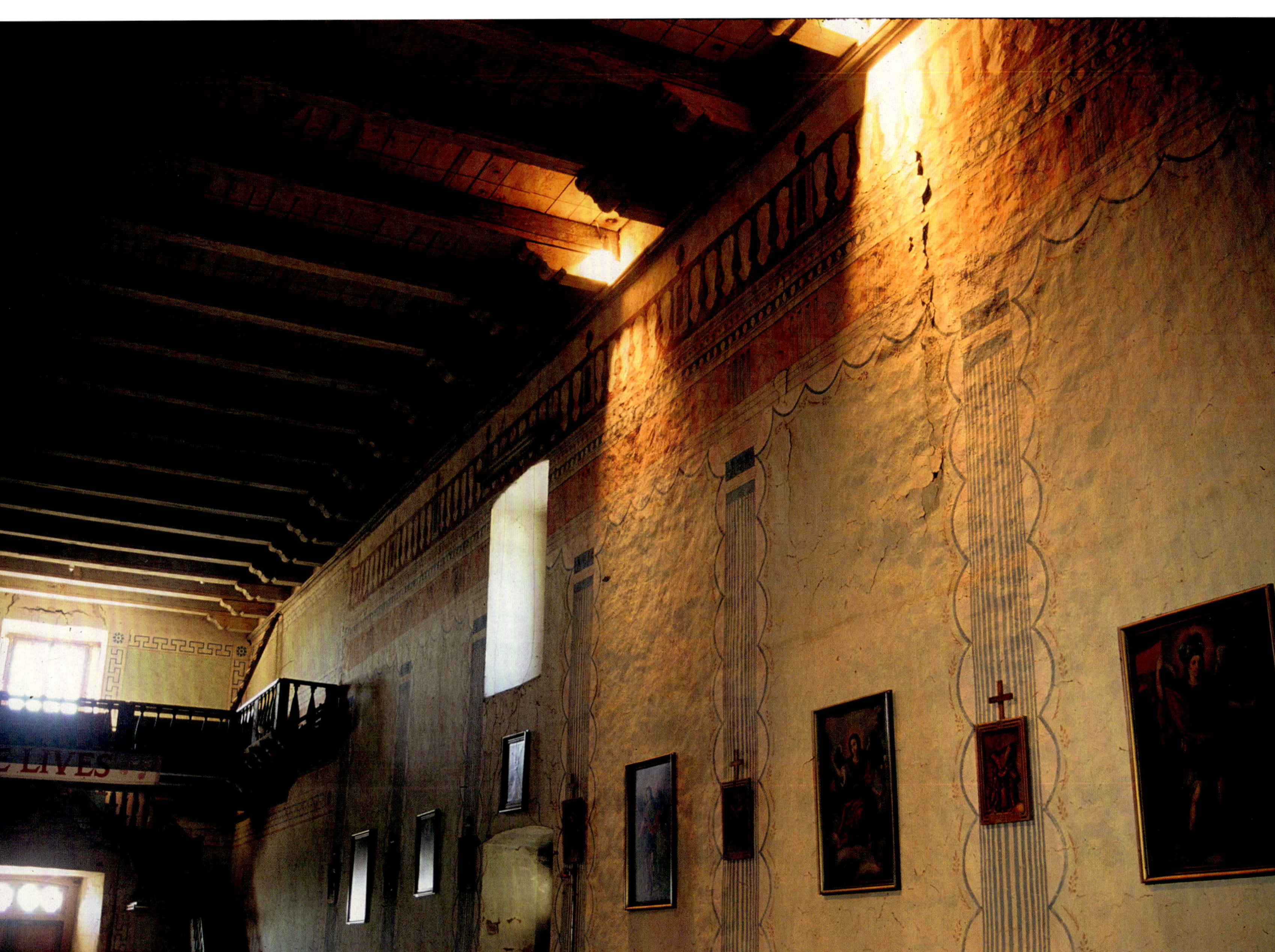

and other quadrangle structures; work on the church building was initiated in 2008 by international seismic and conservation experts, who took measures to protect the painted plaster from the seismic engineering work itself. The mission and its painted walls will be preserved for generations to come.

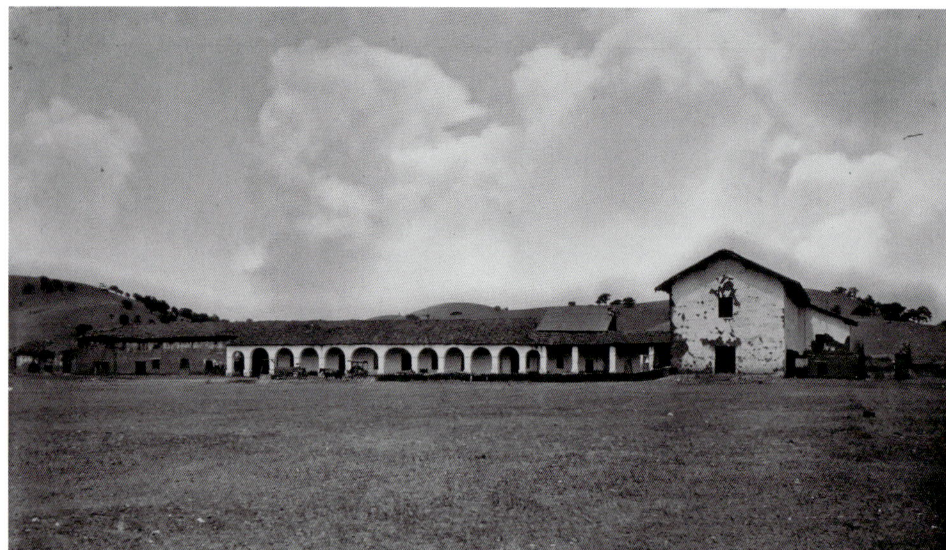

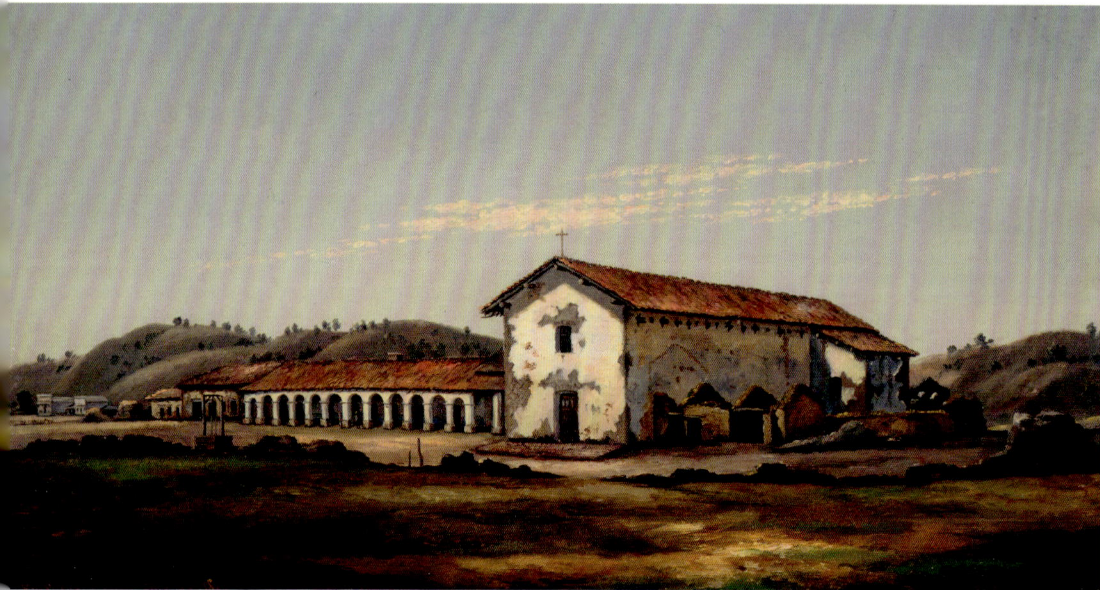

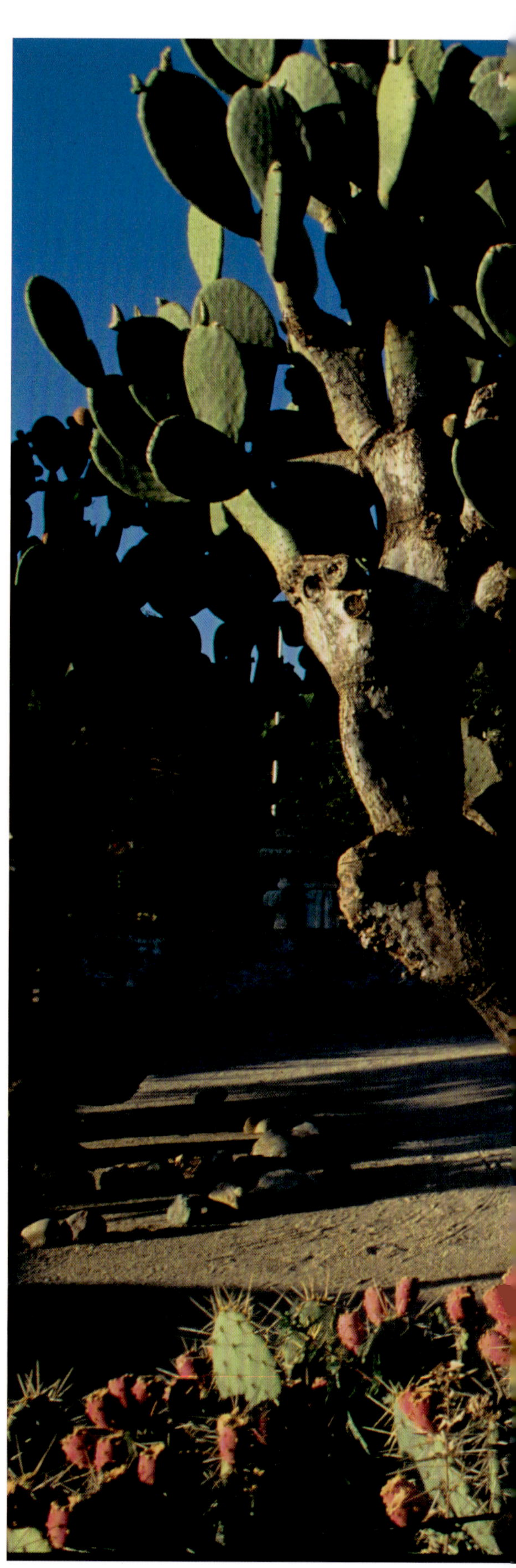

TOP: View of the mission church and *convento*, ca. 1880. Photograph by Frank B. Randolf. Courtesy of The Bancroft Library, University of California, Berkeley

ABOVE: The mission church and *convento* in the late nineteenth century. Henry Chapman Ford, *Mission San Miguel*, 1881. Oil on canvas. Courtesy of the Mission Inn Foundation and Museum, Riverside, California. From the collection of The Historic Mission Inn Corporation

RIGHT: The old plaza of San Miguel, now planted with succulents and desert flora. Photograph by G. Aldana

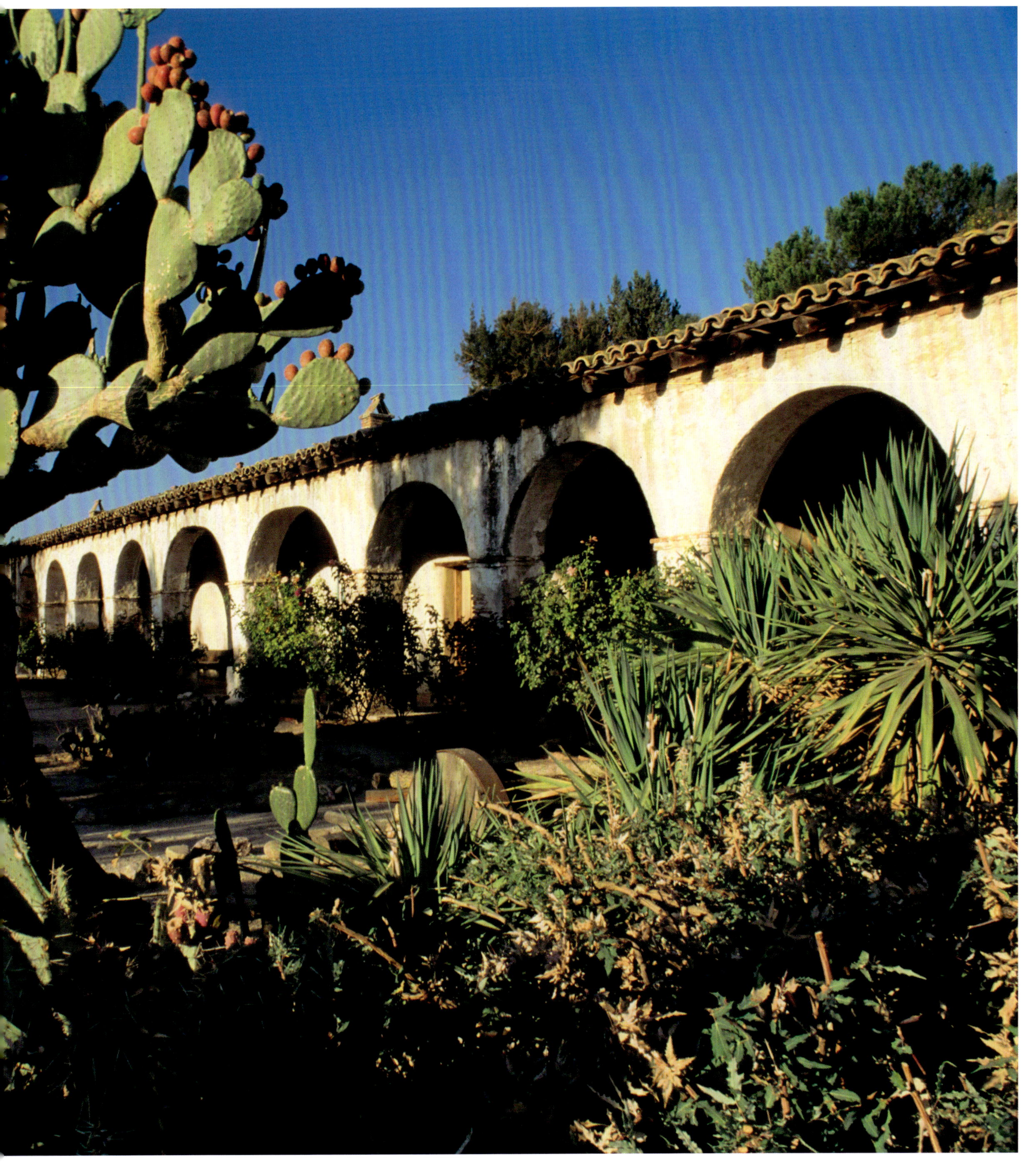

San Fernando Rey de España

FOUNDED SEPTEMBER 8, 1797

LOCATION: *Mission Hills*

FOUNDER: *Father Fermín Lasuén*

PRESIDIO DISTRICT: *Santa Bárbara*

PEAK MISSION POPULATION: *1,081 (1811)*

MAJOR NATIVE GROUPS: *Fernandeño, Tataviam, Ventureño Chumash, Vanyumé, Kitanemuk*

HISTORICAL ASSETS: Convento *building with re-created wall decorations; two original fountains (the Córdoba, or Rosette, fountain was moved); museum with library*

EXISTING CHURCH: *Reconstructed of reinforced concrete in 1974*

OWNERSHIP: *Roman Catholic Church, Archdiocese of Los Angeles*

HISTORICAL STATUS: *California Historical Landmark (No. 157)*

Mission San Fernando Rey de España was the southernmost mission in the Santa Bárbara presidio district. The land was home to Native Americans belonging to the Southern California Takic language group, of whom the Fernandeños, Tataviam, and Vanyumé, along with Chumash to the northwest, were drawn into the mission institution. The mission's agricultural endeavors benefited from its location in a fertile inland valley with year-round water. Like Mission San Buenaventura, it was an active participant in the hide-and-tallow trade, converting cattle herds into trade items for imported commodities. It is unique among the missions for having its *convento* building detached from the closed quadrangle that includes the church. Perhaps this separateness was a benefit, for the lordly two-story *convento* is this mission's lone surviving building from mission days. Occupied by Andrés Pico and his family into the 1870s, it was maintained and therefore survived while surrounding mission buildings crumbled to ruin. In 1874 a room in the *convento* was adapted for use as a church when that building's roof collapsed. The *convento* later served as ranch headquarters for the Porter Land and Water Company, used for storage of equipment and supplies.

Restoration of the church and *convento* was effected by a series of determined locals and luminaries who championed the historic site. In the 1890s the ruins caught the eye of Charles Lummis of the

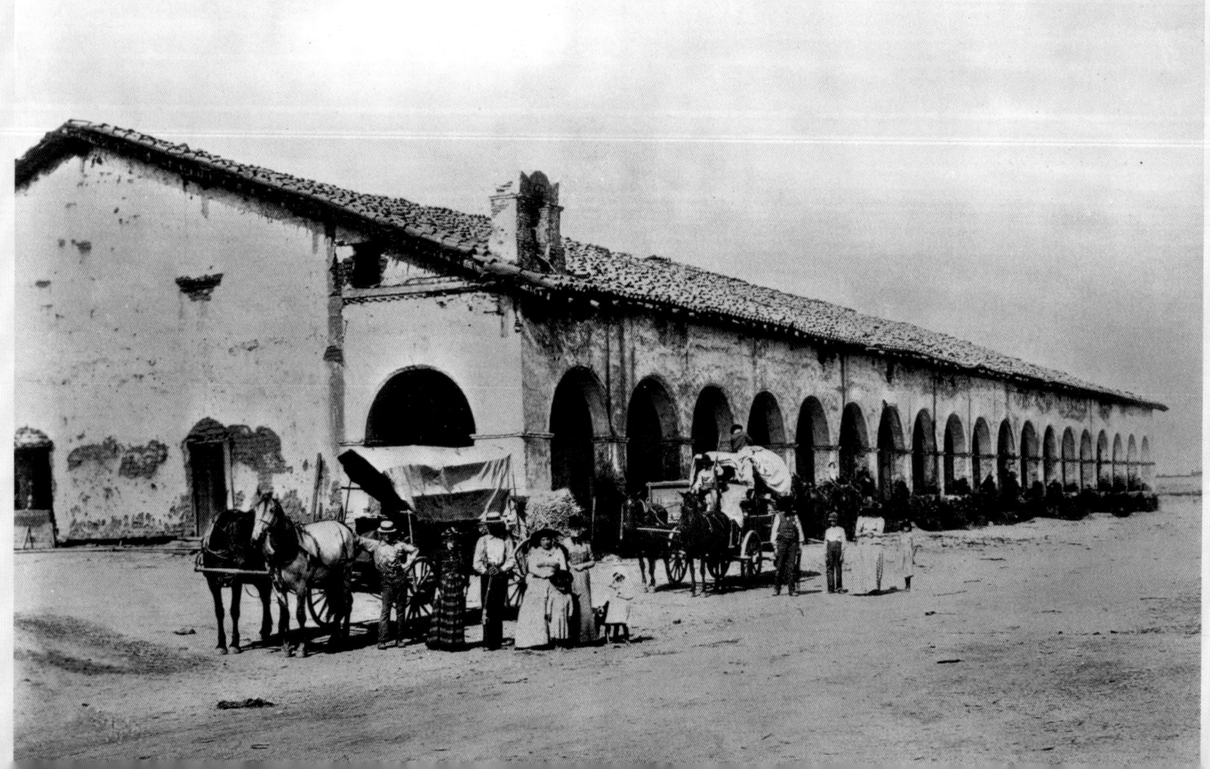

LEFT: Wagon travelers in front of Mission San Fernando Rey's *convento* building, ca. 1895. Photograph by C.C. Pierce. Courtesy University of Southern California, on behalf of the USC Special Collections

OPPOSITE: The church and attached wing, reconstructed following the 1971 Sylmar earthquake. Photograph by G. Aldana

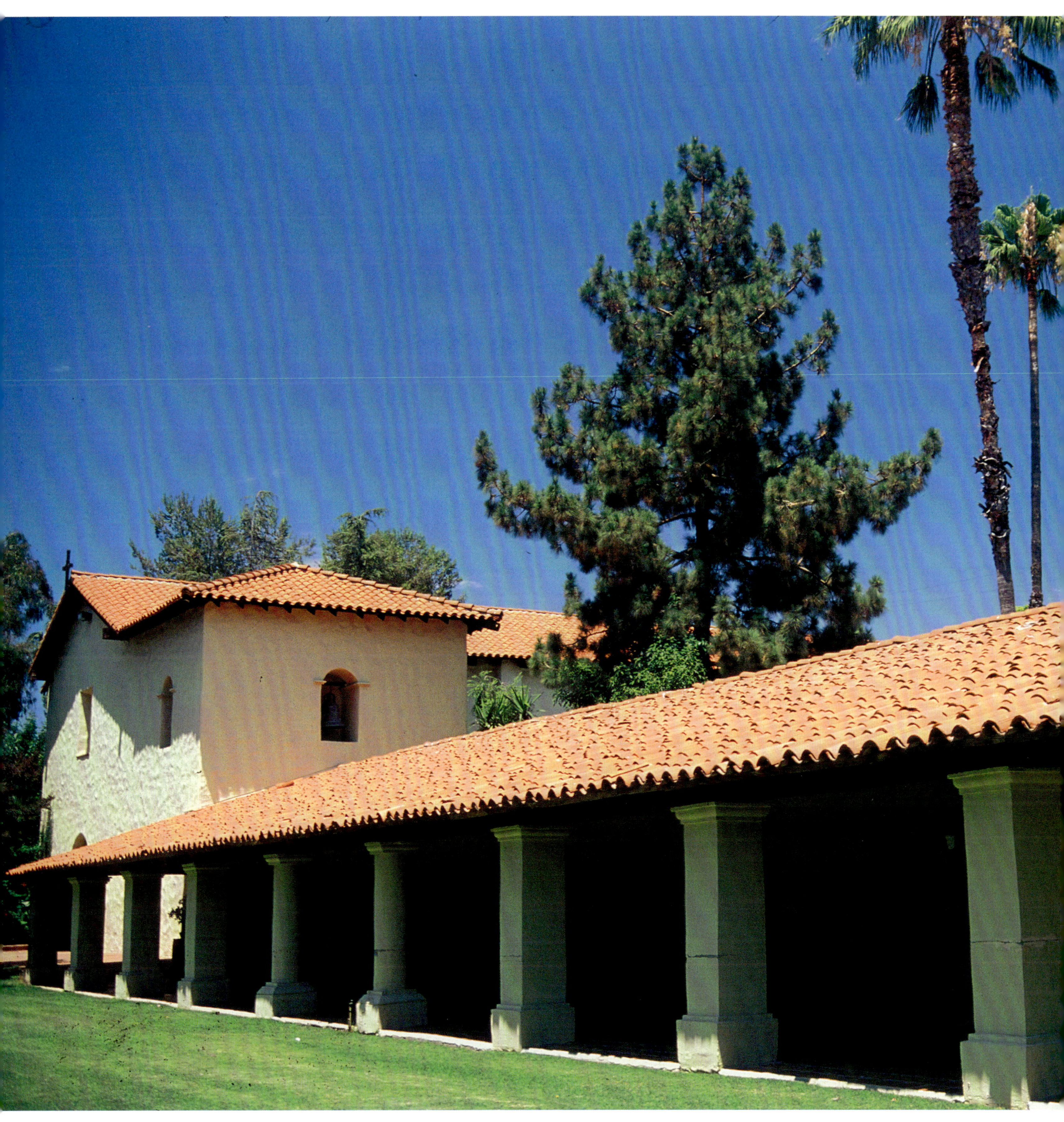

Landmarks Club of Southern California, and by 1897 walls had been stabilized and new roofs installed over both the church and the *convento*, slowing their deterioration. Restoration efforts surged in 1916, and fund-raisers sustained efforts over the subsequent decades when thousands of adobe bricks were made to repair walls and steel braces and concrete columns were inserted in the church. Lummis personally oversaw removal of the Moorish Córdoba fountain to a location closer to the *convento* (a replica was later installed inside the quadrangle). Ultimate success was attained with the involvement of Father Charles Burns and the backing of Mark R. Harrington, curator of the Southwest Museum: on September 7, 1941, the church was rededicated after being inactive for nearly seventy years.[1]

Years of faithful restoration were laid waste in the early morning of February 9, 1971, by the devastating Sylmar earthquake. Damage to the church was deemed irreparable, and the building was red tagged for demolition; the massive walls were battered down and hauled off the site. The church was replaced with one of reinforced concrete, faithfully following the old design. The *convento*, however, was approved for restoration, and great care was taken to preserve as much original fabric of this last mission building as possible. The art historian Norman Neuerburg dedicated himself to repainting many of the original murals on the restored wall surfaces.

The completed complex had only a short reprieve: on January 17, 1994, the Northridge earthquake inflicted extensive damage to the veteran *convento* building; the new church, built to withstand earthquakes, rode out the peril without mishap. This temblor inspired a thorough seismic retrofitting of the *convento*, enabling it to survive future seismic upheavals. And the re-creation of the historic wall paintings ensures that San Fernando Rey will remain famous for its vibrant interpretation of these rare neophyte decorations.

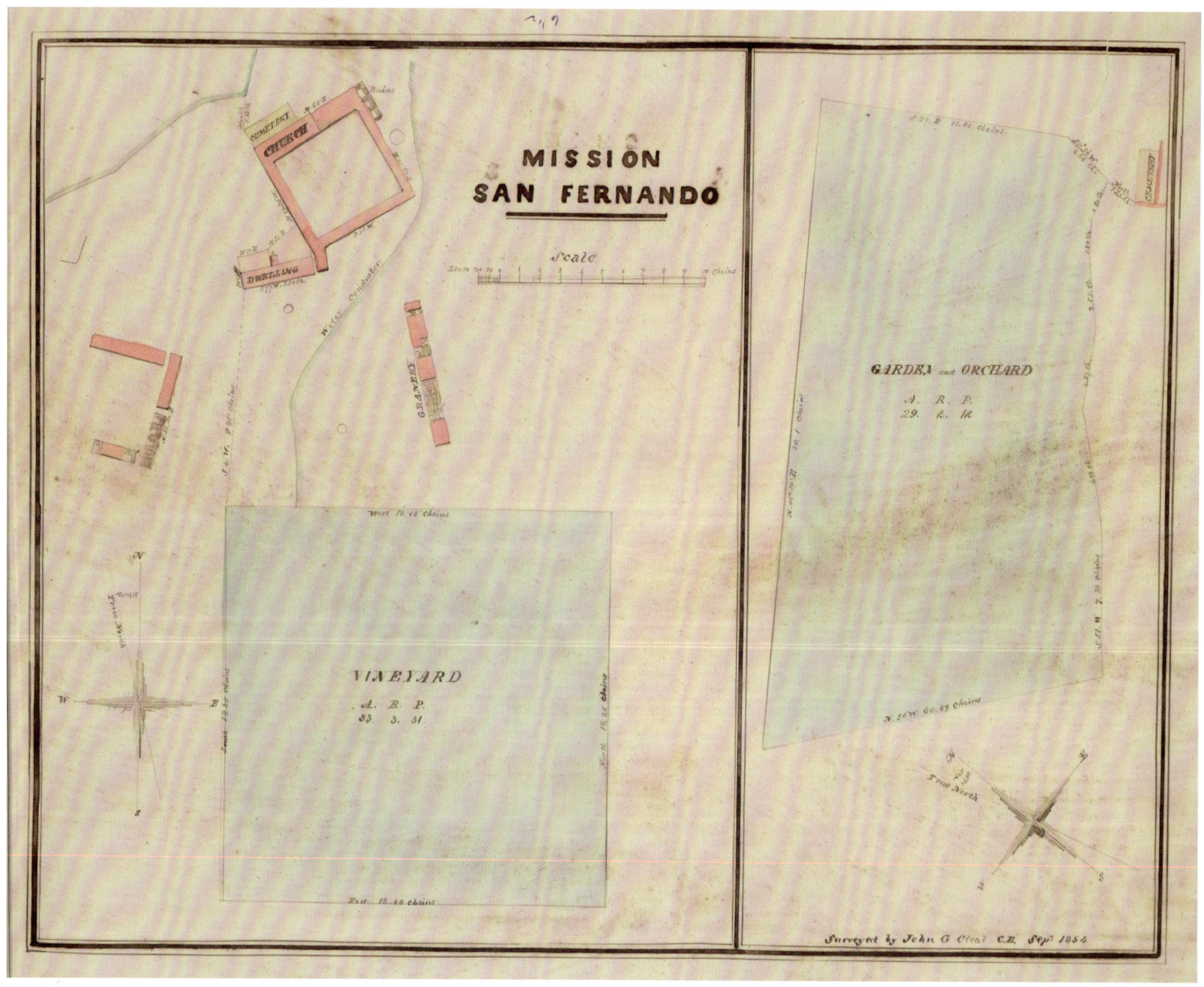

Map of the *casco* of Mission San Fernando by the surveyor John G. Cleal, 1854. The quadrangle is at top; the mission's granary, vineyard, gardens, and orchard are also indicated. Courtesy of The Bancroft Library, University of California, Berkeley

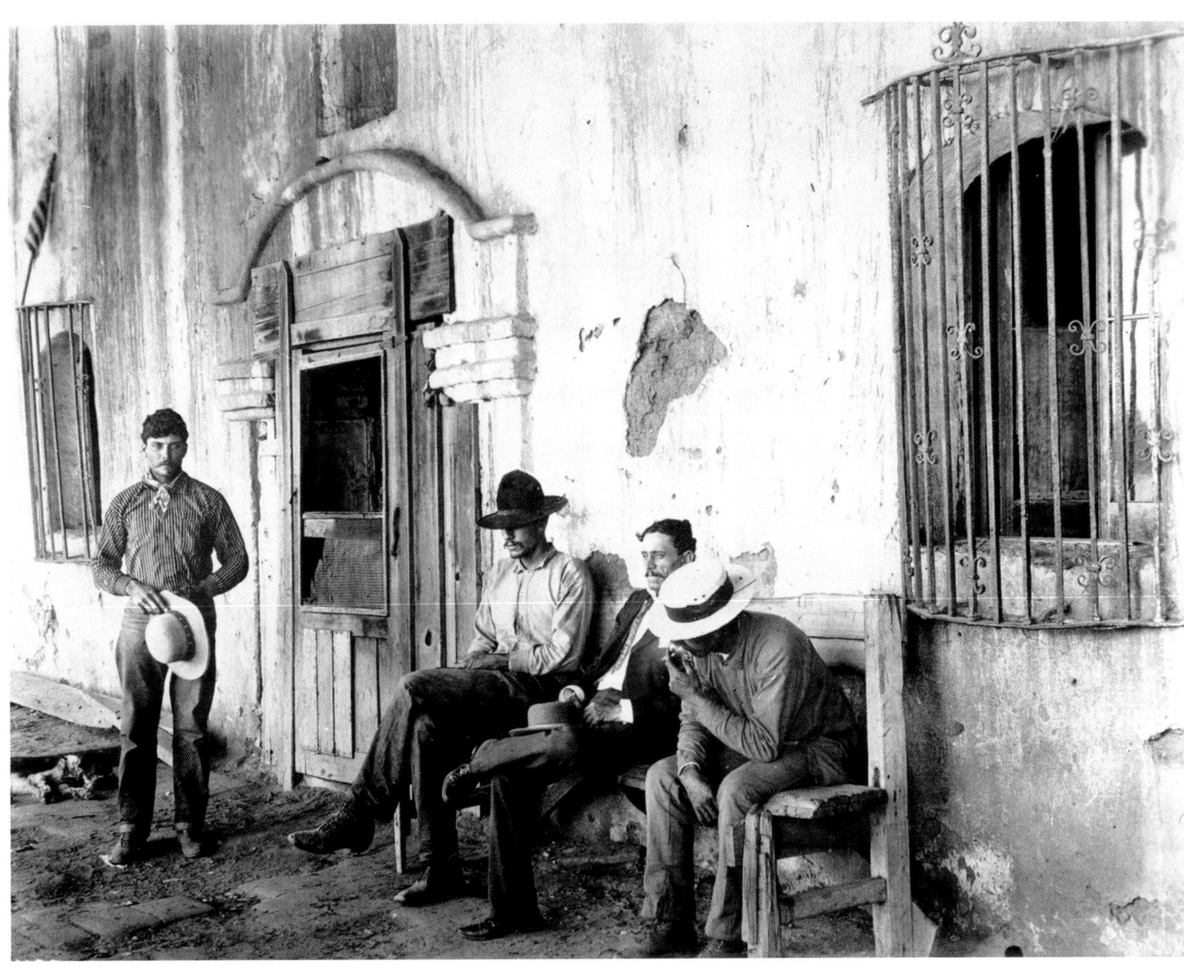

Four Californians in front of the *convento*, ca. 1895. Courtesy University of Southern California, on behalf of the USC Special Collections

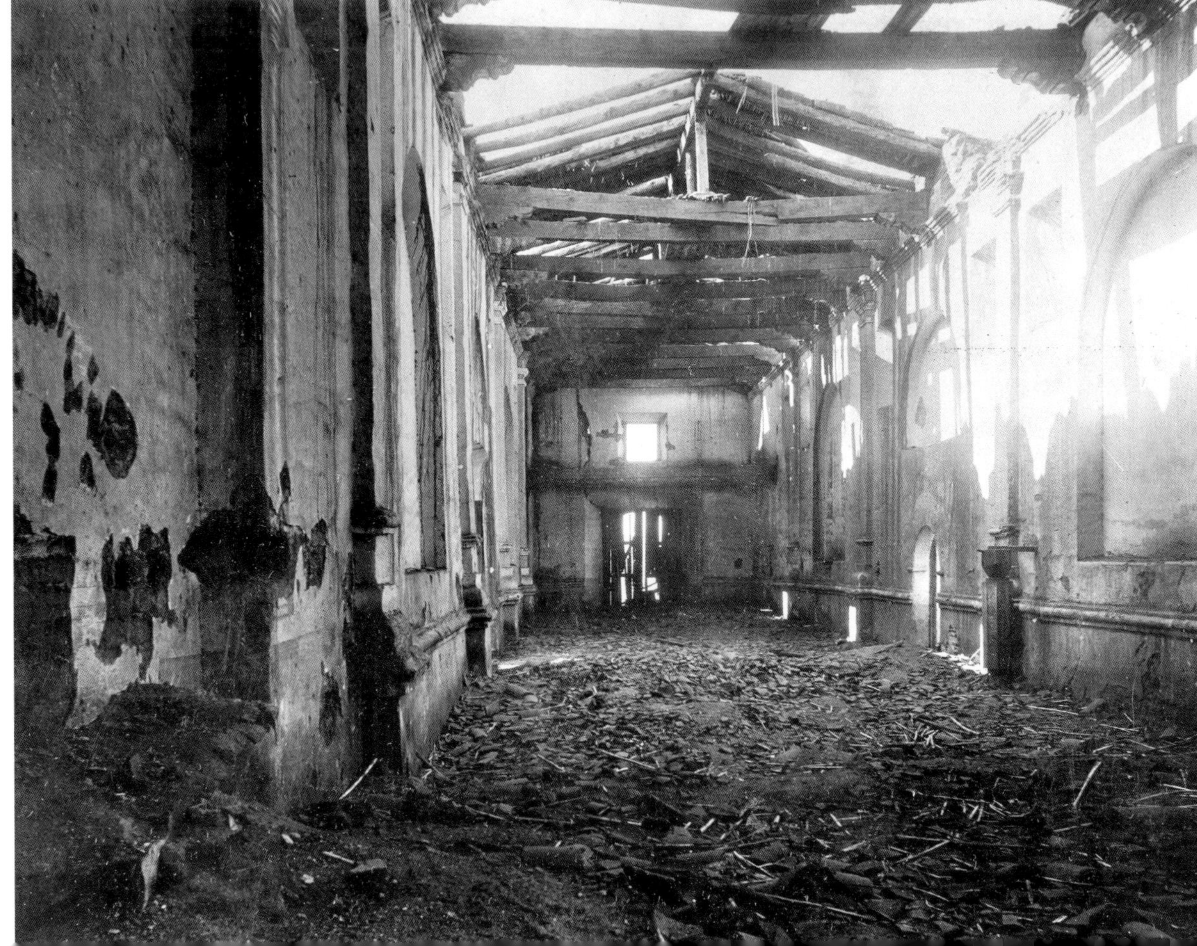

Interior view of the abandoned and roofless mission church, ca. 1887. Although some beams remain intact, many of the roof tiles have fallen to the floor. Courtesy University of Southern California, on behalf of the USC Special Collections

San Luis Rey de Francia

FOUNDED JUNE 13, 1798

LOCATION: *Oceanside*

FOUNDER: *Father Fermín Lasuén*

PRESIDIO DISTRICT: *San Diego*

PEAK MISSION POPULATION: *2,869 (1826)*

MAJOR NATIVE GROUPS: *Luiseño, Ipai, Cupeño, Cahuilla*

HISTORICAL ASSETS: *Cruciform church with octagonal mortuary chapel; sunken garden area with tile* lavanderías, *water systems, and kilns; archaeological remains of neophyte village; museum*

EXISTING CHURCH: *Constructed of adobe and* ladrillo, *completed in 1815*

OWNERSHIP: *Roman Catholic Church, Diocese of San Diego*

HISTORICAL STATUS: *California Historical Landmark (No. 239); National Historic Landmark*

Mission San Luis Rey de Francia was founded late in the mission period among the populous native peoples between long-established Missions San Diego and San Juan Capistrano. Benefiting from this nearby support, the mission grew quickly: fields were developed, adobe buildings constructed, and successful industries established. San Luis Rey was unique in that it not only was the largest mission in California but also housed the healthiest neophyte population. While virtually every other establishment declined in numbers toward the end of the mission period, San Luis Rey retained a considerable population—1,909 neophytes—at secularization in 1834. Recent studies have attributed this to Father Antonio Peyrí's unusual decision to allow nearly half of his baptized neophytes to remain in their traditional villages instead of requiring them to move to the mission community. Healthful practices and this decentralized living pattern allowed the mission to minimize the effects of catastrophic diseases that debilitated other institutions. Continued association of baptized Indians with their traditional villages and lands also resulted in establishment of several reservations in the post-mission period.[1] The *asistencia* at what is now the Pala Reservation, constructed in 1815, is remarkably intact and still serves its Luiseño and Cupeño community.

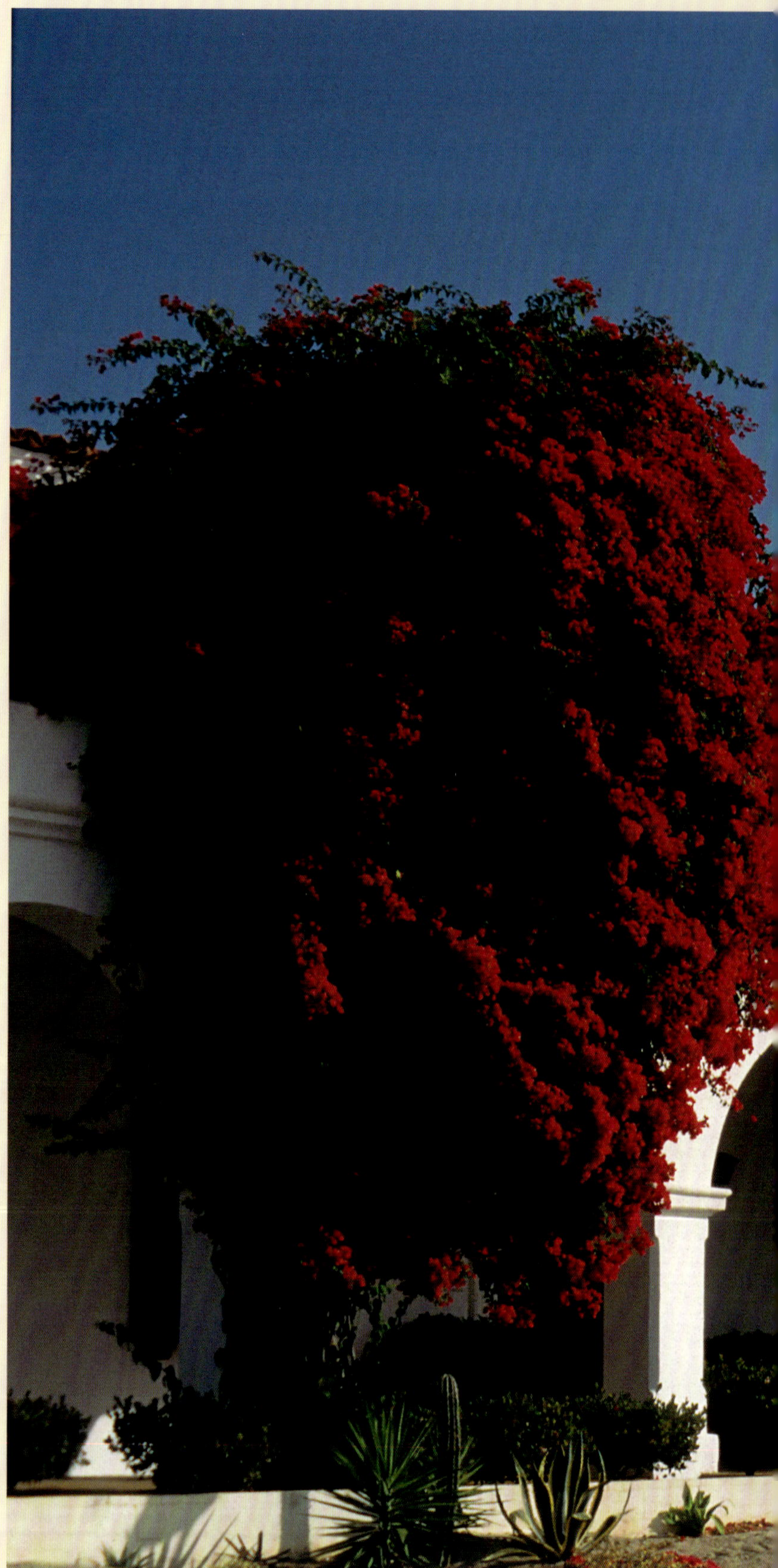

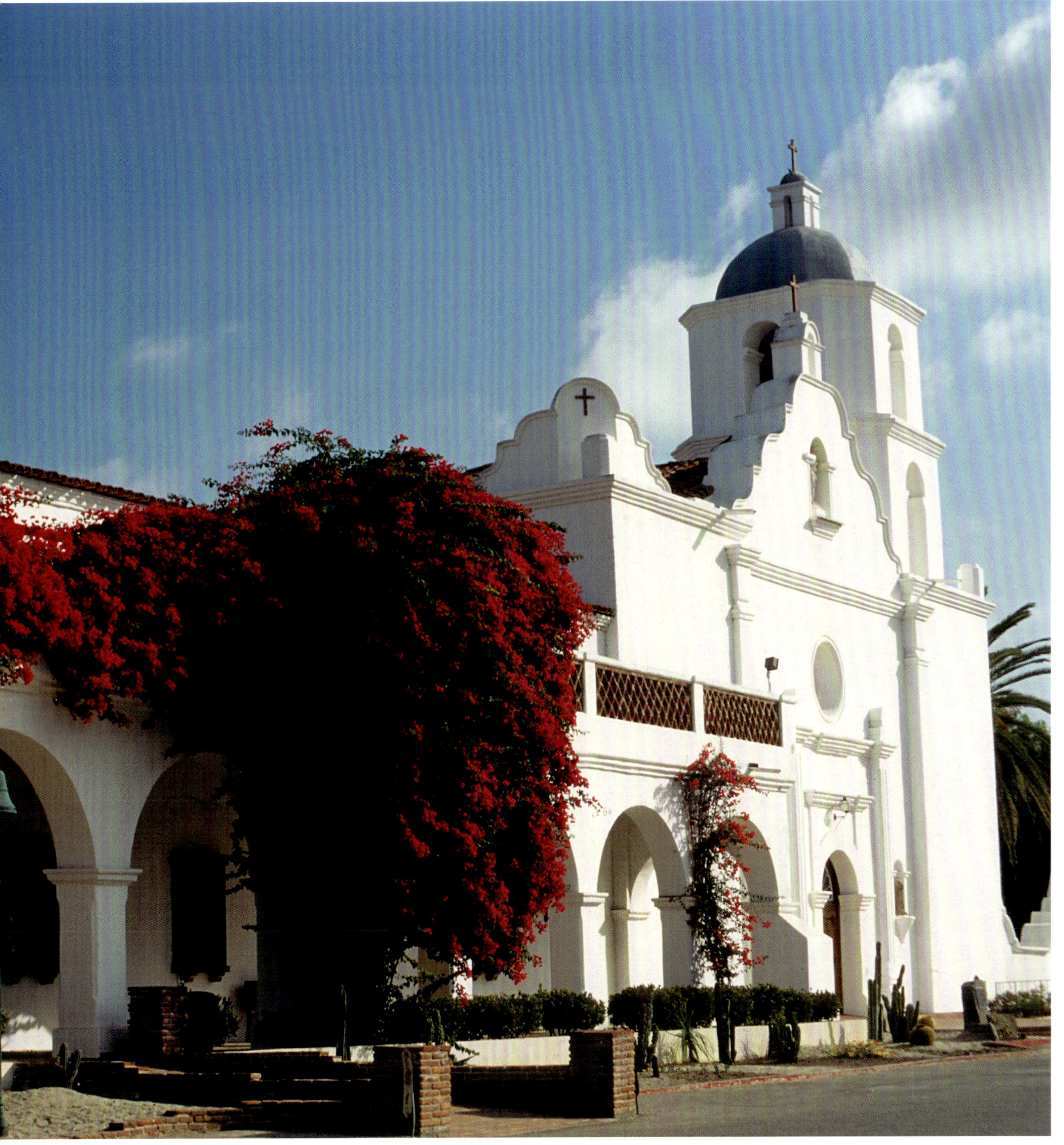

Mission San Luis Rey, distinctive for its facade and bell tower and for the two-story *convento* with the balustrade of *citarilla*, or *ladrillo* latticework.
Photograph by G. Aldana

The distinctive church is the only surviving building at the mission site. Constructed of *ladrillos* and adobe, it was completed in 1815 by "architect and director" José Antonio Ramírez, the well-known master mason who also constructed the churches at Missions Santa Bárbara and San Buenaventura. The building features a cruciform-like plan, with brick pilasters and moldings, and a distinctive stepped gable. The *ladrillo*-faced tower originally had a ground-floor baptistery, which was soon filled in to stabilize the structure. The unique wooden dome with a cupola supported by eight columns had been added by 1829, and a remarkable octagonal room on the east side was added between 1832 and 1844.[2] The historical church structure is largely intact although the interior was thoroughly pillaged during its abandonment during the late 1800s, with even the altar removed. Fortunately, statuary and other religious items had been removed to Pala for safekeeping.

The restoration of Mission San Luis Rey was undertaken by Franciscan friars from Zacatecas who arrived in 1892 to establish a seminary. Traditional techniques were brought by the Zacatecans from Mexico, and much of the adobe material was salvaged from the ruins. With work directed by Father Joseph Jeremiah O'Keefe, the church received a new roof, adobe walls were patched and replastered, the dome was repaired, a new floor was laid, and a portion of the quadrangle was reconstructed.[3] In later years the extraordinary *lavanderías,* cisterns, and kilns in the gardens below the mission were uncovered and restored. Today the mission has recovered its impressive visage, worthy of this largest and most productive of the California institutions.

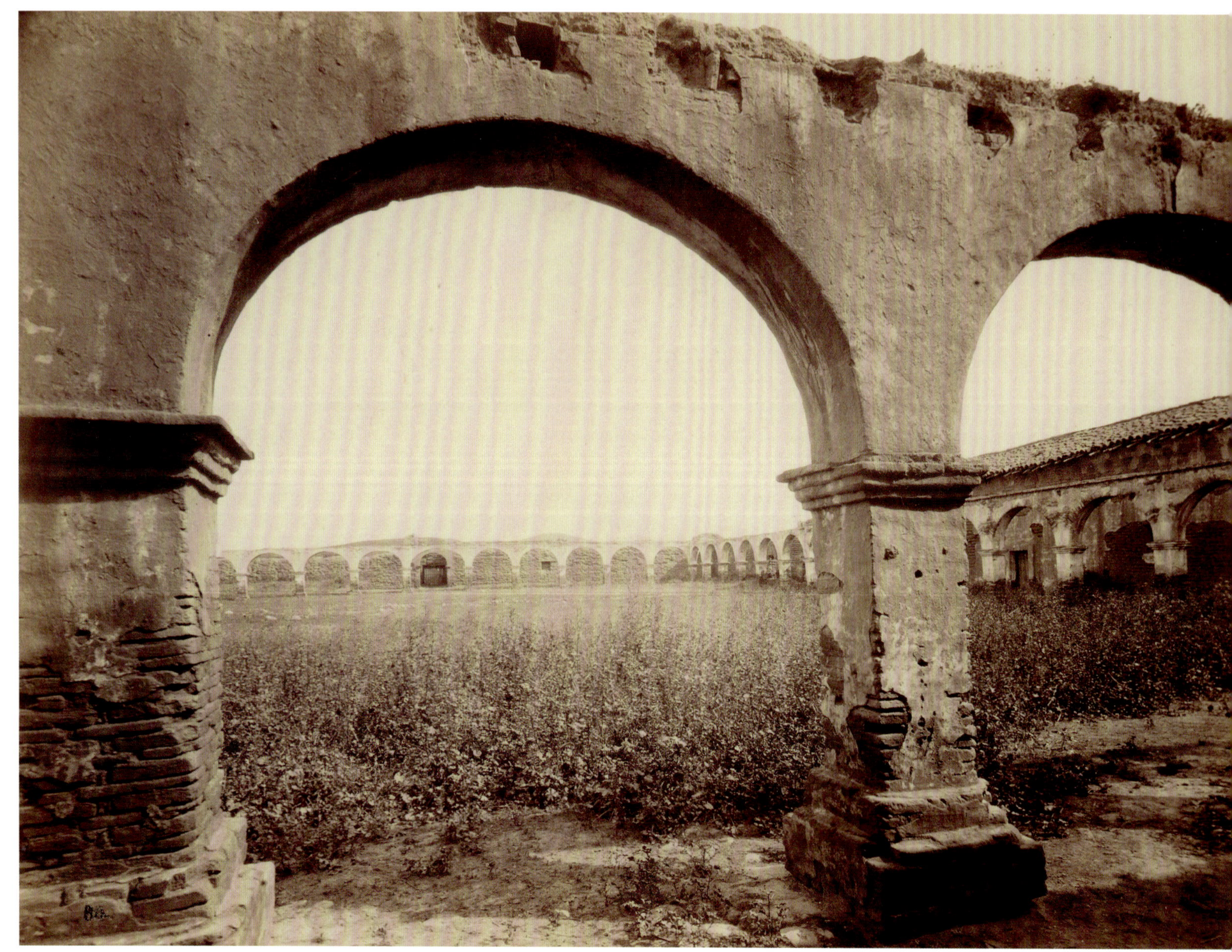

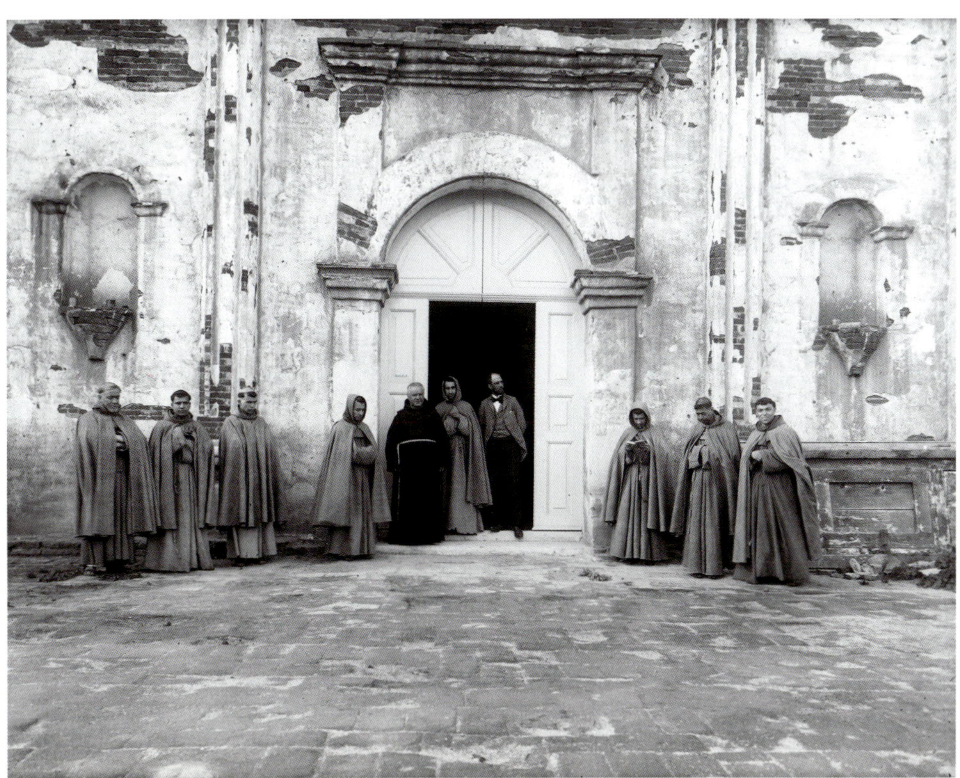

RIGHT: Franciscan monks from Zacatecas, Mexico, in front of the church entrance, ca. 1895. From 1892 to 1903, the monks worked to restore the church and part of the *convento*, under the direction of Father Joseph Jeremiah O'Keefe, seen in the black robe at center. Photograph by C.C. Pierce. Courtesy of the Seaver Center for Western History Research, Los Angeles County Museum of Natural History

OPPOSITE: View of the quadrangle at Mission San Luis Rey, marked by the standing ladrillo columns of its corridors, ca. 1885–90. Photograph by William Henry Jackson. Albumen silver print. This item is reproduced by permission of The Huntington Library, San Marino, California

BELOW: Mission San Luis Rey from the northwest, ca. 1876–80; the arches of the quadrangle mark the outlines of the melted adobe buildings. Photograph by Carleton Watkins. Albumen silver print. Courtesy of The Bancroft Library, University of California, Berkeley

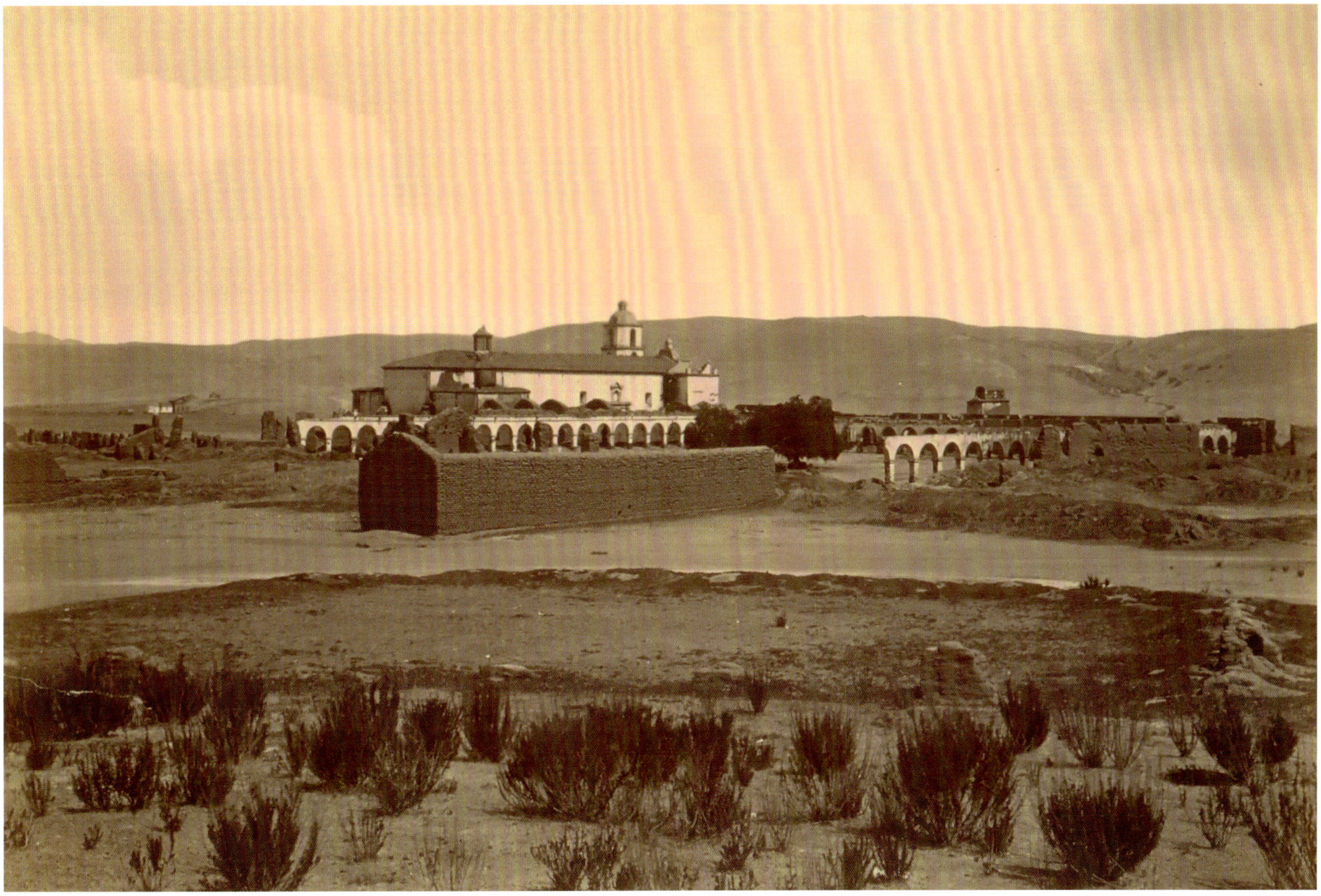

Santa Inés, Virgen y Mártir

FOUNDED 1804

LOCATION: *Solvang*

FOUNDER: *Father Esteban Tapis*

PRESIDIO DISTRICT: *Santa Bárbara*

PEAK MISSION POPULATION: *522 (1822)*

MAJOR NATIVE GROUPS: *Ineseño and Island Chumash, Yokuts*

HISTORICAL ASSETS: *Church, most of the* convento, *reservoir,* lavandería; *archaeological remains of the south and west wings and neophyte village; extensive collection of mission-period art and artifacts. View to the east includes ruins of the mission's reservoir and mills and a remarkably intact historic landscape setting*

OWNERSHIP: *Roman Catholic Church, Archdiocese of Los Angeles*

EXISTING CHURCH: *Constructed in 1817 of adobe with a* ladrillo *facade*

HISTORICAL STATUS: *California Historical Landmark (No. 305); National Historic Landmark District*

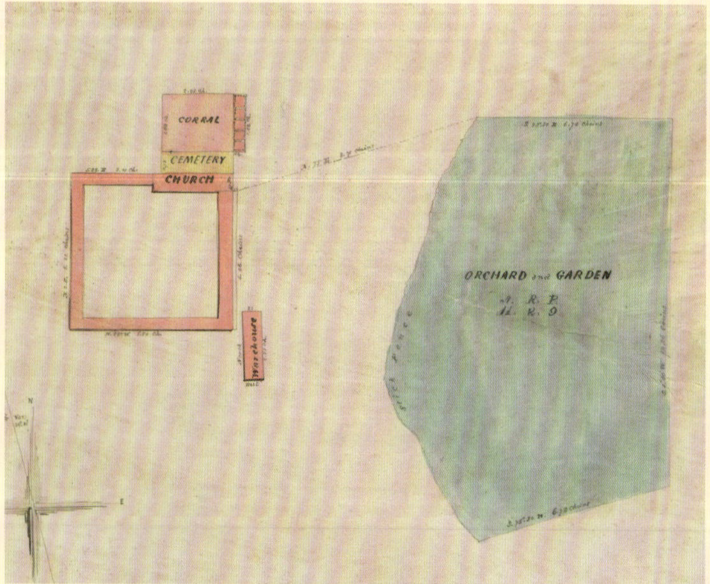

Map of the *casco* by the surveyor John G. Cleal, 1854 (detail). Courtesy of The Bancroft Library, University of California, Berkeley

Mission Santa Inés was established late in the mission period astride El Camino Real. It was carved out of territory served by Mission Santa Bárbara to the east and Mission La Purísima to the west, completing conversion of the Chumash villages in the Santa Ynez Valley. Because of its comparatively small area, about ten miles wide and stretching about twenty miles inland from the coast, Santa Inés did not establish outlying ranch stations common to missions with larger territories. Nevertheless, it was one of the most successful agricultural producers in its district. Santa Inés is famously the birthplace of the 1824 Chumash revolt, one of the largest and most successful uprisings of Native American neophytes in the Spanish West. Mission buildings were burned at Santa Inés, La Purísima was taken by armed neophytes, and hundreds of Santa Bárbara converts fled to Santa Cruz Island and the interior. Peace was eventually restored, the instigators punished, and baptisms resumed, although the steady decline of the missions already under way was inevitable. Although secularized in 1832, the establishment continued to survive: in 1850 some three hundred Chumash were still identified as part of the community, and a priest remained in residence until about 1875. In 1855 the remaining neophytes were removed to a reservation at Zanja de Cota, about two miles to the east.

During the Mexican era, Mission Santa Inés was selected as the location for the first ecclesiastical seminary in California, the College of Our Lady of Refuge, established in 1844 in the mission courtyard. Soon after 1868 the college was moved several miles to a site that came to be known as College Ranch.[1] Isolated and with a small Christian Indian congregation from the nearby reservation, Mission Santa Inés did not have a full-time resident priest again until 1904, when Father Alexander Buckler began his twenty-year residency and implemented needed repairs and stabilization of the buildings. Based on careful historical research, a major restoration was completed in 1950, funded by the Hearst Foundation, with additional efforts continuing through 1962 by Father Timothy O'Sullivan. Reconstruction of the south end of the *convento* in 1990 was preceded by archaeological studies of the original rooms, revealing their complex layers of floors, wall finishing, renovations, and artifacts. The new wing was constructed to preserve these remains under suspended concrete flooring.[2] Santa Inés still serves the local Chumash community, as well as the growing town of Solvang, with its church and school.

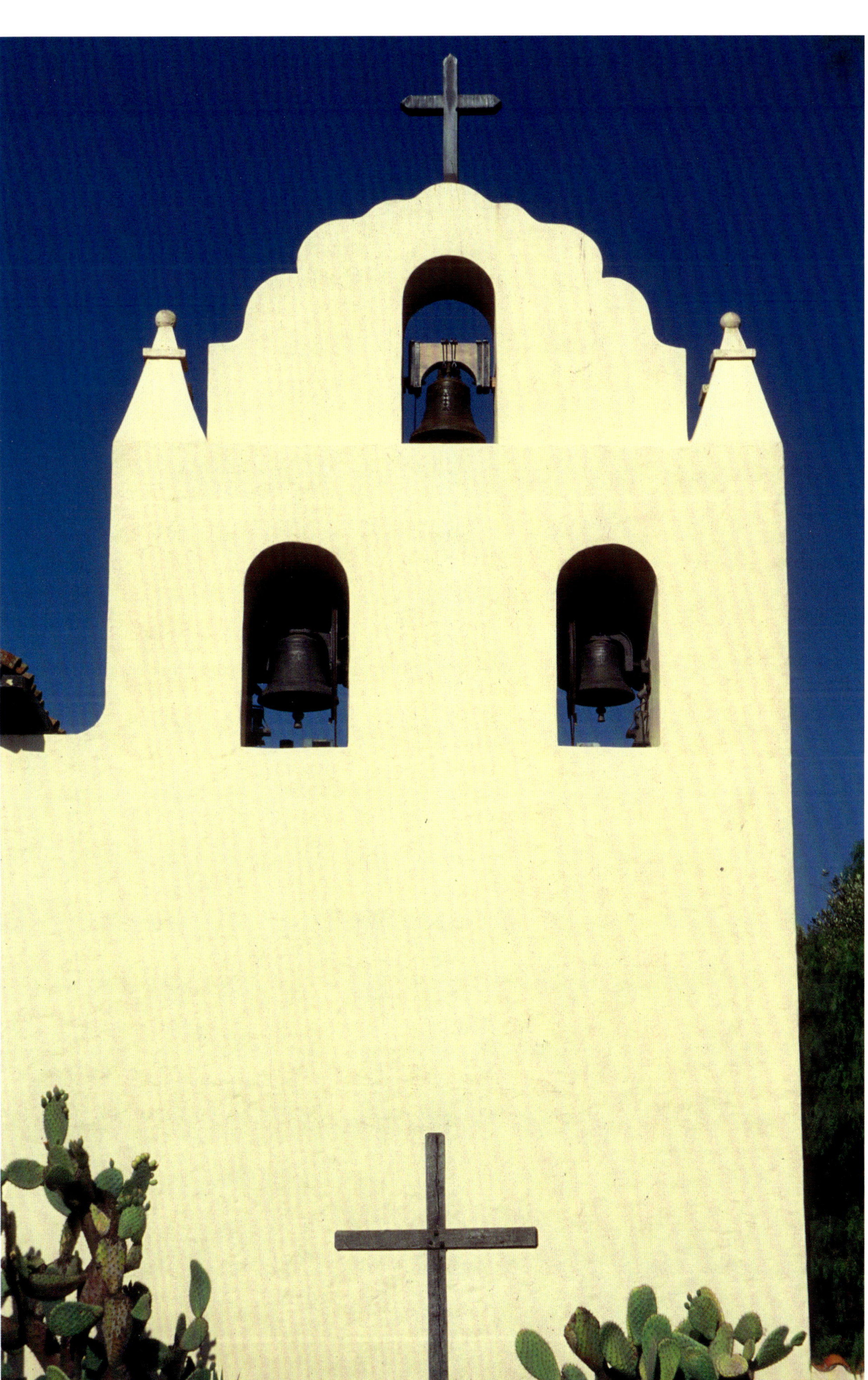

The landmark *espadaña*; the original fell in 1911 and was replaced with an inaccurate replica; it was restored to its earlier appearance in 1947. Photograph by G. Aldana

Never abandoned, Mission Santa Inés is one of the best preserved of California's Spanish missions, containing an impressive combination of landscape setting, original buildings, extant collections of art and interior furnishings, water-related industrial structures, and archaeological remains. The present church was constructed in 1817 of adobe faced with *ladrillos*. Heavy buttresses support its sides,[3] and the simple facade features painted flat pilasters on the corners and an unadorned choir window over the door. The *ladrillo espadaña* has twice been reconstructed (1912, 1947), the last time quite accurately.

Inside the church, original Chumash wall decorations are preserved around the altar, although the walls of the nave have been repainted. The art collections at the mission are among the best in the state, enriched with items brought from neighboring La Purísima when it was abandoned and including the largest and most diverse collection of mission Indian artworks in California. This rich collection is in part a result of the mission's location in the rural Santa Ynez Valley, which fortunately was overlooked during the Americanization of California.

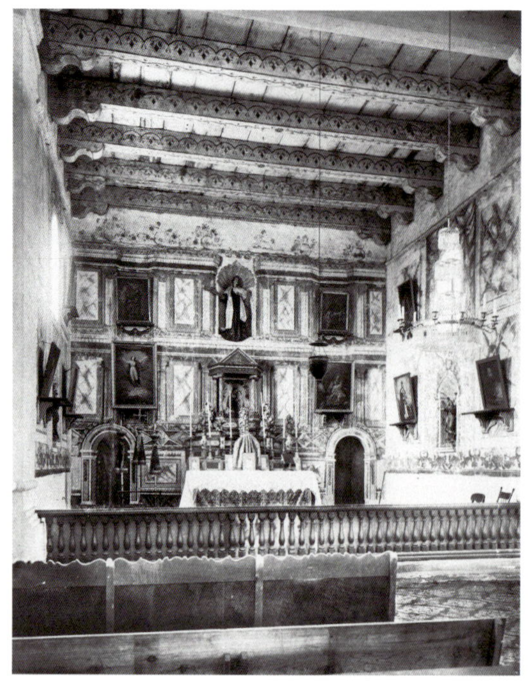

LEFT: View of the wall murals in the church sanctuary, ca. 1904. They have changed little since this photo was taken, and Santa Inés still presides over the altar. Photograph by C. C. Pierce. Courtesy University of Southern California, on behalf of the USC Special Collections

BELOW: The mission church and convento, 1881. When the artist Henry Chapman Ford visited that year, he found the church still intact and serving a small congregation, although only a few rooms of the convento were habitable. Henry Chapman Ford, *Mission Santa Ines*, 1881. Oil on canvas. Courtesy of the Mission Inn Foundation and Museum, Riverside, California. From the collection of The Historic Mission Inn Corporation

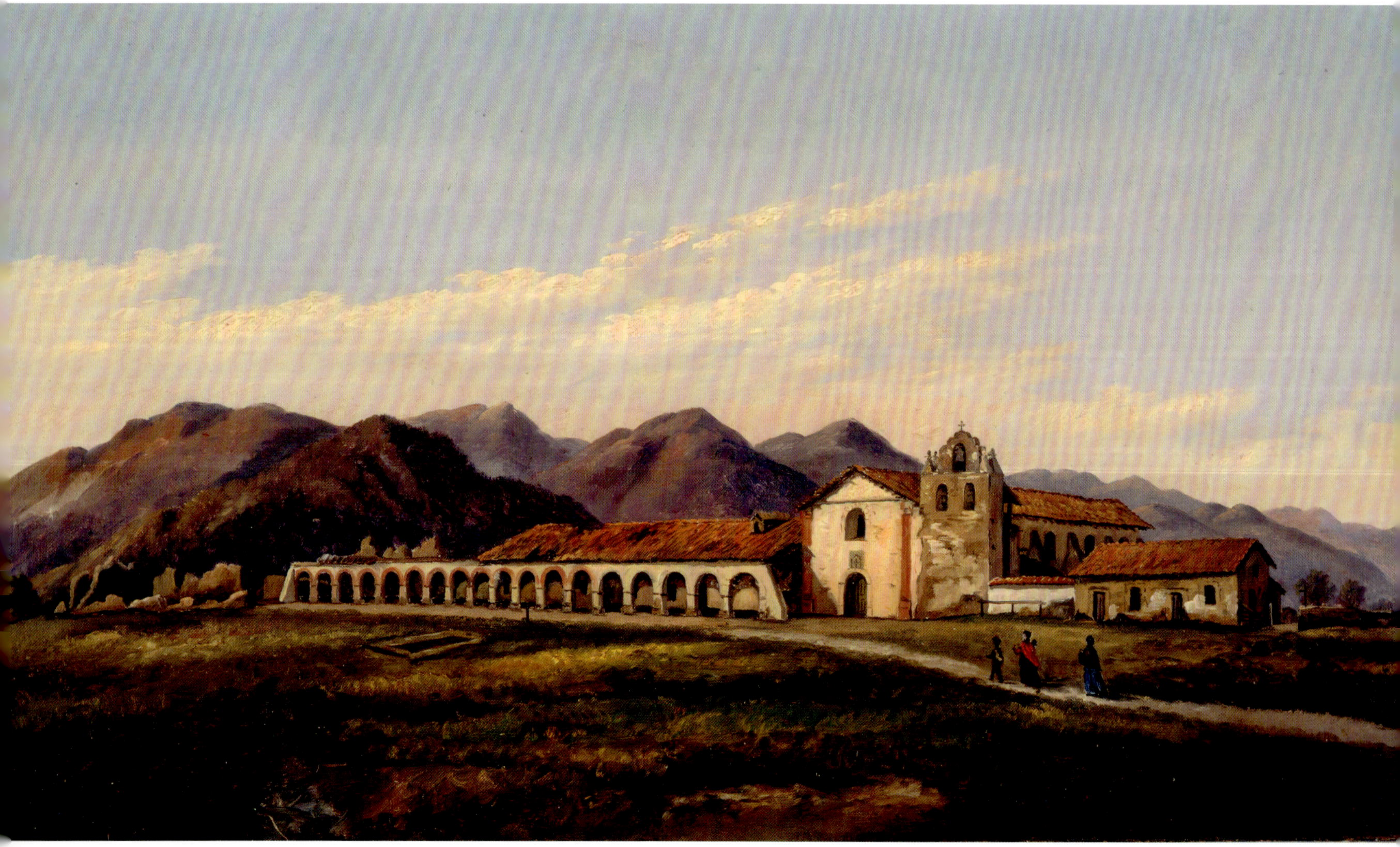

The grounds surrounding the mission buildings preserve important examples of mission-period ruins and archaeological remains. The site of the neophyte village, surrounding the *lavandería*, is marked by low mounds formed by the melted adobe walls. Similar undisturbed mounds can be seen where the south and west wings of the quadrangle once stood. Santa Inés's well-preserved ruins of a reservoir, flour mill, and fulling mill are visible to the south. The southern vista also features agricultural fields footing the Santa Ynez mountain range, forming a remarkably intact historic landscape setting.

View of the church and *convento*, ca. 1876–80, showing traces of painted pillars on the facade; behind the *espadaña*, the platform for the bell-ringer can also be seen. Two figures are standing in front of the entrance. Photograph by Carleton Watkins. Albumen silver print. Courtesy of The Bancroft Library, University of California, Berkeley

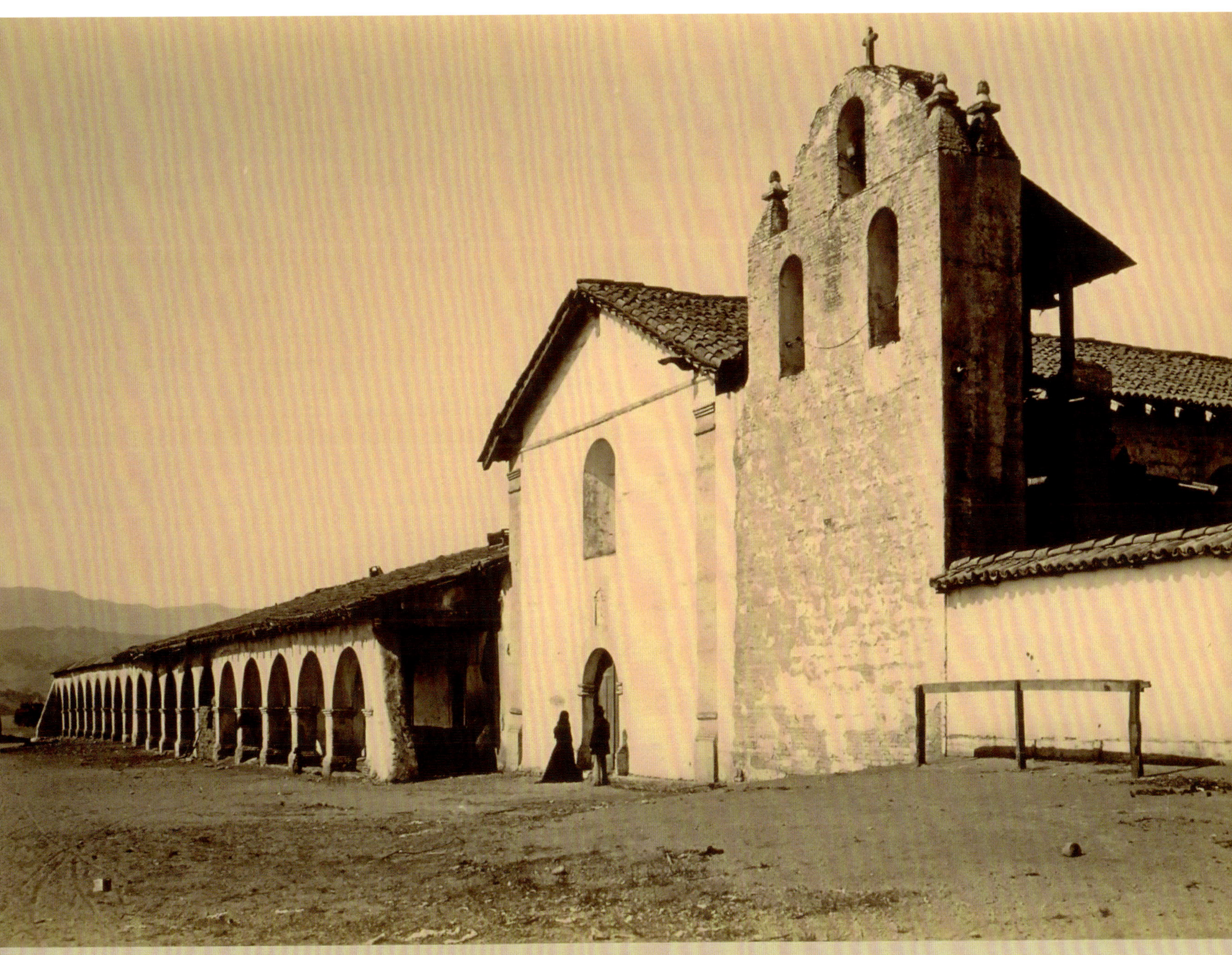

San Rafael, Arcángel

FOUNDED DECEMBER 14, 1817

Location: *San Rafael*

Founder: *Father Vicente Sarría*

Presidio District: *San Francisco*

Peak Mission Population: *1,140 (1828)*

Major Native Groups: *Coast Miwok, Wappo, Pomo*

Historical Assets: *Three original mission bells and a painting of San Rafael Arcángel*

Existing Church: *Replica constructed in 1949 of reinforced concrete, near original location*

Ownership: *Roman Catholic Church, Diocese of San Francisco*

Historical Status: *California Historical Landmark (No. 327)*

In 1817 San Rafael, Arcángel, was established on the Marin peninsula to house and heal neophytes from Mission San Francisco de Asís. That first year some 253 Coast Miwok were transferred to this healthier climate, to lands that were their traditional homeland.[1] Although identified as an *asistencia* (outstation), from the beginning San Rafael had a resident padre, Father Luis Gil y Taboada, and its own birth, marriage, and death records. In 1823 Father Altimira at Mission San Francisco de Asís sought a permanent solution to that mission's unhealthy location, proposing consolidation with San Rafael and moving both to a new site in the Sonoma area. This action was opposed by San Rafael's Father Juan Amorós and by Father President Señán, who quickly declared the actions illegal. It was decided that San Francisco de Asís would remain where it was, San Rafael would achieve mission status, and a new mission would be established at Sonoma.

San Rafael prospered both because of the oversight of Father Amorós and because it was located on land rich in resources. The

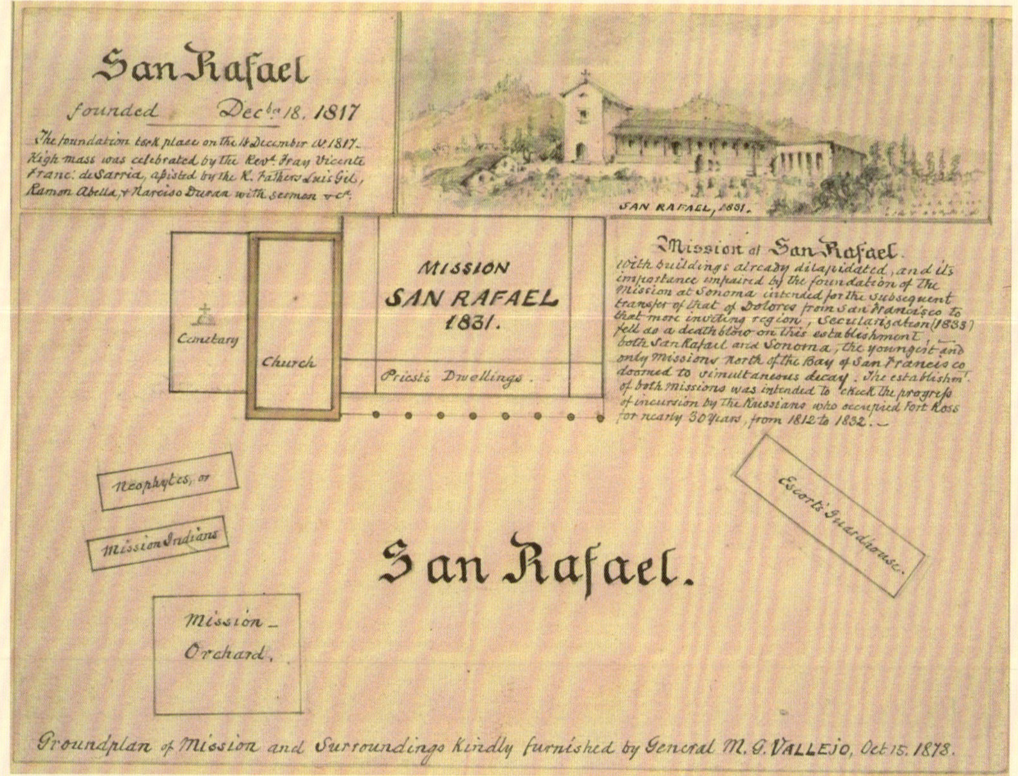

LEFT: Ground plan of the mission, along with an 1878 rendering by Edward Vischer. It was based on a memory sketch of the mission by General Mariano Guadalupe Vallejo, showing the establishment as it appeared in 1831. Watercolor on paper. Courtesy of The Bancroft Library, University of California, Berkeley

OPPOSITE: The small replica chapel was built in 1949 to commemorate the mission, which had long since disappeared. The Church of Saint Raphael, completed in 1919, can also be seen. Photograph by G. Aldana

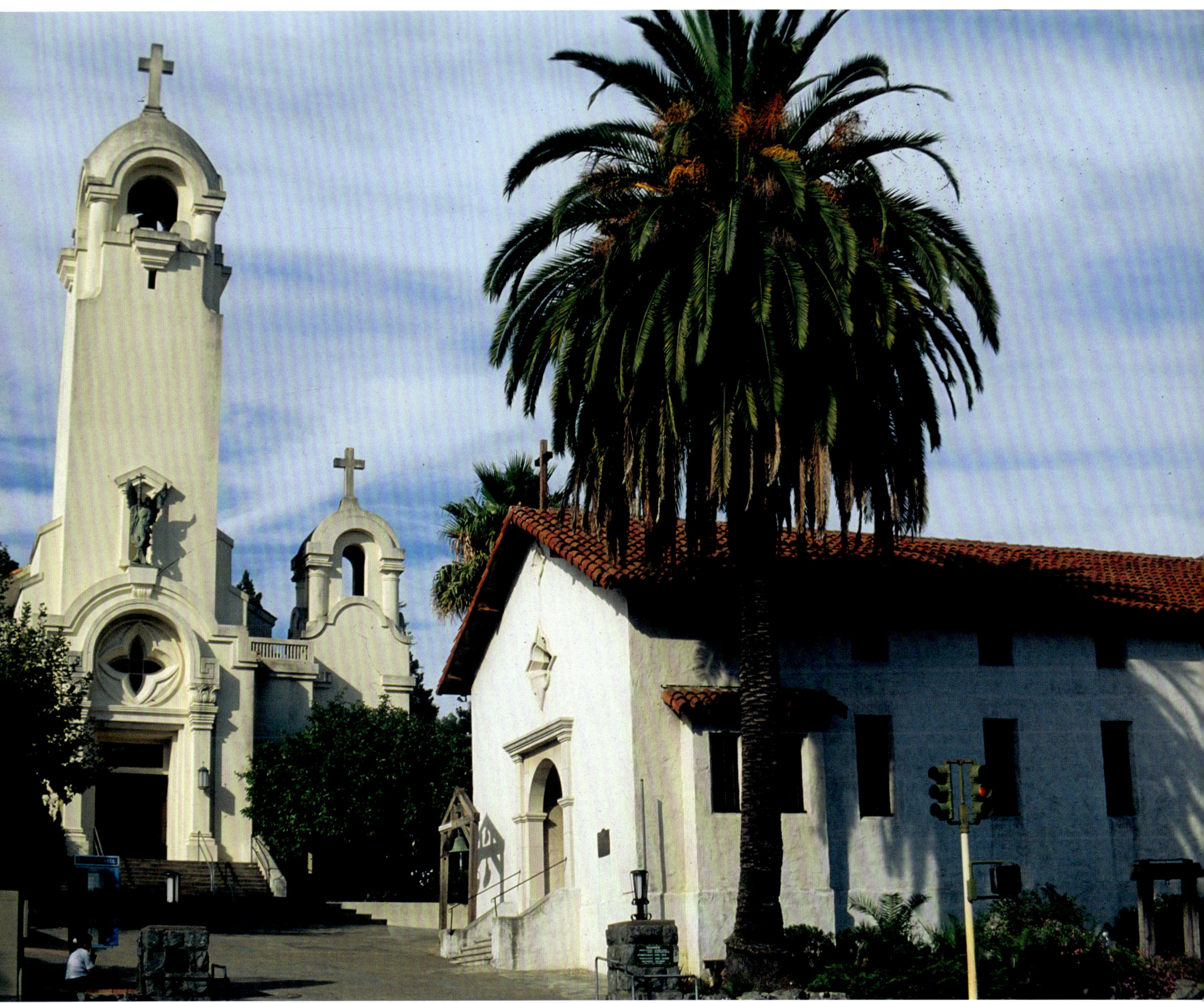

population eventually exceeded one thousand, as the sick from other missions were sent to be healed there and new converts were attracted. All the buildings at San Rafael were constructed by neophyte artisans baptized and trained at San Francisco de Asís; it was the first mission to be completely constructed by native builders. Among the names recorded are masons Januario and Pascual; carpenters Ygnacio, Gudelio, Elzeario, Nemesio, Mateo, Lozano, Ligorio, and Luis Gonzaga; and blacksmiths Gervasio and Rogerio.[2] Little is known about the physical appearance of Mission San Rafael, as it was short-lived and remote. The only surviving depictions are the survey map by C. E. Black in 1854 and a memory sketch by General Mariano Guadalupe Vallejo in 1878 for the artist Edward Vischer.

Following the Mexican secularization decree in 1834, Mission San Rafael was one of the first establishments to be confiscated. The mission's assets, as throughout California, were diverted from former neophytes by unscrupulous actions. Rancho Nicasio, for example, consisting of 56,620 acres of San Rafael lands, was granted in 1835 to a group of Indians led by Mission San Francisco de Asís neophyte

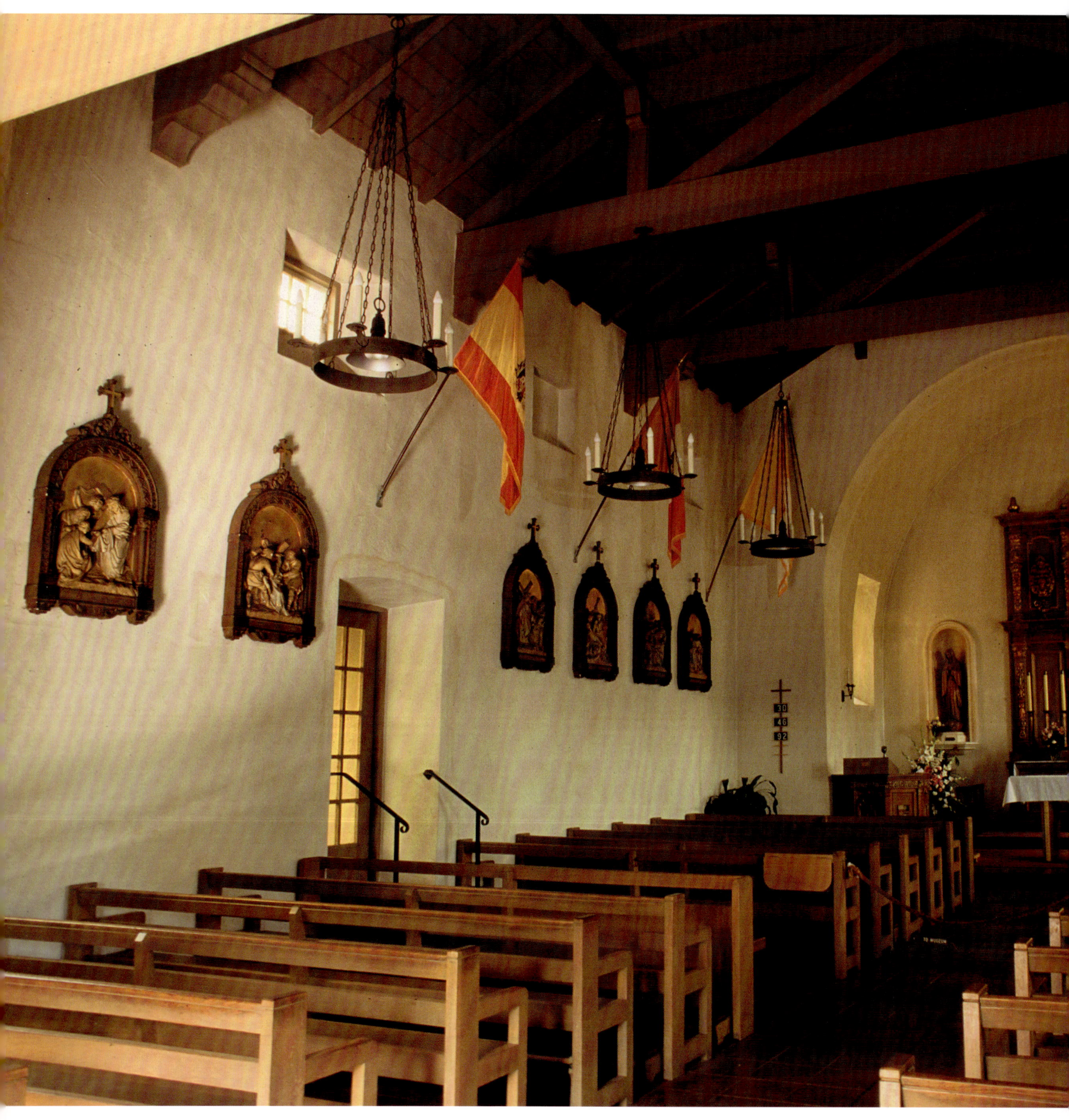
30
46
92

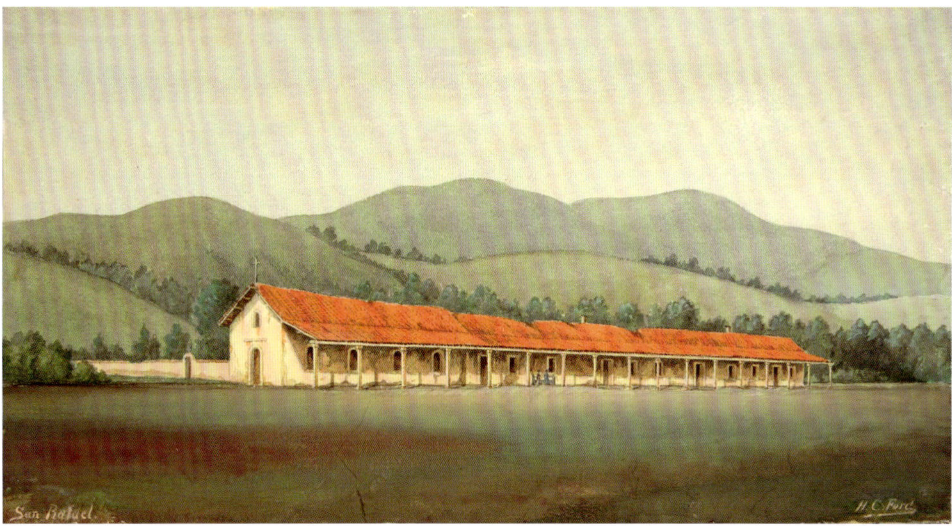

ABOVE: When the artist Henry Chapman Ford visited the site in 1881, "not a solitary wall was standing." This painting is based on the same memory sketch by General M.G. Vallejo that Vischer had used for the drawing seen on p. 246. Ford, however, misinterpreted Vellejo's sketch; the *convento* was perpendicular to the church, not part of a continuous building, as portrayed here. Henry Chapman Ford, *Mission San Rafael*, ca. 1881. Watercolor on canvas. Iris & B. Gerald Cantor Center for Visual Arts at Stanford University, Stanford Family Collections

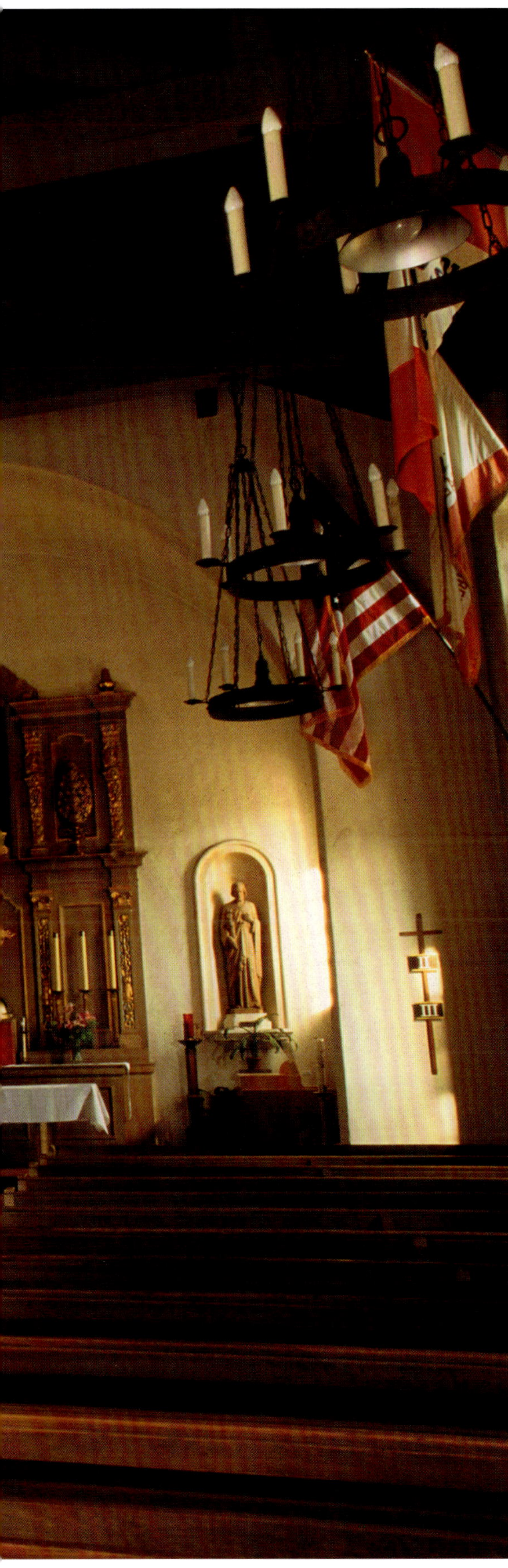

LEFT: Interior view of the replica church. Photograph by G. Aldana

Teodorico Quilaguequi. In 1837, Vallejo took control of the land "in trust," returning only one square league (4,428 acres) to them in 1840. Four years later Governor Manuel Micheltorena assigned the entire Nicasio grant to Pablo de la Guerra and Juan Cooper, with no reference to the prior Indian claim. And, as an ultimate injustice, in 1855 the U.S. Land Commission rejected the claim of Teodorico and his Indian associates for the one league of land Vallejo had left them.

In 1846 the abandoned buildings were occupied by General John C. Frémont, who used the mission as a headquarters during his Bear Flag Revolt. In 1881 the artist Henry Chapman Ford visited the mission site and observed "that not a solitary wall was standing. The space formerly devoted to the mission structures was occupied by a public park in which stood a few of the neglected pear and olive trees of the former garden."[3] Six and a half acres of mission *casco* land was returned to the Catholic Church in 1863, and in 1884 a large gothic church and parish hall were erected on this property by the congregation. Destroyed by fire in 1917, the church was replaced by the current Church of St. Raphael, completed two years later. In 1949, adjacent to this church, a small-sized replica of a simple adobe chapel was constructed of concrete to commemorate the mission origins of the modern parish. Surviving from the original mission facility are three bells and an *enrollado* (scroll) painting of San Rafael Arcángel that once hung behind the mission altar.

San Francisco Solano

FOUNDED JULY 4, 1823

LOCATION: *Sonoma*

FOUNDER: *Father José Altimira*

PRESIDIO DISTRICT: *San Francisco*

PEAK MISSION POPULATION: *996 (1832)*[1]

MAJOR NATIVE GROUPS: *Coast Miwok, Wappo, Lake Miwok, Patwin, Pomo*

HISTORICAL ASSETS: *Adobe walls of part of the* convento *building, constructed in 1825*

EXISTING CHURCH: *1913 restoration of 1841 adobe chapel*

OWNERSHIP: *State of California, Department of Parks and Recreation*

HISTORICAL STATUS: *California Historical Landmark (No. 3)*

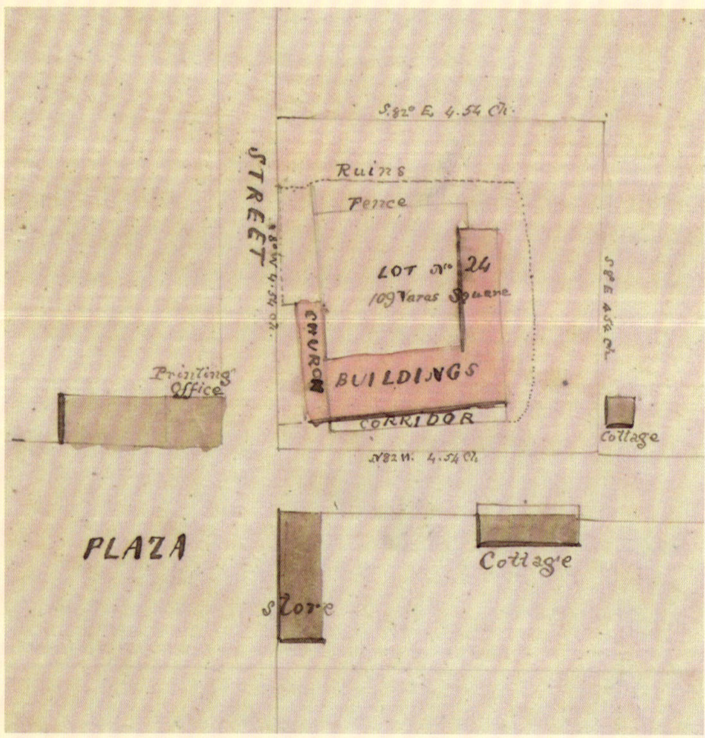

Map of the *casco* by the surveyor George Black, 1854 (detail). Courtesy of The Bancroft Library, University of California, Berkeley

In 1823 the lands of the Napa and Sonoma areas were empty as the tribes had been brought in to Mission San Francisco de Asís in previous years. When the newly arrived friar, Father José Altimira, decided to relocate his mission to this area—for its abundant resources and healthier climate—Father President Señán declared the action illegal. A compromise was reached whereby Mission San Francisco de Asís would remain in place, San Rafael would achieve mission status, and San Francisco Solano would be established at Sonoma with Father Altimira as its friar. In addition, any mission Indians at San Rafael, San Francisco de Asís, or San José who were from the Sonoma area were free to transfer to the new establishment. Some 482 converts from these institutions had settled at San Francisco Solano by the end of 1823, and the first church was dedicated the following year.[2]

The initial workforce at San Francisco Solano, drawn from older institutions, was already skilled, and work began immediately constructing buildings, gardens, and water systems and establishing mission industries. The strong-willed Father Altimira, however, did not get along well with his neophytes and was replaced in 1826 by Father Buenaventura Fortuny from Mission San José. Under his leadership, Mission San Francisco Solano improved its agricultural production and, in 1832, reached a population of nearly one thousand residents. In six years he brought the mission facilities to a par with those of most of the California establishments; these facilities included a quadrangle with a church, a *convento,* a *monjerío,* shops, and storage areas, all of adobe and roofed with tiles; adobe quarters for soldiers' families; and tanning vats and granaries. In 1833 the mission celebrated completion of the large new adobe church that formed the eastern side of the quadrangle, replacing the smaller wooden one on the southwest corner, which was then used for storage. Father Fortuny was eventually succeeded by the popular friar Father José Lorenzo Quijas, from San Francisco de Asís, who left in 1835.

In 1834 Lt. Mariano Guadalupe Vallejo was appointed mission administrator and authorized to establish both a town and a presidio at this northern outpost to rebuff local warring tribes and keep the Russians at bay. He laid out a grid of streets, commandeered mission buildings, moved in the San Francisco Presidio garrison, and encouraged settlers. He also formed an important alliance and friendship with Sem-Yeto (baptized Francisco Solano), a powerful local chief who assisted in defeating neighboring Indian tribes and served as an *alcalde* at the mission.[3]

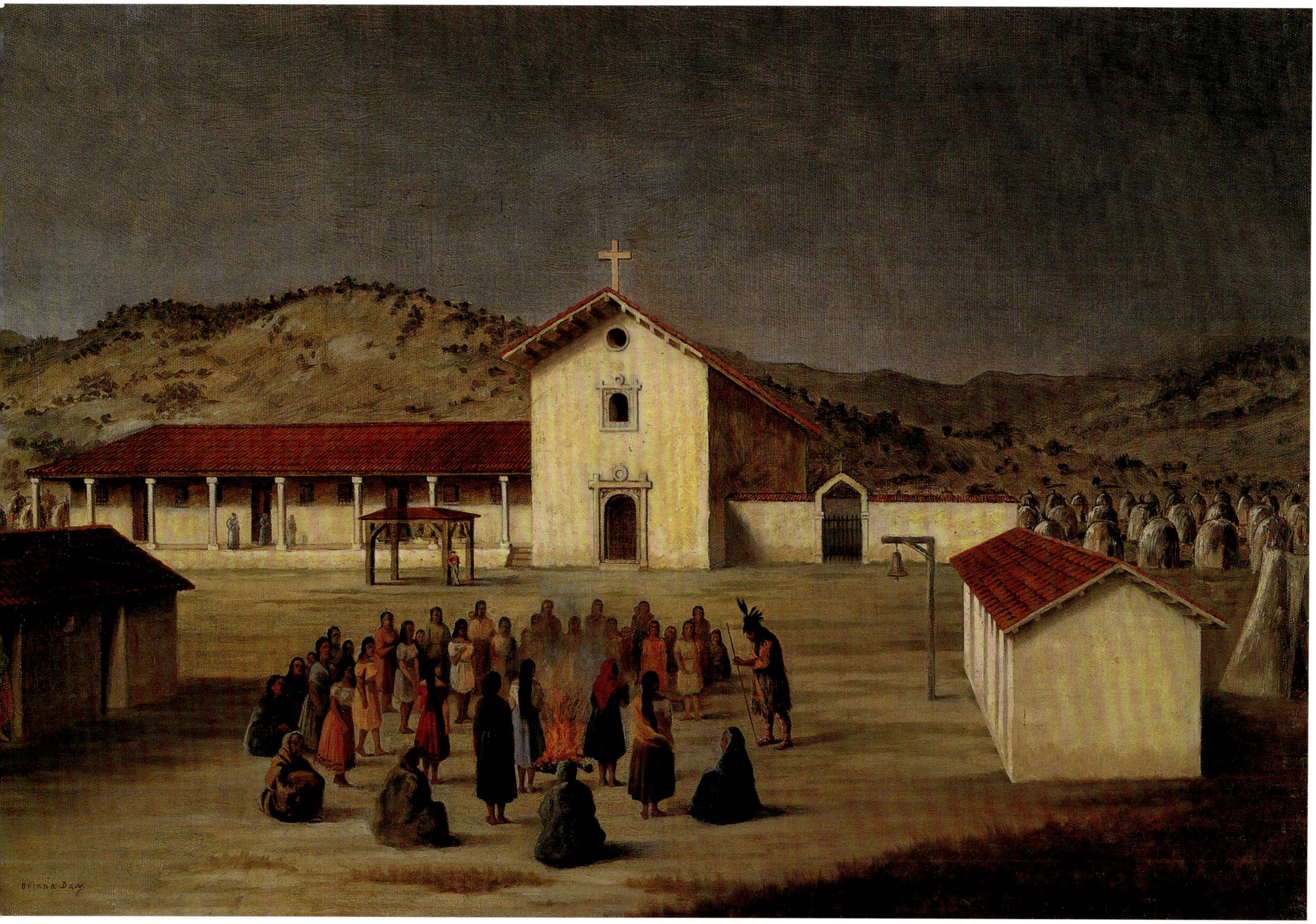

In 1836 Vallejo was appointed commander general of California, and within a few years the former mission lands were virtually all owned or managed by Vallejo's family and friends. Vallejo's own Rancho Petaluma prospered with a workforce of former mission neophytes estimated to number from several hundred to a thousand.[4] Vallejo had established his own small fiefdom on California's northern frontier.

By 1839 the six-year-old San Francisco Solano mission church was in ruins, as were all but a few of the mission buildings, as residents of the growing town helped themselves to roof tiles and other building materials. Benicia Vallejo, General Vallejo's wife, was likely the force behind construction of a new adobe chapel with an American-style rooftop belfry. It was completed in 1841 at the southwest corner of the old mission quadrangle, the site of the original wooden church and adjacent to the surviving *convento.* A refurbishing of the chapel by Vallejo in the 1850s included the addition of arches to the windows and doors, brick sheathing on the facade, and a wooden belfrey. The mission buildings were inconveniently located in the burgeoning

ABOVE: A depiction of the mission complex as a later artist imagined it looked in the 1830s. At center is the large 1833 church, which had fallen to ruin by 1839. To the right is the neophyte *ranchería*. Neophytes listen to a speaker in the plaza. Oriana Weatherbee Day, *Mission San Francisco Solano de Sonoma*, 1877–1884. Oil on canvas, 20 × 30 in. Fine Arts Museums of San Francisco. Gift of Mrs. Eleanor Martin, 37573

BELOW: The 1841 church, damaged by the great 1906 earthquake, lost its facade in 1909. Photograph by C.C. Pierce. Courtesy University of Southern California, on behalf of the USC Special Collections

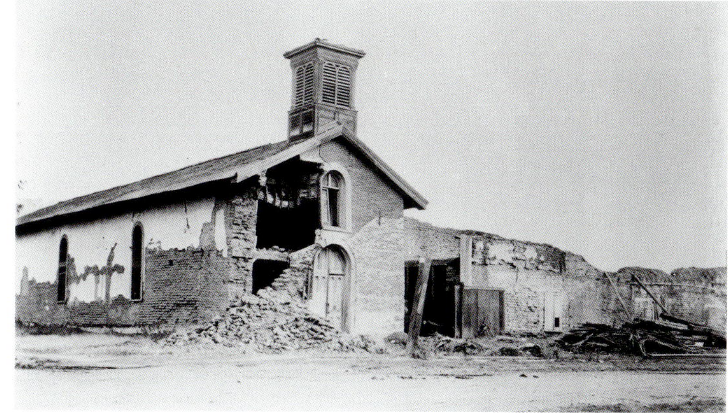

business district, however, and in 1881 the Catholic Church sold the church and the *convento* to finance a new chapel elsewhere in town. The 1841 adobe chapel was subsequently employed as a warehouse and the *convento* leased to businesses until 1903, when the California Historic Landmarks League purchased both properties. By 1906 the League had deeded the property to the state. Restoration efforts were set back by the effects of the 1906 San Francisco earthquake; with assistance from William Randolph Hearst, the first phase was finally completed in 1913. The 1841 adobe chapel had its walls repaired and square windows reinstated, the wooden belfry and brick facade removed, and a tile roof laid; the front half of the *convento* was also roofed and stabilized. Additional restoration efforts continued over time, along with purchase of portions of the old quadrangle until the entire site was owned by the state by 1958. Archaeological studies were carried out on the new parcels, revealing previously unknown rooms and facilities. These and later findings have contributed to current interpretive exhibits that include descriptions of how restoration practices have evolved over time.[5] In 1999 a granite plaque was dedicated, listing the baptismal names of the 837 neophytes buried at the site, the only such memorial at any California mission.

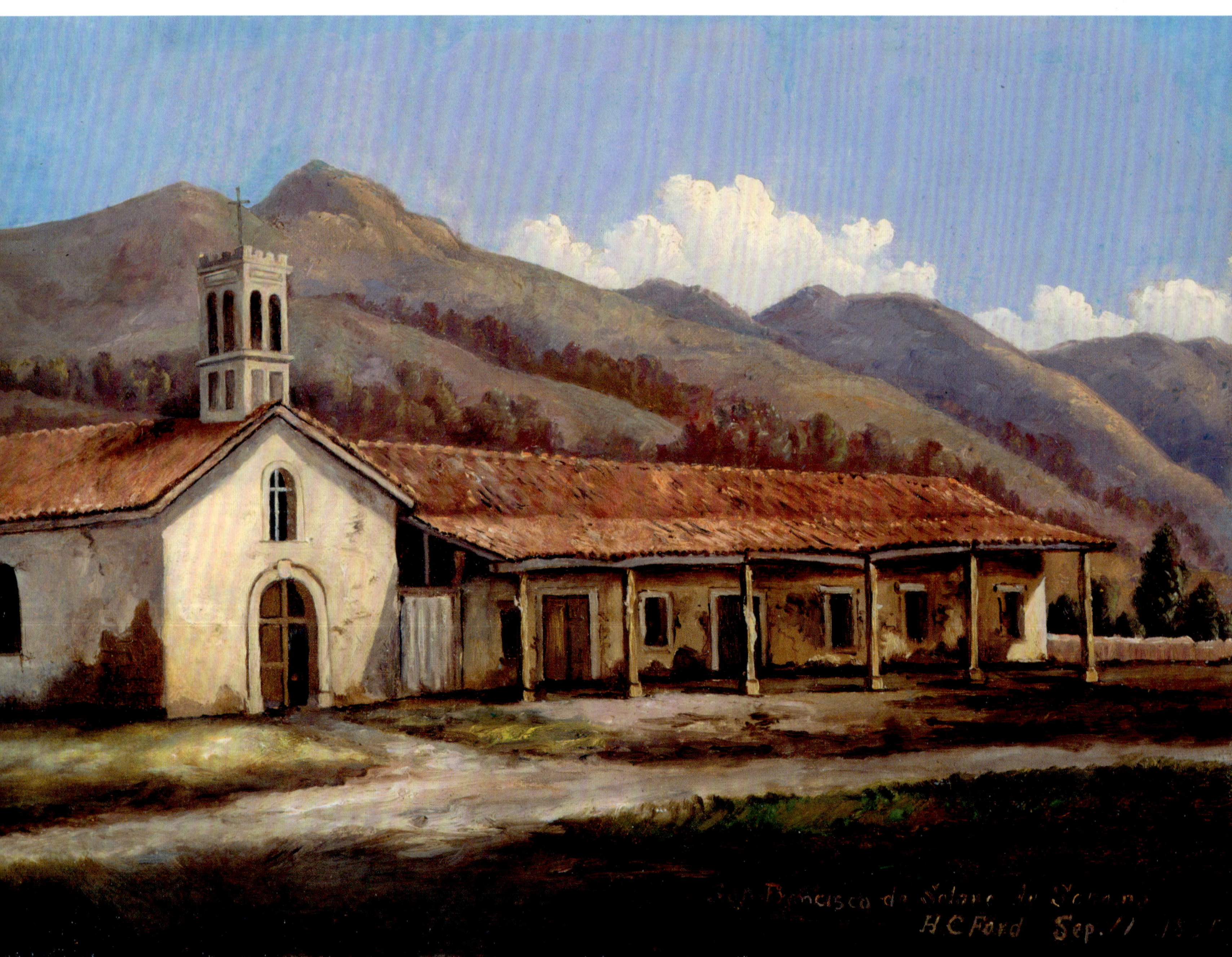

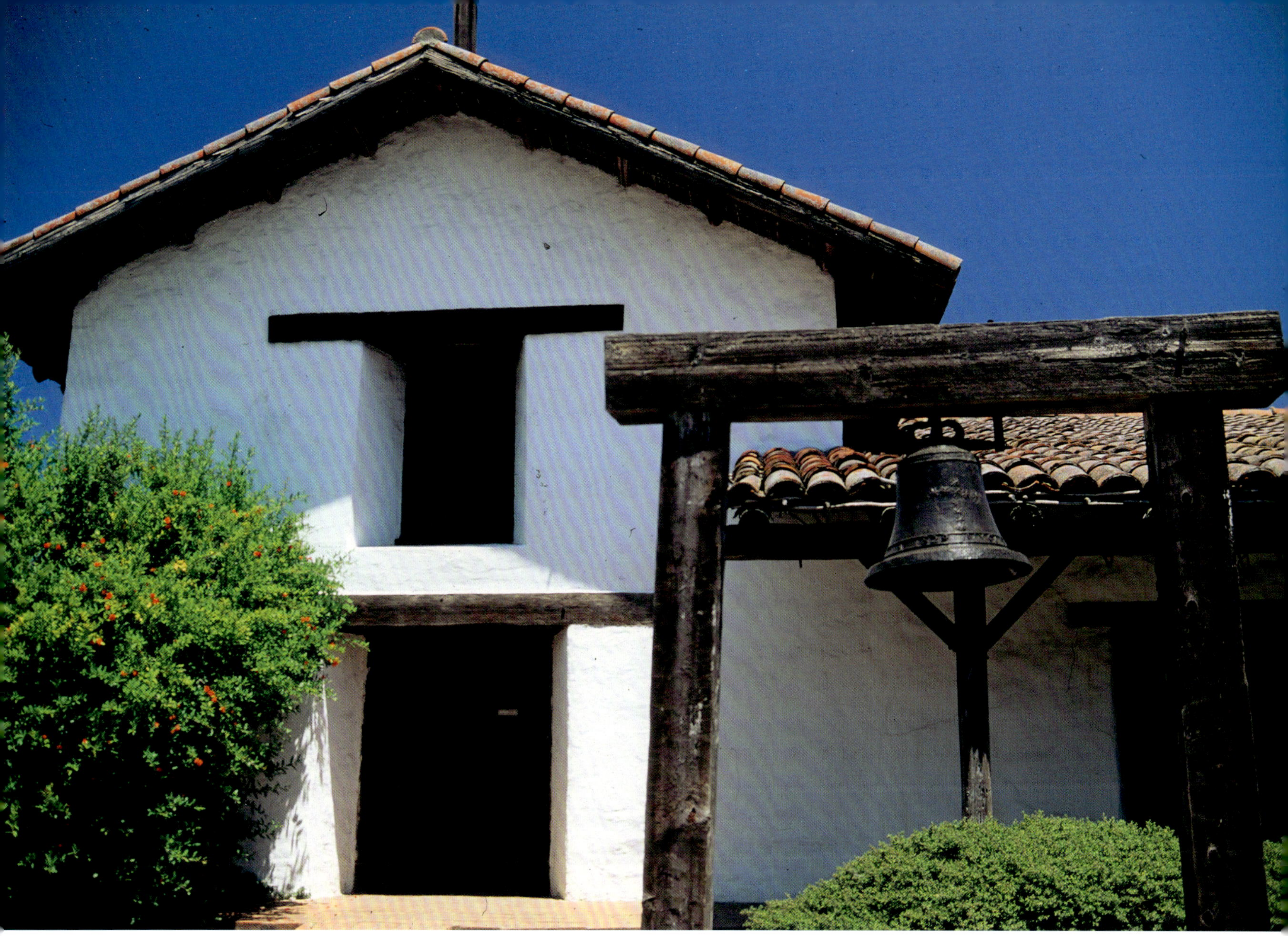

ABOVE: Recent view of the front of the restored mission. Photograph by G. Aldana

OPPOSITE: The mission as it may have appeared in the 1850s, with the American-style belfry. Henry Chapman Ford, *Mission San Francisco de Solano de Sonoma*, 1881. Oil on canvas. Courtesy of the Mission Inn Foundation and Museum, Riverside, California. From the collection of The Historic Mission Inn Corporation

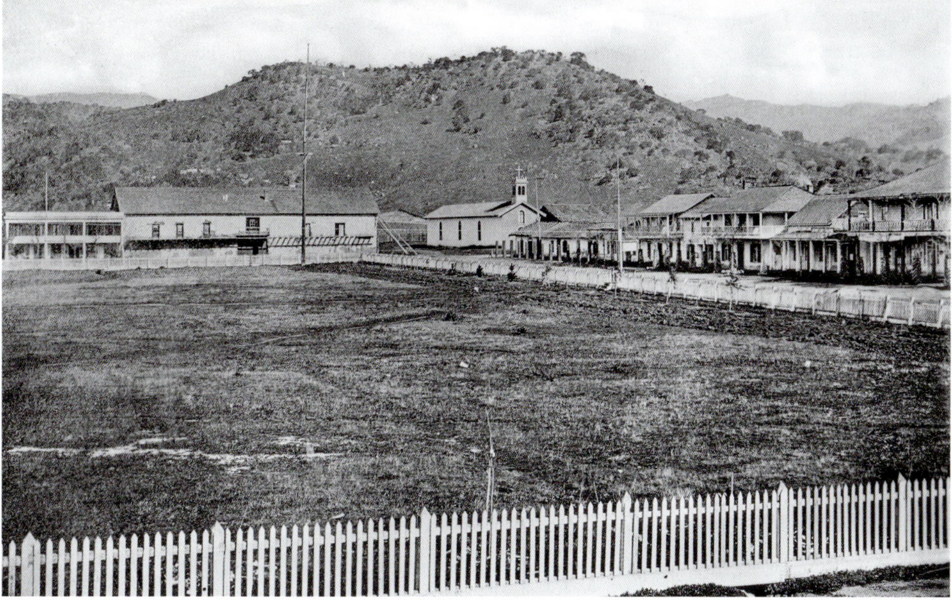

LEFT: View of the young town of Sonoma and Mission San Francisco Solano, ca. 1865. The 1841 church can be seen at rear center. Courtesy University of Southern California, on behalf of the USC Special Collections

Glossary

Some of the historical terms below have had different meanings over time and in different places; the definitions given here are specific to their use in Alta California.

adobe
Building constructed of sun-dried bricks of earth and straw; also, the bricks themselves

alcalde
Local magistrate, usually a member of the municipal council; chief executive officer of a pueblo; or the highest-ranking neophyte in the mission hierarchy

Alta California
Upper California; Spanish and Mexican province including most of the coastal portions of the modern state of California

asistencia
Mission ranch outpost with a chapel that a priest would occasionally visit to conduct religious services

atole
Cooked mixture of water and ground grain; a staple food at the missions

ayuntamiento
Municipal corporation in charge of administering and governing a town; a town council

azoteas
Flat roofs with barrel vaulting or terracing

Baja California
The peninsula of Lower California; now part of Mexico

bajareque
Construction of earth and sticks

balustrade
Railing with distinctive rounded posts

bulto
Carved wooden religious figure

Californio
Regional name for a non-Indian, *gente de razón* (see below) inhabitant of California prior to U.S. annexation

Camino Real
Primary roads between missions; routes varied over time

campanario
General designation for the structure holding a church's bells

camposanto
Church cemetery

canales
Drains, as along a roof

carretas
Long, narrow cart or wagon

casco
Literally, "head"; at a mission the term refers to the central portion where the church, *convento*, neophyte *ranchería*, soldiers' quarters, workshops, and storehouses are located

catechism
Religious instruction

cement
Generic name given to materials that can bind other materials together by setting and hardening independently

chalice
Sacred vessel holding the wine during Mass

ciborium
Device for holding the host during Mass

citarilla
Lattice work of *ladrillos* along a balustrade or railing

comisionado
Noncommissioned soldier (usually a sergeant or corporal) appointed by the commander of the presidio to serve as a liaison between the presidio and the towns or missions. Duties included supervising the *alcalde* and exercising military and judicial authority. With secularization, the *comisionado* also became the temporary supervisor of former missions.

concrete
Composite of coarse granular materials (varying sizes of rocks, gravel, and sand) embedded in a hard matrix of material (binder or cement)

conservation
See **preservation** below. Both *conservation* and *preservation* are used in this volume and in the United States, although *conservation* is the preferred term internationally.*

conservator
Professional concerned with the preservation of an object. Factors considered include determining structural stability, counteracting chemical and physical deterioration, and performing conservation treatment based on an evaluation of the object's aesthetic, historic, and scientific characteristics. Because of the increasingly technical nature of modern conservation, conservators usually specialize in a particular type of object, such as paintings, textiles, sculpture, photographs, or archaeological materials.*

convento
Wing of rooms at a mission housing the priests, and including a *sala*, library, kitchen, and rooms for visitors

criollo
Person born in the New World of peninsular Spanish ancestry

dado
Decoration on the lower part of an interior wall

enconchado
Decorative use of opalescent shell

enrollado
Painting designed to be rolled up, often carried in a leather case during travel

escolta
Group of soldiers assigned to protect, guard, and assist the mission priests

espadaña
Type of *campanario*: a gable or projecting wall pierced with openings where bells are hung

estofado
Decorative technique used on statuary wherein layers of paint or gilding are scratched or pricked to reveal patterns underneath, simulating brocade cloth

fresco
Painting executed on wet plaster, which allows the paint to bond with the wall surface and results in a durable finish

frieze
Decoration on the upper portion of an interior wall

gente de razón
Non-Indian people; literally, "people with the capacity to reason"

gentile
Any non-Christian Indian

gesso
Plaster of paris, gypsum, or chalk prepared with glue for use in painting or making bas-reliefs

host
Wafer used during Mass

imagen para vestir
Statue with moveable joints that can be dressed in different costumes

intervention
Conservation or preservation actions that require removal of or change to historic material

jacal
Construction of closely placed vertical stick framing filled with mud and grasses

ladrillo
Fired, flat tile used for construction; usually rectangular

lavandería
Basin with flowing water for washing clothes

lienzo
Painted canvas altar screen depicting a *retablo*

lime plaster
Coating for walls and ceilings made of quick-lime and sand mixed with water that hardens when dry

matanza
Large, often seasonal slaughtering of herd animals

mayordomo
Foreman or supervisor of a mission under the priest, or of a ranch under the owner

mercantilism
Economic policy restricting trade to the home country

mestizo
Person of mixed European and Indian heritage

missal
Book containing the text and songs for Mass

mission
Community of Roman Catholic clergy, baptized Native American converts, and guards, and encompassing grazing and agricultural lands and local industries; also the physical buildings

monjerío
Separate living quarters at a mission for single Indian women

monstrance
Decorated metal vessel with a transparent section used to display the host

mudéjar
Refers to Moorish influences reflected in the art and architecture of Spain

mural
Paintings executed directly on walls or ceilings

nave
The large portion of the church in front of the altar where the congregation gathers

neophyte
Term used to describe the Christian mission Indians

nichos
Recessed openings or open-sided containers holding representations of saints

plaza
Open area in the center of towns for public gatherings, usually in front of the church

portland cement
Most common hydraulic cement (i.e., capable of hardening underwater) used in the early twentieth century, popular because of its strength and impermeability

preservation
The act or process of applying measures necessary to sustain the existing form, integrity, and materials of a historic site or object. Work generally focuses on the ongoing maintenance and repair of original materials and features rather than extensive replacement and new construction.†

presidio
Fort; military installation housing soldiers, their arms and equipment, their families, and a church

pueblo
Town; a secular community established by the government to promote civilian settlement

ranchería
Indian village or settlement, usually used by the Spanish to refer to non-Christian Indians, but the term became widely used for any Native American community

ranchero
Owner of a rancho

rancho
Ranch; designates both specialized areas of mission lands and private landholdings

reconstruction
The act or process of depicting by means of new construction the form, features, and detailing of a nonsurviving site, landscape, building, structure, or object for the purpose of replicating its appearance at a specific period in time and in its historic location.†

reducción
Colonial process of resettling baptized neophytes at the mission *casco*

reliquary
Container holding a relic of a saint

render
Typically refers to an exterior plaster

reredos
French term for *retablo*

restoration
The act or process of accurately depicting the form, features, and character of a property as it appeared at a particular period by means of the removal of features from other periods in its history and reconstruction of missing features from the period of its restoration.†

retablo
Elaborate backdrop behind the altar that depicts or holds religious images; made of wood, stone, or plaster, or painted on canvas or directly on the wall

retrofitting
Strengthening a building to withstand earthquakes

reverbero
Wall candleholder backed with fragments of mirror that reflect the flame

sacristy
Room adjoining the church where religious items and vestments are kept

sala
Sitting room for receiving guests

sanctuary
Sacred area in the front of the church, behind the communion rail

Stations of the Cross
Fourteen formalized events that occurred as Jesus walked the road to Calvary; depictions of these events are typically hung along the walls of the church nave

tabernacle
Cupboard-like receptacle on the altar where the consecrated host and wine are kept

teja
Curved, fired tile used for roofing

temescal
Aztec word for a sweathouse used for purification

tomol
Wooden plank canoe made by the Chumash

torre
Four-sided bell tower

vaquero
Horseman who works with cattle; cowboy

Vía Crucis
Set of fourteen Stations of the Cross (see **Stations of the Cross** above)

vidrios
Nicho enclosed in glass, for keeping statues

zaguán
Wide passageway for *carretas*

---

* Source: American Institute for the Conservation of Historic and Artistic Works; http://aic.stanford.edu/.
† Source: Kay D. Weeks and Anne E. Grimmer, *The Secretary of the Interior's Standards for the Treatment of Historic Properties with Guidelines for Preserving, Rehabilitating, Restoring & Reconstructing Historic Buildings* (Washington, D.C.: U.S. Department of the Interior, National Park Service, Cultural Resources Stewardship and Partnership, Heritage Preservation Services, 1995).

Notes

Introduction

1 D. Monroy, "Death and Birth: The Missions of California," in Monroy, *The Border Within: Encounters between Mexico and the U.S.* (Tucson: University of Arizona Press, 2008), 154.

Chapter 1: Colonizing California

1 R. L. Oswalt, *Kashaya Texts,* University of California Publications in Linguistics 36 (Berkeley: University of California Press, 1964), 245–47.

2 R. F. Heizer, ed., *California,* vol. 8 of *Handbook of North American Indians* (Washington, D.C.: Smithsonian Institution Press, 1978), 1; W. F. Shipley, "Native Languages of California," in Heizer, ed., *California;* R. Carrico, *Strangers in the Strange Land: Indians of San Diego County from Prehistory to the New Deal* (San Diego: Sunbelt Publications, 2008), 25.

3 L. J. Bean and H. W. Lawton, "Some Explanations for the Rise of Cultural Complexity in Native California with Comments on Proto-Agriculture and Agriculture," in *Before the Wilderness: Environmental Management by Native Californians,* comp. and ed. T. C. Blackburn and K. Anderson (Menlo Park, Calif.: Ballena Press, 1993), 27–54.

4 B. M. Fagan, *Before California: An Archaeologist Looks at Our Earliest Inhabitants* (Walnut Creek, Calif.: Rowman and Littlefield, 2003), 360; R. Milliken, *A Time of Little Choice: The Disintegration of Tribal Culture in the San Francisco Bay Area, 1769–1810* (Menlo Park, Calif.: Ballena Press, 1995), 219. M. K. Anderson, M. G. Barbout, and V. Whitworth, "A World of Balance and Plenty: Land, Plants, Animals, and Humans in a Pre-European California," in *Contested Eden: California before the Gold Rush,* ed. R. A. Gutiérrez and R. Orsi (Berkeley: University of California Press, 1998), 12–47.

5 Fr. G. Boscana, *Chinigchinich: A Revised and Annotated Version of Alfred Robinson's Translation of Father Gerónimo Boscana's Historical Account of the... Acagchemem Tribe* (Banning, Calif.: Malki Museum Press, 1978), 38.

6 T. Hudson and E. Underhay, *Crystals in the Sky: An Intellectual Odyssey Involving Chumash Astronomy, Cosmology, and Rock Art,* Ballena Press Anthropological Papers No. 10 (Santa Barbara, Calif.: Santa Barbara Museum of Natural History, 1978), 29 and Appendix.

7 M. Margolin, *The Ohlone Way: Indian Life in the San Francisco–Monterey Bay Area* (Berkeley: Heyday Books, 1978).

8 Ibid., 147.

9 T. Hudson, T. Blackburn, R. Curletti, and J. Timbrook, *The Eye of the Flute: Chumash Traditional History and Ritual as Told by Fernando Librado Kitseqawit to John P. Harrington* (Santa Barbara, Calif.: Santa Barbara Museum of Natural History, 1977), 37. Chumash narratives titled "The Three Worlds" and "The Making of Man" in J. Hicks et al., eds., *The Literature of California,* vol. 1, *Native Beginnings to 1945* (Berkeley: University of California Press, 2000), 37.

10 C. W. Meighan and R. F. Heizer, "Archaeological Exploration of Sixteenth-Century Indian Mounds at Drake's Bay," *California Historical Quarterly* 31, no. 2 (1952): 99–100; E. P. Von der Porten, "Drake and Cermeño in California: Sixteenth-Century Chinese Ceramics," *Historical Archaeology* 6 (1972): 1–22; and "The Drake Puzzle Solved," *Pacific Discovery* 37, no. 3 (1984): 22–26; C. Shangraw and E. P. Von der Porten, *The Drake and Cermeño Expeditions' Chinese Porcelains at Drakes Bay, California, 1579 and 1595* (Santa Rosa and Palo Alto, Calif.: Santa Rosa Junior Collect and Drake Navigators Guild, 1981). The Kashaya Pomo, living on the periphery of the reach of the Spanish missions, would suffer their own European encounter when the Russians operated a mercantile colony at Fort Ross from 1812 to 1841. See K.G. Lightfoot, *Indians, Missionaries, and Merchants: The Legacy of Colonial Encounters on the California Frontiers* (Berkeley: University of California Press, 2005).

11 In F. Palóu, *Palóu's Life of Fray Junípero Serra,* trans. and annot. M. J. Geiger, O.F.M. (Washington, D.C.: Academy of American Franciscan History, 1955), 75.

12 His life's work of envisioning, inspiring, and managing the conversion of native peoples has resulted in his recent promotion for sainthood—an honor not without controversy, in view of the devastating impact of the Spanish colony on the native peoples of California.

13 Palóu, *Palóu's Life of Fray Junípero Serra,* 92.

14 Z. Engelhardt, O.F.M., *Mission La Concepción Purísima de Maria Santísima* (Santa Barbara, Calif.: Mission Santa Barbara, 1932), 22, 177. Mission San Francisco de Asís also suffered from the cold and damp that plague today's residents in that modern city. San Rafael was founded as an adjunct where produce would thrive and ill neophytes were sent to recover. It eventually achieved status as an independent mission.

15 Compiled in collaboration with J. Johnson, R. Milliken, and R. Carrico.

16 H. H. Bancroft, *History of California,* vol. 1, *1542–1800* (San Francisco: History Company, 1886), 177.

17 A. Ogden, *The California Sea Otter Trade: 1748–1848* (Berkeley: University of California Press, 1941); R. Archibald, *The Economic Aspects of the California Missions* (Washington, D.C.: Academy of American Franciscan History, 1978).

18 Palóu, *Life of Fray Junípero Serra,* 93–94.

19 In Milliken, *A Time of Little Choice,* 62. On the difference between Spanish and Native American accounts of early encounters at Mission San Gabriel, see D. Monroy, *Thrown Among Strangers: The Making of Mexican Culture in Frontier California* (Berkeley and Los Angeles: University of California Press, 1990), 3–18 and *passim.*

20 S. B. Dakin, *A Scotch Paisano in Old Los Angeles: Hugo Reid's Life in California, 1832–1852, Derived from His Correspondence* (Berkeley: University of California Press, Berkeley, 1939); the quote at the top of p. 20 is from p. 261. The quote at the top of p. 21 is from Palóu, *Life of Fray Junípero Serra,* p. 119.

21 Dakin, *A Scotch Paisano in Old Los Angeles,* 262.

22 R. L. Carrico, "Sociopolitical Aspects of the 1775 Revolt at Mission San Diego de Alcalá: An Ethnohistorical Approach," *Journal of San Diego History* 43, no. 3 (1997).

23 Dakin, *A Scotch Paisano in Old Los Angeles,* 261–62.

24 E. Duflot de Mofras, *Exploration du territoire de l'Orégon, des Californies et de la mer Vermeille, exécuté e pendant les années 1840, 1841, et 1842,* 2 vols. and atlas (Paris: A. Bertrand, 1844), cited in L. T. Burcham, *California Range Land* (California Division of Forestry, Sacramento, 1957; rpt. Center for Archaeological Research at Davis, Publication No. 7, 1982), 120.

25 A single *barjareque* interior partition wall survives in the *tapanco* (loft) of the *convento* of Mission San José.

26 The first adobe churches were generally temporary, until a larger building could be undertaken, and because of their size they were commonly converted to granaries when replaced.

27 No complete *casco* remains today. Extensive reconstructions and re-creations have taken place at Missions La Purísima and San Antonio, but even these are lacking neophyte quarters, granaries, storehouses, and other key facilities.

28 A. B. Duhaut-Cilly, "Duhaut-Cilly's Account of California in the Years 1827–28," trans. C. F. Carter, *California Historical Society Quarterly* 8 (1929): 228.

29 Ibid.

30 J. Bandini, *A Description of California in 1828,* trans. D. M. Wright, Bancroft Library Publications, No. 3 (Berkeley: Friends of the Bancroft Library, 1951).

31 Alfred Robinson, who later married Ana María de la Guerra in Santa Barbara, wrote of his experiences in *Life in California during a Residence of Several Years in That Territory* (New York: Da Capo Press, 1969), 24.

32 G. H. Freiher von Langsdorff, *Voyages and Travels in Various Parts of the World, during the Years*

1803, 1804, 1805, 1806, and 1807; Part II (London: Henry Colburn, 1814), 195. Langsdorff was with the Russian Rezanov party that visited California in 1806 on the *Juno* to try to obtain supplies for the suffering colony in Sitka, Alaska.

33 G. H. Freiher von Langsdorff, *Langsdorff's Narrative of the Rezanov Voyage to Nueva California in 1806...* (San Francisco: Thomas C. Russell, 1927), 66.

34 Langsdorff, *Voyages and Travels*, 195–96.

35 Extensive studies of native languages were made by Father Gerónimo Boscana at Mission San Juan Capistrano (published as *Chinigchinich*) and can be seen in M. S. Beeler, ed., *The Ventureño Confesionario of José Señán, O.F.M.*, University of California Publications in Linguistics No. 47 (Berkeley: University of California, 1967); and Fr. F. Arroyo de la Cuesta, *Grammar of the Mutsun Language Spoken at the Mission of San Juan Bautista, Alta California* (New York 1861).

36 Dakin, *A Scotch Paisano in Old Los Angeles*, 265.

37 Some missions reported using translations in as many as four dialects to serve their varied communities. M. Geiger, trans. and comm., *As the Padres Saw Them: California Indian Life and Customs as Reported by the Franciscan Missionaries, 1813–1815* (Santa Barbara, Calif.: Santa Barbara Mission Archive-Library, 1976), 53–55.

38 Geiger, *As the Padres Saw Them*, 47–51, 57–60.

39 Ibid., 57.

40 J. Sandos, *Converting California: Indians and Franciscans in the Missions* (New Haven: Yale University Press, 2004), 182.

41 A. Schabelski, "Visit of the Russian Warship *Apollo* to California in 1822–1823," *Southern California Quarterly* 75, no. 1 (1993): 6.

42 P. Tac, "Indian Life and Customs at Mission San Luis Rey: A Record of California Mission Life Written by Pablo Tac, an Indian neophyte [Rome, California, 1835]," ed. and trans. M. Hewes and G. Hewes, *The Americas* 9, no. 1 (1952): 99.

43 Lightfoot, *Indians, Missionaries, and Merchants*, 93–96.

44 T. Hudson, ed., *Breath of the Sun: Life in Early California as Told by a Chumash Indian, Fernando Librado to John P. Harrington* (Banning, Calif.: Malki Museum Press, 1979), 17.

45 L. Asisara, "The Assassination of Padre Andrés Quintana by the Indians of Mission Santa Cruz in 1812: The Narrative of Lorenzo Asisara," trans. and introd. E. D. Castillo, *California History* 68, no. 3 (1989): 117–25; R. M. Beebe and R. M. Senkewicz, eds., *Lands of Promise and Despair: Chronicles of Early California, 1535–1846* (Berkeley: Heyday Books, 2001), 284–97; E. D. Castillo, "The Native Response to Colonization," in *Columbian Consequences*, vol. 1, *Archaeological and Historical Perspectives on the Spanish Borderlands West*, ed. D. H. Thomas (Washington, D.C.: Smithsonian Institution Press, 1989), 377–94.

46 A. Forbes, *California: A History of Upper and Lower California* (San Francisco: John Henry Nash, 1937; rpt. New York: Kraus Reprint Co., 1972).

47 J. G. Costello, "Not Peas in a Pod: Documenting Diversity among the California Missions," in *Text-Aided Archaeology*, ed. B. J. Little (Boca Raton, Fla.: CRC Press, 1991), 67–81.

48 Tac, "Indian Life and Customs at Mission San Luis Rey," 100.

49 Robinson, *Life in California*, 34–35, 58, 59, 80.

50 The southern California missions—San Luis Rey, San Juan Capistrano, and San Diego—did not practice *reducción* but allowed their neophytes to continue to reside on their traditional lands. Today these are among the strongest and most intact native groups in California. Lightfoot, *Indians, Missionaries, and Merchants*.

51 J. G. Costello, E. Kimbro, and L. Wilcoxon, *National Historic Landmark, Mission Santa Inés* (Washington, D.C.: National Park Service, 1997).

52 Paolo Emilio Botta, twenty-five-year-old ship's doctor on the visiting ship *Herós*, 1827–28. P. E. Botta, "Paolo Emilio Botta's Observations on the Inhabitants of California," trans. A. M. Appel, *Boletín: The Journal of the California Mission Studies Association* 23, no. 2 (2006) and 24, no. 1 (2007): 59–76.

53 Langsdorff, *Voyages and Travels*, 168.

54 Milliken, *A Time of Little Choice*, 1–2, 136, 219–26; S. W. Hackel, *Children of Coyote, Missionaries of Saint Francis: Indian-Spanish Relations in Colonial California, 1769–1850* (Durham: University of North Carolina Press, 2005).

55 S. W. Hackel, "Land, Labor, and Production: The Colonial Economy of Spanish and Mexican California," in Gutiérrez and Orsi, eds., *Contested Eden*, 132.

56 R. H. Dana, *Two Years before the Mast: A Personal Narrative of Life at Sea* (New York: Macmillan, 1911; rpt. New York: Mayflower Books, 1980), 181.

57 William Hartnell, married to Teresa de la Guerra, was appointed *visitador general* of the secularized former missions of California from 1839 to 1840. W. Hartnell, *The Diary and Copybook of William E. P. Hartnell: Visitador General of the Missions of Alta California in 1839 and 1840*, trans. S. P. Gurcke, ed. with annot., introd., and prol. G. J. Farris (Santa Clara, Calif. and Spokane, Wash.), 45, 60.

58 Beebe and Senkewicz, eds., *Lands of Promise and Despair*, 470.

59 Dana, *Two Years before the Mast*, 142.

60 Hartnell, *Diary and Copybook*, 14.

61 W. A. Beck and Y. D. Haase, *Historical Atlas of California* (Norman: University of Oklahoma Press, 1974).

62 Hartnell, *Diary and Copybook*, 36.

Chapter 2: Ruins, Romance, and Revival

1 Miller did not visit Mission San Francisco Solano (Sonoma) or San Rafael.

2 H. Miller, *Account of a Tour of the California Missions and Towns, 1856: The Journal and Drawings of Henry Miller* (Santa Barbara, Calif.: Bellerophon Books, 1985), 3.

3 The Treaty of Guadalupe Hidalgo was signed on February 2, 1848, in the Cathedral of Guadalupe in Villa Hidalgo, just north of Mexico City.

4 J. S. Holiday, *The World Rushed In: The California Gold Rush Experience* (New York: Simon and Schuster, 1981), 26.

5 The Land Law of 1851 opened up challenges to landownership guaranteed by the Treaty of Guadalupe Hidalgo (L. Pitt, *The Decline of the Californios* [Berkeley: University of California Press, 1966], 65).

6 Earthquakes in 1857 and 1868 would bring down walls at many of the northern California missions, accelerating the effects of abandonment.

7 E. Bryant, *What I Saw in California: Being a Journal of a Tour, by the Emigrant Route and South Pass of the Rocky Mountains, across the Continent of North America, the Great Desert Basin, and through California, in the Years 1846, 1847* (New York: D. Appleton & Co., 1848).

8 F. Walker, *San Francisco's Literary Frontier* (New York: Knopf, 1939), 128–29.

9 Quoted in N. G. Weinberg, "Historic Preservation and Tradition in California: The Restoration of the Missions and the Spanish-Colonial Revival" (Ph.D. dissertation, University of California, Davis, 1976), 92.

10 F. J. Weber, Msgr., *The California Missions* (Strasbourg: Éditions du Signe, 2005), 235. Bishop Alemany, through the U.S. State Department, compelled Mexico to return to the California Diocese some of the Pious Fund moneys obtained from the sale of mission lands and deposited in the Mexican treasury. Final adjudication of this issue, in 1902, was reached by the International Board of Arbitration at The Hague (P. W. Riordan, *Catholic Encyclopedia*: Joseph Sadoc Alemany, www.domcentral.org/trade/ce/alemany.htm, 2007). In addition, Alemany unsuccessfully petitioned the U.S. Land Commission to set up one square league around each mission as a land base for the Indians (J. R. Johnson, *The Chumash Indians after Secularization*, Keepsake Volume [Santa Clara: California Mission Studies Association, 1995], 11).

11 The San Juan Capistrano chapel was leased in the early years for hay storage, which may be why the tile roof remained intact, and not because of any local reverence for the building (P. C. Johnson, ed., *The California Missions: A Pictorial History* [Menlo Park, Calif.: Sunset Books, Lane Book Co., 1964]), 146. Other mission churches, however, such as San Rafael, San Miguel, Santa Cruz, San José, and Solano, deteriorated despite the presence of towns. The Plaza Church in Los Angeles, not actually a mission, also survived as an important church for the surrounding community.

12 Miller, *Account of a Tour of the California Missions*, 37, 48–49.

13 Ibid., 42.

14 The traveler J. Ross Browne, quoted in M. B. Hoover, D. E. Kyle, and H. Rensch, *Historic Spots in California* (Palo Alto, Calif.: Stanford University Press, 2002), 234.

15 Miller, *Account of a Tour of the California Missions and Towns*, 3, 29.

16 Johnson, *The California Missions*, 54.

17 H. Kelsey, *Mission San Luis Rey: A Pocket History* (n.p.: Published by the author, 1993), 24.

18 This practice had begun during the secularization of the Mexican period. In 1834, for example, the new *mayordomo* of Mission La Purísima had delivered to Father Jimeno at Mission Santa Inés the "vestments, sacred vessels, and other treasures of the church," valued at nearly $5,000 (Z. Engelhardt, O.F.M., *Mission Santa Inés, Virgen y Mártir, and Its Ecclesiastical Seminary* [Santa Barbara, Calif.: Mission Santa Barbara, 1932], 57–60).

19 Construction began in 1851; it was dedicated as the Immaculate Conception of the Blessed Virgin Mary in 1858.

20 B. Casey, *Padres and People of Old Mission San*

Antonio (King City, Calif.: Rustler-Herald, 1957; rpt. King City, Calif.: Casey Newspapers, 1976), 82–86.

21 Robert Louis Stevenson, *Across the Plains* (1883; reprint, Albion Press, 1987), chap. 2. Stevenson apparently forgot that the missions were Franciscan, not Jesuit.

22 See S. Shields, *Edwin Deakin: California Painter of the Picturesque* (Sacramento: Crocker Art Museum, 2008), 72–74.

23 N. Neuerburg, "The California Missions in Art, 1786–1890," in J. Stern, G. J. Miller, P. Hallan-Gibson, and N. Neuerburg, *Romance of the Bells: The California Missions in Art* (Irvine, Calif.: Irvine Museum, 1995), 92; J. Stern, "The California Missions in Art, 1890 to 1930," in Stern et al., *Romance of the Bells,* 97.

24 N. Neuerburg, "The California Missions in Art," in Stern et al., *Romance of the Bells,* 88; Shields, *Edwin Deakin.*

25 "The Painter of the California Missions," *Outlook,* January 1904. Other artists included J. Henry Sandham, who accompanied Helen Hunt Jackson on several of her travels around California and illustrated a 1900 edition of *Ramona;* the landscape artists William Keith and Thomas Hill; Oriana Day; and Lemuel Wiles.

26 Quoted in Weinberg, "Historic Preservation and Tradition in California," 93, 94.

27 In *Across the Plains,* 106–7.

28 Stevenson was writing as "The Monterey Barbarian" in the *Monterey Californian,* November 11, 1879. Reprinted in *Scribner's Magazine* 67, no. 2 (August 1920): 209–11.

29 Knowland, in Weinberg, "Historic Preservation and Tradition in California," 86.

30 Weinberg, "Historic Preservation and Tradition in California," 3.

31 Weber, *The California Missions,* 237.

32 Doris Sky, Women's Hall of Fame, Colorado, www.cogreatwomen.org/jackson.htm. September 2007.

33 Jackson's commentaries had previously been published as articles in the *Independent* and *Scribner's Monthly.*

34 S. F. Cook, *Historical Demography*, 92; in Heizer, ed., *California*, 91–98.

35 Cook, *Historical Demography.*

36 V. S. Mathes, "Helen Hunt Jackson and the California Mission Indians: Selected Letters," *Boletín: The Journal of the California Mission Studies Association* 23, no. 2 (2007): 5–23. Jackson and Kinney's 56-page report included specific recommendations: resurvey and marking of reservations, removal of intruders, construction of more schools, and the hiring of a law firm to advocate for the mission Indians. The Jackson/Kinney report was promptly approved by President Chester Arthur and turned into a bill that passed in the House but was defeated in the Senate. Most of its recommendations were finally implemented in the 1891 Act for the Relief of the Mission Indians in the State of California. See also A. May, *Helen Hunt Jackson: A Lonely Voice of Conscience* (San Francisco: Chronicle Books, 1987).

37 K. Starr, *Inventing the Dream: California through the Progressive Era* (New York: Oxford University Press, 1985), 57–63.

38 H. H. Jackson, *Glimpses of California and the Missions* (New York: Little, Brown, 1907), 91.

39 *San Francisco Evening Bulletin*, May 8, 1872.

40 Jackson, *Glimpses of California and the Missions*, 88–100.

41 Mathes, "Helen Hunt Jackson and the California Mission Indians," 20.

42 Jackson did not live to see the full effect of *Ramona*; she died of cancer in August 1885, at the age of fifty-five.

43 D. DeLyser, *Ramona Memories: Tourism and the Shaping of Southern California* (Minneapolis: University of Minnesota Press, 2005), xi.

44 Starr, *Inventing the Dream,* 61. See also D. Fine, *Imagining Los Angeles: A City in Fiction* (Las Vegas: University of Nevada Press, 2004), 30–34; and W. A. McClung, *Landscapes of Desire: Anglo Mythologies of Los Angeles* (Berkeley: University of California Press, 2002), passim.

45 In 1901 the magazine was renamed *Out West.*

46 See M. Thompson, *American Character: The Curious Life of Charles Fletcher Lummis and the Rediscovery of the Southwest* (New York: Arcade Publishing, 2001).

47 Starr, *Inventing the Dream,* 85.

48 K. J. Weitze, *California's Mission Revival,* California Architecture and Architects, No. 3, ed. D. Gebhard (Los Angeles: Hennessey and Ingalls, 1984), 15.

49 Ibid., 16.

50 H. Kirker, *California's Architectural Frontier* (Santa Barbara, Calif.: Peregrine Smith, 1973), 87.

51 N. Hata, *The Historic Preservation Movement in California, 1940–1976* (Sacramento: California Department of Parks and Recreation, 1992), 4.

52 Weitze, *California's Mission Revival,* 141 n. 23.

53 Ibid., 13.

54 Quoted in Thompson, *American Character,* 185–86.

55 Thompson, *American Character*, 186.

56 W. Deverell, *Whitewashed Adobe: The Rise of Los Angeles and the Remaking of Its Mexican Past* (Berkeley: University of California Press, 2005), 49–91.

57 Starr, *Inventing the Dream*, 89. For a thorough account of the *Mission Play*, see Deverell, *Whitewashed Adobe*, 207–49.

58 Weitze, *California's Mission Revival*, 93.

59 Ibid.

60 Ibid., 84.

61 K. E. Pauley and C. M. Pauley, *San Fernando, Rey de España: An Illustrated History* (Santa Clara, Calif. and Spokane, Wash.: CMSA and Arthur H. Clark Company), 275–77.

62 The league consisted of the Society of California Pioneers, Pioneer Women, Daughters of California Pioneers, Young Men's Institute, Women's Press Association, Native Sons of the Golden West, Native Daughters of the Golden West, San Francisco Teachers' Club, Sons of Exempt Firemen, and the California Club. Hata, *Historic Preservation Movement in California*, 5–7.

63 Weinberg, *Historic Preservation*, 142–43.

64 Kelsey, *Mission San Luis Rey*, 30–32. Other notable efforts were carried out by Father Alexander Buckler at Mission Santa Inés, Father Ricardo Valentin Closa at Mission San Juan Bautista, and Father St. John O'Sullivan at Mission San Juan Capistrano. Hata, *Historic Preservation Movement in California*, 7.

65 A. S. C. Forbes, *California Missions and Landmarks* (Los Angeles: Published by the author, 1925), 354–55, cited in Weinberg, *Historic Preservation*, 145.

66 Weinberg, *Historic Preservation*, 146. Weinberg notes that "the original bell guideposts carried a placard" directing tourists to the missions and other historical landmarks, "but this ceased to be practical with the advent of good roads and high speed automobiles."

67 Weinberg, *Historic Preservation*, 124–39.

68 Jackson, *Glimpses of California and the Missions;* D. P Elder, *The Old Spanish Missions of California* (1913).

Chapter 3: Restoration and Reconstruction

1 C. B. Hosmer Jr., *Preservation Comes of Age: From Williamsburg to the National Trust, 1926–1949* (Charlottesville: University Press of Virginia, 1981), 1:427–28.

2 Ibid., 378. In the first group of seventy-eight registered landmarks was Mission San Francisco Solano and the San Diego Presidio. Thirty-three other landmarks were related to Spanish and Mexican California, including explorers (Portolá and Anza), mission-related facilities (aqueducts, *asistencias*), and Californios' casas.

3 S. B. Woodbridge, *California Architecture: Historic American Buildings Survey* (San Francisco: Chronicle Books, 1988). This material is available online at www.cr.nps.gov/hdp/habs. Those missions where HABS drawings were not completed are San Carlos Borromeo, Santa Cruz, Soledad, San José, San Rafael, and Solano. La Purísima drawings were part of the CCC reconstruction discussed below. Documentation was also completed for the Royal Presidio Chapel in Monterey, the Plaza Church in Los Angeles, and the San Francisco de Pala *asistencia.*

4 Engelhardt, *Mission La Concepción Purísima de María Santísima*, 115–21.

5 The site had been deeded briefly to the Landmarks Club by Union Oil in 1906 but was reclaimed after the club did not proceed with restoration; Union Oil later gifted the site to the county; the church and cemetery were deeded to the state by the Catholic Church in 1953 (F. C. Hageman and R. C. Ewing, *An Archeological and Restoration Study of Mission La Purísima Concepción* [Santa Barbara, Calif.: Santa Barbara Trust for Historic Preservation, 1980], xxvi, 13, 220–21).

6 Hageman and Ewing, *An Archeological and Restoration Study.*

7 D. H. Thomas, "Harvesting Ramona's Garden: Life in California's Mythical Mission Past," in *Columbian Consequences,* vol. 3, *The Spanish Borderlands in Pan-American Perspective* (Washington, D.C.: Smithsonian Institution, 1991), 139.

8 Ibid., 133, quoting D. Gebhard, "Architectural Imagery, the Mission, and California," *Harvard Architectural Review* 1 (1980): 137–45.

9 Ibid., 139.

10 Hosmer, *Preservation Comes of Age*, 429.

11 G. Ostergren, "Angels and Saints: Making and Promoting Place in Los Angeles and Southern California, 1890–1932" (Ph.D. dissertation, University of California, Los Angeles, 2005), 44.

12 Ibid., 44–99.

13 C. E. Savage, *New Deal Adobe: The Civilian Conservation Corps and the Reconstruction of Mission La Purísima, 1934–1942* (Santa Barbara, Calif.: Fithian Press, 1991), 60.

14 Thomas, "Harvesting Ramona's Garden," 137–38.

15 Ibid., 140; Hageman and Ewing, *An Archeological and Restoration Study.*

16 Current standards for reconstructions require a clear differentiation between original and new materials.
17 Savage, *New Deal Adobe*, 59.
18 Ibid., 29, 34.
19 Gilbert Ballesterose, in Savage, *New Deal Adobe*, 42.
20 Weinberg, *Historic Preservation*, 215.
21 Savage, *New Deal Adobe*, 125. The project horticulturalist was Ed Rowe.
22 C. Pagliarulo, "Harry Downie and the Restoration of Mission San Carlos Borromeo, 1931–1967," *Southern California Quarterly* 86, no. 1 (2004): 19.
23 Ibid., 45.
24 Ibid., 21.
25 Thomas, "Harvesting Ramona's Garden," 134.
26 Pagliarulo, "Harry Downie and the Restoration of Mission San Carlos Borromeo," 42.
27 Weinberg, *Historic Preservation*, 216–19. Weinberg's interviews with Downie provided interesting insight into Downie's working methods.
28 P. Hallan-Gibson, "Mission San Juan Capistrano," in Stern et al., *Romance of the Bells*, 64–69.
29 Pauley and Pauley, *San Fernando, Rey de España: An Illustrated History*, 281–82.
30 Weber, *The California Missions*, 236.
31 Weinberg, *Historic Preservation*, 222.
32 P. Farnsworth, "The Economics of Acculturation in the California Missions: A Historical and Archaeological Study of Mission Nuestra Señora de la Soledad" (Ph.D. dissertation, University of California, Los Angeles, 1987), 127–333.
33 For these reasons, in the southeastern United States, black slave populations have been a subject of considerable research.
34 Work was carried out by the eminent archaeologists James A. Bennyhoff, Albert B. Elsasser, and Adan E. Treganza.
35 Thomas, "Harvesting Ramona's Garden," 144–45.
36 Ibid., 144.
37 D. L. Felton, "Santa Cruz Mission State Historic Park, Architectural and Archeological Investigations, 1984–1985," report, Cultural Heritage Section, California Department of Parks and Recreation, 1987; R. Allen, *Native Americans at Mission Santa Cruz, 1791–1834*, Perspectives in California Archaeology, vol. 5 (Los Angeles: Institute of Archaeology, University of California, Los Angeles, 1998).
38 Thomas, "Harvesting Ramona's Garden," 147.
39 Greenwood and Associates, "The Changing Faces of Main Street," report submitted to Redevelopment Agency, City of Buenaventura, Calif., 1976; "3500 Years on One City Block," report submitted to Redevelopment Agency, City of Buenaventura, Calif., 1975.

Chapter 4: Artisans and Architecture

1 M. K. Schuetz-Miller, *Building and Builders in Hispanic California, 1769–1850* (Tucson, Ariz.: Southwestern Mission Research Center; Santa Barbara, Calif.: Santa Barbara Trust for Historic Preservation, Presidio Research Publication, 1994). This pioneering work provides much of the detail on which this chapter is based.
2 With the exception of Mission San Gabriel and the church at the second location of Mission La Purísima, which had side entrances.
3 Vestigial *atrios* (enclosed forecourts) have been identified in front of some California missions through early historical photographs and paintings; they may have been used for outdoor pageants and processions (S. Y. Edgerton, *Theaters of Conversion: Religious Architectural and Indian Artisans in Colonial Mexico* [Albuquerque: University of New Mexico Press, 2001], 64); see drawing of San Luis Obispo by Miller in 1856 (*Account of a Tour of the California Missions and Towns*, 28), 186.
4 1960 edition in paperback from Dover Press.
5 Schuetz-Miller, *Building and Builders*, 41.
6 C. R. Ettinger, *Architecture as Order in the California Missions* (Los Angeles: Santa Barbara Mission Archive-Library and Historical Society of Southern California, 2003), 5.
7 Reservoirs and fountains were often rendered with water-resistant *coccio pesto,* hydraulic lime stucco made pink by the admixture of ground terracotta tiles, another Vitruvian formula. *Coccio pesto* was also used on architectural elements, such as the *ladrillo* colonnade columns at Mission Santa Inés.
8 Such roofs were constructed at San Gabriel, San Luis Rey, San Diego, San Buenaventura, and Santa Cruz.
9 In the past, the term *espadaña* has been misapplied to parapet walls without openings for bells.
10 Bell towers are found at San Luis Rey, San Buenaventura, Santa Cruz, San Carlos Borromeo, Santa Clara, San Fernando, Santa Bárbara, San José, and the Great Stone Church of San Juan Capistrano.
11 K. Baer, *Architecture of the California Missions* (Berkeley: University of California Press, 1958), 14, 15.
12 R. Newcomb, *The Old Mission Churches and Historic Houses of California* (Philadelphia: J. P. Lippincott, 1925), 181.
13 Ibid., 109–10.
14 E. Egenhoff, *Fábricas* (Sacramento: California Division of Natural Resources, Division of Mines, 1952), 181.
15 Salvador was briefly assigned to Nootka (Schuetz-Miller, *Building and Builders*, 88).
16 The original *ladrillo espadaña* was damaged by successive earthquakes and removed in 1880, to be reconstructed in 1934.
17 H. C. Ford, *An Artist Records the California Missions*, ed. N. Neuerburg (San Francisco: Book Club of California, 1989), 19.
18 Schuetz-Miller, *Building and Builders*, 163.
19 Newcomb, *The Old Mission Churches*, 270–73.
20 Schuetz-Miller, *Building and Builders*, 93–95.
21 Missions San Buenaventura (1809), San Luis Rey (1815), San Antonio (1813), San Juan Bautista (1812), San Diego (1813), and Santa Inés (1817).
22 Schuetz-Miller, *Building and Builders*, 171, 153–54.
23 The stone church at San Juan Capistrano, however, failed disastrously in the 1812 earthquake.
24 Egenhoff, *Fábricas*, 167.
25 Ibid., 94.
26 Ibid., 26–27.
27 In addition, some artisans employed by the missions were foreigners who arrived uninvited, such as John Mulligan, an Irishman who taught weaving at Monterey Bay area missions, but were tolerated for their skills. These individuals were known as *sirvientes*, or employees of the missions.
28 Schuetz-Miller, *Building and Builders*, 64–65, 83, 12, 33.
29 The anthropologist Georgia Lee and the art historian Norman Neuerburg published an important collaborative essay in the first volume of the Smithsonian Institution's *Columbian Consequences*: G. Lee and N. Neuerburg, "The Alta California Indians as Artists before and after Contact," in *Columbian Consequences*, vol. 1, *Archaeological and Historical Perspectives on the Spanish Borderlands West*, ed. D. H. Thomas (Washington, D.C.: Smithsonian Institution Press, 1989), 467–80. This narrative owes much to their cogent presentation of the subject in this and subsequent publications.
30 A. Wey, "Spanish Drawn-Work," *Land of Sunshine* 4, no. 2 (January 1896): 19–51; Edith Buckland Webb reportedly had a collection of Indian-made lacework.
31 The original has been replaced by a casting on the exterior of the church.
32 Schuetz-Miller, *Building and Builders*, 39.
33 M. K. Schuetz-Miller, *Architectural Practices in Mexico City: A Manual for Journeyman Architects of the Eighteenth Century* (Tucson: University of Arizona Press, 1987), 126. In Central and Latin America today stone is still considered a noble building material, while adobe is considered humble.
34 This mobility suggests the informal operation of an independent guild in this remote colony. Schuetz-Miller, *Building and Builders*, 38–39, 50.
35 Quoted in Engelhardt, *Mission La Concepción Purísima de María Santísima*, 11.
36 The details of Ramírez's life are presented in Schuetz-Miller, *Building and Builders*, 38, 85–87.
37 Schuetz-Miller, *Building and Builders*, 86.
38 Quoted in Schuetz-Miller, *Building and Builders*, 195.
39 Also referred to as Pacomio Poqui/Pogui/Poquis; and, in Monterey, as José Pacomio. Details of Pacomio's life have been drawn from J. R. Johnson, "Pacomio's Chumash Dancing Songs," in *Bulletin of the Santa Barbara Museum of Natural History, 1989*; and G. J. Farris and J. R. Johnson, "Prominent Indian Families at Mission La Purisima Conceptión as Identified in Baptismal, Marriage, and Burial Records," in *California Mission Studies Association Occasional Paper No. 3*, 1999.
40 Schuetz-Miller, *Building and Builders*, 106.
41 Bancroft, *History of California*, vol. 2, *1801–1824*, 527 n. 37.
42 Bancroft, *History of California* vol. 3, *1825–1840*, 675.
43 Schuetz-Miller, *Building and Builders*, 106–7.
44 *History of Santa Barbara and Ventura Counties* (Thompson & West, 1883; rpt. Berkeley: Howell-North Books, 1961), 30.
45 H. H. Bancroft, *History of California*, vol. 2, *1801–1824* (San Francisco: History Company, 1886; rpt. Santa Barbara, Calif.: Wallace Hebberd, 1965), 615–17.
46 Schuetz-Miller, *Building and Builders*, 51–145.
47 Schuetz-Miller, *Building and Builders*.
48 Ibid., 186.
49 R. K. Skowronek, *Situating Mission Santa Clara de Asís* (Berkeley: Academy of American Franciscan History, 2006), 261.
50 Schuetz-Miller, *Building and Builders*, 195.
51 Ibid., 33–34.
52 Ibid., 105, 115, 116, 125.
53 Egenhoff, *Fábricas*, 174–75.

54 Individual churches discussed in the mission profiles in part 2 provide the names of their architects and builders where known.
55 Schuetz-Miller, *Building and Builders*, 198.

Chapter 5: Adorning the Theaters of Conversion

1 Robinson, *Life in California,* quoted in Egenhoff, *Fábricas*, 48.
2 In Egenhoff, *Fábricas*, 51.
3 Forbes, *California: A History*, 132.
4 Edgerton, *Theaters of Conversion*, 156.
5 Lightfoot, *Indians, Missionaries, and Merchants*, 183.
6 K. Baer, "Spanish Colonial Art in the California Missions," *The Americas* 18, no. 1 (1961): 34–35.
7 K. Baer, *Painting and Sculpture at Mission Santa Barbara* (Washington, D.C.: Academy of Franciscan History, 1955), 6.
8 The only completely painted *retablo* that has survived in use in the California missions is at Santa Inés, although these early designs may be preserved behind subsequent *retablo* constructions, as at Mission San Francisco de Asís. N. Neuerburg, *The Decoration of the California Missions* (Santa Barbara, Calif.: Bellerophon Press, 1987), 22.
9 G. F. Giffords, *Sanctuaries of Earth, Stone, and Light: The Churches of Northern New Spain, 1530–1821* (Tucson: University of Arizona Press, 2007), 293–318.
10 Neuerburg, *The Decoration of the California Missions*, 12. Notable extant examples of pulpits with sounding boards can be found at Missions San Juan Bautista, San Juan Capistrano, San Miguel, and San Luis Rey.
11 Morgado, *Junípero Serra's Legacy*, 60.
12 A thorough discussion of the use of prints in the California missions can be found in Neuerburg, "The Function of Prints."
13 N. Neuerburg, "New Light on the Church of Mission San Buenaventura," *Ventura County Historical Society Quarterly* 28, no. 4 (1983): 9.
14 San Carlos, San Miguel, La Purísima, San Fernando Rey, San José, San Luis Rey, San Francisco, and San Diego are identified on the 1809 invoice, San Gabriel on the next year's (Neuerburg, "New Light," 9–11). Only four are thought to be extant, at San Buenaventura, San Gabriel, San Francisco de Asís, and San Luis Rey.
15 The pine was *allacaguite* (*Pinus ayacahuite*) (Neuerburg, "New Light," 9–10).
16 Stunning examples of mission chandeliers may be seen at Santa Inés and Santa Bárbara.
17 Until the mid-twentieth century, Mass was said with the priest's back to the assemblage. Convex mirrors had the potential advantage of allowing the celebrants to observe the activities of the congregation behind them. At the California missions, however, they seem to have been placed too high for effective observance and may have been enjoyed for their reflective qualities.
18 Baer, *Painting and Sculpture at Mission Santa Barbara*, 206.
19 Lee and Neuerburg, "The Alta California Indians as Artists," 471.
20 Ford, *An Artist Records the California Missions*, 58.
21 Alfred Robinson at Mission Santa Bárbara in 1829; quoted in Egenhoff, *Fábricas*, 51.
22 Santa Clara's collection is at the De Saisset Museum, Santa Clara University.
23 J. L. Nolan, "Anglo-American Myopia and California Mission Art: Part Two," *Southern California Quarterly* 58, no. 2 (1976): 164–67.
24 Pagliarulo, "Harry Downie," 32.
25 Lee and Neuerburg, "The Alta California Indians as Artists," 471, 472.
26 An invoice from this work is reportedly at Mission Santa Bárbara. Paisano is also credited with stone sculptures of a horse and a lion. He may also have made the original carved animal spout on the front fountain. Schuetz-Miller, *Building and Builders*, 29, 10; Lee and Neuerburg, "The Alta California Indians as Artists," 470.
27 N. Neuerburg, "Indian Carved Statues at Mission Santa Barbara," *Masterkey* 51, no. 4 (1977): 147–51.
28 By calling the image La Conquistadora, Gálvez compared her with one of that title brought by the Spanish to New Mexico in 1625. When the Pueblo Indians revolted in 1680, the Spanish removed this Conquistadora and brought it back to Santa Fe when New Mexico was reoccupied. The title also evokes the role played by the Virgin of Loreto, who presided over the colonization of Lower California, as well as the original La Conquistadora of Puebla, Mexico, brought by Hernán Cortés. An exhaustive study of Alta California's La Conquistadora can be found in M. J. Morgado, *Junípero Serra's Legacy* (Pacific Grove, Calif.: Mount Carmel, 1987), 44–48.
29 Ibid., 45.
30 Pérouse, quoted in Baer, *Painting and Sculpture at Mission Santa Barbara*, 17.
31 A. Tibesar, O.F.M., ed., *Writing of Junípero Serra*, vol. 2 (Washington, D.C.: Academy of Franciscan History, 1956), 319.
32 Baer, "Spanish Colonial Art," 50.
33 Páez paintings of the baptism of Christ are at Missions San Juan Bautista, San Buenaventura, San Carlos Borromeo, and San Miguel.
34 The famous Vía Crucis painted by neophytes at Mission San Fernando is discussed in chapter 6.
35 The San Rafael *enrollado* painting that hung behind the altar at Mission San Rafael is now preserved in the museum.
36 The sacred cloth is displayed in the Basilica of Our Lady of Guadalupe in Mexico City.
37 Skowronek, *Situating Mission Santa Clara de Asís*, 283.
38 The historian James Sandos, in his study *Converting California: Indians and Franciscans in the Missions* (New Haven: Yale University Press, 2004), discusses this aspect of religious education at length and in depth.
39 Robinson, visiting Mission Santa Bárbara in about 1829; in Egenhoff, *Fábricas*, 51.
40 Skowronek, *Situating Mission Santa Clara de Asís*, 194, 464.
41 Alfred Robinson (1841), in Skowronek, *Situating Mission Santa Clara de Asís*, 308.
42 The painting of Our Lady of Guadalupe was gifted to Mission San Carlos Borromeo in the 1940s.
43 Miller, *Account of a Tour*, 19.

Chapter 6: Painting and Painters in Early California

1 H. W. Evans, *The Hand-Writing on the Walls: Artist-Explorers Uncover Indian Wall Paintings Which Made Old Missions Bright with Colors* (Los Angeles: Index of American Design, ca. 1940), 1–2. MS on file, National Gallery of Art, Washington, D.C.
2 These original documents are archived at the National Gallery of Art, Washington, D.C.
3 The Index artists also recorded extensive painted murals at Missions San Miguel and Santa Inés and elements at Missions La Purísima, San Buenaventura, San Juan Capistrano, and Santa Bárbara.
4 N. Neuerburg, *The Function of Prints in the California Missions* (Los Angeles: Historical Society of Southern California, 1986), 276. Reprint from *Southern California Quarterly* 63 (3).
5 A. B. Duhaut-Cilly, "Duhaut-Cilly's Account of California in the Years 1827–28," trans. C. F. Carter, *California Historical Society Quarterly* 8 (1929): 130–66, 214–50, 306–36; cited in Egenhoff, *Fábricas,* 171.
6 Neuerburg, *Decoration of the California Missions*, 4.
7 The earliest analysis is K. Crist, "American Art Comes Back to America," *Los Angeles Times Sunday Magazine*, October 11, 1936; followed by G. H. Phillips, "The Indian Paintings from Mission San Fernando: An Historical Interpretation," *Journal of California Anthropology* 3, no. 1 (Summer 1976): 96–100. A recent authoritative summary can be found in N. Neuerburg, *The Indian Via Crucis from Mission San Fernando: An Historical Exposition* (Santa Barbara, Calif.: Santa Barbara Mission Archive-Library, 1998); and an answering essay by G. H. Phillips: "The Stations of the Cross Revisited, Reconsidered, and Revised (sort of)," *Boletín: The Journal of the California Mission Studies Association* 24, no. 2 (2007): 76–87.
8 Baptized in 1798 (Schuetz-Miller, *Building and Builders*, 114).
9 The paintings were executed on painting-quality canvas pieced together to form similar-sized formats.
10 Phillips, "The Stations of the Cross Revisited," 79.
11 Ibid., 77.
12 Ibid., 5; Lee and Neuerburg, "The Alta California Indians as Artists," 473; E. B. Webb, *Indian Life at the Old Missions* (Lincoln: University of Nebraska Press, 1952), 232–33.
13 Neuerburg, *Decoration of the California Missions*, 19.
14 Ibid., 20.
15 Ibid.
16 Ibid., 12.
17 Ibid., 10–11.
18 Use of patterns is verified in an 1815 letter to don José de la Guerra, paymaster at the presidio of San Diego, who was asked to send the patterns used to paint the church at San Diego so that they could serve for the decoration of a new church being completed in Baja California. N. Neuerburg, "The Changing Face of Mission San Diego," *Journal of San Diego History* 33, no. 1 (1986): 6.
19 For wall painting techniques, see Giffords, *Sanctuaries of Earth, Stone, and Light*, 276.
20 This physical layering has helped to preserve the original painted designs and allowed researchers to record sequences of decorative phases.
21 Munras married Catalina Manzaneli of Tepic, and their adobe was one of the first built outside the Monterey Presidio walls. He was *alcalde*

in 1837 and *juez* in 1840 and was granted three ranches by the government. H. H. Bancroft, ed., *History of California*, vol. 4, *1840–1845* (San Francisco: History Company, 1886; rpt. Santa Barbara, Calif.: Wallace Hebberd, 1969), 748; A. Fink, *Monterey the Presence of the Past* (San Francisco: Chronicle Books, 1972).

22 Schuetz-Miller, *Buildings and Builders*, 174.

23 Neuerburg, *Decoration of the California Missions*, 64.

24 Ibid., 64–65.

25 Ibid.

26 Ibid., 66.

27 Lee and Neuerburg, "The Alta California Indians as Artists," 476.

28 Neuerburg, *Decoration of the California Missions*, 71–72.

29 Ibid., 7–10; Johnson,*The California Missions*, 237.

30 Neuerburg, *Decoration of the California Missions.*

31 Ibid., 23–25. Dávila apparently applied for a scholarship from the Academy of San Carlos in Mexico to study drawing in Rome; Schuetz-Miller, *Building and Builders*, 65.

32 Schuetz-Miller, *Building and Builders*, 65.

33 Neuerburg, *Decoration of the California Missions*, 10; Schuetz-Miller, *Building and Builders*, 64–65.

34 Neuerburg, *Decoration of the California Missions*, 51.

35 Ibid. The information presented here on mission wall painting is drawn primarily from his work.

36 Schuetz-Miller, *Building and Builders*, 190.

37 Neuerburg, *Decoration of the California Missions*, 55–58.

38 Early California Population Project, Huntington Library: www.huntington.org/Information/ECPPmain.htm.

39 Johnson, *The Chumash Indians.*

40 This information comes from the ethnographer Mark P. Harrington, who extensively interviewed Chumash elder Fernando Librado Kitsepawit, the last-known full-blooded Island Chumash. Librado was born in 1839 at Mission San Buenaventura and died in 1915 in Santa Bárbara. He likely obtained his information about Pacífico from others who had known the painter personally.

41 N. Neuerburg, "Painting in the California Missions," *American Art Review* 4, no. 1 (July 1977): 72–88.

42 It was heavily retouched in 1980. Many of the wall designs were recorded by the Index of American Design. Neuerburg, *Decoration of the California Missions*, 27.

Chapter 7: Preserving California's Missions

1 Father Mariano Payras provides details in a letter dated December 31, 1812 (Englehardt, *Mission La Concepción Purísima de Maria Santisima*, 30–31.

2 Santa Inés is preserved by the Capuchin Franciscan order of the Roman Catholic Church, the city of Solvang, and the Santa Barbara Trust for Historic Preservation as Mission Santa Inés National Historic Landmark District.

3 Some "stabilization" elements can be added to increase its durability. The NPS provides recommendations.

4 The GSAP has produced three volumes on its findings: *Survey of Damage to Historic Adobe Buildings after the January 1994 Northridge Earthquake* (Los Angeles: Getty Conservation Institute, 1996); *Seismic Stabilization of Historic Adobe Structures: Final Report of the Getty Seismic Adobe Project* (Los Angeles: Getty Conservation Institute, 2000); and *Planning and Engineering Guidelines for the Seismic Retrofitting of Historic Adobe Structures* (Los Angeles: Getty Conservation Institute, 2002). See www.getty.edu/conservation/science/seismic for more information on GSAP.

5 Vargas-Neumann, quoted in Tolles, Kimbro, and Ginell, *Planning and Engineering Guidelines for the Seismic Retrofitting of Historic Adobe Structures*, xi.

6 Other historic sites include Rancho Camulos National Historic Landmark (Ventura County), Rancho Las Flores Adobe (San Diego County, Camp Pendleton), and Salvado Vallejo Historic Adobe State Historical Landmark (Sonoma County).

7 A. Crosby, "Recent Discoveries of Interior Finishes on the Interior of the Royal Presidio Chapel," February 2008. Manuscript on file with author and at Royal Presidio Chapel.

8 Baer, *Painting and Sculpture at Mission Santa Barbara*, 19.

9 NPS conservation notes provide useful information on canvas paintings: www.nps.gov/history/museum/publications/MHI/AppenL.pdf.

10 C. Kenyon, "Conservation of Mission Art," *Boletín: The Journal of the California Mission Studies Association* 20, no. 1 (2002): 40.

11 Ibid., 39.

12 Ibid., 38–39.

13 While many projects have received federal or private funding through Save America's Treasures, "Official Project" designation does not necessarily mean that a certain site will be a grantee.

San Diego de Alcalá

1 Several sources were used throughout the mission profiles and are not cited in each instance. Population and production numbers are drawn from the following sources: tables of statistics from Annual Reports found in the series of sixteen studies of individual missions by Father Z. Engelhardt; and, for the five missions not addressed by Engelhardt (Santa Clara, Santa Cruz, San José, San Rafael, and San Francisco Solano), the analysis in R. Milliken, L. H. Shoup, and B. R. Ortiz, "The Costanoan Indians of the San Francisco Peninsula and Their Neighbors, Yesterday and Today," Draft Report, Archaeological and Historical Consultants, Oakland, Calif., submitted to National Park Service, Golden Gate National Recreation Area, San Francisco, 2007. Statements comparing environmental, economic, and institutional circumstances of missions are largely drawn from the analyses by J. G. Costello: "Variability among the Alta California Missions," in *Columbian Consequences*, vol. 1, *Archaeological and Historical Perspectives on the Spanish Borderlands West*, 435–50, ed. D. H. Thomas (Washington, D.C.: Smithsonian Institution Press, 1989); and Costello, "Not Peas in a Pod." References to individual artisans are almost all drawn from Schuetz-Miller's authoritative study, *Building and Builders.* References to archaeological studies carried out at the missions and other Spanish colonial sites can be found in L. R. Barker, R. Allen, and J. Costello, "The Archaeology of Spanish and Mexican Alta California," in *The Archaeology of Spanish and Mexican Colonialism in the American Southwest*, Guides to the Archaeological Literature of the Immigrant Experience in America, No. 3 (Ann Arbor, Mich.: Society for Historical Archaeology, 1995), 3–51.

2 E. D. Castillo, "The Native Response to the Colonization of Alta California," in *Columbian Consequences*, 1:385–86; R. L. Carrico, "Sociopolitical Aspects of the 1775 Revolt at Mission San Diego de Alcalá: An Ethnohistorical Approach," *Journal of San Diego History* 43, no. 3 (1997); R. L. Carrico, "Castigating the Insolent Ones: The Pa'mu Incident and Frontier Justice," ms. in posession of author, 2009.

3 Neuerburg, "The Changing Face of Mission San Diego"; Schuetz-Miller, *Building and Builders*, 153–54.

4 Neuerburg, "The Changing Face of Mission San Diego."

5 A. D. Bevil, "The Sacred and the Profane: The Restoration of Mission San Diego de Alcalá, 1866–1931," *Journal of San Diego History* 38, no. 3 (1992): 138–59.

6 R. Brandes, J. R. Moriarty III, T. Nagle, G. N. Chase, and L. T. Campbell, "Mission San Diego de Alcalá: The Archaeological Design and Fieldwork Conducted by the University of San Diego, 1966 to 1984," Manuscript on file, University of San Diego, San Diego, 1987.

San Carlos Borromeo del Río Carmelo

1 Milliken, Shoup, and Ortiz, "The Costanoan Indians of the San Francisco Peninsula," 148.

2 Schuetz-Miller, *Building and Builders.*

3 R. Newcomb, *Spanish-Colonial Architecture in the United States* (New York: J. J. Augustin, 1937; rpt. New York: Dover Publications, 1990), 22.

San Antonio de Padua

1 J. G. Costello, *The Ranches and Ranchos of Mission San Antonio de Padua*, Keepsake Volume (Santa Clara: California Mission Studies Association, 1994).

2 Schuetz-Miller, *Building and Builders*, 91, 170, 171. Z. Engelhardt notes that an arch was added to the portico in 1821: *San Antonio de Padua: The Mission in the Sierras* (Santa Barbara, Calif.: Mission Santa Barbara, 1929). D. N. Hoover and R. L. Hoover, "Mission San Antonio de Padua: A Chronology of Building," *Boletín: Journal of the California Mission Studies Association* 25, no. 1 (2008): 35–66.

3 R. L. Hoover and J. G. Costello, eds., *Excavations at Mission San Antonio, 1976–1978*, Monograph No. 26 (Los Angeles: Institute of Archaeology, University of California, Los Angeles, 1985); Hoover and Hoover, "Mission San Antonio de Padua."

San Gabriel, Arcángel

1 L. J. Bean and C. R. Smith, "Gabrielino," in *Handbook of North American Indians*, vol. 8, *California*, ed. R. F. Heizer (Washington, D.C.: Smithsonian Institution Press, 1978), 538.

2 Baer, *Architecture of the Old Missions*, 30–31; Newcomb, *Old Mission Churches and Historic Houses*, 181.

3 Schuetz-Miller, *Building and Builders*, 155–57.

San Luis Obispo de Tolosa

1 The new design elements come from the notebooks of Norman Neuerburg.

San Francisco de Asís

1 Milliken, Shoup, and Ortiz, "The Costanoan Indians of the San Francisco Peninsula," 121–38.
2 Z. Engelhardt, O.F.M., *San Francisco or Mission Dolores* (Chicago: Franciscan Herald Press, 1924), 317.

San Juan Capistrano

1 R.C. Kammerer, *Old Mission San Juan Capistrano: History and Tour* (Cincinnati, Ohio: KM Communications, 1980), 59–60.
2 Schuetz-Miller, *Building and Builders*, 51. It is possible that the master carpenter and stonecutter José Antonio Ramírez completed the structure (158–59).

Santa Clara de Asís

1 Skowronek, *Situating Mission Santa Clara*, 167.
2 Saint Clare and Saint Francis were friends from the town of Assisi in Italy.
3 There is no indication of environmental conditions such as drought or forced gathering by soldiers (Milliken, Shoup, and Ortiz, "The Costanoan Indians of the San Francisco Peninsula," 150–51).
4 Neuerburg, *Decoration of the California Missions*, 23–24, 34–35.
5 Candelaria opened a "Fandango" house in the building, which operated through the 1850s, until the Jesuits purchased the building in 1860 for $800. Skowronek, *Situating Mission Santa Clara de Asís*, 333. The treatise has been translated: A.M. Osio, *The History of Alta California: A Memoir of Mexican California*, trans. and ed. R.M. Beebe and R.M. Senkewicz (Madison: University of Wisconsin Press, 1996).
6 Skowronek, *Situating Mission Santa Clara de Asís*, xix, 333, 304.
7 Skowronek, *Situating Mission Santa Clara.*

San Buenaventura

1 Neuerburg, "New Light on the Church of Mission San Buenaventura."
2 Greenwood and Associates, "The Changing Faces of Main Street," report submitted to Redevelopment Agency, City of Buenaventura, Calif., 1976; Greenwood and Associates, "3500 Years on One City Block," report submitted to Redevelopment Agency, City of Buenaventura, Calif., 1975.

Santa Bárbara, Virgen y Mártir

1 Vitruvius, *Vitruvius: The Ten Books on Architecture*, trans. M.H. Morgan (New York: Dover Publications, 1960).
2 Weber, *The California Missions*, 71.
3 St. Anthony's Seminary included the Franciscan School of Theology until 1968.
4 R. Allen and D.L. Felton, *The Water System at Mission Santa Barbara*, Occasional Paper 1 (Santa Clara, Calif.: California Mission Studies Association, 1998).

La Purísima Concepción de María Santísima

1 N. Neuerburg, *The Architecture of Mission La Purísima Concepción* (Santa Barbara, Calif.: Bellerophon Books, 1987), 14.
2 G.J. Farris and E. Wheeler, "The Neophyte Housing and Infirmary at La Purísima Mission SHP: A Review and Remapping of the Site," report, Resource Management Division, California Department of Parks and Recreation, 1998, 4–5. Hageman and Ewing, *An Archeological and Restoration Study.*

La Exaltación de la Santa Cruz

1 E.E. Kimbro, M.E. Ryan, and R.H. Jackson, with R.T. Milliken and N. Neuerburg, "Restoration Research: Santa Cruz Mission Adobe, Santa Cruz Mission State Historic Park," report, Historical Investigations, Davenport, Calif., submitted to Cultural Resource Support Unit, Department of Parks and Recreation, Sacramento, 1985.
2 Schuetz-Miller, *Building and Builders*, 183.
3 A painting by Leon Trousset in 1876 represents the building as described by local residents and as the rear portion of it appeared at that date; Henry C. Ford copied the Trousset painting for his depictions. E.E. Kimbro, "Construction Chronology of the Site of Holy Cross Church, Santa Cruz (Mission Santa Cruz) and Conservation Recommendations for Santa Cruz Mission Ruins," report prepared for Cabrillo Archaeological Technology Program, submitted to the Diocese of Monterey, 1993.
4 Felton, "Santa Cruz Mission State Historic Park"; Allen, *Native Americans at Mission Santa Cruz.*

Nuestra Señora de la Soledad

1 Engelhardt, *Mission Nuestra Senora de la Soledad*, 34–35.
2 Farnsworth, "The Economics of Acculturation in the California Missions," 127–333.

Mission del Gloriosísimo Patriarca San José

1 Milliken, Shoup, and Ortiz, "The Costanoan Indians of the San Francisco Peninsula"; A. Hurtado, *Indian Survival on the California Frontier* (New Haven: Yale University Press, 1988), 43–44, 160; Milliken, *A Time of Little Choice.*
2 Milliken, Shoup, and Ortiz, "The Costanoan Indians of the San Francisco Peninsula," 164; Lightfoot, *Indians, Missionaries, and Merchants,* 202.
3 Schuetz-Miller, *Building and Builders,* 186. See Mission Santa Clara for other examples of Dávila's work.
4 S. Deitz, "Final Archaeological Report of Archaeological Investigations at Mission San Jose," report prepared by Archaeological Consulting and Research Services for Gilbert Arnold Sanchez, Architect/Planner, 1983.

San Juan Bautista

1 Schuetz-Miller, *Building and Builders*, 173–74, 173.

San Miguel, Arcángel

1 Z. Engelhardt, O.F.M., *San Miguel Archangel: Mission on the Highway* (Santa Barbara, Calif.: Mission Santa Barbara, 1929), 91; Ohles, *Lands of Mission San Miguel*, 327–29.
2 Schuetz-Miller, *Building and Builders*, 174.

San Fernando Rey de España

1 Pauley and Pauley, *San Fernando, Rey de España,* 281.

San Luis Rey de Francia

1 J. Johnson and D. Crawford, "Contributions to Luiseño Ethnohistory Based on Mission Register Research," *Pacific Coast Archaeological Society Quarterly* 5, no. 4 (1999): 79–102; Lightfoot, *Indians, Missionaries, and Merchants*, 216–17.
2 Schuetz-Miller, *Building and Builders*, 159. A true cruciform plan has doors at the ends of the transepts; this design and that at the ruined San Juan Capistrano church are more accurately "single-nave churches with deep bays at the transepts" (Baer, *Architecture of the California Missions*, 51).
3 Kelsey, *Mission San Luis Rey*, 30–32.

Santa Inés, Virgen y Mártir

1 The college closed in 1881.
2 J.G. Costello, E. Kimbro, and L. Wilcoxon, *National Historic Landmark, Mission Santa Inés* (Washington, D.C.: National Park Service, 1997); J.G. Costello, *Excavations at Santa Inés Mission, 1986–1988*, California Historical Archaeology, No. 1 (Salinas, Calif.: Coyote Press, 1989), 177–83.
3 Newcomb, *The Old Mission Churches*, 233.

San Rafael, Arcángel

1 Bancroft, *History of California*, 2:229–330; Milliken, Shoup, and Ortiz, "The Costanoan Indians of the San Francisco Peninsula," 128–29, 131–32.
2 Schuetz-Miller, *Building and Builders*, 186–87.
3 Ford, *An Artist Records the California Missions*, 85.

San Francisco Solano

1 R.S. Smilie, *The Sonoma Mission* (Fresno, Calif.: Valley Publishers, 1975), 38.
2 Milliken, Shoup, and Ortiz, "The Costanoan Indians of the San Francisco Peninsula," 131–32; Schuetz-Miller, *Building and Builders*, 187.
3 Milliken, Shoup, and Ortiz, "The Costanoan Indians of the San Francisco Peninsula," 172.
4 S.W. Silliman, *Laborers in Colonial California: Native Americans and the Archaeology of Rancho Petaluma* (Tucson: University of Arizona Press, 2004), 58–60.
5 J.A. Bennyhoff and A.B. Elsasser, *Sonoma Mission: An Historical and Archaeological Study of Primary Constructions, 1823–1913*, Archaeological Survey Reports No. 27 (Berkeley: University of California, Berkeley, 1954); A.E. Treganza, "Sonoma Mission: An Archaeological Reconstruction of the Mission San Francisco de Solano Quadrangle," *Kroeber Anthropological Papers* 14 (1956): 1–18. The mission assets are part of Sonoma Mission State Historic Park, which includes other Mexican- and American-period buildings.

Selected Bibliography

Allen, R. *Native Americans at Mission Santa Cruz, 1791–1834*. Perspectives in California Archaeology 5. Los Angeles: Institute of Archaeology, University of California, Los Angeles, 1998.

Allen, R., and D. L. Felton. *The Water System at Mission Santa Barbara*. Occasional Paper 1. Santa Clara: California Mission Studies Association, 1998.

Anderson, M. K., M. G. Barbout, and V. Whitworth. A world of balance and plenty: Land, plants, animals, and humans in a pre-European California. In *Contested Eden: California before the Gold Rush*, ed. R. A. Gutiérrez and R. Orsi, 12–47. Berkeley: University of California Press, 1998.

Archibald, R. *The Economic Aspects of the California Missions*. Washington, D.C.: Academy of American Franciscan History, 1978.

Arroyo de la Cuesta, Fr. F. *Grammar of the Mutsun Language Spoken at the Mission of San Juan Bautista, Alta California*. New York: Trübner and Co., 1861.

Asisara, L. The assassination of Padre Andrés Quintana by the Indians of Mission Santa Cruz in 1812: The narrative of Lorenzo Asisara. Trans. and introd. E. D. Castillo. *California History* 68, no. 3 (1989): 117–25.

Baer, K. *Architecture of the California Missions*. Berkeley: University of California Press, 1958.

———. *Painting and Sculpture at Mission Santa Barbara*. Washington, D.C.: Academy of American Franciscan History, 1955.

———. Spanish Colonial art in the California missions. *The Americas* 18, no. 1 (1961): 33–54.

Bancroft, H. H. *History of California*, vol. 1, *1542–1800*. San Francisco: History Company, 1886. Rpt. Santa Barbara, Calif.: Wallace Hebberd, 1963.

———. *History of California*, vol. 2, *1801–1824*. San Francisco: History Company, 1886. Rpt. Santa Barbara, Calif.: Wallace Hebberd, 1965.

———. *History of California*, vol. 3, *1825–1840*. San Francisco: History Company, 1886. Rpt. Santa Barbara, Calif.: Wallace Hebberd, 1966.

———. *History of California*, vol. 4, *1840–1845*. San Francisco: History Company, 1886. Rpt. Santa Barbara, Calif.: Wallace Hebberd, 1969.

Bandini, J. *A Description of California in 1828*. Trans. D. M. Wright. Bancroft Library Publications, No. 3. Berkeley: Friends of the Bancroft Library, 1951.

Barker, L. R., R. Allen, and J. Costello. The archaeology of Spanish and Mexican Alta California. In *The Archaeology of Spanish and Mexican Colonialism in the American Southwest*, 3–51. Guides to the Archaeological Literature of the Immigrant Experience in America, No. 3.: Society for Historical Archaeology, 1995.

Bean, L. J., and H. W. Lawton. Some explanations for the rise of cultural complexity in native California with comments on proto-agriculture and agriculture. In *Before the Wilderness: Environmental Management by Native Californians*, comp. and ed. T. C. Blackburn and K. Anderson, 27–54. Menlo Park, Calif.: Ballena Press, 1993.

Bean, L. J., and C. R. Smith. Gabrielino. In *Handbook of North American Indians*, vol. 8, *California*, ed. R. F. Heizer, 538–49. Washington, D.C.: Smithsonian Institution Press, 1978.

Beebe, R. M., and R. M. Senkewicz, eds. *Lands of Promise and Despair: Chronicles of Early California, 1535–1846*. Berkeley: Heyday Books, 2001.

Beeler, M. S., ed. *The Ventureño Confesionario of José Señán, O.F.M.* University of California Publications in Linguistics No. 47. Berkeley: University of California Press, 1967.

Boscana, Fr. G. *Chinigchinich: A Revised and Annotated Version of Alfred Robinson's Translation of Father Gerónimo Boscana's Historical Account of the.... Acagchemem Tribe*. Banning, Calif.: Malki Museum Press, 1978.

Botta, P. E. Paolo Emilio Botta's observations on the inhabitants of California. Trans. A. M. Appel. *Boletín: Journal of the California Mission Studies Association* 23, no. 2 (2007); 24, no. 1 (2007): 59–76.

Brandes, R., J. R. Moriarty III, T. Nagle, G. N. Chase, and L. T. Campbell. Mission San Diego de Alcalá: The archaeological design and fieldwork conducted by the University of San Diego, 1966 to 1984. Manuscript on file, University of San Diego, San Diego, 1987.

Bryant, E. *What I Saw in California: Being a Journal of a Tour, by the Emigrant Route and South Pass of the Rocky Mountains, Across the Continent of North America, the Great Desert Basin, and Through California, in the Years 1846, 1847*. New York: D. Appleton & Co., 1848.

Burcham, L. T. *California Range Land*. California Division of Forestry, Sacramento, 1957. Rpt. Center for Archaeological Research at Davis, Publication No. 7, 1982.

Carrico, R. L. Sociopolitical aspects of the 1775 revolt at Mission San Diego de Alcalá: An ethnohistorical approach. *Journal of San Diego History* 43, no. 3 (1997).

———. Castigating the Innocent Ones: The Pa'mu Incident and Frontier Justice. Ms. in possession of author, 2009.

———. *Strangers in the Strange Land: Indians of San Diego County from Prehistory to the New Deal*. San Diego: Sunbelt Publications, 2008.

Cameron, D. G. Charles Fletcher Lummis and the Landmarks Club of Southern California: Pioneering in Historic Preservation. Paper delivered at the Charles F. Lummis Centennial Symposium, Southwest Museum, Los Angeles, 1985.

Castillo, E. D. The native response to the colonization of Alta California. In *Columbian Consequences*, vol. 1, *Archaeological and Historical Perspectives on the Spanish Borderlands West*, ed. D. H. Thomas, 377–94. Washington, D.C.: Smithsonian Institution Press, 1989.

César, J. Recollections of my youth at San Luis Rey Mission. Ed. and trans. N. Van de Grift Sanchez. *Touring Topics* 22 (1878): 42–43.

Chernykh, E. L. Agriculture in Upper California: A long lost account of farming in California as recorded by a Russian observer at Fort Ross in 1841. Trans. James R. Gibson. *Pacific Historian* 11, no. 1 (1967): 10–28.

Cook, S.F. *The Conflict between the California Indians and White Civilization*. Berkeley and Los Angeles: University of California Press, 1976.

Costello, J. G. *Excavations at Santa Inés Mission, 1986–1988*. California Historical Archaeology, No. 1. Salinas, Calif.: Coyote Press, 1989.

———. Not peas in a pod: Documenting diversity among the California missions. In *Text-Aided Archaeology*, ed. B. J. Little, 67–81. Boca Raton, Fla.: CRC Press, 1991.

———. *The Ranches and Ranchos of Mission San Antonio de Padua*. Keepsake Volume. Santa Clara, Calif.: California Mission Studies Association, 1994.

———. Variability among the Alta California missions. In *Columbian Consequences*, vol. 1, *Archaeological and Historical Perspectives on the Spanish Borderlands West*, 435–50, ed. D. H. Thomas. Washington, D.C.: Smithsonian Institution Press, 1989.

Costello, J. G., E. Kimbro, and L. Wilcoxon. *National Historic Landmark, Mission Santa Inés*. Washington, D.C.: National Park Service, 1997.

Crosby, A. Recent discoveries of interior finishes on the interior of the Royal Presidio Chapel. February 2008. Manuscript on file with author and at Royal Presidio Chapel.

Dakin, S. B. *A Scotch Paisano in Old Los Angeles: Hugo Reid's Life in California, 1832–1852, Derived from His Correspondence*. Berkeley: University of California Press, 1939.

Dana, R. H. *Two Years before the Mast: A Personal Narrative of Life at Sea*. New York: Macmillan, 1911. Rpt. New York: Mayflower Books, 1980.

Deitz, S. Final archaeological report of archaeological investigations at Mission San Jose. Report prepared by Archaeological Consulting and Research Services for Gilbert Arnold Sanchez, Architect/Planner, 1983.

DeLyser, D. *Ramona Memories: Tourism and the Shaping of Southern California*. Minneapolis: University of Minnesota Press, 2005.

Deverell, W. *Whitewashed Adobe: The Rise of Los Angeles and the Remaking of Its Mexican Past*. Berkeley: University of California Press, 2005.

Duhaut-Cilly, A. B. Duhaut-Cilly's account of California in the years 1827–28. Trans. C. F. Carter. *California Historical Society Quarterly* 8 (1929): 130–66, 214–50, 306–36.

Edgerton, S. Y. *Theaters of Conversion: Religious Architectural and Indian Artisans in Colonial Mexico*. Albuquerque: University of New Mexico Press, 2001.

Egenhoff, E. *Fábricas*. Sacramento: California Division of Natural Resources, Division of Mines, 1952.

Engelhardt, Z., O.F.M. *Mission La Concepción Purísima de Maria Santisima*. Santa Barbara, Calif.: Mission Santa Barbara, 1932.

———. *Mission Nuestra Señora de la Soledad*. Santa Barbara, Calif.: Mission Santa Barbara, 1929.

———. *Mission San Carlos Borromeo (Carmelo): The Father of the Missions*. Ramona, Calif: Ballena Press, 1973.

———. *Mission San Juan Bautista: A School of Church Music*. Santa Barbara, Calif.: Mission Santa Barbara, 1931.

———. *Mission San Luis Obispo in the Valley of the Bears*. Santa Barbara, Calif.: Mission Santa Barbara, 1933. Rpt. Santa Barbara, Calif.: W. T. Genns, 1963.

———. *Mission Santa Inés, Virgen y Mártir*. Santa Barbara, Calif.: Mission Santa Barbara, 1932. Rpt. Santa Barbara, Calif.: McNally & Loftin, 1986.

———. *San Antonio de Padua: The Mission in the Sierras*. Santa Barbara, Calif.: Mission Santa Barbara, 1929.

———. *San Buenaventura: The Mission by the Sea*. Santa Barbara, Calif.: Mission Santa Barbara, 1930.

———. *San Diego Mission*. San Francisco: James H. Barry, 1920.

———. *San Fernando Rey: The Mission of the Valley*. Ramona, Calif.: Ballena Press, 1973.

———. *San Francisco or Mission Dolores*. Chicago: Franciscan Herald Press, 1924.

———. *San Gabriel Mission and the Beginnings of Los Angeles*. San Gabriel, Calif.: Mission San Gabriel, 1927.

———. *San Juan Capistrano Mission*. Los Angeles: Standard Printing Co., 1922.

———. *San Luis Rey Mission*. San Francisco: James H. Barry, 1921.

———. *San Miguel Archangel: The Mission on the Highway*. Santa Barbara, Calif.: Mission Santa Barbara, 1929.

———. *Santa Barbara Mission*. San Francisco: James H. Barry, 1923.

Ettinger, C. R. *Architecture as Order in the California Missions*. Los Angeles: Santa Barbara Mission Archive-Library and Historical Society of Southern California, 2003.

Evans, H. W. *The Hand-Writing on the Walls: Artist-Explorers Uncover Indian Wall Paintings Which Made Old Missions Bright with Colors*. Los Angeles: Index of American Design, ca. 1940. Manuscript on file National Gallery of Art, Washington, D.C.

Farnsworth, P. The economics of acculturation in the California missions: A historical and archaeological study of Mission Nuestra Señora de la Soledad. Ph.D. dissertation, University of California, Los Angeles, 1987.

Farris, G. J. and J. R. Johnson. Prominent Indian families at Mission La Purisima Concepción as identified in baptismal, marriage, and burial records. *California Mission Studies Association Occasional Paper No. 3*, 1999.

Farris, G. J., and E. Wheeler. The neophyte housing and infirmary at La Purísima Mission SHP: A review and remapping of the site. Report. Resource Management Division, California Department of Parks and Recreation, 1998.

Felton, D. L. Santa Cruz Mission State Historic Park, architectural and archeological investigations, 1984–1985. Report. Cultural Heritage Section, California Department of Parks and Recreation, 1987.

Forbes, A. *California: A History of Upper and Lower California*. San Francisco: John Henry Nash, 1937. Rpt. New York: Kraus Reprint Co., 1972.

Ford, H. C. *An Artist Records the California Missions*. San Francisco: Book Club of California, 1989. Edit. and introd. by Norman Neuerburg.

Gebhard, D. Architectural imagery, the mission, and California. *Harvard Architecture Review* 1 (1980): 137–45.

Geiger, M., O.F.M., trans. and comm. *As the Padres Saw Them: California Indian Life and Customs as Reported by the Franciscan Missionaries, 1813–1815*. Santa Barbara, Calif.: Santa Barbara Mission Archive-Library, 1976.

Giffords, G. F. *Sanctuaries of Earth, Stone, and Light: The Churches of Northern New Spain, 1530–1821*. Tucson: University of Arizona Press, 2007.

Greenwood and Associates. The changing faces of Main Street. Report submitted to Redevelopment Agency, City of Buenaventura, Calif., 1976.

———. 3500 years on one city block. Report submitted to Redevelopment Agency, City of Buenaventura, Calif., 1975.

Hackel, S. W. *Children of Coyote, Missionaries of Saint Francis: Indian-Spanish Relations in Colonial California, 1769–1850*. Durham: University of North Carolina Press, 2005.

———. Land, labor, and production: The colonial economy of Spanish and Mexican California. In *Contested Eden: California before the Gold Rush*, ed. R. A. Gutiérrez and R. J. Orsi, 111–46. Berkeley: University of California Press, 1998.

Hageman, F. C., and R. C. Ewing. *An Archeological and Restoration Study of Mission La Purísima Concepción*. Santa Barbara, Calif.: Santa Barbara Trust for Historic Preservation, 1980.

Hartnell, W. *The Diary and Copybook of William E. P. Hartnell: Visitador General of the Missions of Alta California in 1839 and 1840*. Trans. S. P. Gurcke. Ed. with annot., introd., and prol. G. J. Farris. Santa Clara, Calif. and Spokane, Wash.: CMSA and the Arthur H. Clark Company, 2004.

Hata, N. *The Historic Preservation Movement in California, 1940–1976*. Sacramento: California Department of Parks and Recreation, 1992.

Heizer, R. F., ed. *Handbook of North American Indians,* vol. 8, *California*. Washington, D.C.: Smithsonian Institution Press, 1978.

Hicks, J., J. D. Houston, M. H. Kingston, and A. Young, eds. *The Literature of California*, vol. 1, *Native Beginnings to 1945*. Berkeley: University of California Press, 2000.

Hoover, R. L., and J. G. Costello, eds. *Excavations at Mission San Antonio, 1976–1978*. Monograph No. 26. Los Angeles: Institute of Archaeology, University of California, Los Angeles, 1985.

Hosmer, C. B., Jr. *Preservation Comes of Age: From Williamsburg to the National Trust, 1926–1949*. 2 vols. Charlottesville: University Press of Virginia, 1981.

Hudson, T., ed. *Breath of the Sun: Life in Early California as Told by a Chumash Indian, Fernando Librado to John P. Harrington*. Banning, Calif.: Malki Museum Press, 1979.

Hudson, T., T. Blackburn, R. Curletti, and J. Timbrook. *The Eye of the Flute: Chumash Traditional History and Ritual as Told by Fernando Librado Kitseqawit to John P. Harrington*. Santa Barbara, Calif.: Santa Barbara Museum of Natural History, 1977.

Hurtado, A. *Indian Survival on the California Frontier*. New Haven: Yale University Press, 1988.

Jackson, H. H. *Glimpses of California and the Missions*. New York: Little, Brown, 1907.

———. *Ramona*. 1884. Rpt. New York: Harper Collins, 1976.

Johnson, J. R. *The Chumash Indians after Secularization*. Keepsake Volume. Santa Clara, Calif.: California Mission Studies Association, 1995.

———. Pacomio's Chumash dancing songs. *Bulletin of the Santa Barbara Museum of Natural History*, 1989.

Johnson, J. R., and D. Crawford. Contributions to Luiseño ethnohistory based on Mission Register research. *Pacific Coast Archaeological Society Quarterly* 5, no. 4 (1999): 79–102.

Johnson, P. C., ed. *The California Missions: A Pictorial History*. Menlo Park, Calif.: Sunset Books, Lane Book Co., 1964.

Kenyon, C. Conservation of mission art. *Boletín: Journal of the California Mission Studies Association* 20, no. 1 (2002): 37–49.

Kimbro, E. E. Construction chronology of the site of Holy Cross Church, Santa Cruz (Mission Santa Cruz) and conservation recommendations for Santa Cruz Mission ruins. Report prepared for Cabrillo Archaeological Technology Program, submitted to the Diocese of Monterey, 1993. www.santacruzpl.org/history/Spanish.

Kimbro, E. E., M. E. Ryan, and R. H. Jackson, with R. T. Milliken and N. Neuerburg. Restoration research: Santa Cruz Mission Adobe, Santa Cruz Mission State Historic Park. Report Historical Investigations, Davenport, Calif., submitted to Cultural Resource Support Unit, Department of Parks and Recreation, Sacramento, Calif., 1985.

Kirker, H. *California's Architectural Frontier*. Santa Barbara, Calif.: Peregrine Smith, 1973.

Kotzebue, O. von. Extract from Kotzebue's report. In *The Visit of the "Rurick" to San Francisco in 1816,* by August C. Mahr, 55–69. Stanford, Calif.: Stanford University, 1932.

Kubler, G. *The Religious Architecture of New Mexico in the Colonial Period and since the American Occupation*. Albuquerque: University of New Mexico Press, 1990.

Langsdorff, G. H., Freiher von. *Langsdorff's Narrative of the Rezanov Voyage to Nueva California in 1806*... San Francisco: Thomas C. Russell, 1927.
———. *Voyages and Travels in Various Parts of the World, during the Years 1803, 1804, 1805, 1806, and 1807; Part II.* London: Henry Colburn, 1814.
Lee, G., and N. Neuerburg. The Alta California Indians as artists before and after contact. In *Columbian Consequences,* vol. 1, *Archaeological and Historical Perspectives on the Spanish Borderlands West,* ed. D. H. Thomas, 467–80. Washington, D.C.: Smithsonian Institution Press, 1989.
Lightfoot, K. G. *Indians, Missionaries, and Merchants: The Legacy of Colonial Encounters on the California Frontiers.* Berkeley: University of California Press, 2005.
Margolin, M. *The Ohlone Way: Indian Life in the San Francisco–Monterey Bay Area.* Berkeley: Heyday Books, 1978.
Mathes, V. S. Helen Hunt Jackson and the California mission Indians: Selected letters. *Boletín: Journal of the California Mission Studies Association* 23, no. 2 (2007): 5–23.
May, A. *Helen Hunt Jackson: A Lonely Voice of Conscience.* San Francisco: Chronicle Books, 1987.
McClung, W. A. *Landscapes of Desire: Anglo Mythologies of Los Angeles.* Berkeley: University of California Press, 2002.
McWilliams, C. *Southern California: An Island on the Land.* 1946. Rpt. Layton, Utah: Peregrine Smith, 1999.
Miller, H. *Account of a Tour of the California Missions and Towns, 1856: The Journal and Drawings of Henry Miller.* Santa Barbara, Calif.: Bellerophon Books, 1985.
Milliken, R. *A Time of Little Choice: The Disintegration of Tribal Culture in the San Francisco Bay Area, 1769–1810.* Menlo Park, Calif.: Ballena Press, 1995.
Monroy, D. *The Borders Within: Encounters Between Mexico and the U.S.* Tucson: University of Arizona Press, 2008.
———. *Thrown Among Strangers: The Making of Mexican Culture in Frontier California.* Berkeley and Los Angeles: University of California Press, 1990.
Morgado, M. J. *Junípero Serra's Legacy.* Pacific Grove, Calif.: Mount Carmel, 1987.
Neuerburg, N. *The Architecture of Mission La Purísima Concepción.* Santa Barbara, Calif.: Bellerophon Books, 1987.
———. The changing face of Mission San Diego. *Journal of San Diego History* 33, no. 1 (1986): 1–26.
———. *The Decoration of the California Missions.* Santa Barbara, Calif.: Bellerophon Press, 1987.
———. The function of prints in the California missions. Reprint from *Southern California Quarterly* 63 (3). Los Angeles: Historical Society of Southern California, 1986.
———. Indian carved statues at Mission Santa Barbara. *Masterkey* 51, no. 4 (1977): 147–51.
———. *The Indian Via Crucis from Mission San Fernando: An Historical Exposition.* Santa Barbara, Calif.: Santa Barbara Mission Archive-Library, 1998.
———. New light on the church of Mission San Buenaventura. *Ventura County Historical Society Quarterly* 28, no. 4 (1983): 000–00.
———. Painting in the California missions. *American Art Review* 4, no. 1 (July 1977): 72–88.
Newcomb, R. *The Old Mission Churches and Historic Houses of California.* Philadelphia: J. P. Lippincott, 1925.
———. *Spanish-Colonial Architecture in the United States.* New York: J. J. Augustin, 1937. Rpt. New York: Dover Publications, 1990.
Nolan, J. L. Anglo-American myopia and California mission art: Part two. *Southern California Quarterly* 58, no. 2 (1976): 143–204.
Nunis, D. B., ed. *Mission San Fernando Rey de España, 1797–1997: A Bicentennial Tribute.* Los Angeles: Historical Society of Southern California, 1997.
Ogden, A. *The California Sea Otter Trade: 1748–1848.* Berkeley: University of California Press, 1941.
Ohles, W. V. *The Lands of Mission San Miguel.* Clovis, Calif.: World Dancer Press, 1997.
Osio, A. M. *The History of Alta California: A Memoir of Mexican California.* Trans. and ed. R. M. Beebe and R. M. Senkewicz. Madison: University of Wisconsin Press, 1996.
Ostergren, G. Angels and saints: Making and promoting place in Los Angeles and southern California, 1890–1932. Ph.D. dissertation, University of California, Los Angeles, 2005.
Oswalt, R. L. *Kashaya Texts.* University of California Publications in Linguistics 36. Berkeley: University of California Press, 1964.
Pagliarulo, C. Harry Downie and the restoration of Mission San Carlos Borromeo, 1931–1967. *Southern California Quarterly* 86, no. 1 (2004): 19–64.
Palóu, Fr. F. *Palóu's Life of Fray Junípero Serra.* Trans. and annot. M. Geiger. Washington, D.C.: Academy of American Franciscan History, 1955.
Pauley, K. E., and C. M. Pauley. *San Fernando, Rey de España: An Illustrated History.* Spokane, Wash.: Arthur H. Clark, 2005.
Phillips, G. H. Indian paintings from Mission San Fernando: An historical interpretation. *Journal of California Anthropology* 3 (Summer 1976): 96–100.
———. The Stations of the Cross revisited, reconsidered, and revised (sort of). *Boletín: Journal of the California Mission Studies Association* 24, no. 2 (2007): 76–87.
Pitt, L. *The Decline of the Californios.* Berkeley: University of California Press, 1966.
Robinson, A. Journal on the Coast of California by A. Robinson, on Board of Ship Brookline, Year 1829, in "Alfred Robinson, New England Merchant," by Adele Ogden. *California Historical Society Quarterly* 23, no. 3 (1944): 203–13.
———. *Life in California during a Residence of Several Years in That Territory.* New York, 1846. Rpt. New York: Da Capo Press, 1969.

Sandos, J. *Converting California: Indians and Franciscans in the Missions.* New Haven: Yale University Press, 2004.
Savage, C. E. *New Deal Adobe: The Civilian Conservation Corps and the Reconstruction of Mission La Purísima, 1934–1942.* Santa Barbara, Calif.: Fithian Press, 1991.
Schuetz-Miller, M. K. *Architectural Practice in Mexico City: A Manual for Journeyman Architects of the Eighteenth Century.* Tucson: University of Arizona Press, 1987.
———. *Building and Builders in Hispanic California, 1769–1850.* Tucson, Ariz.: Southwestern Mission Research Center; Santa Barbara, Calif.: Santa Barbara Trust for Historic Preservation, Presidio Research Publication, 1994.
Shields, S. *Edwin Deakin: California Painter of the Picturesque.* Sacramento: Crocker Art Museum, 2008.
Silliman, S. W. *Laborers in Colonial California: Native Americans and the Archaeology of Rancho Petaluma.* Tucson: University of Arizona Press, 2004.
Skowronek, R. K. *Situating Mission Santa Clara de Asís.* Berkeley: Academy of American Franciscan History, 2006.
Smilie, R. S. *The Sonoma Mission: San Francisco Solano de Sonoma.* Fresno, Calif.: Valley Publishers, 1975.
Starr, K. *Inventing the Dream: California through the Progressive Era.* New York: Oxford University Press, 1985.
Stern, J., G. J. Miller, P. Hallan-Gibson, and N. Neuerburg. *Romance of the Bells: The California Missions in Art.* Irvine, Calif.: Irvine Museum, 1995.
Tac, P. Indian life and customs at Mission San Luis Rey: A record of California mission life written by Pablo Tac, an Indian neophyte [Rome, California, 1835]. Ed. and trans. M. Hewes and G. Hewes. *The Americas* 9, no. 1 (1952): 87–106.
Thomas, D. H. Harvesting Ramona's garden: Life in California's mythical mission past. In *Columbian Consequences*, vol. 3, *The Spanish Borderlands in Pan-American Perspective.* Washington, D.C.: Smithsonian Institution Press, 1991.
Thompson, M. *American Character: The Curious Life of Charles Fletcher Lummis and the Rediscovery of the Southwest.* New York: Arcade Publishing, 2001.
Tibesar, A., O.F.M., ed. *Writings of Junípero Serra.* Vol 2. Washington, D.C.: Academy of Franciscan History, 1956.
Tolles, E.L., E. Kimbro, and W.S. Ginell. *Planning and Engineering Guidelines for the Seismic Retrofitting of Historic Adobe Structures.* Los Angeles: Getty Conservation Institute, 2002.
Treganza, A. E. Sonoma Mission: An archaeological reconstruction of the Mission San Francisco de Solano quadrangle. *Kroeber Anthropological Papers* 14 (1956): 1–18.
Vancouver, G. *Vancouver in California, 1792–1794: The Original Account of George Vancouver.* 3 vols. Ed. and annot. M. E. Wilber. Early California Travel Series, Nos., 9, 10, 11. 1789; Los Angeles: Glen Dawson, 1954.
Vitruvius. *Vitruvius: The Ten Books on Architecture.* Trans. M. H. Morgan. New York: Dover Publications, 1960.
Von der Porten, E. P. Drake and Cermeno in California: Sixteenth-century Chinese ceramics. *Historical Archaeology* 6 (1972): 1–22.
———. The Drake puzzle solved. *Pacific Discovery* 37, no. 3 (1984): 22–26.
Webb, E. B. *Indian Life at the Old Missions.* Lincoln: University of Nebraska Press, 1952.
Weber, F. J., Msgr. *The California Missions.* Strasbourg: Editions du Signe, 2005.
Weinberg, N. G. 1976. Historic preservation and tradition in California: The restoration of the missions and the Spanish-Colonial Revival. Ph.D. dissertation, University of California, Davis.
Weitze, K. J. *California's Mission Revival.* California Architecture and Architects, No. 3, ed. D. Gebhard. Los Angeles: Hennessey and Ingalls, 1984.

Index

Note: Page numbers in *italics* refer to illustrations.

Acknowledgments

The Getty Conservation Institute's interest in the California missions began in the late 1980s with our work in the conservation of earthen architecture. In addition to being extraordinarily rich in cultural significance, these unique buildings—so much a part of the history of the GCI's home state of California—also exemplify many of the challenges faced in preserving historic buildings and, more specifically, buildings of earthen construction, around the world.

In publishing this book we sought to provide readers with an introduction to the cultural significance of the California missions, including their history, architecture, archaeology, and art, as well as the attempts that have been made to preserve them for future generations. We have chosen to accompany the text with a large number of illustrations, ranging from historical site plans and paintings to contemporary photographs, in the hope that they will help convey the complex legacy of these remarkable places.

I am most grateful to the book's original author, the late Edna Kimbro, an architectural conservator and historian who specialized in the preservation of Spanish and Mexican colonial architecture and the material culture of early California. Edna was a tireless advocate for the preservation and interpretation of California's mission past and was a founding member of the California Mission Studies Association. When we invited her to write a book on the California missions, she enthusiastically began revisiting missions, wading through archives, and drafting text for what has become this very special volume. Sadly, Edna passed away in June 2005 and was not able to finish the work she had started.

I would also like to thank Julia Costello, an archaeologist and cultural resource consultant specializing in California's early history, who took on the task of completing the book when Edna knew she could not. Her energy, graciousness, and years of work on this book are a tribute to Edna, her friend and colleague, and their shared love for the California missions.

We also owe a debt of gratitude to the many institutions that supplied illustrations for the book. We would especially like to thank Lynn Bremer, director of the Santa Bárbara Mission Archive-Library, for her generous assistance throughout the course of this project. We would also like to thank the Bancroft Library, University of California, Berkeley; the Mission Inn Foundation and Museum, Riverside, California.; the Seaver Center for Western History Research, Los Angeles County Museum of Natural History; the National Gallery of Art, in Washington, D.C.; the Irvine Museum, Irvine, California, and its director, Jean Stern; Pentacle Press; USC Special Collections, at the University of Southern California; Bellerophon Books, in Santa Barbara; and the South Coast Fine Art Conservation Center, also in Santa Barbara.

Special thanks go to Rose Marie Beebe, Santa Clara University, for her careful attention to this project; and to Guillermo Aldana and Bill Dewey for their fine photography. Thanks also go to longtime GCI collaborator Tony Crosby for his valuable contribution to the discussion of recent conservation at the Royal Presidio Chapel in Monterey.

This book would not have been possible without the support of the GCI's Kristin Kelly, Jemima Rellie, and Cynthia Godlewski, who helped keep Edna's vision and the book alive over the many years of its making. At Getty Publications, we would like to thank Tevvy Ball, editor of the Conservation and Cultural Heritage series, who skillfully helped craft the text and images to create this handsome volume. In addition, our gratitude goes to Ruth Evans Lane, who helped acquire the illustrations for the book; Kurt Hauser, who created its wonderful design; and Anita Keys, who coordinated its production.

Timothy P. Whalen
Director
The Getty Conservation Institute

The heart of this book comes from Edna E. Kimbro, California's unrivaled expert on all things Californio: historian and conservator; authority on art, architecture, and material culture; and member of the Getty Conservation Institute's GSAP team, which was dedicated to saving the state's disappearing adobe buildings. She died far too young, in 2005. Completion of the book was bequeathed to me, her archaeologist friend and colleague, who shared decades of adventures with her in pursuit of California's rich mission history.

The scope and depth of this book can largely be credited to Tevvy Ball. Combining his considerable narrative skills with his knowledge of California history, he developed and shaped the manuscript, ensuring that the mission story was amply and engagingly told. Our friend the historian Charlene Duval provided constant encouragement and support, and the scholar Rose Marie Beebe made many helpful suggestions, while also undertaking the critical task of editing for accurate use of Spanish.

Indeed, the extraordinary number of historical details that constitute California's complex mission story could not have been amassed without generous help from the community of mission scholars and experts, who freely provided knowledge and advice. We are greatly indebted to Sheila Benedict, Alexander Bevil, Lynn Bremer, Julianne Burton-Carvajal, Richard Carrico, Bradford Claybourn, Kathleen Conti, Bruce Coons, Anthony Crosby, Glenn Farris, David L. Felton, John Fonz, Kristina Foss, Andy Galvin, Lisbeth Haas, Karen Hildebrand, Sasha Honig, Robert L. Hoover, Michael Imwale, John Johnson, Carol Kenyon, Dan Krieger, Susan La Montagne, Ruben Mendoza, Randall Milliken, Douglas Monroy, Therese Muranaka, Richard Ochs, Ken Pauley, Debora Rodriguez, Louis Sanna, Mardith Schuetz-Miller, Robert Senkewicz, William Short, Russell K. Skowronek, Fred Webster, and Patricia West.

We are also profoundly grateful to those at each mission who opened their doors, museums, and archives to aid our research. The staff at the Santa Bárbara Mission Archive-Library and the National Gallery of Art in Washington, D.C., are owed a particular debt of gratitude.

At the Getty Conservation Institute, I would like to thank Tim Whalen, for initiating this book, and Kristin Kelly, for her support of the book from its inception. Cynthia Godlewski provided invaluable assistance throughout the long life of this project, and she and Gail Ostergren made many helpful comments on an early draft of the manuscript. We would also like to thank the staff at Getty Publications for bringing our efforts to fruition, particularly the book's designer, Kurt Hauser, and its production coordinator, Anita Keys.

All of us hope that this story of California's missions, past and present, will provide its readers with information, enjoyment, and an appreciation for the profound legacy that we have inherited.

Julia G. Costello

The Getty Conservation Institute works internationally to advance conservation and to enhance and encourage the preservation and understanding of the visual arts in all of their dimensions—objects, collections, architecture, and sites. The Institute serves the conservation community through scientific research; education and training; field projects; and the dissemination of the results of both its work and the work of others in the field. In all its endeavors, the Institute is committed to addressing unanswered questions and promoting the highest possible standards of conservation practice.

This is the eighth volume in the Conservation and Cultural Heritage series, which aims to provide information in an accessible format about selected culturally significant sites throughout the world. Previously published are *Tunisian Mosaics: Treasures from Roman Africa* (2006), *World Rock Art* (2003), *El Pueblo: The Historic Heart of Los Angeles* (2002), *Cave Temples of Mogao: Art and History on the Silk Road* (2000), *Palace Sculptures of Abomey: History Told on Walls* (1999), *The Los Angeles Watts Towers* (1997), and *House of Eternity: The Tomb of Nefertari* (1996).

Getty Publications
1200 Getty Center Drive, Suite 500
Los Angeles, California 90049-1682
www.getty.edu

Gregory M. Britton, *Publisher*
Mark Greenberg, *Editor in Chief*

Tevvy Ball, *Series Editor*
Sheila Berg, *Copy Editor*
Kurt Hauser, *Designer*
Anita Keys, *Production Coordinator*

Printed in China through Asia Pacific Offset, Inc.

BACK COVER, TOP TO BOTTOM: The ruins of the quadrangle at Mission San Luis Rey, ca. 1885–90 (see p. 240). Alexander Harmer, *Mission San Juan Capistrano, 1886* (see p. 48). Perfecta Encinal, former neophyte of Mission San Antonio de Padua, and her family, ca. 1890 (see p. 178).

HALF TITLE PAGE: Facade of Mission Santa Bárbara, reflected in fountain. Photograph by Kurt Hauser.

TITLE PAGE: Native Californian dancers at Mission San Francisco de Asís, 1816 (see pp. 24–25).

CONTENTS PAGES: Native Californians playing traditional gambling games at Mission San Francisco de Asís, 1816 (see pp. 28–29). Priests restoring Mission San Luis Rey, ca. 1900 (see p. 64).

Library of Congress Cataloging-in-Publication Data

Kimbro, Edna E.
The California missions : history, art, and preservation / Edna E. Kimbro and Julia G. Costello with Tevvy Ball.
p. cm. — (Conservation and cultural heritage series ; 8th v.)
Includes bibliographical references (p.) and index.
ISBN 978-0-89236-983-6 (hardcover)
1. Missions, Spanish—California. 2. Spanish mission buildings—California. 3. Cultural property—Protection—California. I. Costello, Julia G. II. Ball, Tevvy. III. Title.
F862.K55 2009
917.9404'2—dc22

2009016115

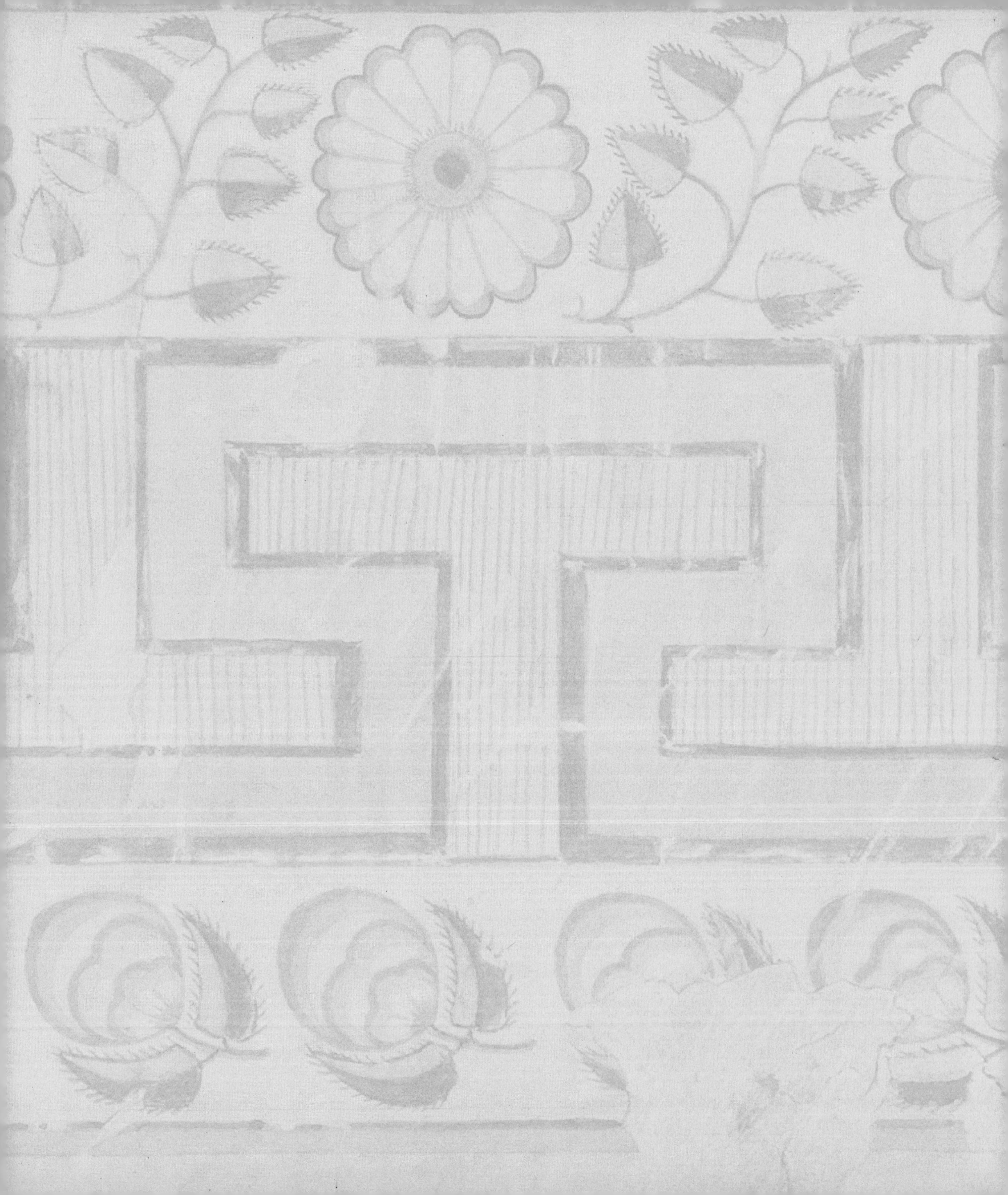